AQA Science

Exclusively endorsed and approved by AQA

Teacher's Book

Sam Holyman

Series Editor: Lawrie Ryan

GCSE Chemistry

Nelson Thornes
a Wolters Kluwer business

Text © Geoff Carr, Darren Forbes, Sam Holyman, Ruth Miller 2006
Original illustrations © Nelson Thornes Ltd 2006

The right of Geoff Carr, Darren Forbes, Sam Holyman and Ruth Miller to be identified as authors of this work has been asserted by them in accordance with the Copyright, Designs and Patents Act 1988.

All rights reserved. No part of this publication may be reproduced or transmitted in any form or by any means, electronic or mechanical, including photocopy, recording or any information storage and retrieval system, without permission in writing from the publisher or under licence from the Copyright Licensing Agency Limited, of Saffron House, 6–10 Kirby Street, London EC1N 8TS.

Any person who commits any unauthorised act in relation to this publication may be liable to criminal prosecution and civil claims for damages.

Published in 2006 by:
Nelson Thornes Ltd
Delta Place
27 Bath Road
CHELTENHAM
GL53 7TH
United Kingdom

07 08 09 10 / 10 9 8 7 6 5 4

A catalogue record for this book is available from the British Library

ISBN 978 0 7487 9645 8

Cover bubble illustration by Andy Parker
Illustrations by Bede Illustration

Page make-up by Wearset Ltd

Printed in Croatia by Zrinski

> The following people have made an invaluable contribution to this book:
>
> Pauline Anning, Jim Breithaupt, Nigel English, Ann Fullick, Patrick Fullick, Richard Gott, Keith Hirst, Paul Lister, Niva Miles, John Scottow, Glenn Toole.

GCSE Chemistry — Contents

How science works — 2
- H1 How science works
- H2 Fundamental ideas about how science works
- H3 Starting an investigation
- H4 Building an investigation
- H5 Making measurements
- H6 Presenting data
- H7 Using data to draw conclusions
- H8 Scientific evidence and society
- H9 How is science used for everybody's benefit?
- Summary answers — 20

C1a Products from rocks — 22

1 Rocks and building — 24
- 1.1 Atoms, elements and compounds
- 1.2 Limestone and its uses
- 1.3 Decomposing carbonates
- 1.4 Quicklime and slaked lime
- 1.5 Cement, concrete and glass
- 1.6 Building materials – from old to new
- Summary, Exam-style, How science works answers — 36

2 Rocks and metals — 38
- 2.1 Extracting metals
- 2.2 Extracting iron
- 2.3 Properties of iron and steels
- 2.4 Alloys in everyday use
- 2.5 Transition metals
- 2.6 Aluminium and titanium
- 2.7 Using metals
- Summary, Exam-style, How science works answers — 52

3 Crude oil — 54
- 3.1 Fuels from crude oil
- 3.2 Fractional distillation
- 3.3 Burning fuels
- 3.4 Cleaner fuels
- 3.5 Alternative fuels
- Summary, Exam-style, How science works answers — 64

End of unit exam answers — 66

C1b Oils, Earth and atmosphere — 68

4 Products from oil — 70
- 4.1 Cracking hydrocarbons
- 4.2 Making polymers from alkenes
- 4.3 The properties of plastics
- 4.4 New and useful polymers
- 4.5 Plastics, polymers and packaging food
- Summary, Exam-style, How science works answers — 80

5 Plant oils — 82
- 5.1 Extracting vegetable oils
- 5.2 Cooking with vegetable oils
- 5.3 Everyday emulsions
- 5.4 What is added to our food?
- 5.5 Vegetable oils as fuels
- 5.6 Vegetable oils
- Summary, Exam-style, How science works answers — 94

6 The changing world — 96
- 6.1 Structure of the Earth
- 6.2 The restless Earth
- 6.3 The Earth's atmosphere in the past
- 6.4 Gases in the atmosphere
- 6.5 The carbon cycle
- 6.6 Earth issues
- Summary, Exam-style, How science works answers — 108

End of unit exam answers — 110

C2 Additional chemistry — 112

1 Structures and bonding — 114
- 1.1 Atomic structure
- 1.2 The arrangement of electrons in atoms
- 1.3 Chemical bonding
- 1.4 Ionic bonding
- 1.5 Covalent bonding
- 1.6 Bonding in metals
- 1.7 The history of the atom
- Summary, Exam-style, How science works answers — 128

2 Structures and properties — 130
- 2.1 Ionic compounds
- 2.2 Simple molecules
- 2.3 Giant covalent substances
- 2.4 Giant metallic structures
- 2.5 Nanoscience and nanotechnology
- Summary, Exam-style, How science works answers — 140

3 How much? — 142
- 3.1 Mass numbers
- 3.2 Masses of atoms and moles
- 3.3 Percentages and formulae
- 3.4 Equations and calculations
- 3.5 Making as much as we want
- 3.6 Reversible reactions
- 3.7 Making ammonia – the Haber process
- 3.8 Aspects of the Haber process
- Summary, Exam-style, How science works answers — 158

4 Rates of reaction — 160
- 4.1 How fast?
- 4.2 Collision theory
- 4.3 The effect of temperature
- 4.4 The effect of concentration
- 4.5 The effect of catalysts
- 4.6 Catalysts in action
- Summary, Exam-style, How science works answers — 172

5 Energy and reactions — 174
- 5.1 Exothermic and endothermic reactions
- 5.2 Energy and reversible reactions

5.3 More about the Haber process
5.4 Industrial dilemmas
Summary, Exam-style, How science works answers 182

6 Electrolysis 184
6.1 Electrolysis – the basics
6.2 Changes at the electrodes
6.3 Electrolysing brine
6.4 Purifying copper
6.5 To build or not to build?
Summary, Exam-style, How science works answers 194

7 Acids, alkalis and salts 196
7.1 Acids and alkalis
7.2 Making salts from metals or bases
7.3 Making salts from solutions
7.4 It's all in the soil
Summary, Exam-style, How science works answers 204

End of unit exam answers 206

C3 Further chemistry 208

1 Development of the periodic table 210
1.1 The early periodic table
1.2 The modern periodic table
1.3 Group 1 – the alkali metals
1.4 Group 7 – the halogens
1.5 The transition elements
1.6 Finding and creating new elements
Summary, Exam-style, How science works answers 222

2 More about acids and bases 224
2.1 Strong and weak acids/alkalis
2.2 Titrations
2.3 Titration calculations
2.4 How ideas about acids and bases developed
Summary, Exam-style, How science works answers 232

3 Water 234
3.1 Water and solubility
3.2 Solubility curves
3.3 Hard water
3.4 Removing hardness
3.5 Water treatment
3.6 Water fit to drink
Summary, Exam-style, How science works answers 246

4 Energy calculations 248
4.1 Comparing the energy produced by fuels
4.2 Energy changes in reactions
4.3 Calculations using bond energies
4.4 Energy balance – how much energy do you use?
Summary, Exam-style, How science works answers 256

5 Analysis 258
5.1 Tests for positive ions
5.2 Tests for negative ions
5.3 Testing for organic substances
5.4 Instrumental analysis 1
5.5 Instrumental analysis 2
5.6 Chemical analysis
Summary, Exam-style, How science works answers 270

End of unit exam answers 272

GCSE Chemistry

Welcome to AQA Chemistry

AQA Science for GCSE is the only series to be endorsed by AQA. The *GCSE Chemistry* Teacher Book is written by experienced science teachers and is designed to make planning the delivery of the specification easy – everything you need is right here! Information is placed around a reduced facsimile of the Student Book page, allowing you quick reference to features and content that will be used in the lesson.

LEARNING OBJECTIVES

These tell you what the students should know by the end of the lesson, linking directly to the Learning Objectives in the Student Book, but providing teachers with extra detail. The Learning Objectives for 'How Science Works' are all listed in Chapter 1. These should be integrated into the lessons chosen to teach various aspects of 'How Science Works' throughout the course.

LEARNING OUTCOMES

These tell you what the students should be able to do to show they have achieved the Learning Objectives. These are differentiated where appropriate to provide suitable expectations for all your students.

How science works

This is covered in the section at the beginning of the Student Book, in the main content, in the end of chapter spreads, and in the exam-style questions and 'How Science Works' questions. The corresponding teacher's notes give you detailed guidance on how to integrate 'How Science Works' fully into your lessons and activities.

Exam-Style Questions

There are multiple-choice questions for Chemistry A and structured questions for Chemistry B. They are ranked in order of difficulty. All questions are useful to complete, no matter which specification is being taken, as they cover the same content. 'How Science Works' is integrated into some exam-style questions and there are separate 'How Science Works' questions to give additional practice in this area.

Lesson structure

This feature provides ideas for the experienced teacher, support for the newly qualified teacher and structure for cover lessons. Available for every double page lesson spread, it contains a variety of suggestions for how the spread could be taught, including starters and plenaries of varying lengths, as well as suggestions for the main part of the lesson.

Teaching suggestions

Ideas on how to use features in the Student Book, suggestions for Gifted and Talented, Special Needs, ICT activities and different learning styles are all covered here, and more.

Practical support

For every practical in the Student Book you will find this corresponding feature which gives a list of equipment needed, safety references and further guidance to carry out the practical. A worksheet is provided on the e-Science CD ROM for each practical.

Activity notes

Each activity in the Student Book has background information notes on how to organise it effectively.

Icons

- appears in the text where opportunities for investigational aspects of 'How Science Works' are signposted in the AQA specification.
- appears in the text where AQA have signposted opportunities to cover societal aspects of 'How Science Works' in the specification.

e-Science CD ROM

This contains a wide range of resources – animations, simulations, photopluses, Powerpoints, activity sheets, practical skill sheets, homework sheets – which are linked to Student Book pages and help deliver the activities suggested in the Teacher Book.

Answers to questions

They're all here! All the questions in the Student Book are answered in the Teacher Book. Each answer is located in the corresponding feature in the Teacher Book. For example, answers to yellow in-text questions in the Student Book can be found in the yellow feature in the Teacher Book.

Key Stage 3 curriculum links:

This expands the 'What you already know' unit opener of the Student Book and gives QCA Scheme of Work references for relevant knowledge that may need revisiting before starting on the unit.

ACTIVITIES & EXTENSIONS

This highlights opportunities to extend a lesson or add activities, providing notes and tips on how to carry them out.

SPECIFICATION LINK-UP

This gives clear references to the AQA specification for the lesson, with additional notes and guidance where appropriate.

KEY POINTS

This feature gives ideas on how to consolidate the key points given in the Student Book, and how to use the key points as a basis for homework, revision or extension work.

1

H1 | How science works

Key Stage 3 Link-up

Sc1 Scientific enquiry

How Science Works does not relate directly to the individual statements in the Key Stage 3 Programme of Study. However, it builds on all of the knowledge, understanding and skills inherent in Sc1.

It is expected that students will be familiar with:
- the need to work safely
- making a prediction
- controls
- the need for repetition of some results
- tabulating and analysing results
- making appropriate conclusions
- suggesting how they might improve methods.

RECAP ANSWERS

1. Ed predicted, 'The hotter the water the more sugar will dissolve in it'.
2. The temperature of the water.
3. The mass of sugar dissolved.
4. E.g. the volume of the water.
5. E.g. the final temperature of the water/amount of stirring.
6.

Temperature of the water (°C)	Mass of sugar dissolved (grams)
8	10
18	32
25	50
45	95

7. A suitable graph, with temperature on X axis and mass of sugar on Y axis. Points plotted correctly, axes labelled (including units) and line of best fit drawn.
8. E.g. as the temperature increased, the mass of sugar dissolved increased/an increased temperature of the water dissolved more sugar.
9. E.g. Ed could have repeated his results.

Teaching suggestions

Finding out what they know

Students should begin to appreciate the 'thinking behind the doing' developed during KS3. It would be useful to illustrate this by a simple demonstration (e.g. metals reacting with water or acid) and posing questions that build into a flow diagram of the steps involved in a whole investigation. This could lead into the recap questions to ascertain each individual student's progress. Emphasis should be placed on an understanding of the following terms: prediction, independent, dependent and control variables and reliability.

The recap questions should identify each individual student's gaps in understanding. Therefore it is best carried out as an assessment. It might be appropriate to do questions 7, 8 and 9 for homework.

Revealing to the students that they are using scientific thinking to solve problems during their everyday life can make their work in science more relevant. Other situations could illustrate this and should be discussed in groups or as a class.

Activity notes

There is a great deal of information on many easily used websites. The information includes: the history of fireworks, the chemistry of fireworks, the structure of large display fireworks and how the placement of chemicals relates to the display, how different metals are used for different colours, including their fuses, and why they continue to burn inside the firework without air, and the electronic organisation of large displays.

KEY POINTS

- Students should appreciate the need for safety in the laboratory.
- Students should be aware of the processes involved in the design of an investigation.
- Students should have notes that bring out the meaning of key words related to the design of an investigation.
- Students should be aware of the importance of observation to starting an investigation.
- Students should be aware of the small steps that science makes towards more certain theories.

H1 | How science works

This first chapter looks at 'How Science Works'. It is an important part of your GCSE because the ideas introduced here will crop up throughout your course. You will be expected to collect scientific evidence and to understand how we use evidence. These concepts will be assessed as the major part of your internal school assessment. You will take one or more 45-minute tests on data you have collected previously plus data supplied for you in the test. These are called Investigative Skills Assignments. The ideas in 'How Science Works' will also be assessed in your examinations.

What you already know

Here is a quick reminder of previous work with investigations that you will find useful in this chapter:

- You will have done some practical work and know how important it is to keep yourself and others safe.
- Before you start investigating you usually make a prediction, which you can test.
- Your prediction and plan will tell you what you are going to change and what you are going to measure.
- You will have thought about controls.
- You will have thought about repeating your readings.
- During your practical work you will have written down your results, often in a table.
- You will have plotted graphs of your results.
- You will have made conclusions to explain your results.
- You will have thought about how you could improve your results, if you did the work again.

RECAP QUESTIONS

Ed wrote this account of a practical he did:

I wanted to find out how much sugar would dissolve in water at different temperatures. I thought that the hotter the water the more sugar would dissolve.

So I took 100 cm³ of tap water, measured its temperature (18°C) and stirred in as much sugar as I could. I dissolved 32 grams. I then took the same amount of water out of the fridge, the water was at 8°C. This time only 10 grams dissolved. I did exactly the same with 100 cm³ of water at 25°C and at 45°C. The first one of these dissolved 50 grams. The second one dissolved 95 grams.

1. What was Ed's prediction?
2. What was the variable he chose to change? (We call this the independent variable.)
3. What was the variable he measured to judge the effect of varying the independent variable? (We call this the dependent variable. Its value **depends** on the value chosen for the independent variable.)
4. Write down a variable that Ed controlled.
5. Write down a variable that Ed did not say he had controlled.
6. Make a table of Ed's results.
7. Draw a graph of his results.
8. Write a conclusion for Ed.
9. How do you think Ed could have improved his results?

For example:
'How can I get the potatoes to cook quickly? Large potatoes are always harder than the smaller ones (observation). I know that smaller pieces of solid increase the rate of reactions.' (knowledge)

You can use your observations and your knowledge to make a prediction that decreasing the size of the potatoes will make them cook quicker. You can then test your prediction and see what the results are. You check again the next day to see if you get the same results (reliability). Perhaps you could use a different ring on the

How science works

SPECIFICATION LINK-UP

This opening chapter covers the complete specification for 'How science works – the procedural content'.

'How science works' is treated here as a separate chapter. It offers the opportunity to teach the 'thinking behind the doing' as a discrete set of procedural skills. However, it is of course an integral part of the way students will learn about science and those skills should be nurtured throughout the course.

It is anticipated that sections of this chapter will be taught as the opportunity presents itself during the teaching programme. The chapter should also be referred back to at appropriate times when these skills are required and in preparation for the internally assessed ISAs.

Section 10.1

The thinking behind the doing

Science attempts to explain the world in which we live. It provides technologies that have had a great impact on our society and the environment. Scientists try to explain phenomena and solve problems using evidence. The data to be used as evidence must be reliable and valid, as only then can appropriate conclusions be made.

A scientifically literate citizen should, amongst other things, be equipped to question, and engage in debate on, the evidence used in decision-making.

The reliability of evidence refers to how much we trust the data. The validity of evidence depends on the reliability of the data as well as whether the research answers the question. If the data is not reliable, the research cannot be valid.

To ensure reliability and validity in evidence, scientists consider a range of ideas which relate to:

- *how we observe the world;*
- *designing investigations so that patterns and relationships between variables may be identified;*
- *making measurements by selecting and using instruments effectively;*
- *presenting and representing data;*
- *identifying patterns, relationships and making suitable conclusions.*
- *These ideas inform decisions and are central to science education.*

They constitute the 'thinking behind the doing' that is a necessary complement to the subject content of biology, chemistry and physics.

Checking for misconceptions

Some common misconceptions that can be dealt with here and throughout the course are:

- The purpose of controls – some students believe that it is about making accurate measurements of the independent variable.
- The purpose of preliminary work – some believe that it is the first set of results.
- That the table of results is constructed after the practical work – students should be encouraged to produce the table before carrying out their work and complete it during their work.
- That anomalies are identified after the analysis – they should preferably be identified during the practical work or at the latest before any calculation of a mean.
- They automatically extrapolate the graph to its origin.
- Lines of best fit must be straight lines.
- Some will think you repeat readings to make sure your investigation is a fair test.

Special needs

Cloze statements can be used for essential notes.

Gifted and talented

Discussion could range into the importance of chance in scientific discoveries. Louis Pasteur called it 'chance favouring the prepared mind'. Viagra is a good example. Patients in the clinical trial designed to improve their heart problems refused to return unused tablets, even though it had no effect on their heart condition! Art Fry tried to develop a superglue. He failed so miserably with one mixture that it worked perfectly for sticking paper temporarily. The Post-it had arrived and made massive profits for 3Ms (Minnesota Mining and Manufacturing Company).

Learning styles

Kinaesthetic: Constructing a table and graph of results.
Visual: Observing the demonstration.
Auditory: Listening to ideas of others on scientific opinions.
Interpersonal: Discussing the firework problem.
Intrapersonal: Reviewing personal knowledge from KS3.

cooker – will this work better? Does it help to use less water? This could lead to a discussion of the need for controls. Scientists work in exactly the same way – this is 'How science works'.

Collect newspaper articles and news items from the television to illustrate good and poor uses of science. There are some excellent television programmes illustrating good and poor science. Have a competition for who can bring in the poorest example of science used to sell products – shampoo adverts are a very good starter!

H2 HOW SCIENCE WORKS
Fundamental ideas about how science works

LEARNING OBJECTIVES
Students should learn:
- The difference between continuous, discrete, ordered and categoric variables.
- That evidence needs to be valid and reliable.
- That variables can be linked causally, by association or by chance.
- To distinguish between opinion based on scientific evidence and non-scientific ideas.

LEARNING OUTCOMES
Students should be able to:
- Recognise variables as continuous, ordered, discrete or categoric.
- Suggest how an investigation might demonstrate its reliability and validity.
- State that variables can be linked causally, by association or by chance.
- Identify when an opinion does not have the support of valid and reliable science.

SPECIFICATION LINK-UP   How Science Works
Section 10.2
Fundamental ideas

Evidence must be approached with a critical eye. It is necessary to look closely at how measurements have been made and what links have been established. Scientific evidence provides a powerful means of forming opinions. These ideas pervade all of 'How science works'.

Students should know and understand:
- *It is necessary to distinguish between opinion based on valid and reliable evidence and opinion based on non-scientific ideas (prejudice, whim or hearsay).*
- *Continuous variables (any numerical values) give more information than ordered variables, which are more informative than categoric variables. A variable may also be discrete, that is, restricted to whole numbers.*
- *Scientific investigations often seek to identify links between two or more variables. These links may be:*
  - *causal, in that a change in one variable causes a change in another*
  - *due to association – changes in one variable and a second variable are linked by a third variable*
  - *due to chance occurrence.*

Lesson structure

STARTER
Crazy science – Show a video clip of one of the science shows that are aimed at entertainment rather than education or an advert that proclaims a scientific opinion. This should lead into a discussion of how important it is to form opinions based on sound scientific evidence. (5–10 minutes)

MAIN
- From a light-hearted look at entertainment science, bring the thalidomide example into contrast (if appropriate with video clips) and discuss how tragic situations can be created by forming opinions that are not supported by valid science.
- Show how some metals bend more easily than others. Discuss, in small groups, the different ways in which the dependent variable could be measured, identifying these in terms of continuous, ordered and categoric measurements.
- Discuss the usefulness in terms of forming opinions of each of the proposed measurements.
- Consider that this might be a commercial proposition and the students might be advising an architect on which metal to use for a particular construction.
- Discuss how they could organise the investigation to demonstrate its validity and reliability to a potential investor.
- Discuss whether the relationship shows a causal link, a chance link or a link by association.

PLENARIES
Evidence for opinions – Bring together the main features of scientific evidence that would allow sound scientific opinions to be formed from an investigation. (5 minutes)

Analyse conclusions – Use an example of a poorly structured investigation and allow the students to critically analyse any conclusions drawn, e.g. data from an investigation into different forms of insulation, using calorimeters and cooling curves. (10 minutes)

How science works

Teaching suggestions

- **Special needs.** Lists of possible variables could be made from which to select the most appropriate. Cloze statements can be used for essential notes.
- **Gifted and talented.** Discussion could range into how important accurate measurement is to scientists. Historically, with the absence of the technology needed for accurate measurement of continuous variables, chemists used categoric and ranked variables more often. Today, data collecting is far more sophisticated because the technology is available. The first vulcanised rubber was tested by nailing it to the outside of a doorpost to see if it went brittle overnight! In contrast, in the eighteenth century, M and Mme Lavoisier were able to establish that, rather than lose weight, a rusting piece of iron gained weight.
- **Learning styles**

Visual: Observing metal bending experiment.

Auditory: Listening to ideas of others on scientific opinions.

Interpersonal: Discussing the variables associated with the metal bending experiment.

Intrapersonal: Considering the ethics of the thalidomide case and possibly the use of animals for testing human drugs.

Practical support

Equipment and materials required
Thin strips of different metals that bend to differing degrees. Some standard technique for bending the metals. If they are of different shapes then this will complicate the task – but could be more appropriate to higher attaining students.

HOW SCIENCE WORKS

H2 Fundamental ideas about how science works

LEARNING OBJECTIVES
1 How do you spot when a person has an opinion that is not based on good science?
2 What is the importance of continuous, ordered and categoric variables?
3 What is meant by reliable evidence and valid evidence?
4 How can two sets of data be linked?

NEXT TIME YOU…
…read a newspaper article or watch the news on TV ask yourself if that research is valid and reliable. (See page 5.) Ask yourself if you can trust the opinion of that person.

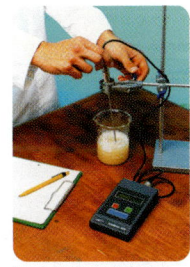

Science is too important for us to get it wrong

Sometimes it is easy to spot when people try to use science poorly. Sometimes it can be funny. You might have seen adverts claiming to give your hair 'body' or sprays that give your feet 'lift'!

On the other hand, poor scientific practice can cost lives.

Some years ago a company sold the drug thalidomide to people as a sleeping pill. Research was carried out on animals to see if it was safe. The research did not include work on pregnant animals. The opinion of the people in charge was that the animal research showed the drug could be used safely with humans.

Then the drug was also found to help ease morning sickness in pregnant women. Unfortunately, doctors prescribed it to many women, resulting in thousands of babies being born with deformed limbs. It was far from safe.

These are very difficult decisions to make. You need to be absolutely certain of what the science is telling you.

a) Why was the opinion of the people in charge of developing thalidomide based on poor science?

Deciding on what to measure

You know that you have an independent and a dependent variable in an investigation. These variables can be one of four different types:

- A **categoric variable** is one that is best described by a label (usually a word). The type of gas given off in a reaction is a categoric variable, e.g. the gas given off was carbon dioxide gas.
- A **discrete variable** is one that you describe in whole numbers. The number of lumps of marble chip used.
- An **ordered variable** is one where you can put the data into order, but not give it an actual number. The amount of gas given off in one reaction compared to another is an ordered variable, e.g. more carbon dioxide was given off by the hydrochloric acid.
- A **continuous variable** is one that we measure, so its value could be any number. Volume of gas given off (as measured by a gas syringe or an upturned measuring cylinder of water) is a continuous variable, e.g. 45 cm^3; 43 cm^3; 37 cm^3; 56 cm^3; 33 cm^3 of carbon dioxide were given off.

When designing your investigation you should always try to measure continuous data whenever you can. This is not always possible, so you should then try to use ordered data. If there is no other way to measure your variable then you have to use a label (categoric variable).

b) Imagine you were testing the heat given out in three different reactions (A, B and C). Would it be best to say i) reactions A and B felt warm, but C felt hot, or ii) reaction C got hottest, followed by A and and finally B, or iii) the rise in temperature in reaction C was 31°C, in A it was 16°C and in B it was 14°C?

Figure 1 Student recording a range of temperatures – an example of a continuous variable

Making your investigation reliable and valid

When you are designing an investigation you must make sure that others can get the same results as you – this makes it **reliable**.

You must also make sure you are measuring the actual thing you want to measure. If you don't, your data can't be used to answer your original question. This seems very obvious but it is not always quite so easy. You need to make sure that you have **controlled** as many other variables as you can, so that no-one can say that your investigation is not **valid**. A valid investigation should be reliable and answer the original question.

c) State one way in which you can show that your results are valid.

Figure 2 The aftermath of an earthquake

How might an independent variable be linked to a dependent variable?

Variables can be linked together for one of three reasons:

- It could be because one variable has caused a change in the other, e.g. the higher the temperature the quicker the glue will set. This is a **causal link**.
- It could be because a third variable has caused changes in the two variables you have investigated, e.g. the denser iron ore is, the more valuable it is. This is because there is an **association** between the two variables. Both of the variables are caused by the increased proportion of iron in the rock.
- It could be due simply to **chance**, e.g. a link between the number of deaths and the strength of an earthquake in a built-up area may be weak but still cause many deaths – the link was just by chance.)

d) Describe a causal link that you have seen in chemistry.

DID YOU KNOW?
At any time there are only about twenty atoms of francium in the entire planet. Better make sure any investigations are valid!

SUMMARY QUESTIONS
1 Students were asked to find the solubility of three different solids – D, E and F.
Name each of the following types of dependent variable described by the students in a), b) and c):
a) D and E were 'soluble', whereas F was 'very soluble'.
b) F was most soluble, D was second and E was least soluble.
c) 59.8 g of F dissolved in 100 cm^3 of water, 30.2 g of D dissolved in 100 cm^3 of water, 25.9 g of F dissolved in 100 cm^3 of water.
2 Some people believe that the artificial sweetener aspartame causes headaches and dizziness. Do you trust these opinions? What would convince you not to use aspartame?

KEY POINTS
1 Be on the lookout for non-scientific opinions.
2 Continuous data give more information than other types of data.
3 Check that evidence is reliable and valid.
4 Be aware that just because two variables are related it does not mean that there is a causal link between them.

SUMMARY ANSWERS

1 a) Categoric
   b) ordered
   c) continuous

2 If the investigation can be shown to be reliable; if other scientists can repeat their investigations and get the same findings. Because it is reliable, opinions formed from it are more useful.

Answers to in-text questions

a) The original animal investigation did not include pregnant animals/was not carried out on human tissue, and so was not valid, when the opinion was formed that it could be given to pregnant women.

b) iii

c) Control all (or as many as possible) of the other variables.

d) A simple causal link described.

KEY POINTS

- Students should appreciate the need for sound science before opinions can be valued. They could challenge others in their group by presenting deliberately unfair tests and ask the others to spot the mistakes.

- Students should have notes that bring out the meaning of the key words, including 'continuous, discrete, categoric, ordered, valid and reliable'.

HOW SCIENCE WORKS

H3 Starting an investigation

LEARNING OBJECTIVES

Students should learn:

- How scientific knowledge can be used to observe the world around them.
- How good observations can be used to make hypotheses.
- How hypotheses can generate predictions that can be tested.
- That investigations must produce valid results.

LEARNING OUTCOMES

Students should be able to:

- State that observation can be the starting point for an investigation.
- State that observation can generate hypotheses.
- Recall that hypotheses can generate predictions and investigations.
- Show that the design of an investigation must allow results to be valid.

Teaching suggestions

- **Learning styles**

  Kinaesthetic: Practical activities.

  Visual: Observations made.

  Auditory: Listening to group discussions.

  Interpersonal: Discussing hypotheses and predictions.

  Intrapersonal: Answering question c.

- **Teaching assistant.** The teaching assistant could be primed to ask appropriate questions and to prompt thought processes in line with the theme of the lesson.

SPECIFICATION LINK-UP How Science Works

Section 10.3

Observation as a stimulus to investigation

Observation is the link between the real world and scientific ideas. When we observe objects, organisms or events we do so using existing knowledge. Observations may suggest hypotheses and lead to predictions that can be tested.

Students should know and understand:

- *Observing phenomena can lead to the start of an investigation, experiment or survey. Existing theories and models can be used creatively to suggest explanations for phenomena (hypotheses). Careful observation is necessary before deciding which are the most important variables. Hypotheses can then be used to make predictions that can be tested.*
- *Data from testing a prediction can support or refute the hypothesis or lead to a new hypothesis.*
- *If the theories and models we have available to us do not completely match our data or observations, then we need to check the validity of our observations or data, or amend the theories or models.*

Lesson structure

STARTER

Linking observation to knowledge – Show students some photographs of corrosion, erosion or pollution. Get them to discuss in groups their observations. Try to link observations to their scientific knowledge. They are more likely to notice events that they can offer some scientific explanation for. This may well need prompting with some directed questions. Once students have got used to making observations get them to start to ask questions about those observations. (10 minutes)

Demo observation – Begin the lesson with a demonstration – as simple as lighting a match or more involved such as a bell ringing in a bell jar, with air gradually being withdrawn. Students should, in silence and without further prompting, be asked to write down their observations. These should be collated and questions be derived from those observations. (10 minutes)

MAIN

- Work through the first section and allow time for students to discuss question a.
- If in the lab, allow students to participate in a 'scientific happening' of your choice, e.g. blowing large and small bubbles or dropping paper cups with different masses in. Preferably something that they have not met before, but which they will have some knowledge of.
- If students need some help at this point, they should try question b.
- Making bubbles: In groups they should discuss possible explanations for one agreed observation. Encourage a degree of lateral thinking. You might need to pose the questions for some groups, e.g. why were some bubbles larger than others? They could be told how the bubble mixture was made. Ask the group to select which of their explanations is the most likely, based on their own knowledge of science.
- Work these explanations into a hypothesis.
- Individually each student should try question c). Gather in ideas and hypotheses. Use a hypothesis that suggests that the metal lock is rusting due to its proximity to water and air (oxygen) or the proportion of iron in the alloy or any other plausible hypothesis.
- Students, working in groups, can now turn this into a prediction.
- They could suggest ways in which their prediction could be tested. Identify independent, dependent and control variables and the need to make sure that they are measuring what they intend to measure.
- Go over question c) as a class.

PLENARIES

Poster – Students to design a poster that links 'Observation + knowledge – hypothesis – prediction – investigation. (10 minutes)

A chemist called Karl Scheele illustrates a good example of how observation without knowledge can be a dangerous thing. He brilliantly discovered many elements including chlorine, nitrogen and oxygen, none of which he got credit for. He was keen to 'observe' as many properties of his discoveries as he could. His method included tasting them. His discovery of hydrocyanic acid probably led to his death aged 43! Priestley 'discovered' oxygen two years after Scheele. Davy discovered chlorine 36 years after Scheele!

How science works
Practical support

Equipment and materials required
Distilled water, washing up liquid, glycerine, possibly different sized loops.

Details
Fill container three-quarters full with water, add some detergent and glycerine.

HOW SCIENCE WORKS

H3 Starting an investigation

LEARNING OBJECTIVES
1 How can you use your scientific knowledge to observe the world around you?
2 How can you use your observations to make a hypothesis?
3 How can you make predictions and start to design an investigation?

Observation
As humans we are sensitive to the world around us. We can use our many senses to detect what is happening. As scientists we use observations to ask questions. We can only ask useful questions if we know something about the observed event. We will not have all of the answers, but we know enough to start asking the correct questions.

If we observe that the weather has been hot today, we would not ask if it was due to global warming. If the weather was hotter than normal for several years then we could ask that question. We know that global warming takes many years to show its effect.

When you are designing an investigation you have to observe carefully which variables are likely to have an effect.

a) Would it be reasonable to ask if the iron in Figure 1 is rusting because of acid rain? Discuss your answer.

Amjid noticed that the driveway up to his house had cracks in the concrete on the left side of the driveway (observation). He was concerned because the driveway had only been laid for ten weeks. The work had been done last December. Before the builder came to look at it, Amjid thought of a few ideas to put to the builder.
- Did he have the correct amount of water in the concrete?
- Did he use the correct amount of cement?
- Could it be the car that was causing the damage?
- Did the builder dig the foundations deep enough?
- Did the builder put the same depth of foundations on both sides?
- Could the frost have caused the damage?
- Could the bushes growing next to the drive have caused the problem?

b) Discuss all of these good ideas and choose three that are the most likely.

Observations, backed up by really creative thinking and good scientific knowledge can lead to a hypothesis.

What is a hypothesis?
A hypothesis is a 'great idea'. Why is it so great? – well because it is a great observation that has some really good science to try to explain it.

For example, you observe that small, thinly sliced chips cook faster than large, fat chips. Your hypothesis could be that the small chips cook faster because the heat from the oil has a shorter distance to travel before it gets to the potato in the centre of the chips.

DID YOU KNOW?
Mendeleev knew of only 63 elements. He put his observations and knowledge together to predict that others would be found. He was correct, but what he couldn't predict was that others would be made, some of which only exist for a few millionths of a second!

c) Check out the photograph of the rusting object in Figure 1 and spot anything that you find interesting. Use your knowledge and some creative thought to suggest a hypothesis for each observation you can make.

When making hypotheses you can be very imaginative with your ideas. However, you should have some scientific reasoning behind those ideas so that they are not totally bizarre.

Remember, your explanation might not be correct, but you think it is. The only way you can check out your hypothesis is to make it into a prediction and then test it by carrying out an investigation.

Observation + knowledge → hypothesis
prediction → investigation

Figure 1 Rusting lock

Starting to design a valid investigation
An investigation starts with a prediction. You, as the scientist, predict that there is a relationship between two variables.
- An **independent variable** is one that is changed or selected by you, the investigator.
- A **dependent variable** is measured for each change in your independent variable.
- All other variables become **control variables**, kept constant so that your investigation is a fair test.

If your measurements are going to be accepted by other people then they must be valid. Part of this is making sure that you are really measuring the effect of changing your chosen variable. For example, if other variables aren't controlled properly, they might be affecting the data collected.

d) Look at Figure 2. Darren was investigating the temperature change when adding anhydrous copper sulfate to water. He used a test tube for the reaction. What is wrong here?

Figure 2 Darren investigating the temperature change

SUMMARY QUESTIONS
1 Copy and complete using the words below:
   controlled   dependent   hypothesis   independent
   knowledge   prediction
   Observations when supported by scientific …… can be used to make a ……. This can be the basis for a …… . A prediction links an …… variable to a …… variable. Other variables need to be …… .
2 Explain the difference between a hypothesis and a prediction.

KEY POINTS
1 Observation is often the starting point for an investigation.
2 Hypotheses can lead to predictions and investigations.
3 You must design investigations that produce valid results if you are to be believed.

SUMMARY ANSWERS

1 Observations when supported by scientific *knowledge* can be used to make a *hypothesis*. This can be the basis for a *prediction*. A prediction links an *independent* variable to a *dependent* variable. Other variables need to be *controlled*.

2 A hypothesis seeks to explain an observation – it is a good idea. A prediction tests the hypothesis in an investigation.

Answers to in-text questions

a) Yes – because you know that much of our rain is acidic and you know that some metals react with acids. However . . .

b) Did he have the correct amount of water in the concrete?
Did he use the correct amount of cement?
Did the builder put the same depth of foundations on both sides?
Could the bushes growing next to the drive have caused the problem?
All of the suggestions are possible, but any three of these would be the more likely.

c) e.g. Observation: of where the rust is. Hypothesis: related to type of metal.

d) Darren's hand could be heating or cooling the solution. The thermometer is not in the solution. The results would not be valid.

KEY POINTS

- Students should have notes relating observations to knowledge to hypothesis to prediction and to investigation. They should also have some notes on what it means to design validity into an investigation.

HOW SCIENCE WORKS

H4 Building an investigation

LEARNING OBJECTIVES

Students should learn:
- How to design a fair test.
- The purpose of a trial run.
- How to ensure accuracy and precision.

LEARNING OUTCOMES

Students should be able to:
- Design a fair test and understand the use of control groups.
- Manage fieldwork investigations.
- Use trial runs to design valid investigations.
- Design accuracy into an investigation.
- Design precision into an investigation.

Teaching suggestions

- **Learning styles**
  Kinaesthetic: Carrying out experiment.
  Visual: Reading instruments.
  Auditory: Listening to the outcomes of experiments from different groups.
  Interpersonal: Discussing the quality of results.
  Intrapersonal: Considering fair tests in relation to athletics.

- **Teaching assistant.** The teaching assistant could support pupils who have physical or coordination difficulties with practical work. The purpose of the experiment will need reinforcing for lower attaining students.

KEY POINTS

- The students must be able to appreciate the difference between accuracy and precision. Ask students for their own definitions without the use of the textbook.
- They sometimes confuse accuracy with the sensitivity of an instrument. Also, in calculations, some students will write irrelevant places of decimals. Ask students to comment on an example.

SPECIFICATION LINK-UP   How Science Works

Section 10.4
Designing an investigation

An investigation is an attempt to determine whether or not there is a relationship between variables. Therefore it is necessary to identify and understand the variables in an investigation. The design of an investigation should be scrutinised when evaluating the validity of the evidence it has produced.

Students should know and understand:
- An independent variable is one that is changed or selected by the investigator. The dependent variable is measured for each change in the independent variable.
- Any measurement must be valid in that it measures only the appropriate variable.

Fair test
- It is important to isolate the effects of the independent variable on the dependent variable. This may be achieved more easily in a laboratory environment than in the field where it is harder to control all variables.
- A fair test is one in which only the independent variable affects the dependent variable, as all other variables are kept the same.
- In field investigations it is necessary to ensure that variables that change their value do so in the same way for all measurements of the dependent variable.
- When using large-scale survey results, it is necessary to select data from conditions that are similar.
- Control groups are often used in biological and medical research to ensure that observed effects are due to changes in the independent variable alone.

Choosing values of a variable
- Care is needed in selecting values of variables to be recorded in an investigation. A trial run will help to identify appropriate values to be recorded, such as the number of repeated readings needed and their range and interval.

Accuracy and precision
- Readings might be repeated to improve the reliability of the data. An accurate measurement is one that is close to the true value..
- The design of an investigation must provide data with sufficient accuracy.
- The design of an investigation must provide data with sufficient precision to form a valid conclusion.

Lesson structure

STARTER

Head start – Start, for example, with a video clip of a 100 m race. This has to be a fair test. How is this achieved? Then show the mass start of the London marathon and ask if this is a fair test. Then move on to ask why there is no official world record for a marathon. Instead they have world best times. This could lead discussion into how difficult it is to control all of the variables in the field. You could go back to suggest that athletes can break the 100 m world record and for this not to be recognised because of a helping wind. (10 minutes)

That's not fair! – Challenge students with a test you set up in an 'unfair' way e.g. burning fuels to establish energy released. You can differentiate by making some errors obvious and some more subtle. Students can observe then generate lists of mistakes in small groups. Ask each group to give one error from their list and record what should have been done to ensure fair testing until all suggestions have been considered. (10 minutes)

Answers to in-text questions

a) Ensure that the different paints are exposed to exactly the same environmental factors.

b) Diagram of thermometer showing the true value with 4 readings tightly grouped around it.

How science works

MAIN

- Move into group discussion of question a. Other examples of field testing might include testing durability of paints, corrosion of metals at sea or durability of different plastics.
- Group discussions on how and why we need to produce survey data. Use a topical issue here. It might be appropriate to see how it should *not* be done by using a vox pop clip from a news programme.
- Students will be familiar with the idea of a placebo, but possibly not with how it is used to set up a control group. This might need explanation.
- Consider the case of whether it is possible to tell the difference in taste if the milk is put in before or after the tea. R.A. Fisher tested this, using a double-blind test and went on to devise 'Statistical Methods for Research Workers'.
- Students should work in groups to discuss question b. One person in each group should have the responsibility of reporting their answers to the class in a brief plenary.
- It is important that students appreciate the difference between accuracy and precision. They could be given a challenge to set up a water bath to be at a constant temperature and the teacher will check the temperature at an unknown time. The group with the temperature closest to the required temperature wins. Listening to excuses for failure will illustrate the ways in which reliability can be achieved! For this part of the lesson you will need various materials for constructing water baths, this probably will include material to insulate the beaker.
- Try finding the average of the whole class and see how reliable the methods are.
- Award a prize to the group showing the greatest accuracy.
- Find the maximum range for the whole class – who got the highest reading/who got the lowest? Can we explain why? Gather suggestions.

PLENARIES

Prize giving! – The winning group should explain why they think they got the most accurate results. (5 minutes)

Precision and accuracy – Discuss precision and accuracy in small groups then gather feedback. (10 minutes)

ACTIVITY & EXTENSION

The water bath test could be extended to commercial water baths or thermostat heaters. They could be tested to check their effectiveness in maintaining a 'constant' accurate temperature.

SUMMARY ANSWERS

1 Trial runs give you a good idea of whether you have the correct *conditions*; whether you have chosen the correct *range*; whether you have enough *readings*; if you need to do *repeat* readings.

2 Any example that demonstrates understanding of the two terms. e.g. I measured the loss in mass as 3.5 g, 4.8 g, 2.2 g, 3.8 g, 3.2 g. The average of my results is 3.5 g and the calculated value is 3.5 g.
So the set of repeat measurements were not precise, but the mean was accurate.

3 Control all the variables that might affect the dependent variable, apart from the independent variable whose values you select.

HOW SCIENCE WORKS

H4 Building an investigation

LEARNING OBJECTIVES
1 How do you design a fair test?
2 How do you make sure that you choose the best values for your variables?
3 How do you ensure accuracy and precision?

Fair testing

A **fair test** is one in which only the independent variable affects the dependent variable. All other variables are controlled.

This is easy to set up in the laboratory, but almost impossible in fieldwork. Imagine you were studying the quality of the water from wells at different distances from a factory. To make your investigation valid, you would want to take many samples from similar rock formations. You would choose sites where all of the many variables change in much the same way, except for the one you are investigating.

a) How would you set up an investigation to see how exposure to different amounts of sunlight affected different types of paint?

If you are investigating two variables in a large population then you will need to do a survey. Again it is impossible to control all of the other variables. Imagine you were investigating the effect of salt on blood pressure. You would have to choose people of the same age and same family history to test. The larger the sample size you test, the more reliable your results will be.

Control groups are used in investigations to try to make sure that you are measuring the variable that you intend to measure. When investigating the effects of a new drug, the control group will be given a placebo.

Figure 1 Different types of paint

The control group think they are taking a drug but the placebo does not contain the drug. This way you can control the variable of 'thinking' that the drug is working' and separate out the effect of the actual drug.

Choosing values of a variable

Trial runs will tell you a lot about how your early thoughts are going to work out.

Do you have the correct conditions?
Suppose you are finding out how much gas was produced when different masses of a chemical were added to some water. Only very small amounts of gas were produced.
- There might not have been enough chemical added.
- It might not have been left long enough.

Have you chosen a sensible range?
If there is enough gas produced, but the results all look about the same:
- you might not have chosen a wide enough range of masses of the chemical.

Have you got enough readings that are close together?
If the results are very different from each other:
- you might not see a pattern if you have large gaps between readings over the important part of the range.

DID YOU KNOW?
Schonbein a German chemist was so keen on his beloved chemistry that he used to take home experiments that he couldn't do in the lab. One day he spilt a hot mixture of two strong acids on the kitchen table. Seizing the first thing that he could see he mopped it up with his wife's cotton apron. Naturally he washed it and hung it out to dry. Soon after the apron exploded and disappeared into thin air. Schonbein had discovered gun cotton.

Accuracy
Accurate measurements are very close to the **true value**.

Your investigation should provide data that is accurate enough to answer your original question.

However, it is not always possible to know what the true value is.

How do you get accurate data?
- You can repeat your measurements and your mean is more likely to be accurate.
- Try repeating your measurements with a different instrument and see if you get the same readings.
- Use high quality instruments that measure accurately.
- The more carefully you use the measuring instruments, the more accuracy you will get.

Precision and reliability
If your repeated measurements are closely grouped together then you have precision and you have improved the reliability of your data.

Your investigation must provide data with sufficient precision. It's no use measuring the time for a fast reaction to finish using the seconds hand on a clock! If there are big differences within sets of repeat readings, you will not be able to make a valid conclusion. You won't be able to trust your data!

How do you get precise and reliable data?
- You have to use measuring instruments with sufficiently small scale divisions.
- You have to repeat your tests as often as necessary.
- You have to repeat your tests in exactly the same way each time.

A word of caution!
Be careful though – just because your results show precision does not mean your results are accurate. Look at the box opposite.

b) Draw a thermometer scale showing 4 results that are both accurate and precise.

The difference between accurate and precise results

Imagine measuring the temperature after a set time when a fuel is used to heat a fixed volume of water. Two students repeated this experiment, four times each. Their results are marked on the thermometer scales below:

Student A — Precise (but not accurate)
Student B — Accurate (but not precise)

- A precise set of repeat readings will be grouped closely together.
- An accurate set of repeat readings will have a mean (average) close to the true value.

SUMMARY QUESTIONS

1 Copy and complete using the following terms:

   range   repeat   conditions   readings

Trial runs give you a good idea of whether you have the correct ......; whether you have chosen the correct ......; whether you have enough ......; if you need to do ...... readings.

2 Use an example to explain how a set of repeat measurements could be accurate, but not precise.

3 Briefly describe how you would go about setting up a fair test in a laboratory investigation. Give your answer as general advice.

KEY POINTS
1 Care must be taken to ensure fair testing – as far as is possible.
2 You can use a trial run to make sure that you choose the best values for your variables.
3 Careful use of the correct equipment can improve accuracy.
4 If you repeat your results carefully they are likely to become more reliable.

HOW SCIENCE WORKS

H5 Making measurements

LEARNING OBJECTIVES

Students should learn:

- That they can expect results to vary.
- That instruments vary in their accuracy.
- That instruments vary in their sensitivity.
- That human error can affect results.
- What to do with anomalies.

LEARNING OUTCOMES

Students should be able to:

- Differentiate between results that vary and anomalies.
- Explain why it is important to use equipment properly.
- Explain that instruments vary in their accuracy and sensitivity.
- State the difference between random and systematic errors.

Teaching suggestions

- **Special needs.** Students will need support when interpreting data on oil and identifying evidence for random and systematic error.
- **Gifted and talented.** Demonstrate a different experiment in which there is a built-in systematic error, e.g. measuring the effect of temperature on the rate of an exothermic reaction.
- **Learning styles**
  Kinaesthetic: Taking measurements.
  Visual: Observing systematic error.
  Auditory: Listening to explanations of differences between random and systematic errors.
  Interpersonal: Group discussions to determine how to accurately measure the volume of gas.
  Intrapersonal: Answering questions d and e.
- **ICT link-up.** Using data logging to exemplify minor changes in dependent variables provides a good opportunity to include ICT in the lesson.

SPECIFICATION LINK-UP How Science Works

Section 10.5

Making measurements

When making measurements we must consider such issues as inherent variation due to variables that have not been controlled, human error and the characteristics of the instruments used. Evidence should be evaluated with the reliability and validity of the measurements that have been made in mind

A single measurement

- There will always be some variation in the actual value of a variable no matter how hard we try to repeat an event.
- When selecting an instrument, it is necessary to consider the accuracy inherent in the instrument and the way it has to be used.
- The sensitivity of an instrument refers to the smallest change in a value that can be detected.
- Even when an instrument is used correctly, human error may occur which could produce random differences in repeated readings or a systematic shift from the true value which could, for instance, occur due to incorrect use or poor calibration.
- Random error can result from inconsistent application of a technique. Systematic error can result from consistent misapplication of a technique.
- Any anomalous values should be examined to try to identify the cause and, if a product of a poor measurement, ignored.

Lesson structure

STARTER

Demonstration – Demonstrate different ways of measuring the volume of a gas produced in a chemical reaction. These could include displacement of water in a test tube, measuring cylinder or burette. Gas syringes could also be used. Bubbles could be counted. Conclude that the most accurate method is likely to be the burette or the gas syringe. (10 minutes)

MAIN

- In small groups, devise a method for testing the accuracy of the two methods, e.g. using a known volume of air pumped into each device.
- Choose a person to try out this technique. Stress that we do not have a true answer. We trust the instrument and the technique that is most likely to give us the most accurate result – the one nearest the true value.
- In groups, answer question a).
- Individually answer questions b) and c).
- Demonstrate an experiment in which there is a built-in systematic error, e.g. weighing some chemicals using a filter paper without using the tare or measuring radioactivity without taking background radiation into account.
- Point out the difference between this type of systematic error and random errors. Also, how you might tell from results which type of error it is. You can still have a high degree of precision with systematic errors.
- Complete questions d and e individually.

PLENARIES

Check list – Draw up a check list for an investigation so that every possible source of error is considered. (10–15 minutes)

Human vs computer – Class discussion of data logging compared to humans when collecting data. Stress the importance of data logging in gathering data over extended or very short periods of time.

How science works

Answers to in-text questions

a) Generally a failure to control variables, e.g. temperature of the oil might have changed. Tile might have moved slightly, temperature of tile might have changed, tile might not be as clean as it was, some oil might have remained from previous test, detergent might remain on tile, might not view finish line from same angle, student might not react as quickly when stopping watch.

b) Student is standing too far away and at the wrong angle to see when the oil reaches the line.

c)

Used to measure	Sensitivity of weighing machine
Cornflakes delivered to a supermarket	kilograms
Carbohydrate in a packet of cornflakes	grams
Vitamin D in a packet of cornflakes	micrograms
Sodium chloride in a packet of cornflakes	milligrams

d) First attempt for b is the random error.

e) Average results are close to individual results, which are consistently different to the calculated time.

ACTIVITY & EXTENSION IDEAS

Use data logging to illustrate how detailed measurements taken frequently can show variation in results that would not have been seen by other methods. It can increase considerably the accuracy of readings that can be taken where other readings might not be possible to take accurately. It can also illustrate a surfeit of data that might detract from the data required.

HOW SCIENCE WORKS

H5 Making measurements

LEARNING OBJECTIVES
1 Why do results always vary?
2 How do you choose instruments that will give you accurate results?
3 What do we mean by the sensitivity of an instrument?
4 How does human error affect results and what do you do with anomalies?

Using instruments

Do not panic! You cannot expect perfect results.

Try measuring the temperature of a beaker of water using a digital thermometer. Do you always get the same result? Probably not. So can we say that any measurement is absolutely correct?

In any experiment there will be doubts about actual measurements.

a) Look at Figure 1. Suppose, like this student, you tested the time it takes for one type of oil to flow down the tile. It is unlikely that you would get two readings exactly the same. Discuss all the possible reasons why.

When you choose an instrument you need to know that it will give you the accuracy that you want. That is, it will give you a true reading.

If you have used an electric water bath, would you trust the temperature on the dial? How do you know it is the true temperature? You could use a very expensive thermometer to calibrate your water bath. The expensive thermometer is more likely to show the true temperature. But can you really be sure it is accurate?

You also need to be able to use an instrument properly.

b) In Figure 1 the student is measuring the time it takes for the oil to reach the line. Why is the student unlikely to get a true measurement?

When you choose an instrument you need to decide how accurate you need it to be. Instruments that measure the same thing can have different sensitivities. The **sensitivity** of an instrument refers to the smallest change in a value that can be detected. This determines the precision of your measurements.

Choosing the wrong scale can cause you to miss important data or make silly conclusions, for example 'The amount of gold was the same in the two rings – they both weighed 5 grams.'

c) Match the following weighing machines to their best use:

Used to measure	Sensitivity of weighing machine
Cornflakes delivered to a supermarket	milligrams
Carbohydrate in a packet of cornflakes	grams
Vitamin D in a packet of cornflakes	micrograms
Sodium chloride in a packet of cornflakes	kilograms

Figure 1 Student reading the arrival of the oil

DID YOU KNOW?
Professor Hough was investigating possible uses of sucrose (ordinary sugar) in industry. He had created a molecule of sucrose with three atoms of chlorine in it. He asked his new assistant to 'test' it. His assistant thought he had said 'taste' it. Fortunately for his assistant it did him no harm, but he noticed how incredibly sweet it was – a thousand times sweeter than sugar!

Errors

Even when an instrument is used correctly, the results can still show differences.

Results may differ because of **random error**. This is most likely to be due to a poor measurement being made. It could be due to not carrying out the method consistently.

The error might be a **systematic error**. This means that the method was carried out consistently but an error was being repeated.

Check out these two sets of data that were taken from the investigation that Mark did. He tested 5 different oils. The third line is the time calculated from knowing the viscosity of the different oils:

Type of oil used	a	b	c	d	e
Time taken to flow down tile (seconds)	23.2	45.9	49.5	62.7	75.9
	24.1	36.4	48.7	61.5	76.1
Calculated time (seconds)	18.2	30.4	42.5	55.6	70.7

d) Discuss whether there is any evidence for random error in these results.
e) Discuss whether there is any evidence for systematic error in these results.

Anomalies

Anomalous results are clearly out of line. They are not those that are due to the natural variation you get from any measurement. These should be looked at carefully. There might be a very interesting reason why they are so different. If they are simply due to a random error, then they should be discarded (rejected).

If anomalies can be identified while you are doing an investigation, then it is best to repeat that part of the investigation.

If you find anomalies after you have finished collecting data for an investigation, then they must be discarded.

DID YOU KNOW?
Ludwig Mond was a very important industrial chemist. He was passing carbon monoxide over heated nickel powder. One evening after experimenting with this apparatus, his assistant noticed that as the equipment cooled it left a green flame rather than the usual blue flame. Mond really couldn't understand this and rather than ignoring this anomaly started to investigate. He eventually discovered that it was nickel carbonyl. This gave rise to a new way of extracting nickel from nickel ore and a whole new industry which was set up in Swansea.

SUMMARY QUESTIONS

1 Copy and complete using the words below:

accurate   discarded   random   sensitivity   systematic
use   variation

There will always be some …… in results. You should always choose the best instruments that you can to get the most …… results. You must know how to …… the instrument properly. The …… of an instrument refers to the smallest change that can be detected. There are two types of error – …… and …… . Anomalies due to random error should be …… .

2 Which of the following will lead to a systematic error and which to a random error?
a) Using a weighing machine, which has something stuck to the pan on the top.
b) Forgetting to re-zero the weighing machine.

KEY POINTS
1 Results will nearly always vary.
2 Better instruments give more accurate results.
3 Sensitivity of an instrument refers to the smallest change that it can detect.
4 Human error can produce random and systematic errors.
5 We examine anomalies; they might give us some interesting ideas. If they are due to a random error, we repeat the measurements. If there is no time to repeat them, we discard them.

SUMMARY ANSWERS

1 There will always be some *variation* in results. You should always choose the best instruments that you can to get the most *accurate* results. You must know how to *use* the instrument properly. The *sensitivity* of an instrument refers to the smallest change that can be detected. There are two types of error, *random* and *systematic*. Anomalies due to random error should be *discarded*.

2 a) systematic, b) random

KEY POINTS

- The students need to demonstrate an appreciation that accuracy and precision of measurement is a key feature in a successful investigation.

HOW SCIENCE WORKS

H6 Presenting data

LEARNING OBJECTIVES
Students should learn:
- What is meant by the range and the mean of a set of data.
- How to use tables of data.
- How to display data.

LEARNING OUTCOMES
Students should be able to:
- Express accurately the range and mean of a set of data.
- Distinguish between the uses of bar charts and line graphs.
- Draw line graphs accurately.

Teaching suggestions

- **Gifted and talented.** These students could be handling two dependent variables in the table and graph, e.g. temperature of reactants of volume of CO_2 produced.
- **Learning styles**
  Kinaesthetic: Practical activities.
  Visual: Making observations and presenting data.
  Auditory: Listening to group discussions.
  Interpersonal: Participating in group discussions on the choice of suitable tables/graphs.
  Intrapersonal: Produce own table and graph.
- **ICT link-up.** Students could use a set of data with, e.g., Excel to present the data in different ways, such as pie charts, line graphs, bar charts, etc. Allow them to decide on the most appropriate form. Care needs to be given to 'smoothing' which does not always produce a line of best fit.

SPECIFICATION LINK-UP   How Science Works

Section 10.6

Presenting data

To explain the relationship between two or more variables, data may be presented in such a way as to make the patterns more evident. There is a link between the type of graph used and the variable they represent. The choice of graphical representation depends upon the type of variable they represent.

Students should know and understand:
- The range of the data refers to the maximum and minimum values.
- The mean (or average) of the data refers to the sum of all the measurements divided by the number of measurements taken.
- Tables are an effective means of displaying data but are limited in how they portray the design of an investigation.
- Bar charts can be used to display data in which the independent variable is categoric and the dependent variable continuous.
- Line graphs can be used to display data in which both the independent and dependent variables are continuous.

Lesson structure

STARTER

Excel – Prepare some data from a typical investigation that the students may have recently completed. Use all of the many ways of presenting the data in Excel to display it. Allow students to discuss and reach conclusions as to which is the best method. (10 minutes)

Newspapers – Choose data from the press – particularly useful are market trends where they do not use 0,0. This exaggerates changes. This could relate to the use of data logging which can exaggerate normal variation into major trends. (5 minutes)

MAIN

- Choose an appropriate topic to either demonstrate or allow small groups to gather data. E.g., production of CO_2 from 0.5M HCl and $CaCO_3$ over 1 minute; using food labels to determine saturated oil content of different foods. Any topic that will allow rapid gathering of data. Be aware that some data will lead to a bar chart, this might be more appropriate to groups struggling to draw line graphs.
- Students should be told what their task is and therefore know how to construct an appropriate table. This should be done individually prior to collecting the data. Refer to the first paragraph under 'Table'.
- Group discussion on the best form of table.
- Carry out data gathering, putting data directly into table. Refer to the second paragraph under 'Table'.
- Individuals produce their own graphs. Refer to the 'Next time you . . .'. box.
- Graphs could be exchanged and marked by others in the group, using the criteria in the paragraph mentioned above.

PLENARIES

Which type of graph? – Give students different headings from a variety of tables and ask them how best to show the results graphically. This could be done as a whole class with individuals showing answers as the teacher reveals each table heading. Each student can draw a large letter 'L' (for line graph) on one side of a sheet of paper and 'B' (for bar chart) on the other, ready to show their answers. (5 minutes)

Key words – Students should be given key words to prepare posters for the lab. Key words should be taken from the summary questions in the first six sections. (10 minutes)

Crossword – The students should complete a crossword based on the previous five lessons. (15 minutes)

How science works

ACTIVITY & EXTENSION

Lower-attaining students should start with bar charts and move on to line graphs. Higher-attaining students ought to be practising the skills learned earlier whilst gathering their data. They could also be given more difficult contexts that are more likely to produce anomalies. They could, for example, be given a context that produces both random and systematic errors, e.g. dropping ball bearings through oils with different viscosities.

HOW SCIENCE WORKS

H6 Presenting data

LEARNING OBJECTIVES
1. What do we mean by the 'range' and the 'mean' of the data?
2. How do you use tables of results?
3. How do you display your data?

For this section you will be working with data from this investigation:

Mel took a litre (1 dm^3) of tap water. She shook it vigorously for exactly 2 minutes. She tried to get as much oxygen to dissolve in it as possible. Then she took the temperature of the water. She immediately tested the oxygen concentration, using an oxygen meter.

Tables

Tables are really good for getting your results down quickly and clearly. You should design your table **before** you start your investigation.

Your table should be constructed to fit in all the data to be collected. It should be fully labelled, including units.

In some investigations, particularly fieldwork, it is useful to have an extra column for any notes you might want to make as you work.

While filling in your table of results you should be constantly looking for anomalies.

- Check to see if a repeat is sufficiently close to the first reading.
- Check to see if the pattern you are getting as you change the independent variable is what you expected.

Remember a result that looks anomalous should be checked out to see if it really is a poor reading or if it might suggest a different hypothesis.

Figure 1 Student using an oxygen meter

Planning your table

Mel knew the values for her independent variable. We always put these in the first column of a table. The dependent variable goes in the second column. Mel will find its values as she carries out the investigation.

So she could plan a table like this:

Temperature of water (°C)	Concentration of oxygen (mg/dm^3)
5	
10	
16	
20	
28	

Or like this:

Temperature of water (°C)	5	10	16	20	28
Concentration of oxygen (mg/dm^3)					

All she had to do in the investigation was to write the correct numbers in the second column to complete the top table.

Mel's results are shown in the alternative format in the table below:

Temperature of water (°C)	5	10	16	20	28
Concentration of oxygen (mg/dm^3)	12.8	11.3	9.9	9.1	7.3

The range of the data

Pick out the maximum and the minimum values and you have the range. You should always quote these two numbers when asked for a range. For example, the range is between .... (the lowest value) and .... (the highest value) – and don't forget to include the units!

a) What is the range for the independent variable and for the dependent variable in Mel's set of data?

The mean of the data

Often you have to find the mean of each repeated set of measurements. You add up the measurements in the set and divide by how many there are. Miss out any anomalies you find.

The repeat values and mean can be recorded as shown below:

Temperature of water (°C)	Concentration of oxygen (mg/dm^3)			
	1st test	2nd test	3rd test	Mean

Displaying your results

Bar charts
If you have a categoric or an ordered independent variable and a continuous dependent variable then you should use a bar chart.

Line graphs
If you have a continuous independent and a continuous dependent variable then a line graph should be used.

Scatter graphs or scattergrams
Scatter graphs are used in much the same way as line graphs, but you might not expect to be able to draw such a clear line of best fit. For example, if you wanted to see if people's lung capacity was related to how long they could hold their breath, you would draw a scatter graph with your results.

SUMMARY QUESTIONS

1. Copy and complete using the words below:

   categoric   continuous   mean   range

   The maximum and minimum values show the ...... of the data. The sum of all the values divided by the total number of the values gives the .... Bar charts are used when you have a ...... independent variable and a continuous dependent variable.
   Line graphs are used when you have ...... independent and dependent variables.

2. Draw a graph of Mel's results from the top of this page.

NEXT TIME YOU...
... make a table for your results remember to include:
- headings,
- units,
- a title.

... draw a line graph remember to include:
- the independent variable on the x-axis,
- the dependent variable on the y-axis,
- a line of best fit,
- labels, units and a title.

GET IT RIGHT!
Marks are often dropped in the ISA by candidates plotting points incorrectly. Also use a line of best fit where appropriate – don't just join the points 'dot-to-dot'!

KEY POINTS
1. The range states the maximum and the minimum values.
2. The mean is the sum of the values divided by how many values there are.
3. Tables are best used during an investigation to record results.
4. Bar charts are used when you have a categoric or an ordered independent variable and a continuous dependent variable.
5. Line graphs are used to display data that are continuous.

SUMMARY ANSWERS

1. The maximum and minimum values show the *range* of the data. The sum of all the values divided by the total number of the values gives the *mean*. Bar charts are used when you have a *categoric or ordered* independent and a *continuous* dependent variable. Line graphs are used when you have *continuous* independent and dependent variables.

2. Student graph.

Answers to in-text question

a) Independent variable: 5°C to 28°C, dependent variable: 7.3 mg/dm^2 to 12.8 mg/dm^2.

KEY POINTS

- The students should be able to produce their own correctly labelled table and graph.

HOW SCIENCE WORKS

H7 Using data to draw conclusions

LEARNING OBJECTIVES
Students should learn:
- How to use charts and graphs to identify patterns.
- How to draw accurate conclusions from relationships.
- How to improve the reliability of an investigation.

LEARNING OUTCOMES
Students should be able to:
- Identify patterns using charts and graphs.
- Develop patterns and relationships into conclusions.
- Evaluate the reliability of an investigation.

Teaching suggestions

- **Special needs.** Provide a flow diagram so that students can see the process as they are going through it.
- **Gifted and talented.** Students could take the original investigation then design out some of the flaws, producing an investigation with improved validity and reliability. Summary question 2 could be examined in some detail and the work researched on the web.
- **Learning styles**
  Kinaesthetic: Drawing graphs.
  Visual: Observing tests.
  Auditory: Discussing the concepts of reliability and validity of whole investigations.
  Interpersonal: Generating a flow diagram together.
  Intrapersonal: Evaluating the reliability and validity of their own tests.
- **ICT link-up/activity.** ICT can be used to quickly create data for graphs in the lesson and this will generate a good volume of data for discussion. Some ICT support is needed for rapid production of graphs.
  Data logging will be useful for gathering data from two dependent variables for the gifted and talented.

SPECIFICATION LINK-UP   How Science Works
Section 10.7
Using data to draw conclusions

The patterns and relationships observed in data represent the behaviour of the variables in an investigation. However, it is necessary to look at patterns and relationships between variables with the limitations of the data in mind.

Students should know and understand:
- *Patterns in tables and graphs can be used to identify anomalous data that require further consideration.*
- *A line of best fit can be used to illustrate the underlying relationship between variables.*
- *The relationships that exist between variables can be linear (positive or negative), directly proportional, predictable curves, complex curves and relationships not easily represented by a mathematical relationship.*
- *Conclusions must be limited by the data available and not go beyond them.*

Evaluation
- *In evaluating a whole investigation, the reliability and validity of the data obtained must be considered. Reliability and validity of an investigation can be increased by looking at data obtained from secondary sources, through using an alternative method as a check and by requiring that the results are reproducible by others.*

Lesson structure

STARTER

Starter graphs – Prepare a series of graphs that illustrate the various types of relationships in the specification. Each graph should have fully labelled axes. Students should, in groups, agree statements that describe the patterns in the graphs. Gather feedback from groups and discuss. (10 minutes)

MAIN

- Using the graphs from the previous lesson, students should be taught how to produce lines of best fit. (Develop own data if this is not available or in the form of a bar graph.) Students could work individually with help from the first section of H6 'Presenting data'.
- They should identify the pattern in their graph.
- They now need to consider the reliability and validity of their results. They may need their understanding of reliability and validity reinforced. How this is achieved will depend on the investigation chosen in H6 'Presenting data'. Questions can be posed to reinforce their understanding of both terms. If the investigation was not carefully controlled, then it is likely to be unreliable and invalid, thus posing many opportunities for discussion. There is also an opportunity to reinforce other ideas such as random and systematic errors.
- If the previous activity is unlikely to yield these opportunities, then a brief demonstration of a test, e.g. finding the energy transfer when burning fuel of different mass could be used. Students should observe the teacher and make notes as the tests are carried out. They should be as critical as they can be, and in small groups discuss their individual findings. One or two students could be recording the results and two more plotting the graph as the teacher does the tests. These could be processed immediately onto the screen.
- Return to the original prediction. Look at the graph of the results. Ask how much confidence the group has in the results.
- Review the links that are possible between two sets of data. Ask them to decide which one their tests might support.
- Now the word 'conclusion' should be introduced and a conclusion made – if possible! It is sometimes useful to make a conclusion that is 'subject to . . . e.g. the reliability being demonstrated'.

14

PLENARIES

Flow diagram – When pulling the lesson together, it will be important to emphasise the process involved – graph – line of best fit – pattern – question the reliability and validity – consider the links that are possible – make a conclusion – summarise evaluation. This could be illustrated with a flow diagram generated by a directed class discussion.
(5 minutes)

Key words – Students should be given key words to complete the posters for the lab.
(10 minutes)

ACTIVITY & EXTENSION IDEAS

Students should be able to transfer these skills to examine the work of scientists and to become critical of the work of others. Collecting scientific findings from the press and subjecting them to the same critical appraisal is an important exercise. They could be encouraged to collect these or be given photocopies of topical issues suitable for such appraisal.

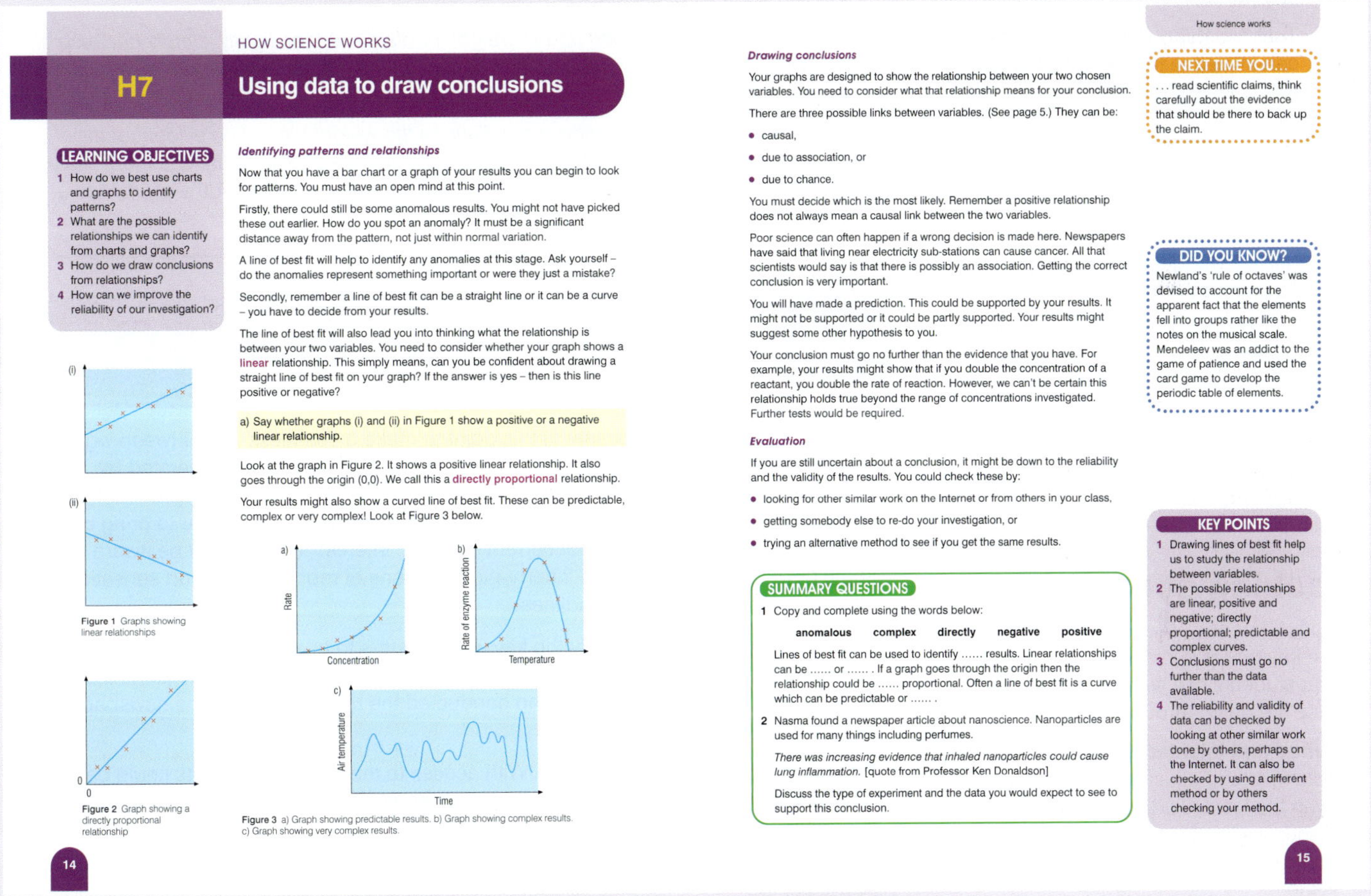

HOW SCIENCE WORKS

H7 Using data to draw conclusions

LEARNING OBJECTIVES
1. How do we best use charts and graphs to identify patterns?
2. What are the possible relationships we can identify from charts and graphs?
3. How do we draw conclusions from relationships?
4. How can we improve the reliability of our investigation?

Identifying patterns and relationships

Now that you have a bar chart or a graph of your results you can begin to look for patterns. You must have an open mind at this point.

Firstly, there could still be some anomalous results. You might not have picked these out earlier. How do you spot an anomaly? It must be a significant distance away from the pattern, not just within normal variation.

A line of best fit will help to identify any anomalies at this stage. Ask yourself – do the anomalies represent something important or were they just a mistake?

Secondly, remember a line of best fit can be a straight line or it can be a curve – you have to decide from your results.

The line of best fit will also lead you into thinking what the relationship is between your two variables. You need to consider whether your graph shows a **linear** relationship. This simply means, can you be confident about drawing a straight line of best fit on your graph? If the answer is yes – then is this line positive or negative?

a) Say whether graphs (i) and (ii) in Figure 1 show a positive or a negative linear relationship.

Look at the graph in Figure 2. It shows a positive linear relationship. It also goes through the origin (0,0). We call this a **directly proportional** relationship.

Your results might also show a curved line of best fit. These can be predictable, complex or very complex! Look at Figure 3 below.

Figure 1 Graphs showing linear relationships

Figure 2 Graph showing a directly proportional relationship

Figure 3 a) Graph showing predictable results. b) Graph showing complex results. c) Graph showing very complex results.

Drawing conclusions

Your graphs are designed to show the relationship between your two chosen variables. You need to consider what that relationship means for your conclusion.

There are three possible links between variables. (See page 5.) They can be:
- causal,
- due to association, or
- due to chance.

You must decide which is the most likely. Remember a positive relationship does not always mean a causal link between the two variables.

Poor science can often happen if a wrong decision is made here. Newspapers have said that living near electricity sub-stations can cause cancer. All that scientists would say is that there is possibly an association. Getting the correct conclusion is very important.

You will have made a prediction. This could be supported by your results. It might not be supported or it could be partly supported. Your results might suggest some other hypothesis to you.

Your conclusion must go no further than the evidence that you have. For example, your results might show that if you double the concentration of a reactant, you double the rate of reaction. However, we can't be certain this relationship holds true beyond the range of concentrations investigated. Further tests would be required.

Evaluation

If you are still uncertain about a conclusion, it might be down to the reliability and the validity of the results. You could check these by:
- looking for other similar work on the Internet or from others in your class,
- getting somebody else to re-do your investigation, or
- trying an alternative method to see if you get the same results.

SUMMARY QUESTIONS

1. Copy and complete using the words below:

   anomalous   complex   directly   negative   positive

   Lines of best fit can be used to identify ...... results. Linear relationships can be ...... or .... If a graph goes through the origin then the relationship could be ...... proportional. Often a line of best fit is a curve which can be predictable or ....

2. Nasma found a newspaper article about nanoscience. Nanoparticles are used for many things including perfumes.

   There was increasing evidence that inhaled nanoparticles could cause lung inflammation. [quote from Professor Ken Donaldson]

   Discuss the type of experiment and the data you would expect to see to support this conclusion.

NEXT TIME YOU...
...read scientific claims, think carefully about the evidence that should be there to back up the claim.

DID YOU KNOW?
Newland's 'rule of octaves' was devised to account for the apparent fact that the elements fell into groups rather like the notes on the musical scale. Mendeleev was an addict to the game of patience and used the card game to develop the periodic table of elements.

KEY POINTS
1. Drawing lines of best fit help us to study the relationship between variables.
2. The possible relationships are linear, positive and negative; directly proportional; predictable and complex curves.
3. Conclusions must go no further than the data available.
4. The reliability and validity of data can be checked by looking at other similar work done by others, perhaps on the Internet. It can also be checked by using a different method or by others checking your method.

SUMMARY ANSWERS

1. Lines of best fit can be used to identify *anomalous* results. Linear relationships can be *positive* or *negative*. If a graph goes through the origin then the relationship could be *directly* proportional. Often a line of best fit is a curve which can be predictable or *complex*.

2. Some of the following ideas: two large groups of people, one using the perfume without nanoparticles, others using nanoparticle perfume – both groups not identified as having any inflammation of the lung – each participant given questionnaire to be completed daily – questionnaire asks about clinical symptoms related to lung inflamation – [control group idea – fieldwork idea]. Data expected would include range and means (averages) of clinical factors for the two groups. Opportunity to discuss medical ethics and whether trials with animals should first be carried out.

KEY POINTS

- The students should appreciate the process involved from the production of a graph to the conclusion and evaluation.

Answers to in-text questions

a) (i) Positive linear relationship
   (ii) Negative linear relationship

HOW SCIENCE WORKS

H8 Scientific evidence and society

LEARNING OBJECTIVES

Students should learn:

- That science must be presented in a way that takes into account the reliability and the validity of the evidence.
- That science should be presented without bias from the experimenter.
- That evidence must be checked to appreciate whether there is any political influence.
- That the status of experimenter can influence the weight attached to a scientific report.

LEARNING OUTCOMES

Students should be able to:

- Make judgements about the reliability and the validity of scientific evidence.
- Identify when scientific evidence might have been influenced by bias or political influence.
- Judge scientific evidence on its merits, taking into account the weight given to it by the status of the experimenter.

Teaching suggestions

- **Special needs.** Provide a diagram with the key points in order of discussion so that students can see the process as they are going through it.
- **Gifted and talented.** Students might be able to attend a local public enquiry or even the local town council as it discusses local issues with a scientific context or consider the report of a local issue.
- **Learning styles**
  Kinaesthetic: Role play.
  Visual: Researching data.
  Auditory: Class and small group discussion on possible bias in newspaper reporting of scientific issues.
  Interpersonal: Class and small group discussion on siting of cement works.
  Intrapersonal: Considering the influences on research to personal life.
- **ICT link-up.** The Internet exercise on researching the issue of waste incinerators in the main part of the lesson is a good ICT activity. This could considerably increase the volume and improve the presentation of data for discussion. Some students may require support for downloading data from the Internet.

SPECIFICATION LINK-UP   How Science Works

Section 10.8

Societal aspects of scientific evidence

A judgement or decision relating to social-scientific issues may not be based on evidence alone, as other societal factors may be relevant.

Students should know and understand:

- *The credibility of the evidence is increased if a balanced account of the data is used rather than a selection from it which supports a particular pre-determined stance.*
- *Evidence must be scrutinised for any potential bias of the experimenter, such as funding sources or allegiances.*
- *Evidence can be accorded undue weight, or dismissed too lightly, simply because of its political significance. If the consequences of the evidence might provoke public or political disquiet, the evidence may be downplayed.*
- *The status of the experimenter may influence the weight placed on evidence; for instance, academic or professional status, experience and authority. It is more likely that the advice of an eminent scientist will be sought to help provide a solution to a problem than a scientist with less experience.*

Lesson structure

STARTER

Ask a scientist – It is necessary at this point to make a seamless join between work which has mostly been derived from student investigations to work generated by scientists. Students must be able to use their critical skills derived in familiar contexts and apply them to second-hand data. One way to achieve this would be to bring in newspaper cuttings on a topic of current scientific interest. They should be aware that some newspaper reporters will 'cherry-pick' sections of reports to support sensational claims that will make good headlines.

Students could be prompted by the key word posters to question some of the assumptions being made. This could be presented as a 'wish-list' of questions they would like to put to the scientists who conducted the research and to the newspaper reporter. (10 minutes)

Researching scientific evidence – With access to the Internet, students could be given a topic to research. They should use a search engine and identify the sources of information from, say, the first six web pages. They could then discuss the relative merits of these sources in terms of potential for bias.

MAIN

- The following points are best made using topics that are of immediate importance to your students. The examples used are only illustrative. Some forward planning is required to ensure that there is a plentiful supply of newspaper articles, both local and national, to support the lesson. These could be displayed and/or retained in a portfolio for reference.
- Working in pairs, students should answer question a). They should write a few sentences about the advert and what it means to them. Follow this with a class discussion, building up many more questions that need to be answered.
- It might be possible to follow this article on the Internet to find out what folic acid is used for in the body. It should lead to a balanced discussion of the possible benefits and hazards of folic acid being added to the diet. What is the daily-required amount? Do we need it as a supplement in our diet?
- Use the next section to illustrate the possibility of bias in reporting science. Again use small group discussions followed by whole class plenary.

If you have access to the Internet for the whole class, then it is worth pursuing the issue of waste incinerators. Pose the question: 'What would happen to waste disposal if it was determined that incineration was too dangerous?' Would different people come together to suppress that information? Should they be allowed to suppress scientific evidence? Stress that there is some evidence for and some against, and some people have that fear. Why do they have that fear? Should scientists have the task of reducing that fear to proper proportions? There is much to discuss.

- Small groups can imagine that they are preparing a case against the siting of a cement works close to their village. They could be given data that relates to pollution levels from similar companies. Up-to-date data can be obtained from the web, e.g. from the DEFRA website. Students could be given the data as if it were information provided at a public enquiry for the cement works. They should be asked to prepare a case that questions, e.g., the reliability and the validity of the data. This links with work covered in the first chapter of C1 on limestone.

ACTIVITY & EXTENSION

Students could role play a public enquiry. They could be given roles and asked to prepare a case for homework. The data should be available to them so that they all know the arguments before preparing their case. Possible link here with the English department.

PLENARIES

Group report – Groups should report their findings on the cement works case to the class. (10 minutes)

Scientific data posters – Groups could prepare posters that use scientific data to present their case for or against any of the developments discussed. (10–15 minutes)

KEY POINTS

- The students should show in discussions that they can apply the skills developed in their own investigative work to scientific evidence generated by professional scientists.

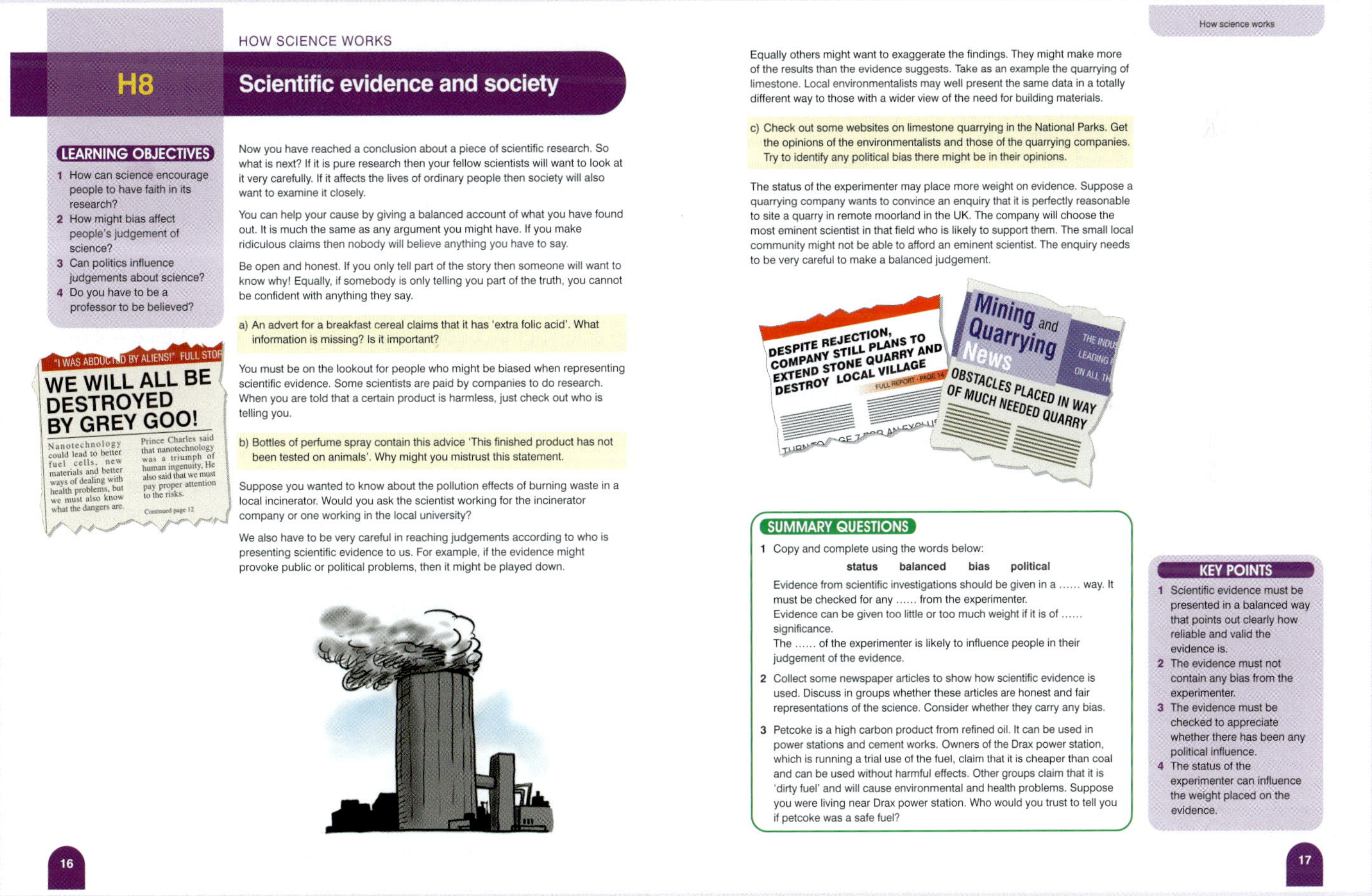

H8 Scientific evidence and society

LEARNING OBJECTIVES
1. How can science encourage people to have faith in its research?
2. How might bias affect people's judgement of science?
3. Can politics influence judgements about science?
4. Do you have to be a professor to be believed?

Now you have reached a conclusion about a piece of scientific research. So what is next? If it is pure research then your fellow scientists will want to look at it very carefully. If it affects the lives of ordinary people then society will also want to examine it closely.

You can help your cause by giving a balanced account of what you have found out. It is much the same as any argument you might have. If you make ridiculous claims then nobody will believe anything you have to say.

Be open and honest. If you only tell part of the story then someone will want to know why! Equally, if somebody is only telling you part of the truth, you cannot be confident with anything they say.

a) An advert for a breakfast cereal claims that it has 'extra folic acid'. What information is missing? Is it important?

You must be on the lookout for people who might be biased when representing scientific evidence. Some scientists are paid by companies to do research. When you are told that a certain product is harmless, just check out who is telling you.

b) Bottles of perfume spray contain this advice 'This finished product has not been tested on animals'. Why might you mistrust this statement.

Suppose you wanted to know about the pollution effects of burning waste in a local incinerator. Would you ask the scientist working for the incinerator company or one working in the local university?

We also have to be very careful in reaching judgements according to who is presenting scientific evidence to us. For example, if the evidence might provoke public or political problems, then it might be played down.

Equally others might want to exaggerate the findings. They might make more of the results than the evidence suggests. Take as an example the quarrying of limestone. Local environmentalists may well present the same data in a totally different way to those with a wider view of the need for building materials.

c) Check out some websites on limestone quarrying in the National Parks. Get the opinions of the environmentalists and those of the quarrying companies. Try to identify any political bias there might be in their opinions.

The status of the experimenter may place more weight on evidence. Suppose a quarrying company wants to convince an enquiry that it is perfectly reasonable to site a quarry in remote moorland in the UK. The company will choose the most eminent scientist in that field who is likely to support them. The small local community might not be able to afford an eminent scientist. The enquiry needs to be very careful to make a balanced judgement.

SUMMARY QUESTIONS
1. Copy and complete using the words below:

   status   balanced   bias   political

   Evidence from scientific investigations should be given in a ...... way. It must be checked for any ...... from the experimenter.
   Evidence can be given too little or too much weight if it is of ...... significance.
   The ...... of the experimenter is likely to influence people in their judgement of the evidence.

2. Collect some newspaper articles to show how scientific evidence is used. Discuss in groups whether these articles are honest and fair representations of the science. Consider whether they carry any bias.

3. Petcoke is a high carbon product from refined oil. It can be used in power stations and cement works. Owners of the Drax power station, which is running a trial use of the fuel, claim that it is cheaper than coal and can be used without harmful effects. Other groups claim that it is 'dirty fuel' and will cause environmental and health problems. Suppose you were living near Drax power station. Who would you trust to tell you if petcoke was a safe fuel?

KEY POINTS
1. Scientific evidence must be presented in a balanced way that points out clearly how reliable and valid the evidence is.
2. The evidence must not contain any bias from the experimenter.
3. The evidence must be checked to appreciate whether there has been any political influence.
4. The status of the experimenter can influence the weight placed on the evidence.

SUMMARY ANSWERS

1. Evidence from scientific investigations should be given in a *balanced* way. It must be checked for any *bias* from the experimenter. Evidence can be given too little or too much weight if it is of *political* significance. The *status* of the experimenter is likely to influence people in their judgement of the evidence.

2. Identification of any bias in reports.

3. Should be independent. Should have the necessary skills as a scientist. Should not be capable of being influenced politically.

Answers to in-text questions

a) E.g. what level of folic acid is required; is there a safe limit?; what evidence is there that folic acid is required?; how much do we get in a normal diet?

b) It might not be safe for humans to use. The constituents of the perfume might have been tested on animals before being made into the final product.

c) Identification of any political bias, this could be from companies and individuals as well as governments.

HOW SCIENCE WORKS

H9 How is science used for everybody's benefit?

LEARNING OBJECTIVES

Students should learn:

- That scientific enquiry can result in technological developments.
- That scientific and technological developments can be exploited by different people in different ways.
- That scientific and technological developments can raise ethical, social, economic and environmental issues.
- That different decisions concerning these issues are made by different groups of people.
- That there are many scientific questions unanswered and some questions that can never be answered by science.

LEARNING OUTCOMES

Students should be able to:

- Recognise links between science and technology.
- Recognise when people exploit scientific and technological developments.
- Recognise ethical, social, economic and environmental issues raised by scientific and technological developments.
- Show how scientific and technological developments raise different issues for different groups of people.
- Discuss how scientific questions remain unanswered and recognise the limitations of science for answering some questions.

KEY POINTS

- The students should show in their discussions that they appreciate the link between science and technology.
- Students should be more aware that science and technology raises different issues for different people.

SPECIFICATION LINK-UP How Science Works

Section 10.8 continued

- *Scientific knowledge gained through investigations can be the basis for technological developments.*
- *Scientific and technological developments offer different opportunities for exploitation to different groups of people.*
- *The uses of science and technology developments can raise ethical, social, economic and environmental issues.*
- *Decisions are made by individuals and by society on issues relating to science and technology.*

Section 10.9

Limitations of scientific evidence

Science can help us in many ways but it cannot supply all the answers.

We are still finding out about things and developing our scientific knowledge. There are some questions that we cannot answer, maybe because we do not have enough reliable and valid evidence.

And there are some questions that science cannot answer at all. These tend to be questions where beliefs and opinions are important or where we cannot collect reliable and valid scientific evidence.

Lesson structure

STARTER

Technological development Part 1 – Choose a technological development where students can appreciate the science that underpins its operation. Your choice will be largely based on the students' level of scientific knowledge. Examples might include: electrolysis, water softeners, cement, steel, alloys, antacid tablets or a catalytic converter. They might research the science for homework. Provide a variety of appropriate pieces of technology to be available, enough for one per small group

Asking students to offer any scientific knowledge that they have related to that technological development can generate discussions. The knowledge can then be evaluated in terms of its importance to the technological development. (10 minutes)

Science as a basis for technological development – Choose a topic that the students have studied from the substantive content or KS3. Or demonstrate a simple phenomenon such as neutralisation. Allow the students to generate their own ideas as to how this scientific knowledge could be used to develop a range of technologies. (10 minutes)

MAIN

- Divide the students into small groups and give each group a different technological development. They should be asked to discuss the different uses to which they have been put. They could offer other ideas for which they might not have been used. They do not have to stay with that actual example but can drift into other developments.
- A plenary session in which one of the group reports their findings to the others. Discussions could then include whether these uses were of general benefit or not.
- If any groups come up with novel ideas as to how to make better use of some of the technology then you could spin the idea of economic development.
- Do any of the ideas raise environmental issues?
- Do any of the ideas raise ethical issues?
- Do any of the ideas raise social issues?
- At this point it might be appropriate to cut to the example in the book. Students could read through this on their own or it could be read and explained as a class or in small groups with support. It might be appropriate to intervene at points to make sure the relevance of each of the learning objectives is appreciated.
- How the discussion is handled will depend on how the reading was organised. It would be useful to allow small group discussion for questions 3 and 4.

Teaching suggestions

- **Special needs.** Small groups will need sympathetic support to work their way through these ideas. It might be more appropriate to separate the lesson in two, dealing with the science behind the technologies separately from the issues raised.
- **Gifted and talented**
  - Students could research their own scientific story and respond to the same issues, e.g. oil industry.
  - The scientific research that led to an understanding of the uses of coal led to the technological development of the steam engine. This could be contrasted with the invention of a steam-powered temple door opener by Egyptians, without prior scientific work. Definitions of science as opposed to technology could be explored. The Egyptians also had weighing scales, cosmetics, inks, locks and, at the time, were well ahead of the Greeks in terms of these technological developments.
- **Learning styles**

Kinaesthetic: Examining the technology.

Visual: Observing equipment.

Auditory: Class and small group discussion on uses of science and technological developments.

Interpersonal: Class and small group discussion.

Intrapersonal: Reflecting on the issues related to energy issues.

ACTIVITY & EXTENSION IDEAS

Could visit a local museum to see how local industry might have used science for its technologies.

How science works

H9 — How is science used for everybody's benefit?

LEARNING OBJECTIVES
1. How does science link to technology?
2. How is science used and abused?
3. How are decisions made about science?
4. What are the limitations of science?

Coal has been burned for centuries as a source of energy. Experiments to capture the energy from burning coal were being carried out in the early 18th century. Thomas Newcomen's experimentation led to him inventing a steam engine.

James Watt was asked to repair an engine that used steam and realised that it would only go a few strokes at a time. He experimented still further to increase the efficiency of the steam engine. The unit of 'power' was named in his honour.

These investigations and their development into technologies were the foundation of the industrial revolution. At this time it seemed to ordinary people that the only problems with coal were the smell and the soot. The people who were making the most money out of these new developments could live well away from the pollution.

Coal remains a very important fuel – 38% of electricity is generated from coal. World-wide coal consumption is expected to grow by 40% before 2025.

Investigations into the effect of carbon dioxide on the atmosphere have shown that increased amounts of carbon dioxide are leading to global warming. Burning coal produces 9 billion tonnes of CO_2 each year, about a third of all CO_2 emissions world-wide.

Investigations have shown that new ways of burning coal, e.g. fluidised bed, mean that less CO_2 per kWh is produced. However CO_2 is still produced. It is too expensive to separate from the waste gases and so still contributes to global warming.

There are two approaches to cutting down CO_2 production. We can burn less fossil fuel or we can remove carbon dioxide from the waste gases of power stations and motor vehicles.

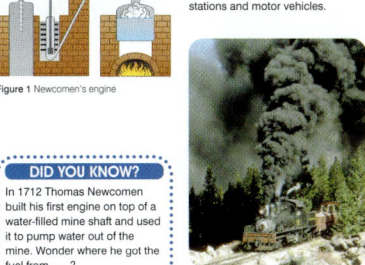

Experiments have taken place to change coal into CO_2 and H_2. The carbon from the coal is reacted with hot water to produce CO and H_2, then the CO and H_2O gives CO_2 and H_2. The hydrogen has five times the energy per kilogram as coal. It could be used to drive cars as well as power stations. Burning hydrogen in oxygen produces water.

The waste CO_2 is separated from the hydrogen. The CO_2 can then be piped into underground caverns left by oil and gas extraction. Here it cannot cause global warming – until it escapes!

The world's first large-scale CO_2 storage technology is being used in Norway. It is in an old gas field called Sleipner, and can store 600 billion tonnes of CO_2.

This technology was developed for removing CO_2 from natural gas using hot potassium carbonate. This process is still very expensive.

Experimentation suggests that the overall efficiency will be 60%.

There are many questions still to be answered. Can this technology be developed to allow all countries to be able to afford it?

There are questions which science cannot answer. For example, 'Should we develop technology or reduce energy use to reduce the effects of global warming?' Questions like this will have to be answered by the politicians that we elect.

Figure 1 Newcomen's engine

DID YOU KNOW?
In 1712 Thomas Newcomen built his first engine on top of a water-filled mine shaft and used it to pump water out of the mine. Wonder where he got the fuel from . . . ?

Figure 2 A smoky steam engine

Figure 3 A coal-fired power station

Figure 4 Changing coal into CO_2 and H_2

Figure 5 Sleipner field oil rig

SUMMARY QUESTIONS

Use the account of the development of coal technology to answer these questions:
1. What early scientific work enabled James Watt to improve on the steam engine?
2. Use your own knowledge and that in the account above to describe some of the different ways in which the energy from coal has been used.
3. a) Identify some of these issues raised by the use of coal as a fuel source:
   i) ethical, ii) social, iii) economic, iv) environmental.
   b) Which of these issues are decided by individuals and which by society?

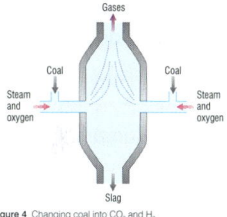

KEY POINTS
1. Scientific knowledge can be used to develop technologies.
2. People can exploit scientific and technological developments to suit their own purposes.
3. The uses of science and technology can raise ethical, social, economic and environmental issues.
4. These issues are decided upon by individuals and by society.
5. There are many questions left for science to answer. But science cannot answer questions that start with 'Should we .... ?'

PLENARIES

Technological development Part 2 – Take another technological development, such as smart alloys, and use it as an example to help the group discuss all of the issues raised by the lesson. (5 minutes)

SUMMARY ANSWERS

1. James Watt experimented on the efficiency of the steam engine.
2. Energy from coal has been used for, e.g., transport, industrial devices such as pumps, farming devices, electricity generation.
3. a) i) E.g. should we be destroying so much of the environment in pursuit of more energy? ii) E.g. focussed populations on the sources of coal in early industrial revolution. iii) E.g. has given work to a wide range of differently skilled people. iv) E.g. global warming, open cast mining.
   b) i) Decided by individuals. ii) By individuals and society iii) and iv) decided by society.

HOW SCIENCE WORKS

SUMMARY ANSWERS

1 a) Could be some differences which would be fine, e.g. prediction; design; safety; controls; method; table; results; repeat; graph; conclusion; improve.

2 a) Scientific opinion is based on reliable and valid evidence, an opinion might not be.

  b) Continuous variable because it is more informative than an ordered or a categoric variable.

  c) A causal link is where only one independent variable has an effect on one dependent variable, an association has a third variable involved.

3 a) A hypothesis is an idea that fits an observation and the scientific knowledge that is available.

  b) Increasing concentrations of sulfuric acid increases the rate of decomposition of marble.

  c) A prediction can be tested.

  d) The hypothesis could be supported or refuted or it might cause you to change your hypothesis.

  e) The theory on which you based the hypothesis might have to be changed.

4 a) When all variables but the one being used as the independent variable are kept constant.

  b) Do you have the correct conditions?; have you chosen a sensible range?; have you got enough readings that are close together?; will you need to repeat the readings?

  c) If repeat results are close enough together.

  d) See how close the actual results are to the predicted results.

5 E.g. was the clock started correctly?; was it stopped correctly?; was the oil measured out accurately?; was it put onto the correct spot?; was there a clear line at the bottom?; was the tile thoroughly washed and dried?

6 a) Take the highest and the lowest.

  b) The sum of all the readings divided by the number of readings.

  c) When you have an ordered or categoric independent variable and a continuous dependent variable.

  d) When you have a continuous independent variable and a continuous dependent variable.

7 a) Examine to see if it is an error, if so, repeat it. If identified from the graph, it should be ignored.

  b) Identify a pattern.

  c) That it does not go further than the data, the reliability and the validity allow.

  d) By repeating results, by getting others to repeat your results and by checking other equivalent data.

8 a) The science is more likely to be accepted.

  b) They might be biased due to who is funding the research or because they are employed by a biased organisation. There might be political influences, the public might be too alarmed by the conclusions.

9 a) For many scientific developments there is a practical outcome which can be used – a technological development. Many technological developments allow further progress in science.

  b) Society.

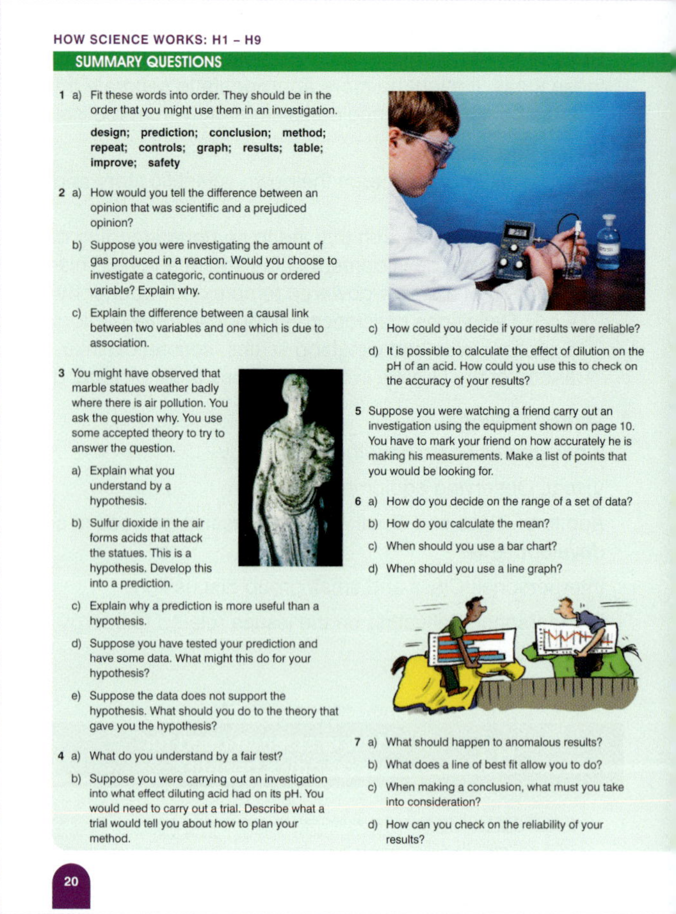

10 a) Increasing the load would increase the bending of the glass.

  b) Line load added.

  c) Bending of the glass.

  d) E.g. same thickness of glass, line load always in the same place.

  e) The two readings are consistently 2 mm apart, except at 5 kN/m.

  f) The 5 kN/m reading could be a random error.

  g) Improved measuring devices.

  h) Yes because there was a difference between each of the chosen line loads and no overlap between them, e.g. at 1 kN/m it bent 18 mm and at 2 kN/m it bent 37 mm.

  i) 95 mm.

  j) Graph drawn with all units and labels, the line load on the X axis – it would be appropriate to plot 0.0.

  k) Appropriate line of best fit.

  l) Directly proportional.

  m) Increasing the line load increases the degree of bending, up to a line load of at least 5 kN/m.

  n) Measure different thicknesses of polymer, using the same thicknesses of glass and test in the same way up until the glass breaks.

  o) Architects will be aware of the forces that the glass will be required to withstand and can choose an appropriate thickness of polymer for the task.

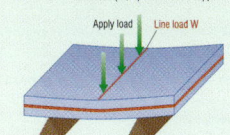

How science works teaching suggestions

- **Literacy guidance.** The externally set test for every ISA has a question in which the scoring of marks is in part dependent on skills such as presenting information, developing an argument and drawing a conclusion.
- Where students are asked for an explanation, they have the opportunity to write answers in continuous prose and practise their literary skills. Look for good grammar, clear expression and the correct spelling of scientific terms. Question 5, for example, would encourage the development of an argument. Question 6 – how to present data and question 7c) – drawing a conclusion. Questions relating to terms used in How Science Works should allow students to express their understanding of those terms, e.g. question 3a.
- **Higher- and lower-level answers.** Clear understanding is needed for the answer to question 3a) and higher attaining students would be expected to include reference to the hypothesis matching observations to accepted theory. Lower-attaining candidates should be able to say that a hypothesis is a 'good idea'. The most demanding question is question 9.
- **Special needs.** Students may be able to cope with question 1 if provided with the words on flash cards and asked to assemble them in the best order, and with question 4a). Lower-ability students would be generally better served by considering these questions in class where they can have access to support, texts and group discussion. Some of the questions could be altered and put into a context taken from the text.
- **How and when to use these questions**
  - The questions are page referenced and most could be used as summary questions for homework or for discussion and plenary sessions in the lesson.
  - Question 1 is a summary of the design of an investigation and, together with a clear diagram, would make an excellent Revision card.
  - Questions 2, 3, 5 and 8 could be used for class discussion.
  - Question 10 should be prepared for homework and discussed in small groups. It brings together many of the skills that have/will have been learned throughout the course.

CHEMISTRY

C1a | Products from rocks

Key Stage 3 curriculum links

The following link to **'What you already know'**:

- That the elements are shown in the periodic table and consist of atoms, which can be represented by symbols.
- How elements vary widely in their physical properties, including appearance; state at room temperature, magnetic properties and thermal and electrical conductivity, and how these properties can be used to classify elements as metals or non-metals.
- How elements combine through chemical reactions to form compounds [for example, water, carbon dioxide, magnesium oxide, sodium chloride, most minerals] with a definite composition.
- To represent compounds by formulae and to summarise reactions by word equations.
- That mixtures [for example, air, sea water and most rocks] are composed of constituents that are not combined.
- How to separate mixtures into their constituents using distillation, chromatography and other appropriate methods.
- How metals react with oxygen, water, acids and oxides of other metals, and what the products of these reactions are and the displacement reactions that take place between metals and solutions of salts of other metals.
- How a reactivity series of metals can be determined by considering these reactions, and used to make predictions about other reactions.
- About some everyday applications of neutralisation [for example, the treatment of indigestion, the treatment of acid soil, the manufacture of fertiliser].

QCA Scheme of Work
8E Atoms and elements
8F Compounds and mixtures
9F The reactions of metals and metal compounds

CHEMISTRY

C1a | Products from rocks

What you already know

Here is a quick reminder of previous work that you will find useful in this unit:

- The chemical elements consist of atoms, which we represent by symbols.
- We can arrange the chemical elements in the periodic table.
- The substances in a mixture are not joined together chemically, so we can separate them again.
- We can represent chemicals using chemical formulae.
- We can summarise what happens in a chemical reaction using a word equation.
- The mass of the products formed in a chemical reaction is the same as the mass of the reactants they were formed from.
- When we burn fossil fuels we may produce new substances that can affect the environment.
- We can place the metals in a reactivity series. Metals higher up the series can displace metals lower down the series.

Rocks, such as limestone from this quarry, provide us with many useful materials

RECAP QUESTIONS

1. How many different types of atom are there in a jar of pure sulfur?
2. What are the symbols for the following elements: iron, oxygen, copper, sodium, chlorine, aluminium, calcium?
3. How could you separate a mixture of sand and salt?
4. Iron and chlorine react together to make iron chloride. Write a word equation for this reaction.
5. a) Describe in words what happens in this reaction:

   magnesium + oxygen → magnesium oxide

   b) In the reaction between magnesium and oxygen, the mass of magnesium and oxygen was 2.5 grams. How much magnesium oxide was formed?
6. When fossil fuels burn in plenty of air, what new substances are produced?
7. Magnesium ribbon is put into blue copper sulphate solution. The solution becomes colourless and a pinkish metal is produced.

   Then copper metal is put into a solution of silver nitrate. The solution turns blue and silver metal is produced.

   Arrange the three metals, copper, silver and magnesium, in order of reactivity. Put the most reactive first.

RECAP ANSWERS

1. 1
2. Fe, O, Cu, Na, Cl, Al, Ca.
3. Dissolve the salt and sand mixture. Filter, collect and dry the sand from the filter paper. Evaporate the water from the filtrate leaving salt crystals.
4. iron + chlorine → iron chloride
5. a) Shiny, magnesium metal burns in oxygen gas to make a white powder of magnesium oxide.
   b) 2.5 grams
6. Carbon dioxide and water.
7. Magnesium, copper, silver.

Products from rocks

SPECIFICATION LINK-UP
Unit: Chemistry C1a

Products from rocks

How do rocks provide building materials?

The exploitation of rocks provides essential building materials. Limestone is a naturally occurring resource that provides a starting point for the manufacture of cement, concrete and glass. Throughout C1, candidates should know that atoms are held together in molecules and lattices by chemical bonds, but no detailed knowledge of the types of chemical bonding is required. Candidates should be able to interpret chemical equations in symbol form and should be able to balance equations in terms of number of atoms.

How do rocks provide metals and how are metals used?

Metals are very useful in our everyday lives. Ores are naturally occurring rocks that provide an economic starting point for the manufacture of metals. Iron ore is used to make iron and steel; limestone plays an important part in this process. Copper can be easily extracted but copper rich ores are becoming scarce. Aluminium and titanium are useful metals but are expensive to produce.

How do we get fuels from crude oil?

Crude oil is an ancient biomass from which many useful materials can be produced. Crude oil can be fractionally distilled. Some of the fractions can be used as fuels.

Chapters in this unit

- Rocks and building
- Rocks and metals
- Crude oil

Teaching suggestions

What you already know

- **Definitions** – Students often struggle with the definitions of atoms, elements, compounds and mixtures. These words could be written on the board and students could volunteer to draw a picture to represent each of them.

- **Key points** – They may be summarised using this text in no more than three sentences. Further guidance could be given to encourage students to use scientific language, such as using the key words: atoms, mixture, and chemical reaction, at least once in their sentences.

- **Explain** – Students could be encouraged to explain the word 'oxygen' in terms of these statements (e.g. it is an **element** on the right of the periodic table, and is a reactant in combustion reaction reactions that form oxides – **compounds**. It is found in the **mixture** of gases we call air, as **molecules** made up of two **atoms**, O_2).

Recap questions

- **Question and answer** – These could be used with laminated A3 white paper, paper towel and washable markers. You could read out the question, the students write the answer on the paper and hold it up. Then give feedback instantly.

- **Revision** – At the end of the topic, the questions could be set as a homework task to review the section of completed work.

Making connections

- **Observations** – Encourage the students to look at the pictures of the airport staff. They could create lists of elements, compounds, mixtures, metals, non-metals and products from crude oil. Some items can be in more than one list. As an extension activity, the students could be asked to consider why each material is used for a particular job.

Activity

- **Environmental impact** – Students should be encouraged to consider the environmental impact of the airport buildings on the landscape and economy, as well as the environmental consequences of the production of the building materials and the burning of fossil fuels for transport. Students should consider ways that this impact has already been reduced (e.g. low-sulfur fuels) and as an extension activity how further advances could be possible if money was no object (e.g. hydrogen fuels).

CHEMISTRY   ROCKS AND BUILDING

C1a 1.1 Atoms, elements and compounds

LEARNING OBJECTIVES

Students should learn that:
- Elements are made of only one type of atom.
- Symbols are used to represent atoms of a particular element.
- Elements are shown in the periodic table.
- Atoms may bond to form compounds.

LEARNING OUTCOMES

Most students should be able to:
- State a definition for elements.
- Recognise names, symbols, formulae and diagrams of elements or compounds.
- Label the sub-atomic structure of an atom, when the key words are given.
- Find symbols for elements in the periodic table.
- Describe briefly what a chemical bond is.

Some students should also be able to:
- Give examples and draw diagrams to explain the difference between elements and compounds.
- Draw and fully label an atom and its structure.

Teaching suggestions

- **Special needs.** Students could use worksheets' information about elements and compounds. They can cut these up and stick them in their books in the correct sequence.
- **Learning styles**
  Kinaesthetic: Handling different elements, some need to be in sealed containers if they are liquids, gases or hazardous.
  Visual: Show Simulation C1a 1.1 'The Periodic Table' on the GCSE Chemistry CD ROM on a large screen. Use it to highlight different sections such as metals and non-metals.
  Auditory: Playing the elements song.
  Intrapersonal: Using information from the lesson and their personal experiences to decide on their favourite element.
  Interpersonal: Working in groups to sort the elements.
- **Homework.** Students could find out a fascinating fact about an element of their choice.
- **ICT link-up.** Play the elements song (this also has a flash animation): www.privatehand.com/flash/elements.html

SPECIFICATION LINK-UP   C1a.11.1

- *All substances are made of atoms. A substance that is made of only one sort of atom is called an element. There are about 100 different elements. Elements are shown in the periodic table. The groups contain elements with similar properties.*
- *Atoms of each element are represented by a chemical symbol, e.g. O represents an atom of oxygen, Na represents an atom of sodium.*
- *Atoms have a small central nucleus around which there are electrons.*
- *When elements react, their atoms join with other atoms to form compounds. This involves giving, taking or sharing electrons and the atoms held together by chemical bonds. (No further knowledge of ions, ionic or covalent bonding is required for this unit.)*

Lesson structure

STARTER

5,4,3,2,1 – Ask students to list 5 solid elements, 4 metal elements, 3 non-metal elements, 2 gaseous elements at room temperature, and 1 liquid element at room temperature. This task draws on the idea that most elements are solids at room temperature and most are metals. (10 minutes)

Anagrams – Students could try to create as many 'scientific' words as they can using the letters from the term 'periodic table'. (5 minutes)

MAIN

- Some students may not have had the opportunity to handle elements, apart from metals that they use in their everyday life. Separate the class into groups of about 5 students. Give each group of students sealed samples of different elements. The students should then be instructed to order them in different ways. Each group can feed-back to the class how they ordered the elements (possible orders include: state, colour, metal/non-metal, hazard). Draw out from the students, using questions and answers, that there is a finite number of elements – about 100. Challenge the students to think about how we get the infinite variety of materials in the world. This should lead onto a discussion of compounds and bonding.
- Students often struggle with defining elements and compounds. A kinaesthetic, cut-and-stick activity could be used. The student should create a two-column (element, compound) table in their book. Different images representing elements and compounds and the definitions of these two words, can then be given to the student to put into their table.

PLENARIES

Favourite – Ask students to think about their favourite element and why (e.g. copper, because it makes spiders' blood blue). Students should then share their idea with a partner. The teacher could then ask a few pairs what their favourite element is and why. (10 minutes)

Code breaker – Ask the students to use the periodic table to decode this hidden message:

Carbon, radon, carbon, potassium, thorium, einsteinium, yttrium, M, boron, oxygen, L, sulfur. (CRaCKThEsYMBOLS) (5 minutes) This could be extended by getting the students to write their own secret message. (10 minutes)

24

ACTIVITY & EXTENSION IDEAS

- Each student can be assigned a different element. They are then given a piece of card to draw a diagram of that atom, labelling the sub-atomic particles and a fascinating fact about that element. These cards can then be used to make a display in the classroom.
- Mobiles of atoms can be created. A 5 cm diameter circle and a ring should be drawn onto a piece of card. The rings need to be drawn so that the circle fits inside and a gap is left between them e.g. inner diameter of 13 cm and outer diameter of 15 cm. The student cuts out the template, and draws on sub-atomic particles, using colours to highlight the charges. They could be encouraged to find out an interesting fact and write it on another piece of card (10 cm × 5 cm). String and tape is then used to join the fact to the ring (electron shell), the ring to the circle (nucleus) and that to the top part of the ring. Excess string should be available at the top to suspend the mobile. *Note* to be chemically correct, the students can only complete a mobile of H or He at this stage; to complete large atoms, additional rings need to be added.

Products from rocks

DID YOU KNOW?

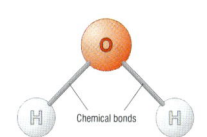

Most of the f-block elements were only discovered when nuclear reactors were invented. Under these conditions, these heavy elements have been synthesised. However, a number decay with very short half-lives and they are difficult to study.

For example, the element Lawrencium (atomic number 103) was first discovered in 1961 in California. Lawrencium-260 has a half-life of 3 minutes.

SUMMARY ANSWERS

1 Atoms, molecule, sharing, bonds.

2 The different substances in a mixture are not joined to each other by chemical bonds, but in a compound the atoms are held together tightly by chemical bonds – this makes them difficult to separate.

3 a)

Element
e.g. hydrogen

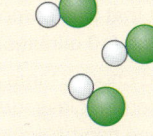

Compound
e.g. hydrogen chloride

b) See diagram of atom on p. 25 in Student Book.

Answers to in-text questions

a) About 100.

b) Because you can combine them together in millions of different ways.

c) Because an element may have different names in different languages.

d) They are also likely to be reactive metals.

KEY POINTS

Begin to make a spider diagram using the key points on this spread. Then at the end of each lesson during this unit, or as a homework activity, the other key points from the topic can be added. Therefore, at the end of the topic a powerful revision resource will have been created.

CHEMISTRY — ROCKS AND BUILDING

C1a 1.2 Limestone and its uses

LEARNING OBJECTIVES

Students should learn that:

- Limestone is used to make a variety of building materials.
- Limestone will undergo thermal decomposition.

LEARNING OUTCOMES

Most students should be able to:

- Recognise that limestone is a building material and state that it can also be used to make glass, cement and concrete.
- Complete a word equation for the thermal decomposition of limestone.
- Write the formula of calcium carbonate.

Some students should also be able to:

- Explain the process of thermal decomposition of limestone.

Teaching suggestions

- **Special needs.** Key-word bingo can be used to reinforce the key words.
- **Learning styles**
  Kinaesthetic: Handling limestone, calcium carbonate, sand, mortar, cement and glass to physically compare the properties.
  Visual: Creating an A-map, the resulting diagram is a useful aid for visual learners.
  Auditory: Giving feedback to other students about their work.
  Intrapersonal: Assimilating information to make their own A-map.
  Interpersonal: Looking at other students' work and giving feedback.
- **Examiner's tips.** Recognise and understand the formulae of the compounds and the symbol equations.
- **Homework.** Find a picture of limestone being used as a building material.
- **ICT link-up.** Excel can be used to create pie charts to show the composition of different types of glass. See for example www.britglass.org.uk

SPECIFICATION LINK-UP C1a.11.1

- The formula of a compound shows the number and type of atoms that are joined together to make the compound.
- Limestone, containing the compound calcium carbonate ($CaCO_3$), is quarried and can be used as a building material.
- Calcium carbonate can be decomposed by heating (thermal decomposition) to make quicklime (calcium oxide) and carbon dioxide.
- Limestone and its products have many uses, including slaked lime, mortar, cement, concrete and glass.

Students should use their skills, knowledge and understanding of 'How Science Works':

- to consider and evaluate the environmental, social and economic effects of exploiting limestone and producing building materials from it.

Lesson structure

STARTER

- **Characteristics** – Ask the students to consider what the following substances have in common: limestone, marble, chalk and calcium carbonate. [They are all made up mainly of the same compound – calcium carbonate.] This task could be expanded to think about other groupings of these substances, e.g. chalk and limestone are sedimentary rocks, whereas marble is metamorphic and calcium carbonate is a pure compound, and not a mixture and therefore not a rock. (5 minutes)
- **Classify** – Students could read through the pages in the Student Book and classify the chemicals that are named as elements [calcium, oxygen, carbon], compounds [calcium carbonate, sodium carbonate, calcium oxide, carbon dioxide, water] and mixtures [limestone, chalk, cement, concrete, sand, clay, coal]. (15 minutes)

MAIN

- Using the text book for information, students create an A-map to demonstrate how limestone can be used to create different building materials. They should select three colours. In the centre of the page, in one colour only, they should write the word 'limestone' and draw a small image that might help them to remember this word. This colour is then not used again. The second colour then is used to create four long wavy lines. Following the contour of the line, they should write 'formation, glass, cement, thermal decomposition' on separate lines, each including an image. The idea is then added to, with a third colour, again with wavy lines. Each line should contain key words or phrases to summarise that branch of thought, and include an image to help them remember. Encourage the students to complete one branch before moving to the next.
- Often it is clear that students are confused about the scientific language, what it means and how it can be used. Students could write the key words (highlighted in the text) in their exercise book. They then need to summarise the explanation of that word to just one sentence. As an extension, they could be encouraged to use each of the key words in a sentence.

PLENARIES

AfL (Assessment for Learning) – Ask students to look at and comment on other students' A-maps. (15 minutes)

Fact finder – Ask students to think about one fact that they already knew before the lesson that had been reviewed and one fact that was completely new to them. Then select a few students to feedback to the class. (10 minutes)

Play key-word bingo – The students should choose three of the following key words: 'limestone, calcium carbonate, cement, concrete, glass, quicklime, calcium oxide, thermal decomposition, calcium oxide'. These can be written in the back of their exercise books, or on a pre-made bingo card that has spaces for the students to write in. Explain the word, and the student crosses it off (if they chose it). The first student to cross off all of the words may get a reward! (10 minutes)

ACTIVITY & EXTENSION IDEAS

- Flash cards of the key words could be created. Hold up the key word, and a student tries to describe it to you, without saying the word.
- As a data research piece, students could be encouraged to find out how Pyrex glass is different to soda glass.
- Students could be encouraged to find some old windows and look closely at them to notice any differences between new and old glass. [Hopefully they will notice that the old glass is thicker at the bottom than the top, due to the glass having been pulled down by gravity over many years.]
- Students could find out where limestone comes from [quarrying]. The students could then detail positives and negatives about where quarries are sited. This can be extended to carry out a debate, with different students given the role of different interest groups presenting their character's views on whether or not a quarry needs to be expanded in an area of outstanding natural beauty.
- A PhotoPLUS resource, C1a 1.2 'Limestone', is available to use on the GCSE Chemistry CD ROM.

FOUL FACTS

Quicklime was also spread over plague victims in their mass graves and over executed prisoners, as people thought it helped their bodies decompose quicker. However, it did help to kill microbes.

CHEMISTRY — ROCKS AND BUILDING

C1a 1.2 Limestone and its uses

LEARNING OBJECTIVES
1. What are the uses of limestone?
2. What happens when we heat limestone?

Uses of limestone

Limestone is a rock that is made mainly of *calcium carbonate*. Some types of limestone were formed from the remains of tiny animals and plants that lived in the sea millions of years ago. We dig limestone out of the ground in quarries all around the world. It has many important uses, including use as a building material.

Many important buildings around the world are made of limestone. We can cut and shape the stone taken from the ground into blocks. These can be placed one on top of the other, like bricks in a wall. We have used limestone in this way to make buildings for hundreds of years.

We can also process limestone to make other building materials. Powdered limestone can be heated to high temperatures with a mixture of sand and sodium carbonate (soda) to make *glass*.

Powdered limestone can also be heated with powdered clay to make *cement*. When we mix cement powder with water, sand and crushed rock, a slow chemical reaction takes place. The reaction produces a hard, stone-like building material called *concrete*.

a) What is limestone made of?
b) How do we use limestone to make buildings?

Figure 1 These white cliffs are made of chalk. This is one type of limestone, formed from the shells of tiny sea plants.

Figure 2 St Paul's Cathedral in London is built from limestone blocks

Figure 3 This building contains plenty of concrete which is made from limestone

Figure 4 Glass gives us buildings that let in natural light and which protect us from the weather

Heating limestone

The chemical formula for calcium carbonate is $CaCO_3$. This tells us that for every calcium atom (Ca) there is one carbon atom (C) and three oxygen atoms (O).

When we heat limestone strongly it breaks down to form a substance called *quicklime* (calcium oxide). Carbon dioxide is also produced in this reaction. Breaking down a chemical by heating is called *thermal decomposition*.

To make lots of quicklime this reaction is done in a furnace called a *lime kiln*. We fill the kiln with crushed limestone and heat it strongly using a supply of hot air. Quicklime comes out of the bottom of the kiln, while waste gases leave the kiln at the top.

We can show the thermal decomposition reaction by a word equation:

$$\text{calcium carbonate} \xrightarrow{\text{heat}} \text{calcium oxide} + \text{carbon dioxide}$$
$$\text{(quicklime)}$$

A rotary lime kiln

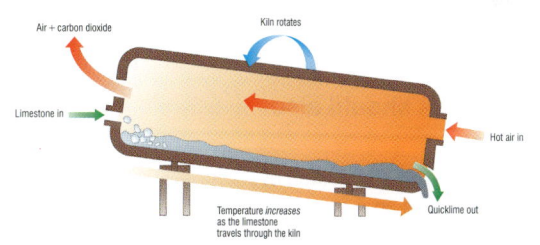

Figure 5 Quicklime is produced in a lime kiln. It is often produced in a *rotary kiln*, where the limestone is heated in a rotating drum. This makes sure that the limestone is thoroughly mixed with the stream of hot air so that it decomposes completely.

FOUL FACTS
Some murderers (and some authors of murder stories) have used quicklime to help get rid of a dead body, thinking that it would 'dissolve' it. Unfortunately for the criminal, quicklime often slows down the rate at which a body decomposes — which makes the job of the detective easier rather than harder.

SUMMARY QUESTIONS

1. Copy and complete using the words below:

   $CaCO_3$ calcium   cement   concrete   glass

   Limestone is mostly made of ...... carbonate (whose chemical formula is ......). As well as being used to produce blocks of building material, limestone can be used to produce ...... , ... and ...... that can also be used in building.

2. Produce a poster to show how limestone is used in building.

3. The stone roof of a building is supported by columns made of limestone. Why might this be unsafe after a fire in the building? Explain the chemical process involved in weakening the structure.

KEY POINTS
1. Limestone is made mainly of calcium carbonate.
2. Limestone is widely used in building.
3. Limestone breaks down when we heat it strongly (thermal decomposition) to make quicklime and carbon dioxide.

SUMMARY ANSWERS

1. Calcium, $CaCO_3$, glass, cement, concrete.

2. Poster.

3. The calcium carbonate in the column may have undergone thermal decomposition, making it weaker. The calcium oxide formed is much softer than the original calcium carbonate present in the columns.

Answers to in-text questions

a) Limestone is mainly made of calcium carbonate.

b) Limestone can be cut into blocks or processed to make materials like cement or concrete.

KEY POINTS

Before the lesson, write three famous characters or people in the public eye (e.g. pop or film stars) and using tape stick them to the underside of three desks. Ask the students to look under their desks, if they have a name, they could read the key points out trying to mimic that person.

CHEMISTRY   ROCKS AND BUILDING

C1a 1.3 Decomposing carbonates

LEARNING OBJECTIVES

Students should learn that:
- Most metal carbonates will undergo thermal decomposition.
- Atoms are rearranged in a chemical reaction.
- Conservation of mass occurs in a chemical reaction.

LEARNING OUTCOMES

Most students should be able to:
- List examples of metal carbonates that react similarly to limestone, when they are heated, and the general products that they make.
- Write word equations to describe thermal decomposition of a metal carbonate.
- Identify that mass is conserved during a chemical reaction.

Some students should also be able to:
- Detail thermal decomposition of metal carbonates, in a balanced symbol equation.

Teaching suggestions

- **Gifted and talented.** These students could be encouraged to make predictions about other metal carbonates and how they would react. Students could be encouraged to use the reactivity series to make a more in depth prediction.
- **Learning styles**
  Kinaesthetic: Completing the practical on heating metal carbonates.
  Visual: Observing the reaction and noting down their observations in a table.
  Auditory: Listening to the teacher demonstrating how to balance symbol equations.
  Intrapersonal: Balancing symbol equations.
  Interpersonal: Evaluating and giving feedback about experiments.
- **Homework.** Give students some more symbol equations to balance.
- **ICT link-up.** Flexi-cam, or a webcam, can be used to film the reactions and show them on an interactive whiteboard. An exercise is available on balancing equations from the GCSE Chemistry CD ROM.

SPECIFICATION LINK-UP   C1a.11.1

- *No atoms are lost or made during a chemical reaction so the mass of the products equals the mass of the reactants and we can write balanced equations showing the atoms involved.*
- *Carbonates of other metals decompose on heating in a similar way.*
- *Atoms and symbols are used to represent and explain what is happening to the substances in chemical reactions.*

Lesson structure

STARTER

Recap – Ask students to recall:
- A definition for thermal decomposition. [Using heat to break down a substance.]
- The two products when limestone is thermally decomposed. [Calcium oxide and carbon dioxide.]
- The lab test for carbon dioxide. [Lime water turns cloudy.] (5 minutes)

Anagram title – Tell students that today's lesson is about: 'acdeehiimmnnotolports' – what does this mean? [Thermal decomposition – using heat to break down a chemical.] (5 minutes)

MAIN

- Split the class into groups of two or three. Give each group two different types of carbonate to study. Initially ask the students to look at them and describe their appearance. They could then complete the thermal decomposition practical and record their results in an appropriate table. Students could then share their results with other groups to obtain a full set of results.
- Encourage students to attempt to write a general equation for the reaction.

    [metal carbonate → carbon dioxide + metal oxide]

- You can carry out the practical as an investigation to see which carbonates decompose most easily when heated. This will introduce students to the parts of 'How Science Works' dealing with different types of variable, taking measurements and evaluating experimental design. For example, you could ask 'How can you time exactly when the lime water goes milky? Is it possible to make this consistent for each carbonate tested?' Students could be encouraged to consider if the practical was a fair test, and how it could be improved.
- Students should have been introduced to balancing equations in Year 9. However this skill remains problematic to many. Therefore, demonstrate balancing equations on the board and give the students some examples to attempt themselves. They could also annotate what observations they would expect to note if they were doing the reaction.
- For students struggling with atoms being rearranged in a chemical reaction, molecular model kits can be used. Using the molecular model kits, a model of a metal carbonate could be made and put on the left of the table (reactant). Then carbon dioxide and the metal oxide can be made and put on the right of the table (products). Explain that atoms can't be created or destroyed, only rearranged to make the actual products formed.

PLENARIES

Chemical equations – Ask students to complete the following equations (answers in brackets):

calcium carbonate → [calcium oxide + carbon dioxide]
[magnesium carbonate] → magnesium oxide + carbon dioxide
[$CuCO_3$] → CuO + CO_2 (5 minutes)

Summary – Ask the students to write down a summary of thermal decomposition of metal carbonates, this should include a definition and general equation. (10 minutes)
[For example, thermal decomposition is using heat to break down a substance. The general equation for the thermal decomposition of a metal carbonate is:

metal carbonate → metal oxide + carbon dioxide]

Practical support

Investigating carbonates

Equipment and materials required
Boiling tube, bung with delivery tube, spatula, test tube, Bunsen burner and safety equipment, eye protection, test tube holder, stand, boss, clamp, samples of metal carbonates (e.g. calcium carbonate, sodium carbonate – irritant, potassium carbonate – harmful, magnesium carbonate, zinc carbonate and copper carbonate – harmful); lime water – irritant. An electric balance and measuring cylinders will be needed if the practical is to be carried out as an investigation into the ease of thermal decomposition.

Details
Put about 1 spatula of a metal carbonate to be tested in a boiling tube. Clamp into position, and fit the bung and delivery tube. Half fill the test tube with lime water and place into the rack. Angle the end of the delivery tube into the test tube.

Using the Bunsen burner heat the carbonate, and observe the lime water. If the lime water goes cloudy, then carbon dioxide has been produced and thermal decomposition has taken place. Repeat with other carbonates to compare results. Wear eye protection throughout the practical and be aware that the boiling tube will still be hot when heating is ceased. Remove end of delivery tube from lime water when heating is stopped to prevent 'suck back'.

Safety: CLEAPSS Hazcards 61, 108, 26. Lime water – CLEAPSS Student Safety Sheet 32.

ACTIVITY & EXTENSION IDEAS

- Give each group of students a molecular model kit. Ask them to show you an oxygen atom (one red sphere), then a carbon atom (one black sphere), then the compound carbon dioxide (two red spheres joined to one black sphere). This activity can reinforce scientific language, and many other examples could be made for this subject spread.
- Students could find out one use for each of the metal carbonates studied in the lesson.

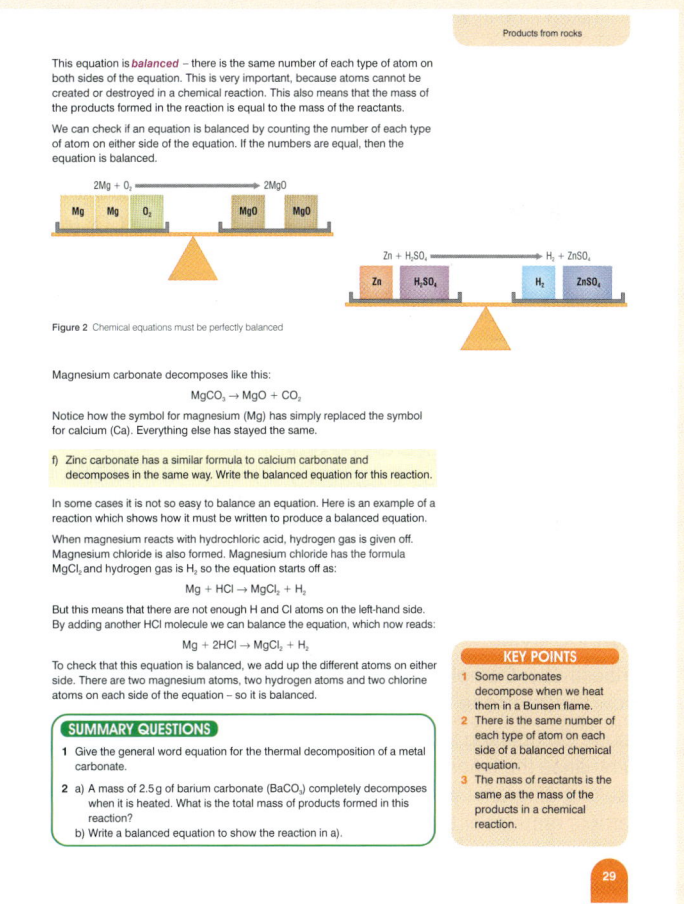

SUMMARY ANSWERS

1. metal carbonate → metal oxide + carbon dioxide

2. a) 2.5 g
   b) $BaCO_3 \rightarrow BaO + CO_2$

Answers to in-text questions

a) Magnesium and calcium are in the same group of the periodic table.

b) Group 1.

c) Group 2.

d) Group 2 carbonates decompose on heating in a Bunsen flame while Group 1 carbonates do not.

e) No – because we haven't tested all of the carbonates of Group 1 and 2 metals.

f) $ZnCO_3 \rightarrow ZnO + CO_2$

KEY POINTS

Ask the students to write three questions, each question should be answered by one of the key points. The questions and answers could then be written in their books, or shared with the class.

CHEMISTRY | ROCKS AND BUILDING

C1a 1.4 Quicklime and slaked lime

LEARNING OBJECTIVES

Students should learn:
- What slaked lime is and how it is produced.
- The processes involved to make lime mortar.

LEARNING OUTCOMES

Most students should be able to:
- Give an example of a use of slaked lime and mortar.
- Describe the production of slaked lime in word equations.
- Recall how mortar is made.

Some students should also be able to:
- Write a balanced symbol equation for the production of slaked lime.
- Give a balanced symbol equation for the production of mortar when reactants and products are named.

Teaching suggestions

- **Special needs.** Provide diagrams of each stage of the limestone cycle, but in the wrong order. Before students start the practical, they cut and stick these to create a pictorial method.
- **Learning styles**
  Kinaesthetic: Completing the practical to show the limestone cycle.
  Visual: Completing a flow chart to summarise the limestone cycle, the resulting diagrams will help visual learners remember the complex steps.
  Auditory: Playing Taboo with key words (where students try to verbally explain a key word, without saying the forbidden vocabulary).
  Interpersonal: Generating symbol and word equations from observed reactions.
  Intrapersonal: Evaluating and giving feedback about experiments.
- **Homework.** Ask students to draw a labelled diagram of a limekiln and write full equations to demonstrate what is happening.
- **ICT link-up.** Search the web and show students images of limekilns.

SPECIFICATION LINK-UP   C1a.11.1
- *Quicklime (calcium oxide) reacts with water to produce slaked lime (calcium hydroxide).*
- *Limestone and its products have many uses, including slaked lime, mortar, cement and glass.*
- *Atoms and symbols are used to represent and explain what is happening to the substances in chemical reactions.*

Lesson structure

STARTER

Spot the mistake – Write the following sentence on the board, and ask the students to spot the deliberate mistake(s):
  'Limestone is a metamorphic rock and made of the pure element, calcium carbonate.'
[The mistakes are that limestone is a <u>sedimentary</u> rock. It is made up mainly of calcium carbonate (which is a <u>compound</u>, not an element) but contains other substances, and so the rock is a <u>mixture</u> of substances, not an element.] (5 minutes)

Chemical formula – Ask students to look at the following formulae and find their chemical and common names:
- $CaCO_3$ [calcium carbonate, limestone/chalk/marble]
- CaO [calcium oxide, quicklime]
- $Ca(OH)_2$ [calcium hydroxide, slaked lime/lime water when in solution]
- CO_2 [carbon dioxide] (10 minutes)

MAIN

- Introduce the idea of a limestone cycle. Draw a brief outline of the cycle on the board or use the animation C1a 1.4 'Quicklime and Slaked lime' from the GCSE Chemistry CD ROM. Explain to the students that they are going to complete a number of experiments to follow the cycle.
- Split the class into groups of two or three and ask each group to complete the practical. Encourage students to note down any important observations and try to label the type of reaction occurring in each part of the cycle.
- Once the practical has been completed, or using the textbook for information, a comprehensive flow chart of labelled diagrams to show the limestone cycle completed as a practical in a lab could be made. Higher attaining students may wish to add on balanced symbol equations for each reaction.
- Create a set of cards (7 cm by 3 cm), each card having a different title (slaked lime, lime water, mortar). Using the textbook, students then state the chemical name, formula and how it is made in a symbol or word equation on each appropriate card. They can also be asked to add any more information that they think is important. This is a revision technique that will help them to discriminate and select key information from text. The cards can be hole-punched in one corner, and joined using a piece of string. This can then be attached to their book or taken home as a learning resource.

PLENARIES

Taboo – Make sets of three cards, each card containing a different key word (quicklime, mortar, slaked lime) and under the key words are lists of words that can't be used to explain the key word (e.g. quicklime: taboo words – slaked lime, limestone, fast). Then in groups a student tries to explain the key word, without using the taboo words. (5 minutes)

Chemical equations – Ask a student to come to the front and put on eye protection, then blow through a straw into a conical flask containing a liquid (lime water). Ask the students to describe what is happening in terms of an equation. (5 minutes)

Cycle – Ask the students to draw a cycle to connect the words: limestone, quicklime, slaked lime, lime water and calcium carbonate. Onto their diagram [which should be limestone → quicklime → slaked lime → lime water and then back to limestone], they could include a colour code, e.g. each time heat is used write it in red, water in blue. Also the chemical names and formula may be added. (15 minutes)

Practical support

Reactions of limestone

Equipment and materials required
Gauze, tripod, Bunsen burner and safety equipment, eye protection, tongs, water, two boiling tubes, fluted filter paper, filter funnel, glass rod, test tube rack, calcium carbonate, dropping pipette, straw.

Details
Place a piece of calcium carbonate onto the gauze, which should be mounted on a tripod. Turn the Bunsen burner to a blue flame, and direct the tip of the blue cone onto a corner of the calcium carbonate. As the Bunsen burner will need to be directed at the calcium carbonate, it will need to be picked up off the bench so extra care should to be taken. First calcium carbonate will glow red/orange, then a whiter orange. Once part of the material glows white for a few minutes, turn off the Bunsen.

After heating, the thermally decomposed calcium carbonate holds its heat for a long period of time. Also the calcium products are all basic and should not be touched with hands. Using the tongs, transfer the product to a boiling tube, add a few drops of water and observe. Then add about a third of the boiling tube of water and shake gently. When water is added to the calcium oxide, it will often spit calcium hydroxide, so eye protection must be worn, and if the compound touches the skin it must be washed off immediately.

Filter the mixture, and keep the filtrate (lime water – irritant). Carefully take a straw and submerge into the lime water and blow gently. The solution should turn cloudy, completing the limestone cycle.

Safety: CLEAPSS Hazcard 19. Lime water CLEAPSS Student Safety Sheet 32.

- Water is produced as steam.
- Small particles of insoluble calcium carbonate are formed and are suspended in the solution.

ACTIVITY & EXTENSION IDEAS

- Students could find out how parts of the limestone cycle are carried out in industry, e.g. thermal decomposition of limestone occurs in a limekiln.
- Mortar is a mixture. Challenge the students to find out why a mixture is used [to improve the mortar's properties] and what proportions of different materials are added to the cement to make mortar. Possible sources of information are DIY shops.
- Gypsum is added to cement, ask the students to find out what it is [calcium sulfate, $CaSO_4$] and why it is added [increases the setting time].

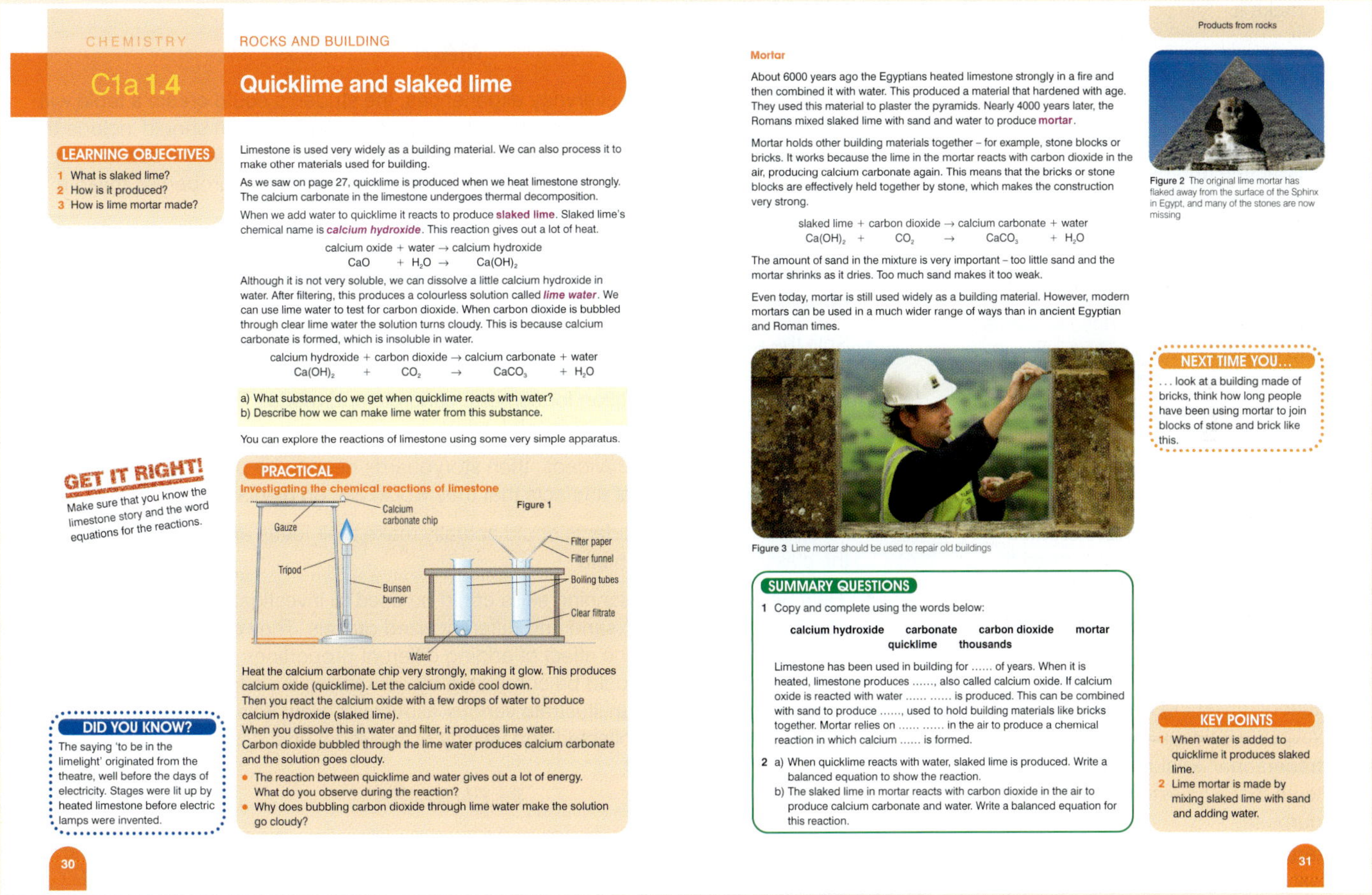

SUMMARY ANSWERS

1. Thousands, quicklime, calcium hydroxide, mortar, carbon dioxide, carbonate.
2. a) $CaO + H_2O \rightarrow Ca(OH)_2$
   b) $Ca(OH)_2 + CO_2 \rightarrow CaCO_3 + H_2O$

GET IT RIGHT!
Make sure that students know the word/symbol equations for making slaked lime.

DID YOU KNOW?
Mortar reacts with carbon dioxide in the air. Sometimes, when old buildings are demolished, the mortar in some places still has not set. This is because the centre of the mortar was not exposed to carbon dioxide.

Answers to in-text questions

a) Slaked lime (or hydrated lime), calcium hydroxide.

b) Dissolve it in water.

KEY POINTS
Add an extra card to the hole punched pack and add the key points about this topic.

CHEMISTRY   ROCKS AND BUILDING

C1a 1.5 Cement, concrete and glass

LEARNING OBJECTIVES

Students should learn:
- How cement is made.
- What is used to make concrete.
- How glass is made.

LEARNING OUTCOMES

Most students should be able to:
- List some uses of cement and the materials needed to make it.
- Describe how concrete is made and list the properties of this material.
- Describe how glass is made and identify the materials needed to make it.

Some students should also be able to:
- Evaluate uses of cement, concrete and glass over other materials to do a particular job.

SPECIFICATION LINK-UP C1a.11.1

- *Limestone and its products have many uses, including slaked lime, mortar, cement, concrete and glass.*

Students should use their skills, knowledge and understanding of 'How Science Works':
- *to evaluate the developments in using limestone, cement, concrete and glass as building materials, and their advantages and disadvantages over other materials.*

Lesson structure

STARTER

List – Ask students to list the properties of cement [opaque, hard], concrete [opaque, hard, can be load bearing i.e. strong] and glass [can be transparent or translucent, brittle, hard, semi-solid]. (5 minutes)

Anagrams – meetcn [cement], noteccre [concrete], Plantdor [Portland], sslag [glass], toneemils [limestone]. (5 minutes)

MAIN

- Using the textbook and everyday experiences, the students could create a table with three columns labelled cement, concrete and glass. Each column should include the raw materials to make the product, a use and which properties make it suitable for that particular use. This encourages students to evaluate which properties make a material fit for each purpose.
- For a more creative approach to this work, students could pretend to work for Portland museum and that they have been asked to design a historical/scientific museum display.
- Split the students into four groups: one is responsible for the historical development of cement, glass and concrete; the other groups detail the properties, uses and outline the basic production for cement, concrete and mortar. They must design their part of the display including visuals/scripts.
- If they are to use speech/videos, then storyboards need to be produced. Also they need to produce a list of artefacts that they would like on display.
- As an extension, the students could actually make their ideas and it could be used in the classroom as an exhibit.
- 'How Science Works' planning skills could be used to investigate concrete. Students could be given cement, sand and different sized gravels. They could design an experiment to find out the effect of adding different proportions of each to the mix. Another investigation could be completed by comparing the effect of different gravel sizes in the mix. This can illustrate various aspects of 'How Science Works', e.g. reliability of data collected and validity of investigational design.

PLENARIES

Predict – Ask students to think about life without limestone products. Which limestone product would they miss the most and why? Ask the students to feedback into small groups and then encourage groups to share their ideas with the whole class. (10 minutes)

True or false – Read out these statements and ask if they're true or false:
- Lime mortar can set under water. [False]
- The Roman method for making underwater mortar was used in the seventeenth century. [True]
- Portland cement is a mixture. [True]
- Recent developments in glass are allowing building innovations. [True]
- Concrete is poor at resisting forces. [False] (5 minutes)

Teaching suggestions

- **Gifted and talented.** These students could be encouraged to make predictions about the effect of different compositions on the properties of cement and mortar.
- **Learning styles**
  Kinaesthetic: Students acting out the storyboards that they have created. (Lower ability students may need to have storyboards provided by the teacher, and they could improvise.)
  Visual: Trying to unscramble the anagrams written on the board.
  Auditory: Listening to other students giving presentations.
  Intrapersonal: Evaluating properties to ensure that a limestone product is fit for a purpose.
  Interpersonal: Working in teams to create a museum display.
- **Homework.** Find out examples of different types of glass and their contents, e.g. soda-lime [65% sand, 13% sodium carbonate, 12% limestone and 10% cullet/re-cycled glass].
- **ICT link-up.** Using the Internet, look at the range history of cement making, e.g. www.castlecement.co.uk

Practical support

Which mixture makes the strongest concrete?
Equipment and materials required
Cement, sand, gravel, spatulas, yoghurt pots, card templates to make concrete moulds, measuring cylinders (plus equipment requested by students to test strength of concrete, e.g. slotted masses, G-clamps) eye protection.

Details
Students make moulds and fill them with various concrete mixes, trying to ensure fair testing. Next lesson, they test the strength of different mixes.
Safety: Avoid skin contact with cement. Wear eye protection when making AND testing concrete.

Making a glass-like substance
Equipment and materials required
Bunsen burner and safety equipment, eye protection, wire loop (about 4 mm diameter) attached to an insulated handle, borax – irritant, transition metal oxides (e.g. manganese oxide – harmful and copper oxide – harmful).

Details
Put a crystal of borax into the metal loop. Heat over a blue Bunsen flame, and it forms a structure similar to glass. When molten, add a tiny amount of one transition metal oxide and note the colour change. Allow the bead to cool. Wear eye protection.
Safety: CLEAPSS Hazcards 14, 60, 26.

ACTIVITY & EXTENSION
- Encourage students to make their own glass-like substance using borax. (See practical support.)
- Ask students to consider the impact of this type of industry in an area. Different students could be given characters (e.g. local resident, local councillor, local unemployed person, MP, cement company, local glass artist, etc.). They then could critically consider whether the character would be for or against the industry, and a debate could be held.

Answers to in-text questions
a) Carbon dioxide.
b) Because water prevents carbon dioxide getting to the mortar.

CHEMISTRY — ROCKS AND BUILDING
C1a 1.5 Cement, concrete and glass

LEARNING OBJECTIVES
1. How do we make cement?
2. What is concrete?
3. How is glass made?

Cement
Although lime mortar holds bricks and stone together very strongly it does not work in all situations. In particular, lime mortar does not harden very quickly. It will not set at all where water prevents it from reacting with carbon dioxide.

The Romans realised that they needed to add something to lime mortar to make it set in wet conditions. They found that adding brick dust or volcanic ash to the mortar mixture enabled the mortar to harden even under water. This method remained in use until the 18th century.

Then people found that heating limestone with clay in a kiln produced **cement**. Much experimenting led to the invention of **Portland cement**. We make this from a mixture of limestone, clay and other minerals which are heated and then ground into a fine powder.

This type of cement is still in use today. The mortar used to build a modern house consists of a mixture of Portland cement and sand. This sets when it is mixed thoroughly with water and left for a few days.

Figure 1 Lime mortar is not suitable for building pools since it will not harden when in contact with water

Figure 2 Portland cement was invented nearly 200 years ago. It is still in use all around the world today.

a) What does lime mortar need in order to set hard?
b) Why will lime mortar not set under water?

Concrete
Sometimes builders add stones or crushed rocks to the mixture of water, cement and sand. When this sets, it forms a hard, stone-like building material called **concrete**.

This material is very strong. It is especially good at resisting forces which tend to squeeze or crush it. We can make concrete even stronger by pouring it around steel rods or bars and then allowing it to set. This makes **reinforced concrete**, which is also good at resisting forces that tend to pull it apart.

PRACTICAL
Which mixture makes the strongest concrete?
Try mixing different proportions of cement, gravel and sand, then adding water, to find out how to make the strongest concrete.
- How did you test the concrete's strength?
- How could you improve the reliability of your data?

Figure 3 Badly designed reinforcement caused the concrete roof of this terminal building at Charles de Gaulle Airport in France to collapse in May 2004

Figure 4 Glass can produce some spectacular buildings

Glass
We can also use limestone to make a very different kind of building material. When powdered limestone is mixed with sand and sodium carbonate and then heated strongly it produces **glass**.

Glass is very important in buildings since it allows us to make them both weatherproof and light. Hundreds of years ago only very rich people could afford glass for their windows. So ordinary people's buildings must have been very cold and very dark during the winter!

Modern chemists have developed glass with many different properties. This makes it possible to design buildings that would have been impossible to build even 50 years ago.

SUMMARY QUESTIONS
1. Write down three ways that limestone is used in building other than as limestone blocks.
2. List the different ways in which limestone has been used to build your home or school.
3. Glass has been advertised as 'insulation you can see through!' Explain what the advertiser meant by this.
4. Concrete and glass are commonly used building materials. Evaluate the use of:
   a) concrete to make a path rather than using bricks
   b) glass to make a window pane rather than using perspex.

GET IT RIGHT!
You don't need to know the details of the industrial processes for making glass – just how it is made.

KEY POINTS
1. Cement is made by heating limestone with clay in a kiln.
2. Concrete is made by mixing crushed rocks, cement and sand with water.
3. Glass is made by heating powdered limestone, sand and sodium carbonate together very strongly.

SUMMARY ANSWERS
1. Concrete, mortar (cement), glass.
2. List.
3. A transparent material that prevents heat travelling through an area. [Strictly, this isn't really insulation.]
4. a) Concrete is strong in compression and can be set in large slabs. Bricks can be dislodged, creating an uneven surface, and soil gathers in gaps producing problems with weeds.
   b) Glass is harder than perspex and more resistant to scratching. On the other hand, perspex is tougher than the brittle glass.

GET IT RIGHT!
Students don't need to know the details of the industrial processes for making glass – just how it is made. They should also be able to describe how they would test the properties of different materials.

DID YOU KNOW?
Glass is a super-cooled liquid and continues to flow even when it is used in windows or other glass objects.

KEY POINTS
Make a poem with three verses, one to reflect each key fact.

CHEMISTRY — ROCKS AND BUILDING
C1a 1.6 Building materials – from old to new

SPECIFICATION LINK-UP
C1a.11.1

Students should use their skills, knowledge and understanding of 'How Science Works':

- to evaluate the developments in using limestone, cement, concrete and glass as building materials, and their advantages and disadvantages over other materials.

CHEMISTRY — ROCKS AND BUILDING
C1a 1.6 Building materials – from old to new

Out of the past...

Since ancient times people have always needed somewhere to shelter. In hot countries people need to find somewhere cool during the day. In cold countries they need somewhere warm – and in wet, windy Britain we often need somewhere to get out of the rain!

In the past, people often had to move around since they did not work in one place. People who looked after animals or who worked in different places at different times of the year built shelters. They used wood and any other natural materials that they could find at that place. They built very simple homes that could be put up quickly. They did not use large amounts of material that had to be carried over long distances.

Once people started to settle down and live in one place, it was worth building a house which was bigger and which took longer to build. People began to use materials like stone, and to develop new materials like bricks and concrete. It was more difficult to build well with these new materials. This meant it was often necessary for people with special skills to be involved in building.

Figure 1 A charcoal burner's hut. The charcoal burner had to watch the kiln constantly, so it was necessary to live right next to it. Charcoal was sold as a fuel. It burned with an intense heat, much hotter than wood.

QUESTIONS
1. Why did ancient people use local materials for building rather than materials that had to be brought from a long distance away?
2. Why did people need special skills to work with materials like bricks and mortar?

...and into the future

As new building materials were developed, new ways of using them were found. Buildings could be made bigger and taller, and new designs were possible. People could live in big houses, grand houses, small houses – and even flats and bungalows.

As our understanding of the chemistry of materials grew, artificial materials like plastics and metals began to replace natural materials like wood. Because the properties of these new materials can be controlled, they can be made to order. They are produced to have exactly the right strength for the job they have to do. As materials scientists continue to produce exciting new materials, who knows what homes in the future may look like?!

ACTIVITY
a) Find some pictures of old houses. Find out what they are made of and think about why people chose these materials.
b) Design a house of the future. Clearly label the materials you use and their properties. Be creative – you can use materials that haven't been invented yet!

Teaching suggestions

Activities

Comparing building materials – Students need to develop an appreciation of the use of building materials and their development. You could give them a piece of A3 paper and ask them to fold it in half. On one side of the paper they could draw a diagram of an ancient house. This image could then be annotated with the building materials used. The second half of the page could be a drawing of a modern building, again annotated with the building materials. To extend the activity, the materials used in both diagrams could be underlined in blue, whereas ancient-only materials in yellow, and modern materials in red. Also, samples of the different building materials could be given to the students to allow them to be handled. An electronic resource, C1a 1.6 'What did people build with first', from the GCSE Chemistry CD can be used here.

Spider diagram – Using the Student Book as a source of information, a spider diagram entitled 'Building materials' could be created. The students should be encouraged to detail the strengths and drawbacks of each material, stating if it is modern or ancient and giving an example of a use.

Guess the material – Separate the class into groups of seven and give out a pack of cards. Each card should be like a name card for a party with one of the following words written on: stone, concrete, wood, glass, mortar, cement, plastic. The students should not look at their card they have been given, but secure it, so that it faces the rest of their group. They then must ask questions, to which the others can only answer, 'yes/no' in order to guess which material they are.

Extension

Makeover advice – Small groups could work on producing advice for a couple on how to makeover their house. This could then be acted out, or a magazine article prepared.

Homework

Timeline – Students could create a timeline, to show the advances in building materials. They could surf the Internet to print-off images to illustrate each building material.

ANSWERS TO QUESTIONS

1. They needed to build shelters quickly, and did not have the means to easily carry building materials from place to place.
2. They were more difficult to build with.

---

lifestyle

Ancient or Modern?

Anna and Simon are buying their second house. It's a modern one, on a big estate. They're hoping to make it look a bit different, to reflect their personalities and lifestyle.

> We'd really like an old house, but there's nothing like that around here. So we want to use old building materials to make the house look older than it really is. We think that we might use natural limestone to cover up the bricks, and we're going to put an old wooden door in to replace the PVC front door. We might even take out the modern windows too. We want it to look more like a cottage than a house on a big estate.

Roger and Su moved into their house a while ago. It's old, and needs some work done on it. Some of the windows leak, and there's a lot of painting to do! They want to try to make the house easy to maintain.

> This house is very old, and it really needs updating. With our children growing up, we really don't have time to look after the house. If we put modern doors and windows in, we won't have to worry about painting them. The windows will be double-glazed too, so the house will be much warmer in winter. And that old metal gutter round the roof – we'll replace that with white PVC plastic. So much more modern!

ACTIVITY

Imagine that you are the host of a TV makeover show. Both couples in the magazine are guests on the show. They need your advice about how they should makeover their houses. Write and present a short script for the programme, presenting your advice to each couple. Remember that you'll not only need to tell them what they should do but why they should do it.

ACTIVITY

Decisions, decisions

There's a huge choice of building materials available for people who want to update their homes – modern scientists have seen to that!

Discuss the issues below:
- Should people just 'do want they fancy' when they decide to update a house?
- Are Anna and Simon right to think about making their modern house look old? Why?
- Should Roger and Su try to make their house as easy as possible to maintain? What advice would you give them?

Learning styles

Kinaesthetic: Handling different building materials.

Visual: Drawing their own spider diagram that will aid visual learners to memorise this topic.

Auditory: Listening to responses in 'Guess the material'.

Intrapersonal: Making the timeline.

Interpersonal: Small groups working on producing advice for a makeover.

Gifted and talented

Groups of students could be given the task to design the next new advancement in building materials. They should produce a specification card, including its advantages, disadvantages, dimensions and an image. This activity is useful for all types of learners.

Special needs

A partially finished spider diagram could be provided.

ICT link-up

There are Internet sites that contain balanced views about limestone quarries, such as: www.bbc.co.uk/scotland/education/int/geog/ limestone/people_bank. This could be used to allow a debate about limestone quarry sites.

CHEMISTRY   ROCKS AND BUILDING

SUMMARY ANSWERS

1. a) 1
   b) Groups.
   c) They have similar reactions.
   d) The atoms are joined by chemical bonds.

2. a) For example: 'When the handwarmer is squeezed it breaks the capsule. Water comes into contact with the quicklime. The chemicals react to produce slaked lime. This reaction also releases energy, making the handwarmer warm.'
   b) $CaO + H_2O \rightarrow Ca(OH)_2$
   c) It is disposable – there is no easy way to reverse the reaction, and the capsule containing the water is broken when the handwarmer is activated.

3. a)

Ingredient	gravel	sand	cement	water
Number of buckets	4	3	1	0.5
Percentage	47	35	12	6

   b) Vary the composition of the mixtures, keeping e.g. dimensions of concrete moulds, volume of mixture placed in the moulds and method of testing, the same.
   Suitable method for testing strength need to be described, e.g. dropping a weight on a concrete block until it breaks, increasing the height of drop systematically.

Summary teaching suggestions

- **Special needs**
  - A lot of students often know the science but can't understand the question, and therefore fail to gain marks that they can answer orally to a teacher. Teachers, or LSAs, could read out each question in turn and allow the students time to answer before reading the next. More competent students could carry on without having the questions read out.

- **Learning styles**
  Visual: Question 2 involves students using previous knowledge to solve a problem, drawing a diagram is excellent for visual learners.
  Interpersonal: Question 3 lends itself to class discussions before the answers are written.

- **When to use the questions?**
  - As a revision resource.
  - Each question relates to a different lesson spread, e.g. question 1 relates to C1a1.1. The relevant question could be given as part of a plenary session.

- **Gifted and talented**
  Question 2b) involves balancing a symbol equation. This is an advanced skill for higher attaining students. Students could also add state symbols to their equation.

- **Misconceptions**
  Question 1 depends on students understanding terminology for particles. Students often substitute: atom, element, compound and particle freely and do not understand the differences between them. Give each student a sheet with these definitions on. Encourage them to use the correct term rather than 'it' in their answers.

ROCKS AND BUILDING: C1a 1.1 – C1a 1.6

SUMMARY QUESTIONS

1. a) Jim has a sample of a pure element. How many different types of atom are there in it?
   b) What do we call the vertical columns of elements in the periodic table?
   c) Three elements are in the same column of the periodic table. What does this tell us about the reactions of these three elements?
   d) The atoms of two different elements react together to form a compound. Why is it difficult to separate the two elements when this has happened?

2. The diagram shows a design for a handwarmer which uses quicklime and water. To activate the handwarmer you squeeze the container. This breaks the capsule containing the water so that it mixes with the quicklime.

   a) Using complete sentences, describe how the handwarmer works.
   b) Write down a balanced chemical equation for the reaction in the handwarmer, using the correct symbols.
   c) Is the handwarmer re-usable or disposable? Give reasons for your answer.

3. a) A set of instructions for making concrete reads:
   'To make good, strong concrete, thoroughly mix together 4 buckets of gravel, 3 buckets of sand and one bucket of cement. When you have done this, add half a bucket of water.'
   Copy and complete the table showing the percentage of each ingredient in the concrete mixture. Give your answers to the nearest whole number.

Ingredient	gravel	sand	cement	water
Number of buckets				
Percentage				

   b) Describe an investigation you could try to see which particular mixture of gravel, sand and cement makes the strongest concrete. What would you vary, what would you keep the same and how would you test the 'strength' of the concrete?

EXAM-STYLE QUESTIONS

1. The diagram shows a molecule of ammonia, NH_3.

   H—N—H
       |
       H

   Match the words **A, B, C** and **D** with spaces **1** to **4** in the sentences.
   A bonds
   B electrons
   C elements
   D symbols
   Ammonia is a compound made from two ......**1**..... .
   The atoms in the molecule are represented by ......**2**..... .
   The atoms in ammonia are held together by chemical ......**3**..... .
   Each atom has a nucleus surrounded by ......**4**..... .   (4)

2. The diagram shows stages in making cement and concrete.

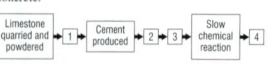

   Limestone quarried and powdered → **1** → Cement produced → **2** → **3** → Slow chemical reaction → **4**

   Match statements **A, B, C** and **D** with the numbers **1** to **4** to describe what happens in this process.
   A cement mixed with sand and crushed rock
   B concrete produced
   C limestone heated in a kiln with clay
   D water added to mixture   (4)

3. (a) Slaked lime is made by reacting quicklime with:
   A carbon dioxide
   B oxygen
   C sulfuric acid
   D water   (1)

   (b) The chemical name for slaked lime is:
   A calcium chloride
   B calcium hydroxide
   C calcium oxide
   D calcium sulfate   (1)

   (c) Slaked lime can be used to make:
   A bricks
   B clay
   C mortar
   D quicklime   (1)

EXAM-STYLE ANSWERS

1 1 **C**
   2 **D**
   3 **A**
   4 **B**   (4 marks)

2 1 **C**
   2 **A**
   3 **D**
   4 **B**   (4 marks)

3 a) **D**
   b) **B**
   c) **C**
   d) **A**   (4 marks)

4 a) *Two from:*
   - Transparent.
   - Water/weather proof.
   - Good (thermal) insulator.
   - Can be moulded to shape.   (2 marks)

   b) *One mark for disadvantage and one mark for correctly linked explanation, e.g.*
   - Can break easily, because it is brittle.
   - Expensive, because high energy cost of manufacture.
   - Can produce high temperatures inside buildings, greenhouse effect.   (2 marks)

5 *Three from:*
   - Unsightly/damage to scenery.
   - Noise.
   - Dust.
   - Air pollution (machinery/traffic fumes).
   - Traffic/heavy lorries.
   - Damage to wildlife/habitats.
   - Provides jobs.   (3 marks)

(d) Lime water goes cloudy when reacted with carbon dioxide. Which substance is produced?
  A calcium carbonate
  B calcium chloride
  C calcium oxide
  D calcium sulfate (1)

4 Glass is used in almost all buildings.
  (a) Suggest **two** properties of glass that make it useful in buildings. (2)
  (b) Suggest and explain one disadvantage of using glass in buildings. (2)

5 One of the largest limestone quarries in the United Kingdom is near the town of Buxton. It is in the Peak District National Park, an area popular with tourists.

Suggest **three** social or environmental issues involved in quarrying limestone in the Peak District. (3)

6 Mortars used in most modern buildings are made using cement.
A student tested the strength of a ready-mixed mortar. He did this by dropping a mass onto a small mortar beam from increasing heights until the beam broke in half. He tested 4 beams made from the mortar. His results were 20 cm, 50 cm, 65 cm and 15 cm.
  (a) What was the range of the student's results? (2)
  (b) Work out the mean of his results. (1)
  (c) Comment on the precision of his results. (1)
  (d) (i) Besides cement, what was the other solid in the ready-mixed mortar? (1)
      (ii) What other solid is needed to make concrete instead of mortar? (1)

HOW SCIENCE WORKS QUESTIONS

Look at the standards for the testing of cement shown below and answer the questions that follow.

Standards for the testing of cement

Cement must be tested to the following standards:
- After 7 days use compressive test standard equipment to test the strength of the cement.
- Three batches of already tested cement must also be treated in the same way.
- The bowl must be wiped clean and 400 g of test cement added during 30 seconds. Add 400 g of the sand and mix for 120 seconds. Add 200 g of water and mix for 240 seconds.
- The sand being used must be washed, heated in a kiln at 110°C and then passed through a sieve with holes of diameter 1 mm.
- The mixing bowl used must be between 20 cm wide at the top, narrowing in a curve to 8 cm at the bottom and made of stainless steel.
- The apparatus used must conform to that described in CTM19.

a) What was the dependent variable in this testing? (1)
b) What was the 'control group' in this testing? (1)
c) Why is it important to test cement that has already been tested? (1)
d) Why is it important to test the cement? (1)
e) Why is it important to give so much detail of how to test the cement? (1)
f) Who should NOT carry out these tests? Explain your answer. (2)
g) Who should carry out these tests? Explain your answer. (2)

HOW SCIENCE WORKS ANSWERS

a) The (compressive) strength of the cement was the dependent variable.
b) Three batches of already-tested cement was the 'control group'.
c) It is important to test cement that has already been tested to make sure that the technique is being used properly.
d) Poor cement could cause structural faults and lead to deaths.
e) So that the test is reliable.
f) The following should not carry out these tests:
   - people who do not understand the scientific procedures
   - people who might be biased, such as the owners of the cement factory or builders using the cement.
   The results could be inaccurate or the results presented in a biased way.
g) Independent scientists should carry out the tests so that the tests are carried out correctly and the results presented without bias.

How science works teaching suggestions

- **Literacy guidance**
  - Key terms that should be clearly understood are: dependent variable, control group, bias.
  - Questions expecting longer answers, where students can practise their literacy skills are f) and g).
- **Higher- and lower-level questions.** Questions c), e) and f) are higher-level questions. Questions a) and b) are lower-level questions. Answers for all these have been provided at these levels.
- **Gifted and talented.** Discuss how to present complex procedures in a way that can be followed successfully. This could be practised on a laboratory procedure that is agreed and, working in pairs, students follow implicitly the instructions of their partner.
- **How and when to use these questions.** When wishing to develop the idea that people who do not fully understand the science, but who can do a very effective job if given the correct support. They can often carry out complex scientific procedures. Also, the importance of building-in safety into the use of materials by constant testing.
- **Homework.** Draw up a list of structures and materials in the house which might have been tested prior to sale.
- **Special needs.** Some help will be needed by some students to interpret the language used.
- **ICT link-up.** Students could use the Internet to find examples of how different materials are tested, e.g. glass.

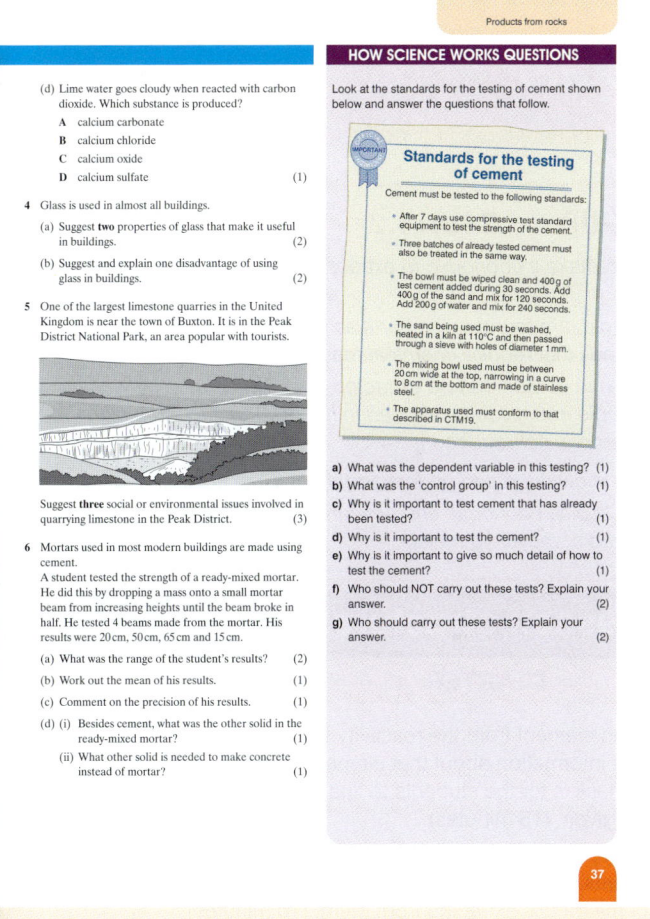

6 a) 15 cm–65 cm *(2 marks – give 1 mark if student does not give maximum and minimum values, i.e. 50 cm)*

  b) 37.5 cm *(1 mark – do not penalise lack of unit if a mark has already been lost in part a))*

  c) Not (very) precise because range is wide/large or there is a large spread about the mean, (OWTTE) *(1 mark)*

  d) i) Sand. *(1 mark)*
     ii) Crushed rock or stones or aggregate or gravel. *(1 mark)*

Exam teaching suggestions

The exam questions could be used on completing the chapter, or individual questions could be set as lessons are completed. Questions could be attempted by students working alone, as homework or in class. There is a total of 25 marks, and it should take about 25 minutes to complete if done as a test. Questions could also be used in lessons by pairs or small groups working together, discussing and refining their answers.

Q1 could be used to check learning after completing spread 1.1, Q2 after 1.2, Q3 after 1.4, etc.

Literacy skills are important in Q4 and Q5. 'Suggest' implies there is more than one correct answer, and that students should use information from the question together with their own knowledge. While learning, they should be encouraged to refer to other sources (such as the chapter in the Student Book).

Students should be encouraged to check that they have written enough to gain all the available marks, e.g. in Q4b) the disadvantage must be explained for the second mark. Students should not write all they know about a topic, e.g. in Q5 they should give no more than **three** points or they may contradict themselves.

Students cannot always distinguish between atoms, molecules and elements. Their understanding can be checked using Q1. Use Q2 to reinforce understanding of the differences between cement, concrete and mortar, which many students confuse.

CHEMISTRY · ROCKS AND METALS

C1a 2.1 Extracting metals

LEARNING OBJECTIVES

Students should learn:
- Where metals are obtained from.
- Examples of how metals are extracted from the Earth.

LEARNING OUTCOMES

Most students should be able to:
- List examples of native metals and metals found in ores.
- Relate the method of extraction to the reactivity of a metal.
- Identify a reduction process from a description of a reaction.

Some students should also be able to:
- Write a balanced equation to show the reduction of a metal oxide.

Teaching suggestions

- **Special needs.** Ask these students only to reduce one metal ore, e.g. copper carbonate as copper is studied later on in the specification. Reducing lots of different ores will just confuse them.
- **Learning styles**
  Kinaesthetic: Lining up in order of reactivity.
  Visual: Observing reduction of metal ores.
  Auditory: Listening to answers in questions and answers.
  Intrapersonal: Completing the sentences.
  Interpersonal: Looking at different ores and discussing their composition.
- **Homework.** Find out the names of copper ore [malachite], iron ore [haematite] and gold ore [trick question, it is a native metal].
- **ICT link-up.** There are some interactive exercises about metal extraction on: www.chemit.co.uk

Answers to in-text questions

a) In the Earth's crust.
b) A metal ore.
c) Because they are very unreactive.
d) Above carbon.
e) Reactions that involve the removal of oxygen.

SPECIFICATION LINK-UP   C1a.11.2

- *Ores contain enough metal to make it economic to extract the metal and this changes over time.*
- *Unreactive metals, such as gold, are found in the Earth as the metal itself, but most metals are found as compounds that require chemical reactions to extract the metal.*
- *Metals that are less reactive than carbon can be extracted from their oxides by reduction in carbon, for example iron oxide is reduced in the blast furnace to make iron. (Details of the blast furnace is not required.)*

Students should use their skills, knowledge and understanding of 'How Science Works':
- *to consider and evaluate the social, economic and environmental impacts of exploiting metal ores, of using metals and of recycling metals.*

Lesson structure

STARTER

'Line up' – Give each student an element from the reactivity series printed on a piece of card. On the back of the card is information about that element's reaction with water, acid and oxygen in the air. The task is for the students to line themselves up in order of reactivity using the information given. (15 minutes)

Prediction – Show students samples of ores and ask them to guess the metal that they contain. This should help students see that ores are usually mixtures of compounds and do not share the properties of the metals extracted from them. (10 minutes)

Key words – Ask students to look at each definition and to match it to its key word.
1. Removal of oxygen from a compound. [reduction] 2. A list of elements from the most reactive to the least reactive. [reactivity series] 3. A rock containing enough metal to make it economic to extract. [ore] 4. Unreactive metals, found as elements in nature. [native] (5 minutes)

MAIN

- Show students a selection of ores and explain that the metal is locked up in a compound, often an oxide. Ask the students to suggest how the metal could be released [through a chemical reaction, some might mention reduction].
- Explain that carbon can be used to 'displace' the metal as long as carbon is more reactive than the metal you wish to extract.
- Ask the students to consult the reactivity series and suggest which metals could be extracted using this technique [e.g. zinc, iron, copper, lead].
- Students, in small groups, can extract a metal from its oxide. They should be encouraged to share their results and compare evidence collected by others. (This could be useful in helping to explain why different people observing the same event 'see' different things – 'How Science Works'.)
- Ask students to make a poster detailing the reactivity series. On the poster, they could highlight which metals can be reduced using carbon and include word equations for the metal oxide being reduced.
- The native metals should also be detailed. At a later date, this poster could be re-visited and the metals that are electrolysed could also be added.

PLENARIES

Random questions and answers – Create a PowerPoint® presentation, with each student's name on a different slide. Set the slide show so that it is continuous. Then start the slide show, the students' names will appear one by one quickly on the screen. Press pause and one slide will hold into position, choosing a student to ask a question to. Then to return to the 'name generator' press pause again. (10 minutes)

Complete the sentences – Ask the students to complete the following sentences [suggested answers in brackets]:
- Metal ores are rocks that . . . [contain enough metal to make it economic to extract].
- Gold, platinum and silver are . . . [native metals].
- Reduction reactions are used . . . [to remove oxygen from a metal oxide]. (5 minutes)

Practical support

Equipment and materials required
Bunsen burner and safety equipment, eye protection, test tube/ignition tube plus test tube holders (alternatively, tripod, pipe-clay triangle), evaporating dish, spatula, carbon powder, crucible, 1 mol/dm³ HCl – irritant), selection of metal oxides (e.g. copper oxide – harmful, magnesium oxide – irritant, lead oxide – toxic).

Safety: Wear eye protection, ventilate room well, but use a fume cupboard if it is available. Acid is an irritant and hands should be washed after the practical. CLEAPSS Hazcards 47, 26, 56.

Details
Mix the metal oxide thoroughly with carbon powder as a 1:1 ratio. Put the mixture into a test tube (or crucible secured in a pipe-clay triangle) and heat strongly in a blue Bunsen flame. Allow cooling and observe to see metal pieces. The pieces can be washed, and almost 'pan' for the pure metal.

Alternately, if the reduced metal would react with acid e.g. magnesium, add acid and, if fizzing occurs, then the metal was produced. Heating magnesium oxide with carbon will prove negative – no fizzing. Allow the mixture to cool before adding dilute acid.

- The carbon is more reactive than copper (or lead) so it can reduce the metal oxide, leaving the metal element:

$$\text{copper oxide} + \text{carbon} \rightarrow \text{copper} + \text{carbon dioxide}$$
$$2\text{CuO} + \text{C} \rightarrow 2\text{Cu} + \text{CO}_2$$

ACTIVITY & EXTENSION IDEAS

- Ask students to find examples of different ores and which compound it is mainly made of, and so state which metal is produced from it.

- Ask students to consider the environmental impact of metal extraction (e.g. mining produces pollution; a greenhouse gas is produced during the reduction process). This could be extended to include a discussion about the social impact (e.g. local jobs, noise pollution) and economic impact (e.g. increase in local tax payment, a lot of mining is completed by international companies and the money often goes outside the mining country's economy). This is useful for introducing the societal aspects of 'How Science Works'.

CHEMISTRY — ROCKS AND METALS

C1a 2.1 Extracting metals

LEARNING OBJECTIVES
1 Where do metals come from?
2 How do we extract metals from the Earth?

Metals have been important to people for thousands of years. You can follow the course of history by the materials people used – from the Stone Age to the Bronze Age and then on to the Iron Age.

Where do metals come from?
Metals are found in the Earth's crust. We find most metals combined with other chemical elements, often with oxygen. This means that the metal must be chemically separated from its compounds before you can use it.

In some places there is enough of a metal or metal compound in a rock to make it worth extracting the metal. Then we call the rock a metal *ore*.

Whether it is worth extracting a particular metal depends on:
- how easy it is to extract it from its ore,
- how much metal the ore contains.

A few metals, such as gold and silver, are so unreactive that they are found in the Earth as the metals (elements) themselves. We say that they exist in their *native* state.

Sometimes a nugget of gold is so large it can simply be picked up. At other times tiny flakes have to be physically separated from sand and rocks by panning.

a) Where do we find metals in nature?
b) If there is enough metal in a rock to make it economic to extract it, what do we call the rock?
c) Why are silver and gold found as metals rather than combined with other elements?

Figure 1 The Angel of the North stands 20 metres tall, and is made of steel which contains a small amount of copper

Figure 2 Panning for gold. Mud and stones are washed away while the dense gold remains in the pan.

DID YOU KNOW…
… that gold in Wales is found in seams, just like coal – although not as thick, unfortunately! Gold jewellery was worn by early Welsh princes as a badge of rank. Welsh gold has been used in modern times to make the wedding rings of Royal brides.

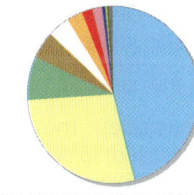

Oxygen 46%
Silicon 28%
Aluminium 8%
Iron 5%
Calcium 4%
Sodium 3%
Magnesium 2%
Potassium 2%
Titanium 0.5%
Hydrogen 0.5%
All other elements 1%

Figure 3 There are many different elements that go to make up the Earth's crust

How do we extract metals?
The way in which we extract a metal depends on its place in the *reactivity series*. The reactivity series lists the metals in order of their reactivity. The most reactive are placed at the top and the least reactive at the bottom.

A more reactive metal will displace a less reactive metal from its compounds. Carbon (a non-metal) will also displace less reactive metals from their oxides. We use carbon to extract metals from their ores commercially.

d) A metal cannot be extracted from its ore using carbon. Where is this metal in the reactivity series?

You can find many metals, such as copper, lead, iron and zinc, combined with oxygen. The compounds are called *metal oxides*. Because carbon is more reactive than each of these metals, you can use it to extract them from their ores.

When you heat the metal oxide with carbon, the carbon removes the oxygen from the metal oxide to form carbon dioxide. The reaction leaves the metal, as the element, behind:

$$\text{metal oxide} + \text{carbon} \rightarrow \text{metal} + \text{carbon dioxide}$$

For example:
$$\text{lead oxide} + \text{carbon} \rightarrow \text{lead} + \text{carbon dioxide}$$
$$2\text{PbO} + \text{C} \rightarrow 2\text{Pb} + \text{CO}_2$$

We call the removal of oxygen in this way a *reduction reaction*.

e) What do chemists mean by a reduction reaction?

PRACTICAL
Reduction by carbon
Heat some copper oxide with carbon powder strongly in a test tube.
Empty the contents into an evaporating dish.
You can repeat the experiment with lead oxide and carbon if you have a fume cupboard to work in.
- Explain your observations. Include a word equation or balanced symbol equation.

SUMMARY QUESTIONS
1 Copy and complete using the words below:
    crust   extracted   native   reduction
Metals come from the Earth's …… . Some metals are very unreactive and are found in their …… state. Metals, such as zinc and iron, are found combined with oxygen and can be …… using chemical reactions. These are known as …… reactions, as oxygen is removed from the oxide.
2 Make a list of all the metal objects found in your classroom or at home. Try to name the metal(s) used to make each object.
3 Platinum is never found combined with oxygen. What does this tell you about its reactivity? Give a use of platinum that depends on this property.
4 Zinc oxide (ZnO) can be reduced to zinc by heating it in a furnace with carbon. Carbon monoxide (CO) is given off in the reaction. Write a word equation and a balanced equation for the reduction of zinc oxide.

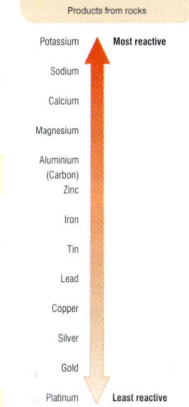

Products from rocks

Potassium — Most reactive
Sodium
Calcium
Magnesium
Aluminium
(Carbon)
Zinc
Iron
Tin
Lead
Copper
Silver
Gold
Platinum — Least reactive

Figure 4 This reactivity series shows how reactive each element is compared to the other elements

KEY POINTS
1 The Earth's crust contains many different elements.
2 A metal ore contains enough of the metal to make it economically worth extracting the metal.
3 We can find gold and other unreactive metals in their native state.
4 The reactivity series is useful in deciding the best way to extract a metal from its ore.
5 Metals more reactive than carbon cannot be extracted from their ores using carbon.

SUMMARY ANSWERS

1 Crust, native, extracted, reduction.

2 List.

3 Platinum is very unreactive. It is used in jewellery and in special wires.

4 zinc oxide + carbon → zinc + carbon monoxide
   ZnO + C → Zn + CO

DID YOU KNOW?

Gold is not just used for jewellery – pure gold is used on the insides of astronauts' helmet sun-visors and in some electrical circuits. A gold compound is also used to treat arthritis suffers.

KEY POINTS

Ask the students to 'translate' the key points into text language. Artistic students could draw a mobile phone and write their message onto the face.

CHEMISTRY   ROCKS AND METALS

C1a 2.2 Extracting iron

LEARNING OBJECTIVES

Students should learn:

- That metals less reactive than carbon can be extracted by reducing their oxides with carbon.
- That iron is extracted in a blast furnace.

LEARNING OUTCOMES

All students should be able to:

- State that iron(III) oxide and coke are used in the blast furnace.
- Explain, in terms of word equations the reduction of iron ore in a blast furnace.

Some students should also be able to:

- Explain, in terms of a balanced symbol equation, the reduction of iron(III) oxide in a blast furnace by carbon.

Teaching suggestions

- **Special needs.** These students would probably benefit from making a model blast furnace. This could be made using cardboard boxes and paint. Velcro can be used to attach labels to different parts of the model.
- **Learning styles**
  Kinaesthetic: Making a mind map (using the cards will appeal to kinaesthetic learners). Also they might find that, as the mind map develops, they may need to change the positions of some key words as they become fundamental in the diagram.
  Visual: Watching a video on metal extraction.
  Auditory: Listening to feedback.
  Intrapersonal: Completing the paragraph.
  Interpersonal: Giving feedback to other students on their mind map.
- **Homework.** Create a poster on the blast furnace.
- **ICT link-up.** See how iron was and is extracted in the blast furnace game at: http://www.bbc.co.uk/history/games/blast/blast.shtml or ask students to search www.bbc.co.uk for the game.

SPECIFICATION LINK-UP   C1a.11.2

- Metals that are less reactive than carbon can be extracted from oxides by reduction with carbon, for example iron oxide is reduced in the blast furnace to make iron. (Details of the blast furnace are not required).

Students should use their skills, knowledge and understanding of 'How Science Works':

- to consider and evaluate the social, economic and environmental impacts of exploiting metal ores, of using metals and of recycling metals.

Lesson structure

STARTER

Chemical equation – Ask students to look at the following equation and decide which substance is being oxidised and which is reduced and say how they decided:

iron oxide + carbon monoxide → iron + carbon dioxide

[Iron oxide is being reduced, as it loses oxygen; whereas carbon monoxide is being oxidised, as it gains oxygen.] (5 minutes)

Chemical formulae – Ask students to find the chemical names of:

- Fe_2O_3 [iron oxide/haematite]
- $CaCO_3$ [calcium carbonate/limestone]
- C [carbon/coke] (5 minutes)

MAIN

- Studying the blast furnace introduces a lot of new words and ideas. However, stress the reduction of iron oxide in the furnace and the role of carbon (as no details of the blast furnace itself are required).
- Often the scale of industrial chemistry is difficult to bring into the classroom, but videos or site visits will help. Students could watch a video on iron production, such as *Industrial Chemistry for Schools and Colleges* (RSC).
- Then the students could interpret information from the textbook and video to create a flow chart to summarise the chemical reactions involved in the reduction of iron ore to extract iron.

PLENARIES

AfL (Assessment for Learning) – Ask students to view another group's mind-map and comment on their map. (See Activity and Extension ideas.) (10 minutes)

Complete a prose – Ask students to complete the paragraph:

A [blast] furnace is used to reduce [iron ore (haematite)]. The solid raw materials are iron ore, [limestone] and [coke]. Coke is first [oxidised] to carbon dioxide. This reacts with more [coke] to make carbon monoxide, and this gas [reduces] the iron ore. Limestone is added to remove the [impurities]. (10 minutes)

Products from rocks

ACTIVITY & EXTENSION IDEAS

- Students could research the historical development of the blast furnace.
- Students could compare and contrast the reduction of iron ore and tungsten ore/zinc ore (which are also reduced using carbon).
- Students could colour in a map of the world to represent the production of iron. They could use a darker colour for a high tonnage of iron produced per annum.
- Students could make their own model blast furnace.
- Students often compartmentalise information, so mind maps help them to make links. Make cards 7 cm by 3 cm with key words: blast furnace, limestone, coke, haematite, calcium carbonate, carbon, iron oxide, hot air, reduction, oxidation, slag, impurities, iron, carbon dioxide, carbon monoxide. Split the class into groups, and give them felt pens, a pack of key words and some Blu-Tack. The students should then work as a team to produce a mind map. They should stick a key word onto the sheet, then select another key word. This becomes the first and last word of a sentence, which the students should then connect with an arrow and write onto the arrows to create the sentence. Each word can be connected to as many words as relevant.

Answers to in-text questions

a) Iron ore (haematite/iron oxide), coke, limestone.

b) Carbon monoxide.

CHEMISTRY — ROCKS AND METALS

C1a 2.2 Extracting iron

LEARNING OBJECTIVES
1. What are the raw materials for making iron?
2. How is iron ore reduced?

Extracting iron from its ore is a huge industry. Iron is the second most common metal in the Earth's crust. Iron ore contains iron combined with oxygen. Iron is less reactive than carbon. So we can extract iron by using carbon to remove oxygen from the iron oxide in the ore.

We extract iron using a **blast furnace**. This is a large container made of steel. It is lined with fireproof bricks to withstand the high temperatures inside. There are solid raw materials which we use in the blast furnace, as well as lots of air. They are:

- **Haematite** – this is the most common iron ore. It contains mainly iron(III) oxide (Fe_2O_3) and sand.
- **Coke** – this is made from coal and is almost pure carbon. It will provide the reducing agent to remove the oxygen from iron(III) oxide.

We also add limestone to remove impurities.

a) List the three solid raw materials for making iron.

Hot air is blown into the blast furnace. This makes the coke burn, which heats the furnace and forms carbon dioxide gas.

$$C + O_2 \rightarrow CO_2$$

At the high temperatures in the blast furnace, this carbon dioxide reacts with more coke to form carbon monoxide gas.

$$CO_2 + C \rightarrow 2CO$$

The carbon monoxide reacts with the iron oxide, removing its oxygen, and reducing it to molten iron. This flows to the bottom of the blast furnace.

$$Fe_2O_3 + 3CO \rightarrow 2Fe + 3CO_2$$

Figure 1 Making iron is a hot, dirty process – and it can be quite spectacular too!

DID YOU KNOW?
The oldest iron smelting plants that we know about were built in China over 2000 years ago. Iron goods around 500 years older than this have been found in China, so it seems likely that iron-making in China goes back at least 2500 years. The first iron smelter in Europe was not built until about 1200 CE.

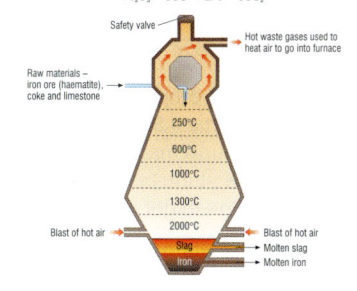

Figure 2 A blast furnace produces molten iron. Impurities from the iron ore are removed as slag.

Some of the molten iron is left to solidify in moulds – we call this **cast iron**. It contains about 96% iron. Most of the iron is kept molten to be turned into **steel**.

We make steel by removing more of the impurities from the iron. Then we mix it with other elements to change its properties.

b) What is the name of the substance that reduces the iron oxide to iron?

Iron – an important metal

Iron played a vital part in the Industrial Revolution, which happened in Britain during the 1700s and 1800s. Three generations of the same family – all called Abraham Darby – improved and developed new ways of making iron.

Up until this time charcoal had been used as the source of carbon for reducing the iron oxide. The Darby family replaced this with coke. They developed the blast furnace as a way of making iron continuously rather than in batches.

Most of the world's steel is now made in Asia. That's because the cost of making it is much lower than in Europe and North America. Iron and steel-making used to employ many thousands of people in the UK but now employs far fewer. Other jobs for these people have had to be made in other industries.

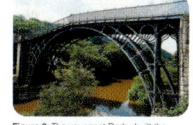

Figure 3 The youngest Darby built the world's first cast-iron bridge in 1779. It still spans the River Severn at Coalbrookdale in Shropshire. Coalbrookdale is now much better known as Ironbridge Gorge.

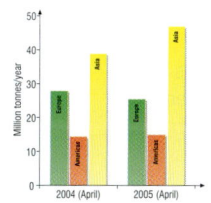

Figure 4 World steel output in April 2004 and April 2005

SUMMARY QUESTIONS

1. Copy and complete using the words below:

   carbon   coke   haematite   limestone

   We can extract iron from iron ore using .... The most common type of iron ore is .... Other raw materials for making iron are .... and ....

2. How is steel different from cast iron?

3. **a)** Some of the iron(III) oxide (Fe_2O_3) in the blast furnace is reduced by carbon, giving off carbon dioxide. Write a word equation for this reaction.
   b) Write a balanced symbol equation for the reaction described in part a).

KEY POINTS

1. We extract iron from iron ore by reducing it with carbon in a blast furnace.
2. The solid raw materials used to make iron are iron ore (haematite), coke and limestone.
3. Molten iron is tapped off from the bottom of the blast furnace.

SUMMARY ANSWERS

1. Carbon, haematite, coke, limestone.
2. Steel contains fewer impurities and has had other elements added.
3. **a)** iron(III) oxide + carbon → iron + carbon dioxide
   b) $2Fe_2O_3 + 3C \rightarrow 4Fe + 3CO_2$

DID YOU KNOW?

Molten iron is needed to fuse sections of railway track together. The molten iron is achieved not through the blast furnace, but a solid displacement reaction between aluminium and iron oxide. This chemical change is called the Thermit reaction.

KEY POINTS

Make cards containing parts of the sentences. The students could then arrange the word tiles to make up the key points. This activity can be made easier by splitting each sentence into just three parts.

CHEMISTRY — ROCKS AND METALS

C1a 2.3 Properties of iron and steels

LEARNING OBJECTIVES

Students should learn:

- The properties of pig iron and how this limits its usefulness.
- That iron can be alloyed to make it more useful.

LEARNING OUTCOMES

Most students should be able to:

- List the properties of iron produced from the blast furnace.
- Explain why steels are produced.

Some students should also be able to:

- Explain why alloying changes the properties of a pure metal in terms of its structure.
- Give examples of different types of steels, their chemical content and how their properties differ.

Teaching suggestions

- **Gifted and talented.** Ask students to find out the compositions of different steels and then to identify a pattern in composition and properties.
- **Learning styles**
  Kinaesthetic: Making model metal structures from polystyrene balls and Blu-Tack.
  Visual: Demonstrating the different compositions of steel in a recipe book format.
  Auditory: Explaining metal properties using the soap bubble model.
  Interpersonal: Working in a group looking at a bubble raft.
  Intrapersonal: Reflecting on the variety of uses for different steels.
- **Homework.** Ask the students to list the properties that both iron and steel share and then to list the desirable properties that make steel more useful than iron.
- **ICT link-up.** A number of resources are available from the Corus Group: www.coruseducation.com and other iron and steel industry web sites.

SPECIFICATION LINK-UP C1a.11.2

- *Iron from the blast furnace contains about 96% iron. The impurities make it brittle and so it has limited uses.*
- *Removing all impurities would produce pure iron. Pure iron has a regular arrangement of atoms, with layers that can slide over each other, and so is soft and easily shaped, but too soft for many uses.*
- *Most iron is converted into steels. Steels are alloys, since they are mixtures of iron with carbon and other metals. The different sized atoms distort the layers in the structure of the pure metal, making it more difficult for them to slide over each other, and so alloys are harder. Alloys can be designed to have properties for specific uses. Low carbon steels are easily shaped, high carbon steels are hard, and stainless steels are resistant to corrosion.*

Students should use their skills, knowledge and understanding of 'How Science Works':
- *to explain how the properties of alloys (but not smart alloys) are related to models of their structures.*

Lesson structure

STARTER

Model – Give students 12 marbles/polystyrene balls/table tennis balls and Blu-Tack. Ask them to make a model of a solid metal. The KS3 link word is 'solid', which students should link to the particle model. Once students have made their model, show a model that has already been made, where the balls in each layer are fixed with permanent glue. Show how the layers slide over each other easily. Ask which property this refers to [ductility and malleability]. Then give each group a different sized ball to add to their model by replacing one of their atoms, and explain that this is an alloy. (15 minutes)

List – Ask students to list as many properties of iron as they can think of, and one use that draws specifically on that property [e.g. conductor of heat – saucepans; malleable – sculptures]. (10 minutes)

MAIN

- Students need to appreciate that different proportions of constituents are used to make steels with a great variety of properties. Show students a recipe book, then a recipe card such as ones given free in supermarkets. Ask students to create a recipe card for making steel, include variations at the bottom of the card, to make different types of steel. You need to follow a recipe to get a repeatable result.

- Ask students to create a 'lonely hearts' column for each type of steel. More artistic students could create the articles and a display could be made.

- Often students can list the properties of metals, but cannot fully explain how a metal's structure changes while it is being manipulated. This concept can be demonstrated with soap bubbles. Give each set of students a Petri dish with a soap solution in. Each student should then use a dropping pipette to create bubbles of about the same size, these represent the atoms in a pure metal. There should be darting black lines formed if you gently push the bubbles, this demonstrates the metal behaving in a malleable and ductile fashion. Then add bubbles of a different size to demonstrate an alloy and the effect on properties of the metal.

- You could develop the concept of alloys by testing the suitability of different metal wires in making springs. Students can coil the wires into springs then test with slotted masses. Their investigations can provide data to plot extension against load graphs and to determine when elastic limit is exceeded. This can address any of the investigative aspects of How Science Works.

Answers to in-text questions

a) It contains carbon.
b) It is too soft.
c) By adding other elements.

GET IT RIGHT!

Students should know how the hardness of steels is related to the carbon content.

Products from rocks

PLENARIES

List uses – For each type of steel, ask the class to give an example of a use. Then ask each table to come up with a different use for each type of steel, and finally the individual to come up with a use for each type of steel. (10 minutes)

True or false? – Give each student a red and a green card. If the students think a statement is true, they hold up the green card; if they think it is false, they hold up the red card. Ask them these true/false statements:
- Steel is a mixture. [True]
- All steels contain cobalt. [False]
- Stainless steels are expensive. [True]
- Stainless steels rust because they contain iron. [False]
- The chemical formula for steel is St. [False] (5 minutes)

ACTIVITY & EXTENSION

- Ask students to find out about BOC steel production and draw a labelled diagram of the vessel needed to make steel.

CHEMISTRY — ROCKS AND METALS

C1a 2.3 Properties of iron and steels

LEARNING OBJECTIVES
1 Why is iron from a blast furnace not very useful?
2 How is iron changed to make it more useful?

The iron produced by a blast furnace, called pig iron, is not very useful. It is about 96% iron and contains impurities, mainly of carbon. This makes pig iron very brittle. However, we can treat the iron from the blast furnace to remove some of the carbon.

Figure 1 The iron which has just come out of a blast furnace contains about 96% iron. The main impurity is carbon.

If we remove all of the carbon and other impurities from pig iron, we get pure iron. This is very soft and easily-shaped. But it is too soft for most uses. If we want to make iron really useful we have to make sure that it contains tiny amounts of other elements, including carbon and certain metals.

We call a metal that contains other elements an **alloy**.

Iron that has been alloyed with other elements is called **steel**. By adding elements in carefully controlled amounts, we can change the properties of the steel.

a) Why is iron from a blast furnace very brittle?
b) Why is pure iron not very useful?
c) How do we control the properties of steel?

Figure 2 The atoms in pure iron are arranged in layers which can easily slide over one another. In alloys the layers cannot slide so easily because atoms of other elements change the regular structure.

Look at Figure 2:
The atoms in pure iron are arranged in layers. Because of this regular arrangement, the atoms can slide over one another very easily. This is why pure iron is so soft and easily shaped.

Steels
Steel is not a single substance. There are lots of different types of steel. All of them are alloys of iron with carbon and/or other elements.

The simplest steels are the **carbon steels**. We make these by alloying iron with small amounts of carbon (from 0.03% to 1.5%). These are the cheapest steels to make. We use them in many products, like the bodies of cars, knives, machinery, ships, containers and structural steel for buildings.

Often these carbon steels have small amounts of other elements in them as well. High carbon steel, with a relatively high carbon content, is very strong but brittle. On the other hand, low carbon steel is soft and easily shaped. It is not as strong, but it is much less likely to shatter.

Mild steel is one type of low carbon steel. It contains less than 0.1% carbon. It is very easily pressed into shape. This makes it particularly useful in mass production, for example, making car bodies.

Low-alloy steels are more expensive than carbon steels because they contain between 1% and 5% of other metals. Examples of the metals used include nickel, chromium, manganese, vanadium, titanium and tungsten. Each of these metals gives a steel that is well-suited for a particular use. We use nickel–steel alloys to build long-span bridges, bicycle chains and military armour-plating. That's because they are very resistant to stretching forces. Tungsten steel operates well under very hot conditions so it is used to make high-speed tools.

Even more expensive are the **high-alloy steels**. These contain a much higher percentage of other metals. For example, chromium steels have between 12% and 15% chromium mixed with the iron, and often some nickel is mixed in too – this provides strength and chemical stability.

These chromium–nickel steels are more commonly known as **stainless steels**. We use them to make cooking utensils and cutlery. They are also used to make chemical reaction vessels because they combine hardness and strength with great resistance to corrosion. Unlike most other steels, they do not rust!

Figure 3 The properties of steel alloys make them ideal for use in suspension bridges

DID YOU KNOW?
The iron that comes out of a blast furnace is called 'pig iron' because the metal used to be cast into sand moulds that ran off a central channel. This looked like piglets suckling from their mother.

GET IT RIGHT!
Know how the hardness of steels is related to their carbon content.

SUMMARY QUESTIONS
1 Complete the following sentences using the terms below:
   carbon steel   pure iron   steel
   If all of the carbon and other impurities are removed from pig iron we get ....
   Iron that has been alloyed with other elements is called ....
   Iron that has been alloyed with a little carbon is called ....

2 a) What is the difference between high-alloy and low-alloy steels?
   b) Why are surgical instruments made from steel containing chromium and nickel?
   c) Make a table to summarise the composition and properties of different types of steel.
   d) Using diagrams, explain how alloying a metal with atoms of another element changes its properties.

KEY POINTS
1 Pure iron is too soft for it to be very useful.
2 Carefully controlled quantities of elements are added to iron to make alloys of steel with different properties.

SUMMARY ANSWERS

1 Pure iron, steel, carbon steel.

2 a) High-alloy steels contain a higher percentage of other elements in them than low-alloy steels.

   b) This is stainless steel, which is very resistant to corrosion.

   c)

Type of steel	Properties
low carbon	soft, not easily shattered (malleable)
high carbon	very strong but brittle
low alloy nickel	resistant to stretching forces (high tensile strength)
low alloy tungsten	works well at high temperatures
high alloy chromium	strong and chemically stable
stainless steels	hard, strong, corrosion resistant

   d) Answers should show that students understand how adding atoms of a different size into the lattice of metal atoms stops layers from sliding over each other, making the metal harder to deform.

Practical support

Observing bubbles

Equipment and materials required
One half of a Petri dish, dropping pipette, soap solution.

Details
Using the pipette, blow similar-sized bubbles into the Petri dish. Observe. Then blow different-sized bubbles and observe.

Investigating alloys

Equipment and materials required
Variety of wires (same gauge needed for fair testing), slotted 10 g masses, clamp stand, ruler.

Details
Students choose wires of same gauge to make springs by winding the wire around a pencil. Then they test the wires by measuring extension as successive masses are added.

KEY POINTS

Create a limerick to remember the two key points.

CHEMISTRY — ROCKS AND METALS

C1a 2.4 Alloys in everyday use

LEARNING OBJECTIVES

Students should learn that:
- Alloys are more useful than pure metals.
- Smart alloys are shape-memory metals.

LEARNING OUTCOMES

Most students should be able to:
- List reasons why alloys are more suitable than pure metals for specified applications.
- Recognise smart alloys and recall their main property.

Some students should also be able to:
- Give an application and critically compare a pure metal and an alloy in order to decide which material is best for the job.
- Give examples of uses of smart alloys, explaining why the smart alloy is used.

Teaching suggestions

- **Special needs.** The metals and alloys listed in the text could be provided on separate cards. Students could physically sort them into two groups and then copy them into their book.
- **Learning styles**
  Kinaesthetic: Passing around the paper and unfolding it in the game 'consequences' (this will appeal to kinaesthetic learners).
  Visual: Observing the comedy spoon.
  Auditory: Listening to presentations from other students.
  Intrapersonal: Listing metals/alloys from the textbook.
  Interpersonal: Working at speed with a group to pass on the paper during 'consequences'.
- **Homework.** Ask students to explain why alloys are more useful than pure metals.
- **ICT link-up.** The Science Enhancement Programme produce information for teachers on new materials: www.sep.org.uk

SPECIFICATION LINK-UP C1a.11.2

- Many metals in everyday use are alloys. Pure copper, gold and aluminium are too soft for many uses and so are mixed with small amounts of similar metals to make them harder for everyday use.
- Smart alloys can return to their original shape after being deformed.

Students should use their skills, knowledge and understanding of 'How Science Works':
- to evaluate the benefits, drawbacks and risks of using metals as structural materials and as smart materials.

Lesson structure

STARTER

Smart demonstration – Obtain a comedy spoon from a joke shop. These are made from a smart alloy, when you submerge them into warm water they change from looking like a 'normal' teaspoon to being a twisted spoon. Demonstrate this action in a glass beaker of warm water, asking a student to stir. Then when the spoon has become twisted, ask the students to try to explain what has happened. (10 minutes)

Listing – Ask the students to look into the Student Book and make two lists: one of all the metals listed and one of all the alloys. [Metals – copper, tin, zinc, gold, aluminium, iron and silver. Alloys – bronze, brass and shape memory alloys (SMAs).] (5–10 minutes)

What's in an alloy? Students research the constituents of common alloys. This activity could be extended by linking which metals are in which alloys. (5–10 minutes)

MAIN

- Many different alloys exist, but the students need to focus on specific types. Split the class into three groups. Each group is going to become the 'experts' on a different part of this spread:
  – Copper and its alloys
  – Gold, aluminium and their alloys
  – SMAs.
- Each group should produce an A5 set of notes about their topic, and a puzzle to check that the class have understood their work. They could also create a small presentation on the topic, maybe using PowerPoint®.
- In the following lesson, each group could deliver their presentation and their handout can be given to the class. The 'experts' are then on-hand to help with the activities.
- Alternatively, using the textbook for their information, ask the students to create a poster about alloys. On their poster the students should include a definition for an alloy, an example of an alloy, its properties and a few uses. Their poster should also include information about SMAs and a use.

PLENARIES

Consequences – Give each student a piece of paper about half of A4 portrait. Ask the students to write down a definition of alloys at the top of the paper, fold it over and pass it to the right. Then they should write their favourite alloy and why, fold and pass to the right, then a 'boring' fact about alloys, fold and pass to the right and finally then a fascinating fact about alloys. Ask the student to unfold their current piece of paper and read the comments. Ask a few students to feedback into the group. (15 minutes)

Summarise – Ask the students to write one sentence to include the following key terms: alloy, metal, SMA. [For example, SMAs, which are mixtures of metals, are the latest development in alloys.] Get feedback from different students. (5–10 minutes)

ACTIVITY & EXTENSION IDEAS

- Ask students to come up with an innovative use for a SMA.
- Give students other examples of alloys, e.g. solder and cupronickel. Ask the students to find out their composition, properties and uses.

FOUL FACTS

You can still drink gold today – certain alcoholic drinks (some lagers and wines) contain gold leaf. You can even get chocolate containing gold leaf!

CHEMISTRY — ROCKS AND METALS

C1a 2.4 Alloys in everyday use

LEARNING OBJECTIVES
1. Why are alloys more useful than pure metals?
2. What are smart alloys?

As we saw on page 42, pure iron is not very useful because it is too soft. In order to use the iron, we must turn it into an alloy by adding other elements. Other metals must also be turned into alloys to make them as useful as possible.

Copper

Copper is a soft, reddish coloured metal. It conducts heat and electricity very well. We have used copper for thousands of years. In fact some people think that it was the first metal to be used by humans. Copper articles have been found which are well over ten thousand years old.

Just like pure iron, pure copper is very soft.

Figure 1 The Statue of Liberty in New York contains over 80 tonnes of copper

Bronze was probably the first alloy made by humans, about 5500 years ago. It is usually made by mixing copper with tin, but small amounts of other elements can be added as well. For example, we can add phosphorus. This gives the alloy properties which make it ideal to use for bearings where we want very low friction.

We make **brass** by alloying copper with zinc. Brass is much harder than copper and it is workable.

It can be hammered into sheets and bent into different shapes. This property is used to make musical instruments.

a) What are the names of two common alloys of copper?
b) Why are copper alloys more useful than pure copper?

DID YOU KNOW?
Bronze makes an excellent material for the barrels of cannons. The low friction between the bronze barrel and the iron cannon ball makes it unlikely that the ball will stick in the barrel and cause an explosion.

Gold and aluminium

Just like copper and iron, we can make gold and aluminium harder by adding other elements. We usually alloy gold with copper and silver when we want to use it in jewellery. By varying the proportions of the two metals added we can get differently coloured 'gold' objects. They can vary from yellow to red, and even a shade of green!

Aluminium is a metal with a low density. It can be alloyed with a wide range of other elements – there are over 300 alloys of aluminium! These alloys have very different properties. We can use some to build aircraft while others can be used as armour plating on tanks and other military vehicles.

c) Apart from making gold harder, what else can alloying change?
d) What property of aluminium makes it useful for making alloys in the aircraft industry?

Smart alloys

Some alloys have a very special property. If we bend (or *deform*) them into a different shape and then heat them, they return to their original shape all by themselves. These alloys are sometimes called **smart alloys**. Their technical name is *shape memory alloys* (SMAs), which describes the way they behave. They seem to 'remember' their original shape!

We can use the clever properties of shape memory alloys in many ways. Some of the most interesting uses of SMAs have been in medicine. Doctors treating a badly broken bone can use smart alloys to hold the bones in place while they heal. They cool the alloy before it is wrapped around the broken bone. When it heats up again the alloy goes back to its original shape. This pulls the bones together and holds them while they heal. Dentists have made braces to push teeth into the right position using this technique.

Figure 2 This dental brace pulls the teeth into the right position as it warms up. That's smart!

SUMMARY QUESTIONS

1 Copy and complete using the words below:

aluminium   brass   bronze   smart   soft   thousands

Copper has been used by people for …… of years. Like pure iron, pure copper is too …… to be very useful. Copper can be alloyed with tin to make ……, and with zinc to make …… . There are over 300 alloys of …… . Some alloys can 'remember' their shape when they are heated after they have been bent – they are called …… alloys.

2 Why can aluminium alloys be used in so many different ways?

3 a) Explain the advantages of a dental brace made of 'smart' alloy over one made of a conventional alloy.
   b) Do some research to find some other uses of smart alloys, explaining why they are used.

FOUL FACTS
In the Middle Ages rich people thought that drinking molten gold would make them better when they were ill. It probably didn't work – and imagine what it did to their insides!

KEY POINTS
1 Copper, gold and aluminium are all alloyed with other metals to make them more useful.
2 We can control the properties of alloys by adding different amounts of different elements.
3 Smart alloys are also called shape memory alloys. When deformed they return to their original shape on heating.
4 Shape memory alloys can be used in medicine and dentistry.

SUMMARY ANSWERS

1 Thousands, soft, bronze, brass, aluminium, smart.

2 Because there are so many of them, with a wide range of properties.

3 a) A brace made from a smart material can be made with a 'memory' of exactly where the teeth should be. It will pull the teeth into this shape and then stop, whereas a conventional brace will keep pulling on the teeth and must be monitored carefully.

  b) Explanation of other uses of smart alloys from research activity, e.g. stent to open arteries, frames for spectacles.

Answers to in-text questions

a) Bronze and brass.
b) They are harder.
c) Colour.
d) Its low density.

KEY POINTS

Split the students into four groups and give each group a different key point. The groups could then create a persuasive argument why their key point is the most important and the debate could flow!

CHEMISTRY ROCKS AND METALS

C1a 2.5 Transition metals

LEARNING OBJECTIVES

Students should learn:

- What transition metals are and their properties.
- That copper is used extensively in modern life.
- Examples of how we extract copper.

LEARNING OUTCOMES

Most students should be able to:

- Recognise transition metals and list their properties.
- Give uses for copper and explain its importance to modern life.
- State two methods for extracting copper.

Some students should also be able to:

- Explain briefly the processes involved in copper extraction.
- Compare, in terms of environmental impact, different methods for extracting copper.

Teaching suggestions

- **Learning styles**
  Kinaesthetic: Removing key words from fun bags.
  Visual: Observing the experiments.
  Auditory: Listening to the other half of the class explaining their method of extraction.
  Intrapersonal: Completing sections of the word search.
  Interpersonal: Working in small groups marking fictitious student responses to examination questions.

- **Homework.** Ask students to list five items around the home, four items around school, three items in the street, two items in a school bag and one item used every day, all made of some copper. All items should be different!

- **ICT link-up.** A copper mine case study can be found at: www.mining-technology.com/projects/zaldivar/. The Simulation, C1a 2.5 'Transition metals', is available on the GCSE Chemistry CD ROM to consider the position of these elements in the periodic table.

- **Teaching assistant.** The teaching assistant could support one method of extraction, while the teacher supports the other method. (This effectively halves the class size.)

SPECIFICATION LINK-UP C1a.11.2

- *The elements in the central block of the periodic table are known as transition metals. Like other metals they are good conductors of heat and electricity and can be bent or hammered into shape. They are useful as structural materials and for making things that must allow heat or electricity to pass through them easily.*
- *Copper has properties that make it useful for electrical wiring and plumbing. Copper can be extracted by electrolysis of solutions containing copper compounds. (No details are required of the extraction process.) The supply of copper-rich ores is limited. New ways of extracting copper from low-grade ores are being researched to limit the environmental impact of traditional mining.*

Students should use their skills, knowledge and understanding of 'How Science Works':

- *to consider and evaluate the social, economic and environmental impacts of exploiting metal ores, of using metals and of recycling metals.*

Lesson structure

STARTER

Word search – Give students a word search containing a variety of elements from the periodic table (don't include the f-block, as students will not be given this in their GCSE examinations). Ask students to only find the transition metals. (There is no need to distinguish between the transition metals and d-block elements at GCSE level.) (10 minutes)

Data interpretation – Give a list of transition metal symbols; ask the students what the symbols mean and to identify any common factors. Hopefully, students will discover that all the symbols relate to elements in the central block of the periodic table, they are all metals and have metallic properties, e.g. conduct heat. (15 minutes)

MAIN

- Students should recognise, from earlier work in this unit, that the reactivity of metals affects the type of extraction method used. Split the class in half, and ask each half to complete a different method of extraction.
- Feedback the two methods and their results, using questions and answers, to the whole class.
- Concepts from 'How Science Works' can be used to evaluate which method is better. Discuss energy requirements and impact on the environment, as well as efficiency.
- Copper is a very important metal. However, the high quality ores are running out. Therefore scientists are developing new ways to extract copper from low-grade ores.
- Ask the students to write a magazine article for a students' science magazine about copper extraction. The article needs to include why copper is an important material and the new developments in extraction. Students may also wish to produce their articles using a desktop publishing program.

PLENARIES

Key words – Get a fun bag and put in key words: copper, smelting, electrolysis, bacteria. Ask students to volunteer and pick out a key word, which then they explain to the rest of the class. (10 minutes)

AfL (Assesment for Learning) – Give the students an examination question with a fictitious student's answer. Ask the students to work as individuals or in small groups to mark the questions. Then ask students to feedback on each question part saying what mark they would award and why. Photocopying can be reduced by producing a PowerPoint® presentation; on the first slide have the question, on the second slide the question and answer, then on each click an additional piece of marking and examiner's comment can appear. (15 minutes)

NEXT TIME YOU . . .

Consider people living in other countries, e.g. Bangladesh, who scour rubbish dumps for metals and plastics that they can trade.

Practical support

Method 1:

Equipment and materials required

Copper oxide powder (harmful), spatula, 1 mol dm^{-3} sulfuric acid (irritant), fluted filter paper, filter funnel, 2 conical flasks, magnesium ribbon (highly flammable), eye protection.

Details

Add one spatula of copper oxide and add about 25 ml of acid to a conical flask and swirl. Sulfuric acid is an irritant, copper sulfate is hazardous, therefore eye protection must be worn. Filter the mixture into a separate conical flask and collect the blue filtrate. Add magnesium metal to perform a displacement reaction to liberate copper. (NB In industry a cheaper, less reactive metal e.g. iron would be used, but this reaction would be slow and not as visual, so magnesium is a better choice.)

Safety: CLEAPSS Hazcards, 26, 59, 98.

Method 2:

Refer to page 39 in this Teacher Book.

ACTIVITY & EXTENSION

- Students could use the Internet and science periodicals to research the bacteria, fungi and plants now being used in copper extraction.
- Complete a case study on a specific copper extraction plant, e.g. Zaldivar copper mine in Chile and how it has affected the environment.
- Show students some transition metal compounds and their solutions. Encourage them to find some uses [for example, pottery glazes].

KEY POINTS

Ask students to write an acrostic poem with the first lines beginning with the letters from 'copper'. Students should incorporate the key points into their poem.

CHEMISTRY — ROCKS AND METALS

C1a 2.5 Transition metals

LEARNING OBJECTIVES
1. What are transition metals and why are they useful?
2. Why do we use so much copper?
3. How can we produce enough copper?

In the centre of the periodic table there is a large block of metallic elements. Here we find the elements called the *transition metals* or *transition elements*. Many of them have similar properties.

Like all metals, the transition metals are very good conductors of electricity and heat. They are also hard, tough and strong. Yet we can easily bend or hammer them into useful shapes. We say they are *malleable*. With the exception of mercury, which is a liquid at room temperature, the transition metals have very high melting points.

a) In which part of the periodic table do we find the transition metals?
b) Name **three** properties of these elements.

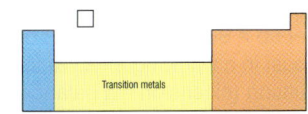

Figure 1 The transition metals

The properties of the transition metals mean that we can use them in many different ways. You will find them in buildings and in cars, trains and other types of transport. Their strength makes them useful as *construction materials*. We use them in heating systems and for electrical wiring because heat and electricity pass through them easily.

One of the transition metals is copper. Although copper is not particularly strong, we can bend and shape it easily. It also conducts electricity and heat very well and it does not react with water. So it is ideal where we need pipes that will carry water or wires that will conduct electricity.

c) Why do we use transition metals so much?
d) What makes copper so useful?

Figure 2 Transition metals are used in many different ways because of their properties. Copper is particularly useful because it is such a good conductor of heat and electricity.

Figure 3 Mining copper ores can leave huge scars on the landscape. This is called open cast mining.

We extract copper from *copper ore*. There are two main methods used to remove the copper from the ore. In one method we use sulfuric acid to produce copper sulfate solution, before extracting the copper.

The other process is called *smelting*. We heat copper ore very strongly in air to produce crude copper. Then we use the impure copper as anodes in electrolysis cells to make pure copper. 85% of copper is still produced by smelting.

e) What chemical do we use to treat copper ore in order to form copper sulfate?

Processing copper ore uses huge amounts of electricity, and costs a lot of money. If we have to smelt an ore, the heating also requires a lot of energy.

New ways to extract copper

Instead of extracting copper using chemicals, heat and electricity, scientists are developing new ways to do the job. They can now use bacteria, fungi and even plants to help extract copper.

If we could extract metals like this on a large scale, it could be a lot cheaper than the way we do it now. It could be a lot 'greener' too.

We would also be able to extract copper from ores which contain very little copper. At the moment it is too expensive to process these 'low grade' ores using conventional methods.

NEXT TIME YOU…

…take a walk in your garden or go onto the school field, think about the transition metals under your feet. Although they might be too expensive to extract now, new ways of extracting metals could mean that you are literally standing on a goldmine!

Figure 4 In Australia Dr Jason Plumb looks for bacteria that can extract metals from ores. His search takes him to some exciting places – including volcanoes!

SUMMARY QUESTIONS

1. Write a few words describing the following: a) transition metals, b) properties of copper, c) smelting.
2. Silver and gold are transition metals that conduct electricity even better than copper. Why do we use copper to make electric cables instead of either of these metals?
3. a) Explain briefly two ways of extracting copper metal.
   b) Explain the advantages of extracting copper using bacteria or fungi rather than the way most is extracted now.

KEY POINTS

1. The transition metals are found in the middle block of elements in the periodic table.
2. Transition metals have properties that make them useful for building and making things.
3. Copper is a very useful transition metal because of its high conductivity.
4. Scientists are looking for new ways to extract copper that will use less energy.

SUMMARY ANSWERS

1. a) Transition metals are the block of elements in the middle of the periodic table.
   b) Copper is a good conductor of heat/electricity and is able to be bent and shaped into pipes and wires.
   c) Smelting is heating a certain type of copper ore to convert it into a form that can then be used to produce pure copper using electrolysis.

2. Silver and gold are much more expensive than copper.

3. a) Add sulfuric acid to ore to produce copper sulfate solution which is electrolysed. Heat copper ore strongly to get crude copper which is purified by electrolysis.
   b) Extracting copper using bacteria or fungi is likely to use much less energy than conventional extraction techniques. However, the technology is at present undeveloped, so the true cost of this method of extraction is unknown. One definite advantage is that it may be useful for extracting copper from ores that would otherwise remain uneconomic. We could also use waste ores, previously dumped because they were low grade, reducing open-cast mining and scars on the landscape.

Answers to in-text questions

a) In the central block (or between Groups 2 and 3).
b) Three of: good conductors of heat/electricity, hard, tough, strong, can be bent/hammered into shapes, have very high melting points (except mercury).
c) Their properties make them useful for building and making things.
d) Its high conductivity (coupled with its cost – silver is a better conductor, as is gold, but they are much rarer and therefore much more expensive – see summary question 2).
e) Sulfuric acid.

47

CHEMISTRY | ROCKS AND METALS

C1a 2.6 Aluminium and titanium

LEARNING OBJECTIVES

Students should learn:

- That aluminium and titanium are useful metals.
- That extracting aluminium and titanium is costly.
- Some reasons for recycling aluminium.

LEARNING OUTCOMES

Most students should be able to:

- List the useful properties of aluminium and titanium.
- Recall the methods of extraction used for aluminium and titanium.
- List reasons for the importance of aluminium recycling.
- Give examples of uses of aluminium and/or titanium and explain which properties makes them fit for purpose.
- Describe why the extraction of aluminium and titanium is costly.

Some students should also be able to:

- Explain the benefits, in terms of social, economic and environmental benefits of aluminium recycling.

Teaching suggestions

- **Special needs.** For these students create a cut and stick activity, where the images showing the use, types of metal and property that makes it fit for that purpose are on separate rectangles. Students cut them out and sort the information.
- **Learning styles**
  Kinaesthetic: Handling different samples of materials.
  Visual: Observing the sparkler experiment.
  Auditory: Listening to explanations of different samples of materials.
  Intrapersonal: Answering their own personal question in 'questions and answers'.
  Interpersonal: Remembering other 'purchases' in 'I went to the shops to buy . . .' and then adding on their own, which was not already in the list.
- **Homework.** Ask students to consider which material they would make an item from and why. They could then think of one use of aluminium or titanium and which property makes it fit for that purpose.

SPECIFICATION LINK-UP   C1a.11.2

- Low density and resistance to corrosion make aluminium and titanium useful metals. These metals cannot be extracted from their oxides by reduction with carbon. Current methods of extraction are expensive because:
  – there are many stages in the processes
  – much energy is needed.
- We should recycle metals because extracting these uses limited resources and is expensive in terms of energy and effects on the environment.

Students should use their skills, knowledge and understanding of 'How Science Works':

- to consider and evaluate the social, economic and environmental impacts of exploiting metal ores of using metals and of recycling metals.
- to evaluate the benefits, drawbacks and risks of using metals as structural materials and as smart materials.

Lesson structure

STARTER

Describing task – In an opaque presentation bag put in a piece of bauxite, aluminium oxide (sealed in a Petri dish), aluminium metal, titanium metal and rutile. Each sample should be labelled. Split the class into five groups and ask a volunteer from each group to come to the bag and remove a sample and return to their group. Give each group 3 minutes to find out information about and describe their sample. Then each group explains, to the whole class, what they have found out about their sample. (15 minutes)

Sparkler! – A demonstration: Set up a Bunsen burner and blow aluminium powder into the flame. The powder will combust in a twinkling effect to form aluminium oxide. Ask the students to generate a word equation (extension – a balanced symbol equation) for the reaction. [Aluminium + oxygen → aluminium oxide $4Al + 3O_2 \rightarrow 2Al_2O_3$] (10 minutes)

MAIN

- Environmental issues, such as the recycling of metals, are a growing concern. Split the class into three groups. Each set of students could produce individual leaflets encouraging people to recycle, but each leaflet could have a different bias; one group could focus on the environment, another on social issues and finally one on economic issues.
- Explain that we should recycle metals because extracting them uses limited resources and is expensive in terms of energy and effects on the environment. Stress the multi-stage process involved in extracting metals such as titanium. Students could look this up to consider cost implications of each step (but no details are required in the specification).
- Students often find it difficult to link specific properties of a material with their use. Search the web to find pictures of various items made of aluminium and titanium, e.g. a bike, a hip replacement joint, aircraft, a saucepan, overhead cables with a pylon, a ring. Ask the students to choose which material it would be made from and give reasons for their choice.

PLENARIES

Questions and answers – Ask all students to stand up. Complete a question and answer session: if a student gets their question correct, then they sit down and they have 'earned the right to leave'; if they are incorrect, they remain standing and a question goes on to another student. A student who answers incorrectly should be given as many questions as needed to get one correct, therefore more questions than students need to be prepared. (15 minutes)

'I went to the shops to buy . . .' – This children's game can be played but the students can only give examples of items made from aluminium or titanium. The teacher could start by saying: 'I went to the shops to buy a titanium aircraft'. The first student then could say: 'I went to the shop to buy a titanium aircraft and some aluminium foil', and so on around the class. (10 minutes)

ACTIVITY & EXTENSION IDEAS

- Students could be given samples of different metals, including aluminium and titanium. They could then design a practical to test the chemical and physical properties of the different metals. This would create an opportunity to teach aspects of 'How Science Works', e.g. designing a fair test.
- Flow charts to shown the main processes in aluminium extraction, titanium extraction and aluminium recycling could be constructed.
- Students could create a bar chart to compare the cost of producing 1 kg of titanium and aluminium from their ore with 1 kg of each respective metal from recycled material.

Products from rocks

Practical support

Investigating aluminium

Equipment and materials required
Bunsen burner, safety equipment, eye protection, spatula and aluminium powder (flammable).

Safety: Wear eye protection and tie back hair and loose clothing. Keep students well away from Bunsen burner.

Details
Set the Bunsen burner up with the blue flame. Hold the Bunsen at an angle. Half-fill the spatula with aluminium powder, and sprinkle into the flame.
This is a very vigorous reaction.

CHEMISTRY — ROCKS AND METALS

C1a 2.6 Aluminium and titanium

LEARNING OBJECTIVES
1. Why are aluminium and titanium so useful?
2. Why does it cost so much to extract aluminium and titanium?
3. Why should we recycle aluminium?

Although they are very strong, many metals are also very dense. This means that we cannot use them if we want to make something that has to be both strong and light. Examples are alloys for making an aeroplane or the frame of a racing bicycle.

Where we need metals which are both strong and light, *aluminium* and *titanium* fit the bill. They are also metals which do not *corrode*.

Aluminium is a silvery, shiny metal which is surprisingly light – it has a relatively low density for a metal. It is an excellent conductor of heat and electricity. We can also shape it and draw it into wires very easily.

Although aluminium is a relatively reactive metal, it does not corrode easily. This is because the aluminium atoms at its surface immediately react with the oxygen in air to form a thin layer of tough aluminium oxide. This layer stops any further corrosion taking place.

Aluminium is not a particularly strong metal, but we can use it to form alloys. These alloys are harder, more rigid and stronger than pure aluminium.

Figure 1 We use aluminium alloys to make aircraft because of their combination of lightness and strength

As a result of these properties, we use aluminium to make a whole range of goods. These range from cans, cooking foil and saucepans through to high-voltage electricity cables, aeroplanes and space vehicles.

a) Why does aluminium resist corrosion?
b) How do we make aluminium stronger?

Titanium is a silvery-white metal, which is very strong and very resistant to corrosion. Like aluminium it has an oxide layer that protects it. Although it is denser than aluminium, it is less dense than most transition metals.

Titanium has a very high melting point – about 1660°C – so we can use it at very high temperatures.

We use it instead of steel and aluminium in the bodies of high-performance aircraft and racing bikes. Here its combination of relative low density and strength is important. We also use titanium to make parts of jet engines because it keeps its strength at high temperatures.

The strength of titanium at high temperatures makes it very useful in nuclear reactors. In reactors we use it to make the pipes and other parts that must stand up to high temperatures. Titanium performs well under these conditions, and its strong oxide layer means that it resists corrosion.

Another use of titanium is also based on its strength and resistance to corrosion – replacement hip joints.

c) Why does titanium resist corrosion?
d) What properties make titanium ideal to use in jet engines and nuclear reactors?

We extract aluminium using electrolysis. Because it is a reactive metal we cannot use carbon to displace it from its ore. Instead we extract aluminium by passing an electric current through molten aluminium oxide at high temperatures.

Titanium is not particularly reactive, so we could produce it by displacing it from its ore with carbon. But carbon reacts with the titanium making it very brittle. So we have to use a more reactive metal. We use sodium or magnesium to do this. However, we have to produce both sodium and magnesium by electrolysis in the first place.

The problem with using electrolysis to extract these metals is that it is very expensive. That's because we need to use high temperatures and a great deal of electricity.

In the UK each person uses around 8 kg of aluminium every year. This is why it is important to *recycle* aluminium. It saves energy, since recycling aluminium does not involve electrolysis.

e) Why do we need electricity to make aluminium and titanium?
f) Why does recycling aluminium save electricity?

Figure 2 We can use titanium inside the body as well as outside. Because it has a low density, is strong and does not corrode, we can use titanium to make alloys that are excellent for artificial joints. These are artificial hip joints, used to replace a natural joint damaged by disease or wear and tear.

DID YOU KNOW?
Titanium dioxide is a brilliant white compound that is used in white paint. It is also used in some sunscreens – tiny particles of titanium dioxide reflect the harmful rays from the Sun, preventing you getting sunburnt.

SUMMARY QUESTIONS

1 Copy and complete using the words below:

corrode   electrolysis   expensive   light   oxide   reactive   strong

Aluminium and aluminium alloys are useful as they are …… and …… . Although aluminium is reactive, it does not …… because its surface is coated with a thin layer of aluminium …… . Titanium does not corrode because it is not very …… and also has its oxide layer to protect it. …… is used in the extraction of both metals from their ores which makes them …… .

2 Why is titanium used to make artificial hip joints?

3 Each person in the UK uses about 8 kg of aluminium each year.
  a) Recycling 1 kg of aluminium saves about enough energy to run a small electric fire for 14 hours. If you recycle 50% of the aluminium you use in one year, how long could you run a small electric fire on the energy you have saved?
  b) Explain the benefits of recycling aluminium.

KEY POINTS
1. Aluminium and titanium are useful because they resist corrosion.
2. Aluminium and titanium are expensive because extracting them from their ores involves many stages in the processes and requires large amounts of energy.
3. Recycling aluminium is important because we need to use much less energy to produce 1 kg of recycled aluminium than we use to extract 1 kg of aluminium from its ore.

SUMMARY ANSWERS

1 Light, strong, corrode, oxide, reactive, electrolysis, expensive.

2 Because of its strength and resistance to corrosion.

3 a) About 56 hours.
  b) Less energy used in recycling, conserving Earth's resources of fuels and ores. Less pollution from metal extraction, e.g. from open-cast mining of aluminium ore.

Answers to in-text questions

a) Because it has a layer of aluminium oxide over its surface that prevents corrosion.
b) By alloying it with other elements.
c) Because it is protected by its oxide layer.
d) It is unreactive and very strong at high temperatures.
e) Because extraction involves electrolysis in both cases.
f) Recycling does not involve extraction.

DID YOU KNOW?
Titanium dioxide is also the white material in correction fluid.

KEY POINTS
Ask students to copy the key points into their books and highlight just the key words, e.g. titanium, aluminium, resist, corrosion, expensive, energy, and recycle.

CHEMISTRY — ROCKS AND METALS
C1a 2.7 Using metals

SPECIFICATION LINK-UP
C1a.11.2

Students should use their skills, knowledge and understanding of 'How Science Works':

- to consider and evaluate the social, economic and environmental impacts of exploiting metal ores, of using metals and recycling metal.
- to evaluate the benefits, drawbacks and risks of using metals as structural materials and as smart materials.

CHEMISTRY — ROCKS AND METALS
C1a 2.7 Using metals

Metals and society

The way we use metals has literally changed the world. Since ancient times metals have enabled us to do things we could never have done without them. These range from making tools to generating electricity; from creating jewellery to flying in aeroplanes.

The timeline below shows some of the main points in the history of the use of metals, up to the beginning of the 20th century.

5000–4000 BCE People mine copper ores and smelt them

3500–3000 BCE People use bronze, an alloy of copper and tin, to make tools and weapons

1000 BCE People have now developed ways of making iron. Iron is much better than bronze for making tools and weapons because it is harder. This means that blades stay sharp for longer

1903 CE The Wright brothers fly their first aeroplane at Kitty Hawk USA. It has an engine made using cast aluminium to make it as light as possible

1825 CE Pure aluminium and titanium are produced for the first time

1400 CE In Europe people can now produce temperatures high enough to melt iron. This means that it can be cast in moulds to make more complicated shapes

QUESTIONS
1. Why was the development of iron so important?
2. Find out about the development of metals in the last 100 years and extend the timeline using this information.

50

Teaching suggestions

Activities

Timeline card sort – Give the students six cards with information from the timeline, but without the dates. Ask the students to put them in order of most recent developments to the oldest development in metal extraction.

A home for an industrial plant – Students can make decisions about where to site industrial plants, looking at economic and social issues involved. Show the students a map of a fictitious island, which includes a small town, a rubbish dump, low-grade mineral ores, high/medium/low tides, high/medium winds, mountains and an electricity station. Ask the students to site a copper extraction plant and a metal recycling plant. They should include the advantages and disadvantages of their chosen sites.

Pros and cons of metals – Ask students to construct a balance sheet of advantages and drawbacks/risks of using metals in the construction and manufacturing industries (including smart alloys).

Homework

Definitions – Ask the students to list all the methods of metal extraction studied in this topic area [smelting, electrolysis, reduction, displacement, phytomining] and to define each word.

Extensions

Web page or poster – Metal extraction techniques are constantly developing, as industry is extracting increasingly from low-grade ores. Ask the students to design and make a web page about advances in metal extraction. Depending on the ability of the students, just a page of text could be made or more advanced students could design the background and images.

Timeline development – Get students to research metal extraction techniques and add additional information to the timeline.

Line graph – Ask students to plot on a line graph the tonnage of different metals produced in the UK over the last 200 years. They could then explain the trends shown.

Products from rocks

Mining with plants

As they grow, plants absorb dissolved chemicals from the ground in the water that they take into their roots. Some plants absorb a lot of one certain chemical, and scientists have found that we can use these plants to help us extract metals from soil.

The technology that we need to do this is quite simple. So we can use plants to mine metals where it would be far too expensive to do it in any other way. Extracting metals like this is called *phytomining*.

1. Complexing agents may be added to enhance metal uptake of crop
   Crop grows on soil containing metal concentration too low for conventional exploitation
   nickel / thallium / gold
2. Possible production of electricity
   Plant material burned
3. Small volume of plant ash (bio-ore) containing high concentration of target metal
   Smelt bio-ore to yield metal

Figure 1 Using plants to mine metals sounds strange – but it's true!

QUESTIONS

3 Why can we use phytomining when it would be too expensive to extract metals in other ways?

4 There is a long time delay between planting the crop and extracting the metal. What might happen if the price of the metal falls before the crop can be harvested?

Recycling fridges

It is nearly always cheaper for us to recycle metals than to extract new metals from their ores. This is especially true for metals like aluminium, where we need to use large amounts of energy to extract them. But sometimes it is not easy to recycle metals because they are combined with other materials. As an example, look at the problems of recycling fridges.

First, we need to remove the chemicals in the cooling system of the fridge

Pliers used to puncture the cooling circuit and extract the liquid coolant

Then we can take out the parts of the fridge like the shelves

Polyurethane foam (PU) and polystyrene (PS)

PU foam dried to reduce water content

Polystyrene

PU foam

Non-ferrous and heavy plastic/glass

Ferrous

After this, the fridge is shredded, and we can separate the metals from other materials like plastics and insulating foam. Some of the metals are **ferrous** metals (they contain iron) while others are **non-ferrous**. Magnets can be used to separate the ferrous metals from the non-ferrous metals

Figure 2 Recycling fridges is difficult but necessary

ACTIVITY

Many people do not realise how important it is to recycle old fridges and other household equipment.
Design a poster to be used in a campaign to persuade people to recycle their old fridge, washing machine, and so on, rather than simply dumping them.

ANSWERS TO QUESTIONS

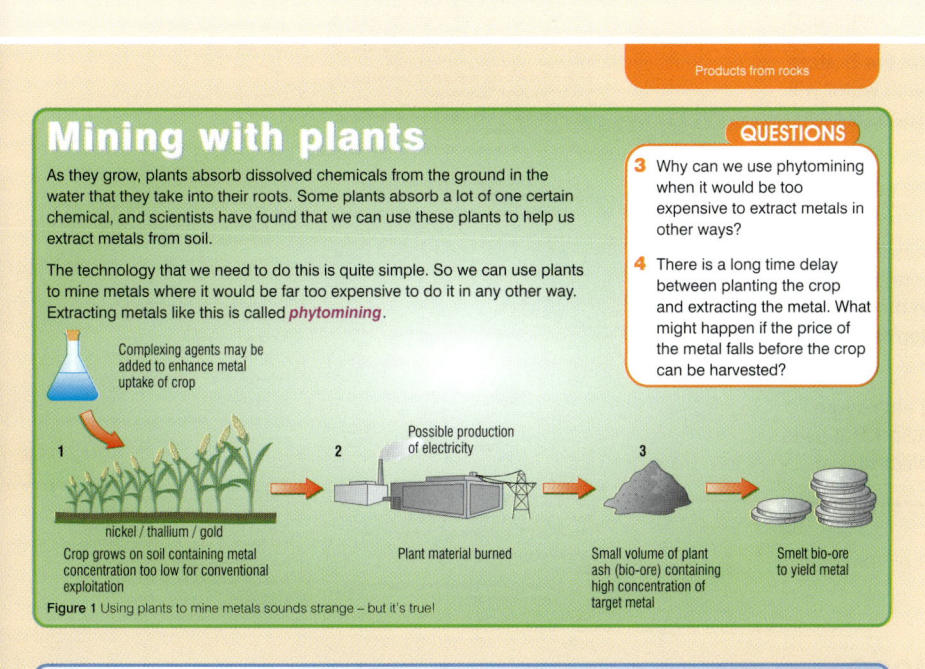

1 It allowed development of better tools and weapons, which stayed sharper for longer than bronze.
2 Extension of timeline.
3 Some plants can absorb a lot of a certain metal from the soil. This makes it economic to extract, whereas other methods would be too costly.
4 This extraction method would become uneconomic and the company would make a financial loss.

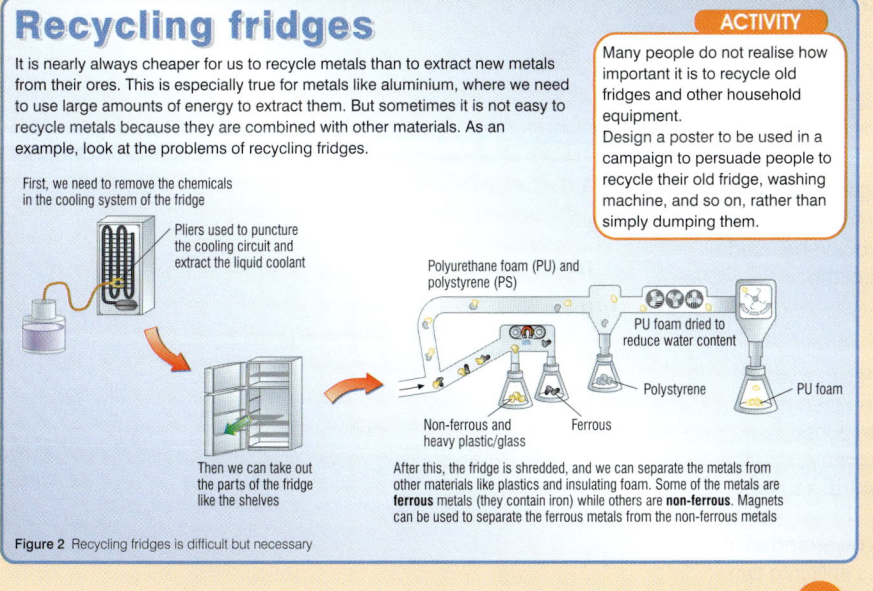

Learning styles

Kinaesthetic: Completing the timeline card sort.

Visual: Making a web page. (These could be shown cased onto the school web site.)

Auditory: Listening to other points of view in the siting of a metal extraction or recycling plant.

Intrapersonal: Defining different methods of metal extraction.

Interpersonal: Working as a group to site a metal extraction or recycling plant.

Gifted and talented

Encourage these students to have an appreciation of the rise and fall of metal extraction and production in the UK, and to understand some of the reasons for this and the effects on local communities.

CHEMISTRY ROCKS AND METALS

SUMMARY ANSWERS

1. **a)** A rock containing enough of a metal to make it economically worthwhile to extract the metal.
   b) Describes a metal found in the earth that has not combined with another element.
   c) A reaction in which oxygen is removed from a compound.

2. Because gold is dense, it will tend to be found at the bottom of the pan. Washing the stones out of the pan with water will leave the much denser gold behind. It can be seen clearly because of its bright colour.

3. **a)** The alloy may be harder, stiffer, and it may be easier to work (shape into different objects).
   b) Different atoms in the metal lattice make it less likely that layers of atoms can slide over each other, changing the way in which the alloy bends. Depending on the exact way in which this happens, the alloy may be stiffer/harder or it may be easier to shape.

4. Recycling uses far less energy, since recycling aluminium does not involve extracting it and it is the extraction that uses energy (to melt the ore and to extract it using electrolysis).

5. Advantage – if they are bent out of shape (if you sit on them!) they can be reshaped by heating.
   Disadvantage – they are more expensive than conventional frames.

Summary teaching suggestions

- **When to use the questions?**
  - As each question links with a lesson spread, set a question as homework at the end of each lesson, e.g. question 1 for homework after C1a 2.1. This will give students frequent practice at examination questions.
  - Question 5 could be used to create a spider diagram on the board about the use of smart alloys.
  - Questions 2, 4 and 5 are lengthy questions that could be used for extended homework assignments at the end of the appropriate spreads.

- **Learning styles**
  Visual: Question 2 allows students to give responses in a variety of different ways. Set up a flexi cam or web cam and then go around the classroom, if a student has a brilliant response, ask their permission to show their work. If they are agreeable, use the camera to show the work on an interactive whiteboard. You can then annotate the work to show why it is so good.
  Intrapersonal: Question 4 would allow a debate to be arranged in the class. A chair should be selected, and the class split into two: half for and half against the motion. Research should be completed and then the chair could hold the debate at the end of the lesson.

- **Special needs**
  - Question 1 is made up of key terms and their definitions. Provide the terms and the definitions on separate pieces of card. Ask the students to match the cards, and then they could be copied or stuck into their book.

- **Misconceptions**
  Students often confuse common alloys, e.g. brass and steel as pure metals (elements). Question 3a) highlights the difference between pure metals and their alloys.

ROCKS AND METALS: C1a 2.1 – C1a 2.7

SUMMARY QUESTIONS

1. Write simple definitions for the following terms:
   a) metal ore
   b) native state
   c) reduction reaction.

2. Gold is a very dense, unreactive metal. Old-fashioned gold prospectors used to 'pan' for gold in streams by scooping up small stones from the stream bed and washing them in water, allowing them slowly to get washed out of the pan. Using words and diagrams, explain how they could find gold by using this technique.

3. We can change the properties of metals by alloying them with other elements.
   a) Write down **three** ways that a metal alloy may be different from the pure metal.
   b) Choose **one** of these properties. Use the two diagrams below to help you to explain why a metal alloy behaves differently to the pure metal.

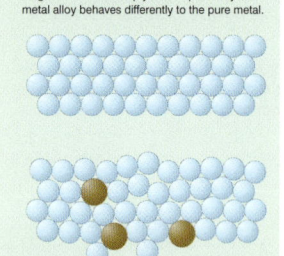

4. One of your fellow students says: 'There is more aluminium in the Earth's crust than any other metal. So why should we bother recycling it?' How would you argue against this point of view?

5. One use of smart alloys is to make spectacle frames. Write down **one** advantage and **one** disadvantage of using a smart alloy like this.

EXAM-STYLE QUESTIONS

1. This question is about the uses of these metals:
   A aluminium   B copper
   C gold   D iron
   Which of these metals is used
   (a) as the main metal in alloys to build aircraft?
   (b) in alloys to make jewellery?
   (c) to make all steels?
   (d) to make water pipes and electrical wiring?   (4)

2. Choose a metal from the list A to D to match each description.
   A aluminium   B chromium
   C gold   D titanium
   (a) A metal that is strong at high temperatures and resists corrosion.
   (b) An unreactive metal found native in the Earth.
   (c) This metal has a low density and is extracted by electrolysis.
   (d) This metal is mixed with iron to make high alloy steels.   (4)

3. Use words from the list A to D to complete the word equations.
   A copper   B iron
   C sodium   D water
   (a) copper oxide + sulfuric acid → copper sulfate + ...
   (b) copper sulfate + iron → ...... + iron sulfate
   (c) iron oxide + carbon → ...... + carbon dioxide
   (d) titanium + ... → titanium + sodium chloride   (4)

4. A student tested the flexibility of four different alloy rods. She suspended a mass from the end of the rods which were fixed at the other end to the edge of a bench. She measured how far each rod bent. Which words describe the 'distance the rod bent'?
   A a categoric, independent variable.
   B a continuous, independent variable.
   C a categoric, dependent variable.
   D a continuous, dependent variable.   (1)

EXAM-STYLE ANSWERS

1. a) **A**
   b) **C**
   c) **D**
   d) **B**   (4 marks)

2. a) **D**
   b) **C**
   c) **A**
   d) **B**   (4 marks)

3. a) **D**
   b) **A**
   c) **B**
   d) **C**   (4 marks)

4. **D**   (1 mark)

5. a) Transition metals/transition elements.   (1 mark)
   b) Ore.   (1 mark)
   c) Alloy.   (1 mark)
   d) Shape memory alloys.   (1 mark)

6. a) Reduction.   (1 mark)
   b) Carbon *or* a named metal more reactive than iron.   (1 mark)
   c) e.g. iron oxide + carbon → iron + carbon dioxide.
      (one mark for reactants, one mark for products)   (2 marks)

7. a) Oxide layer.   (1 mark)
   b) *Two from:*
      - strong,
      - low density/lightweight,
      - non-toxic.   (2 marks)

Products from rocks

HOW SCIENCE WORKS QUESTIONS

How hard is gold?

The following was overheard in a jeweller's shop:

'I would like to buy a 24 carat gold ring for my husband.'

'Well madam, we would advise that you buy one which is lower carat gold. It looks much the same but the more gold there is, the less hard it is.'

Is this actually the case? Let's have a look scientifically at the data.

Pure gold is 24 carat. A carat is a twenty-fourth, so $24 \times 1/24 = 1$ or pure gold. So a 9 carat gold ring will have 9/24ths gold and 15/24ths of another metal, probably copper or silver. Most 'gold' sold in shops is therefore an alloy. How hard the 'gold' is will depend on the amount of gold and on the type of metal used to make the alloy.

Here is some data on the alloys and the maximum hardness of 'gold'.

Gold alloy (carat)	Maximum hardness (BHN)
9	170
14	180
18	230
22	90
24	70

a) The shop assistant said that 'the more gold there is, the less hard it is.' Was this based on science or was it hearsay? Explain your answer. (2)
b) In this investigation which is the independent variable? (1)
c) Which of the following best describes the hardness of the alloy?
    i) continuous
    ii) discrete
    iii) categoric
    iv) ordered. (1)
d) Plot a graph of the results. (3)
e) What is the pattern in your results? (2)
f) You might have expected that the 9 carat gold was much harder than the 14 or the 18 carat gold, but it isn't. Can you offer an explanation for this? (Clue – is there an uncontrolled variable lurking around here?) (1)

---

5 Name the types of substance described in each part of this question.
  (a) These elements are hard, tough and strong, conduct heat and electricity well and are found in the middle of the periodic table.
  (b) These rocks contain enough metal to make it worth extracting.
  (c) This is a metal that contains other elements to give it specific properties.
  (d) These materials are smart because they can return to their original shape when heated and are used by surgeons to hold broken bones while healing. (4)

6 Iron is extracted from iron oxide by removing oxygen.
  (a) What name is given to a reaction in which oxygen is removed from a compound? (1)
  (b) Name an element that could be used to remove oxygen from iron oxide. (1)
  (c) Write a word equation for the reaction that would take place in (b). (2)

7 Titanium is used to make replacement hip joints. One reason why titanium can be used in this way is that it resists corrosion.
  (a) How is titanium protected from corrosion? (1)
  (b) Suggest **two** other properties of titanium that make it suitable for this use. (2)

8 Most of the world's steel is now made in Asia.

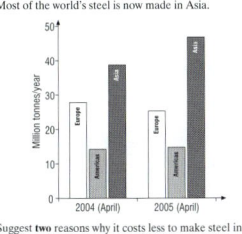

[Bar chart showing Million tonnes/year for 2004 (April) and 2005 (April), with bars for Europe, America, and Asia]

Suggest **two** reasons why it costs less to make steel in Asia than in Europe. (2)

9 New methods using bacteria, fungi and plants are being developed to extract copper. Suggest **three** reasons why these new methods have been developed. (3)

HOW SCIENCE WORKS ANSWERS

a) Hearsay – as it is not as simple as it sounds. The hardness increases up to 18 carat and only then decreases.
b) Gold alloy carat is the independent variable.
c) The hardness of the alloy is a continuous variable.
d) Suitable graph which could be a line graph as both variables are continuous. However, it could be argued that gold is sold in these carats and therefore for public use it might be more suitable as a bar chart. The axes should be fully labelled and the points plotted correctly. The gold alloy (carat) should be on the X axis and the maximum hardness on the Y axis.
e) The pattern in the results: as the proportion of gold in the alloy increases so the hardness increases up to about 18 carat. After this, as the alloy carat increases the hardness decreases.
f) The uncontrolled variable is the type of metal used in the alloy.

How science works teaching suggestions

- **Literacy guidance**
  - Key terms that should be clearly understood are: independent variable, hearsay, continuous variable.
  - Questions expecting a longer answer, where students can practise their literacy skills is f).
- **Higher- and lower-level questions.** Questions c), e) and f) are higher-level and the answers have been provided at this level. Questions a) and b) are lower-level and the answers are also at this level.
- **Gifted and talented.** Able students could begin to gather together other examples of 'hearsay'.
- **How and when to use these questions.** When wishing to develop graph-drawing skills and careful analysis of scientific data. Results do not always support expectations. We should trust good science more than hearsay.
- **Homework.** Students could be asked to find out the carat of gold used in different types of jewellery and relate this to its hardness.
- **Special needs.** Some help will be needed by some students to interpret the language used, particularly BHN (Brinell Hardness Number!). Students should be confident to tackle questions where the units used might not be fully understood, but their meaning can be guessed at.

---

8 Two from:
  - cheaper labour,
  - lower transport costs,
  - raw materials cheaper/more easily obtained/more abundant.
  (2 marks)

9 Three from:
  - Use less energy.
  - Produce less pollution.
  - Can use low-grade ores.
  - High-grade ores running out.
  - Avoids moving large amounts of rock/digging huge areas.
  - Increasing costs of traditional mining/extracting. *(3 marks)*

Exam teaching suggestions

Q1, Q2 and Q3 are best used to check knowledge when the chapter has been completed. Q6 could be used after completing 2.2, Q5 after 2.5, Q7 after 2.6 and Q9 after 2.7. If the questions are done as a complete test, allow 30 minutes (total 29 marks).

In Q5d) the response 'smart alloy' is not sufficient for the mark because 'smart' is given in the question. Question 7b) requires students to apply their knowledge to a situation that they should have met. They should read the question carefully and not repeat the reason given in the question. Also, high melting point is not relevant in this application.

Q7b), Q8 and Q9 are specific in the number of responses required and students should check they have given no more than the correct number. Good answers will be succinct, with distinct points and no repetition or contradictions. Using bullets in answers can help students to identify the number of points they have made.

Many students think that aluminium and titanium are similar in all their properties. Use Q1, Q2 and Q3 to help students clarify the differences between these metals. Economics features in Q8 and Q9, but simple answers like 'cheaper' will not usually gain marks unless qualified further, such as 'cheaper labour'.

CHEMISTRY   CRUDE OIL

C1a 3.1 Fuels from crude oil

LEARNING OBJECTIVES

Students should learn:

- What crude oil is.
- What an alkane is.
- How to represent alkanes.

LEARNING OUTCOMES

Most students should be able to:

- Recognise that crude oil is a mixture and state that it can be separated by distillation.
- Define and recognise simple alkanes.
- Write the correct chemical formula of an alkane represented by a structural formula.

Some students should also be able to:

- Given named examples, draw diagrams and write the formulae of simple alkanes.
- Recall and use the formula C_nH_{2n+2} to give the formula of an alkane, when *n* is given.

Teaching suggestions

- **Special needs.** Create a half-finished table detailing alkane names, molecular and structural formulae. For each row, there should only be one missing piece of information. For very weak students, this task could be created into a cut and stick activity.
- **Learning styles**
  Kinaesthetic: Making model hydrocarbons from molecular model kits.
  Visual: Observing fractional distillation.
  Auditory: Explaining how distillation happens.
  Intrapersonal: Defining key words.
  Interpersonal: Working in small groups to act out hydrocarbons.
- **Homework.** Students could find out the names and work out the formulae for the first ten alkanes.

DID YOU KNOW?

Not all cars run on fossil fuels; alcohol can be used instead of petrol and a diesel alternative can be made from rapeseed oil.

SPECIFICATION LINK-UP   C1a.11.3

- *Crude oil is a mixture of a very large number of compounds.*
- *A mixture consists of two or more elements or compounds not chemically joined together. The chemical properties of each substance in the mixture are unchanged. This makes it possible to separate the substances in a mixture by physical methods including distillation.*
- *Most of the compounds in crude oil consist of molecules made up of hydrogen and carbon atoms only (hydrocarbons). Most of these are saturated hydrocarbons called alkanes, which have the general formula C_nH_{2n+2}.*
- *Alkane molecules can be represented in the following forms:*

$$H-\overset{\overset{\displaystyle H}{|}}{\underset{\underset{\displaystyle H}{|}}{C}}-\overset{\overset{\displaystyle H}{|}}{\underset{\underset{\displaystyle H}{|}}{C}}-H \text{ and } C_2H_6$$

Lesson structure

STARTER

Match definitions and key words – Ask the students to match the definitions with the key words. (10 minutes)

- Hydrocarbon
- Alkane
- Mixture

- A molecule that contains only hydrogen and carbon
- A saturated hydrocarbon
- More than one substance, not chemically joined.

Observations – Draw the structural formula of butane on the board. Ask the students to write down as much information as they can about this molecule. (10 minutes)

MAIN

- Students often struggle with the idea that molecules are three dimensional, but we often represent them in a two-dimensional format. Give each pair of students a molecular model kit. Then show students which atoms represent H and C, noting the size difference and number of holes in each type of atom. Set the students the task of making the first four hydrocarbons, given their structural formula, and writing their molecular formula. Ask them to list the similarities and differences between these molecules. Work out the general formula C_nH_{2n+2}.
- Explain that crude oil is a mixture of hydrocarbons and ask them to suggest how mixtures can be separated into their components and predict the method used to separate crude oil.
- Students should appreciate that the alkanes are a 'chemical family', but that no two alkanes are identical. Show students three different alkane liquids (e.g. pentane, octane, paraffin). Allow the students to note colour, viscosity, ease of lighting and colour of flame. Link here to 'How Science Works' – relationships between variables.
- Show the students the distillation equipment that has been set up and ask them to predict what will happen to the crude oil and why. Develop their ideas of a simple distillation into fractional distillation, using questions and answers. Demonstrate distillation; the fractions from this could then be tested as detailed under 'Practical support.'

PLENARIES

Model a molecule – Split the class into groups. Give each group a different hydrocarbon name and some sport shirts. They could act out a hydrocarbon molecule. The students who represent carbon atoms would need to sit down, so that four bond (holding hands, feet/hands) can be created. (10 minutes)

Complete sentences – Ask students to complete the following sentences:

- Hydrocarbons are . . . [compounds made of carbon and hydrogen only]
- Alkanes are hydrocarbons whose molecules are . . . [saturated]
- Crude oil is a mixture of . . . [hydrocarbons] (5 minutes)

54

Practical support

Investigating alkanes

Equipment and materials required
Three samples of different alkanes (flammable), eye protection, four watch glasses, four pieces of string, four micro-burners (or four spirit burners), heat proof mat, matches, molecular model kits.

Details
Pour each alkane onto a separate watch glass, starting with the smallest carbon chain. Ask students to comment on the viscosity, then the colour. Then, using a micro-burner (or spirit burner), put one end of a 5 cm piece of string into the alkane. Allow some of the liquid to soak up. Light the 'dry' end of the string (which acts as a wick). Ask students to comment on the ease of lighting and the colour of the flame.

Safety: Ensure the stock bottles of alkanes are closed before lighting matches.

Fractional distillation

Equipment and materials required
A boiling tube with side arm, bung with thermometer through, four test tubes (as collecting tubes – ignition tubes can also be used to display small volumes of fractions), two beakers, ice/water mixture, boiling water, mineral wool, 'synthetic' crude oil (for the recipe see CLEAPSS Recipe Card 20 – Crude oil – or CLEAPSS 45 – hydrocarbons – aliphatic, or it can be purchased already made), Bunsen burner and safety equipment, eye protection, six watch glasses.

Details
Soak the mineral wool in the synthetic crude oil and place in the boiling tube. Fix bung and ensure that the bulb of the thermometer is adjacent to the side arm. Put a collecting tube into an ice bath, and the end of the side arm into the top of it. Gently heat the boiling tube with a Bunsen flame, and notice when the temperature reading has stabilised (around 80°C). When the temperature rises again, quickly change the current collecting tube for a new one. Repeat four times, collecting five fractions and leaving a residue in the boiling tube. During this practical, wear eye protection and complete in a well ventilated room. Each fraction can be collected about every 50°C up to about 300°C. The residues will remain on the mineral wool, making the sixth fraction. These fractions can be ignited. Tip them onto mineral wool on a watch glass. Then ignite the mineral wool, taking great care.

Safety: Tie back hair and loose clothing. CLEAPSS Hazcard 45 – Hydrocarbons.

ACTIVITY & EXTENSION

- Show, by pouring them, that crude oils from different oil fields have different viscosities. Ask the students to suggest why this is so. [Different crude oils have different proportions of each type of hydrocarbons.]
- Other homologous series could be considered and compared to alkanes, e.g. alkenes.

Answers to in-text questions

a) Oil affects everything we do – heating and lighting our homes, transporting us around. (Also feedstock for chemical industry)

b) Crude oil is a mixture of chemical compounds.

c) Because the properties of the individual compounds in the mixture remain the same when they are mixed. Distillation relies on the different boiling points of these compounds.

SUMMARY ANSWERS

1. Mixture, carbon, hydrogen hydrocarbons, distillation.
2. Because there are too many substances in it.
3. a) C_6H_{14} (hexane), C_7H_{16} (heptane), C_8H_{18} (octane).
   b) 14 carbon atoms.

KEY POINTS

Ask the students to try to determine the most important word from the lesson that would help them remember all of the key points. Encourage different students to justify their choice, e.g. alkanes as these are saturated hydrocarbons and are contained in crude oil.

CHEMISTRY — **CRUDE OIL**

C1a 3.1 Fuels from crude oil

LEARNING OBJECTIVES
1. What is in crude oil?
2. What are alkanes?
3. How do we represent alkanes?

Some of the 21st century's most important chemistry involves chemicals that are made from crude oil. These chemicals play a major part in our lives. We use them as fuels in our cars, to warm our homes and to make electricity.

Fuels are important because they keep us warm and on the move. So when oil prices rise, it affects us all. Countries that produce crude oil can have an affect on the whole world economy by the price they charge for their oil.

Figure 1 The price of nearly everything we buy is affected by oil because the cost of moving goods to the shops affects the price we pay for them

a) Why is oil so important?

NEXT TIME YOU...
...go anywhere by car, bus, train or even aeroplane, remember that the energy transporting you comes from the sunlight trapped by plants millions of years ago.

Crude oil
Crude oil is a dark, smelly liquid, which is a **mixture** of lots of different chemical compounds. A mixture contains two or more elements or compounds that are not chemically combined together.

Crude oil straight out of the ground is not much use. There are too many substances in it, all with different boiling points. Before we can use crude oil, we have to separate it into its different substances. Because the properties of substances do not change when they are mixed, we can separate mixtures of substances in crude oil by using **distillation**. Distillation separates liquids with different boiling points.

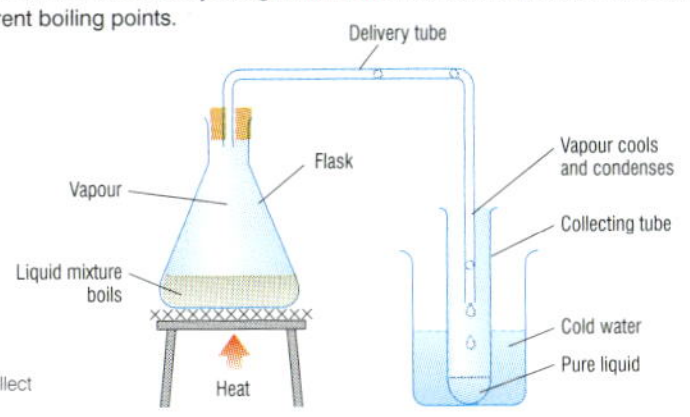

Figure 2 Mixtures of liquids can be separated using distillation. We heat the mixture so that it boils, and collect the vapour that forms by cooling and condensing it.

DEMONSTRATION
Distillation in the lab
Your teacher may show you the simple distillation of a mixture similar to crude oil.

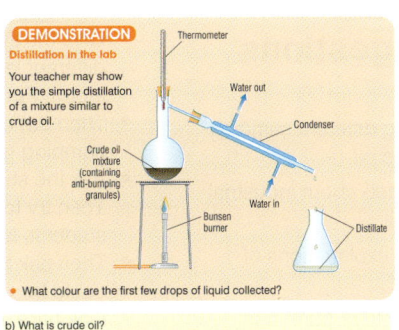

- What colour are the first few drops of liquid collected?

b) What is crude oil?
c) Why can we separate crude oil using distillation?

Nearly all of the compounds in crude oil are made from atoms of just two chemical elements – hydrogen and carbon. We call these compounds **hydrocarbons**. Most of the hydrocarbons in crude oil are **alkanes**. You can see some examples of alkane molecules in Figure 3.

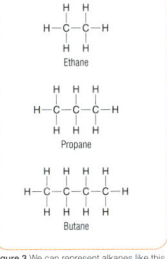

Another way of writing these alkane molecules is like this:

CH_4 (methane); C_2H_6 (ethane); C_3H_8 (propane); C_4H_{10} (butane); C_5H_{12} (pentane).

Can you see a pattern in the formulae of the alkanes? We can write the general formula for alkane molecules like this:

$$C_nH_{2n+2}$$

which means that 'for every n carbon atoms there are $(2n + 2)$ hydrogen atoms'. For example, if an alkane contains 25 carbon atoms its formula will be $C_{25}H_{52}$. We describe alkanes as **saturated** hydrocarbons. This means that they contain as many hydrogen atoms as possible in each molecule. We cannot add any more.

Figure 3 We can represent alkanes like this, showing all of the atoms in the molecule. The line between two atoms in the molecule is the chemical bond holding them together.

SUMMARY QUESTIONS

1. Copy and complete using the words below:

   carbon   distillation   hydrocarbons   hydrogen   mixture

   Crude oil is a ...... of compounds. Many of these contain only atoms of ...... and .... They are called .... The compounds in crude oil can be separated using ....

2. Why is crude oil not very useful before we have processed it?

3. a) Write down the formula of the alkanes which have 6, 7 and 8 carbon atoms. Then find out their names.
   b) How many carbon atoms are there in an alkane which has 30 hydrogen atoms?

KEY POINTS
1. Crude oil is a mixture of many different compounds.
2. Many of the compounds in crude oil are hydrocarbons – they contain only carbon and hydrogen.
3. Alkanes are saturated hydrocarbons. They contain as much hydrogen as possible in their molecules.

CHEMISTRY | CRUDE OIL

C1a 3.2 Fractional distillation

LEARNING OBJECTIVES

Students should learn:

- That crude oil is separated into fractions using fractional distillation.
- The properties of each fraction and how they relate to chain length.
- Which fractions make useful fuels and why.

LEARNING OUTCOMES

Most students should be able to:

- State that crude oil is separated into fractions by fractional distillation.
- List how the properties change from small chain fractions to long chain fractions.
- State which fractions are useful fuels.

Some students should also be able to:

- Explain the key steps involved in fractional distillation.
- Relate the trend in properties to molecular size.

Teaching suggestions

- **Learning styles**

    Kinaesthetic: Handling different samples of fractions from crude oil.

    Visual: Watching a video about industrial separation of crude oil.

    Auditory: Listening to explanations of key words.

    Interpersonal: Finding their partner in the question and answer session.

- **Homework.** Ask students to find out all the different names used for each fraction, e.g. residue may also be called bitumen.

- **Teaching assistant.** Split the class in two. The teacher could demonstrate the properties of the different fractions, while the teaching assistant shows the ampoule samples of the fractions. Then rotate the groups.

- **ICT link-up.** Show the students a model of fractional distillation. Use the Simulation, C1a 3.2 'Fractional Distillation' from the GCSE Chemistry CD ROM, to show how crude oil is separated and demonstrate the properties of the fractions.

SPECIFICATION LINK-UP   C1a.11.3

- *The many hydrocarbons in crude oil may be separated into fractions, each of which contains molecules with a similar number of carbon atoms, by evaporating the oil and allowing it to condense at a number of different temperatures. This process is fractional distillation.*

- *Some properties of hydrocarbons depend on the size of their molecules. These properties influence how hydrocarbons are used as fuels.*

Lesson structure

STARTER

Fuel list – Ask students to consider what they have used today that relies on a fuel. Ask various students to feedback their thoughts to the class. [For example, transport (petrol, diesel and more recently gas), heating (gas, oil), cooking (gas, charcoal for barbecues, lighting (gas, oil).] Even if students state that they use electricity, this is a secondary source, as it must be generated more often than not from the burning of fossil fuels. (10 minutes)

Distil the order – Students could try to put these key words about distillation in order: mixture, separate, boil, heat. [Mixture → heat → boil → separate] (5 minutes)

MAIN

- In order to contrast fractional distillation in a school lab with what happens in industry, students could watch a video on separation of crude oil such as *Industrial Chemistry for Schools and Colleges* (RSC).
- Then the students could be given a drawing of a fractionating column, which they have to add their own notes to. For lower ability students, this activity could be adapted into a cut and stick (where the key points are given as words and diagrams, on a piece of paper and the students assemble a poster).
- Often students do not know what a fraction of crude oil looks like. Ampoules of the different crude oil fractions could be shown to the students (available from BP: www.bpes.com).
- Give the students some string beads. Then ask them to cut or break links to give different lengths to represent the different fractions (each bead represents a carbon atom). Put these onto a demonstration table – one pile for each fraction.
- Then put out samples of different fractions (e.g. light a Bunsen burner or show a camping gas bottle, sample of octane, paraffin, lubricating oil and wax).
- Ask the students to comment on the colour, viscosity and state a room temperature. Then try to ignite some of each fraction (explanation on page 169), and ask the students to note the flame colour and ease of ignition.
- Then ask the students to compare the properties with the chain length. This task could be written up in the form of a results' table.
- Link here to 'How Science Works' – relationships between variables.

PLENARIES

Improvisation – Ask for volunteers to talk about a key word for 30 seconds without 'erms' or pauses. Ask the student to talk about: hydrocarbons, fractions or viscosity – without any preparation! The volunteer is given their word and starts talking, while the rest of the class listens. If they are any misconceptions, ask the other students to pick them out. (5–10 minutes)

Questions and answers – Give each student either a question or an answer. Ask the students to find their partners. (10 minutes)

Practical support

Comparing fractions

Equipment and materials needed

Three samples of different alkanes, e.g. pentane, wax, paraffin (flammable), three watch glasses, mineral wool, heat-proof mat, matches, eye protection, molecular model kits.

Details

Show the alkanes in their bottles or as the candle. Put a small piece of mineral wool on each watch glass, and place them on a heat-proof mat. Then pour each one onto a separate watch glass and allow soaking into the mineral wool. Allow some of the liquid to soak up. Light the mineral wool. Ask students to comment on the ease of lighting and the colour of the flame. Ensure the stock bottles of alkanes are closed before lighting matches.

Safety: Wear eye protection and tie back hair and loose clothing.

ACTIVITY & EXTENSION IDEAS

- Ask students to find out the difference between red diesel and 'normal' diesel. [Brown diesel is used in cars, but red diesel is used in working vehicles, e.g. tractors. The fuel is the same, but a dye is added, as red diesel is tax-free.]
- Students could research alternatives to fossil fuels, e.g. nuclear power; hydrogen fuel cells; renewable resources.

SUMMARY ANSWERS

1 Mixture, fractions, fractional distillation, high, viscosity, easily.

2 a) Hot vapour enters fractionating column which is hottest at the bottom. Vapours rise, condensing at different levels as they reach their boiling point temperature.

b) Table to summarise properties in Figure 1 on page 56 in Student Book.

DID YOU KNOW?

Antarctica has a lot of reserves including oil, but as there are disputes over who owns which parts, and international environmental agreements are in place, this reserve has not been exploited.

Answers to in-text questions

a) Increasing hydrocarbon chain length *increases* both boiling point and viscosity of a hydrocarbon.

b) Short hydrocarbon chains.

c) 'Light' crude oil has more fractions that can be turned easily into fuels.

KEY POINTS

Ask the students to copy down the key points and draw a diagram to represent each one. For example,

1 Sketch of a distillation column.

2 A structural formula of an alkane.

3 CH_4 with a flame coming out of it, on top of a balance with a low reading.

CHEMISTRY | CRUDE OIL

C1a 3.3 Burning fuels

LEARNING OBJECTIVES

Students should learn:

- The combustion products formed from fuels.
- That in a combustion reaction, the amount of oxygen available to react affects the products produced.
- The pollutants produced when we burn fuels.

LEARNING OUTCOMES

Most students should be able to:

- Write word equations for the complete combustion of hydrocarbons.
- Describe differences between incomplete and complete combustion.
- List pollutants formed when we burn fuels.

Some students should also be able to:

- Complete balanced symbol equations for the complete and incomplete combustion of simple alkanes.
- Explain how nitrogen oxides, sulfur dioxide and particulates are produced during the combustion process.

Teaching suggestions

- **Special needs.** For these students, balancing symbol equations is not appropriate. Instead create an activity whereby they need to complete word equations. In the first section, they must always write in oxygen, in the second section, they must always write in water and carbon dioxide. The repetition should help them grasp the concept.
- **Learning styles**
  Kinaesthetic: Moving to find other people's opinions during the true and false game.
  Visual: Watching the demonstration of combustion.
  Auditory: Listening to the group's sentence.
  Intrapersonal: Recalling the combustion triangle.
  Interpersonal: Asking other student's opinions in the true or false game.
- **Homework.** Ask students to find three examples of using combustion in their everyday life. They could then find out the fuel that is used, and decide if it is a fraction of crude oil.

SPECIFICATION LINK-UP C1a.11.3

- Most fuels contain carbon and/or hydrogen and may also contain some sulfur. The gases released into the atmosphere when a fuel burns may include carbon dioxide, water (vapour), and sulfur dioxide. Particles may also be released.

Students should use their skills, knowledge and understanding of 'How Science Works':
- to consider and evaluate the social, economic and environmental impacts of the use of fuels.

Lesson structure

STARTER

True or false? – Give each student one of the following statements:
- Hydrocarbons contain only hydrogen and carbon. [True] • Fuels can only be hydrocarbons. [False] • A fuel is burned to release energy. [True] • Fuel is stored light energy. [False] • Combustion is a reduction reaction. [False] • When hydrocarbons burn in plenty of oxygen, carbon dioxide and water are made. [True] • Carbon dioxide can be tested with a glowing splint. [False] • Oxygen can be tested with lime water. [False] • Water can be tested with blue cobalt chloride paper. [True] • Sulfur dioxide can be made by burning fossil fuels. [True]
Each student then should ask three other students if they think their statement is true or false. The student then makes a final decision about their statement. Finally, the students go around the room to find out which statements are true. To extend the exercise, students could be asked to correct the false statements. (10 minutes)

List fuels – Ask students to list as many fuels as they can think of. (5 minutes)

Triangle – Ask students to recall and draw the combustion triangle, as studied in Key Stage 3. (5 minutes)

MAIN

- Have the demonstration of the combustion products of hydrocarbons (methane) practical already set up. Some students may have already seen this demonstration in Key Stage 3. Ask the students to predict the products, and which section of the apparatus to test for each product.
- Students have frequently used Bunsen burners throughout Key Stage 3, but probably have not considered the combustion process that takes place within the equipment in any detail. Encourage the students to experiment with the Bunsen flame to observe the differences between complete and incomplete combustion. With the yellow Bunsen flame, the oxygen flow is restricted, and incomplete combustion occurs. Therefore, a lower temperature is achieved and soot is produced. With the air-hole open we get the blue flame; oxygen is in excess and complete combustion occurs. Therefore, the combustion is most efficient under these conditions, producing high temperatures and only carbon dioxide and water.

PLENARIES

Equations – Ask students to complete the following equations:
- Wax + oxygen → [carbon dioxide] + water
- Petrol + [oxygen] → carbon dioxide + [water] + carbon + [carbon monoxide]
- $CH_4 + 2O_2 \rightarrow [CO_2] + [2H_2O]$
- $[6]CH_4 + [8]O_2 \rightarrow CO_2 + [12]H_2O + [2]CO + [3]C$

An Animation, C1a 3.3 'Burning propane', can be used here from the GCSE Chemistry CD ROM. (10 minutes)

Summarise – Split the class into groups and give each team a different topic: combustion; nitrogen oxides; sulfur dioxide; particulates. They could develop a sentence that summarises what they have learned in the lesson about their topic. The students then could share their sentences and note them down in their book. (15 minutes)

Practical support
Investigating combustion of methane or wax
Equipment and materials required

A candle, a small Bunsen burner and safety equipment, eye protection, a glass funnel, a boiling tube, a U-tube, lime water, cobalt chloride paper, selection of delivery tubes, a vacuum pump, two bungs with holes in (for the delivery tubes), one bung with two holes in, rubber tubing, matches, three stands, bosses and clamps.

Details

Place the Bunsen burner or candle onto the heat-proof mat, invert the glass funnel and clamp into position about 2 cm above the top of the candle. Using a small piece of rubber tubing, connect an 'n' shaped delivery tube to the filter funnel, put the other end through a bung. Mount a U-tube and put in a few pieces of cobalt chloride paper, seal one end with the bung connected to the funnel. Put a bung in the other end of the U-tube, and connect it to a boiling tube of lime water (irritant), using further bungs and delivery tubes. The test tube bung should have two delivery tubes through it, the final tube should be connected to the vacuum pump. Turn on the pump, and light the Bunsen burner. The cobalt chloride paper should change colour from blue to pink indicating the presence of water and the lime water should turn cloudy, indicating carbon dioxide is produced.

Safety: Eye protection should be worn. Wash hands after handling cobalt chloride paper (CLEAPSS Hazcard 25).

ACTIVITY & EXTENSION IDEAS

- Ask students to find out what fuel and car manufacturing companies are doing to reduce emissions of sulfur dioxide, nitrogen oxides and particulates.
- Cut open a catalytic converter to expose the honeycomb structure. Challenge students to suggest what it is. Share with the students how it works.
- Ask the students to find out why carbon monoxide detectors are important and how they work.

CHEMISTRY — CRUDE OIL

C1a 3.3 Burning fuels

LEARNING OBJECTIVES
1. What do we produce when we burn fuels?
2. When we burn fuels, how do changes in conditions affect what is produced?
3. What pollutants are produced when we burn fuels?

As we saw on page 57, the lighter fractions produced from crude oil are very useful as fuels. When hydrocarbons burn in plenty of air they produce two new substances – carbon dioxide and water.

For example, when propane burns we can write:

propane + oxygen → carbon dioxide + water

or

$C_3H_8 + 5O_2 \rightarrow 3CO_2 + 4H_2O$

Notice how we need five molecules of oxygen for the propane to burn. This makes three molecules of carbon dioxide and four molecules of water. The equation is *balanced*!

Figure 1 On a cold day we can often see the water produced when fossil fuels burn

PRACTICAL
Products of combustion

We can test the products given off when hydrocarbon burns as shown in Figure 2.

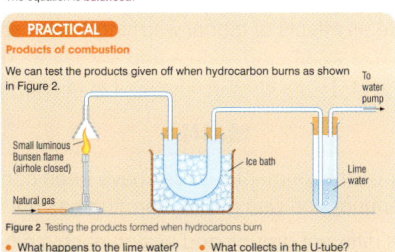

Figure 2 Testing the products formed when hydrocarbons burn

- What happens to the lime water?
- What collects in the U-tube?

a) What are the names of the two substances produced when hydrocarbons burn in plenty of air?
b) Write a balanced equation for methane (CH$_4$) burning in plenty of air.

All fossil fuels – oil, coal and natural gas – produce carbon dioxide and water when they burn in plenty of air. But as well as hydrocarbons, these fuels also contain other substances. These produce different compounds when we burn the fuel, and this can cause problems for us.

Impurities of sulfur cause us major problems. All fossil fuels contain at least some of this element, which reacts with oxygen when we burn the fuel. It forms a gas called **sulfur dioxide**. This gas is poisonous. It is also acidic. This is bad for the environment, as it is a cause of acid rain.

Sulfur dioxide can also cause engine corrosion.

c) When hydrocarbons burn, what element present in the impurities in a fossil fuel may produce sulfur dioxide?
d) Why is it bad if sulfur dioxide is produced?

When we burn hydrocarbons in a car engine, even more substances can be produced. When there is not enough oxygen inside the cylinders of the engine, we get *incomplete combustion*. Instead of all the carbon in the fuel turning into carbon dioxide, we also get **carbon monoxide** (CO).

Carbon monoxide is a poisonous gas. Your red blood cells pick up this gas and carry it around in your blood instead of oxygen. So even quite small amounts of carbon monoxide gas are very bad for you.

The high temperature inside an engine allows the nitrogen and oxygen in the air to react together. This makes **nitrogen oxides**, which are poisonous and which can trigger some people's asthma. They also make acid rain.

Diesel engines burn hydrocarbons with much bigger molecules than petrol engines. When these big molecules react with oxygen in an engine they do not always burn completely. Tiny particles containing carbon and unburnt hydrocarbons are produced. These **particulates** get carried into the air of our towns and cities. We do not understand fully what particulates may do when we breathe them in. However, scientists think that they may damage the cells in our lungs and perhaps even cause cancer.

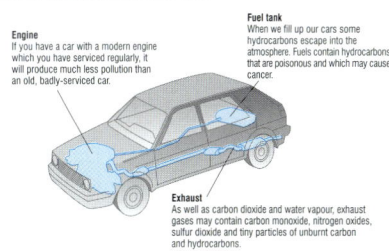

Engine If you have a car with a modern engine which you have serviced regularly, it will produce much less pollution than an old, badly-serviced car.

Fuel tank When we fill up our cars some hydrocarbons escape into the atmosphere. Fuels contain hydrocarbons that are poisonous and which may cause cancer.

Exhaust As well as carbon dioxide and water vapour, exhaust gases may contain carbon monoxide, nitrogen oxides, sulfur dioxide and tiny particles of unburnt carbon and hydrocarbons.

Figure 3 The effect of many cars in a small area. Under the right weather conditions smog can be formed. This is a mixture of SMoke and fOG. Smog formed from car pollution contains many different types of chemicals which can be harmful to us.

DID YOU KNOW...
...in 1996 a three-wheeled diesel car set a record for the lowest amount of fuel used to go a fixed distance? The car could travel 568 miles on one gallon (4.5 litres) of fuel!

SUMMARY QUESTIONS
1. Copy and complete using the words below:

   carbon   carbon dioxide   nitrogen   particulates   sulfur   water

   When we burn hydrocarbons in plenty of air …… …… and …… are made. As well as these compounds other substances like …… dioxide may be made. Other pollutants that may be formed include …… oxides, …… monoxide and …… .

2. a) Natural gas is mainly methane (CH$_4$). Write a balanced equation for the complete combustion of methane.
   b) When natural gas burns in a faulty gas heater it can produce carbon monoxide (and water). Write a balanced equation to show this reaction.
   c) Explain how i) sulfur dioxide ii) nitrogen oxides and iii) particulates are produced when fuels burn in vehicles.

KEY POINTS
1. When we burn hydrocarbon fuels in plenty of air they produce carbon dioxide and water.
2. Impurities in fuels may produce other substances which may be poisonous and/or which may cause pollution.
3. Changing the conditions in which we burn fuels may change the products that are made.

SUMMARY ANSWERS

1. Carbon dioxide, water, sulfur, nitrogen, carbon, particulates.

2. a) $CH_4 + 2O_2 \rightarrow CO_2 + 2H_2O$
   b) $2CH_4 + 3O_2 \rightarrow 2CO + 4H_2O$
   c) i) When sulfur from impurities in fuel burn it reacts with oxygen to form sulfur dioxide.
      ii) At the high temperatures in the engine, nitrogen gas from the air reacts with oxygen to form nitrogen oxides.
      iii) Incomplete combustion of the fuel can produce small particles of carbon and unburnt hydrocarbons.

Answers to in-text questions

a) Carbon dioxide and water (vapour).
b) $CH_4 + 2O_2 \rightarrow CO_2 + 2H_2O$
c) Sulfur.
d) It is poisonous and it causes pollution (acid rain).

KEY POINTS

Ask the students to write a word equation (more advanced students could write a balanced symbol equation) to represent each key point, e.g.

1. Hydrocarbon + (excess) oxygen → water + carbon dioxide
2. Sulfur + oxygen → sulfur dioxide
3. Hydrocarbon + (limited) oxygen → carbon dioxide + water + carbon monoxide + carbon

CHEMISTRY | CRUDE OIL

C1a 3.4 Cleaner fuels

LEARNING OBJECTIVES

Students should learn:
- That burning fuels has a negative environmental impact.
- How we can reduce the pollution from burning fuels.

LEARNING OUTCOMES

Most students should be able to:
- State what causes global warming, global dimming and acid rain.
- List some ways of reducing pollutants released when we burn fuels.

Some students should also be able to:
- Explain how acid rain is produced, and how it can be reduced.
- Discuss the relationship between global dimming and global warming.
- Explain methods of reducing pollutants from fuels.

Teaching suggestions

- **Special needs.** To make the crossword a little easier, add the first letter of each word into the grid.
- **Learning styles**
  Kinaesthetic: Making the square-based pyramid with information about environmental issues.
  Visual: Looking at the photographs and making a link.
  Auditory: Listening to feedback.
  Intrapersonal: Individually completing the crossword.
  Interpersonal: Working as groups to become experts and then disseminating their knowledge to answer questions.
- **Homework.** Students could summarise the difference between global warming and the greenhouse effect.

SPECIFICATION LINK-UP   C1a.11.3

- Sulfur dioxide causes acid rain, carbon dioxide causes global warming, and particles cause global dimming.
- Sulfur can be removed from fuels before they are burned, for example in vehicles. Sulfur dioxide can be removed from the waste gases after combustion, for example in power stations.

Students should use their skills, knowledge and understanding of 'How Science Works':
- to evaluate the impact on the environment of burning hydrocarbon fuels.
- to consider and evaluate the social, economic and environmental impacts of the use of fuels.

Lesson structure

STARTER

Demonstration – Ignite sulfur in oxygen to demonstrate the production of sulfur dioxide, wearing eye protection.
Ask the students to write a word (or balanced symbol equation) for the reaction [sulfur + oxygen → sulfur dioxide]. Then ask them how this relates to burning fuels. [Sulfur is an impurity in fossil fuels; as the fuel is burned, this reaction can occur which leads to the production of acid rain.] (10 minutes)

Photographs – Show the students an image of a drought area, polar ice caps and flooding. Topical pictures can be found on the web. Ask the students to link the pictures. [Scientists believe these are all effects of global warming.] Then show the students a forest damaged by acid rain, a weathered statute and a weathered building. Again ask the students to link the images. [They are the effects of acid rain.] (5 minutes)

MAIN

- During Year 9 a number of environmental issues have been considered, but global dimming and its interdependence with global warming has not been studied.
- Split the class into three different groups and assign each a different environmental issue:
  – acid rain   – global warming   – global dimming.
  The group could be given access to different research materials e.g. the Internet and library books, and each member of the team should become an expert on their environmental issue. Then make teams of three, each team should have one specialist on each issue. Each new group should then answer the questions set out in the objectives.
- Students already have a large body of background knowledge gained form KS3 science, geography and citizenship about environmental issues. Give each student a square-based pyramid net. Each triangular face should contain information about a different environmental issue (as detailed above), using the textbook to ensure that the science content is correct. The base should contain information about what can be done to reduce these problems.
- Once the information has been drawn and written, the students could cut it out and assemble the pyramid. For lower attaining students some information could already be printed on the net, e.g. the start of a diagram, a prose with missing words or just a title. Encourage students to use lots of colour as this aids their learning, they might even want to include a key e.g. each time they mention the word acid, or an example of an acid, they write it in red.

PLENARIES

Crossword – Give the students a crossword to complete in pairs. These can be tailor made if a puzzle generator is used e.g. www.discoveryschool.com. (10 minutes)

AfL (Assessment for Learning) – Give students an examination question with fictitious answers: a weak, an average and an excellent answer. Students could then order them to show which they think is the worst and best answer, and why they think this. Then feed back to the class the group ideas through a question and answer session. (15 minutes)

ACTIVITY & EXTENSION

- Each student could be asked to write a letter to their local MP outlining their concerns about environmental issues. They could also include ways in which they believe our government could reduce these problems. Students could search for 'Climate Change' at www.wmnet.org.uk for information.
- A debate could be held, with the motion posed: 'There are no environmental problems, just normal changes in the Earth's environment'. Split the class into two groups. One group could be 'green' protestors, who believe the worst-case scenario regarding these environmental issues. The second group could be politicians and an elect group of scientists who believe that these issues are within the natural range for the Earth or are under control, and pose no threat.

Practical support

Equipment and materials needed
Gas jar of oxygen, sulfur flowers, spatula, combustion spoon, Bunsen burner, eye protection.

Details
Put half a spatula of sulfur in a combustion spoon. Heat in a blue Bunsen flame, until it begins to combust (blue flame is visible). Put into a gas jar of oxygen.

Safety – Complete in a fume hood, as sulfur dioxide is harmful, wear eye protection and wash hands after use. CLEAPSS Hazcards 69, 96, 97.

CHEMISTRY — CRUDE OIL

C1a 3.4 Cleaner fuels

LEARNING OBJECTIVES
1 When we burn fuels, what are the consequences?
2 What can we do to reduce the problems?

When we burn hydrocarbons, as well as producing carbon dioxide and water, we produce other compounds. Many of these are not good for the environment, and can affect our health.

Pollution from our cars does not stay in one place but spreads through the whole of the Earth's atmosphere. For a long time the Earth's atmosphere seemed to cope with all this pollution. But the increase in the number of cars in the last 50 years means that pollution is a real concern now.

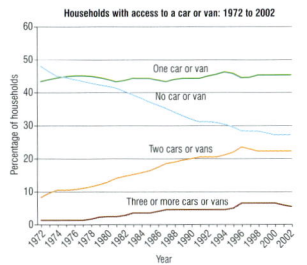

Figure 1 In 1972, about 50% of people had a car they could use. Now around 75% of people have access to a car.

a) Why is there more pollution from cars now than there was 50 years ago?
b) Why is pollution from cars in Moscow as important as pollution from cars in London?

What kinds of pollution?
When we burn any fuel it makes carbon dioxide. Carbon dioxide is a **greenhouse gas**. It collects in the atmosphere and reduces the amount of heat lost by radiation from the surface of the Earth. Most scientists think that this is causing **global warming**, which changes temperatures around the world.

Burning fuels in engines also produce other substances. One group of pollutants is called the **particulates**. These are tiny particles made up of unburnt hydrocarbons, which scientists think may be especially bad for young children. Particulates may also be bad for the environment too – they travel into the upper atmosphere, reflecting sunlight back into space, causing **global dimming**.

NEXT TIME YOU...
...use a fuel (or electricity which is usually made from natural gas, coal or oil), think how your action affects the environment.

Other pollutants produced by burning fuels include carbon monoxide, sulfur dioxide and nitrogen oxides. Carbon monoxide is formed when there is not enough oxygen present for the fuel to react with oxygen to form carbon dioxide. Carbon monoxide is a serious pollutant because it affects the amount of oxygen that our blood is able to carry. This is particularly serious for people who have problems with their hearts.

Sulfur dioxide and nitrogen oxides damage us and our environment. In Britain scientists think that the number of people who suffer from asthma and hayfever have increased because of air pollution.

Sulfur dioxide and nitrogen oxides also form acid rain. These gases dissolve in water droplets in the atmosphere and form sulfuric and nitric acids. The rain with a low pH can damage plant and animals.

c) Name four harmful pollutants that may be produced when fossil fuels burn.

Cleaning up our act
We can reduce the effect of burning fossil fuels in several ways. The most obvious way is to remove the pollutants from the gases that are produced when we burn fuels. For some time the exhaust systems of cars have been fitted with **catalytic converters**.

The exhaust gases from the engine travel through the catalytic converter where they pass over transition metals. These are arranged so that they have a very large surface area. This causes the carbon monoxide and nitrogen oxides in the exhaust gases to react. They produce carbon dioxide and nitrogen:

carbon monoxide + nitrogen oxides → carbon dioxide + nitrogen

In power stations, sulfur dioxide is removed from the flue gases by reacting it with quicklime. This is called **flue gas desulfurisation** or FGD for short.

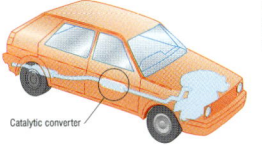

Figure 2 A catalytic converter greatly reduces the carbon monoxide and nitrogen oxides produced by a car engine

The methods described here reduce pollution by tackling it after it has been produced. The next page shows how we can also reduce the pollution that fuels produce if we start using alternative fuels.

SUMMARY QUESTIONS
1 Write definitions for the following terms:
   a) greenhouse gas, b) global warming, c) global dimming, d) acid rain
2 A molecule of carbon monoxide requires another atom of oxygen if it is to become a molecule of carbon dioxide. How does a catalytic converter supply this?
3 a) Explain how acid rain is formed and how we are reducing the problem.
   b) Compare the effects of global warming and global dimming.

KEY POINTS
1 Burning fuels releases substances that spread throughout the atmosphere.
2 Some of these substances dissolve in droplets of water in the air, which then fall as acid rain.
3 Carbon dioxide produced from burning fuels is a greenhouse gas. It reduces the rate at which energy is lost from the surface of the Earth by radiation.
4 The pollution produced by burning fuels may be reduced by treating the products of combustion. This can remove substances like nitrogen oxides, sulfur dioxide and carbon monoxide.

SUMMARY ANSWERS

1 a) Greenhouse gas – a gas that reduces the energy lost from the Earth by radiation.
   b) Global warming – an increase in the world's temperatures due to humans releasing extra greenhouse gases.
   c) Global dimming – occurs when particulates reflect sunlight back into space.
   d) Acid rain – rain containing dissolved gases, lowering its pH below natural levels.

2 By using the carbon monoxide as a reducing agent. It removes the oxygen from nitrogen oxides, producing harmless nitrogen and oxidises carbon monoxide to carbon dioxide.

3 a) Acidic gases (sulfur dioxide and nitrogen oxides) react with oxygen and water to form sulfuric and nitric acids which fall to ground in rain, snow, hail or mist. Reduce by removing sulfur from fuels/removing SO_2 from gases released/removing nitrogen oxides by catalytic converters.
   b) Global warming is the increase in average temperature of the Earth (due to an increase in greenhouse gases) whereas global dimming will decrease temperatures (as particulates reduce the energy reaching the Earth's surface from the Sun).

Answers to in-text questions

a) There are more cars than there were 50 years ago; and even though cars now are less polluting than cars 50 years ago, the increase in number more than compensates for this.

b) Because pollution doesn't just stay in one place but spreads throughout the Earth's atmosphere.

c) Particulates, sulfur dioxide, nitrogen oxides, carbon monoxide, carbon dioxide.

NEXT TIME YOU ...

Electricity is a secondary fuel source, as it must first be generated. Very little of the UK's energy comes from renewable resources, e.g. wind and wave, most comes from the burning of fossil fuels. Some also is produced by nuclear power, which doesn't contribute to acid rain, the greenhouse effect or global dimming. However it does produce highly radioactive and dangerous waste.

KEY POINTS

Give the students a word search using key words from the key points, e.g. burning, but, do not give the students the list of words to find.

CHEMISTRY — CRUDE OIL

C1a 3.5 Alternative fuels

SPECIFICATION LINK-UP
C1a.11.3

Students should use their skills, knowledge and understanding of 'How Science Works':

- to consider and evaluate the social, economic and environmental impacts of the use of fuels
- to evaluate developments in the production and uses of better fuels, for example ethanol and hydrogen.

CHEMISTRY — CRUDE OIL

C1a 3.5 Alternative fuels

Fuel from plants . . .

The fossil fuels that we use to produce electricity and to drive our cars have some big disadvantages. They produce carbon dioxide, which is a greenhouse gas, and they produce other pollutants too. What's more, once they have all been used there will be no other similar fuels that we can use to replace them – unless we think about the problem and do something about it.

Plants may be one answer to the problem of fuels. For thousands of years people have burned wood to keep themselves warm. Obviously we cannot use wood as a fuel for cars, but there are two ways that plants may be able to keep us on the road. These are explained in Figures 1 and 2.

Figure 1 We can use plants that make sugar to produce ethanol by fermenting the sugar using yeast. We can then add the ethanol to petrol, making **gasohol**. Not only does this reduce the amount of oil needed, it also produces less pollution because gasohol burns more cleanly than pure petrol.

Figure 2 Another new fuel is **biodiesel**. Some plants, like this oilseed rape, produce oils which can be used in diesel engines. We hardly need to make any changes to the engine to do this, and the biodiesel burns very cleanly, like gasohol. These bio-fuels also help tackle global warming. That's because the plants take in carbon dioxide gas during photosynthesis. They still give off carbon dioxide when we burn the bio-fuel – but overall they make little contribution to the greenhouse effect compared with burning fossil fuels.

ACTIVITY

One problem with switching to a new fuel for cars is that people may not trust it, preferring to stick with what they know. One way of convincing them to switch may be to produce advertising material like stickers. People who have switched fuels can then use these on their cars to show other people that the new fuel works just as well as the old fuel.
Design a set of stickers which can be used to make other people think about switching fuels.

Teaching suggestions

Activities

Guide to Fuels – Students can often list fuel names and uses, but do not consider which would be the optimum fuel for a situation. Ask students to create a 'Guide to Fuels'. This should be in alphabetical order, with the name of the fuel, what/how it is made and advantages and disadvantages. The students could then rate each fuel with a 0–5 star to represent how good a fuel they think it is.

Spider diagram – Ask students to complete a spider diagram in the back of their book about fuels. Then, in turn, ask each student to write one point onto the class diagram on the board or projector (each point should be different). Then ask the students to consider all the points written and see if they agree or disagree and why. If students highlight any misconceptions, change any incorrect statements.

Adverts – Despite the energy crisis, people are often resistant to change. Ask the students to create persuasive adverts to encourage people to change from using petrol/diesel to using newer fuels in their cars. Persuasive argument should have been studied at KS3 English. Students could script a radio advert and record it onto a computer, a TV commercial, which could be recorded on a web cam, a magazine advert, a billboard poster, or other promotional material, e.g. car stickers. All of these materials would create excellent displays or could be used on the school web site.

Homework

Properties of Fuels – Ask the students to list the properties that make a good fuel. Encourage students to discuss their lists with other students. Obtain feedback from the class to produce a class list of properties and explore the reasons for their choice. [Affordable, easy to transport, easy to store, ignites easily, produces little waste, easy to make.]

Extension

Role plays – Students are often good at explaining their point of view, but struggle with empathy of others. Ask students to prepare role plays of these (either writing a script or improvising after some research into the issues):

- Somebody resistant to changing the fuel type in their car/a scientist pro fuel change.
- Rubbish disposal company/local resident.
- Commuter/environmentalist.
- Person whose garden backs onto a rubbish dump/local council.

A room swap to a drama studio or the hall could be negotiated, so that the students could act out their work.

Homework

Ask the students to write key points for this spread.

...fuel from rubbish

Another way that we could reduce the amount of fuels we use is to replace them with something else – and rubbish seems a good answer! By burning rubbish we could produce some of the energy we need to heat our homes, and we would get rid of a big problem too.

Figure 3 Getting rid of all our rubbish usually means burying it in holes in the ground. This is not a good solution since it is messy, smelly and produces pollution.

Figure 4 We can burn rubbish in an incinerator like this. We can use the energy to heat water which can then heat our homes – or the energy can be used to make electricity.

But producing energy from rubbish is not straightforward. Unless the incinerator is run very carefully, dangerous chemicals called *dioxins* may be produced when the rubbish burns. Although no-one is exactly certain what dioxins do, many people think that they may cause cancer, and that they may damage us in other ways too. So there are arguments on both sides about the benefits of building incinerators.

ACTIVITY

You are going to take part in a planning enquiry which will decide whether or not an incinerator should be built. Choose one of the following rôles:

Director of incinerator company
You believe that incinerating waste is the best option – better for the environment (getting rid of waste and producing energy), and better for the local economy. The incinerator would bring real benefits.

Environmental campaigner
You argue that an incinerator is not good. Although the energy produced would replace fossil fuels, you believe that the pollutants the incinerator would produce will be harmful to local people, especially children.

Parent of young children
Although you like the idea of cheap heating and electricity you are concerned that the pollutants, which may be given off by the incinerator, may harm your children.

Local resident
You have lived and worked in the area for years. You feel that the incinerator will bring many benefits to the local area, and that the cheap energy will be a real bonus for local people.

Chair of enquiry
It is your job to manage the enquiry. You will have to give everyone a chance to speak, and you must ensure that everyone gets a fair hearing.

ACTIVITY & EXTENSION IDEAS

- Hold a fictitious public enquiry meeting about the site of an incinerator.
- Students could research other types of fuel currently being used in other countries (e.g. ethanol in Brazilian cars) and those that are under development (hydrogen fuel cells).
- Write an article for a top car magazine about how car fuel has developed and continues to develop. The article could include details of lead additives, unleaded petrol, diesel, gas, ethanol and fuel cells. ICT literate students could write up the article using a desk-top publishing package and could source images from the Internet.
- Students could find information on the percentage use of different fuels in the UK and draw a pie chart to show the data.

Learning styles

Kinaesthetic: Acting out promotional material.

Visual: Observing the fuel guide, an excellent visual resource.

Auditory: Listening to feedback from other students about the spider diagram.

Interpersonal: Making individual promotional material.

Intrapersonal: Working as a group on role plays.

Special needs

Role plays could already be written, so that these students just act them out.

Gifted and talented

Ask the students to make 'Top Trump' cards about the different types of fuel. They need to decide on the categories and rating systems. Then the game could be played as a plenary.

CHEMISTRY — CRUDE OIL

SUMMARY ANSWERS

1. **a)** Carbon dioxide and water.
   b) Carbon dioxide – it is a greenhouse gas that is linked to global warming.
   c) Sulfur dioxide.
   d) Nitrogen oxides and carbon monoxide.
   e) Nitrogen oxides make acid rain, carbon monoxide is a toxic gas.
   f) Tiny particles of carbon and unburnt hydrocarbon, thought to be associated with global dimming.

2. **a)** Light crude is more expensive than heavy crude.
   b) Light crude contains more fractions that can be used as fuels.
   c) The effect of war in the Middle East on oil supplies.
   d) In the summer people use their cars more (holidays, picnics etc.). This requires more fuels, so the price goes

Summary teaching suggestions

- **When to use these questions?**
  - Students can find it difficult to decide how to write answers and whether they would be given a mark. Ask students to write a mark scheme for the questions. They should identify the marking points and consider alternative responses and what must not be awarded a mark.
  - Question 2 is a good data response question that doesn't require any chemical understanding and could be used anytime during the topic.

- **Gifted and talented**
  Give the students fictitious answers to the questions. Ask the students in small groups to mark the answers and give 'examiner's comments'. Then ask each group to feedback to the class what they thought about each answer. Encourage discussion between other groups about the marks that have been awarded.

- **ICT Link-up**
  Scan the questions in and add the fictitious students' answers. Protect the image onto the interactive whiteboard and ask the groups to come to the front and 'mark' the work. This can then be saved by taking a screen shot and importing into another program.

- **Learning styles**
  Visual: Reading graphs (question 2).

- **Special needs**
  Question 1a) to d) could be turned into a card sort, where students cut out and match up the chemical names with each part of the question. This activity could also be put into interactive whiteboard software and completed virtually.

CRUDE OIL: C1a 3.1 – C1a 3.5

SUMMARY QUESTIONS

1. The following questions are about using hydrocarbons from crude oil as fuels.
   a) When hydrocarbon fuels burn in plenty of air, what are the **two** main products?
   b) One of these products is particularly bad for the environment – which one, and why?
   c) What other substance may be produced when hydrocarbon fuels burn in plenty of air?
   d) When hydrocarbon fuels burn inside an engine, what **two** other substances may be produced?
   e) What effect do these two substances have on the environment?
   f) Diesel engines produce **particulates**. What are they and what effect may they have on the environment?

2. Look at the graph of crude oil prices:

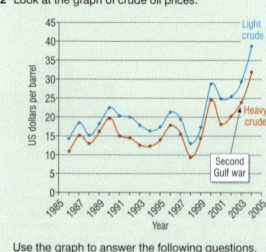

   Use the graph to answer the following questions.
   a) How do the prices of light crude and heavy crude differ?
   b) Why is there this price difference?
   c) Why did the price of crude oil rise sharply in 2003?
   d) Light crude oil is particularly expensive during summer in the Northern Hemisphere. Suggest **one** possible reason for this.

EXAM-STYLE QUESTIONS

1. The following compounds are found in crude oil:
   A C_5H_8 B C_5H_{10}
   C $C_{12}H_{26}$ D C_nH_{34}
   You can use A, B, C or D once, more than once or not at all when answering the questions below.
   Which of these compounds
   (a) has the highest boiling point?
   (b) catches fire most easily?
   (c) is collected at the top of the fractionating column when crude oil is distilled?
   (d) is the thickest liquid? (4)

2. Crude oil is a mixture of many different hydrocarbons. Match the words **A**, **B**, **C** and **D** with spaces **1** to **4** in the sentences.
   A alkanes B compounds
   C fractions D molecules
   (a) Crude oil is separated by distillation into ...... containing hydrocarbons with similar boiling points.
   (b) Hydrocarbons with the smallest ...... have the lowest boiling points.
   (c) Hydrocarbons are ...... of hydrogen and carbon only.
   (d) Crude oil contains mostly saturated hydrocarbons called .... (4)

3. The table shows the number of carbon atoms in the molecules of four fuels obtained from crude oil.

Fuel	Number of carbon atoms in molecules
petroleum gases	2–4
petrol	4–10
kerosene	10–15
diesel oil	14–19

   (a) The fuel with the highest boiling point is ...
   A petroleum gases B petrol
   C kerosene D diesel oil (1)
   (b) Petrol ...
   A has a higher boiling point than diesel oil.
   B is a thinner liquid than diesel oil.
   C ignites less easily than kerosene.
   D has larger molecules than kerosene. (1)

EXAM-STYLE ANSWERS

1. a) **D** b) **A** c) **A** d) **D** (4 marks)
2. a) **C** b) **D** c) **B** d) **A** (4 marks)
3. a) **D** b) **B** c) **C** d) **C** (4 marks)
4. a) Oxygen. (1 mark)
   b) pentane + oxygen → carbon dioxide + water
   (one mark for reactants, one for products) (2 marks)
   c) $C_5H_{12} + 8O_2 \rightarrow 5CO_2 + 6H_2O$
   (one mark for correct formulae, one mark for correct balance) (2 marks)
   d) Carbon monoxide. (1 mark)
   e) Accept any balanced equation with some CO as product, e.g.:
   - $C_5H_{12} + 5.5O_2 \rightarrow 5CO + 6H_2O$
   - $C_5H_{12} + 7O_2 \rightarrow 2CO + 3CO_2 + 6H_2O$
   - $C_5H_{12} + 6O_2 \rightarrow 4CO + CO_2 + 6H_2O$
   (one mark for correct formulae, one mark for correct balance) (2 marks)

5. One mark each for any two reasonable suggestions of alternative fuels, one mark for a reasonable advantage and one mark for a reasonable disadvantage for each fuel, e.g.

Fuel	Advantages	Disadvantages
Ethanol	Renewable/can be used in existing petrol engines/less pollution.	Only partly replaces fossil fuel/competition with food crops.
Biodiesel/ plant or vegetable oil	Renewable/can be used in existing diesel engines/cleaner burning.	Using possible food source/cannot be used in all engines.
Hydrogen	No pollution.	Difficult to store or distribute/leaks easily/engines need modification.
Biogas	Renewable/less pollution.	More difficult to store or distribute/engines need modification.

   (6 marks)

Products from rocks

(c) The molecule C₅H₁₀ could be in ...
A petrol only.
B petrol and kerosene.
C petrol and petroleum gases.
D petroleum gases only. (1)

(d) Which one of the following is a saturated hydrocarbon that could be in diesel oil?
A C₁₂H₂₆
B C₁₅H₁₂
C C₁₅H₃₆
D C₁₆H₃₆O (1)

4 Pentane, C₅H₁₂, is a hydrocarbon fuel. It burns completely in plenty of air.
(a) Name the gas in air that pentane reacts with when it burns. (1)
(b) Write a word equation for the combustion of pentane in plenty of air. (2)
(c) Write a balanced symbol equation for this reaction. (2)
(d) When the air supply is limited a poisonous gas is produced. Name this gas. (1)
(e) Write a balanced symbol equation for the combustion of pentane in a limited supply of air. (2)

5 Suggest two fuels that could be used in place of fossil fuels. Give one advantage and one disadvantage for each of the fuels you have named. (6)

6 Oil companies promote the use of low sulfur fuels.
(a) Explain why it is better to use low sulfur fuels. (3)
(b) Suggest one other reason why oil companies advertise that their fuels are low in sulfur. (1)

7 Crude oil is separated by fractional distillation. In oil refineries this is done in tall towers called fractionating columns. Give the main steps in this process and explain how the different fractions are separated in a fractionating column. (4)

HOW SCIENCE WORKS QUESTIONS
Calculating energy from different fuels

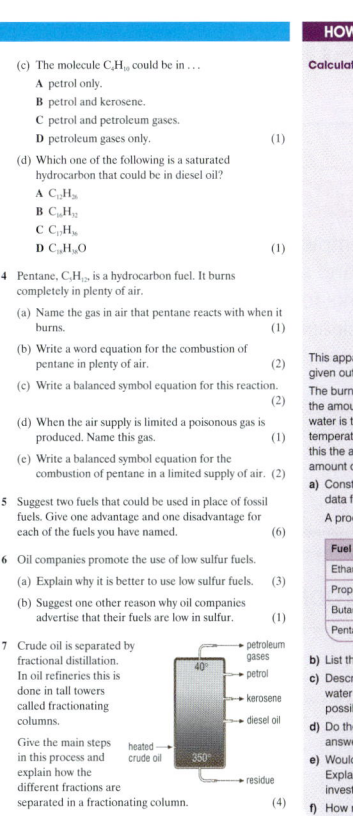

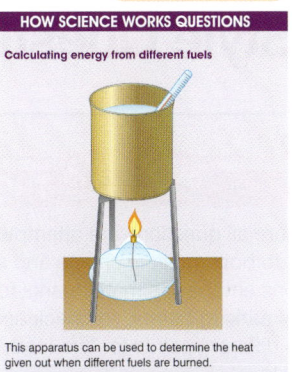

This apparatus can be used to determine the heat given out when different fuels are burned.

The burner is weighed before and after to determine the amount of fuel burned. The temperature of the water is taken before and after, so as to calculate the temperature rise. The investigation was repeated. From this the amount of heat produced by burning a known amount of fuel can be calculated.

a) Construct a table that could be used to collect the data from this experiment. (3)
A processed table of results is given below.

Fuel	Mass burned (g)	Temperature rise (°C)
Ethanol	4.9	48 47
Propanol	5.1	56 56
Butanol	5.2	68 70
Pentanol	5.1	75 76

b) List three variables that need to be controlled. (3)
c) Describe how you would take the temperature of the water to get the most accurate measurement possible. (2)
d) Do these results show precision? Explain your answer. (2)
e) Would you describe these results as accurate? Explain your answer. (Clue – look at the way the investigation was carried out.) (2)
f) How might you present these results? (1)

65

---

6 a) *Three from*:
- Produces less sulfur dioxide.
- Sulfur dioxide causes acid rain.
- Sulfur dioxide/acid rain is harmful to living things – plants damaged/effects on humans, e.g. asthma or respiratory problems.
- Sulfur dioxide corrodes metals/engines/exhaust systems.

(3 marks)

b) *Any reasonable suggestion, e.g.*:
- to justify higher costs,
- good company image,
- to increase sales/market share. *(1 mark)*

7 One mark for each of the following:
- Crude oil is **vaporised/vapour** fed into tower.
- Vapours **condense** in the column.
- Temperature in column is higher at the bottom/lower at the top.
- Different substances condense or are collected at different levels according to their boiling points/heavier or larger molecules condense or are collected near the bottom/lighter or smaller molecules condense or are collected near the top.

(4 marks)

Exam teaching suggestions

Q1 could be used after completing spread 3.1, Q2, Q3 and Q7 after 3.2, Q4 after 3.3, Q5 and Q6 at the end of the chapter. The questions should take about 30 minutes altogether (total 34 marks).

In questions that involve matching answers the four letters will all be used only once, but in other multiple-choice questions, like Q1 and Q3, the letters may be used once, more than once or not at all.

Students should use the information in the table in Q3 together with their own knowledge to answer the questions. Students should be able to organise information and communicate their ideas effectively in Q5, Q6 and Q7. Higher-Tier candidates should be able to use symbols and equations in Q4.

Most students should be able to name two alternative fuels in Q5. Good answers will include advantages and disadvantages correctly related to each named fuel in a clearly organised response. Students could be encouraged to tabulate their answers or to use bullets to make presentation clearer in this type of question.

Q6a) asks students to explain why, so reasons are required. Most students should know that less sulfur dioxide would be produced. To gain two or three marks they should describe the harmful effects of sulfur dioxide.

Some students confuse distillation and cracking, thinking that when crude oil is distilled the molecules are broken down. Some students find it difficult to relate boiling points to the temperature gradient in the fractionating column, thinking that low boiling fractions are collected near the bottom of the column. Q2, Q3 and Q7 should help identify these misconceptions.

HOW SCIENCE WORKS ANSWERS

a)

Fuel	Mass burned (g) 1	Mass burned (g) 2	Temperature (°C) Before 1	Temperature (°C) After 1	Temperature (°C) Before 2	Temperature (°C) After 2
Ethanol						
Propanol						
Butanol						
Pentanol						

b) Variables that need to be controlled include:
distance from burner to beaker
volume of water in beaker
starting temperature of the water
insulation on beaker
time left to burn
size of flame
draughts
how the temperature was recorded.

c) Stir the water before recording the temperature.
Use a well-calibrated thermometer.

d) The repeats are consistent so this would suggest that they are precise.

e) The results are not accurate – because large amounts of fuel are not being used to heat the water.

f) As a bar graph of the mean temperature rise for each fuel.

How science works teaching suggestions

- **Higher- and lower-level questions**
  - Questions b), d) and e) are higher-level and answers for these questions have been provided at this level.
  - Lower-level questions are a) and c) and the answers are also at this level.

65

CHEMISTRY   PRODUCTS FROM ROCKS

C1a   Examination-Style Questions

Examiner's comments
Maximum coverage of the specification will be achieved if your students do both multiple choice and structured questions whichever exam they are doing.

BUMP UP THE GRADE
Make sure all questions are attempted and answers given – applies to both multiple choice and structured. In structured questions emphasise that 2 marks for a question means there are two marking points, so check answers to make sure there are two different points for two marks, three points for three marks etc.

Answers to Questions

Chemistry A

1   1   D
    2   C
    3   B
    4   A   *(1 mark each)*

2   1   B
    2   C
    3   A
    4   D   *(1 mark each)*

3   D   *(1 mark)*

continues opposite ›

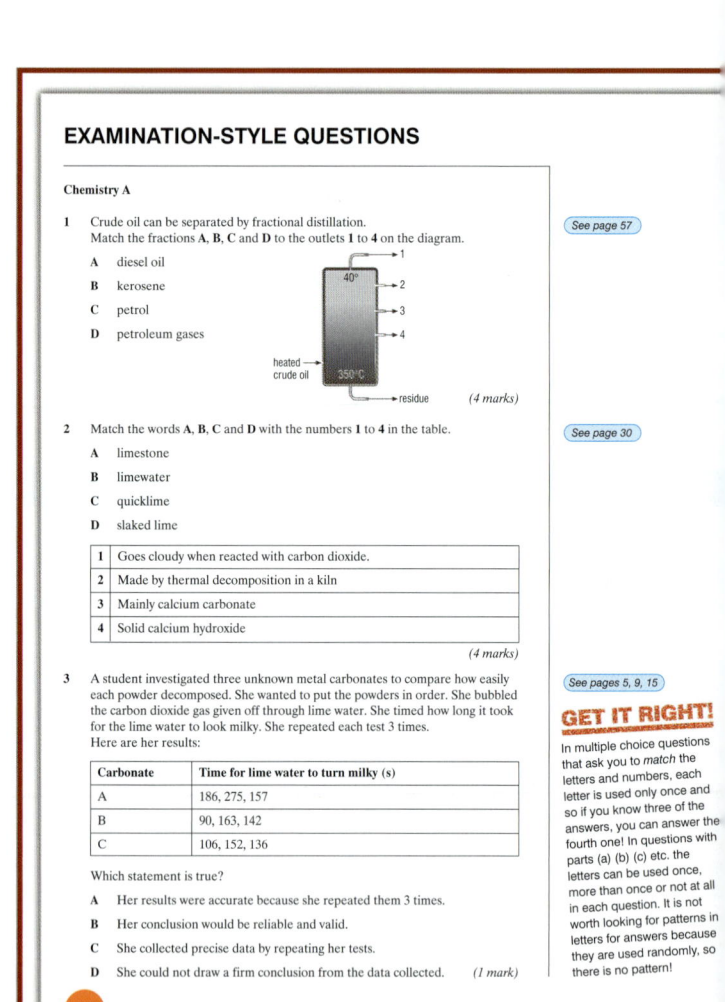

EXAMINATION-STYLE QUESTIONS

Chemistry A

1   Crude oil can be separated by fractional distillation.   *See page 57*
    Match the fractions **A, B, C** and **D** to the outlets **1** to **4** on the diagram.
    A   diesel oil
    B   kerosene
    C   petrol
    D   petroleum gases
    (4 marks)

2   Match the words **A, B, C** and **D** with the numbers **1** to **4** in the table.   *See page 30*
    A   limestone
    B   limewater
    C   quicklime
    D   slaked lime

    | 1 | Goes cloudy when reacted with carbon dioxide. |
    | 2 | Made by thermal decomposition in a kiln |
    | 3 | Mainly calcium carbonate |
    | 4 | Solid calcium hydroxide |

    (4 marks)

3   A student investigated three unknown metal carbonates to compare how easily each powder decomposed. She wanted to put the powders in order. She bubbled the carbon dioxide gas given off through lime water. She timed how long it took for the lime water to look milky. She repeated each test 3 times.
    Here are her results: *See pages 5, 9, 15*

Carbonate	Time for lime water to turn milky (s)
A	186, 275, 157
B	90, 163, 142
C	106, 152, 136

    Which statement is true?
    A   Her results were accurate because she repeated them 3 times.
    B   Her conclusion would be reliable and valid.
    C   She collected precise data by repeating her tests.
    D   She could not draw a firm conclusion from the data collected.   *(1 mark)*

GET IT RIGHT!
In multiple choice questions that ask you to *match* the letters and numbers, each letter is used only once and so if you know three of the answers, you can answer the fourth one! In questions with parts (a) (b) etc. the letters can be used once, more than once or not at all in each question. It is not worth looking for patterns in letters for answers because they are used randomly, so there is no pattern!

GET IT RIGHT!

Encourage students to answer every question – no answer = no marks! In multiple choice questions get them to shorten the odds by eliminating answers they know are wrong if they have to resort to a guess.

Get students to make notes when working through these questions, because you probably do not want them writing on their books. This will help to identify problems with understanding or exam technique. In the real exam they should be encouraged to write on, underline, highlight their exam question paper to help them get it right. It is their paper and should be used as effectively as possible.

Encourage them to read and use information in questions. Many are put off by text or what appear to be difficult questions. Use whatever techniques they have been shown when dealing with text. This may mean photocopying for those who cannot make notes. Their aim should be no blank spaces!

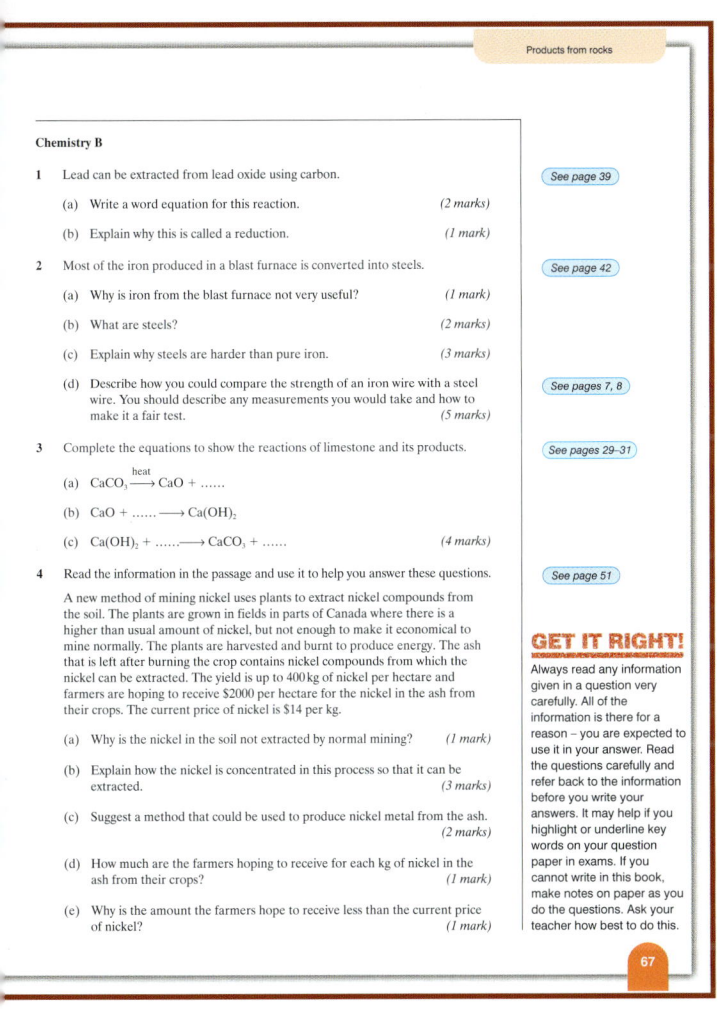

Chemistry B

1 Lead can be extracted from lead oxide using carbon. *(See page 39)*
  (a) Write a word equation for this reaction. *(2 marks)*
  (b) Explain why this is called a reduction. *(1 mark)*

2 Most of the iron produced in a blast furnace is converted into steels. *(See page 42)*
  (a) Why is iron from the blast furnace not very useful? *(1 mark)*
  (b) What are steels? *(2 marks)*
  (c) Explain why steels are harder than pure iron. *(3 marks)*
  (d) Describe how you could compare the strength of an iron wire with a steel wire. You should describe any measurements you would take and how to make it a fair test. *(5 marks)* *(See pages 7, 8)*

3 Complete the equations to show the reactions of limestone and its products. *(See pages 29–31)*
  (a) $CaCO_3 \xrightarrow{heat} CaO + \ldots$
  (b) $CaO + \ldots \longrightarrow Ca(OH)_2$
  (c) $Ca(OH)_2 + \ldots \longrightarrow CaCO_3 + \ldots$ *(4 marks)*

4 Read the information in the passage and use it to help you answer these questions. *(See page 51)*
  A new method of mining nickel uses plants to extract nickel compounds from the soil. The plants are grown in fields in parts of Canada where there is a higher than usual amount of nickel, but not enough to make it economical to mine normally. The plants are harvested and burnt to produce energy. The ash that is left after burning the crop contains nickel compounds from which the nickel can be extracted. The yield is up to 400kg of nickel per hectare and farmers are hoping to receive $2000 per hectare for the nickel in the ash from their crops. The current price of nickel is $14 per kg.
  (a) Why is the nickel in the soil not extracted by normal mining? *(1 mark)*
  (b) Explain how the nickel is concentrated in this process so that it can be extracted. *(3 marks)*
  (c) Suggest a method that could be used to produce nickel metal from the ash. *(2 marks)*
  (d) How much are the farmers hoping to receive for each kg of nickel in the ash from their crops? *(1 mark)*
  (e) Why is the amount the farmers hope to receive less than the current price of nickel? *(1 mark)*

GET IT RIGHT!

Always read any information given in a question very carefully. All of the information is there for a reason – you are expected to use it in your answer. Read the questions carefully and refer back to the information before you write your answers. It may help if you highlight or underline key words on your question paper in exams. If you cannot write in this book, make notes on paper as you do the questions. Ask your teacher how best to do this.

> continues from previous page

Chemistry B

1 (a) lead oxide + carbon → lead + carbon dioxide
      (all correct = 2 marks, one side correct = 1 mark, accept carbon monoxide instead of carbon dioxide)

  (b) Oxygen is removed. *(1 mark)*

2 (a) Too brittle/too hard/breaks easily. *(1 mark)*

  (b) Alloys of iron *(1 mark)*
      with other elements. *(1 mark)*

  (c) *Three from:*
      • Pure iron has a regular structure/regular layers.
      • Steels contain atoms other than iron/different atoms.
      • These distort the layers/change the regular structure.
      • Layers cannot slide easily. *(3 marks)*

  (d) *Five from:*
      • Support the wires (firmly/in a clamp).
      • Attach a hanger/weights (to the wires).
      • Add weights until wire breaks.
      • Record weight when it breaks.
      • Same length of wire.
      • Same thickness of wire. *(5 marks)*

3 (a) CO_2 *(1 mark)*

  (b) H_2O *(1 mark)*

  (c) CO_2 *(1 mark)*
      H_2O *(1 mark)*

4 (a) Not economic OR not enough metal in the ore/soil. *(1 mark)*

  (b) *Three from:*
      • Plants take up nickel from the soil.
      • Plants are burnt.
      • Burning removes organic matter.
      • Burning produces ash which has less bulk/volume/mass.
      • Metal compounds remain in the ash/are not volatile. *(3 marks)*

  (c) EITHER: *two from:*
      • Dissolve ash in acid/make a solution,
      • electrolyse
      • using nickel electrodes.
      OR:
      • Displace the metal with/heat ash with/make a solution of the ash and add
      • a (named) more reactive metal. *(2 marks)*

  (d) $5 *(1 mark)*

  (e) *One from:*
      • Cost of extracting the metal.
      • The metal is a compound in the ash.
      • The metal still has to be extracted. *(1 mark)*

CHEMISTRY

C1b | Oils, Earth and atmosphere

Key Stage 3 curriculum links

The following link to 'What you already know':

- That mixtures [for example, air, sea water and most rocks] are composed of constituents that are not combined.
- How to separate mixtures into their constituents using distillation, chromatography and other appropriate methods.
- How materials can be characterised by melting point, boiling point and density.
- How forces generated by expansion, contraction and the freezing of water can lead to the physical weathering of rocks.
- About the formation of rocks by processes that take place over different timescales, and that the mode of formation determines their texture and the minerals they contain.
- How igneous rocks are formed by the cooling of magma; sedimentary rocks by processes including the deposition of rock fragments or organic material, or as a result of evaporation; and metamorphic rocks by the action of heat and pressure on existing rocks.
- About possible effects of burning fossil fuels on the environment [for example, production of acid rain, carbon dioxide and solid particles] and how these effects can be minimised.
- To use indicators to classify solutions as acidic, neutral or alkaline, and to use the pH scale as a measure of the acidity of a solution.

QCA Scheme of work
7E Acids and alkalis
7G Particles
8E Atoms and elements
8F Compounds and mixtures
8G Rocks and weathering
8H The rock cycle
9H Using chemistry

CHEMISTRY

C1b | Oils, Earth and atmosphere

What you already know

Here is a quick reminder of previous work that you will find useful in this unit:

- We can characterise materials by melting point, boiling point and density.
- Mixtures are made up of different substances that are not chemically combined to each other.
- We can separate a mixture of liquids into its different parts using distillation.
- Changes of state involve energy transfers.
- Rocks are formed by processes that take place over different timescales.
- Burning fossil fuels affects our environment.
- We can use indicators to classify solutions as acidic, neutral or alkaline.

The face of the Earth has changed over millions of years

RECAP QUESTIONS

1. Where does the water in a puddle go as the puddle dries out when the Sun shines?
2. A car engine will not work properly if there is dirt in the petrol. The dirty petrol is passed through a funnel containing filter paper. How does this clean the petrol?
3. The tea-leaves in a tea bag contain colours and flavours that dissolve in water. Why is it difficult to make iced tea using a tea bag dipped in very cold water?
4. When you put a tray of water in the freezer its temperature drops. At 0°C the water starts to freeze. The temperature then stays the same until all the water is frozen. What is happening?
5. Two fossils are found in two different layers of rocks, one above the other. Which fossil is likely to be the older one – the one found in the upper layer of rock, or the one found in the lower layer? Explain your answer.
6. When we burn fossil fuels, how can it affect the environment?
7. A solution turns universal indicator red – what does this tell you about the solution?

68

RECAP ANSWERS

1. Water evaporates into the air.
2. The solid dirt gets trapped in the filter. Only the clean liquid petrol can pass through to the engine.
3. When a solvent (water) is heated the solutes (from tea-leaves) dissolve more quickly than in cold water.
4. The temperature stays at 0°C as the process of forming new bonds between water molecules gives out energy.
5. The lower fossil is likely to be older as this would have been laid down first to be covered by other material that eventually turned to rock as the layers built up.
6. Acid rain, global warming.
7. The solution is strongly acidic, pH ≈ 0 → 2 (depending on the colour chart of the indicator).

Oils, Earth and atmosphere

SPECIFICATION LINK-UP
Unit: Chemistry C1b

Oils, Earth and atmosphere

How are polymers and ethanol made from oil?

Fractions from the distillation of crude oil can be cracked to make smaller molecules including unsaturated hydrocarbons such as ethene. Unsaturated hydrocarbons can be used to make polymers and ethene can be used to make ethanol.

How can plant oils be used?

Many plants produce useful oils that can be converted into consumer products including processed foods. Vegetable oils can be hardened to make margarine. Biodiesel fuel can be produced from vegetable oils.

What are the changes in the Earth and its atmosphere?

The Earth and its atmosphere provide everything we need. The Earth has a layered structure. Large-scale movements of the Earth's crust can cause changes in the rocks. The Earth's atmosphere was originally very different from what it is today. It has been much the same for the last 200 million years and provides the conditions needed for life on Earth. Recently human activities have produced further changes.

Chapters in this unit
- Products from oil
- Plant oils
- The changing world

Teaching suggestions

What you already know

- **Definitions** – Students often struggle with the definitions of melting/boiling point and how these relate to changes of state and freezing point. Ask the students to draw a vertical thermometer and then add two horizontal lines to split it into thirds. Label the line closest to the bulb of the thermometer as melting/freezing point, and the higher line as boiling point. Ask the students to define these key terms, and decide which section(s) of the thermometer would have a substance as a solid, liquid and gas. Higher attaining students could then draw an arrow facing upwards at the side of the thermometer and mark this with the word 'energy'. This would represent that as temperature increases, so does the energy content in the substance.

- **Questions** – Ask students to consider each statement in turn. Each statement should be used as an answer, and the students should generate questions for them. As an assessment for learning opportunity, students could be asked to swap their questions with other groups and they could then try to answer them.

- **Diagram** – Students at Key Stage 3 should have studied the rock cycle and this will form the basis for the later stages of this section of work. Give students a diagram of the cycle and ask them to label the arrows with what they think are key words.

Recap questions

- **Timed questions** – For each marking point, students could be given 1 minute to answer the question. The teacher could have a stopwatch on an interactive whiteboard, or at the front of the class. They start the timer, and students begin to answer the questions, they should stop when the teacher asks. The question answer should then be read out and the student marks his or her own work.

- **AfL (Assessment for Learning)** – Students could try to answer the questions and then another student marks their work. They then return to their own work, and make corrections as highlighted by their peer.

Making connections

- Encourage students to use the information in the Student Book to create a comprehensive timeline to show the events detailed.

Activity

- Students should be encouraged to consider the environmental impact on the car in terms of pollution, but counterbalance this with reasons why it is popular. Students can use their background knowledge and empathy, coupled with the information in the Student Book to create a script for a short (5 minute) radio programme on how the motor car has affected our lives. The script could then be performed in front of the class, at an assembly or recorded on a computer and could be put on the school web site.

CHEMISTRY | PRODUCTS FROM OIL

C1b 4.1 Cracking hydrocarbons

LEARNING OBJECTIVES

Students should learn:

- Reasons for cracking large hydrocarbon molecules and how it is carried out.
- That alkenes contain double bonds and are called unsaturated hydrocarbons.

LEARNING OUTCOMES

Most students should be able to:

- Explain why cracking is carried out.
- Write a word equation for the cracking reaction.
- List the conditions needed for cracking, stating that it is a thermal decomposition reaction.
- Recognise an alkene from a structural or molecular formula.
- State and carry out the test for alkenes.

Some students should also be able to:

- Write a balanced symbol equation to represent cracking.
- State and use the general formula to work out a molecular formula when n is given.

Teaching suggestions

- **Special needs.** The cracking practical may be too difficult for students with poor manual dexterity; this could be completed as a demonstration instead.
- **Learning styles**
  Kinaesthetic: Completing the practical.
  Visual: Making a poster highlighting the differences between alkanes and alkenes.
  Intrapersonal: Completing their own creative writing.
  Interpersonal: Reflecting on the molecular re-arrangement that takes place in cracking
- **Homework.** Write up the cracking experiment.
- **ICT link-up.** If you have a webcam you might film the cracking experiment for a later discussion on what happens. The Simulation C1b 4.1 'Cracking of hydrocarbons' on the GCSE Chemistry CD ROM helps students visualise how the atoms can be rearranged.
- **Teaching assistant.** Split the class into two groups. The teacher and teaching assistant can then help small groups to test for alkenes.

SPECIFICATION LINK-UP   C1b.11.4

- Hydrocarbons can be broken down (cracked) to produce smaller, more useful molecules. This process involves heating the hydrocarbons to vaporise them and passing the vapours over a hot catalyst. A thermal decomposition reaction occurs.
- The products of cracking include alkanes and unsaturated hydrocarbons called alkenes. Alkenes have the general formula C_nH_{2n} and can be represented in the following forms:

$$C_2H_4 \qquad \begin{array}{c} H \quad H \quad H \\ | \quad\; | \quad\; | \\ H-C-C=C \\ | \quad\; | \\ H \quad H \end{array}$$

- Some of the products of cracking are useful as fuels.

Lesson structure

STARTER

Comparing – On the board, draw the structural formulae of ethane and ethene. Ask the students to list the similarities and differences. [**Similarities:** Same number of C atoms / H atoms all have one bond / C atoms all have 4 bonds / both are hydrocarbons. (5 minutes) **Differences:** Different number of H atoms / ethane is saturated, ethene is unsaturated / ethane has C—C but ethene has C=C.] (5 minutes)

Recap – Ask students to consider the phrase 'thermal decomposition' (recall limestone work). Ask them to define it and give an example [using heat to break down a substance, heating of calcium carbonate]. (10 minutes)

MAIN

- Cracking can be done at a laboratory scale in the classroom. Groups of about three are best, as one student can heat the boiling tube, and often it takes two students to collect the gas over water.
- Bromine water can be used to test the product and contrast this with the reactant. Ethene is flammable; this can be demonstrated by putting a lighted splint into the test tube and a flame should be seen travelling down the tube (eye protection must be worn). The flame should be smokier than the equivalent alkane (ethane) as there is a higher percentage of carbon.
- Use the Interactive/Simulation C1b 4.1 'Cracking of hydrocarbons' from the GCSE Chemistry CD. See how important it is to control the conditions in the refinery. Particularly note what goes in and what comes out of the cracking unit. Ask why cracking is useful to us.
- Students often find the idea of atoms rearranging themselves during chemical reactions a difficult concept. Encourage the students to imagine that they are a carbon atom in a molecule of paraffin. They could then write a creative story about their journey from being in paraffin, through being cracked and finally being tested with bromine water.
- For lower attaining students, statements of each 'scene' could be given. Then students put them into the correct order and then draw a cartoon/picture to represent that section of the story.
- Some students can find it difficult to notice the differences between alkanes and alkenes. Encourage them to compare alkanes and alkenes in terms of their structures and how to test them. They could be given a piece of coloured paper to fold in half and make a poster comparing the two families of hydrocarbons.

PLENARIES

Chemical formula – Ask the students to use the general formula for an alkene to work out the molecular and displayed formula if $n = 2, 3, 4$ [C_2H_4, C_3H_6, C_4H_8]. For quick workers, ask if there are alternative structures for any of the formulae. [There are two alternatives for C_4H_8.] (10 minutes)

Models – Give students a molecular model kit, A3 sheet of paper and a pen. Ask them, in groups, to represent cracking in model form. Students should make a long-chain alkane, e.g. decane, and place on the left of the paper. They should then draw an arrow, with heat and catalyst written on. They should then make a small alkene, e.g. ethene, and a smaller alkane, e.g. octane. (10 minutes)

Practical support

Cracking

Equipment and materials required
Bunsen burner and safety equipment, S-shaped delivery tube (with bung on one end and Bunsen valve on the other), pneumatic trough, boiling tube, mineral wool, three test tubes with bungs, test-tube rack, stand, boss and clamp, a hydrocarbon (medicinal paraffin, petroleum jelly or decane – flammable), broken ceramic pot/aluminium oxide powder (catalyst), bromine water (irritant and harmful – see CLEAPSS Hazcard 15).

Details
Soak the mineral wool in paraffin and put at the bottom of the boiling tube. About 2 cm from the bung put in the catalyst (about 1 spatula full) and clamp in position. Heat the catalyst strongly (with a blue flame), then flash the flame towards the mineral wool, so that the hydrocarbon evaporates and reaches the catalyst. Students should collect the gas over water. The Bunsen valve will help prevent suck back within the apparatus but get students to remove the end of the delivery tube from the trough of water by lifting the clamp stand as soon as they finish heating. Eye protection should be worn throughout. The collected gas can be tested with bromine water (as detailed below). The gas collected is highly flammable and this can be demonstrated by igniting it with a burning splint in the test tube.

Equipment and materials required
A selection of hydrocarbons (e.g. hexane, hexene, octane – flammable), dropping pipettes, test tubes, bromine water (hazardous), bungs, test-tube rack.

Details
Students should pipette about 1 ml of each liquid into separate test tubes, stored in a rack. About the same amount of bromine water should be added to each test tube, and each bunged and shaken. Ensure that the students wear eye protection, hold the bung and base of the test tube when they shake it. Bromine vapour may be given off, therefore a well ventilated area is necessary.

Only use weak solutions of bromine water (yellow, not orange) otherwise you are unlikely to see complete discoloration (and there will be less bromine vapour released).

ACTIVITY & EXTENSION IDEAS

- Students could be asked to explain why bromine water decolourises in alkenes and to display the reaction using molecular modelling kits.
- Students could be given the chemical formula of decane, and asked to generate as many balanced equations as possible to demonstrate all the possible combinations of alkanes and alkenes that could be generated in the cracking reaction.
- Students could use the bromine water test for margarine. They should find that the margarine decolourises the bromine water, showing that it is unsaturated.

Answers to in-text questions

a) Because we can use it to make smaller, more useful hydrocarbon molecules from larger ones.

b) By heating them strongly and passing the gas over a catalyst.

KEY POINTS

Ask students to match up the key points with suitable objective questions.

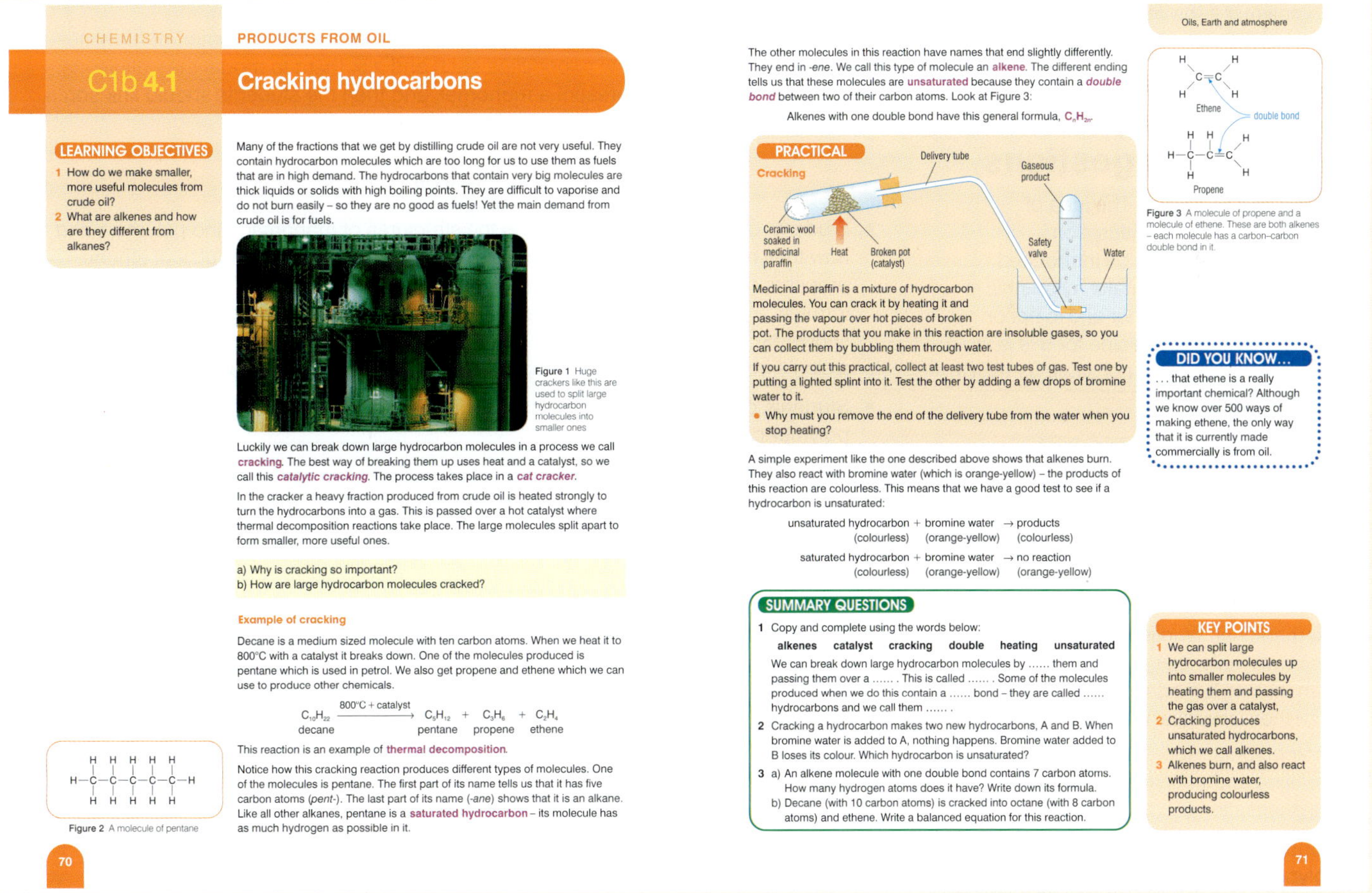

CHEMISTRY — **PRODUCTS FROM OIL**

C1b 4.1 Cracking hydrocarbons

LEARNING OBJECTIVES
1. How do we make smaller, more useful molecules from crude oil?
2. What are alkenes and how are they different from alkanes?

Many of the fractions that we get by distilling crude oil are not very useful. They contain hydrocarbon molecules which are too long for us to use them as fuels that are in high demand. The hydrocarbons that contain very big molecules are thick liquids or solids with high boiling points. They are difficult to vaporise and do not burn easily – so they are no good as fuels! Yet the main demand from crude oil is for fuels.

Figure 1 Huge crackers like this are used to split large hydrocarbon molecules into smaller ones

Luckily we can break down large hydrocarbon molecules in a process we call **cracking**. The best way of breaking them up uses heat and a catalyst, so we call this **catalytic cracking**. The process takes place in a **cat cracker**.

In the cracker a heavy fraction produced from crude oil is heated strongly to turn the hydrocarbons into a gas. This is passed over a hot catalyst where thermal decomposition reactions take place. The large molecules split apart to form smaller, more useful ones.

a) Why is cracking so important?
b) How are large hydrocarbon molecules cracked?

Example of cracking
Decane is a medium sized molecule with ten carbon atoms. When we heat it to 800°C with a catalyst it breaks down. One of the molecules produced is pentane which is used in petrol. We also get propene and ethene which we can use to produce other chemicals.

$$C_{10}H_{22} \xrightarrow{800°C + catalyst} C_5H_{12} + C_3H_6 + C_2H_4$$
decane → pentane + propene + ethene

This reaction is an example of **thermal decomposition**.

Notice how this cracking reaction produces different types of molecules. One of the molecules is pentane. The first part of its name tells us that it has five carbon atoms (pent-). The last part of its name (-ane) shows that it is an alkane. Like all other alkanes, pentane is a **saturated hydrocarbon** – its molecule has as much hydrogen as possible in it.

Figure 2 A molecule of pentane

The other molecules in this reaction have names that end slightly differently. They end in -ene. We call this type of molecule an **alkene**. The different ending tells us that these molecules are **unsaturated** because they contain a **double bond** between two of their carbon atoms. Look at Figure 3:

Alkenes with one double bond have this general formula, C_nH_{2n}.

PRACTICAL
Cracking

Medicinal paraffin is a mixture of hydrocarbon molecules. You can crack it by heating it and passing the vapour over hot pieces of broken pot. The products that you make in this reaction are insoluble gases, so you can collect them by bubbling them through water.

If you carry out this practical, collect at least two test tubes of gas. Test one by putting a lighted splint into it. Test the other by adding a few drops of bromine water to it.

- Why must you remove the end of the delivery tube from the water when you stop heating?

A simple experiment like the one described above shows that alkenes burn. They also react with bromine water (which is orange-yellow) – the products of this reaction are colourless. This means that we have a good test to see if a hydrocarbon is unsaturated.

unsaturated hydrocarbon + bromine water → products
(colourless)   (orange-yellow)   (colourless)

saturated hydrocarbon + bromine water → no reaction
(colourless)   (orange-yellow)   (orange-yellow)

Figure 3 A molecule of propene and a molecule of ethene. These are both alkenes – each molecule has a carbon–carbon double bond in it.

DID YOU KNOW...
... that ethene is a really important chemical? Although we know over 500 ways of making ethene, the only way that it is currently made commercially is from oil.

SUMMARY QUESTIONS

1. Copy and complete using the words below:
   alkenes catalyst cracking double heating unsaturated
   We can break down large hydrocarbon molecules by …… them and passing them over a …… . This is called …… . Some of the molecules produced when we do this contain a …… bond – they are called …… hydrocarbons and we call them …… .

2. Cracking a hydrocarbon makes two new hydrocarbons, A and B. When bromine water is added to A, nothing happens. Bromine water added to B loses its colour. Which hydrocarbon is unsaturated?

3. a) An alkene molecule with one double bond contains 7 carbon atoms. How many hydrogen atoms does it have? Write down its formula.
   b) Decane (with 10 carbon atoms) is cracked into octane (with 8 carbon atoms) and ethene. Write a balanced equation for this reaction.

KEY POINTS
1. We can split large hydrocarbon molecules up into smaller molecules by heating them and passing the gas over a catalyst.
2. Cracking produces unsaturated hydrocarbons, which we call alkenes.
3. Alkenes burn, and also react with bromine water, producing colourless products.

Practical – Give students a selection of different hydrocarbons labelled with letters and some bromine water. Their task is to identify which liquids are alkenes and which are alkanes. Any alkenes tested should decolourise the bromine water, alkanes will not. (10 minutes).

SUMMARY ANSWERS

1. Heating, catalyst, cracking, double, unsaturated, alkenes.

2. Hydrocarbon B is unsaturated.

3. a) 14 hydrogen atoms. C_7H_{14}
   b) $C_{10}H_{22} \rightarrow C_8H_{18} + C_2H_4$

CHEMISTRY PRODUCTS FROM OIL

C1b 4.2 Making polymers from alkenes

LEARNING OBJECTIVES

Students should learn:

- That monomers join together to make polymers.
- About some uses of polymers.

LEARNING OUTCOMES

Most students should be able to:

- State definitions of monomers and polymers.
- Determine the polymer name if the monomer name is given.
- Determine the monomer name if the polymer name is given.
- List some uses of polymer products.

Some students should also be able to:

- Draw the structural formula of a polymer if the monomer is given.
- Explain polymerisation in terms of bond breaking and making.

Teaching suggestions

- **Gifted and talented.** The idea of another type of polymerisation – condensation – could be introduced. Students could then make nylon (this is a condensation polymer and is not on the specification). A recipe for this is in *Classic Chemistry Demonstrations* (RSC).

- **Learning styles**

    Kinaesthetic: Making models of polymers.

    Visual: Observing how the monomers change their bonds to become polymers.

    Auditory: Listening to students explain their polymer models.

    Interpersonal: Working in groups to make their own molecular model of ethene and then making a model of poly(ethene) from their individual models.

    Intrapersonal: Appreciating the bond breaking and making a model of polymerisation.

- **Homework.** For polyethene and polypropene, find two uses and explain which property makes it suitable for that application.

- **ICT link-up.** Show the students an animation of simple addition polymerisation from the GCSE Chemistry CD ROM.

SPECIFICATION LINK-UP   C1b.11.4

- Alkenes can be used to make polymers such as poly(ethene) and poly(propene). In these reactions, many small molecules (monomers) join together to form very large molecules (polymers).

Students should use their skills, knowledge and understanding of 'How Science Works':

- *to evaluate the social and economic advantages and disadvantages of using products from crude oil as fuels or as raw materials for plastics and other chemicals*
- *to evaluate the social, economic and environmental impacts of the use, disposal and recycling of polymers.*

Lesson structure

STARTER

List – Ask the students to look around the classroom and write a list of all the things that are made from plastics. Encourage the students to think about more unusual applications, such as elastic in clothes, fillings in teeth and natural polymers like proteins and DNA. (10 minutes)

Odd one out – On the board, write: 'protein, rubber, DNA, polyethene'. Ask the students to name the odd one out. [All of these are polymers, but polyethene is not a naturally occurring polymer.] (5 minutes)

Models – Ask the students to use the Student Book to define 'monomer' or 'polymer'. Then give the students a few paper clips each and ask them to model the definitions. Each paper clip should represent a monomer, and then the students should link some paper clips together to represent a polymer. (15 minutes)

MAIN

- Students often struggle with drawing the structures of monomers and polymers and how they relate to each other. Provide students with structural formulae of ethene, propene, chloroethene and tetrafluoroethene; give three cards of each structural formula. All of the cards should be laminated, and washable pens and paper towels should be given to the students. They could then line up the same monomers and draw a single bond between each carbon, joining the monomers to make the polymers.
- Students could then record the names and structural formula of each monomer and polymer couple.
- A kinaesthetic approach to polymerisation would be to use molecule kits to represent the polymerisation process.
- Students could then be encouraged to create their own model of polymerisation but using people as monomers.
- Show students the Simulation C1b 4.2 'Making polymers' from the GCSE Chemistry CD ROM. Here they can see the process of joining monomers as well as appreciate that different monomers can be involved.

PLENARIES

Models – Students act out their polymer models and explain them to the class. (10 minutes)

Matching – Ask the students to generate the polymer names from these monomer names:

– Ethene → [poly(ethene)]
– Propene → [poly(propene)]
– Styrene → [poly(styrene)]
– Vinyl chloride → [poly(vinyl chloride)]
– Ethene terephthalate → [poly(ethene terephthalate)] (5 minutes)

Practical support

Modelling polymerisation

Equipment and materials required
Molecular model kit(s).

Details
On the board, draw the structural formula of ethene. Ask each group of students to make an ethene molecule. Then take two molecules and explain that when they are heated with a catalyst the double bond breaks (show this on the two models) and the molecules join up (join the two monomers). Get each group to add their monomer onto the growing polymer chain. Explain that scientists are interested in the structure but don't draw the whole chain, as it is thousands of atoms long. Ask the students to suggest what could be done to show this. Explain that the repeating unit is drawn; ask a student to draw this on the board. Then explain that this is shown in brackets with an '*n*' to show that it is repeated lots of times.

ACTIVITY & EXTENSION

- Students could be encouraged to look at the industrial production of polymers. Videos are available on *Industrial Chemistry* (RSC).

CHEMISTRY — PRODUCTS FROM OIL

C1b 4.2 Making polymers from alkenes

LEARNING OBJECTIVES
1 What are monomers and polymers?
2 How do we make polymers from alkenes?

Refining crude oil produces a huge range of hydrocarbon molecules which are very important to our way of life. Oil products are all around us. We simply cannot imagine life without them.

Figure 1 All of these products were manufactured using chemicals made from oil

The most obvious way that we use hydrocarbons from crude oil is as fuels. We use fuels in our transport and at home. We also use them to make electricity in oil-fired power stations.

Then there are the chemicals we make from crude oil. We use them to make things ranging from margarines to medicines, from dyes to explosives. But one of the most important ways that we use chemicals from oil is to make plastics.

Plastics
Plastics are made up of huge molecules made from lots of small molecules that have joined together. We call the small molecules **monomers**. We call the huge molecules they make **polymers** – *mono* means 'one' and *poly* means 'many'. We can make different types of plastic which have very different properties by using different monomers.

a) List three ways that we use fuels.
b) What are the small molecules that make up a polymer called?

NEXT TIME YOU...
... pick up a plastic bag, think how tiny monomers have joined together to make the huge polymer molecules that the bag is made from.

Figure 2 Polymers produced from oil are all around us and are part of our everyday lives

Ethene (C_2H_4) is the smallest unsaturated hydrocarbon molecule. We can turn it into a polymer known as poly(ethene) or polythene. Polythene is a really useful plastic. It is easy to shape, strong and transparent (unless we add colouring material to it). 'Plastic' bags, plastic drink bottles, dustbins and clingfilm are all examples of polythene that are very familiar to us in everyday life.

Propene (C_3H_6) is another alkene. We can also make polymers with propene as the monomer. The plastic formed is called poly(propene) or polypropylene. Poly(propene) is a very strong, tough plastic. We can use it to make many things, including milk crates and ropes.

c) Is ethene an alkane or an alkene?
d) Which plastic can we make from the monomer called propene?

How do monomers join together?
When alkene molecules join together, the double bond between the carbon atoms in each molecule 'opens up'. It is replaced by single bonds as thousands of molecules join together. This is an example of an *addition reaction*. Because a polymer is made, we call it *addition polymerisation*.

Ethene monomers → Poly(ethene)

We can also write this much more simply:
$$n \, C{=}C \longrightarrow {-}[C{-}C]{-}_n$$
Many single ethene monomers → Long chain of poly(ethene), where *n* is a large number

PRACTICAL
Modelling polymerisation
Use a molecular model kit to show the polymerisation of ethene to form poly(ethene).
Make sure you can see how the equation shown above represents the polymerisation reaction you have modelled.
- Describe what happens to the bonds in the reaction.

e) Think up a model to demonstrate the polymerisation of ethene, using people in your class as monomers. Evaluate the ideas of other groups.

SUMMARY QUESTIONS
1 Copy and complete using the words below:
  addition ethene monomers polymers
  Plastics are made out of large molecules called .... We make these by joining together lots of small molecules called .... One example of a plastic is poly(ethene), made from .... Poly(ethene) is formed as a result of an ...... reaction.
2 Why is ethene the smallest unsaturated hydrocarbon molecule?
3 a) Draw a propene molecule.
   b) Draw structures to show how propene molecules join together to form poly(propene).
   c) Explain the polymerisation reaction in b).

DID YOU KNOW?
Twenty-five plastic drinks bottles can be recycled to make one fleece jacket.

GET IT RIGHT!
The double C=C bond in ethene (an alkene) makes it much more reactive than ethane (an alkane).

KEY POINTS
1 Plastics are made of polymers.
2 Polymers are large molecules made when monomers (small molecules) join together.

SUMMARY ANSWERS

1 Polymers, monomers, ethene, addition.

2 It has two carbon atoms, the minimum number for a C=C double bond.

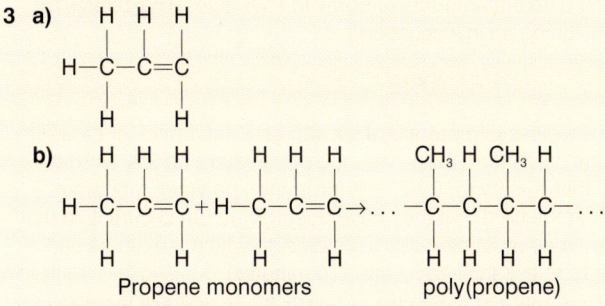

3 a)
$$\begin{array}{c} H \quad H \quad H \\ | \quad\; | \quad\; \\ H{-}C{-}C{=}C \\ | \quad\; | \quad\;| \\ H \quad H \quad H \end{array}$$

b) Propene monomers → poly(propene)

c) The double bond 'opens up' in neighbouring propene molecules and forms single bonds, joining molecules together in a chain.

NEXT TIME YOU . . .

Plastic shopping bags are often polyethene. The polymer's chains are all jumbled up and do not allow light through, meaning that the plastic is opaque. When you stretch the bag, the polymer chains are lining up and this allows light to pass through and the bag often becomes transparent.

KEY POINTS

Begin to make a spider diagram using the key points on this spread. Then at the end of each lesson during the unit, or as a homework activity, the other key points from the topic can be added. Therefore, at the end of the topic a powerful revision tool will have been created.

Answers to in-text questions

a) Transport, heating, generating electricity.
b) Monomers.
c) Ethene is an alkene.
d) Poly(propene) or polypropylene.

CHEMISTRY — PRODUCTS FROM OIL

C1b 4.3 The properties of plastics

LEARNING OBJECTIVES

Students should learn that:

- The properties of plastics depend on the monomers used to make them.
- The properties of plastics depend on the conditions chosen to make them.

LEARNING OUTCOMES

Most students should be able to:

- State that the monomers used to make a plastic will affect its properties.
- Give an example of a plastic whose properties differ when it is formed in different conditions.
- Explain why a given plastic is fit for a purpose.

Some students should also be able to:

- Explain how the intermolecular forces between the polymer molecules in plastics affect their properties.

Teaching suggestions

- **Special needs.** For these students, only choose two plastics – one thermosetting and one thermosoftening to complete the practicals on.
- **Learning styles**
  Kinaesthetic: Carrying out a practical.
  Visual: Completing a card sort about polymers in order to generate a table.
  Auditory: Listening to information to guess their materials.
  Interpersonal: In groups, handling different polymers and discussing which classification they would fall into.
  Intrapersonal: Finding different names for PVC.
- **Homework.** Find the names and uses of two different plastics – one thermosetting and one thermosoftening.

Answers to in-text questions

a) By (strong/covalent) chemical bonds.
b) Intermolecular forces.
c) A thermosoftening plastic.
d) A thermosetting plastic.

SPECIFICATION LINK-UP   C1b.11.4

- *Polymers have properties that depend on what they are made from and the conditions under which they are made. For example, slime with different viscosities can be made from poly(ethenol).*

Students should use their skills, knowledge and understanding of 'How Science Works':

- to evaluate the social and economic advantages and disadvantages of using products from crude oil as fuels or as raw materials for plastics and other chemicals
- to evaluate the social, economic and environmental impacts of the use, disposal and recycling of polymers.

Lesson structure

STARTER

Find – Find all the different names for PVC in the text. [Polymer, plastic, polyvinylchloride, poly(chloroethene).] (5 minutes)

Define – Ask the students to use the Student Book to find out what the two groups of plastics are and what property is used to distinguish between them. [Thermosoftening plastics can be re-heated to become pliable and can be re-moulded, whereas thermosetting plastics will char before they melt.] (5 minutes)

Card sort – Give the students a pack of cards that has sets of information about PVC, PTFE, poly(propene), poly(methyl-2-methylpropenoate). The cards should be sorted into sets of three for each polymer. These would consist of the structural formula of the monomer, the structural formula of the polymer, and the final card would have the name of the polymer classified into thermosoftening/thermosetting and a use. Students could then arrange the cards into a table and copy it into their book. (15–20 minutes)

MAIN

- There is a wide range of different plastics, all with very different properties and uses. Students could be given a selection of plastics and asked to find out their properties and suggest uses for them. They could then note their findings in terms of 'Top Trumps'. Students could be given index cards, where they determine a scale and rate each property of the plastics they studied.
- Students could be given a sample of a thermosetting and a thermosoftening plastic and compare their properties during heating in a fume cupboard. They could also try to remould the thermosoftening plastic. Results could then be recorded as a cartoon strip, drawing images to represent different stages of the practical. Below each image, the students could be encouraged to explain the observations in terms of intermolecular forces of attraction.
- Students could experiment with the consistency of slime made with PVA glue (poly(ethenol)). The polymer strands are H-bond cross linked with borate groups. This cross linking is not permanent and most of the space in the gel is taken up with water molecules. This makes it a pliable polymer.
- Adding different amounts of borax changes the number of cross-links; the more there are, the stiffer the polymer. Ask the students to design and conduct an experiment to find out the effect of adding different amounts of borax to PVA glue. (This relates to 'How Science Works' – designing an investigation.)

PLENARIES

Guess the word – Separate the class into groups of six and give out a pack of cards. Each card should be like name cards for a party with one of the following key words written on: 'thermosoftening, thermosetting, PVC, poly(propene), polymer, monomer'. The students should not look at the card that they have been given, but secure it so that it faces the rest of their group. They must then ask questions, to which the others can only answer 'yes/no' in order to guess their key word. (10 minutes)

Classify – Give the students a number of examples of plastic items and ask them to sort them into thermosoftening or thermosetting. For example, *thermosoftening*: a chocolate box tray, nylon clothes, student's toys, plastic beakers; *thermosetting*: epoxy resin glues, electrical equipment, pan handles. (10 minutes)

Practical support

Making a polymer

Equipment and materials required
100 ml measuring cylinder, 250 ml beaker, dropping pipettes, hot plate, stirring rod, 4 g PVA glue, 4 g borax (irritant), eye protection, (food colouring).

Details
Before the lesson, make up a solution of borax, with 100 ml of warm water in a beaker with the borax. Students should wear eye protection when using borax solution. The solution may need to be warmed for it to fully dissolve. Put 100 ml of water into the 250 ml beaker and heat gently. Add 4 g of PVA slowly, while stirring, the mixture must not boil. When all the PVA has dissolved, remove from the heat, and add a few drops of the borax solution and stir. If too much borax is added, the polymer will be brittle, if not enough is added the slime will be runny. Food colourings can be added to make slime of different colours. This should be done before the borax is added. In time, the slime will dry out. Students can handle the slime, but should wash their hands afterwards, and eye protection should be worn throughout.

Testing different plastics

Equipment and materials required
Samples of different plastics (polystyrene, polyethene, poly(propene), nylon, melamine, phenolic resins, PTFE/Teflon (some could be flammable releasing toxic fumes), Bunsen burner and safety equipment, tongs, water bath, nail varnish remover in a stoppered bottle (flammable), mounted needle, hand lens, eye protection.

Details
Students should first look at the plastic using the hand lens to compare the different textures. Then using the mounted needle, they need to try to scratch the plastic to find out how hard it is and gently pull at the plastic to consider the flexibility of it. To compare the density, they place it in the water bath and record its buoyancy. At this point eye protection must be worn. In a fume cupboard only, take a small piece of the plastic and hold in the Bunsen flame, using tongs, in order to find out if it is flammable, and whether it is a thermosoftening or a thermosetting plastic. Finally, with Bunsens turned off, take a small piece of the plastic, and place on the flame-proof mat. Add a drop of nail varnish remover to see if it is soluble in this substance.

Heating different plastics

Equipment and materials required
Samples of a thermosoftening and thermosetting plastic (flammable and toxic fumes may be released), tin lid, tripod, Bunsen burner and safety equipment, glass rod, eye protection.

Details
Set up the Bunsen burner in a fume cupboard. Put a sample of each plastic on the same tin lid, and position over the Bunsen burner on a tripod. Heat gently, and observe any changes. Then, as the thermosoftening plastic becomes pliable, touch it with a glass rod and gently pull away, drawing a thread of remoulded plastic. Then heat more strongly, and the thermoset should begin to combust. (Be aware that asthmatics may be affected by any fumes that escape.)

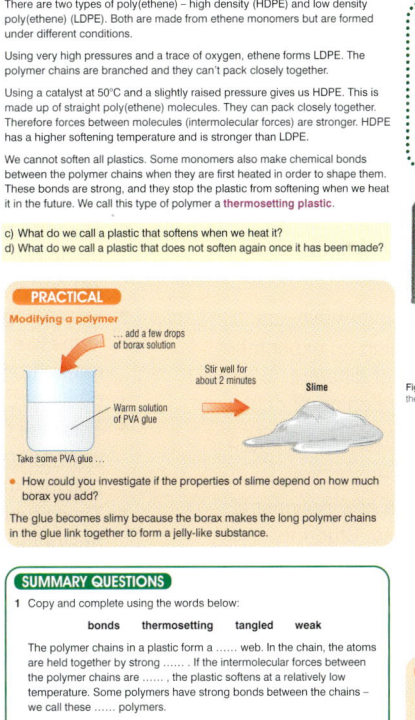

SUMMARY ANSWERS

1 Tangled, bonds, weak, thermosetting.

2 Because the plastic used to make a kettle must not melt when the kettle is heated.

3 Polymer A has a high melting point and therefore strong intermolecular forces; polymer B has a lower melting point and therefore weaker intermolecular forces.

DID YOU KNOW?

The longest recorded sneezing fit lasted 978 days and Donna Griffiths completed an estimated 1 million sneezes!

KEY POINTS

If there are some EFL students, get them or the Learning Support department to translate the key points.

CHEMISTRY PRODUCTS FROM OIL

C1b 4.4 New and useful polymers

LEARNING OBJECTIVES

Students should learn:
- That there are new polymers being developed and being used in innovative ways.
- What smart polymers are and what they are used for.

LEARNING OUTCOMES

Most students should be able to:
- Give an example of a polymer that is used because of its properties.
- Give an example of a polymer that has been designed for a specific job.

Some students should also be able to:
- Evaluate the suitability of different polymers for particular uses.

Teaching suggestions

- **Learning styles**
  Kinaesthetic: Completing tests on different materials.
  Visual: Watching presentations from other students.
  Auditory: Listening to feedback.
  Intrapersonal: Designing an experiment to test the properties of different materials used for packaging of drinks.
  Interpersonal: As a group, designing a new coat.
- **Homework.** Design a new polymer fit for a particular purpose. Students should list its properties and what specific use it is designed for.
- **ICT link-up.** This web site contains information on smart polymers: www.sep.org.uk

SPECIFICATION LINK-UP C1b.11.4

- *Polymers have many useful applications and new ones are being developed, for example: new packaging materials, waterproof coatings for fabrics, dental polymers, wound dressings, hydrogels, smart materials, including shape memory polymers.*
- *Many polymers are not biodegradable, so they are not broken down by microorganisms, and this can lead to problems with waste disposal.*

Students should use their skills, knowledge and understanding of 'How Science Works':
- to evaluate the social and economic advantages and disadvantages of using products from crude oil as fuels or as raw materials for plastics and other chemicals
- to evaluate the social, economic and environmental impacts of the use, disposal and recycling of polymers.

Lesson structure

STARTER

Word game – Ask the students to try to make as many words as they can from: 'poly(ethyleneterephthalate)', with double points for any scientific words. (10 minutes)

Monomer or polymer – Ask the students to categorise the following statements as monomers or polymers. The statements could be written down or read out:
- A very long chain hydrocarbon. [Polymer] • Contains a double bond. [Monomer]
- Reactive molecule. [Monomer] • PET. [Polymer] • Ethene. [Monomer]
- Plastic. [Polymer] • Joins together to make a plastic. [Monomer] (5 minutes)

MAIN

- Plastics are now often developed for a particular purpose. However, new uses for existing plastics are being found. Set the students the task of designing a new waterproof coat. They could work in small teams.
- The students should list the properties of the material that they want the coat to be made out of. They should then complete tests to decide on the best material for the job and why.
- Increasingly society is using more polymers, but often they are used for single-use items like ready meal packaging. Students could be set the task to choose the best to make a drinks container. In this exercise, they should consider the size of the drinks container, aesthetics, recycling and price.
- This task could be completed using secondary data from the Internet (search at www.wikipedia.org). This could be developed further by the students selecting their top polymer choices and designing an experiment to check their suitability for this task.
- These tests will be useful for teaching various aspects of 'How Science Works', e.g. designing investigations, making measurements and societal influences on decisions made.
- Students need to have some understanding of the vast range in new polymers. Split the class into six groups and give each a topic: 'new packaging materials, waterproof coatings for fabrics, dental polymers, wound dressings, hydrogels, shape memory polymers'. Ask each group to come up with a PowerPoint® presentation (no more than 3 minutes long) about their topic. This should include what their material is, its special properties, what it is used for and one fascinating fact.

PLENARIES

AfL (Assessment for Learning) – Split the class into pairs. Give each pair two short examination questions about new and useful polymers. Allow the students 5 minutes to answer a question each. Then ask the students to swap, and encourage them to mark the other student's work. Allow the two students to sit together 'debriefing' each other about their examination work. (15 minutes)

Answers – Ask the students to look back at the objectives in the Student Book and answer the questions that have been posed. (10 minutes)

Presentations – Ask the students to deliver their presentations. Have a stopwatch running, and stop the students when they reach their 3 minutes. (15–20 minutes)

Practical support

Evaluating plastics

Equipment and materials required

Swatches of different polymer fabrics (untreated nylon, treated nylon, Teflon, wool, cotton, polyester and neoprene), sandpaper, water bath, washing powder, two beakers, hairdryer, stand, boss and clamp, fabric dyes, cobalt chloride paper – toxic.

Details

Each fabric can be tested for:

- Wearing – rub the fabric with sandpaper a number of times (set by the students) to see the effect on the wear of the material.
- Water permeability – Carefully place on the surface of a water bath and put a piece of cobalt chloride paper onto the fabric. If water seeps through, the paper will turn from blue to pink.
- Wind permeability – Set up the fabric stretched out in a stand, boss and clamp. Hold the hairdryer on cold blow at one side, and put your hand on the other, in order to feel the air flow through the fabric.
- Dyeing – The coloured dyes could be applied as the instructions to determine how easy it is to change the colour of the fabric.
- Wash test – Measure the fabric swatch, then wash it in washing detergent and dry. Re-measure the material to see if it has shrunk.

ACTIVITY & EXTENSION IDEAS

- Students could research into unusual polymers, e.g. surgical glues.
- Ask which synthetic polymers have not been around for more than a hundred years; students could produce a timeline showing the development of important (e.g. Bakelite) or interesting (e.g. superglue) polymers.
- Encourage students to research into new biodegradable plastics like the ones used for some plastic shopping bags and babies' disposable nappies. Ask students to find out the names of the monomer(s) and the polymer and by what action it breaks down, e.g. by the effects of light, bacteria or water.

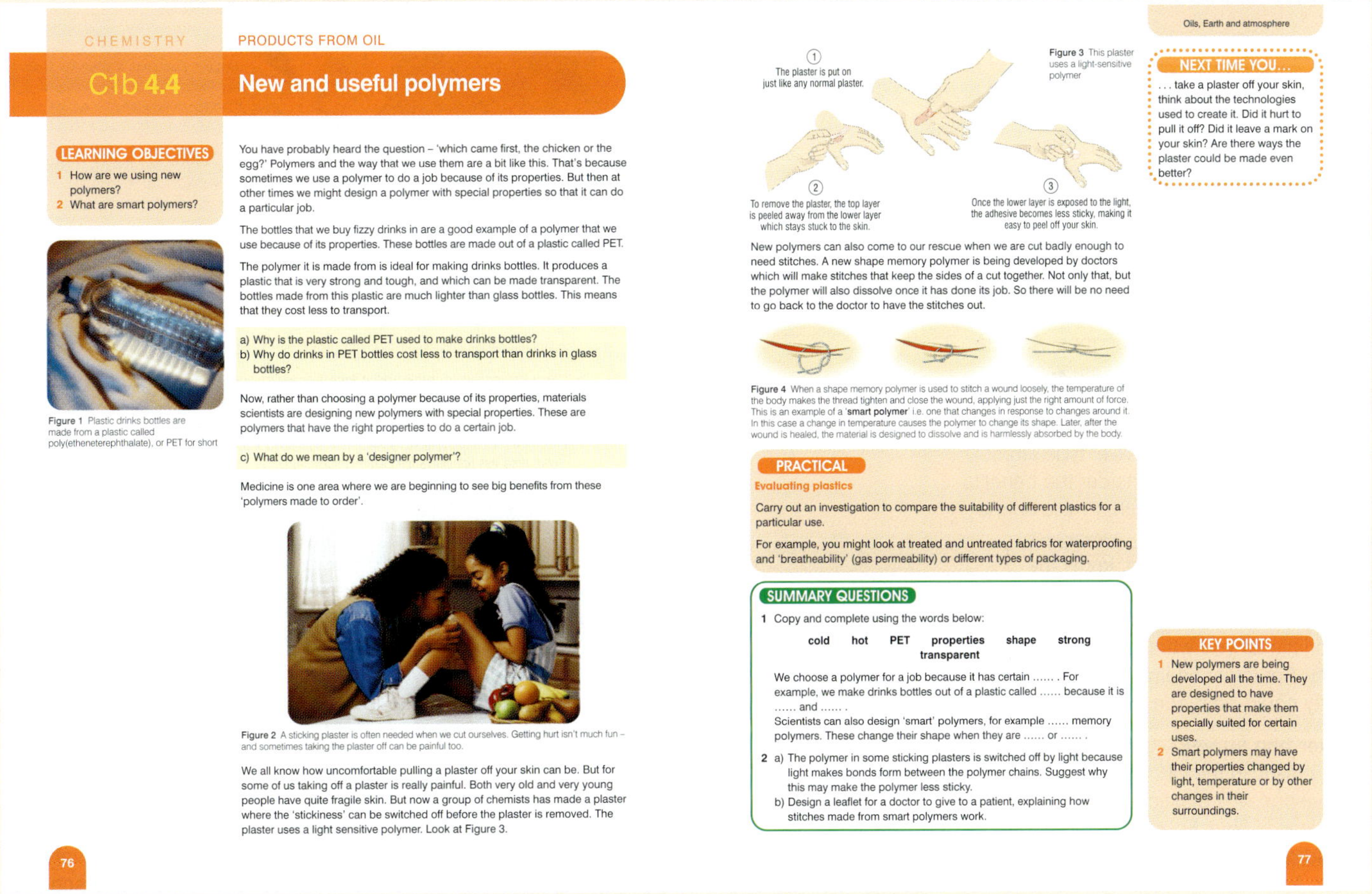

CHEMISTRY — PRODUCTS FROM OIL

C1b 4.4 New and useful polymers

LEARNING OBJECTIVES
1. How are we using new polymers?
2. What are smart polymers?

You have probably heard the question – 'which came first, the chicken or the egg?' Polymers and the way that we use them are a bit like this. That's because sometimes we use a polymer to do a job because of its properties. But then at other times we might design a polymer with special properties so that it can do a particular job.

The bottles that we buy fizzy drinks in are a good example of a polymer that we use because of its properties. These bottles are made out of a plastic called PET.

The polymer it is made from is ideal for making drinks bottles. It produces a plastic that is very strong and tough, and which can be made transparent. The bottles made from this plastic are much lighter than glass bottles. This means that they cost less to transport.

a) Why is the plastic called PET used to make drinks bottles?
b) Why do drinks in PET bottles cost less to transport than drinks in glass bottles?

Now, rather than choosing a polymer because of its properties, materials scientists are designing new polymers with special properties. These are polymers that have the right properties to do a certain job.

c) What do we mean by a 'designer polymer'?

Medicine is one area where we are beginning to see big benefits from these 'polymers made to order'.

Figure 1 Plastic drinks bottles are made from a plastic called poly(ethenetrephthalate), or PET for short

Figure 2 A sticking plaster is often needed when we cut ourselves. Getting hurt isn't much fun – and sometimes taking the plaster off can be painful too.

We all know how uncomfortable pulling a plaster off your skin can be. But for some of us taking off a plaster is really painful. Both very old and very young people have quite fragile skin. But now a group of chemists has made a plaster where the 'stickiness' can be switched off before the plaster is removed. The plaster uses a light sensitive polymer. Look at Figure 3.

① The plaster is put on just like any normal plaster.
② To remove the plaster, the top layer is peeled away from the lower layer which stays stuck to the skin.
③ Once the lower layer is exposed to the light, the adhesive becomes less sticky, making it easy to peel off your skin.

Figure 3 This plaster uses a light-sensitive polymer

New polymers can also come to our rescue when we are cut badly enough to need stitches. A new shape memory polymer is being developed by doctors which will make stitches that keep the sides of a cut together. Not only that, but the polymer will also dissolve once it has done its job. So there will be no need to go back to the doctor to have the stitches out.

Figure 4 When a shape memory polymer is used to stitch a wound loosely, the temperature of the body makes the thread tighten and close the wound, applying just the right amount of force. This is an example of a **smart polymer** i.e. one that changes in response to changes around it. In this case a change in temperature causes the polymer to change its shape. Later, after the wound is healed, the material is designed to dissolve and is harmlessly absorbed by the body.

PRACTICAL
Evaluating plastics

Carry out an investigation to compare the suitability of different plastics for a particular use.

For example, you might look at treated and untreated fabrics for waterproofing and 'breatheability' (gas permeability) or different types of packaging.

NEXT TIME YOU...
... take a plaster off your skin, think about the technologies used to create it. Did it hurt to pull it off? Did it leave a mark on your skin? Are there ways the plaster could be made even better?

SUMMARY QUESTIONS

1 Copy and complete using the words below:

cold	hot	PET	properties	shape	strong
transparent					

We choose a polymer for a job because it has certain ...... For example, we make drinks bottles out of a plastic called ...... because it is ...... and ....
Scientists can also design 'smart' polymers, for example ...... memory polymers. These change their shape when they are ...... or ....

2 a) The polymer in some sticking plasters is switched off by light because light makes bonds form between the polymer chains. Suggest why this may make the polymer less sticky.
b) Design a leaflet for a doctor to give to a patient, explaining how stitches made from smart polymers work.

KEY POINTS
1. New polymers are being developed all the time. They are designed to have properties that make them specially suited for certain uses.
2. Smart polymers may have their properties changed by light, temperature or by other changes in their surroundings.

SUMMARY ANSWERS

1 Properties, PET, strong, transparent, shape, hot/cold, cold/hot.

2 a) Light makes the polymer form bonds between itself making it less sticky. The polymer becomes more brittle and easier to remove. (In the dark the polymer bonds with the collagen in your skin.)
   b) Leaflet.

Answers to in-text questions

a) It is strong and tough, and the bottles can be transparent.
b) PET bottles are much lighter than glass bottles.
c) Polymers that are designed with ideal properties for a particular job.

KEY POINTS

Ask the modern languages department to translate the key points into French and German. Supply the phrases along with the English translation on cards. Ask the students to sort the phrases into threes: the English phrase and the other language alternatives.

CHEMISTRY | PRODUCTS FROM OIL

C1b 4.5 Plastics, polymers and packaging food

SPECIFICATION LINK-UP
C1b.11.4
Students should use their skills, knowledge and understanding of 'How Science Works':

- to evaluate the social and economic advantages and disadvantages of using products from crude oil as fuels or as raw materials for plastics and other chemicals
- to evaluate the social, economic and environmental impacts of the use, disposal and recycling of polymers.

Teaching suggestions

Activities

Is packaging needed? – Set up a display of some food already wrapped, e.g. flour, sugar, cereal, then have the same products in plastic containers with scoops. Ask the students how their families usually buy these sorts of foods, and suggest where they can buy the unpackaged food (e.g. markets and 'shop and save' type stores). Then ask students to consider the benefits and disadvantages of both. Focus on the advantages of each, e.g. *packaged*: hygienic, know the brand, know the amount that you are buying, quick to purchase; *non-packaged*: have as much/little as you want; can easily see the quality. For lower attaining students this activity could be made into a card sort.

Carrier bag survey – Carrier bags are often plastic in the UK. Ask the students to list reasons why plastic is chosen and not paper (as in films from America). Students should recognise that the weather is a large factor. Ask the students to design a questionnaire about the usage of plastic bags. Some question ideas are given in the Student Book. Ask the students to consider what they are going to do with the data, i.e. draw graphs, so they need to ensure that the questions supply quantitative responses. For lower attaining students, the questionnaire could be supplied from the teacher. Students could then practise asking the questions to other members of staff to gain confidence. The sample size needs to be decided, maybe a few questionnaires completed from each student and the results pooled.

The questionnaire could be completed by a street survey. Permission will probably need to be sort from the shop, which is targeted. Also full risk assessment needs to be completed and parental consent with medical forms need to be issued and completed. Alternatively, students could be set the task of asking three people as homework. On returning to school, the data could be pooled in a tally chart and graphs could be drawn either free hand or using Excel. The class could be split into groups and each team could take a different question to report on. The graphs could then be mounted into a display, and each student/group could write their own conclusions from the data collection.

Homework
Environmental poster – List the factors that affect the number of carrier bags that are used during shopping trips. Then make a poster to make shoppers more aware of the environmental impact of their overuse of plastic bags.

Extension
Biodegradable plastics – Ask students to find out the ways in which carrier bags, and plastic nappies, are made increasingly environmentally friendly.

Oils, Earth and atmosphere

Oils, Earth and atmosphere

'Would you like that in a bag, sir?'

When you buy something in a shop, you need to get it home safely. If you're a well-organised kind of person you may have taken a bag with you – but most of us are quite happy to say 'yes' when the shop assistant asks us 'Would you like a bag for that?' And when we get home – what happens to the bag?

So just how many bags do we use in one year? How many bags does one supermarket give out in a year? Is this a problem?

Are the bags *biodegradable* (will they be broken down in nature by microorganisms when we throw them away)? Or will they take up valuable space in land-fill sites for years to come?

ACTIVITY

How many bags?

You are going to carry out a survey to find out how many carrier bags people use.
Design a questionnaire to answer questions like:

- how many carrier bags do you have at home?
- how many carrier bags do you bring home from the supermarket each week?
- do you use re-usable bags for your shopping?
- what happens to the carrier bags once you have used them?

When you have collected the answers to your questions, present the information using tables, graphs and charts. Discuss the questions below:

- What do you think about the number of carrier bags used by people? Should we try to reduce this? Why (not)? How?
- Is your data representative of your local area? How could you be more certain?

What factors, if any, might affect the number of carrier bags used in different parts of the country?
How could you collect data to best reflect the picture in the whole country?

79

Learning styles

Kinaesthetic: Handling packaged and unpackaged foods.

Visual: Viewing the resulting graphs from the carrier bag survey.

Auditory: Listening to responses from questions.

Interpersonal: Discussing conclusions from results to share with the whole class.

Intrapersonal: Evaluating the impact of using plastics on society.

ICT link-up

There are many pieces of information about biodegradable plastics on the Internet. For example, search the web for 'biodegradable nappies'. Also search for 'Biodegradation' at www.wikipedia.org.

CHEMISTRY PRODUCTS FROM OIL

SUMMARY ANSWERS

1. a) The use of heat and a catalyst to break down a longer chained hydrocarbon to form an alkane and alkene.
   b) A method used to separate mixtures of liquids.
   c) To remove impurities.
   d) A molecule with only single bonds that contains only carbon and hydrogen atoms.
   e) A molecule with at least one C=C bond that contains only carbon and hydrogen atoms.

2. a) Contains only hydrogen and carbon.
   b) $CH_2=CH-CH_3$
   c) Unsaturated, as it is an alkene and contains C=C.
   d) Put bromine water into each tube. Shake well, and the tube that decolourises contains the unsaturated hydrocarbon, i.e. propene.
   e) i) Polymerisation.
      ii) Solid at room temperature, gets soft on heating, opaque, insulator.
      iii) They do not biodegrade and remain in landfill sites for many years. If they are burnt, then carbon dioxide gas (which causes global warming) would be released.

3. a) A very long chain molecule made from thousands of repeating units (monomer).
   b) Through (addition) polymerisation.
   c) The type of monomer used; the conditions in which the polymer is made; additives in the plastic.

4. **Agree:** On the whole they are non-biodegradable, take up a lot of space in landfill, when burnt they produce carbon dioxide which is a greenhouse gas.
   Disagree: New biodegradable plastics are being made, plastics can be recycled, plastics can be burnt as a fuel, carbon dioxide can be removed from the waste gases using a gas scrubber.

Summary teaching suggestions

- **Special needs**
  - The key words and definitions used in question 1 could be given to students as a cut and stick activity.
- **When to use these questions?**
  - Students often put down irrelevant information when answering examination questions. Although they have filled the lines with correct information, they do not include any marking points. To help students with this issue, write the question parts onto separate flip chart pages and stick them onto the walls or desks around the classroom. Split the students into small groups and supply them with a felt pen. Give the groups a short amount of time (maybe 3 minutes) at each page. They should jot down their ideas to answer that question and feel free to annotate and change previous scribbles. Students should rotate around most of the sheets. Then give each group a sheet to distil the 'perfect' answer from all the ideas on the page. These answers are then shared with the class, explaining how they feel that they have thoroughly covered the question.
  - Questions 1, 2 and 3 provide a good summary of this section of the work. These questions would be useful as a consolidation task to highlight any misconceptions that need addressing at the end of the topic.
- **Learning styles**
  Interpersonal: Question 4 could be completed as a class activity. The question could be displayed on the board, and students work in groups discussing the question and the points, which they would include in the answer. Then groups could take it in turn to write their ideas on the board. If using an interactive whiteboard, the page could be printed and inserted into the students' books.

Visual: Question 3a) and b) could also be answered using diagrams.
Auditory: Question 4 could be completed through a class discussion.
Kinaesthetic: Students could answer question 3b) using molecular model kits, verbally explaining what is happening.

- **Homework**
  Question 4 is a good extension task for a longer homework assignment, where students can complete research into this topic using secondary research.

EXAM-STYLE ANSWERS

1	1	D	(1 mark)
	2	C	(1 mark)
	3	A	(1 mark)
	4	B	(1 mark)
2	1	D	(1 mark)
	2	C	(1 mark)
	3	B	(1 mark)
	4	A	(1 mark)
3	1	C	(1 mark)
	2	D	(1 mark)
	3	B	(1 mark)
	4	A	(1 mark)
4	a)	B	(1 mark)
	b)	B	(1 mark)
	c)	C	(1 mark)
	d)	C	(1 mark)

Oils, Earth and atmosphere

HOW SCIENCE WORKS QUESTIONS

Biodegradable plastics could be used for growing crops

Non-biodegradable plastic has been used for many years for growing melons. The plants are put into holes in the plastic and their shoots grow up above the plastic. The melons are protected from the soil by the plastic and grow with very few marks on them. Biodegradable plastic has been tested – to reduce the amount of non-recycled waste plastic.

In this investigation two large plots were grown. One using biodegradable plastic, the other using normal plastic. The results were as follows:

Plastic used	Early yield (kg/hectare)	Total yield (kg/hectare)	Average melon weight (kg)
Normal	210	4 829	2.4
Biodegradable	380	3 560	2.2

a) This was a field investigation. Describe how the experimenter would have chosen the two plots. (3)
b) The hypothesis was that the biodegradable plastic would produce less fruit than the normal plastic. Is the hypothesis supported or refuted, or should a new hypothesis be considered? Explain your answer. (2)
c) How could the accuracy of this investigation be improved? (1)
d) How could the reliability of these results be tested? (1)
e) How would you view these results if you were told that they were funded by the manufacturer of the normal plastic? (1)

4 An alkane, $C_{17}H_{36}$, was cracked. The reaction that took place is represented by the equation:
$$C_{17}H_{36} \rightarrow C_7H_{14} + C_5H_6 + \ldots\ldots$$
(a) The formula of the missing compound is ...
  A CH_4 B C_2H_4
  C C_2H_6 D C_3H_8
(b) The compound C_7H_{14} is ...
  A an alkane   B an alkene
  C a poly(alkane)   D a poly(alkene)
(c) Addition polymers can be made from ...
  A $C_{17}H_{36}$ B C_7H_{14}
  C C_5H_6 D C_2H_6
(d) The structure of C_5H_6 could be ...

A H–C=C–C–C–H (with H's)   B H–C–C–C–C–H
C H–C–C–C=C–H   D (structure)   (4)

5 Read the passage about 'Slime' and use the information to help you answer the questions.

'Slime' has some of the properties of a liquid and some of the properties of a solid. It can be poured but it bounces if dropped on the floor. 'Slime' is made by mixing a solution containing a polymer called PVA with borax. When the substances are mixed the borax forms cross-links between the polymer chains. Some of the cross-links are chemical bonds and some are intermolecular forces involving water molecules. Lots of water molecules are held between the polymer chains and these give 'Slime' its flexibility and fluidity.

(a) Describe a molecule of a typical polymer. (2)
(b) Suggest why 'Slime' has the properties of both a solid and a liquid. (3)
(c) Suggest one method that you could use to modify the properties of 'Slime'. (1)
(d) A student tested different types of 'Slime' by measuring how far they stretched before they broke.
  (i) What was the independent variable in the investigation? (1)
  (ii) What type of variable was the dependent variable – categoric, ordered, discrete or continuous? (1)

HOW SCIENCE WORKS ANSWERS

a) The plots should have been chosen to minimise any differences in relation to, for example, soil conditions or weather conditions. Any changes in these conditions should be similar in all plots.

b) The hypothesis needs amending. It is more complicated. The early yield is higher with the biodegradable plastic, but the total yield is much less. The average melon weight is also less with the biodegradable plastic.

c) Accuracy of this investigation could be improved by increasing the number of plots. Repeat the investigation in a second year. Carry out the investigation under controlled conditions in a laboratory.

d) To test the reliability of these results the investigation should be repeated by other scientists.
An investigation could be carried out in more controlled conditions, e.g. in a glasshouse.

e) With scepticism, because they have an interest in selling their plastic and could be using selected results. They might not be telling the whole truth.

How science works teaching suggestions

- **Literacy guidance**
  - Key terms that should be clearly understood are: hypothesis, accuracy, reliability and bias.
  - All questions expect longer answers, students can practise their literacy skills.
- **Higher- and lower-level questions.** Questions b), d) and e) are higher-level and answers for these questions have been provided at this level. Lower-level questions are a) and c) and the answers are also at this level.
- **Gifted and talented.** Able students should appreciate the difficulties inherent to a fieldwork investigation. They should also be able to consider the marketability of crops and that size doesn't always matter.
- **How and when to use these questions.** When wishing to develop the ideas around how reliability can be demonstrated.
- **Homework.** This would be useful as a homework, that might provoke thoughts from other members of the family.
- **Special needs.** The students may need help with the idea of biodegradable and interpretation of the table of results.
- **ICT link-up.** The Internet could be used to check out web sites offering information on agricultural research, such as www.rothamsted.ac.uk.

5 a) *Two from:*
  - Long (chain) molecule.
  - Atoms held together by chemical bonds.
  - Made from many monomers joined together. *(2 marks)*

b) *One mark each for:*
  - Chemical bonds between large/polymer molecules (like giant structure/make it solid).
  - Intermolecular forces between chains/polymer molecules (like a liquid).
  - Lots of water molecules between the chains (like liquid water). *(3 marks)*

c) Change the concentration of solution(s)/change temperature of solutions/change other conditions/change PVA/add other substances before mixing. *(1 mark)*

d) i) Types of 'Slime'. *(1 mark)*
   ii) Continuous. *(1 mark)*

Exam teaching suggestions

Q1 is best left until the chapter has been completed. Q2 and Q4 could be used after spread 4.2 and Q3 and Q5 after spread 4.3. The total mark is 24, and altogether the questions should take about 25 minutes to complete.

In Q5 students should be encouraged to read the passage carefully and to refer to it when writing their answers. Part b) is a demanding question aimed at Higher-Tier students. Good answers to parts a) and b) will be succinct and well organised, using appropriate scientific terms. This question could be used as the basis for small group or class discussions.

Q4 will reveal students' understanding of formulae. Students who find this question difficult should be encouraged to count the atoms of each element and to draw out the structures in alternative forms.

Foundation-Tier students aiming for grade C should be able to gain most of the marks in Q1 to Q4, and in 5a) and 5c).

81

CHEMISTRY   **PLANT OILS**

C1b 5.1 Extracting vegetable oils

LEARNING OBJECTIVES

Students should learn:
- That oils can be extracted from plants.
- That vegetable oils are important foods.
- What unsaturated oils are and how we can test for them.

LEARNING OUTCOMES

Most students should be able to:
- Describe how oils can be extracted from plants.
- Recognise an unsaturated oil.
- Describe why plant oils are important in foods.

Some students should also be able to:
- Detail a method for testing unsaturated oils.

Teaching suggestions

- **Learning styles**

  Kinaesthetic: Completing a distillation of plant oil or crushing plant material to extract oil.

  Visual: Making a flow chart to show the different methods for extracting plant oils.

  Auditory: Listening to questions and responses from other students.

  Intrapersonal: Completing sentences with increasing scientific information.

  Interpersonal: Working in question and answer pairs.

- **Homework.** Ask students to answer the questions posed in the learning objectives.

SPECIFICATION LINK-UP   C1b.11.5

- *Some fruits, seeds and nuts are rich in oils that can be extracted. The plant material is crushed and the oil removed by pressing or, in some cases by distillation. Water and other impurities are removed.*
- *Vegetable oils are important foods as they provide a lot of energy. They also provide us with nutrients.*
- *Vegetable oils that are unsaturated contain double carbon carbon bonds. These can be detected by reacting with bromine or iodine.*

Students should use their skills, knowledge and understanding of 'How Science Works':
- *to evaluate the effects on using vegetable oils in foods and the impacts on diet and health.*

Lesson structure

STARTER

List – Ask students to make a list of oily foods. Then ask them to consider where the oil comes from, e.g. crisps – sunflower seeds; chocolate spread – nuts; olive oil – seeds. (10 minutes)

Sentences – Ask students to finish the sentence:

'Plants get their energy from . . .'

Encourage students to try to finish it three times, each sentence getting progressively more scientific, e.g.

1. Plants get their energy from the Sun.
2. Plants get their energy from sugar that is made by using sunlight.
3. Plants get their energy according to the following equation:

   carbon dioxide + water → sugar + oxygen   (10 minutes)

MAIN

- Some plants quickly release oil when they are crushed, e.g. nuts and seeds. Other oils are more difficult to extract and steam distillation needs to be used.
- Students can complete steam distillation on a micro-scale or crush plant material to extract oil (be aware of nut allergies, eye protection must be worn) using mortar and pestle (see if you get a translucent stain on filter paper).
- Fats are an important part of the human diet. In the media we often hear terms like 'saturated, unsaturated, polyunsaturated fats'. Students often do not realise that these terms have a scientific meaning. Ask them to consider these words and define them [saturated – no double bonds, unsaturated – contains double bonds, polyunsaturated – contains many double bonds]. They can then practically classify different fats as saturated or unsaturated using bromine water.

PLENARIES

Questions and answers – Ask a student to pick a number from 1 to the number of students in the class. Look at which number this corresponds to in the register. Then ask that student to generate a question about the topic studied and choose a person to answer it. The question maker then decides if the answer is correct. If misconceptions are highlighted, then you should take over the question and answer in order to correct them. (10 minutes)

Flow chart – Ask the students to make a flow chart to demonstrate two different ways of extracting plant oils. (15 minutes)

Practical support

Extracting plant oil by distillation

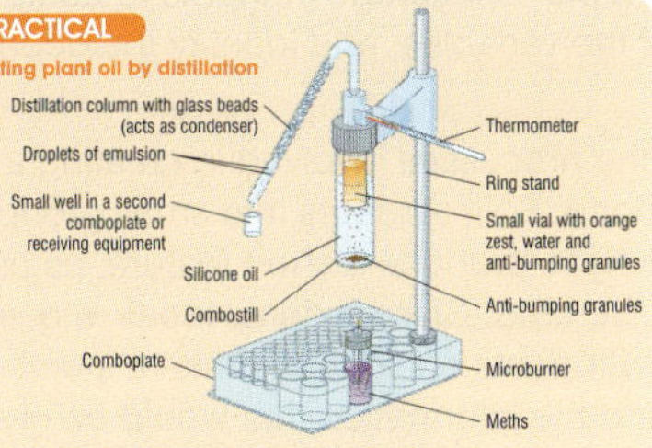

Equipment and materials required

Orange, grater, antibumping granules, methylated spirits, silicone oil, microscale distillation apparatus (see Student Book).

Details

Grate the zest from part of an orange and place in a small vial in the apparatus shown – one quarter full. Mix with water to half fill the vial and add a few antibumping granules. Heat gently, to avoid the mixture boiling over. Collect a few drops of the 'orange oil' emulsion in a small well. Note its smell and cloudy appearance. (The apparatus is available from Edulab, Karoo Close, Bexwell, Norfolk PE38 9GA.)

Testing for unsaturation

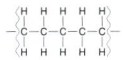

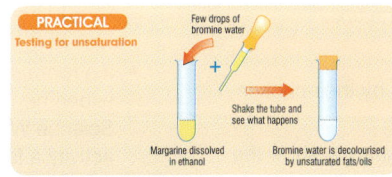

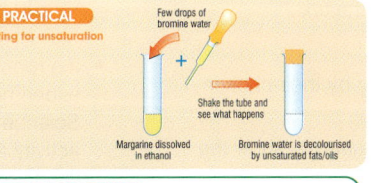

Equipment and materials required

A selection of fats (e.g. butter, margarine, dripping, lard, olive oil, vegetable oil), dropping pipettes, test tubes, bromine water (irritant and harmful – see CLEAPSS Hazcard 15), bungs, test-tube rack, water bath, ethanol (flammable – see CLEAPSS Hazcard 40), eye protection.

Details

Students should pipette about 1 ml of each liquid into separate test tubes, stored in a rack. If a solid fat is to be tested, e.g. dripping, then it needs to be dissolved in ethanol. About the same amount of bromine water should be added to each test tube, and each bunged and shaken. Ensure that the students wear eye protection and hold the bung and base of the test tube when they shake it. Bromine vapour may be given off (so use pale yellow bromine water), therefore a well-ventilated area is necessary and students should wash their hands after the practical. Asthmatics may experience problems with any bromine vapour present.

ACTIVITY & EXTENSION IDEAS

- Students could extract oils from petals in order to make their own 'perfume'.
- Students could find the calorific content of a variety of fats that humans eat. They could then make a bar chart to compare the values. An extension of this would be to encourage students to look at nutritional labels of different foods, and represent the percentage calories from fat in a graphical form.

Answers to in-text questions

a) Pressing and (steam) distillation.

b) The iodine water will decolorise.

SUMMARY ANSWERS

1. Pressing, distillation, energy, unsaturated, bromine, iodine.

2. Because vegetable oils contain a lot of energy which if not used up becomes stored as fat in the body.

3. Answer c) – we can be certain that the sample contains unsaturated oils (because it decolourises iodine solution) but we cannot be certain whether or not it contains saturated oils because these have no effect on iodine solution.

DID YOU KNOW?

Sunflower oil is made from pressed sunflower seeds. The biggest recorded sunflower head had a diameter of 82 cm and was grown in Canada in 1983.

KEY POINTS

Ask the students to imagine that they work for a marketing company. They are to make a poster to encourage students to think about science in their everyday lives (like the RSC posters 'scientists don't always wear white coats'). Their poster should include all the key points.

83

CHEMISTRY   PLANT OILS

C1b 5.2 Cooking with vegetable oils

LEARNING OBJECTIVES

Students should learn:

- Reasons why people cook with vegetable oils.
- What is meant by 'to harden' vegetable oils.
- How vegetable oils are turned into spreads.

LEARNING OUTCOMES

Most students should be able to:

- List reasons for why vegetable oils are used for cooking.
- Define the term 'harden'.
- State how oils are turned into spreads.

Some students should also be able to:

- Explain how oils are turned into spreads in terms of the bonding and forces between molecules.

Teaching suggestions

- **Special needs.** The flow chart could be made as a cut and stick activity. Or the flow chart could be given in words, and the students could them draw a picture for each stage below the text.
- **Learning styles**

  Kinaesthetic: Standing by their chosen answer.

  Visual: Making a flow chart to show the method of hydrogenation of fats.

  Auditory: Listening to different questions and answers.

  Interpersonal: Working in groups to make a segment in a news programme.

  Intrapersonal: Writing their own question and answer.

- **Homework.** Find out about the risks of a high fat diet.

Answers to in-text questions

a) The boiling point of vegetable oils is much higher.

b) Food cooked in oil cooks more quickly, the outside often turns a different colour and becomes crisper, the food absorbs some of the oil and that increases its energy content.

c) Hardening.

SPECIFICATION LINK-UP   C1b.11.5

- *Vegetable oils that are unsaturated can be hardened by reacting them with hydrogen in the presence of a nickel catalyst at about 60°C. The hydrogenated oils have higher melting points so they are solids at room temperature, making them useful as spreads and in cakes and pastries.*

Students should use their skills, knowledge and understanding of 'How Science Works':
- *to evaluate the effects on using vegetable oils in foods and the impacts on diet and health.*

Lesson structure

STARTER

Thermometer – Draw a thermometer on the board. Draw two lines to approximately divide it into thirds. Ask the students to label the states of matter, and state changes on the diagram. Before the first line (melting/freezing point), students should notice that the substance would be a solid; between the two lines, it would be a liquid; above the last line (boiling point) a gas. (10 minutes)

Stand-by – Put the key words: 'saturated' and 'unsaturated' onto two large pieces of paper and pin them at opposite sides of the room. Read out different examples of chemicals, students should decide whether they are saturated or unsaturated and stand by the appropriate sign, e.g.

- Sunflower oil [unsaturated] • Butter [saturated] • Lard [saturated]
- Alkenes [unsaturated] • Alkanes [saturated] (5 minutes)

MAIN

- When foods are cooked at different temperatures, they have different flavours, appearances, smells and nutritional content. Students could compare different potatoes that have been prepared in different ways. Encourage the students to design their own results table to record their observations. Lower attaining students may need to copy a previously prepared one.
- If a room swap can be completed into a home economics suite, then additional experiments can be completed about cooking time. This will help to integrate 'How Science Works' into this topic. Encourage students to contemplate how to make this activity a fair test and list the variables, and identify the dependent and independent variables.
- Students need to know the processes involved in creating a spread from an oil and the reasons why this is done. Split students into small groups and ask them to imagine that they are going to produce a short feature, as part of a TV programme, about how food is manufactured. Give students ideas, e.g. interview a chemical engineer at the oil plant. Students could then make a storyboard to show what would happen in each scene and the information that would be given.
- Students often struggle with empathy; being able to argue from another viewpoint is a valuable skill particularly in essay writing. Give students different roles:
  – Chemical engineer.   – Lay person.
  – Science teacher.   – Top chef.
  – Spread company.   – Campaigner for health.
  – Host of the show.

  Students could then get into character and think about what each person would think about using oils and fats to cook. Then a debate (similar to a talk show) could be chaired. People without specific roles could be the audience and pose questions to the panel.
- Students could investigate the degree of saturation in a variety of oils using bromine water. 'How Science Works' concepts of fair testing and measurement can be practised. Some might try a colorimeter or a light sensor and data logger to get quantitive data on how much bromine remains after reaction with the oils. A little ethanol will help the oil and aqueous layers to mix for the test.
- An Animation, C1b 5.2 'Making oils into solid fat', is available to use on the GCSE Chemistry CD ROM.

Practical support

Investigating cooking

Equipment and materials required

Raw potato cores, boiled potato cores, fried potato cores, mounted needle, magnifying glass. Cooker, chip pan, cooking oil, saucepan, water, stopwatch, knife.

Details

Ask the students to study the appearance of the three different samples, using the magnifying glass. They should note the colour and smell. Then using a mounted needle, they can scratch the surface and comment on the textures.

Students should carefully cook the potato cores in cooking oil (this may be completed as a demonstration as boiling oil can be dangerous) and boiling water. They should time how long it takes for each. They could repeat the test three times to gain an average, or pool the class results in order to gain more reliable evidence. Once the potatoes have been cooked, they could be tasted, and students could comment on their different taste and texture in the mouth due to the cooking conditions.

Safety: Know how to extinguish a fat fire.

Comparing oils for degree of saturation

Equipment and materials required

Iodine solution or bromine water (irritant and harmful – see CLEAPSS Hazcard 15), variety of plant oils, ethanol (highly flammable – no naked flames) test tubes, bungs, dropping pipettes (possibly colorimeter, light sensor, data logging equipment), eye protection.

Details

Mix the oil and bromine water or iodine solution. Stopper and shake. Judge degree of decolorisation.

ACTIVITY & EXTENSION IDEAS

- Give students the nutritional information for different potato products. Ask them to draw a graph to compare different cooking techniques and their fat/calorie contents.
- Ask students to find out the boiling points of different fats used in cooking and to show this information in an appropriate diagram, e.g. bar chart.

KEY POINTS

Ask students to write a limerick that includes the key points.

CHEMISTRY — **PLANT OILS**

C1b 5.2 Cooking with vegetable oils

LEARNING OBJECTIVES
1. Why do we cook with vegetable oils?
2. What does it mean when we 'harden' vegetable oils?
3. How do we turn vegetable oils into spreads?

The temperature that a liquid boils at depends on the size of the forces between its molecules. The bigger these forces are, the higher the liquid's boiling point.

The molecules in vegetable oils are much bigger than water molecules. This makes the forces between the molecules in vegetable oils much larger. So the boiling points of vegetable oils are much higher than the boiling point of water.

When we cook food we heat it to a temperature where chemical reactions cause permanent changes to happen to the food. When we cook food in vegetable oil the result is very different to when we cook it in water. This is because vegetable oils can be used at a much higher temperature than boiling water.

So the chemical reactions that take place are very different. The food cooks more quickly, and very often the outside of the food turns a different colour, and becomes crisper.

a) How does the boiling point of vegetable oils compare to the boiling point of water?

Cooking food in oil also means that the food absorbs some of the oil. As you know, vegetable oils contain a lot of energy. This can make the energy content of fried food much higher than that of the same food cooked by boiling it in water. This is one reason why too much fried food can be bad for you!

Figure 1 An electric fryer like this one enables vegetable oil to be heated safely to a high temperature.

Figure 2 Boiled potatoes and fried potatoes are very different. One thing that probably makes chips so tasty is the contrast of crisp outside and soft inside, together with the different taste produced by cooking at a higher temperature. The different colour may be important too.

PRACTICAL
Investigating cooking

Compare the texture and appearance of potato pieces after equal cooking times in water and oil.

You might also compare the cooking times for boiling, frying and oven baking chips.

If possible carry out some taste tests in hygienic conditions.

b) How is food cooked in oil different to food cooked in water?

Unsaturated vegetable oils are usually liquids at room temperature. This is because the carbon–carbon double bonds in their molecules stop the molecules fitting together very well. This reduces the size of the forces between the molecules.

The boiling and melting points of these oils can be increased by adding hydrogen to the molecules. The reaction replaces some or all of the carbon–carbon double bonds with carbon–carbon single bonds. This allows the molecules to fit next to each other better. So the size of the forces between the molecules increases and the melting point is raised.

With this higher melting point, the liquid oil becomes a solid at room temperature. We call changing a vegetable oil like this *hardening* it.

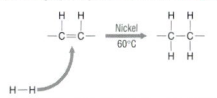

Figure 3 We harden a vegetable oil by reacting it with hydrogen. To make the reaction happen, we must use a nickel catalyst, and carry it out at about 60°C.

c) What do we call it when we add hydrogen to a vegetable oil?

Oils that we have treated like this are sometimes called *hydrogenated oils*. Because they are solids at room temperature, it means that they can be made into spreads to be put on bread. We can also use them to make cakes, biscuits and pastry.

Figure 4 We can use hydrogenated vegetable oils in cooking to make a huge number of different, and delicious, foods!

SUMMARY QUESTIONS

1 Copy and complete using the words below:

   energy   hardening   higher   hydrogen   melting   tastes

The boiling points of vegetable oils are …… than the boiling point of water. This means that food cooked in oil …… different to boiled food. It also contains more …… .
The boiling and …… points of oils may also be raised by adding …… to their molecules. We call this …… the oil.

2 a) Why are hydrogenated vegetable oils more useful than oils that have not been hydrogenated?
   b) Explain how we harden vegetable oils and why the melting point is raised.

GET IT RIGHT!
No chemical bonds are broken when vegetable oils melt or boil – these are physical changes.
When oils are hardened with hydrogen, a chemical change takes place, producing margarine (which has a higher melting point than the original oil).

KEY POINTS
1. Vegetable oils are useful in cooking because of their high boiling points.
2. Vegetable oils are hardened by reacting them with hydrogen to increase their boiling and melting points.

PLENARIES

Question loop – Small pieces of paper are given to each student. They write a question and its answer. They then separate the question from the answer and all the papers are collected and shuffled. Each student is then given a question and an answer. The first student reads their question; the student with the correct answer reads their answer, then their question and so on. (10 minutes)

Flow chart – Students could summarise the hydrogenation of fats in a flow chart format. Lower attaining students could be encouraged to show this in a diagrammatic format. (5–10 minutes)

SUMMARY ANSWERS

1. Higher, tastes, energy, melting, hydrogen, hardening.

2. a) They have a higher melting point.
   b) Heat the oil and hydrogen at 60°C with a nickel catalyst. The oil becomes more saturated and its molecules can fit next to each other better – increasing the forces between molecules.

CHEMISTRY | PLANT OILS

C1b 5.3 Everyday emulsions

LEARNING OBJECTIVES

Students should learn:

- What emulsions are and how they are made.
- That emulsions made from vegetable oils have many uses.

LEARNING OUTCOMES

Most students should be able to:

- Describe what an emulsion is.
- Give an example of an emulsion.

Some students should also be able to:

- Explain why emulsifiers are an important addition to some foods.
- Explain how emulsifiers work in terms of intermolecular forces.

Teaching suggestions

- **Gifted and talented.** Students could be told that emulsions are part of a group of mixtures called 'colloids'. These students could then be encouraged to define and give examples of other colloids, e.g. sol, gel, foam.
- **Learning styles**
  Kinaesthetic: Students lining up in order of fat content/making emulsions.
  Visual: Drawing a diagram of the microscope slide.
  Auditory: Listening to other group members explain about their food additives.
  Interpersonal: Working in groups to look at and make emulsions.
  Intrapersonal: Making a list of different emulsions.
- **ICT link-up.** Connect a flexi-cam to the head of the microscope. The image of the different milk emulsions could then be projected or shown on a TV screen.
- **Homework.** Ask students to find some names/E-numbers of emulsifiers in foods, e.g. soya lecithin, E471.

SPECIFICATION LINK-UP C1b.11.5

- *Oils do not dissolve in water. They can be used to produce emulsions. Emulsions are thicker than oil or water and have many uses that depend on their special properties. They provide better texture, coating ability and appearance, for example in salad dressings and ice creams.*

Students should use their skills, knowledge and understanding of 'How Science Works':
- *to evaluate the effects of using vegetable oils in foods and the impacts on diet and health.*

Lesson structure

STARTER

List – Ask students to list as many emulsions that they can think of. [For example, salad dressing, mayonnaise, salad cream, milk, ice cream. Please note that emulsion paint is a colloid but not an emulsion.] (5 minutes)

Prediction – Give each student a bung and a test tube with water and oil in it (about 1 ml of each). Ask the students how you could make the oil and water mix. Some might say that it is possible to shake it. Encourage the class to shake their tubes and make a prediction as to what will happen. Allow the students time to observe. Ask the students what has happened [the oil and water have separated, they are immiscible liquids (do not mix)]. Ask the students to think of a way of keeping oil and water mixed. Encourage them to think about doing the washing up or clothes washing, i.e. what happens to the fat from plates or on clothes? [Students will hopefully realise that another chemical – an emulsifier – needs to be added to make immiscible liquids mix and make an emulsion.] (10 minutes)

Microscope – For lower attaining students, provide a diagram of a microscope and ask them to label the key parts. This could be turned into a kinaesthetic activity, by giving each pair of students a microscope and reading out the parts, while the students point to them. (5 minutes)

MAIN

- Students come into contact with many emulsions in everyday life. One of the most common is milk, which is fat suspended in water. Ask the students what type of fat is in milk [animal fat and therefore saturated]. Then encourage the students to make wet slides of different types of milk to see the different emulsions.
- Students could record their results in the form of a diagram, but they should also work out the magnification on the microscope (eye lens × object lens).
- Students could make another common emulsion – mayonnaise. If a room swap can be completed into a home economics room, the students could take the mayonnaise home. Ask the students to try to identify the emulsifier in this mixture [egg yolk].

PLENARIES

Order – Split the students into groups of six students. Give each group a set of cards with 'whole milk, Jersey milk, skimmed milk, semi-skimmed milk, whole goat milk and semi-skimmed goat milk'. On the back of each card, have the nutritional information for that type of milk. Ask the students to line up in order of the most to the least fat content. [The order should be: Jersey milk, whole milk, whole goat milk, semi-skimmed milk, semi-skimmed goat milk.] (10 minutes)

Explain – Split the students into groups of three. Give each member a different food additive from 'emulsifiers, stabilisers and thickeners'. Give the students 2 minutes to find an example of its use and why it is used. Then the students feedback their ideas in their groups. (5 minutes)

Practical support

A closer look at milk

Equipment and materials required

Samples of different milks (whole, semi-skimmed, skimmed) – be aware of lactose-intolerant students, microscope, slides, mounted needle, cover slip, dropping pipette.

Details

Put a drop of one type of milk in the centre of the microscope slide. Place a cover slip at the edge, and support it with the mounted needle. Gently, lower onto the liquid in order to minimise air bubbles. Put the slide onto the microscope stage, and adjust for the lowest magnification and bring into focus. Repeat for other milk samples.

Making mayonnaise

Equipment and materials required

Two egg yolks (be aware of students with an egg allergy), salt, pepper, oil, vinegar, mustard, bowl, whisk, measuring jug, tablespoon, teaspoon.

Details

Beat the eggs with a pinch of salt. Add the oil 1–2 teaspoons at a time, while continuing to beat the mixture. After a quarter of the oil has been added, add 1–2 teaspoons of vinegar. Continue to add oil slowly and beat the mixture. Add mustard and pepper to taste.

Safety: Wash hands before and after handling eggs.

ACTIVITY & EXTENSION IDEAS

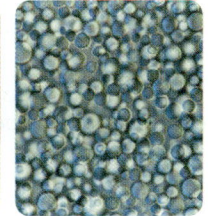

- The different types of milk could be purchased and the students could taste them in a Food Technology room or outside the laboratory to see what difference fat makes to the milk (be aware of lactose-intolerant students).
- If there is access to an ice-cream machine, then this emulsion could also be made.

SUMMARY ANSWERS

1. Mix, small, emulsion, separating, emulsifier, mayonnaise, ice cream.

2. Salad cream is thick (viscous) and is not transparent.

3. a) To prevent the oil and water in the emulsion from separating.
   b) The 'tails' of the emulsifier molecules dissolve into the oil, leaving 'heads' of the molecules lining the surface of the oil droplet. These droplets then repel each other and remain spread throughout the water.

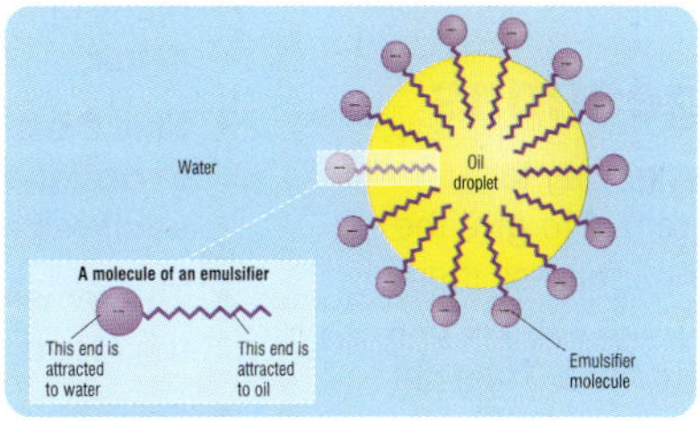

Answers to in-text questions

a) A substance that stops oil and water separating out into layers.

b) It keeps the sauce thick and smooth.

DID YOU KNOW?

Eating the most ice cream in 30 seconds, with a teaspoon, is a world record. The current holder is Portuguese (Jamie Andre Sargento da Silva) who ate 167 g!

KEY POINTS

Ask the students to re-write the key points into their own words. This could be in a paragraph, or questions and answers format or by changing the bullet points so that it is not just copied.

CHEMISTRY | PLANT OILS

C1b 5.4 What is added to our food?

LEARNING OBJECTIVES

Students should learn:
- The importance of food additives.
- List the purposes of food additives.
- How to detect coloured food additives.

LEARNING OUTCOMES

Most students should be able to:
- Describe why an additive with an E-number might be used and state one example.
- Describe one test to show coloured additives.

Some students should also be able to:
- Explain why a range of different types of food additives are used.
- Explain how coloured food additives can be detected and identified.

SPECIFICATION LINK-UP C1b.11.5

- *Processed foods may contain additives to improve appearance, taste and shelf-life. These additives must be listed in the ingredients and some permitted additives were given E-numbers.*
- *Chemical analysis can be used to identify additives in food. Artificial colours can be detected and identified by chromatography.*

Students should use their skills, knowledge and understanding of 'How Science Works':
- *to evaluate the use, benefits, drawbacks and risks of ingredients and additives in food.*

Lesson structure

STARTER

Spot the E-number – Give the students different food packaging. Ask them to note the E-numbers and which families of additives they belong to. Then complete a tally chart to show which additives was most frequently found in the foods studied. (10 minutes)

Dominoes – Give the students a card sort with the key words: 'preserve, food additive, E-number, chromatography' written on. Each card should also have a definition. Students should work in pairs to match the ends up, as in a domino game. (10 minutes)

MAIN

- A lot of people are now very concerned about food additives, but do not realise that many of them are naturally occurring chemicals such as pectin (E440), which is found in fruit.
- Split the class into half and give each group a different task. Ask half of the students to design and make a leaflet to be put in doctors' surgeries to explain that food additives aren't necessarily harmful.
- The remaining students should design a leaflet warning people about additives in their food and their effects.
- Food colourings are often added to food to make them more appealing. Colours can be added to sweets and savoury foods. Students can complete chromatography experiments of different food colourings. Then the chromatograms could be stuck into their book and conclusions drawn from their results.
- Students can evaluate the reliability and validity of the experiment as a means of detecting and identifying artificial colourings. (How Science Works opportunity.)

PLENARIES

AfL (Assessment for Learning) – Pair students with the two different styles of leaflet (not harmful and warning). Ask each student to read their partner's work, then to decide if additives are necessary in foods or not. Take a class vote on whether additives should be banned or not. This could be extended into a debate. (10 minutes)

Explain – Ask the students to explain how chromatography works. Then pick three students randomly from the register to read their explanations. Reward the best explanation. (15 minutes)

Teaching suggestions

- **Special needs.** An easier way to generate a chromatogram is to give the students a disk of filter paper. Ask them to use a paintbrush to put a sample of a food colouring into the centre. Then cut a wick (a wedge shape towards the centre). Then balance the paper over a beaker with water in it. The wick must be submerged. The colours will then separate into rings.
- **Learning styles**
  Kinaesthetic: Manipulating information cards during the domino game and making a chromatogram.
  Visual: Looking at the chromatograms and interpreting the information.
  Auditory: Listening to peers and explaining how chromatography works.
  Interpersonal: Comparing leaflets with arguments about food additives and debating the need for food additives.
  Intrapersonal: Understanding how chromatography works.
- **Homework.** Ask students to choose their favourite convenience food (could be a sweet or frozen pizza, etc.). Encourage them to list all the additives in that food, and what they are used for.
- **ICT link-up.** A PhotoPlus, C1b 5.4 'Detecting additives', is available on the GCSE Chemistry CD ROM.

KEY POINTS

Before the lesson begins, pick six famous people and write their names on separate pieces of paper. Stick the names under six different chairs. Ask the students to check under their chairs. If they have a name attached, they should be encouraged to read the Key Points 'in character'.

Practical support

Detecting dyes in food colourings

Equipment and materials required
Different food colourings, capillary tubes, boiling tube, boiling tube rack, ruler, pencil, strips of chromatography paper that fit into the boiling tube.

Details
Draw a pencil line 2 cm from the bottom of the chromatography paper when it is in a portrait position. Draw three pencil crosses on the base line, of equal distance apart. Dip a clean capillary tube into a food colouring, the colour will suck into the tube. Gently dot one of the crosses, trying to add only a small amount of colouring. Repeat with two further colours. Put a small amount of water in the boiling tube (about 1 cm deep). Lower the chromatography paper into the tube and place in the rack. Leave the chromatogram to develop, until the solvent line is past the last coloured dot. Try not to move the chromatograms while they develop, or they will not be easy to compare.

- Students will see which colourings were pure substances and which were mixtures of dyes, and can list the component colours in any mixtures.

ACTIVITY & EXTENSION IDEAS

- Students could investigate the dye in Smarties. Different coloured Smarties could be put into dimple dishes. Students wet a paintbrush to remove the dye and complete a chromatogram.
- In recent years, there have been a number of food scares involving additives, e.g. Sudan 1 dye. Students could look into these using the Internet (e.g. search newspaper web sites for 'food scare') and newspaper clippings kept in the school library. They could look at the economic and social effect of scares such as this and the impact on the British food industry.

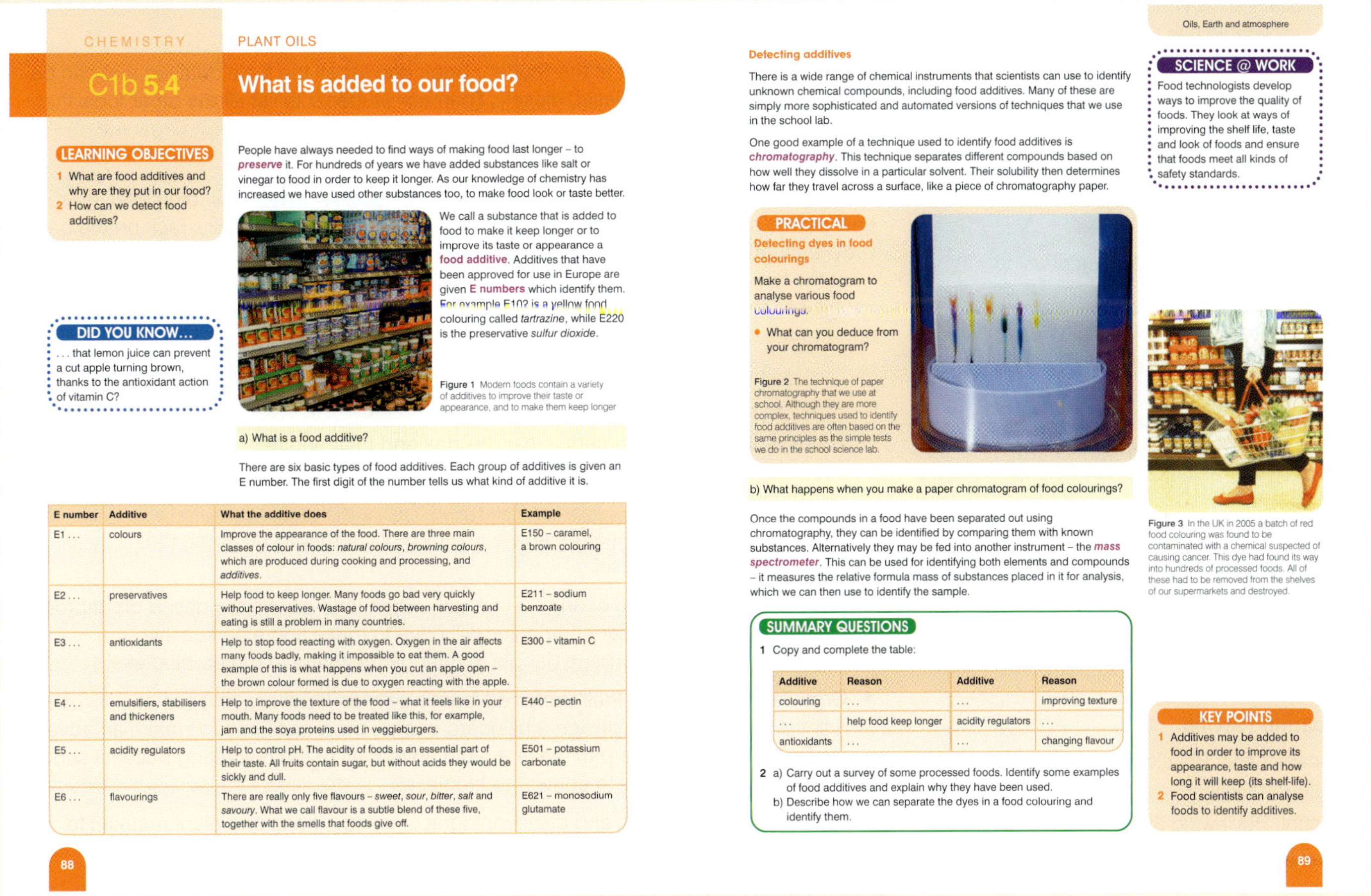

CHEMISTRY — PLANT OILS
C1b 5.4 What is added to our food?

LEARNING OBJECTIVES
1. What are food additives and why are they put in our food?
2. How can we detect food additives?

People have always needed to find ways of making food last longer – to *preserve* it. For hundreds of years we have added substances like salt or vinegar to food in order to keep it longer. As our knowledge of chemistry has increased we have used other substances too, to make food look or taste better.

We call a substance that is added to food to make it keep longer or to improve its taste or appearance a **food additive**. Additives that have been approved for use in Europe are given **E numbers** which identify them. For example E102 is a yellow food colouring called *tartrazine*, while E220 is the preservative *sulfur dioxide*.

DID YOU KNOW...
...that lemon juice can prevent a cut apple turning brown, thanks to the antioxidant action of vitamin C?

Figure 1 Modern foods contain a variety of additives to improve their taste or appearance, and to make them keep longer

a) What is a food additive?

There are six basic types of food additives. Each group of additives is given an E number. The first digit of the number tells us what kind of additive it is.

E number	Additive	What the additive does	Example
E1...	colours	Improve the appearance of the food. There are three main classes of colour in foods: *natural colours*, *browning colours*, which are produced during cooking and processing, and *additives*.	E150 – caramel, a brown colouring
E2...	preservatives	Help food to keep longer. Many foods go bad very quickly without preservatives. Wastage of food between harvesting and eating is still a problem in many countries.	E211 – sodium benzoate
E3...	antioxidants	Help to stop food reacting with oxygen. Oxygen in the air affects many foods badly, making it impossible to eat them. A good example of this is what happens when you cut an apple open – the brown colour formed is due to oxygen reacting with the apple.	E300 – vitamin C
E4...	emulsifiers, stabilisers and thickeners	Help to improve the texture of the food – what it feels like in your mouth. Many foods need to be treated like this, for example, jam and the soya proteins used in veggieburgers.	E440 – pectin
E5...	acidity regulators	Help to control pH. The acidity of foods is an essential part of their taste. All fruits contain sugar, but without acids they would be sickly and dull.	E501 – potassium carbonate
E6...	flavourings	There are really only five flavours – *sweet, sour, bitter, salt* and *savoury*. What we call flavour is a subtle blend of these five, together with the smells that foods give off.	E621 – monosodium glutamate

Detecting additives
There is a wide range of chemical instruments that scientists can use to identify unknown chemical compounds, including food additives. Many of these are simply more sophisticated and automated versions of techniques that we use in the school lab.

One good example of a technique used to identify food additives is **chromatography**. This technique separates different compounds based on how well they dissolve in a particular solvent. Their solubility then determines how far they travel across a surface, like a piece of chromatography paper.

PRACTICAL
Detecting dyes in food colourings
Make a chromatogram to analyse various food colourings.
- What can you deduce from your chromatogram?

Figure 2 The technique of paper chromatography that we use at school. Although they are more complex, techniques used to identify food additives are often based on the same principles as the simple tests we do in the school science lab.

b) What happens when you make a paper chromatogram of food colourings?

Once the compounds in a food have been separated out using chromatography, they can be identified by comparing them with known substances. Alternatively they may be fed into another instrument – the **mass spectrometer**. This can be used for identifying both elements and compounds – it measures the relative formula mass of substances placed in it for analysis, which we can then use to identify the sample.

SCIENCE @ WORK
Food technologists develop ways to improve the quality of foods. They look at ways of improving the shelf life, taste and look of foods and ensure that foods meet all kinds of safety standards.

Figure 3 In the UK in 2005 a batch of red food colouring was found to be contaminated with a chemical suspected of causing cancer. This dye had found its way into hundreds of processed foods. All of these had to be removed from the shelves of our supermarkets and destroyed.

SUMMARY QUESTIONS
1. Copy and complete the table:

Additive	Reason	Additive	Reason
colouring	...	...	improving texture
...	help food keep longer	acidity regulators	...
antioxidants	...	...	changing flavour

2. a) Carry out a survey of some processed foods. Identify some examples of food additives and explain why they have been used.
   b) Describe how we can separate the dyes in a food colouring and identify them.

KEY POINTS
1. Additives may be added to food in order to improve its appearance, taste and how long it will keep (its shelf-life).
2. Food scientists can analyse foods to identify additives.

SUMMARY ANSWERS

1.

Additive	Reason	Additive	Reason
colouring	**improves appearance**	**emulsifiers**	improving texture
preservatives	help food keep longer	acidity regulators	**control pH**
antioxidants	**stops food reacting with oxygen**	**flavourings**	changing flavour

2. a) Examples of additives in some packaged food and why they have been added.
   b) Description of using chromatography then comparing chromatogram with known substances or using an instrument, such as a mass spectrometer, to identify each substance separated.

Answers to in-text questions

a) A substance that is added to food to make it keep longer or to improve its taste or appearance.

b) Each dye separates into spots of pure colour.

DID YOU KNOW?
Scientists at Birmingham University were the first people to synthesise vitamin C (ascorbic acid).

CHEMISTRY — **PLANT OILS**

C1b 5.5 Vegetable oils as fuels

LEARNING OBJECTIVES

Students should learn that:
- Vegetable oils can be used as fuels.
- There are advantages of using vegetable oils as fuels.
- Ethanol can be made from ethene.

LEARNING OUTCOMES

Most students should be able to:
- List an example of vegetable oil being used as a fuel.
- State an advantage of using vegetable oils as fuels.
- Write the word equation and conditions for the production of ethanol from ethene.

Some students should also be able to:
- Explain the advantages of using vegetable oils as fuels.
- Evaluate different fuels in terms of their advantages and disadvantages.
- Write the symbol equation for the reaction of ethene with steam.

Teaching suggestions

- **Special needs.** Role-plays could be given to the students to perform the radio advert/TV advert. The billboard poster could be half-finished and given to the students.
- **Learning styles**
  Kinaesthetic: Physically sorting the different fuels.
  Visual: Reviewing the billboard poster.
  Auditory: Listening to the prepared radio advert.
  Interpersonal: Working in teams to produce marketing material.
  Intrapersonal: Reflecting on what they have revised and learnt.
- **ICT link-up.** Students could type up their newspaper article in a publishing or presentation package. The sorting activity could also be completed using an interactive whiteboard.
- **Homework.** Ask students to summarise the advantages of using biodiesel compared to petrol. Give the students a maximum number of words (40) to encourage them to summarise, rather than regurgitate.

SPECIFICATION LINK-UP C1b.11.5 (and 11.4)

- Vegetable oils are important foods and fuels as they provide a lot of energy. They also provide us with nutrients.
- Ethene can be reacted with steam in the presence of a catalyst to produce ethanol. (11.4)

Students should use their skills, knowledge and understanding of 'How Science Works':
- to evaluate the advantages and disadvantages of making ethanol from renewable and non-renewable sources. (11.4)
- to evaluate the benefits, drawbacks and risks of using vegetable oils to produce fuels.

Lesson structure

STARTER

List – Ask students to look at the Student Book and list all the fuels detailed that can be used to run a car [oil, biodiesel, diesel]. Then ask students to list all the other fuels that they know can be used to power cars [petrol, gas, alcohol, hydrogen]. Organise feedback from the class into two lists on the board. (10 minutes)

Sorting – Get pictures of different fuels for cars at least A4 in size (oil, biodiesel, diesel, gas, petrol, alcohol and hydrogen). Laminate the pictures, and put Blu-Tack on the back. Draw a table with two columns (renewable, non-renewable). Ask two students to explain what the two words in the table mean. Then ask seven students, in turn, to move one image into renewable or non-renewable. They should take the image and stick it in the appropriate column. (5–10 minutes)

MAIN

- There is always development in car designs and their engines. Cars were run using petrol for many years; it has been relatively recently that other fuels have started to be investigated and used in the UK, e.g. gas power.
- Ask students to write a feature article in a glossy car magazine about the developments in biodiesel.
- People are often slow to change, especially when innovations are based on unproven technology. Therefore car companies will have to make some persuasive advertisements to encourage people to change their cars to run on biodiesel.
- Organise students into their preferred learning styles (auditory, kinaesthetic, visual). Ask the visual group to design a billboard poster; the kinaesthetic to make an advert for TV; the auditory group to make a radio advert. All of the marketing material should aim to persuade drivers to convert to biodiesel.
- Discuss the advantages and disadvantages of using ethene and plant material to manufacture ethanol for use as a fuel.

PLENARIES

AfL (Assessment for Learning) – Each group displays/acts out their marketing material. Question the students about any misconceptions in the adverts. Then students vote for the most persuasive advert, that group could be given a prize. (15 minutes)

Reflection – Ask the students to think about one thing that they have learned today, and one thing that they have revised. These could be facts or skills. Ask a selection of students to share their thoughts with the rest of the class. (5 minutes)

ACTIVITY & EXTENSION IDEAS

- Encourage students to find out about other developments in fuels for cars. This could involve completing an Internet search.
- Students could be played TV adverts about fuel/engine developments, e.g. the Honda campaign 2005 'Hate something . . .', as stimulus material for producing their own marketing material.
- Ask students to consider why electric cars are not as environmentally friendly as using biodiesel. Students should have the idea that electricity is a secondary source and, therefore, pollution is occurring elsewhere to fuel the car.

Answers to in-text questions

a) The name for any fuel made from vegetable oils.

b) Vegetable oils.

c) Ethanol from sugar cane comes from a plant source whereas the ethene used to make ethanol comes from crude oil (from the cracking of heavier fractions).

CHEMISTRY — **PLANT OILS**

C1b 5.5 Vegetable oils as fuels

LEARNING OBJECTIVES
1. How can we use vegetable oils as a fuel?
2. What are the advantages of using vegetable oils as fuels?

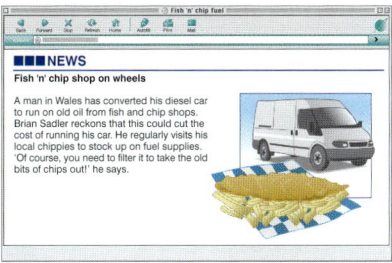

NEWS — Fish 'n' chip shop on wheels

A man in Wales has converted his diesel car to run on old oil from fish and chip shops. Brian Sadler reckons that this could cut the cost of running his car. He regularly visits his local chippies to stock up on fuel supplies. 'Of course, you need to filter it to take the old bits of chips out!' he says.

Figure 1 A true story of recycling

Running our cars on the old oil from fish and chip shops isn't realistic for most of us. But it is possible to make fuel for cars using vegetable oils, even used cooking oil. We just need to use a little bit of clever chemistry.

Biodiesel is the name we give to any fuel made from vegetable oils. We can use these fuels in any car or van that has a diesel engine.

Most modern biodiesel is made by treating vegetable oils to remove some unwanted chemicals. The biodiesel made like this can be used on its own, or mixed with diesel fuel made from refining crude oil.

When we make biodiesel we also produce other useful products. For example, we get a solid waste material that we can feed to cattle as a high-energy food. We also get glycerine which we can use to make soap.

a) What is biodiesel?
b) What is biodiesel made from?

There are some very big advantages in using biodiesel as a fuel. First, biodiesel is much less harmful to animals and plants than diesel made from crude oil. If it is spilled, it breaks down about five times faster than 'normal' diesel. Also, when we burn biodiesel in an engine it burns much more cleanly. It makes very little sulfur dioxide and other pollutants.

DID YOU KNOW...
. . . that the largest factory for turning used cooking oil into biodiesel was opened in Scotland in 2005? The plant can produce up to 5% of Scotland's diesel fuels requirements.

But using biodiesel has one really big advantage over petrol and diesel. It is the fact that the crops used to make biodiesel absorb carbon dioxide gas as they grow. So biodiesel is effectively 'CO₂ neutral'. That means the amount of carbon dioxide given off is nearly balanced by the amount absorbed. Therefore, biodiesel makes little contribution to the greenhouse gases in our atmosphere.

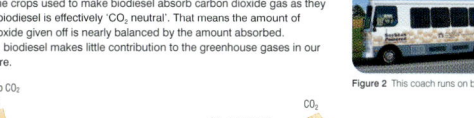

Figure 2 This coach runs on biodiesel

Figure 3 Cars run on biodiesel produce very little CO₂ overall, as CO₂ is absorbed by plants as the fuel is made

Using ethanol as a bio-fuel

Another bio-fuel is ethanol. We can make it by fermenting the sugar from sugar beet or sugar cane. In Brazil they can grow lots of sugar cane. They add the ethanol to petrol, saving our dwindling supplies of crude oil. The ethanol gives off carbon dioxide (a greenhouse gas) when it burns, but the sugar cane absorbs the gas during photosynthesis.

Ethanol can also be made from the ethene we get by cracking the heavier fractions from crude oil (see page 70):

$$C_2H_4 + H_2O \xrightarrow[\text{high pressure}]{\text{catalyst}} C_2H_5OH$$
ethene   steam   ethanol

c) Why is ethanol from sugar cane known as a 'bio-fuel' whereas ethanol from ethene isn't?

Figure 4 Ethanol can be made from sugar cane

SUMMARY QUESTIONS

1 Copy and complete using the words below:

   carbon dioxide   cattle   diesel   plants   soap

   Biodiesel is a fuel made from …… . Making the fuel also produces some other useful products, including …… and food for …… . Biodiesel produces less pollution than …… , and absorbs nearly as much …… …… when it is made as it does when it burns.

2 Where does the energy in biodiesel come from?

3 a) How is ethene converted into ethanol? Include a balanced equation in your answer.
   b) When can we describe ethanol as a bio-fuel?
   c) Write an article for a local newspaper describing the arguments for using biodiesel instead of other fuels made from crude oil.

KEY POINTS
1. Vegetable oils can be burned as fuels.
2. Vegetable oils are a renewable source of energy that could be used to replace some fossil fuels.

SUMMARY ANSWERS

1 Plants, soap, cattle, diesel, carbon dioxide.

2 From the Sun through photosynthesis.

3 a) Ethene and steam are passed over a catalyst at high pressure.

   $$C_2H_4 + H_2O \rightarrow C_2H_5OH$$

   b) When the ethanol has been produced by fermenting plant material.

   c) Article [mark this based on the appropriate use of facts about biodiesel used to support arguments].

DID YOU KNOW?

The most fuel-efficient car was developed by a team in Japan. The team built a car which managed to move 3624.5 km/litre in 2001. This was during the Scottish Eco Marathon, where their speed could not drop below 10 mph or they would be disqualified.

KEY POINTS

Give the students a crossword, where the key words and ideas can be found in this section.

CHEMISTRY   PLANT OILS

C1b 5.6 Vegetable oils

SPECIFICATION LINK-UP
C1b.11.5
Students should use their skills, knowledge and understanding of 'How Science Works':

- to evaluate the effects of using vegetable oils in foods and the impact on diet and health
- to evaluate the benefits, drawbacks and risks of using vegetable oils to produce fuels.

CHEMISTRY   PLANT OILS

C1b 5.6 Vegetable oils

GO FASTER!

Plant-powered performance

BIO BLEND DIESEL – Cheaper Eco Friendly Fuel SOLD HERE

Whatever will those ace scientists come up with next? Just when you think you've seen everything, the idea of filling up your car with plant power comes along! The latest idea by those who want us all to save the planet is to take oil made from oilseed rape plants (you know, that yellow stuff you see growing all over the countryside in springtime), mix it with diesel and then shove it in the tank of your motor! And they call it ... biodiesel!

So why would anyone want to do this? Well, mainly, because biodiesel is better for the environment. Not only does it burn just like ordinary diesel fuel, but it doesn't produce as much pollution. And what's more, it's a 'green fuel' which doesn't contribute as much to global warming – though we couldn't quite see why ... there's a year's free subscription on offer to anyone who can explain it to us!

ACTIVITY

Imagine that you are a presenter on a popular television programme about cars and driving. Write and present an article for this programme about biodiesel.

Make your article fun and informative. Include as much factual information as you can so that people can decide whether they would like to use this fuel in their car.

Look after your family's hearts

Everyone knows the benefits of a healthy diet. But do you know the benefits of ensuring that you eat vegetable oils as part of your diet?

Scientists have found that eating vegetable oils instead of animal fats can do wonders for the health of your heart. The saturated fats you find in things like butter and cheese can make the blood vessels of your heart become clogged up with fat.

However, the unsaturated fats in vegetable oils (like olive oil and corn oil) are especially good for you. They help to keep your arteries clear and reduce the chance of you having heart disease.

The levels of a special fat called **cholesterol** in your blood give doctors an idea about your risk of heart disease. People who eat lots of vegetable oils tend to have a much healthier level of cholesterol in their blood.

92

Teaching suggestions

Activities

Article – Fats are an important part of our diet. Without them, for example, we would not have any cell walls! Set the students the task of writing an article for a lifestyle magazine. Students should be encouraged to include quotes from fictitious people, e.g. a GP, a dieter etc. They should endeavour to create a balanced article explaining how the body needs fat, but there are effects of having too much fat.

Poster – Whenever people go into health centres there are a number of thought provoking health posters on the wall. Try to get some of the posters (e.g. from the school nurse) to show the students. Then set the students the task of designing and making their own poster to highlight vegetable oils in our diet.

Homework

Alternative fuels – Ask students to complete a storyboard for a segment on a popular car show. The section should be about 5 minutes long and be about biodiesel as a fuel for cars.

Extension

Presenting – Ask students to act out their storyboard. They may need to go into groups, and choose their favourite from their group, as the storyboard may have more than one character.

Bias – There is a lot of bias media about fat in our diet. Split the class into groups. Supply each group with different written materials about fat in our diet, e.g. a leaflet available from the NHS, healthy eating books, lifestyle magazine articles, adverts for low fat foods. Encourage the students to read the articles and list the facts in the work, then to list the incorrect statements. Finally, ask the students to decide if the work was balanced or biased.

Fat definitions – In everyday language there are a lot of scientific words used, but people often do not know what they mean. Encourage the students to define all the science words used to define fat (e.g. saturate, unsaturated, cholesterol, trans fats) and the effects on our body if they are eaten in large quantities. They could display this work as a leaflet, poster or a booklet.

Oils, Earth and atmosphere

Online Health Encyclopaedia
Trans fats

Trans unsaturated fatty acids, or ***trans fats***, are solid fats. They are produced artificially by heating liquid vegetable oils with metal catalysts and hydrogen. Trans fats are made in huge quantities when we harden vegetable oils to make margarine.

The fats used to cook French fries and other fast foods usually contain trans fats. Concerns have been raised for several decades that eating trans fats might have contributed to the 20th century epidemic of coronary heart disease.

Studies have shown that trans fats have adverse effects on cholesterol in the blood – increasing 'bad' cholesterol while decreasing 'good' cholesterol. Trans fats have also been associated with an increased risk of coronary heart disease in other studies.

Changes in food labelling are very important. But many products, including fast food, often contain extremely high levels of trans fats. Yet these are exempt from labelling regulations and may have labels such as 'cholesterol-free' and 'cooked in vegetable oil'.

For example, a person eating one doughnut for breakfast and a large order of French fries for lunch would eat 10 g of trans fats, or 5 per cent of the total energy of an 1800-calorie diet. Thus, simple labelling changes alone will not be sufficient.

ACTIVITIES

a) Write an article for a family lifestyle magazine about 'feeding your family'. Include in this article reasons for including vegetable oils in a balanced diet and their effect on people's health.

b) Design a poster with the title 'Vegetable oils – good or bad?'

Learning styles

Kinaesthetic: Presenting a segment on a popular car show.

Visual: Making a poster for the use in a health centre about fat and diet.

Auditory: Discussion about articles that could be biased.

Interpersonal: Working as a group to present a segment in a car show.

Intrapersonal: Completing definitions about fats.

ICT link-up

Students could record their presentations using a camcorder. Then using a firewire card, the data could be manipulated and images/text added using Windows Movie Maker. The video could then be used on the school web site, or shown at a 'New Parents Evening' or in an assembly.
A PhotoPlus is available for C1b 5.6 on the GCSE Chemistry CD ROM.

CHEMISTRY — PLANT OILS

SUMMARY ANSWERS

1 a) Substances produced by plants containing long hydrocarbon chains.

b) Oils containing one or more C=C bonds.

c) Oils containing as much hydrogen as possible in which there are no C=C bonds.

2 Bromine (which is orange-brown) reacts with C=C bonds when the vegetable oil is unsaturated. When it has been hardened, the oil is saturated; there are no C=C bonds so no reaction occurs.

3 a) The ice cream emulsion has separated, so that there are parts of the mixture which contain pure water instead of water with droplets of fat in it. When the mixture is refrozen the water freezes and forms ice that is 'crunchy' when compared to the frozen emulsion.

b) To prevent the emulsion from separating out.

4 a) So that we know how the food has been treated when it has been processed. Some people are allergic to some additives.

b) i) 4
   ii) 1
   iii) 5
   iv) 6

5 This is impossible. Even if making biodiesel involved no use of energy produced by burning carbon (e.g. if all the energy used to make biodiesel was made using nuclear or renewable energy sources) the CO_2 produced when the biodiesel was burnt will always at least equal the CO_2 absorbed by the plant in making the oil in the first place.

6 Reasoned argument by student.

7 a) No. (Some natural substances have been assigned E-numbers and could be present in the food but can't be described as artificial.)

b) Any example from the Student Book (page 88) supported with reasons for using it.

c) Answers that include reasoned explanation of chosen position: yes because some additives are bad for you; no because some additives improve the food by preventing it from going off, for example.

Summary teaching suggestions

- **When to use these questions?**
  Questions 1, 2 and 4 could be set as homework near the end of the chapter.

- **Terminology**
  Students can struggle with the terminology of questions. Give the students a sheet detailing the key things that examiners ask of them, e.g. recall, explain, define, sketch, and then an explanation of what each of these words mean. Encourage students to read the examination question and consult the explanation sheet before starting their response.

- **Misconceptions**
  Question 4 is concerned with E-numbers. A lot of people think that all substances represented by an E-number are unnatural and not necessary in foods. Encourage students to understand that some E-numbers are naturally occurring chemicals already in foods, e.g. pectin from fruit, and that pectin can be refined and used to make jelly. Also, students should realise that pre-made meals do require additives to maintain their quality.

- **Learning styles**
  Visual: Students could annotate an image of the carbon cycle to show how humans can alter the carbon content in the atmosphere.
  Auditory: Questions 3 and 5 lend themselves to being discussed in small groups, or as a class, with ideas jotted onto the board. Then students can tackle the question individually using the ideas generated by the class/group.

PLANT OILS: C1b 5.1 – C1b 5.6

SUMMARY QUESTIONS

1 Write simple definitions for the following words:
a) vegetable oils
b) unsaturated oils
c) saturated oils.

2 A vegetable oil removes the colour from bromine solution. When the oil has been hardened it does not react with bromine solution. Explain these observations.

3 a) Some ice cream is left standing out on a table during a meal on a hot day. It is then put back in the freezer again. When it is taken out of the freezer a few days later, people complain that the ice cream tastes 'crunchy'. Why is this?
b) A recipe for ice cream says: 'Stir the ice cream from time to time while it is freezing.' Why must you stir ice cream when freezing it?

4 a) Why is it important to be able to identify food additives in food?
b) What is the first number of the E number of the following additives?
   i) lecithin (an emulsifier)
   ii) quinoline yellow (a food colouring)
   iii) calcium oxide (an acidity regulator)
   iv) inosinic acid (a flavour enhancer)

5 Biodiesel is almost 'carbon neutral'. Explain, using your knowledge of the carbon cycle, whether it would ever be possible to produce biodiesel that produces less carbon dioxide when burnt than was absorbed by the plants which made it.

6 'Alternative fuels like biodiesel and gasohol are all very well for countries like Brazil and India – but no good in countries like the UK!' Do you agree with this statement? Give your reasons.

7 Some food are marketed as 'free from artificial additives'.
a) Does this mean that the food contains no added substances?
b) Give an example of a substance that is added to food, and outline the reasons for using it.
c) Is 'additive-free food' better than food which contains additives?

EXAM-STYLE QUESTIONS

1 The energy values of chips depend on their fat content. Match the energy values **A**, **B**, **C** and **D** with the numbers **1** to **4** in the table.
A 687 kJ/100 g
B 796 kJ/100 g
C 1001 kJ/100 g
D 1174 kJ/100 g

	Description of type of chips	Fat content (g/100 g)
1	Fish and chip shop, fried in blended oil	12.4
2	French fries from burger outlet	15.5
3	Homemade fried in blended oil	6.7
4	Oven chips, frozen, baked	4.2

(4)

2 Match the words **A**, **B**, **C** and **D** with spaces **1** to **4** in the sentences.
A cooking oils
B emulsifiers
C emulsions
D hydrogenated oils

Mayonnaise and salad dressings are ......**1**...... that are made by mixing oil and vinegar with other ingredients such as egg yolk.
In mayonnaise the egg yolk contains ......**2**...... that stop the oil and water separating.
Vegetable oils can be converted into ......**3**...... by reacting with hydrogen and a catalyst.
Biodiesel is a fuel that can be made from waste ......**4**...... (4)

3 The table on the next page gives some information about four different vegetable oils. Smoke point is the temperature at which the oil begins to smoke when heated. Match descriptions **A**, **B**, **C** and **D** with numbers **1** to **4** in the table.
A The oil that contains the most monounsaturated fat.
B The oil that reacts with the largest volume of bromine water.
C The oil with the highest melting point.
D The oil with the widest range of smoke point.

- **Homework**
  Question 4 focuses on E-numbers. Students could be encouraged to find examples of different substances for each category of E-number (i–iv).

- **Gifted and talented**
  Question 2 can be explained using a mechanism. Students could find this in an Post-16 textbook.

EXAM-STYLE ANSWERS

1 1 C (1 mark)
    2 D (1 mark)
    3 B (1 mark)
    4 A (1 mark)

2 1 C (1 mark)
    2 B (1 mark)
    3 D (1 mark)
    4 A (1 mark)

3 1 D (1 mark)
    2 A (1 mark)
    3 B (1 mark)
    4 C (1 mark)

4 a) They absorb it when cooked. (1 mark)
b) Largest surface area. (1 mark)
c) *One each for:*
   - Not cooked in oil/cooked by baking/not absorbed in cooking.
   - Amount of oil is controlled/already on chips. (2 marks)
d) *One each for:*
   - Oil has higher boiling point than water.
   - So chips are cooked at higher temperature. (2 marks)
e) i) Bar chart. (1 mark)
   ii) Categoric independent variable; continuous dependent variable. (1 mark)
   (Or to allow easy comparison across categories.)

Oils, Earth and atmosphere

The information in Q5 should be read carefully and used when answering, together with students' own knowledge. Answers should always add something to the stem of the question. Merely repeating the question in another form does not gain credit, for example in part b).

Q6 requires good organisation and communication to achieve full marks. Students who find this difficult could work in pairs or small groups with a higher attaining student taking the lead, acting as mentor.

HOW SCIENCE WORKS ANSWERS

a) So that the results could be compared. The instructions acted as a control.

b) Controls that should have been included in the instructions:
The amount of oil used.
How the bromine water was added.
What to look for as an end point.

c) There are no anomalies. The variation in results is to be expected.

d) The repeats are very close to each other, and they have been done by two different groups.

e) Accuracy could be further increased or checked by obtaining data from the manufacturers or doing a third titration.

f) Results best presented as a bar graph.

How science works teaching suggestions

- **Literacy guidance**
  - Key terms that should be clearly understood are: accuracy and anomalies.
  - Question expecting a longer answer, where students can practise their literacy skills is b).
- **Higher- and lower-level questions.** Questions a) and e) are higher-level and answers for these questions have been provided at this level. Lower-level questions are b) and f) and the answers are also at this level.
- **Gifted and talented.** Able students might consider the relative merits, in terms of end points of using iodine or bromine for these tests.
- **How and when to use these questions.** When wishing to consolidate an appreciation of the importance of designing reliability into an investigation.
- **Homework.** As a homework exercise ask students to find out the relative amounts of unsaturated or saturated fats in various food products – see who can find the highest percentage and the highest likely daily intake.
- **Special needs.** These students will need some help to interpret the use of bromine water in this context.

---

5 a) *Two from:*
- Heat/high temperatures:
- damages oil
- destroys enzymes
- changes flavour
- causes more rapid oxidation
- increases rate of reactions (that cause spoilage). *(2 marks)*

b) *Two from:*
- Not contaminated by solvent/does not contain solvent residues.
- Solvent (residues) may be harmful to health.
- High temps/removing solvent may modify properties/change flavour.
(Not just they prefer the flavour/taste) *(2 marks)*

6 One mark each for:
- Put spot of colour onto chromatography paper.
- Dip bottom of paper into solvent.
- Allow solvent to rise to top of paper.
Plus one mark for any other detail, e.g.
- Pencil line near bottom of paper.
- Place into (tall) beaker.
- Cover the container with a lid. *(4 marks)*

Exam teaching suggestions

Q5 could be used after completing spread 5.1, and Q1, Q3 and Q4 could follow spread 5.2. Use Q6 after spread 5.4 or at the end of the chapter. The questions altogether should take about 30 minutes for a total of 28 marks.

Some students find tables of data off-putting. They should be encouraged to read the questions and to look carefully at the headings in the table before starting their answers. Q1 is a very simple matching exercise, while Q3 is a little more challenging. The data in these questions could be used as a basis for further questions and discussions, for example it could be checked against other sources for reliability and validity.

CHEMISTRY | THE CHANGING WORLD

C1b 6.1 Structure of the Earth

LEARNING OBJECTIVES

Students should learn:

- The basic structure of the Earth.
- That theories have changed about how mountains and valleys were formed.

LEARNING OUTCOMES

Most students should be able to:

- Label the basic structure of the Earth.
- Describe how people used to think that mountains and valleys were formed (the 'Shrinking Earth' hypothesis).

Teaching suggestions

- **Learning styles**

  Kinaesthetic: Making a model of the Earth's structure.

  Visual: Labelling a diagram of the Earth's structure.

  Auditory: Discussing the creation of the Earth.

  Interpersonal: Listening and interacting with other students during a discussion.

  Intrapersonal: Creating questions to the answers that have been supplied. (See Plenaries.)

- **ICT link-up.** An image of the Earth can be placed into interactive whiteboard software and labelled. The labels can be covered with boxes and used as a class quiz exercise.

- **Homework.** Find out how old scientists believe the Earth to be [about 4 600 000 000 years old].

SPECIFICATION LINK-UP   C1b.11.6

- *The Earth consists of a core, mantle and crust.*
- *Scientists once thought that the features of the Earth's surface were the result of the shrinking of the crust as the Earth cooled down following its formation.*

Lesson structure

STARTER

Citizenship – Write on the board: 'How was the Earth made?' Encourage the students to list as many ideas as they can – scientific, religious and cultural. Then hold a discussion about all of these ideas. Explain that most scientists believe in the 'Big Bang' theory, although no-one can be absolutely certain. (15 minutes)

Brainstorm – Ask the students to think about geography and rocks in science. Ask them to complete a brainstorm about the structure of the Earth in the back of their books. Ask one student to be a scribe and write on the board. They could pick students from the class to add ideas to the whole class brainstorm. (20 minutes)

Questions – Write the following questions on the board for the students to answer while they enter the room and the register is being taken:

- What is the crust? [The solid outer layer of the Earth.]
- What is a feature? [Details on the Earth's surface, e.g. mountain ranges.]
- How did scientists first think features were made? [The crust shrinking as the early molten Earth cooled.] (10 minutes)

MAIN

- It is important that the students recognise a diagram of the Earth and that they could label its structure. Ask them to use secondary sources, e.g. the Internet (search for 'Earth structure' at www.bbc.co.uk) and the Student Book, to make a poster about the Earth's structure.

- To ensure that students include the relevant information, state that their poster must include at least one diagram, one measurement, and the key terms: 'core, mantle, crust'.

- For kinaesthetic and artistic students, a model of the Earth and its structure could be made, although this may take a couple of lessons to be completed fully.

- The students could use papier mâché to make the model of the Earth. Blow up balloons to act as a framework, and then mix wallpaper paste (some students may be allergic to this – cellulose paste can be purchased which does not contain a fungicide). Tear newspaper and stick onto the balloon – the paper must be at least three layers thick; once dried (overnight should be enough if they are put in a warm place) they can be cut in half. The shell can then be decorated to show the Earth and its layers. Small pieces of coloured paper or card could be used to add information about the layer and then stuck to the model. By using a knitting needle or similar a small hole could be made in the top of the model, string can then be threaded through and knotted, so it can be suspended, e.g. from the ceiling.

PLENARIES

Label – Give the students a laminated diagram of the Earth's structure. Supply a paper towel and a washable pen. Ask the students to label as much as they can remember onto their diagram. Then show them a fully labelled (this should include a section of the Earth, depth, properties and materials) image via a projector or a photocopied sheet. Ask the students to count how many pieces of information that they collected. For feedback, ask students to put their hand up if they got all, half, or a quarter of the labels. (10 minutes)

Questions and answers – Instead of asking a question and the students putting hands up to answer it, reverse this idea. Give the students answers that are key terms and they should put up their hand with a question that matches the answer. Some answers could be 'Earth, crust, mantle, core, iron, nickel, features, cooled and shrank'. (5 minutes)

ACTIVITY & EXTENSION IDEAS

- Compare the Earth's structure with that of other planets in our solar system. Information for this can be found on the Internet or probably in the school library.

Answers to in-text questions

a) Crust or lithosphere.
b) Mantle.
c) Two – the inner core and outer core.

FOUL FACTS

In a volcanic smoke vent (fumarole), the greatest temperature recorded was 941°C in Russia.

CHEMISTRY
THE CHANGING WORLD
C1b 6.1 Structure of the Earth

LEARNING OBJECTIVES
1. What is below the surface of the Earth?
2. How did people used to think that mountains and valleys were formed?

The deepest mines go down to about 3500 m, while geologists have drilled down to more than 12 000 m in Russia. Although these figures seem large, they are tiny compared with the diameter of the Earth. The Earth's diameter is about 12 800 km. That's more than one thousand times the deepest hole ever drilled!

The Earth is made up of layers that formed many millions of years ago, early in the history of our planet. Heavy matter sank to the centre of the Earth while lighter material floated on top. This produced a structure consisting of a dense **core**, surrounded by the **mantle**. Outside the mantle there is a thin layer called the **crust**.

The uppermost part of the mantle and the crust make up the Earth's **lithosphere**.

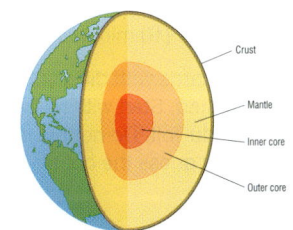

Figure 1 The structure of the Earth

We call the outer layer of the Earth the crust. This layer is very thin compared to the diameter of the Earth (thinner than the outer layer of a football!). Its thickness can vary from as thin as 5 km under the oceans to as much as 70 km under the continents.

Underneath the crust is the mantle. This layer is much, much thicker than the crust – nearly 3000 km. The mantle behaves like a solid, but it can flow in parts very slowly.

Finally, inside the mantle lies the Earth's core. This is about half the radius of the Earth, and is made of a mixture of nickel and iron. The core is actually two layers. The outer core is a liquid, while the inner core is solid.

a) What is the outer layer of the Earth called?
b) What is the next layer of the Earth called?
c) How many parts make up the Earth's core?

How do we know the structure inside the Earth if we have never seen it? Scientists use evidence from earthquakes. Following an earthquake, seismic waves travel through the Earth. The way in which seismic waves travel through the Earth is affected by the structure of the Earth. By observing how seismic waves travel, scientists have built up the detailed picture of the inside of the Earth described here.

Also, by making careful measurements, physicists have been able to measure the mass of the Earth, and to calculate its density. The density of the Earth as a whole is much greater than the density of the rocks found in the crust. This suggests that the centre of the Earth must be made from a different material to the crust. This material must have a much greater density than the material that makes up the crust.

Crust	Mantle	Core
Averages: about 6 km under the oceans about 35 km under continental areas	Starts underneath crust and continues to about 3000 km below Earth's surface. Behaves like a solid, but is able to flow very slowly	Radius of about 3500 km Made of nickel and iron Outer core is liquid, inner core is solid

At one time scientists thought that features like mountain ranges on the surface of the Earth were caused by the crust shrinking as the early molten Earth cooled down. They thought of it rather like the skin on the surface of a bowl of custard shrinks then wrinkles as the custard cools down.

However, scientists now have a better explanation for the features on the Earth's surface, as we shall see later in this chapter.

Figure 2 All of the minerals that we depend on in our lives – iron, aluminium and copper, for example, as well as oil and gas – come from the thin crust of the Earth

FOUL FACTS
The temperature at the centre of the Earth is between 5000°C and 7000°C – enough to burn a person to a crisp in a fraction of a second!

SUMMARY QUESTIONS

1. Copy and complete using the words below:
   core   crust   mantle   slowly   solid   thin
   The structure of the Earth consists of three layers – the ...., the .... and the .... The outer layer of the Earth is very .... compared to its diameter. The layer below this is .... but can flow in parts very ....

2. Why do some people think that the mantle is best described as a 'very thick syrupy liquid'?

3. Why do scientists think that the core of the Earth is made of much denser material than the crust?

KEY POINTS
1. The Earth consists of a series of layers.
2. Scientists originally thought that the features on the Earth's surface were caused as the crust cooled and shrank.

SUMMARY ANSWERS

1. Crust, mantle, core, thin, solid, slowly.
2. It can flow, but only very slowly.
3. Because the density of the Earth as a whole is greater than the density of the crust and mantle.

DID YOU KNOW?

The largest geological feature that can be seen from space is a sedimentary basin. The 50 km diameter basin is in the Sahara desert and has been eroded, but still can be seen and was discovered in 1965 during the *Gemini IV* mission.

KEY POINTS

Ask the students to choose actions for the key terms, e.g. Earth, layer(s), crust, features, cooled. Then ask the students in small groups to read and 'act out' the key points.

CHEMISTRY **THE CHANGING WORLD**

C1b 6.2 The restless Earth

LEARNING OBJECTIVES

Students should learn:
- What tectonic plates are.
- Why tectonic plates move.
- That earthquakes and volcanic eruptions are difficult to predict.

LEARNING OUTCOMES

Most students should be able to:
- State that the outer layer of the Earth is made up of tectonic plates.
- List the reasons to support plate tectonics as a theory.
- State why the tectonic plates move.
- List what happens at plate boundaries.

Some students should also be able to:
- Explain how convection currents cause the plates to move.
- Explain why Wegener's ideas on continental drift were not generally accepted in his time.
- Explain why earthquake and volcano activity is difficult to predict.

Teaching suggestions

- **Learning styles**
  Kinaesthetic: Completing the experiment to show convection currents.
  Visual: Looking at a lava lamp and relating this to the lesson.
  Auditory: Listening to presentations.
  Interpersonal: Interacting with other students during group activities.

- **ICT link-up.** The Internet could be used to show news reports and videos of earthquakes, volcanoes and tsunamis. Students' work could be scanned and displayed on the school web site.

- **Homework**
  - Find out by how much the Atlantic Ocean is increasing each year and why. [About 10 cm per annum due to sea floor spreading.]
  - Students could research the job of a seismologist and find out what their 'tools of the trade' are.

SPECIFICATION LINK-UP   C1b.11.6

- *The Earth's crust and upper part of the mantle are cracked into a number of large pieces (tectonic plates). Convection currents with the Earth's mantle, driven by heat released by natural radioactive processes, cause the plates to move at relative speeds of a few centimetres per year.*
- *The movements can be sudden and disastrous. Earthquakes and/or volcanic eruptions occur at the boundaries between tectonic plates.*

Students should use their skills, knowledge and understanding of 'How Science Works':
- *to explain why the theory of crustal movement (continental drift) was not generally accepted for many years after it was proposed*
- *to explain why scientists cannot accurately predict when earthquakes and volcanic eruptions will occur.*

Lesson structure

STARTER

Pictionary – Ask for five volunteers. They are each given a key word (crust, lithosphere, mantle, core, Earth). They should draw a picture: no noise, symbols, numbers or text are allowed; the image should explain to the class their key word. The first student in the remainder of the class to guess the word (hand up, or write the word on small whiteboards and hold up) could win a prize. (10 minutes)

Card sort – Give the students a pack of cards with different theories about how the features on the Earth's surface were created. Start with religious viewpoints, e.g. God created them, and finish with Alexander du Toit. Do not put dates onto the cards. Ask the students to sort them into date order, and guess the dates. Feedback to the class with questions and answers. (15 minutes)

MAIN

- Students should have an appreciation of how theories were developed and others disproved. Ask students to imagine that they are Wegener and that they are going to attend an international conference for scientists. They are to have a 'slot' to explain his new theory and explain why previous theories were incorrect. Students should prepare a presentation that is about 5 minutes long. If the class is a large group, then the students could work in groups. (This relates to 'How Science Works' – developing theories.)

- The tectonic plates move on convection currents. These should have been studied in KS3. However, students may benefit from seeing the convection current demonstration. Students could be encouraged to draw a diagram of the experiment and label the demonstration labels (e.g. beaker, potassium manganate(VII), convection current, Bunsen burner) in blue. Then ask students to relate this to the Earth, and label these in red (e.g. mantle, magma, heat spot, tectonic plates).

- This can be completed as a demonstration or a class practical. Pieces from a polystyrene tile can be floated in larger beakers to model the tectonic plate movement. Discuss the limitations of this model.

- Students need to know what happens at plate boundaries and the effects of natural disasters. This topic is excellent to show visual images of plate boundaries, and the students are often very enthralled by it. Split the class into three groups: one group researches volcanoes, another earthquakes and the third looks at prediction and prevention.

- Each group should be supplied with video footage of natural disasters caused by earthquakes and volcanoes. For examples see Volcano World at www.volcano.und.nodak.edu. Students then use this information, coupled with textbooks, to write a revision page for an imaginary textbook. The pages could be collected and selected ones photocopied and given to each student.

Practical support

Convection currents

Equipment and materials required

Potassium manganate crystals (oxidising agent and harmful), tweezers, large glass beaker, cold water, Bunsen burner and safety equipment, tripod and gauze, eye protection.

Details

Fill the beaker about 75% with cold water and put onto a tripod. With a set of tweezers, add no more than three crystals to the bottom of the beaker. Put the Bunsen burner under the beaker at the point where the crystal is and heat on the blue flame. The convection current should become visible.

Safety: Potassium manganate(VII) – see CLEAPSS Hazcard 56. Handle carefully as crystals will stain hands and clothing.

Oils, Earth and atmosphere

DID YOU KNOW?

The earliest evidence for plate tectonics was discovered in 2002 by US/Chinese scientists. They found rocks, near the Great Wall of China, that show plates were moving 2.5 billion years ago – this is about 500 million years earlier than scientists first thought.

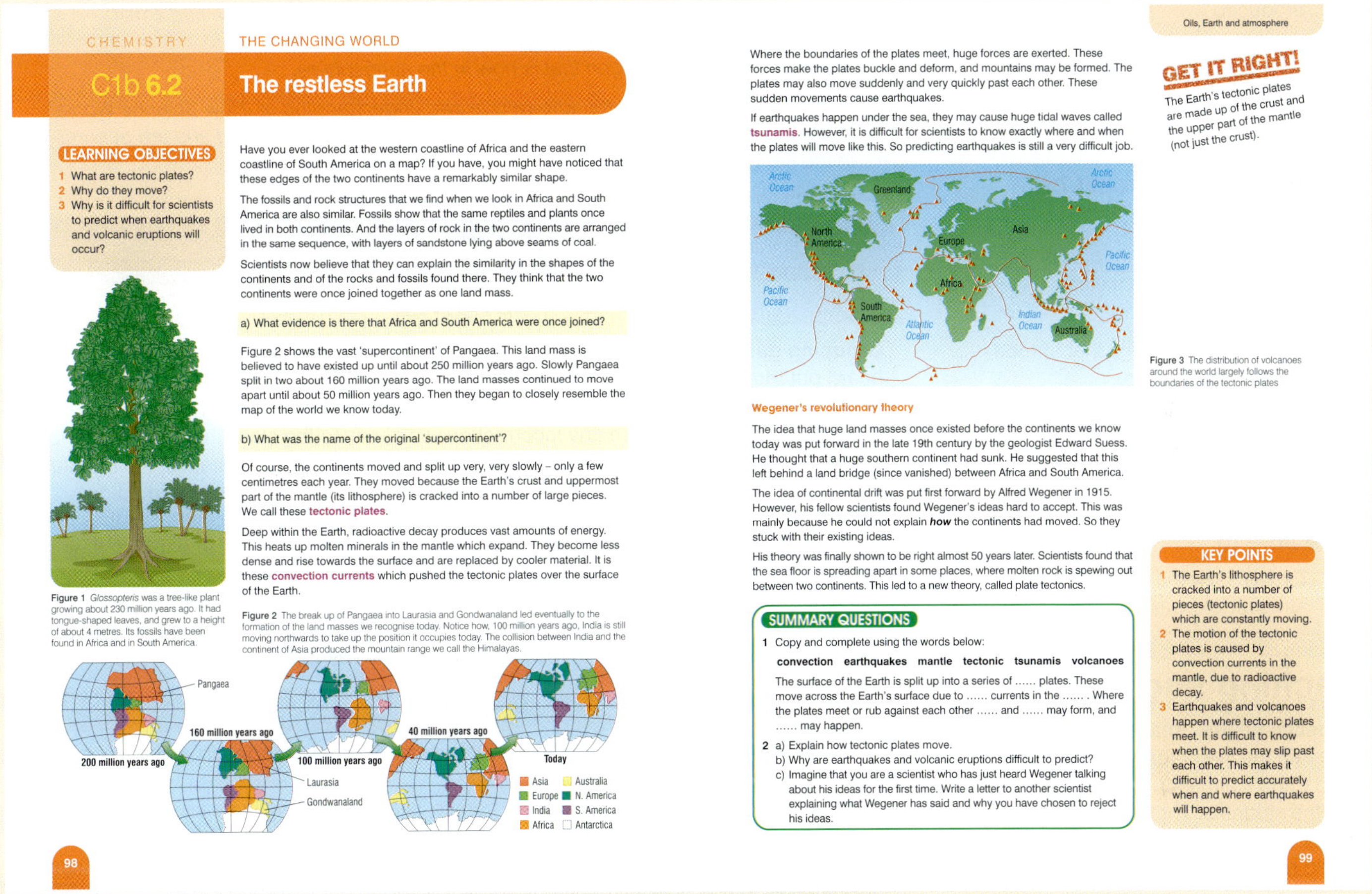

CHEMISTRY — THE CHANGING WORLD

C1b 6.2 The restless Earth

LEARNING OBJECTIVES
1. What are tectonic plates?
2. Why do they move?
3. Why is it difficult for scientists to predict when earthquakes and volcanic eruptions will occur?

Have you ever looked at the western coastline of Africa and the eastern coastline of South America on a map? If you have, you might have noticed that these edges of the two continents have a remarkably similar shape.

The fossils and rock structures that we find when we look in Africa and South America are also similar. Fossils show that the same reptiles and plants once lived in both continents. And the layers of rock in the two continents are arranged in the same sequence, with layers of sandstone lying above seams of coal.

Scientists now believe that they can explain the similarity in the shapes of the continents and of the rocks and fossils found there. They think that the two continents were once joined together as one land mass.

a) What evidence is there that Africa and South America were once joined?

Figure 2 shows the vast 'supercontinent' of Pangaea. This land mass is believed to have existed up until about 250 million years ago. Slowly Pangaea split in two about 160 million years ago. The land masses continued to move apart until about 50 million years ago. Then they began to closely resemble the map of the world we know today.

b) What was the name of the original 'supercontinent'?

Of course, the continents moved and split up very, very slowly – only a few centimetres each year. They moved because the Earth's crust and uppermost part of the mantle (its lithosphere) is cracked into a number of large pieces. We call these **tectonic plates**.

Deep within the Earth, radioactive decay produces vast amounts of energy. This heats up molten minerals in the mantle which expand. They become less dense and rise towards the surface and are replaced by cooler material. It is these **convection currents** which pushed the tectonic plates over the surface of the Earth.

Figure 1 Glossopteris was a tree-like plant growing about 230 million years ago. It had tongue-shaped leaves, and grew to a height of about 4 metres. Its fossils have been found in Africa and in South America.

Figure 2 The break up of Pangaea into Laurasia and Gondwanaland led eventually to the formation of the land masses we recognise today. Notice how, 100 million years ago, India is still moving northwards to take up the position it occupies today. The collision between India and the continent of Asia produced the mountain range we call the Himalayas.

Where the boundaries of the plates meet, huge forces are exerted. These forces make the plates buckle and deform, and mountains may be formed. The plates may also move suddenly and very quickly past each other. These sudden movements cause earthquakes.

If earthquakes happen under the sea, they may cause huge tidal waves called **tsunamis**. However, it is difficult for scientists to know exactly where and when the plates will move like this. So predicting earthquakes is still a very difficult job.

Figure 3 The distribution of volcanoes around the world largely follows the boundaries of the tectonic plates.

Wegener's revolutionary theory

The idea that huge land masses once existed before the continents we know today was put forward in the late 19th century by the geologist Edward Suess. He thought that a huge southern continent had sunk. He suggested that this left behind a land bridge (since vanished) between Africa and South America.

The idea of continental drift was put first forward by Alfred Wegener in 1915. However, his fellow scientists found Wegener's ideas hard to accept. This was mainly because he could not explain *how* the continents had moved. So they stuck with their existing ideas.

His theory was finally shown to be right almost 50 years later. Scientists found that the sea floor is spreading apart in some places, where molten rock is spewing out between two continents. This led to a new theory, called plate tectonics.

SUMMARY QUESTIONS

1. Copy and complete using the words below:

   convection   earthquakes   mantle   tectonic   tsunamis   volcanoes

   The surface of the Earth is split up into a series of …… plates. These move across the Earth's surface due to …… currents in the …… . Where the plates meet or rub against each other …… and …… may form, and …… may happen.

2. a) Explain how tectonic plates move.
   b) Why are earthquakes and volcanic eruptions difficult to predict?
   c) Imagine that you are a scientist who has just heard Wegener talking about his ideas for the first time. Write a letter to another scientist explaining what Wegener has said and why you have chosen to reject his ideas.

GET IT RIGHT!

The Earth's tectonic plates are made up of the crust and the upper part of the mantle (not just the crust).

KEY POINTS

1. The Earth's lithosphere is cracked into a number of pieces (tectonic plates) which are constantly moving.
2. The motion of the tectonic plates is caused by convection currents in the mantle, due to radioactive decay.
3. Earthquakes and volcanoes happen where tectonic plates meet. It is difficult to know when the plates may slip past each other. This makes it difficult to predict accurately when and where earthquakes will happen.

SUMMARY ANSWERS

1. Tectonic, convection, mantle, volcanoes, earthquakes, tsunamis.

2. a) Convection currents, caused by heat from natural radioactive processes, form in the mantle beneath the plates.
   b) Although we know where plate boundaries lie, we cannot tell exactly when and where the forces building up will cause the sudden movement that produces an earthquake or when the magma building up in a volcano will cause an explosive eruption
   c) Letter. [Mark based on ideas from description of Wegener's ideas in the spread.]

PLENARIES

Lava lamps – Set up a lava lamp (this may need to be done at least 30 minutes before the end of the lesson). Ask the students to look at the lava lamp and relate it to the lesson. Some students should make the connection with the name 'lava'. Hopefully, most students will notice that the wax moves in a convection current, which is the same process that we use to explain how tectonic plates move. (5 minutes)

Presentations – Students could show their presentations to the class. (20 minutes)

Definitions – Ask students to define the key terms used in the lesson e.g. plate, plate tectonics, Pangaea, convection currents. (5 minutes)

ACTIVITY & EXTENSION

- Ask the students to think of questions or arguments that Wegener could have been facing from the scientific community. A volunteer or group of volunteers could pretend to be Wegener, then other students could pose their questions/arguments for Wegener and his team to answer.

Answers to in-text questions

a) The similar shapes of their coastlines, similar rock types, similar fossils.

b) Pangaea.

KEY POINTS

Turn the key points to a bullet point list of vital information.

CHEMISTRY — THE CHANGING WORLD

C1b 6.3 The Earth's atmosphere in the past

LEARNING OBJECTIVES

Students should learn:

- What the Earth's atmosphere was like in the past.
- How the mixture of gases in the Earth's atmosphere was produced.
- How oxygen was released into the Earth's atmosphere.

LEARNING OUTCOMES

Most students should be able to:

- Name the gases that probably made up the Earth's early atmosphere.
- List the major events that formed today's atmosphere.
- State how oxygen entered the Earth's atmosphere.

Some students should also be able to:

- Explain how the Earth and its atmosphere was formed.

Teaching suggestions

- **Special needs.** Images and text to explain the five stages of development of the Earth's atmosphere could be given to the students. They could then cut and stick them into the appropriate cartoon strip boxes.

- **Learning styles**

  Kinaesthetic: Ordering the statements from the specification.

  Visual: Creating a cartoon strip to show atmospheric development.

  Auditory: Listening to other students' sketches.

  Interpersonal: Working in a group to create a sketch.

  Intrapersonal: Making a personal list of gases.

- **Homework.** Find some examples of organisms that probably produced the first oxygen. Students could be encouraged to find images, not just names.

- **ICT link-up.** A background for each part of the atmosphere's development could be made for the students if a data projector is available. Get images of the different stages from the Internet and put one per page in PowerPoint®, then project behind the students while they perform their sketch.

SPECIFICATION LINK-UP C1b.11.6

- During the first billion years of the Earth's existence there was intense volcanic activity. The activity released the gases that formed the early atmosphere and water vapour that condensed to form the oceans.
- Some theories suggest that during this period the Earth's atmosphere was mainly carbon dioxide and there would have been little or no oxygen gas (like the atmosphere of Mars and Venus today). There may also have been water vapour, and small proportions of methane and ammonia.
- Plants produced the oxygen that is now in the atmosphere.

Students should use their skills, knowledge and understanding of 'How Science Works':
- to explain and evaluate theories of the changes that have occurred and are occurring in the Earth's atmosphere.

Lesson structure

STARTER

Grouping gases – Ask students to list as many gases as they can think of. Then on the board put three titles: 'element, compound and mixture'. Then encourage each student to go to the board and add a gas from their list under the correct column heading. Look at the board, and if there are any incorrect answers, say to the class there are 'x' number of mistakes. Then ask the students to see if they can pick out the mistakes. (10 minutes)

Pass it on – Give each student a piece of paper with the same question printed on: 'Where does oxygen come from?' On the piece of paper the first student starts the answer, and is timed for 30 seconds. Then ask the students to pass the paper to their left (even if they are mid-sentence) and give the next student 1 minute, then pass the paper again and give the final student 1.5 minutes. Each student should read the answer so far, change anything that they feel is incorrect and add further information if they think they can. Then pick a few students to read their papers. (10 minutes)

MAIN

- Students need to have an idea of how the atmosphere developed from the newly formed Earth to the present day.
- Give students a cartoon strip with five frames, with space to draw a picture and write notes. Encourage students to use a textbook to detail five stages in the development of the atmosphere. They should draw an image and write text to explain the atmosphere's composition and how it compares to other planets in our current solar system.
- Separate the class into groups. Ask the groups to imagine that they are astronauts who had landed on the planet in the different stages of atmospheric development. Ask them to design a sketch or role-play to describe the surroundings.
- Not all students need be involved in the acting side, but all students should collect research about the development. This activity could encourage students to manage their own time and group dynamics.
- The activity could include a predictive stage in which students consider the atmosphere in five hundred years time.
- Alternatively, each student could be given a role by the teacher e.g. chair person, resource manager, etc., and encourage the students to stick to their role, allowing them to experience a different role in a group compared to their preferred choice.

PLENARIES

Ordering – Copy out the specification link-up, and cut out each sentence separately. Ask the students to arrange the information into chronological order in small groups. (15 minutes)

Chemical equations – Ask students to copy out the word equation for photosynthesis. Then set them the task of completing the balanced symbol equation. Some students may need the formulae put on the board. Then they could be asked why this is an important equation. [It was how oxygen came to be part of the Earth's atmosphere.] (5 minutes)

Sketch – Groups of students could act out their sketch. The rest of the class comment on misconceptions in the sketch and then vote on the best, and a prize could be awarded. (15 minutes)

ACTIVITY & EXTENSION IDEAS

- Students could display the composition of the Earth's atmosphere at different stages in the form of charts and graphs.
- Students could contrast the Earth's atmospheric development with that of other planets. Venus would be a good example, as some scientists believe that it has had a runaway greenhouse effect that has caused its current atmosphere. (This links to the greenhouse effect, featured previously in C1a.)
- A PhotoPLUS, C1b 6.3 'Earth's atmosphere', is available on the GCSE Chemistry CD ROM for individuals, groups or the whole class to use.

CHEMISTRY
THE CHANGING WORLD

C1b 6.3 The Earth's atmosphere in the past

LEARNING OBJECTIVES
1. What was the Earth's atmosphere like in the past?
2. How were the gases in the Earth's atmosphere produced?
3. How was oxygen produced?

Scientists think that the Earth was formed about 4.5 billion years ago. To begin with it was a molten ball of rock and minerals. For its first billion years it was a very violent place. The Earth's surface was covered with volcanoes belching fire and smoke into the atmosphere.

Figure 1 Volcanoes moved chemicals from inside the Earth to the surface and the newly forming atmosphere

The volcanoes released carbon dioxide, water vapour and nitrogen gas, which formed the early atmosphere. Water vapour in the atmosphere condensed as the Earth gradually cooled down, and fell as rain. This collected to form the first oceans.

Comets also brought water to the Earth. As icy comets rained down on the surface of the Earth they melted, adding to the water supplies. Even today many thousands of tonnes of water fall onto the surface of the Earth from space every year.

So as the Earth began to stabilise, the early atmosphere was probably mainly carbon dioxide, with some water vapour, nitrogen and traces of methane and ammonia. There was very little or no oxygen. This is very like the atmospheres which we know exist today on the planets Mars and Venus.

Figure 2 The surface of one of Jupiter's moons called Io, with its small atmosphere and active volcanoes. This photograph probably gives us a reasonable glimpse of what our own Earth was like billions of years ago.

a) What was the main gas in the Earth's early atmosphere?
b) How much oxygen was there in the Earth's early atmosphere?

After the initial violent years of the history of the Earth, the atmosphere remained relatively stable. That's until life first appeared on Earth.

Scientists think that life on Earth began about 3.4 billion years ago, when simple organisms like bacteria appeared. These could make food for themselves, using the breakdown of other chemicals as a source of energy.

Later, bacteria and other simple organisms such as algae evolved. They could use the energy of the Sun to make their own food by photosynthesis, and oxygen was produced as a waste product.

By two billion years ago the levels of oxygen were rising steadily as algae and bacteria filled the seas. More and more plants evolved, all of them also photosynthesising, removing carbon dioxide and making oxygen.

$$\text{carbon dioxide} + \text{water} \xrightarrow{\text{(energy from sunlight)}} \text{sugar} + \text{oxygen}$$

As plants evolved and successfully colonised most of the surface of the Earth, the atmosphere became richer and richer in oxygen. Now it was possible for animals to evolve. These animals could not make their own food and needed oxygen to respire.

On the other hand, many of the earliest living microorganisms could not tolerate oxygen (because they had evolved without it). They largely died out, as there were fewer and fewer places where they could live.

Figure 3 Some of the first photosynthesising bacteria probably lived in colonies like these stromatolites. They grew in water and released oxygen into the early atmosphere.

Figure 4 Bacteria such as these not only do not need oxygen – they die if they are exposed to it. But they can survive and breed in rotting tissue and other places where there is no oxygen.

SUMMARY QUESTIONS

1 Copy and complete using the words below:

    carbon dioxide   methane   oxygen   volcanoes   water

The Earth's early atmosphere probably consisted mainly of the gas ……… ……… . There could also have been ……… vapour and nitrogen, plus small amounts of ……… and ammonia. These gases were released by ……… as they erupted. Plants removed carbon dioxide from the atmosphere and produced ……… .

2 How was the Earth's early atmosphere formed?

3 Why was there no life on Earth for several billion years?

4 Draw a chart that explains the early development of the Earth's atmosphere.

DID YOU KNOW…
…that scientists have reconstructed what they think the atmosphere must have been like based on evidence from gas bubbles trapped in rocks and from the atmospheres of other planets in the Solar System?

KEY POINTS
1 The Earth's early atmosphere was formed by volcanic activity.
2 It probably consisted mainly of carbon dioxide. There may also have been water vapour together with traces of methane and ammonia.
3 As plants colonised the Earth, the levels of oxygen in the atmosphere rose.

SUMMARY ANSWERS

1 Carbon dioxide, water, methane, volcanoes, oxygen.

2 From gases emitted by volcanoes.

3 The temperature was too high.

4 Student chart showing development from early volcanic atmosphere to the first plant-produced oxygen and the removal of carbon dioxide during photosynthesis.

Answers to in-text questions

a) Carbon dioxide.
b) Very little or none.

DID YOU KNOW?

The oldest volcanic rock known is nearly 4 billion years old and was found in Canada.

KEY POINTS

Give students a pyramid. They should put the main idea at the top (Earth's atmosphere), and draw a line underneath it. Then they write the main points and draw a line. This continues until all the information has been summarised.

CHEMISTRY   THE CHANGING WORLD

C1b 6.4 Gases in the atmosphere

LEARNING OBJECTIVES

Students should learn:

- The main gases in the current atmosphere.
- The percentage composition of the current atmosphere.
- About noble gases and their uses.

LEARNING OUTCOMES

Most students should be able to:

- List the main gases in the atmosphere and the approximate percentage composition of the atmosphere.
- List the noble gases and state some uses.

Some students should also be able to:

- Explain how ammonia and methane were probably removed from the Earth's atmosphere.
- Give examples of noble gases and explain some specific uses.

Teaching suggestions

- **Special needs.** The class could write the story about the changing Earth's atmosphere together and the learning support assistant could act as scribe using the board. Alternatively, the story could be written into discrete sentences and the students could order them and stick them into their book.

- **Learning styles**
  Visual: Creating a spider diagram.
  Auditory: Listening to other students explaining their key term.
  Interpersonal: Working as a group on a story.
  Intrapersonal: Breaking the code to reveal the mystery sentence.

- **Homework.** Ask students to find out what scientists predict will happen to the composition of the Earth's atmosphere. It is important that the students list their sources. Then next lesson the information can be compared and consider whether bias has crept into the evidence gathered. (This relates to 'How Science Works' – societal aspects.)

- **ICT link-up.** Students could draw their pie chart using Excel.

SPECIFICATION LINK-UP   C1b.11.6

- For 200 million years the properties of different gases in the atmosphere have been much the same as they are today:
  – About four-fifths (80%) nitrogen   – About one-fifth (20%) oxygen
  – Small proportions of various other gases, including carbon dioxide, water vapour and noble gases.
- The noble gases are in Group 0 of the periodic table. They are all chemically unreactive gases and are used in filament lamps and electric discharge tubes. Helium is much less dense than air and is used in balloons.

Students should use their skills, knowledge and understanding of 'How Science Works':
- to explain and evaluate theories of the changes that have occurred and are occurring in the Earth's atmosphere.

Lesson structure

STARTER

Pie chart – Ask the students to find the percentage of each gas in the current atmosphere. Encourage the students to represent this information as a pie chart. (15 minutes)

Code breaker – Ask students to decipher the following code:

1, 9, 18, 9, 19, 1, 13, 9, 24, 20, 21, 18, 5, 15, 6, 7, 1, 19, 5, 19

The key to the code is that each letter is represented by its position in the alphabet, e.g. A=1, Z=26. [Air is a mixture of gases.] (10 minutes)

Reflection – Give the students an A4 sheet of paper and ask them to make three columns. The first should be headed with 'what I already know', then 'what I want to know' and finally 'what I know now'. Ask the students to consider the title of the double page spread and complete the first two columns with bullet points of information. (10 minutes)

MAIN

- Students may not know what a noble gas 'looks' like. Get four gas jars, and seal them with tape. Label them as the first four noble gases. Put these out onto the tables and ask the students to describe their chemical.
- Then bring in a helium balloon and ask the students what it contains, and list reasons why the gas is suitable for filling balloons [less dense than air, cheap, inert].
- Then show students a filament bulb and ask them to think about what is inside it and why it is fit for that purpose [stops the tungsten reacting with oxygen when it gets hot]. Students could then complete a spider diagram to explain what noble gases are, their uses and properties.
- The percentage composition of gases in the Earth's atmosphere has changed over time, but has remained relatively static in the last 200 million years. Ask students to imagine that they are Earth and to write a creative story about how its 'clothes', i.e. atmosphere, has changed and why. Students could be encouraged to share ideas and storyboards to create a group story.
- Alternatively, the class could be split into three. One group writes the beginning of the story, another the middle and the final one writes the end. In order to complete this last suggestion, a link sentence from each section needs to be provided to the groups so they know where/how to start and/or finish their part of the story.

PLENARIES

Guess what – Ask the students to break off into pairs. Give each pair a pack of cards with separate key words per card, e.g. oxygen, nitrogen, air, gas, carbon dioxide, photosynthesis, methane, ammonia, Earth, noble gas, helium, argon. The students should take it in turns to pick a card and look at the key term. They should explain it to their partner without using the key word and the other student should guess the word. Play one pair against another. The pair with the most correct guesses in a set time wins! (5–10 minutes)

Reflection part 2 – Ask the students to return to their A4 table. Ask them to add information to the last column, 'what I now know', that isn't included in the middle column. They should also correct any misconceptions from the middle column and ask for help if they have not found out some information that they wanted. (10 minutes)

ACTIVITY & EXTENSION

- Encourage students to think about other examples of noble gases and their uses e.g. Kr for lasers.
- Students could compare the fractional distillation of crude oil to the fractional distillation of liquid air. A video of this process is available from *Industrial Chemistry* (RSC).

NEXT TIME YOU...

Noble gases are also used in packaging of some foods, e.g. salads to keep them fresh for longer.

Answers to in-text questions

a) Into carbonate rocks.
b) Oxygen.

CHEMISTRY — THE CHANGING WORLD

C1b 6.4 Gases in the atmosphere

LEARNING OBJECTIVES

1. What are the main gases in the atmosphere?
2. What are their relative proportions?
3. What are the noble gases and why are they useful?

We think that the early atmosphere of the Earth contained a great deal of carbon dioxide. Yet the modern atmosphere of the Earth has only around 0.04% of this gas. Where has it all gone? The answer is mostly into living organisms and into materials formed from living organisms.

Carbon dioxide is taken up by plants during photosynthesis and the carbon can end up in new plant material. Then animals eat the plants and the carbon is transferred to the animal tissues, including bones, teeth and shells.

Over millions of years the dead bodies of huge numbers of these living organisms built up at the bottom of vast oceans. Eventually they formed sedimentary carbonate rocks like limestone.

Some of these living things were crushed by movements of the Earth and heated within the crust. They formed fossil fuels such as coal and oil. In this way much of the carbon from carbon dioxide in the ancient atmosphere became locked up within the Earth's crust.

a) Where has most of the carbon dioxide in the Earth's early atmosphere gone?

Carbon dioxide also dissolved in the oceans. It reacted and made insoluble carbonate compounds. These fell to the sea-bed and helped to form carbonate rocks.

At the same time, the ammonia and methane, from the Earth's early atmosphere, reacted with the oxygen formed by the plants. This got rid of these poisonous gases and increased the nitrogen and carbon dioxide levels:

$$CH_4 + 2O_2 \rightarrow CO_2 + 2H_2O$$
$$4NH_3 + 3O_2 \rightarrow 2N_2 + 6H_2O$$

By 200 million years ago the proportions of the different gases in the Earth's atmosphere were much the same as they are today.

Look at the pie chart in Figure 2.

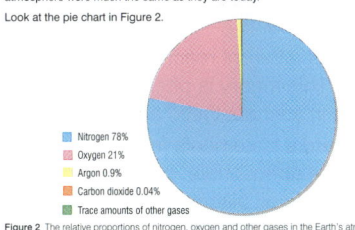

Figure 1 There is clear evidence in carbonate rocks of the organisms which lived millions of years ago, now preserved with their ancient carbon in the structure of our rocks

Figure 2 The relative proportions of nitrogen, oxygen and other gases in the Earth's atmosphere
- Nitrogen 78%
- Oxygen 21%
- Argon 0.9%
- Carbon dioxide 0.04%
- Trace amounts of other gases

b) What gas did plants produce that changed the Earth's atmosphere?

The noble gases

The Earth's atmosphere contains tiny amounts of a group of gases that we call the **noble gases**. They are all found in Group 0 of the periodic table.

Helium, neon and argon, along with krypton, xenon and radon are the least reactive elements known. It is very difficult to make them react with any other elements. They don't even react with themselves to form molecules. They exist as single atoms. We say that they are monatomic.

Because the noble gases are very unreactive, we cannot use them to make useful materials. Instead, we use them in situations where they are useful because of their extreme lack of reactivity.

Uses of the noble gases

Helium is used in airships and in party balloons. Its low density means that balloons filled with the gas float in air. It is also safer than the only alternative gas, hydrogen, because its low reactivity means that it does not catch fire. We also use it with oxygen as a breathing mixture for deep-sea divers. The mixture reduces their chances of suffering from the 'bends'.

Figure 3 The noble gases are all found in Group 0 of the periodic table

We use **neon** in electrical discharge tubes – better known as **neon lights**. When we pass an electrical current through the neon gas it gives out a bright light. Neon lights are familiar as street lighting and in advertising.

We use **argon** in a different type of lighting – the everyday light bulb (or filament lamp). The argon provides an inert atmosphere inside the bulb. When the electric current passes through the metal filament, the metal becomes white hot. If any oxygen was inside the bulb, it would react with the hot metal. However, no chemical reaction takes place between the metal filament and argon gas. This stops the filament from burning away and makes light bulbs last longer.

Figure 4 These brightly coloured balloons are filled with helium, which makes them float upwards through the air

SUMMARY QUESTIONS

1. Copy and complete the table showing the proportion of gases in the Earth's atmosphere today.

nitrogen	oxygen	argon	carbon dioxide	other gases
%	%	%	%	%

2. How did the evolution of plants change the Earth's atmosphere?
3. a) Explain how ammonia and methane were probably removed from the Earth's atmosphere.
   b) Find out how the noble gases are used and make a list that explains at least one use of each gas.

KEY POINTS

1. The main gases in the Earth's atmosphere are oxygen and nitrogen.
2. About four-fifths (80%) of the atmosphere is nitrogen, and one-fifth (20%) is oxygen.
3. The noble gases are unreactive gases found in Group 0 of the periodic table. Their lack of reactivity makes them useful in many ways.

SUMMARY ANSWERS

1

nitrogen	oxygen	argon	carbon dioxide	other gases
78%	21%	0.9%	0.04%	trace

2 They produced oxygen. Not only was this available for life, it also reacted with ammonia and methane, removing these from the atmosphere to produce nitrogen, water and carbon dioxide.

3 a) Ammonia and methane probably reacted with oxygen produced by plants.
e.g. $CH_4 + 2O_2 \rightarrow CO_2 + 2H_2O$
$4NH_3 + 3O_2 \rightarrow 2N_2 + 6H_2O$

b) He – balloons, airships, diving gases for deep diving.
Ne – glowing advertising signs.
Ar – filament lamps, welding.
Kr – fluorescent lamps, flash bulbs, lasers.
Xe – fluorescent lamps, flash bulbs, lasers.
Rn – cancer treatment.

KEY POINTS

Ask students to generate questions for which each key point is the answer. Then cut up each question and give them to another student. Their task is to match the question with the key point. The pairs then feed back to each other about where their sorting was correct and about how the question was phrased.

CHEMISTRY · THE CHANGING WORLD

C1b 6.5 The carbon cycle

LEARNING OBJECTIVES

Students should learn that:
- Carbon moves in and out of the atmosphere.
- The amount of carbon dioxide is increasing in the atmosphere.

LEARNING OUTCOMES

Most students should be able to:
- Describe the main parts of the carbon cycle.
- State that burning fossil fuels increases the amount of carbon dioxide in the atmosphere.

Some students should also be able to:
- Explain why there is a general trend that the amount of carbon dioxide in the air is increasing.

Teaching suggestions

- **Special needs.** Key words could be supplied on the board to help students label the carbon cycle. Alternatively, the exercise could be turned into a cut and stick activity.
- **Learning styles**
  Kinaesthetic: Completing a range of experiments to find out the properties of carbon dioxide.
  Visual: Labelling the carbon cycle.
  Auditory: Listening to statements from other students about the carbon cycle.
  Interpersonal: Working as a class to make a carbon cycle model.
  Intrapersonal: Appreciating the mechanism of carbon recycling on Earth.
- **Homework.** List the ways that humans are changing the composition of carbon dioxide in the atmosphere.
- **ICT link-up.** The semi-finished diagram of the carbon cycle could be projected using a data projector. Alternatively, the diagram could be put into specialist interactive whiteboard software with the labels at the bottom of the screen. Students can then drag the labels to the appropriate positions on the diagram.

SPECIFICATION LINK-UP   C1b.11.6

- *Most of the carbon from the carbon dioxide in the air gradually becomes locked up in the sedimentary rocks as carbonates and fossil fuels.*
- *Nowadays the release of carbon dioxide by burning of fossil fuels increases the level of carbon dioxide in the atmosphere.*

Students should use their skills, knowledge and understanding of 'How Science Works':
- to explain and evaluate theories of the changes that have occurred and are occurring in the Earth's atmosphere
- to explain and evaluate the effects of human activities on the atmosphere.

Lesson structure

STARTER

Describe – Supply carbon dioxide gas in a gas jar to each table. Ask the students to describe its physical appearance [colourless, transparent gas]. (5 minutes)

Demonstration – If solid carbon dioxide can be obtained, e.g. from a spare black carbon dioxide fire extinguisher, put it into water and dry ice will be created. Be careful not to handle the solid for too long or burns will be caused, but tweezers could be used to manipulate it. Students can then put their hands briefly into the water (as long as they do not touch the solid) and it will feel really cold. Ask the students to suggest what is happening [the solid carbon dioxide is boiling in the water]. (5 minutes)

Model – Ask students to make a model of a molecule of CO_2, given a molecular model kit. Describe the bonds holding the black carbon and red oxygen atoms together. (5 minutes)

MAIN

- The carbon cycle is a network of different reactions, which remove and add carbon out of or into the atmosphere. This theory is often represented in diagrammatic form, but it can also be represented in a kinaesthetic activity.
- Make laminated cards with different statements for sections of the carbon cycle, e.g. *on blue paper:* carbon dioxide in the atmosphere, fossil fuel, carbonate rocks, carbon in plants, carbon in animals (these are all places where carbon can be found); *on yellow paper:* combustion, photosynthesis, dissolved in oceans, chemical reactions, heating, decay, fossilisation, feeding, respiration (processes that involve carbon dioxide).
- Hole punch each card and put string around it, so that students can wear the labels. Take the students into a large space, e.g. a playground or hall, and give them a ball of string. Then make a web to show the carbon cycle, where the yellow students are joined by string, then the blue labels go and stand by the sections that represent their process. Some of the yellow labels, e.g. respiration, will need to hold more than one string.
- Students could then discuss which parts of the cycle humans are changing.
- All animals breathe out carbon dioxide gas, and students often talk about it, but rarely can they explain the physical and chemical properties of the gas. They could complete a series of experiments and note their observations; they then summarise the properties of this chemical.

PLENARIES

Agree? – Ask for a volunteer to stand in the centre of the classroom. They should say a statement about the content of the lesson (it could be correct or deliberately incorrect) e.g. 'carbon can be found in rocks'. The rest of the class decides how much they agree or not with this statement. The more they agree the closer they should stand to the person who spoke. Then ask a few students why they are positioned as they are and feedback whether the statement is correct. Ask all the students to sit down and for another volunteer to repeat the idea. (5–10 minutes)

PhotoPLUS – Show and discuss this resource from the GCSE Chemistry CD ROM. (10 minutes)

Practical support

The properties of carbon dioxide

Equipment and materials required
Lime water (irritant), straws, test tube, carbon dioxide filled balloon, bucket of water, sealed test tubes of carbon dioxide gas, Bunsen burner and safety equipment, splints, universal indicator solution, water, eye protection.

Details
Set up five stations each with a separate activity card to explain to students what to do. Students must wear eye protection.

Station 1: Students should blow gently through the straw into lime water and note their observations. Ask the students to explain the chemical reaction that is occurring (link back to the limestone cycle in C1a).

Station 2: Students should investigate the density of carbon dioxide. They should release the balloon in air (it will sink – more dense) and into water (float – less dense).

Station 3: Light a splint and put it into a test tube of carbon dioxide and observe.

Station 4: Students should blow through a straw into a test tube of diluted universal indicator solution and observe the colour change. Eye protection must be worn.

Answers to in-text questions

a) The carbon cycle.

b) Carbon dioxide is released as the rocks break down.

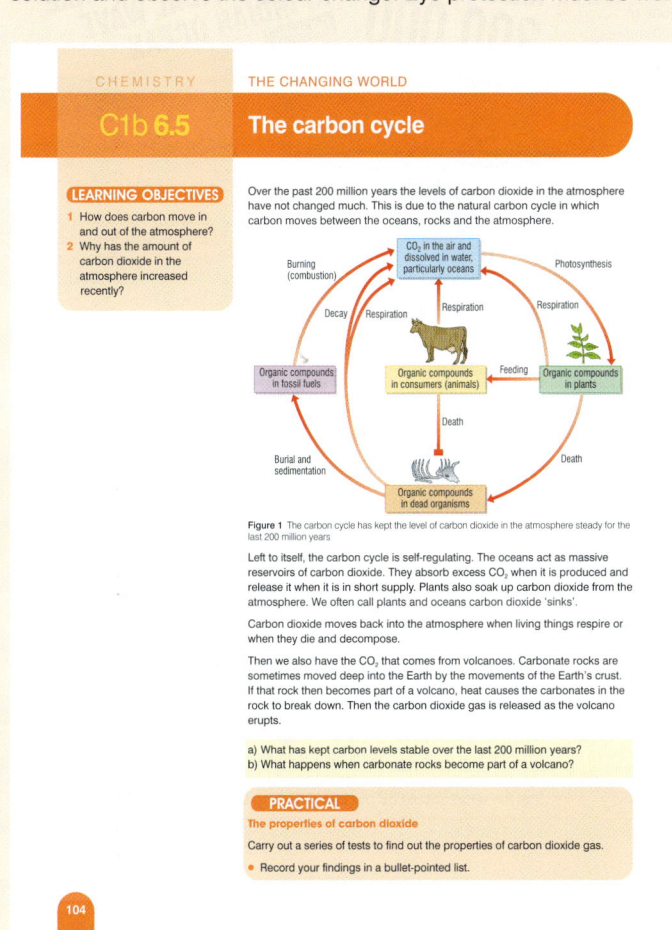

C1b 6.5 The carbon cycle

LEARNING OBJECTIVES
1. How does carbon move in and out of the atmosphere?
2. Why has the amount of carbon dioxide in the atmosphere increased recently?

Over the past 200 million years the levels of carbon dioxide in the atmosphere have not changed much. This is due to the natural carbon cycle in which carbon moves between the oceans, rocks and the atmosphere.

Figure 1 The carbon cycle has kept the level of carbon dioxide in the atmosphere steady for the last 200 million years

Left to itself, the carbon cycle is self-regulating. The oceans act as massive reservoirs of carbon dioxide. They absorb excess CO_2 when it is produced and release it when it is in short supply. Plants also soak up carbon dioxide from the atmosphere. We often call plants and oceans carbon dioxide 'sinks'.

Carbon dioxide moves back into the atmosphere when living things respire or when they die and decompose.

Then we also have the CO_2 that comes from volcanoes. Carbonate rocks are sometimes moved deep into the Earth's crust. If that rock then becomes part of a volcano, heat causes the carbonates in the rock to break down. Then the carbon dioxide gas is released as the volcano erupts.

a) What has kept carbon levels stable over the last 200 million years?
b) What happens when carbonate rocks become part of a volcano?

PRACTICAL
The properties of carbon dioxide
Carry out a series of tests to find out the properties of carbon dioxide gas.
- Record your findings in a bullet-pointed list.

The changing balance
Over the last fifty years or so we have increased the amount of carbon dioxide released into the atmosphere tremendously. We burn fossil fuels to make electricity, heat our homes and drive our cars. This has enormously increased the amount of carbon dioxide we produce.

There is no doubt that the levels of carbon dioxide in the atmosphere are increasing.

We can record annual changes in the levels of carbon dioxide which are due to seasonal differences in the plants. The variations within each year show how important plants are for removing CO_2 from the atmosphere. But the overall trend for the last 30 years has been ever upwards.

The balance between the carbon dioxide produced and the carbon dioxide absorbed by 'CO_2 sinks' is very important.

Think about what happens when we burn fossil fuels. Carbon, which has been locked up for hundreds of millions of years in the bodies of once-living animals, is released as carbon dioxide into the atmosphere. For example:

propane + oxygen → carbon dioxide + water
C_3H_8 + $5O_2$ → $3CO_2$ + $4H_2O$

As carbon dioxide levels in the atmosphere go up, so the reaction between carbon dioxide and sea water increases. This reaction makes insoluble carbonates (mainly calcium carbonate). These are deposited as sediment on the bottom of the ocean. It also produces soluble hydrogencarbonates – mainly calcium and magnesium – which simply remain dissolved in the sea water.

In this way the seas and oceans act as a buffer, absorbing excess carbon dioxide but releasing it if necessary. However this buffering system probably cannot cope with all the additional carbon dioxide that we are currently pouring out into the atmosphere.

Figure 2 Most of the electricity that we use in the UK is made by burning fossil fuels. This releases carbon dioxide into the atmosphere. One solution would be to pump the CO_2 deep underground to be absorbed into porous rocks. This would increase the cost of producing electricity by about 10%.

DID YOU KNOW...
...that scientists predict that global warming may mean that the Earth's temperature could rise by as much as 5.8°C by the year 2100?

SUMMARY QUESTIONS
1 Match up the parts of sentences:

a) Carbon dioxide levels in the Earth's atmosphere	A ...... carbon locked up long ago is released as carbon dioxide.
b) Plants and oceans are known as	B ...... were kept steady by the carbon cycle.
c) When we burn fossil fuels	C ...... the reaction between carbon dioxide and sea water increases.
d) As carbon dioxide levels rise	D ...... carbon dioxide sinks.

2 Draw a labelled diagram to illustrate how boiling an electric kettle may increase the amount of carbon dioxide in the Earth's atmosphere.

3 Why has the amount of carbon dioxide in the Earth's atmosphere risen in the last 50 years?

KEY POINTS
1. Carbon moves into and out of the atmosphere due to plants, the oceans and rocks.
2. The amount of carbon dioxide in the Earth's atmosphere has risen due to the amount of fossil fuels we burn.

SUMMARY ANSWERS

1 a) B b) D c) A d) C

2 Diagram to show how an electric kettle may use energy produced by burning fossil fuels.

3 Due to increased burning of fossil fuels.

KEY POINTS

Ask students to copy out the key points onto a flash card. On the other side, draw an image that will help them remember/represent the key point.

CHEMISTRY — THE CHANGING WORLD

C1b 6.6 Earth issues

SPECIFICATION LINK-UP
C1b.11.6

Students should use their skills, knowledge and understanding of 'How Science Works':

- to explain why scientists cannot accurately predict when earthquakes and volcanic eruptions will occur
- to explain and evaluate the effects of human activities on the atmosphere.

CHEMISTRY — THE CHANGING WORLD

C1b 6.6 Earth issues

EARTHQUAKES

The tsunami that tore across the Indian Ocean on 26 December 2004 left nearly 300 000 people dead. It was caused when a huge earthquake – the second biggest ever recorded – lifted billions of tonnes of sea water over 20 metres upwards. This produced a huge wave that travelled thousands of miles at speeds of several hundred miles an hour.

The earthquake was detected thousands of miles away by the Pacific Tsunami Warning Centre, but no-one could tell that it would produce such devastation. In the aftermath of the disaster, people discussed the lessons that had been learnt.

DEATH TOLL FROM TSUNAMI MAY REACH 300,000

MASSIVE EARTHQUAKE CAUSES TIDAL WAVE IN INDIAN OCEAN

What we need to do is to build an early warning system that would tell us when a tidal wave is coming. A system like this already exists in the Pacific Ocean – but now we need one in the Indian Ocean.

Any early warning system would cost millions of dollars. Tidal waves don't happen that often. The money would be better spent on feeding people who are starving and buying medicines to treat people who are sick.

Rather than detect tidal waves it would be better to predict when an earthquake was going to happen – then we could help to protect people against earthquakes and tidal waves.

ACTIVITY

Set up a discussion between three people on a TV news show or a radio phone-in. Each person should take one of the viewpoints described above, and should argue for their particular point of view.
Try to find as much factual information as you can to back up your view:

- whether you think a tsunami early warning system is needed, or
- that money is better spent on food and health, or
- that the effort should be put into detecting earthquakes.

106

Teaching suggestions

Activities

Earthquakes news report – Show the students footage of an earthquake, maybe the 2004 Boxing Day tsunami (search for 'tsunami video'). Ask the students to imagine that they are a reporter for a news show. They are to imagine that there is an earthquake – anywhere in the world of their choice (encourage them to pick a place near a plate boundary). Then they should prepare a news report – live from the scene of the earthquake. Students could then present their news reports to the class. Their reports should include the difficulty in predicting earthquakes.

The Carbon Problem Diary – Ask students to look at the different characters in the Student Book and read their speech bubbles. Students should try to get into character and write a diary for a short period of time. Then ask the students to review the diary and underline the parts that require fossil fuels to be burned. The students could write a personal recommendation to the character about how to reduce their carbon emissions.

Homework

Kyoto – Ask students to find out what the Kyoto agreement is. They could also find out about how the UK has met/tried to meet this agreement and contrast this with the reluctance from the USA. Research could include subsequent meetings, e.g. Montreal 2005, and any progress made.

Extension

Flip-book – Students could create separate frames of an earthquake from the focus, showing the p and s waves as they extend from the focus. Then fix the frames together with a binding on the left-hand side. Then students flip the books and get a moving image of the waves from the focus of an earthquake.

Map – Give the students a map of the world and ask them to chart the plate boundaries. Then give them data for the occurrence of large earthquakes and volcanoes in the last few years. Students should then add a key, and plot the positions of the natural disasters in order to see a pattern.

Oils, Earth and atmosphere

THE CARBON PROBLEM

Our lifestyles all affect the Earth – and in particular, the amount of carbon dioxide we produce from the fuels we burn and the electricity we use. Here are four different people – you might even know one or two of them ...

It's sooo difficult just keeping up these days. The right clothes, makeup and hair – not to mention being seen at all the right places. Fortunately Mummy has lots of time to take me to where I have to be in her new car ... cool isn't it? Must dash – I hear they've got some new jeans in at that lovely little shop, only 30 miles drive away! Mummy ... !

It's alright round here I suppose – but not a lot to do except watch telly and play computer games. I'd like to go up to London to see the football at the weekend but I can't afford it and Dad says it's too far for him to drive. S'pose I'll just have to listen to it on the radio ...

It's amazing what cheap air tickets you can get now ... I'm just off to see a mate in California! Spent time in Spain, Morocco and Eastern Europe so far this year – and if I can get the money together, I might even manage to get to Australia. Brilliant gap year!

Haven't got much time to stop and talk – just on my way to the 'save the whale' rally. It's 20 miles away, but it won't take me long to get there on my trusty bike. Like my new jeans – cool label, but from the charity shop! Wanna share a tofu sandwich ... !

ACTIVITY

Look at each of these characters. Choose **one** of them and write a 'diary' for what they do and where they go in a typical week. When you have done this, think about the amount of fossil fuels this character uses, not just in travel but in everything they do and buy. Make a list of ways that they could reduce their fossil fuel consumption – and so reduce the amount of carbon dioxide they produce.

Learning styles

Kinaesthetic: Acting out their news report.

Visual: Completing a map to chart earthquakes and volcanoes.

Auditory: Listening to students' news reports.

Interpersonal: Discussing earthquakes – difficulty in predicting them and the consequences of earthquakes.

Special needs

Each student could be given a diagram to form a flick book of a natural disaster and colour it. Then the class could put them into order and make the flick book.

CHEMISTRY — THE CHANGING WORLD

SUMMARY ANSWERS

1. **a)** Middle layer of the Earth, about 3000 km thick and lying about 100 km under the surface.
   b) Innermost layer of the Earth.
   c) Outermost layer of the Earth.
   d) Part of the Earth's crust that moves and causes continental drift, earthquakes, volcanoes and mountains.

2. Shape of coastline, similarity of fossils, similarity of rock types.

3. **a)** Amount of oxygen, methane and ammonia decreased, nitrogen increased.
   b) Reaction of oxygen with ammonia and methane.
   c) i) methane + oxygen → carbon dioxide + water
   ii) ammonia + oxygen → nitrogen + water

4. [Mark answer on the basis of arguments in the Student Book.] Other scientists were slow to accept Wegener's ideas partly because he had no way of explaining *how* continental drift happened, and he was not a geologist.

5. Mark poster based on facts about Earth's early atmosphere, how this has changed, the atmosphere today and how this continues to change.

Summary teaching suggestions

- **Special needs**
  - Question 3 contains a number of sections, sometimes these students can be phased by long examination questions. Give the students a piece of A4 paper, and encourage the students to only look at the part of the question that they are tackling.

- **When to use these questions?**
  - Question 4 is a longer question that students might face. Students need to be aware of mark schemes and how they can maximise their grades during examinations. Ask the students to look at this and, instead of answering them, try to write a mark scheme. They should consider what the marks will be awarded for, and also what terminology will not gain marks. Students could work in groups discussing the mark scheme, or they could complete this as individuals and then compare and rationalise their schemes.
  - Question 4 lends itself to a homework assignment. Statements to explain plate tectonics and criticisms that Wegener may have faced could be given to the students on cards. They then order the cards into two piles: evidence and criticisms.

- **Gifted and talented**
  Students could turn question 3c) from word equations into balanced symbol equations.

- **Learning styles**
  Visual: Creating a poster in question 5.
  Interpersonal: Working in pairs to create a bullet-pointed list of the evidence for Wegener's theory in question 4.

THE CHANGING WORLD: C1b 6.1 – C1b 6.6

SUMMARY QUESTIONS

1. Write simple definitions for the following words describing the structure of the Earth:
   a) mantle
   b) core
   c) lithosphere
   d) tectonic plate.

2. Write down **three** pieces of evidence that suggest that South America and Africa were once joined together.

3. The pie charts show the atmosphere of a planet shortly after it was formed (A) and then millions of years later (B).

   A: Nitrogen 5%, Ammonia 25%, Oxygen 40%, Methane 30%
   B: Ammonia (trace), Methane (trace), Oxygen 25%, Nitrogen 75%

   a) How did the atmosphere of the planet change?
   b) What might have caused this change?
   c) Copy and complete the word equations showing the chemical reactions that may have taken place in the atmosphere.
   i) methane + ... → carbon dioxide + ...
   ii) ammonia + ... → nitrogen + ...

4. Wegener suggested that all the Earth's continents were once joined in a single land mass.
   a) Describe the evidence for this idea, and explain how the single land mass separated into the continents we see today.
   b) Why were other scientists slow to accept Wegener's ideas?

5. The Earth and its atmosphere are constantly changing. Design a poster to show this, that would be suitable for displaying in a classroom with children aged 10–11 years.
   Use diagrams and words to describe and explain ideas and to communicate them clearly to the children.

EXAM-STYLE QUESTIONS

1. Match words **A**, **B**, **C** and **D** with the numbers **1** to **4** in the table.
   A atmosphere
   B core
   C crust
   D mantle

	Description
1	Almost entirely solid, but can flow very slowly
2	Contains mainly the elements nitrogen and oxygen
3	Has an average thickness of about 6 km under oceans and 35 km under continents
4	Part liquid and part solid, with a radius of about 3500 km

   (4)

2. Match words **A**, **B**, **C** and **D** with the spaces **1** to **4** in the sentences.
   A believed
   B dismissed
   C produced
   D published

   In 1912 Alfred Wegener ......**1**...... a theory that a single land mass had split apart into continents that moved to their current positions.
   At the time geologists ......**2**...... that the continents moved up and down – not sideways.
   Wegener's theory was ......**3**...... by geologists because he could not explain how the continents moved.
   In 1944 an English geologist explained that heat from radioactivity ......**4**...... convection currents strong enough to move continents. (4)

3. Match words **A**, **B**, **C** and **D** with spaces **1** to **4** in the sentences.
   A ammonia
   B carbon dioxide
   C noble gases
   D oxygen

   The Earth's early atmosphere consisted mainly of ......**1**...... with some nitrogen, water vapour, methane and ......**2**......
   The Earth's atmosphere now contains 78% nitrogen, 21% ......**3**......, about 1% ......**4**...... and 0.04% carbon dioxide. (4)

EXAM-STYLE ANSWERS

1. **1** D **2** A **3** C **4** B (4 marks)

2. **1** D **2** A **3** B **4** C (4 marks)

3. **1** B **2** A **3** D **4** C (4 marks)

4. a) Less dense/lighter than air. (1 mark)
   Not flammable. (1 mark)

   b) *Two from:*
   - Unreactive/does not react with hot filament/wire.
   - Replaces oxygen/air in light bulb.
   - So filament/wire does not burn. (2 marks)

   c) *One each for:*
   - Used in electric discharge tubes/neon lights.
   - Glows red/brightly when electricity is passed through.
   (2 marks)

5. a) The variables are
   i) Continuous. (1 mark)
   ii) A line of best fit. (1 mark)

   b) 0.077%/0.08% (allow any value from 0.075 to 0.085). (1 mark)

   c) Any value from 24% to 26%. (1 mark)

   d) *One each for:*
   - Increased use of fossil fuels.
   - Deforestation/fewer trees. (2 marks)

   e) *Three from:*
   - Plants/photosynthesis.
   - (Dissolving in) oceans.
   - Formation of sediments in oceans.
   - Formation of coral/shells/fossils. (3 marks)

   f) *Two from:*
   - Causes global warming.
   - Increasing at alarming rate (25% in 45 years).
   - Natural processes not coping/removing it fast enough.
   (2 marks)

Oils, Earth and atmosphere

HOW SCIENCE WORKS QUESTIONS

4 This question is about three of the noble gases, helium, neon and argon.
   (a) Why is helium used in balloons and airships rather than hydrogen? (2)
   (b) Explain how argon allows you to use an electric light bulb for many hours. (2)
   (c) Explain how neon is used for advertising. (2)

5 The graph shows the percentage of carbon dioxide in the atmosphere in recent years.

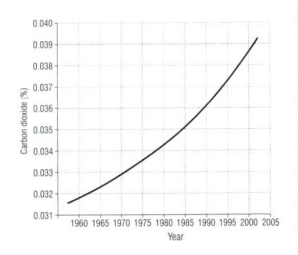

(a) (i) Could the 'percentage of carbon dioxide in the atmosphere' be described as a categoric, discrete or continuous variable? (1)
   (ii) There is considerable variation in the percentage of carbon dioxide within each 5 year period. What do we call the line that 'smooths out' these variations on the graph? (1)
(b) By how much has the percentage of carbon dioxide increased from 1960 to 2005? (1)
(c) What is this increase as a percentage of the 1960 figure? (2)
(d) Suggest **two** reasons for this increase. (2)
(e) What natural processes remove carbon dioxide from the atmosphere? (3)
(f) Why should we be concerned about the increase in carbon dioxide? (2)

Core samples have been taken of the ice from Antarctica. The deeper the sample the longer it has been there. It is possible to date the ice and to take air samples from it. The air was trapped when the ice was formed. It is possible therefore to test samples of air that have been trapped in the ice for many thousands of years.

This table shows some of these results. The more recent results are from actual air samples taken from a Pacific island.

Year	CO_2 concentration (ppm)	Source
2005	379	Pacific island
1995	360	Pacific island
1985	345	Pacific island
1975	331	Pacific island
1965	320	Antarctica
1955	313	Antarctica
1945	310	Antarctica
1935	309	Antarctica
1925	305	Antarctica
1915	301	Antarctica
1905	297	Antarctica
1895	294	Antarctica
1890	294	Antarctica

a) If you have access to a spreadsheet, enter this data and produce a line graph. (3)
b) Draw a line of best fit. (1)
c) What pattern can you detect? (2)
d) What conclusion can you make? (1)
e) Should the fact that the data came from two different sources affect your conclusion? Explain why. (2)

109

HOW SCIENCE WORKS ANSWERS

a) Graph should have the axes correctly and fully labelled. The points should be accurately plotted. The date should be on the X axis and the CO_2 concentration on the Y axis.

b) The line of best fit should be a curve.

c) Slow increase in the concentration of CO_2 at the start of the data, followed by more rapid increases in more recent years. Some might spot the anomalies around 1945. This might prompt a debate about the causes, which could prove very interesting. Remember these probably represent global figures and they might conclude that they would like more detailed data between 1935 and 1955 to try to sort out what might have happened. This is given in Table 1 below.

d) That the concentration of carbon dioxide in the atmosphere has increased.
That it has increased at a faster rate in more recent years. Caution here about taking conclusions too far and resist the conclusion that therefore this alone is evidence for the greenhouse effect or global warming.

e) Yes – they are two totally different ways of deriving the data. Students might want to know of any overlap between the two sets of data and the correlation between the two. The data is given in Table 2 below.

How science works teaching suggestions

- **Literacy guidance**
  - Key terms that should be clearly understood are: line of best fit, pattern, conclusion.
  - Questions expecting a longer answer, where students can practise their literacy skills are c) and d).
- **Higher- and lower-level questions.** Questions c) and d) are higher-level and answers for these questions have been provided at this level. Question e) is a lower-level question – the answer is also at this level.
- **Gifted and talented.** Higher attaining students should be critical of the collection of the data, e.g. how representative is it of global CO_2 concentrations. The additional data given in Tables 1 and 2 below should provide information for an informed debate on the reliability of the two sources of information.
- **How and when to use these questions.** When wishing to develop graph drawing skills using a database and careful analysis of scientific data. We should be critical of good science as well as poor science.
- **Homework.** Ask students to present data to their family and record the responses.
- **Special needs.** The graph could be drawn to allow speedy access to the rest of the argument.
- **ICT link-up.** ICT could be used to review other sources of the same data and check its reliability.

Exam teaching suggestions

Each of the questions on this chapter could be used after the corresponding spread. Altogether, the questions should take about 25–30 minutes to complete for 29 marks.

These questions concentrate on students' knowledge of the content in this chapter. Many students confuse parts of the Earth and the relative amounts of gases in the atmosphere. If Q1 and Q3 are poorly answered, students should be encouraged to memorise the amounts and descriptions given in the specification using a variety of learning techniques.

Q2 could be used as a basis for discussing how scientific theories develop. The passage is incomplete and students could research and finish the story and then set further questions on the additional information.

In Q5 students should be able to interpret the graph and Higher-Tier students should be able to calculate the percentage increase. This is a demanding question, but most students should be able to gain some marks. In part e), students should use the number of marks to guide them in the number of points in their answer.

Table 1

Year	'35	'36	'37	'38	'39	'40	'41	'42	'43	'44	'45
CO_2 conc. (ppm)	309.4	309.8	310.0	310.2	310.3	310.4	310.4	310.3	310.2	310.1	310.1
Year	'46	'47	'48	'49	'50	'51	'52	'53	'54	'55	
CO_2 conc. (ppm)	310.1	310.2	310.3	310.5	310.7	311.1	311.5	311.9	312.4	313.0	

Table 2

Year	'78	'77	'76	'75	'74	'73	'72	'71	'70	'69
Pacific island CO_2 conc. (ppm)	335.5	333.9	332.1	331.1	330.2	329.7	327.5	326.3	325.7	324.6
Antarctica CO_2 conc. (ppm)	333.7	332.6	331.5	330.3	329.2	328.0	326.9	325.8	324.8	323.8

CHEMISTRY — OILS, EARTH AND ATMOSPHERE

C1b Examination-Style Questions

Examiner's comments

Maximum coverage of the specification will be achieved if your students do both multiple choice and structured questions whichever exam they are doing.

Answers to Questions

Chemistry A

1.
  1. D
  2. B
  3. A
  4. C   *(1 mark each)*

2.
  (a) C
  (b) D
  (c) B
  (d) B   *(1 mark each)*

EXAMINATION-STYLE QUESTIONS

Chemistry A

1. Match the polymers **A, B, C** and **D** with the numbers **1** to **4** in the table.

   A high density poly(ethene)
   B low density poly(ethene)
   C poly(chloroethene)
   D poly(propene)

	Density (g/cm³)	Monomer
1	0.90	C_3H_6
2	0.92	C_2H_4
3	0.96	C_2H_4
4	1.30	C_2H_3Cl

   (4 marks)   *See pages 72–5*

2. Alfred Wegener first suggested his theory of continental drift in 1915. He suggested that the continents had once been a single large land mass that had split apart. He showed that fossils and rocks were similar on the parts of America and Africa that fitted together. He produced a lot of evidence to support his theory but other scientists did not accept his ideas for over 50 years.

   (a) One of the main reasons why other scientists did not accept his ideas was ...
       A America and Africa are too far apart.
       B Fossils are similar all over the Earth.
       C He could not explain how the continents moved.
       D He had no evidence that the continents were moving.

   (b) Geologists did not like his ideas because ...
       A they could not understand his fossil evidence.
       B they did not know enough about the rocks of Africa and America.
       C they did not like German scientists.
       D they would have to change all their own long established ideas.

   (c) What new evidence was found in the 1960s?
       A Land bridges had existed between the continents.
       B The sea floor was spreading on either side of deep ocean ridges.
       C The polar ice-caps were shown to be melting.
       D The Earth had been shrinking since it had been formed.

   (d) What new theory was developed using Wegener's ideas?
       A convection currents
       B plate tectonics
       C radioactive decay
       D seismic activity

   (4 marks)   *See pages 98–9*

BUMP UP THE GRADE

Questions will often be set across the topics in a unit. The best students will be able to link the ideas from one section with another. Developing this understanding can make a big difference in how they cope with questions in the exam.

GET IT RIGHT!

Students often omit or avoid questions that seem unfamiliar to them or that contain a lot of information. Although they may be put off by what seems like a lot of work, the questions are often quite straightforward. They should be trained to read information carefully and should be encouraged to try out their understanding in new contexts.

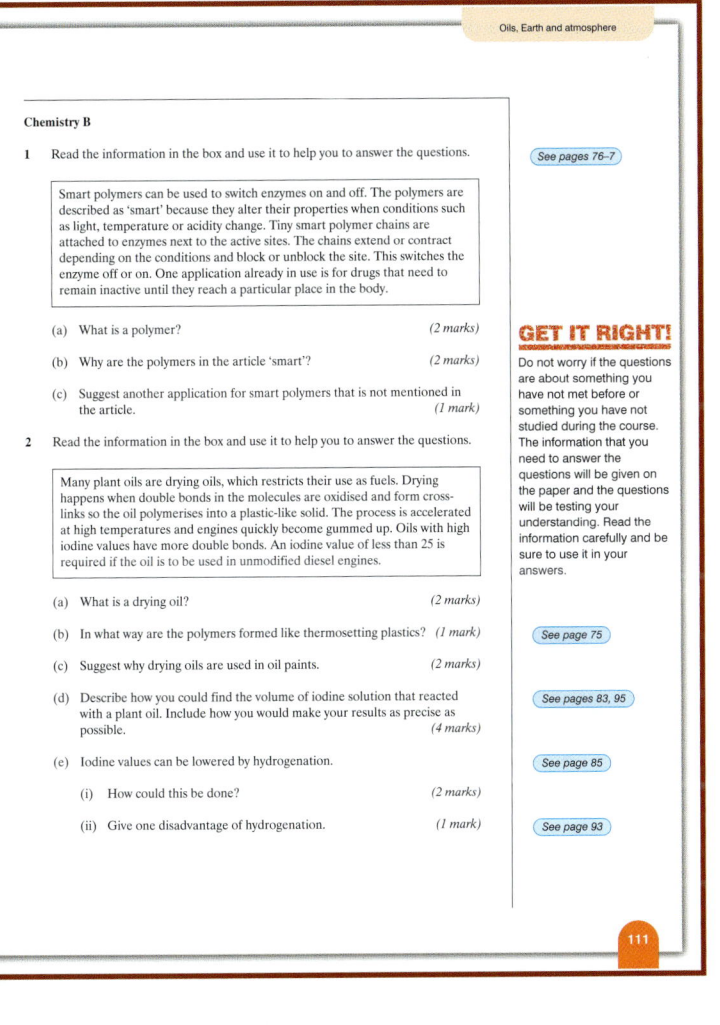

Chemistry B

1 Read the information in the box and use it to help you to answer the questions. *(See pages 76–7)*

> Smart polymers can be used to switch enzymes on and off. The polymers are described as 'smart' because they alter their properties when conditions such as light, temperature or acidity change. Tiny smart polymer chains are attached to enzymes next to the active sites. The chains extend or contract depending on the conditions and block or unblock the site. This switches the enzyme off or on. One application already in use is for drugs that need to remain inactive until they reach a particular place in the body.

(a) What is a polymer? *(2 marks)*

(b) Why are the polymers in the article 'smart'? *(2 marks)*

(c) Suggest another application for smart polymers that is not mentioned in the article. *(1 mark)*

2 Read the information in the box and use it to help you to answer the questions.

> Many plant oils are drying oils, which restricts their use as fuels. Drying happens when double bonds in the molecules are oxidised and form cross-links so the oil polymerises into a plastic-like solid. The process is accelerated at high temperatures and engines quickly become gummed up. Oils with high iodine values have more double bonds. An iodine value of less than 25 is required if the oil is to be used in unmodified diesel engines.

(a) What is a drying oil? *(2 marks)*

(b) In what way are the polymers formed like thermosetting plastics? *(1 mark)* *(See page 75)*

(c) Suggest why drying oils are used in oil paints. *(2 marks)*

(d) Describe how you could find the volume of iodine solution that reacted with a plant oil. Include how you would make your results as precise as possible. *(4 marks)* *(See pages 83, 95)*

(e) Iodine values can be lowered by hydrogenation.
  (i) How could this be done? *(2 marks)* *(See page 85)*
  (ii) Give one disadvantage of hydrogenation. *(1 mark)* *(See page 93)*

GET IT RIGHT!
Do not worry if the questions are about something you have not met before or something you have not studied during the course. The information that you need to answer the questions will be given on the paper and the questions will be testing your understanding. Read the information carefully and be sure to use it in your answers.

Oils, Earth and atmosphere

Chemistry B

1 (a) *Two from:*
  • A long/very large molecule
  • made from many small molecules/monomers
  • joined together in a chain. *(2 marks)*

(b) *One each for:*
  • They alter/change their properties
  • when conditions change. *(2 marks)*

(c) *Any one from:*
  • New type of stitches for wounds.
  • Easy release sticking plasters.
  • Any use of shape memory polymers.
  • Any type of sensor.
  • Microprocessors.
  • Liquid crystal displays/fibre optics. *(1 mark)*

2 (a) *Two from:*
  • an oil which oxidises
  • has many double bonds
  • polymerises
  • forms cross links
  • turns into a solid. *(2 marks)*

(b) They have cross links/chemical bonds joining chains or polymer molecules *(just goes solid is not enough)*. *(1 mark)*

(c) *Two from:*
  • They set hard.
  • They bind the paint/pigment/colour.
  • They fix the paint to the paper/canvas/surface.
  • *Accept* they are waterproof. *(2 marks)*

(d) *Four from:*
  • measure or use known volume or mass of oil
  • add iodine solution gradually
  • from a burette
  • until colour remains/appears in oil/no longer goes colourless
  • measure volume of iodine solution used
  (4 marks)

(e) (i) React with hydrogen. *(1 mark)*
  Using a catalyst (at high temperature). *(1 mark)*

  (ii) Turns oil solid/increases melting point/hardens the oil. *(1 mark)*

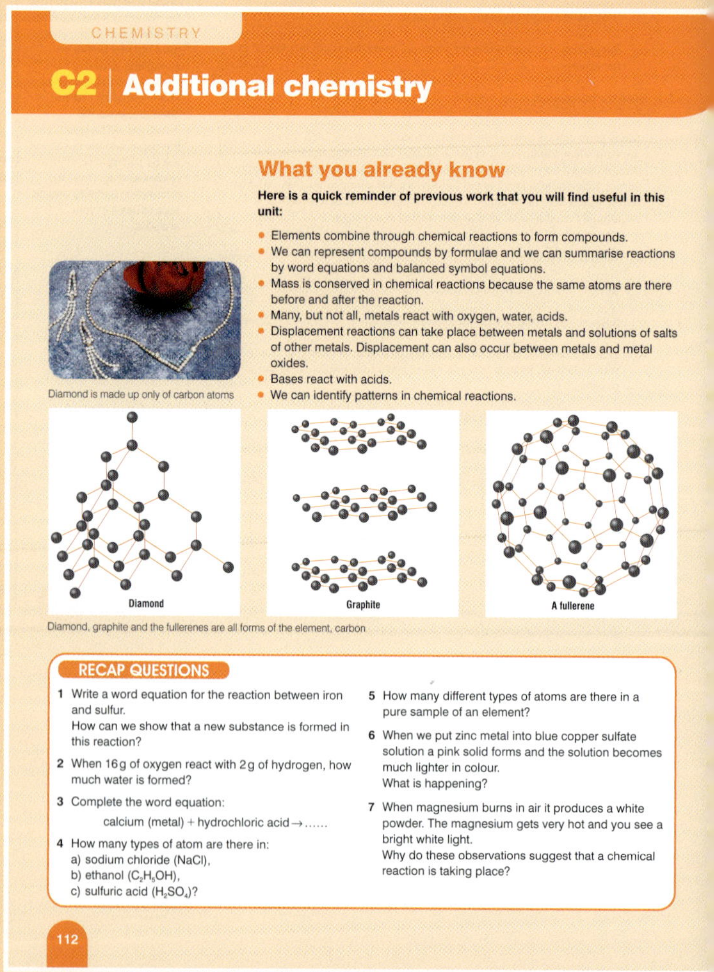

CHEMISTRY

C2 | Additional chemistry

Key Stage 3 curriculum links

The following link to 'What you already know':

- How elements combine through chemical reactions to form compounds [for example, water, carbon dioxide, magnesium oxide, sodium chloride, most minerals] with a definite composition.
- To represent compounds by formulae and to summarise reactions by word equations.
- How mass is conserved when chemical reactions take place because the same atoms are present, although combined in different ways.
- How metals react with oxygen, water, acids and oxides of other metals, and what the products of these reactions are.
- About the displacement reactions that take place between metals and solutions of salts of other metals.
- How metals and bases, including carbonates, react with acids, and what the products of these reactions are.
- To identify patterns in chemical reactions.

QCA Scheme of work
8E Atoms and elements
8F Compounds and mixtures
9H Using chemistry

Activity notes

- **Poster** – Students should be encouraged to make a poster explaining the recent advances in our knowledge of the atom. They could think about why most advances have been made in the last 200 years (since the advent of electricity).
- To extend students, they could research CERN on the Internet.
- To encourage group work, they could work as a class, if each student were given a different aspect of the topic to study. Then a giant (display board) sized poster could be generated.

RECAP ANSWERS

1 iron + sulfur → iron sulfide
   The reaction mixture is magnetic whereas the product of the reaction (iron sulfide) is not magnetic.

2 18g

3 calcium chloride + hydrogen

4 a) Two. b) Three. c) Three.

5 One.

6 A displacement reaction. Zinc displaces the copper in the solution and copper metal forms as the solid.

7 There is a visible change as a new product forms and a large amount of energy is given out.

Teaching suggestions

What you already know

- **Questions** – Students could know this information, but may not be able to think of when they would use it. The students could generate questions that are answered by the bullet points in this section.

112

Additional chemistry

SPECIFICATION LINK-UP
Unit: Chemistry 2

How do sub-atomic particles help us to understand the structure of substances?

Simple particle theory is developed in this unit to include atomic structure and bonding. The arrangement of electrons in atoms can be used to explain what happens when elements react and how atoms join together to form different types of substance.

How do structures influence the properties and uses of substances?

Substances that have simple molecular, giant ionic and giant covalent structures have very different properties. Ionic, covalent, and metallic bonds are strong. The forces between molecules are weaker, e.g. in carbon dioxide and iodine. Nanomaterials have new properties because of their very small size.

How much can we make and how much do we need to use?

The relative masses of atoms can be used to calculate how much to react and how much we can produce because no atoms are gained or lost in a chemical reaction. In industrial processes, atom economy is important for sustainable development.

How can we control the rate of chemical reactions?

Being able to speed up or slow down chemical reactions is important in everyday life and in industry. Changes in temperature, concentration of solutions, surface area of solids, and the presence of catalysts all affect the rates of reactions.

Do chemical reactions always release energy?

Chemical reactions involve energy transfers. Many chemical reactions involve the release of energy. For other chemical reactions to occur, energy must be supplied. In industrial processes, energy requirements and emissions need to be considered both for economic reasons and for sustainable development.

How can we use ions in solutions?

Ionic compounds have many uses and can provide other substances. Electrolysis is used to produce alkalis and elements such as chlorine and hydrogen. Oxidation–reduction reactions do not just involve oxygen. Soluble salts can be made from acids and insoluble salts can be made from solutions of ions.

Additional chemistry

Making connections
Developing ideas about substances

ACTIVITY

The three scientists described here made enormous contributions to our understanding of the behaviour of matter and chemistry. Using this information, produce a poster with a timeline showing how our understanding of the behaviour of matter changed in the period from the early 18th century to the beginning of the 20th century.
You could research these ideas further using the Internet, especially at www.timelinescience.com.

Many people think that Antoine Lavoisier was the father of modern chemistry. If this is so, then his wife, Marie-Anne may well be the mother. She was well educated, and translated documents and illustrated his scientific texts with great skill.

Antoine Lavoisier lived in France between 1743 and 1794. His experiments were some of the first proper chemical experiments involving careful measurements. For example, in chemical reactions he carefully weighed reactants and products. This was an important advance over the work of earlier chemists.

Working with his wife, Lavoisier showed that the quantity of matter is the same at the end as at the beginning of every chemical reaction. Working with other French chemists, Lavoisier invented a system of chemical names which described the structure of chemical compounds. Many of these names are still in use, including names such as sulfuric acid and sulfates.

Michael Faraday came from very humble beginnings, but his work on electricity and chemistry still affects our lives today. His achievements were acknowledged when his portrait was included on the £20 note in 1991.

Born in Yorkshire in 1791, Michael Faraday was one of 10 children. Apprenticed to a bookbinder, Faraday became an assistant to the great chemist Sir Humphry Davy. After hearing some of Davy's lectures in London, he sent him a bound copy of some notes he had made and was taken on.

After much work on electricity, Faraday turned his attention to electrolysis. He produced an explanation of what happens when we use an electric current to split up a chemical compound. Not only did Faraday explain what happens, he also introduced the words we still use today – *electrolysis*, *electrolyte* and *electrode*.

Ernest Rutherford was born in New Zealand in 1871. After his education in New Zealand he worked and studied in England and Canada. Then in 1910 he showed that the structure of the atom consists of a tiny positively charged nucleus that makes up nearly all of the mass of the atom. The nucleus is surrounded by a vast space which contains the electrons – but most of the atom is simply empty space! Rutherford received the Nobel Prize for Chemistry in recognition of his huge contribution to our understanding of the atom.

Ernest Rutherford was responsible for producing the evidence that completely changed our ideas about the structure of atoms

Chapters in this unit

Structures and bonding → Structures and properties → How much? → Rates of reaction → Energy and reactions → Electrolysis → Acids, alkalis and salts

113

- **Word equations** – Most of the key points can be represented as word equations, e.g. bases react with acids:

  copper oxide + hydrochloric acid → copper chloride + water

  Encourage the student to write relevant word equations for the different points, and higher attaining students could attempt to write balanced symbol equations.

Recap questions

- **Starter** – These questions could be used as a starter for appropriate lessons, e.g. question 1 for section C2 1.3 'Chemical bonding'.

- **AfL (Assessment for Learning)** – Give students a set amount of time to answer the questions. Then ask the students to swap their answers with another student. They should mark each others' work, compare answers and annotate corrections.

Making connections

- **Card sort** – Make a pack of cards with the names of the scientists/philosophers and their contribution to the discovery of the structure of the atom on separate cards. Students should then match the names with their discoveries.

- For lower ability groups, pictures of the scientists and their discoveries could be used.

- An extension would be to ask the students to put the discoveries in date order.

- **Mind map** – Students often compartmentalise information and do not link things learned in different topics together. Give them the key words on separate cards, some Blu Tack, felt pens and sugar paper. Working in small groups, they stick two related key words on to their paper and join them with an arrow. The group then adds text so that the two words are the start and end of a sentence. They then add more key words (there may be lots of arrows to or from each card, or just one). This helps students to view the topic as a whole, and any missing links can be quickly identified and teachers can challenge any misconceptions.

Chapters in this unit

- Structures and bonding
- Structures and properties
- How much?
- Rates of reaction
- Energy and reactions
- Electrolysis
- Acids, alkalis and salts

113

CHEMISTRY — STRUCTURES AND BONDING

C2 1.1 Atomic structure

LEARNING OBJECTIVES

Students should learn:

- That there are particles inside an atom.
- That the number of protons equals the number of electrons in an atom.
- That the atoms are arranged on the periodic table.
- The relative charges on sub-atomic particles.

LEARNING OUTCOMES

Most students should be able to:

- Label the sub-atomic particles in an atom.
- State the charge of the sub-atomic particles in an atom.
- Define atomic number (proton number).
- Describe how the elements are ordered in the periodic table.

Some students should also be able to:

- Explain why atoms are electrically neutral.

Teaching suggestions

- **Learning styles**

  Kinaesthetic: Sorting the different elements into groups.

  Visual: Labelling of an atom.

  Auditory: Listening to discussion on thought provoking questions.

  Interpersonal: Working as a group to order different elements.

  Intrapersonal: Evaluating different representations of atoms.

- **Homework.** John Dalton believed that atoms could not be split (*atomos* means 'indivisible'). Students could find out which scientist disproved this and how. [JJ Thompson, in 1897, discovered electrons.]

- **ICT link-up.** Search the web for atom diagrams, then stipulate a type of animation format e.g. applets/flash/macromedia.

SPECIFICATION LINK-UP   Unit: Chemistry 2.12.1

- Atoms have a small central nucleus made up of protons and neutrons around which there are electrons.
- The relative electrical charges are as shown:

Name of particle	Charge
Proton	+1
Neutron	0
Electron	−1

- In an atom, the number of electrons is equal to the number of protons in the nucleus. Atoms have no overall electrical charge.
- All atoms of a particular element have the same number of protons. Atoms of different elements have different numbers of protons.
- The number of protons in an atom is called its atomic number (proton number). Atoms are arranged in the modern periodic table in order of their atomic number (proton number).

Lesson structure

STARTER

Spot the mistake – 'When different compounds join together, atoms of the same element are made.' [Compounds do not join together, atoms join up to make compounds. Also, if all the atoms are the same in a material, then it is an element, not a compound.] (5 minutes)

Define – Ask the students to match these definitions to key words:

- Positive particle in the nucleus of an atom. [Proton]
- Negative particle that orbits the nucleus of an atom. [Electron]
- A sub-atomic particle that carries no charge and is found in the nucleus of the atom. [Neutron] (5 minutes)

MAIN

- Students will need to be able to recognise atom diagrams in a lot of different forms. Some will be two-dimensional dot and cross diagrams, others will be three-dimensional moving representations of the atom. Give each student an element from the first 20 on the periodic table. Encourage them to research their element and represent its structure in as many different ways that they can find.
- Students could compile their diagrams into a poster, with the sub-atomic particles labelled. The posters could be displayed in the classroom.
- Atoms were discovered and grouped in many different ways. Supply students with cards for the first 20 elements. On one side of the card there should be the elements name, symbol, atomic number and electronic structure.
- As an extension, on the reverse general physical and chemical properties could be listed.
- Students should then work in small teams to order the elements in different ways (alphabetically, proton number, number of electrons in the outer shell, physical properties etc.). You should tour the other groups, asking them about their grouping structure and encouraging them to find new ways to group the elements.
- Then ask the students to sort their cards into the order of Mendeleev's periodic table.
- Ask the students what they notice [that the elements are in atomic/proton number order], higher attaining students may notice the links between the group/period number and the electronic structure.
- Then ask students to summarise in one sentence how the atoms are arranged in the periodic table.

Additional chemistry

PLENARIES

Label – On the board draw a diagram of a helium atom (two protons, two neutrons in the nucleus and two electrons in the first shell). Ask the students to copy the diagram and label the particles with their name and their charge. (5 minutes)

Thinking – Ask the students the following thought-provoking questions. Students work in small groups discussing the question, then you could ask them to feedback into a class discussion:

- What mostly makes up atoms? [Space]
- What stops electrons whizzing off into space? [The electrostatic force of attraction between them and the nucleus]
- Which bit of the atom do you think does the chemistry? [Electrons – more specifically the outer shell electrons]
- Which bit of an atom do you think radioactivity comes from? [The nucleus] (10 minutes)

AfL (Assessment for Learning) – Students could look at the different ways of representing the atom, as highlighted on the different posters. They could then evaluate the different diagrams and decide which they think is the most useful way of representing the atom and explain why. (15 minutes)

ACTIVITY & EXTENSION IDEAS

- Ask students to find out who discovered each sub-atomic particle, how and when.
- Instead of organising cards with elements' details on, the elements themselves could be provided in sealed gas jars and Petri dishes. The relevant information could then be stuck onto the container with tape.

CHEMISTRY — STRUCTURES AND BONDING

C2 1.1 Atomic structure

LEARNING OBJECTIVES
1. What is inside atoms?
2. Why is the number of protons in an atom equal to the number of electrons?
3. What is the order in which atoms are arranged in the periodic table?
4. What is the charge on a proton, neutron and electron?

In the middle of an atom is a small nucleus. This contains two types of particles, which we call **protons** and **neutrons**. A third type of particle orbits the nucleus – we call these particles **electrons**. Any atom has the same number of electrons orbiting its nucleus as it has protons in its nucleus.

Protons have a positive charge while neutrons have no charge – they are neutral. So the nucleus itself has an overall positive charge.

The electrons orbiting the nucleus are negatively charged. The size of the negative charge on an electron is exactly the same as the size of the positive charge on a proton. (In other words, the relative charge on a proton is +1, while the relative charge on an electron is −1.)

Because any atom contains equal numbers of protons and electrons, the overall charge on any atom is exactly zero. For example, a carbon atom has 6 protons, so we know it also has 6 electrons.

a) What are the names of the three particles that make up an atom?
b) An oxygen atom has 8 protons – how many electrons does it have?

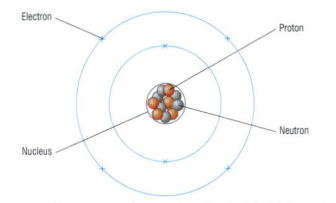

Figure 1 Understanding the structure of an atom gives us important clues to the way chemicals react together

Type of sub-atomic particle	Relative charge
proton	+1
neutron	0
electron	−1

To help you remember the charge on the sub-atomic particles:
Protons are Positive;
Neutrons are Neutral;
so that means Electrons must be Negative!

Atomic number

We call the number of protons in the nucleus of an atom its **atomic number** or **proton number**.

As all of the atoms of a particular element have the same number of protons, they also have the same atomic number. So the atomic number of hydrogen is 1 and it has one proton in the nucleus. The atomic number of carbon is 6 and it has 6 protons in the nucleus. The atomic number of sodium is 11 and it has 11 protons in the nucleus.

Each element has its own atomic number. If you are told that the atomic number of an element is 8, you can identify that element from the periodic table. In this case it is oxygen.

c) Which element has an atomic number of 14?

Elements in the periodic table are arranged in order of their atomic numbers.

Figure 2 The elements in the periodic table are arranged in order of their atomic numbers

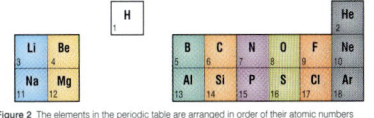

You read the periodic table from left to right, and from the top down – just like reading a page of writing.

Look at the atomic numbers of the elements in the last group of the periodic table:

d) What do you notice about the atomic numbers going from helium to neon to argon?

You will be able to explain this pattern when you learn more about the arrangement of electrons in atoms later in this chapter.

SUMMARY QUESTIONS

1 Copy and complete using the words below:

   atomic   electrons   negative   neutrons   protons

In the nucleus of atoms there are …… and …… . Around the nucleus there are …… which have a …… charge. In the periodic table, atoms are arranged in order of their …… number.

2 Use the periodic table in Figure 2 to find the atomic number of the elements lithium, sulfur, magnesium, chlorine and nitrogen.

3 Atoms are always neutral. Explain why this means that an atom must always contain the same number of protons and electrons.

GET IT RIGHT!
In an atom, the number of protons is always equal to the number of electrons. You can find out the number of protons and electrons in an atom by looking up its atomic number in the periodic table.

DID YOU KNOW?
In 1808, a chemist called John Dalton published a theory of atoms, explaining how these joined together to form new substances. Not everyone liked his theory though – one person wrote 'Atoms are round bits of wood invented by Mr Dalton!'

KEY POINTS
1. Atoms are made of protons, neutrons and electrons.
2. Protons and electrons have equal and opposite electric charges. Protons are positively charged, and electrons are negatively charged.
3. Atoms are arranged in the periodic table in order of their atomic number.
4. Neutrons have no electric charge. They are neutral.

SUMMARY ANSWERS

1 Protons (neutrons), neutrons (protons), electrons, negative, atomic.

2 Li = 3, S = 16, Mg = 12, Cl = 17, N = 7.

3 Because protons and electrons have the same amount of charge but with opposite signs, the charge on a proton is exactly cancelled out by the charge on an electron.

Answers to in-text questions

a) Protons, neutrons and electrons.
b) 8 electrons.
c) Silicon.
d) They increase by 8 between each element.

DID YOU KNOW?

Atoms are very small. Ask students to guess how small this would be [about 0.000 000 000 1 m in diameter].

KEY POINTS

Students could translate the key points into text language.

CHEMISTRY | STRUCTURES AND BONDING

C2 1.2 The arrangement of electrons in atoms

LEARNING OBJECTIVES

Students should learn:

- To represent the electronic structures of the first 20 elements.
- That the number of electrons in the highest energy level relates to the group number in the periodic table.
- That the number of electrons in the highest energy level determines chemical properties.

LEARNING OUTCOMES

Most students should be able to:

- Draw the electronic structure of the first 20 elements of the periodic table, when the atomic/proton number is given.
- State the relationship between the number of electrons in the highest energy level and the group number.

Some students should also be able to:

- Explain how the number of electrons in the highest energy level relates to the chemical properties of an element.

Teaching suggestions

- **Special needs**
  - Give the students the electronic structure of the first 20 elements and their names as a cut and stick activity.
  - Some students may find ordering 40 pieces of information too much, so these students could be given the data in packs of 10 (5 elements at a time).
- **Learning styles**

  Kinaesthetic: Sorting the information on sub-atomic particles into a table.

  Visual: Creating a table to represent the electronic structure of the first 20 elements.

  Auditory: Listening to another student's list on electrons.

  Interpersonal: Working as a class to model different types of atom.

  Intrapersonal: Detailing two facts from the lesson.
- **Homework.** Give each student a different element and ask him or her to find out a fascinating fact about it. Next lesson, encourage the students to share their facts.

SPECIFICATION LINK-UP   Unit: Chemistry 2.12.1

- *Electrons occupy particular energy levels. Each electron in an atom is at a particular energy level (in a particular shell). The electrons in an atom occupy the lowest available energy levels (innermost available shells). (Though only energy levels are referred to throughout this specification, the candidate may answer in terms of shells if they prefer.)*
- *Elements in the same group in the periodic table have the same number of electrons in the highest energy levels (outer electrons).*

Students should use their skills, knowledge and understanding of 'How Science Works':

- *to represent the electronic structure of the first twenty elements of the periodic table.*

Lesson structure

STARTER

Card sort – Give the students a pack of eight cards, each with different information on: proton, electron, neutron, nucleus, shell, +1, 0, −1. Students should also be given a table on a piece of laminated paper, consisting of three columns (labelled: sub-atomic particle, charge, position) and three rows. They then sort the cards, putting them in the appropriate positions on the table. (10 minutes)

List – Ask students to list all the information they can think of about electrons. [For example, have a charge of −1, are very small, are found in shells/energy levels of an atom, are what electricity is made of, there are the same number as protons in an atom.] Then ask students to share their ideas in pairs, then groups of four. Ask each group of four to give a piece of information that a scribe writes onto the board. You should address any misconceptions revealed in this activity. (15 minutes)

MAIN

- Students need to be able to draw diagrams of the first 20 elements, but many kinaesthetic learners find it difficult to use information from the periodic table to draw the structure. If it is possible, try to do a room swap to a hall or playground. Other materials that would be needed are a number of different coloured sports bibs, A3 paper and felt pens. The students will be electrons to act out different atoms.
- Get two volunteers to stand in the centre of the room – a student is a proton (should wear a red bib) and another is a neutron (should wear a green bib). Tell the students which atom they are going to represent, e.g. oxygen.
- Using question and answer, ask them to work out how many protons and neutrons would be in the nucleus and instruct those students to write the appropriate numbers onto paper and hold them up.
- Then ask the students how many electrons the atoms would have and in each shell. Place the students around the nucleus into shells – each shell should be made up of students with bibs of a different colour.
- Ask students to create a table to show the element name, symbol, number of electrons, electronic structure and short-hand notation for the first 20 elements. Students should be encouraged to use the periodic table to get the information to complete this activity.

- **ICT link-up.** Take a digital photograph of the students acting out the atoms. Then, when the group returns to the classroom, project the different images. Ask for volunteers to draw around the atom to show the different shells, they could also draw crosses on top of the students to display the electronic structure as detailed in the specification.

116

Additional chemistry

PLENARIES

Guess the atom – Create flash cards to show the electronic structure of the first 20 elements in a random order. Ask the students to look at the images and work out which atom is being displayed. Students to write their answer on an A4 whiteboard and hold up their response for you to give instant feedback. (10 minutes)

Reflection – Ask students to consider a fact that they have revised in the lesson and a new fact that they have learned in the lesson. As they leave the classroom, ask them for their facts. You should challenge any misconceptions during the reflection plenary of the following lesson. (5 minutes)

ACTIVITY & EXTENSION

Scientists now don't believe that neutrons and protons are indivisible. Ask students to find out what makes up these sub-atomic particles. [Quarks and Leptons.]

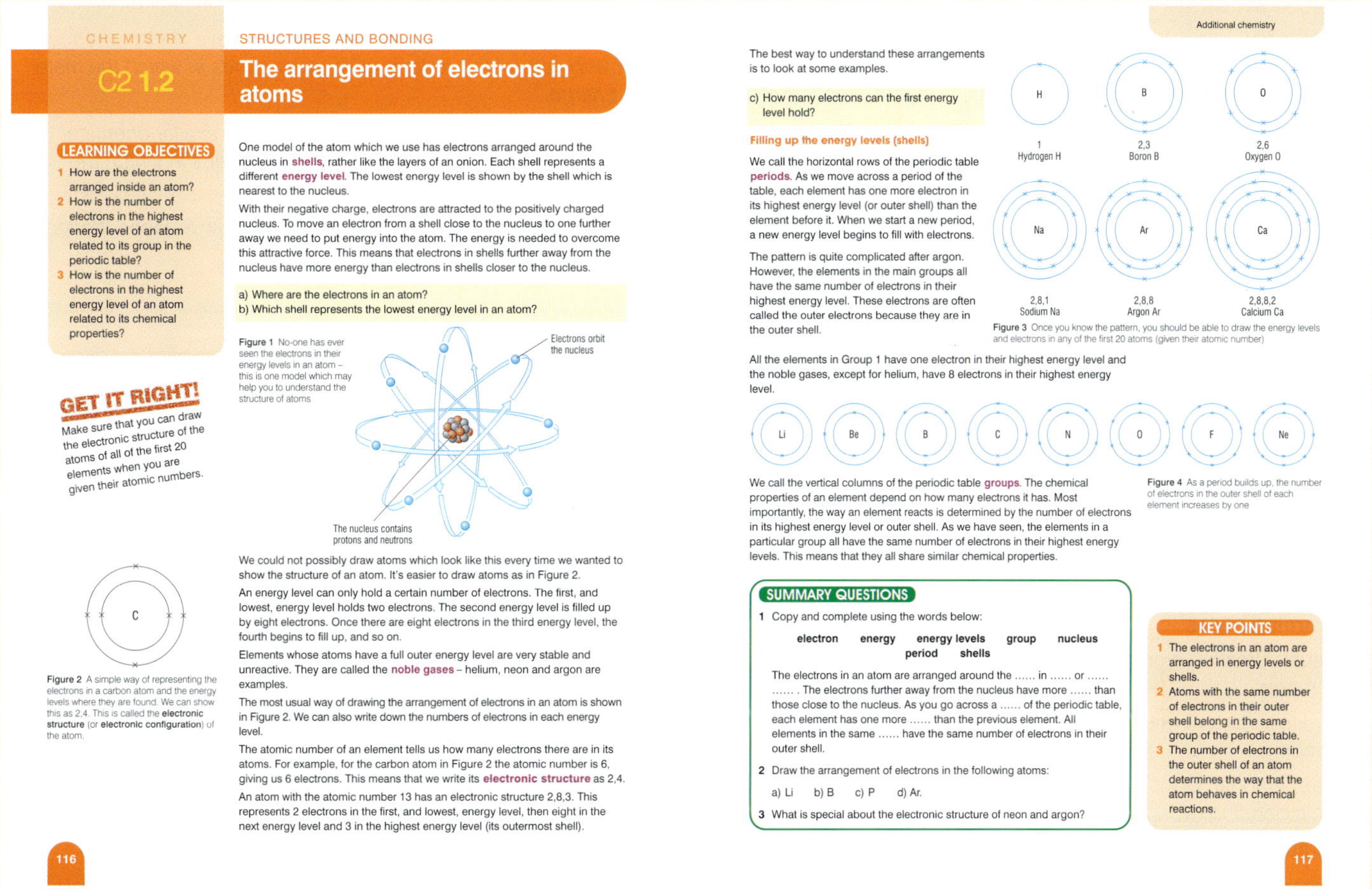

CHEMISTRY — STRUCTURES AND BONDING

C2 1.2 The arrangement of electrons in atoms

LEARNING OBJECTIVES
1 How are the electrons arranged inside an atom?
2 How is the number of electrons in the highest energy level of an atom related to its group in the periodic table?
3 How is the number of electrons in the highest energy level of an atom related to its chemical properties?

GET IT RIGHT!
Make sure that you can draw the electronic structure of the atoms of all of the first 20 elements when you are given their atomic numbers.

One model of the atom which we use has electrons arranged around the nucleus in **shells**, rather like the layers of an onion. Each shell represents a different **energy level**. The lowest energy level is shown by the shell which is nearest to the nucleus.

With their negative charge, electrons are attracted to the positively charged nucleus. To move an electron from a shell close to the nucleus to one further away we need to put energy into the atom. The energy is needed to overcome this attractive force. This means that electrons in shells further away from the nucleus have more energy than electrons in shells closer to the nucleus.

a) Where are the electrons in an atom?
b) Which shell represents the lowest energy level in an atom?

Figure 1 No-one has ever seen the electrons in the energy levels in an atom – this is one model which may help you to understand the structure of atoms.

Electrons orbit the nucleus
The nucleus contains protons and neutrons

We could not possibly draw atoms which look like this every time we wanted to show the structure of an atom. It's easier to draw atoms as in Figure 2.
An energy level can only hold a certain number of electrons. The first, and lowest, energy level holds two electrons. The second energy level is filled up by eight electrons. Once there are eight electrons in the third energy level, the fourth begins to fill up, and so on.
Elements whose atoms have a full outer energy level are very stable and unreactive. They are called the **noble gases** – helium, neon and argon are examples.
The most usual way of drawing the arrangement of electrons in an atom is shown in Figure 2. We can also write down the numbers of electrons in each energy level.
The atomic number of an element tells us how many electrons there are in its atoms. For the carbon atom in Figure 2 the atomic number is 6, giving us 6 electrons. This means that we write its **electronic structure** as 2,4.
An atom with the atomic number 13 has an electronic structure 2,8,3. This represents 2 electrons in the first, and lowest, energy level, then eight in the next energy level and 3 in the highest energy level (its outermost shell).

Figure 2 A simple way of representing the electrons in a carbon atom and the energy levels where they are found. We can show this as 2,4. This is called the **electronic structure** (or **electronic configuration**) of the atom.

The best way to understand these arrangements is to look at some examples.

c) How many electrons can the first energy level hold?

Filling up the energy levels (shells)
We call the horizontal rows of the periodic table **periods**. As we move across a period of the table, each element has one more electron in its highest energy level (or outer shell) than the element before it. When we start a new period, a new energy level begins to fill with electrons.
The pattern is quite complicated after argon. However, the elements in the main groups all have the same number of electrons in their highest energy level. These electrons are often called the outer electrons because they are in the outer shell.

All the elements in Group 1 have one electron in their highest energy level and the noble gases, except for helium, have 8 electrons in their highest energy level.

We call the vertical columns of the periodic table **groups**. The chemical properties of an element depend on how many electrons it has. Most importantly, the way an element reacts is determined by the number of electrons in its highest energy level or outer shell. As we have seen, the elements in a particular group all have the same number of electrons in their highest energy levels. This means that they all share similar chemical properties.

Figure 3 Once you know the pattern, you should be able to draw the energy levels and electrons in any of the first 20 atoms (given their atomic number).

Figure 4 As a period builds up, the number of electrons in the outer shell of each element increases by one

SUMMARY QUESTIONS
1 Copy and complete using the words below:
electron   energy   energy levels   group   nucleus
period   shells
The electrons in an atom are arranged around the …… in …… or …… . The electrons further away from the nucleus have more …… than those close to the nucleus. As you go across a …… of the periodic table, each element has one more …… than the previous element. All elements in the same …… have the same number of electrons in their outer shell.
2 Draw the arrangement of electrons in the following atoms:
a) Li   b) B   c) P   d) Ar.
3 What is special about the electronic structure of neon and argon?

KEY POINTS
1 The electrons in an atom are arranged in energy levels or shells.
2 Atoms with the same number of electrons in their outer shell belong in the same group of the periodic table.
3 The number of electrons in the outer shell of an atom determines the way that the atom behaves in chemical reactions.

SUMMARY ANSWERS

1 Nucleus, shells (energy levels), energy levels (shells), energy, period, electron, group.

2 a) Li   b) B 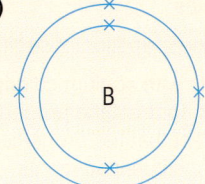   c) P   d) Ar

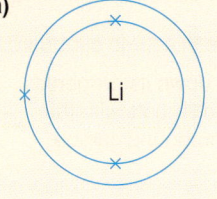

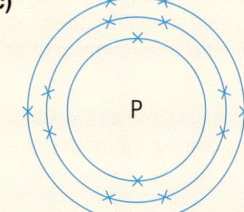

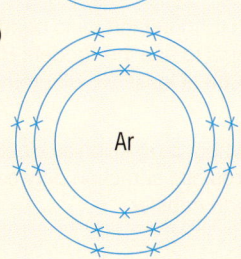

3 They both have full outer shells or energy levels of electrons/ have very stable arrangements of electrons.

Answers to in-text questions

a) Arranged around the nucleus.
b) The energy level closest to the nucleus.
c) 2

KEY POINTS

Match the key points to which learning objective in the Student Book they best answer.

117

CHEMISTRY   STRUCTURES AND BONDING

C2 1.3 Chemical bonding

LEARNING OBJECTIVES

Students should learn that:
- Elements form compounds.
- Elements in Group 1 react with elements in Group 7.

LEARNING OUTCOMES

Most students should be able to:
- State why atoms react.
- Name the two types of bonding present in compounds.
- Represent Cl⁻ and Na⁺ using a diagram.

Some students should also be able to:
- Explain why atoms bond.
- Explain and work out the charge on an ion.
- Explain the formation of ions when a Group 1 and Group 7 element react together.

Teaching suggestions

- **Learning styles**
  Visual: Creating a poster about ionic bonding.
  Auditory: Listening to explanations of bonding.
  Interpersonal: Discussing the nature of ionic bonding.
  Intrapersonal: Reflecting on the lesson.

- **Homework.** Ask students to answer the learning objective questions at the start of the spread in the Student Book.

- **ICT link-up.** Record the demonstration using a web cam. The film can then be played back, annotated and paused on an interactive whiteboard during a discussion about the reaction.

Answers to in-text questions

a) Mixing involves a physical change (easily reversed) while reacting involves a chemical change, which is much less easily reversed.

b) Covalent.

c) Ionic.

SPECIFICATION LINK-UP   Unit: Chemistry 2.12.1

- *Compounds are substances in which atoms of two, or more, elements are not just mixed together but chemically combined.*
- *Chemical bonding involves either transferring or sharing electrons in the highest occupied energy levels (shells) of atoms.*
- *When atoms form chemical bonds by transferring electrons, they form ions. Atoms that lose electrons become positively charge ions. Atoms that gain electrons become negatively charged ions. Ions have the electronic structure of a noble gas (Group 0).*
- *The elements in Group 1 of the periodic table, the alkali metals, have similar chemical properties. They all react with non-metals to form ionic compounds in which the metal ion has a single positive charge.*
- *The elements in Group 7 of the periodic table, the halogens, have similar chemical properties. They react with the alkali metals to form ionic compounds in which the halide ions have a single negative charge.*

Students should use their skills, knowledge and understanding of 'How Science Works':
- *to represent the electronic structure of the ions in sodium chloride . . .*

Lesson structure

STARTER

Think – Ask students to think about why atoms bond. They should talk about the question in pairs and could refer to the Student Book. Then they feedback with questions and answers while you note bullet points on the board. (5 minutes)

True or false – Ask the students to decide if the following are true or false. Encourage them to use the Student Book to help them decide.
- Only compounds contain chemical bonds. [False]
- The nuclei of atoms form chemical bonds. [False]
- Atoms usually bond to get a full shell of electrons. [True]
- Covalent bonds form when pairs of electrons are shared between atoms. [True]
- A chloride ion has a positive charge. [False] (5 minutes)

MAIN

- The formation of sodium chloride from its elements is an exciting and impressive reaction. The elements can be shown to the students in sealed containers – chlorine is toxic and should be stored in a sealed gas jar; sodium is highly flammable and should be stored under oil.
- Students could describe the properties of these elements and the electronic structure could be generated in their notes.
- Then you could demonstrate the formation of sodium chloride in a fume cupboard.
- Following this, provide students with sodium chloride to note down its properties. They should be encouraged to contrast the properties of the elements with the compound and reflect on the fact that the properties of the compound can be completely different from its constituent elements.
- Students need to be able to understand ionic bonding and represent it as dot and cross diagrams. Ask students to use the Student Book to create a poster about ionic bonding. They should include at least two diagrams of ions, and one diagram of an ionic bond.
- Stress to students that ionic bonding involves electron transfer, but the actual ionic bonds arise from the electrostatic attraction between the oppositely charged ions formed as a result of electron transfer.

Additional chemistry

PLENARIES

Reflection – Ask the students to note down:
- What I have seen . . .
- What I have heard . . .
- What I have done . . .

These can be collected in from the class to be used to see what the students have remembered. (10 minutes)

Chemical equation – Ask students to write a word equation for the synthesis of sodium chloride from its elements. (Higher attaining students could write a balanced symbol equation with state symbols.) Then the students should draw the electronic structure of each element and the compound beneath the equation. (15 minutes)

ACTIVITY & EXTENSION IDEAS

- Students could look at and draw models of a salt crystal. They could label the ions.
- Sodium chloride is an important compound in our diet. Ask students to research why humans need to eat salt, and what can happen if we consume too much salt.
- Sodium (a rice grain sized piece) could be put into water (CARE!) to demonstrate that it is a highly reactive metallic element that should not be eaten, and contrast this with sodium chloride. Safety screens all around and above. Wear eye protection (CLEAPSS Hazcard 88).

CHEMISTRY
STRUCTURES AND BONDING

C2 1.3 Chemical bonding

LEARNING OBJECTIVES
1. How do elements form compounds?
2. Why do the elements in Group 1 react with the elements in Group 7?

You already know that we can mix two substances together without either of them changing. For example, we can mix sand and salt together and then separate them again. No change will have taken place. We can even dissolve sugar in tea and separate it out again. But in chemical reactions the situation is very different.

When the atoms of two or more elements react they make a compound. The compound formed is different to both of them and we cannot get either of the elements back again easily. We can also react compounds together to form other compounds, but the reaction of elements is easier to understand as a starting point.

a) What is the difference between **mixing** two substances and **reacting** them?

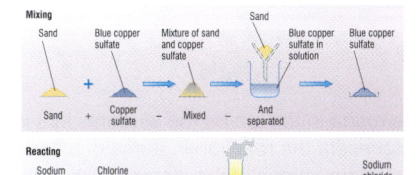

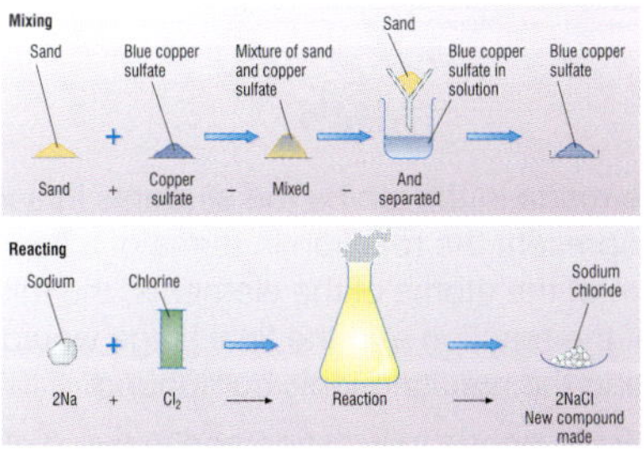

Figure 1 The difference between mixing and reacting. Separating mixtures is usually quite easy, but separating substances once they have reacted can be quite difficult.

Why do atoms react?

When an atom has a full outer shell it is stable and unreactive (like the noble gases in Group 0). However most atoms do not have a full outer shell. When atoms react they take part in changes which give them a stable arrangement of electrons. They may do this by either:

- sharing electrons, which we call **covalent bonding**, or by
- transferring electrons, which we call **ionic bonding**.

In ionic bonding the atoms involved lose or gain electrons so that they have a noble gas structure. So for example, if sodium, 2,8,1 loses one electron it is left with the stable electronic structure of neon 2,8.

However, it is also left with one more proton in the nucleus than there are electrons in orbit around the nucleus. The proton has a positive charge so the sodium atom has now become a positively charged particle. We call this a **sodium ion**. The sodium ion has a single positive charge. We write the formula of a sodium ion as Na$^+$. The electronic structure of the Na$^+$ ion is [2,8]$^+$.

b) When atoms join together by **sharing** electrons, what type of bond is this?
c) When atoms join together as a result of **gaining** or **losing** electrons, what type of bond is this?

Similarly some atoms gain electrons in reactions to achieve a stable noble gas structure. Chlorine, for example, has the electronic structure 2,8,7. By gaining a single electron, it gets the stable electronic structure of argon [2,8,8]. In this case there is now one more electron than there are positive protons in the nucleus. So the chlorine atom becomes a negatively charged particle known as a **chloride ion**. This carries a single negative charge. We write the formula of the chloride ion as Cl$^-$. Its electronic structure is [2,8,8]$^-$.

Representing ionic bonding

When atoms react together to form ionic bonds, atoms which need to lose electrons react with elements which need to gain electrons. So when sodium reacts with chlorine, sodium loses an electron and chlorine gains that electron so they both form stable ions.

We can show this in a diagram. Look at Figure 4:

The electrons of one atom are represented by dots, and the electrons of the other atom are represented by crosses.

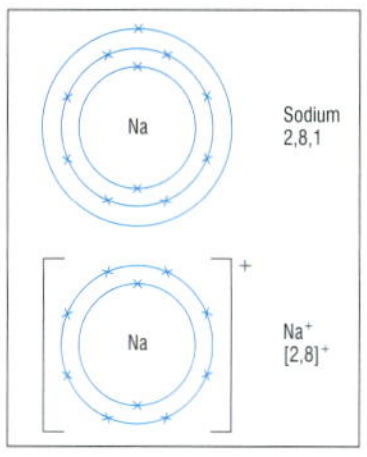

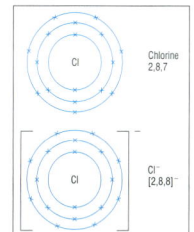

Figure 2 A positive sodium ion (Na$^+$) is formed when a sodium atom loses an electron during ionic bonding with another element

Figure 3 A negative chloride ion (Cl$^-$) is formed when a chlorine atom gains an electron during ionic bonding with another element

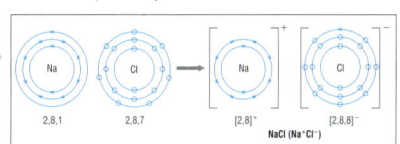

Figure 4 The formation of sodium chloride (NaCl) – an example of ion formation by transferring a single electron

SUMMARY QUESTIONS

1 Copy and complete using the words below:
  covalent   difficult   gaining   ionic   losing   new   noble   sharing

When two substances react together they make a …… substance and it is …… to separate them. Some atoms react by …… electrons – we call this …… bonding. Other atoms react by …… or …… electrons we call this …… bonding. When atoms react in this way they tend to get the electronic structure of a …… gas.

2 Draw diagrams to show the ions that would be formed when the following atoms are involved in ionic bonding. For each one, state whether electrons have been lost or gained and show the charge on the ions formed.
a) aluminium (Al)   b) fluorine (F)
c) potassium (K)   d) oxygen (O)

KEY POINTS
1. Elements react to form compounds by gaining or losing electrons or by sharing electrons.
2. The elements in Group 1 react with the elements in Group 7 because Group 1 elements can lose an electron to gain a full outer shell. This electron can be given to an atom from Group 7, which then also gains a full outer shell.

SUMMARY ANSWERS

1 New, difficult, sharing, covalent, losing (gaining), gaining (losing), ionic, noble.

2 a) Al^{3+} ion, electrons lost.
  b) F$^-$ ion, electron gained. 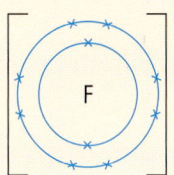
  c) K$^+$ ion, electron lost.
  d) O^{2-} ion, electrons gained.

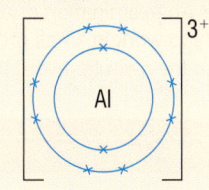

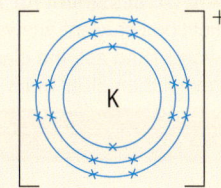

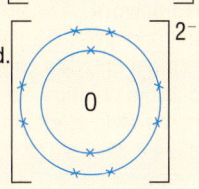

KEY POINTS

Note the points onto flash cards.

CHEMISTRY STRUCTURES AND BONDING

C2 1.4 Ionic bonding

LEARNING OBJECTIVES

Students should learn:

- How ions are held together in a giant structure.
- That elements which aren't in Groups 1 and 7 can also form ions.

LEARNING OUTCOMES

Most students should be able to:

- Describe ionic bonding as electrostatic forces of attraction.
- Draw the dot and cross diagram for magnesium oxide and calcium chloride.

Some students should also be able to:

- Describe an ionic lattice.
- Apply their knowledge of ionic bonding to draw dot and cross diagrams for other ionic compounds.

SPECIFICATION LINK-UP Unit: Chemistry 2.12.1

- An ionic compound is a giant structure of ions. Ionic compounds are held together by strong forces of attraction between oppositely charged ions. These forces act in all directions in the lattice and this is called ionic bonding.

Students should use their skills, knowledge and understanding of 'How Science Works':

- to represent the electronic structure of the ions in sodium chloride, magnesium oxide and calcium chloride.

Lesson structure

STARTER

Define – Give students the following definitions and ask them to decide which key word it is relating to:

- A charged particle formed by an atom losing or gaining electrons. [Ion]
- All the atoms are the same. [Element]
- More than one type of atom chemically bonded together. [Compound]
- A chemical bond formed as electrons are transferred. [Ionic bond]
- A section of the periodic table whose elements all form 1+ ions. [Group 1/Alkali metals] (5 minutes)

Guess the ion – Give the students a diagram of chlorine, sodium, calcium, oxygen and calcium ions. Encourage them to use the periodic table and the textbook to name each ion. (10 minutes)

MAIN

- Magnesium oxide can be made in the lab by the students in a variety of ways. Encourage students to represent the reaction in terms of a flow chart. The first stages should detail the structure of the atoms of the elements, the middle stages could show the observations of the reaction and the final stage would include a dot and cross diagram representing the resulting ionic compound.
- Often students consider ionic bonds in isolation and in two-dimensional particle diagrams or in dot and cross diagrams. Show students already made-up structures of calcium chloride and magnesium oxide.
- Students could then compare the structures to the actual substances (crystalline powders).
- Then give students molecular model kits and ask them to generate a sodium chloride crystal. Using question and answer, encourage students to understand which part of the model represents ions and bonds and what the bonds are (an electrostatic force of attraction between oppositely charged ions).

PLENARIES

Question – Split the class into four groups and give each team a different key term: 'ions', 'ionic bond', 'lattice', 'charge'. Each group should write a question which matches their answer. Students then share their questions with the rest of the class. (5 minutes)

AfL (Assessment for Learning) – Give students an examination question with a fictitious student answer. Encourage the students to work in small groups to mark the work. Then ask the class to say how many marks they would award the student, and reveal the actual mark. (10 minutes)

Teaching suggestions

- **Special needs.** Give these students a sheet with dot and cross diagrams of a sodium ion, magnesium ion, calcium ion, oxide ion and two chloride ions. Encourage them to represent sodium chloride, magnesium oxide and calcium chloride by cutting out the ions and sticking them into the correct arrangement.
- **Gifted and talented**
  - Students could be encouraged to research and find out the charges of transition metals and to find out different examples of ionic lattices involving these elements.
  - Students could compare copper oxide produced with the two differently charged copper ions.
- **Learning styles**

  Kinaesthetic: Completing the practical to form magnesium oxide.

  Visual: Creating a flow chart to represent the formation of magnesium oxide.

  Auditory: Listening to different students' opinions on the marking of fictitious student answers.

  Interpersonal: Working in groups to generate questions for which answers are provided.

  Intrapersonal: Individually naming the ions.

- **Homework.** Ask students to draw the dot and cross diagrams to represent sodium chloride, magnesium oxide and calcium chloride. To extend this homework, students could research and draw a diagram to represent the ionic lattice for each compound.

Practical support
Burning magnesium
Equipment and materials required

Magnesium ribbon (flammable – CLEAPSS Hazcard 59), magnesium powder (flammable), spatula, tongs, Bunsen burner and safety equipment, eye protection, blue plastic.

Details

Safety: During both of these reactions, eye protection must be worn. Magnesium oxide powder will aspirate, so it is advisable to complete this in a well-ventilated area, or demonstrate.

Students hold a small piece (<1 cm) of magnesium ribbon in tongs. The metal should be held at the top of the blue gas cone in the Bunsen flame. As soon as it ignites, they need to remove it from the flame. This reaction produces a bright light that can blind if looked at directly, so either encourage the students to look past the reaction or through the special blue plastic.

Then ask the students to sprinkle about half a spatula of magnesium powder directly into the blue Bunsen flame and observe. As the surface area is greater, it will combust more quickly and produces a twinkling effect. Make sure that they hold the Bunsen at an angle or the magnesium powder may fall down the Bunsen chimney and fuse the collar to the chimney.

ACTIVITY & EXTENSION

- Students could be encouraged to draw more complex dot and cross diagrams, e.g. aluminium oxide.
- Students could research into elements that can have more than one charge, e.g. manganese.
- Students could evaluate dot and cross diagrams as a means of representing ionic compounds.

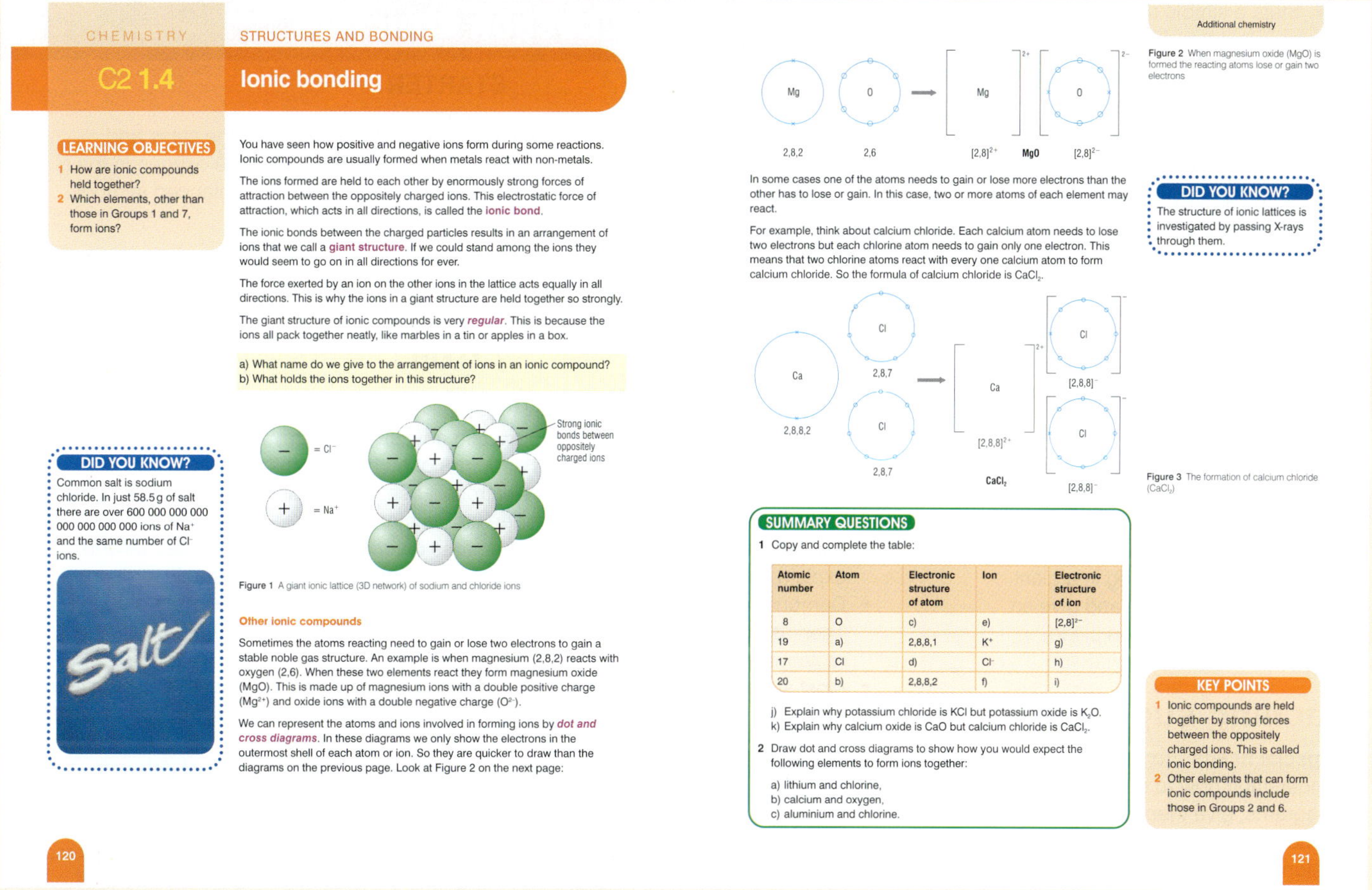

CHEMISTRY — STRUCTURES AND BONDING
C2 1.4 Ionic bonding

LEARNING OBJECTIVES
1. How are ionic compounds held together?
2. Which elements, other than those in Groups 1 and 7, form ions?

You have seen how positive and negative ions form during some reactions. Ionic compounds are usually formed when metals react with non-metals.

The ions formed are held to each other by enormously strong forces of attraction between the oppositely charged ions. This electrostatic force of attraction, which acts in all directions, is called the **ionic bond**.

The ionic bonds between the charged particles results in an arrangement of ions that we call a **giant structure**. If we could stand among the ions they would seem to go on in all directions for ever.

The force exerted by an ion on the other ions in the lattice acts equally in all directions. This is why the ions in a giant structure are held together so strongly.

The giant structure of ionic compounds is very **regular**. This is because the ions all pack together neatly, like marbles in a tin or apples in a box.

a) What name do we give to the arrangement of ions in an ionic compound?
b) What holds the ions together in this structure?

DID YOU KNOW?
Common salt is sodium chloride. In just 58.5 g of salt there are over 600 000 000 000 000 000 000 000 ions of Na+ and the same number of Cl– ions.

Figure 1 A giant ionic lattice (3D network) of sodium and chloride ions

Other ionic compounds

Sometimes the atoms reacting need to gain or lose two electrons to gain a stable noble gas structure. An example is when magnesium (2,8,2) reacts with oxygen (2,6). When these two elements react they form magnesium oxide (MgO). This is made up of magnesium ions with a double positive charge (Mg^{2+}) and oxide ions with a double negative charge (O^{2-}).

We can represent the atoms and ions involved in forming ions by **dot and cross diagrams**. In these diagrams we only show the electrons in the outermost shell of each atom or ion. So they are quicker to draw than the diagrams on the previous page. Look at Figure 2 on the next page:

Figure 2 When magnesium oxide (MgO) is formed the reacting atoms lose or gain two electrons

In some cases one of the atoms needs to gain or lose more electrons than the other has to lose or gain. In this case, two or more atoms of each element may react.

For example, think about calcium chloride. Each calcium atom needs to lose two electrons but each chlorine atom needs to gain only one electron. This means that two chlorine atoms react with every one calcium atom to form calcium chloride. So the formula of calcium chloride is $CaCl_2$.

DID YOU KNOW?
The structure of ionic lattices is investigated by passing X-rays through them.

Figure 3 The formation of calcium chloride ($CaCl_2$)

SUMMARY QUESTIONS

1 Copy and complete the table:

Atomic number	Atom	Electronic structure of atom	Ion	Electronic structure of ion
8	O	c)	e)	$[2,8]^{2-}$
19	a)	2,8,8,1	K+	g)
17	Cl	d)	Cl–	h)
20	b)	2,8,8,2	f)	i)

j) Explain why potassium chloride is KCl but potassium oxide is K_2O.
k) Explain why calcium oxide is CaO but calcium chloride is $CaCl_2$.

2 Draw dot and cross diagrams to show how you would expect the following elements to form ions together:
a) lithium and chlorine,
b) calcium and oxygen,
c) aluminium and chlorine.

KEY POINTS
1. Ionic compounds are held together by strong forces between the oppositely charged ions. This is called ionic bonding.
2. Other elements that can form ionic compounds include those in Groups 2 and 6.

SUMMARY ANSWERS

1

Atomic number	Atom	Electronic structure of atom	Ion	Electronic structure of ion
8	O	2,6	O^{2-}	$[2,8]^{2-}$
19	K	2,8,8,1	K+	$[2,8,8]^+$
17	Cl	2,8,7	Cl–	$[2,8,8]^-$
20	Ca	2,8,8,2	Ca^{2+}	$[2,8,8]^{2+}$

j) K forms K+ and Cl forms Cl–. Therefore one type of each ion is needed to make the compound electrically neutral. But O forms O^{2-}, so two K+ are needed.

k) Ca forms Ca^{2+} and O forms O^{2-}. Therefore one type of each ion is needed to make the compound electrically neutral. But Cl forms Cl–, so two Cl– are needed.

2 Dot and cross diagrams in style of those shown on page 121 in the Student Book, showing:
a) Li+ $[2]^+$ and Cl– $[2,8,8]^-$
b) Ca^{2+} $[2,8,8]^{2+}$ and O^{2-} $[2,8]^{2-}$
c) Al^{3+} $[2,8]^{3+}$ and $3 \times Cl^-$ $[2,8,8]^-$

Answers to in-text questions

a) Lattice.
b) Attractive forces between oppositely charged ions.

DID YOU KNOW?

Using X-rays, scientists have discovered that ionic lattices aren't perfect. There are sections where the ions aren't perfectly arranged, and if you tap the crystal they will break along cleavage planes.

KEY POINTS

Begin to make a spider diagram using the key points on this spread. Then at the end of each lesson during the unit, or as a homework activity, the other key points from the topic can be added. Therefore, at the end of the topic, a powerful revision tool will have been created.

CHEMISTRY | STRUCTURES AND BONDING

C2 1.5 Covalent bonding

LEARNING OBJECTIVES

Students should learn:

- How a covalent bond is formed.
- The types of substances formed from covalent bonds.

LEARNING OUTCOMES

Most students should be able to:

- State a simple definition for a covalent bond.
- Draw a dot and cross diagram for simple covalent bonds (hydrogen, chlorine, hydrogen chloride, water).
- Name an element that has a giant covalent structure (carbon, diamond).

Some students should also be able to:

- Explain the formation of a covalent bond.
- Draw dot and cross diagrams for more complex covalent substances (methane, ammonia and oxygen).
- Explain the bonding in a giant covalent structure and give an example e.g. silicon oxide.

Teaching suggestions

- **Special needs.** To help the students understand how to draw dot and cross diagrams, give them the electronic structures of key atoms (hydrogen, chlorine) OHTs. Then ask them to arrange the images so that each atom has a full outer shell of electrons, by overlapping one image onto another. When they have the correct arrangement of electrons they can copy the diagram into their book. This process can be demonstrated on an OHP in front of the class.
- **Learning styles**
  Kinaesthetic: Completing a card sort.
  Visual: Watching the demonstration of the exploding hydrogen balloon.
  Auditory: Listening to explanations of covalent bonding.
  Interpersonal: Working in groups to model different substances.
  Intrapersonal: Drawing dot and cross diagrams.

SPECIFICATION LINK-UP   Unit: Chemistry 2.12.1

- When atoms share pairs of electrons, they form covalent bonds. These bonds between atoms are strong. Some covalently bonded substances consist of simple molecules such as H_2, Cl_2, O_2, HCl, H_2O and CH_4. Others have giant covalent structures (macromolecules), such as diamond and silicon dioxide.

Students should use their skills, knowledge and understanding of 'How Science Works':

- to represent the covalent bonds in molecules such as water, ammonia, hydrogen, hydrogen chloride, chlorine, methane and oxygen and in giant structures such as diamond and silicon dioxide.

Lesson structure

STARTER

Demonstration – Ignite a hydrogen balloon to get the attention of the class and generate excitement. The hydrogen will explode, as it reacts with the oxygen in the air to make water (steam). Encourage the students to write a word and balanced symbol equation for this reaction. (10 minutes)

Card sort – Give the students separate cards with images (just coloured circles and dot and cross diagrams) and words on: 'compound', 'element', 'molecule', 'mixture', 'ionic bond', 'ion'. Students should then try to match the image with the key term. (10 minutes)

MAIN

- Students need to be able to draw dot and cross diagrams for certain molecules and some students should be able to explain how and why they are formed. Ask for volunteers to draw the electronic structure of hydrogen on the board.
- Then ask the students how many electrons it needs to obtain a complete outer shell [1]. Then explain how and why hydrogen atoms make diatomic molecules.
- Ask the students to draw the dot and cross diagram of a chlorine molecule and explain, in no more than two sentences, why chlorine forms a diatomic molecule.
- Demonstrate how hydrogen and chlorine atoms bond to form hydrogen chloride. Then ask students to draw the other dot and cross diagrams for the appropriate molecules in their books.
- Most substances that form covalent bonds make discrete molecules, however there are some macromolecules, e.g. carbon and silicon oxide, that the students need to be aware of.
- Give students molecular model kits and ask them to make models of different molecules. Then focus on carbon, and ask them to make a carbon molecule using only single bonds – hopefully the students will find that the structure is never-ending.
- Explain to students that this is an example of a macromolecule and that it too is made of covalent bonds.
- To extend this, students could brainstorm the properties of diamond and try to explain them in terms of the structure.

PLENARIES

Model – Split the class into teams and give each team a different covalent compound to represent. In their team, students should represent atoms and their hands and feet can make up to four bonds (e.g. C in methane). Each team should 'act out' their molecule and explain it to the class. (10 minutes)

Ionic/covalent – Give the students a piece of paper. Ask them to write in large letters 'ionic bonding' and 'covalent bonding', one on each side of the paper. Then read out the following substances, and the students should hold up which type of bonding is present:

- Methane [Covalent]
- Sodium chloride [Ionic]
- Oxygen [Covalent]
- Water [Covalent]
- Magnesium oxide [Ionic]
- Carbon [Covalent]
- Silicon oxide [Covalent]
- Ammonia [Covalent]
- Calcium chloride [Ionic]
- Hydrogen chloride [Covalent] (5 minutes)

Definitions – Ask the students to define the term 'covalent bonding' in one sentence and explain this using a labelled diagram. (5 minutes)

Practical support

Burning hydrogen

Materials and equipment required
Rubber balloon, string, hydrogen gas cylinder (pressurised gas), metre rule, splint, tape, matches.

Details
Fill a rubber balloon with hydrogen from a gas cylinder. Tie the balloon with a piece of string onto a tap or 1 kg mass, so that it is clear of any flammable materials, students and the ceiling.

Then light a splint taped to the end of a metre ruler. Hold the lighted splint onto the stretched part of the rubber.

Safety: It is advised that the demonstrator wears eye protection and should be aware that hot rubber can fly from the balloon. Hydrogen is flammable – CLEAPSS Hazcard 48.
NB Soap bubbles filled with hydrogen are an alternative here.

Answers to in-text questions
a) Covalent.
b) Two electrons.
c) A giant covalent structure (macromolecule).

ACTIVITY & EXTENSION
- Students could define the term 'allotrope' and look up other allotropes of carbon [fullerenes].
- Students could draw dot and cross diagrams of other covalent compounds.

KEY POINTS
- Ask students to draw diagrams or pictures to illustrate each key point.
- Alternatively, ask them to imagine that each key point is an answer, then to write the question to match it.

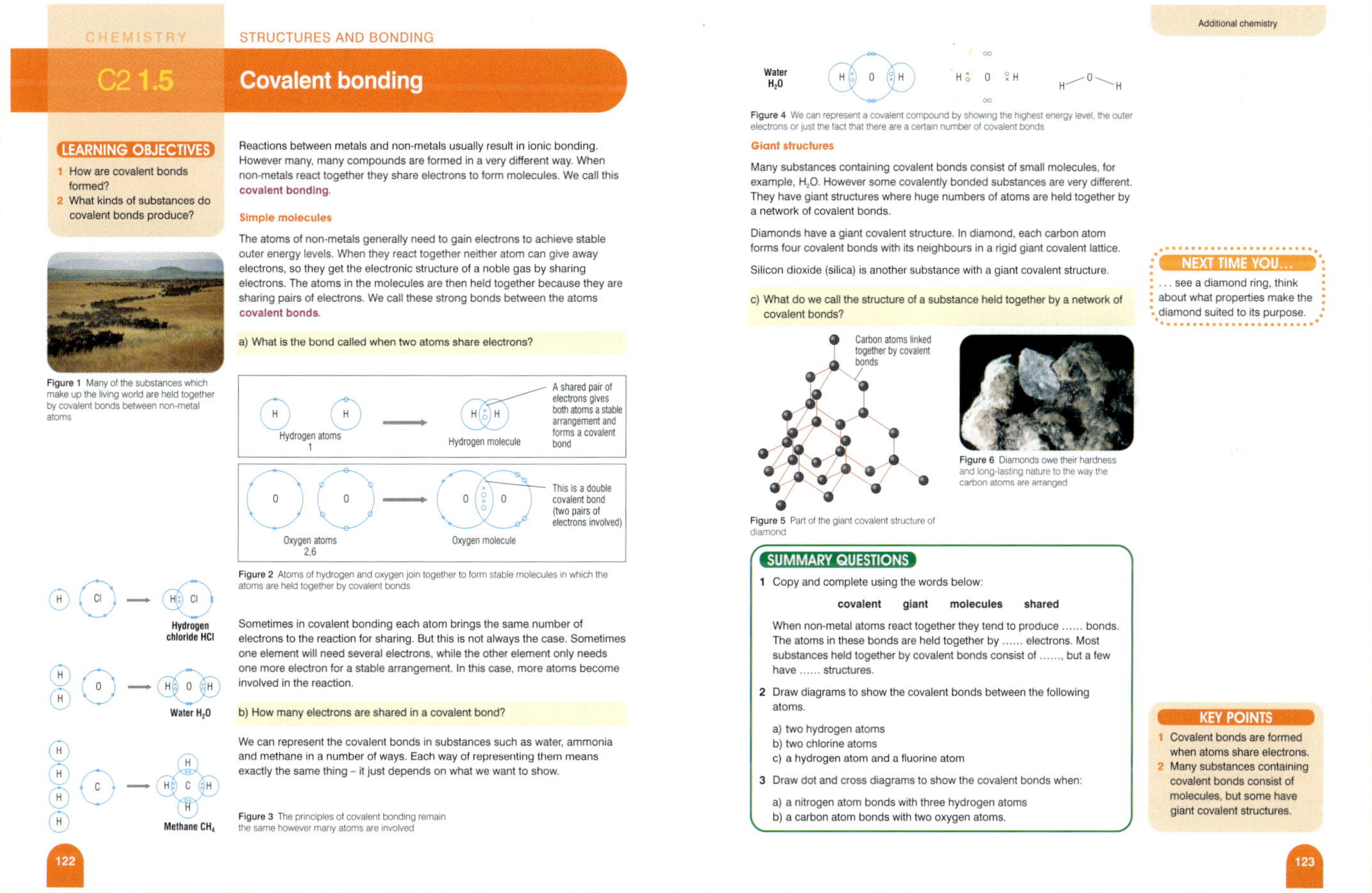

CHEMISTRY — STRUCTURES AND BONDING

C2 1.5 Covalent bonding

LEARNING OBJECTIVES
1. How are covalent bonds formed?
2. What kinds of substances do covalent bonds produce?

Reactions between metals and non-metals usually result in ionic bonding. However many, many compounds are formed in a very different way. When non-metals react together they share electrons to form molecules. We call this **covalent bonding**.

Simple molecules
The atoms of non-metals generally need to gain electrons to achieve stable outer energy levels. When they react together neither atom can give away electrons, so they get the electronic structure of a noble gas by sharing electrons. The atoms in the molecules are then held together because they are sharing pairs of electrons. We call these strong bonds between the atoms **covalent bonds**.

Figure 1 Many of the substances which make up the living world are held together by covalent bonds between non-metal atoms

a) What is the bond called when two atoms share electrons?

Figure 2 Atoms of hydrogen and oxygen join together to form stable molecules in which the atoms are held together by covalent bonds

Sometimes in covalent bonding each atom brings the same number of electrons to the reaction for sharing. But this is not always the case. Sometimes one element will need several electrons, while the other element only needs one more electron for a stable arrangement. In this case, more atoms become involved in the reaction.

b) How many electrons are shared in a covalent bond?

We can represent the covalent bonds in substances such as water, ammonia and methane in a number of ways. Each way of representing them means exactly the same thing – it just depends on what we want to show.

Figure 3 The principles of covalent bonding remain the same however many atoms are involved

Figure 4 We can represent a covalent compound by showing the highest energy level, the outer electrons or just the fact that there are a certain number of covalent bonds

Giant structures
Many substances containing covalent bonds consist of small molecules, for example, H_2O. However some covalently bonded substances are very different. They have giant structures where huge numbers of atoms are held together by a network of covalent bonds.

Diamonds have a giant covalent structure. In diamond, each carbon atom forms four covalent bonds with its neighbours in a rigid giant covalent lattice.

Silicon dioxide (silica) is another substance with a giant covalent structure.

c) What do we call the structure of a substance held together by a network of covalent bonds?

Figure 5 Part of the giant covalent structure of diamond

Figure 6 Diamonds owe their hardness and long-lasting nature to the way the carbon atoms are arranged

NEXT TIME YOU...
...see a diamond ring, think about what properties make the diamond suited to its purpose.

SUMMARY QUESTIONS
1. Copy and complete using the words below:

   covalent   giant   molecules   shared

   When non-metal atoms react together they tend to produce ...... bonds. The atoms in these bonds are held together by ...... electrons. Most substances held together by covalent bonds consist of ......, but a few have ...... structures.

2. Draw diagrams to show the covalent bonds between the following atoms.
   a) two hydrogen atoms
   b) two chlorine atoms
   c) a hydrogen atom and a fluorine atom

3. Draw dot and cross diagrams to show the covalent bonds when:
   a) a nitrogen atom bonds with three hydrogen atoms
   b) a carbon atom bonds with two oxygen atoms.

KEY POINTS
1. Covalent bonds are formed when atoms share electrons.
2. Many substances containing covalent bonds consist of molecules, but some have giant covalent structures.

SUMMARY ANSWERS

1. Covalent, shared, molecules, giant.

2. a) H–H   b) Cl–Cl   c) H–F

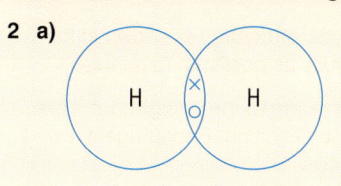

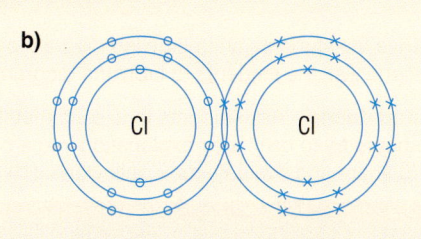

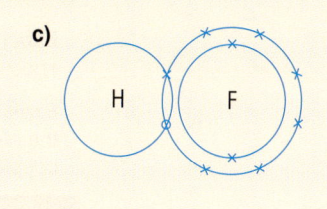

3. a) $H:\overset{\times\times}{\underset{H}{N}}:H$ (with dots and crosses around N)
   b) O=C=O (dot and cross diagram)

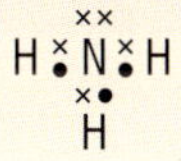

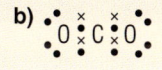

CHEMISTRY   STRUCTURES AND BONDING

C2 1.6 Bonding in metals

LEARNING OBJECTIVES

Students should learn:

- How atoms in metals are arranged.
- What holds metal atoms (ions) together. [**HT** only]

LEARNING OUTCOMES

Most students should be able to:

- Describe the bonding in metals. [**HT** only]
- List examples of elements that have a giant metallic structure.

Some students should also be able to:

- Explain metallic bonding and structures in words and a labelled diagram, including delocalised electrons. [**HT** only]

SPECIFICATION LINK-UP   Unit: Chemistry 2.12.1

- *Metals consist of giant structures of atoms arranged in a regular pattern. The electrons in the highest occupied energy levels (outer shell) of metal atoms are delocalised and so free to move through the whole structure. This corresponds to a structure of positive ions with electrons between the ions holding them together by strong electrostatic attractions.* [**HT** only]

Students should use their skills, knowledge and understanding of 'How Science Works':

- to represent the bonding in metals in the following form: [**HT** only]

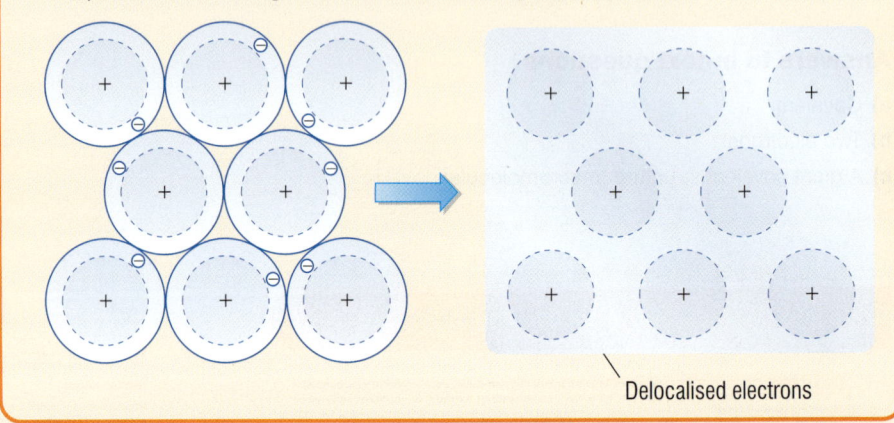

Delocalised electrons

Teaching suggestions

- **Learning styles**

  Kinaesthetic: Finding different examples of metal crystals.

  Visual: Labelling a metallic structure.

  Auditory: Listening to explanations of metallic bonding.

  Interpersonal: Working in groups to find different examples of metal crystals.

  Intrapersonal: Deciding which metal is the odd one out and why.

- **Homework.** Ask students to answer the following question:

  'Which metal do you think would have the strongest bonding: sodium or aluminium, and why?' [Al has more delocalised electrons]

- **ICT link-up.** Digital images taken by students or from the Internet could be used by the students to create a PowerPoint® about metal crystals and where you can find them. They could then show their presentations to their classmates.

Lesson structure

STARTER

5,4,3,2,1 – Ask students to write a list of: 5 metal symbols, 4 metal properties, 3 magnetic elements, 2 metals used in jewellery, 1 liquid metal at room temperature. Build up a class list on the board through questions and answers. (10 minutes)

Odd one out – Ask students to look at the list and decide which metal doesn't fit the pattern and why. The metals are: 'nickel, cobalt, iron and steel'. [Steel is the odd one out as it is an alloy, whereas nickel, cobalt and iron are elements.] (5 minutes)

MAIN

- Metals are made up of grains, which can be seen using very powerful microscopes. Show students images of the grains and grain boundaries. The grains order themselves in metals and form crystals.
- Students can grow their own metal crystals by completing a solution displacement reaction. Students could be encouraged to record the metal crystal in the form of a diagram in their book.
- Visible metal crystals can be found in a variety of structures in and around the school site. Students could go out and about in small teams, armed with digital cameras to find examples.
- When students return to the class, they could display the photographs to the rest of the class.

PLENARIES

Label – Give the students an unlabelled diagram of a metal structure (as shown in the specification). Ask the students to label the diagram as fully as possible. (5 minutes)

Explain and define – Ask students to explain metallic bonding to their neighbour. Then the pair should try to distil their explanation into a concise definition. Encourage a few couples to share and evaluate their definitions. (10 minutes)

Practical support

Growing silver crystals

Equipment and materials required

Boiling tube, boiling tube rack, copper wire, silver nitrate solution <0.5 M (irritant – CLEAPSS Hazcard 87), eye protection.

Details

- Wrap the copper wire into a spring shape and put into a boiling tube. Eye protection should be worn and silver nitrate solution added to the boiling tube so that it is about half full.
- Leave to allow displacement to occur: it would be best if the experiment were left until next lesson and reviewed as a starter.

Survey of metallic crystals

Equipment and materials required

Clipboards, digital camera, stationery.

Details

- Split the class into small groups. Take the students to an example of a metal crystal e.g. a galvanised dustbin on the school site.
- Give the students a time limit (10 minutes) to find further examples around the school of metal crystals. They should record, in a table, the photograph number, place and item that the metal crystal was found on.

ACTIVITY & EXTENSION IDEAS

- Students could electrolyse copper sulfate solution in order to grow copper crystals or grow lead crystals from zinc foil suspended in lead nitrate solution.
  [**Safety:** Copper sulfate is harmful (CLEAPSS Hazcard 27) and lead nitrate is toxic (CLEAPSS Hazcard 57).]
- If the school has any examples, students could be shown different metal crystals and metal structural models.
- Students could try to make a three-dimensional model of a metallic structure using art materials, e.g. polystyrene balls, string, paint and a shoe box.

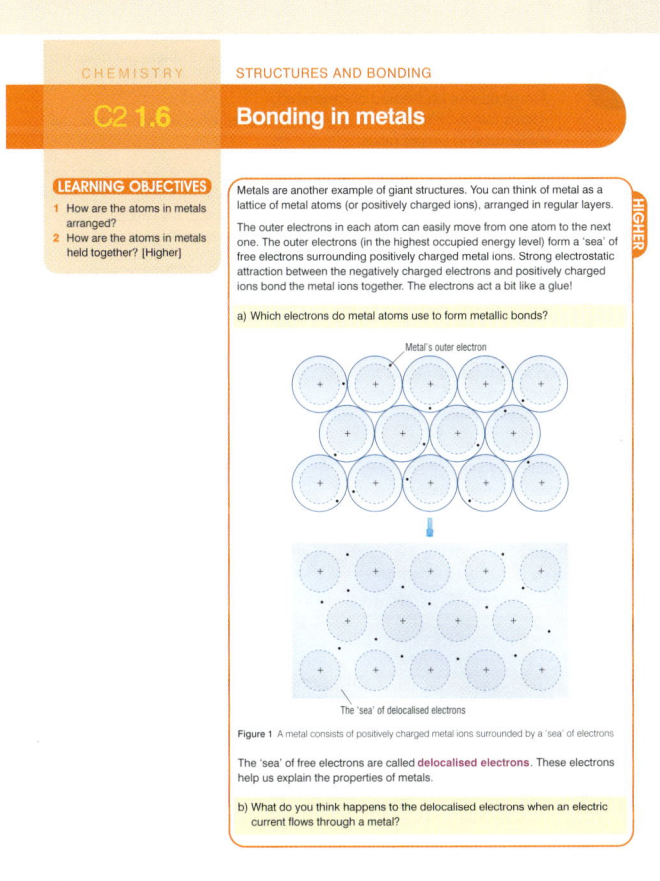

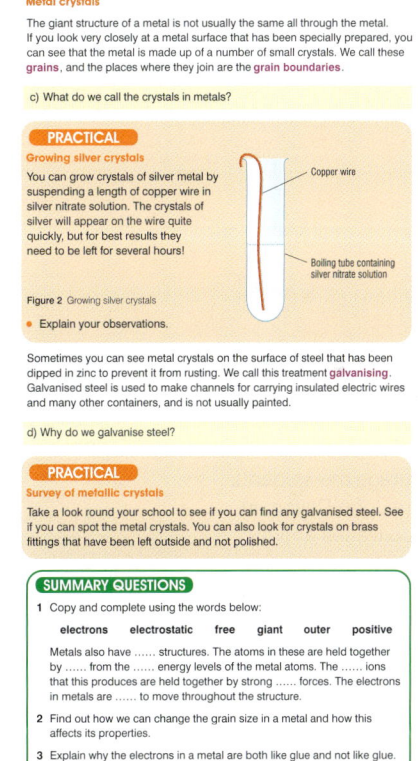

SUMMARY ANSWERS

1. Giant, electrons, outer, positive, electrostatic, free.
2. Student research – e.g. cold working, annealing.
3. Like glue – because they hold the atoms together.
   Unlike glue – because atoms can still move/flow past each other when force is applied. The electrons can also move freely through the structure.
   [**HT** only]

Answers to in-text questions

a) Outer electrons.
b) They drift towards the positive terminal.
c) Grains.
d) To prevent rusting.

KEY POINTS

Answer each learning objective from Student Book page 124 using a key point.

CHEMISTRY | STRUCTURES AND BONDING

C2 1.7 The history of the atom

SPECIFICATION LINK-UP
Unit: Chemistry 2.12.1

This spread provides the opportunity to revisit the following substantive content already covered in this chapter:

- *Compounds are substances in which atoms of two, or more, elements are not just mixed together but chemically combined.*

CHEMISTRY | STRUCTURES AND BONDING

C2 1.7 The history of the atom

John Dalton's atomic theory

John Dalton was born in 1766 in the Lake District in England. His father was a weaver who taught John at home before sending him to a Quaker school in Eaglesfield, where they lived. John was amazingly clever – by the time he was 12 he was teaching other children!

He was interested in almost everything. He made observations of the weather as well as being the first person to study colour-blindness. (John was colour-blind himself – see the photo below.)

But Dalton is best-remembered for his ideas about chemistry – and in particular his theories about atoms. As a result of a great deal of work, Dalton suggested that:

- All matter is made up of indivisible particles called atoms.
- Atoms of the same element are similar in mass and shape but differ from the atoms of other elements.
- Atoms cannot be created or destroyed.
- Atoms join together to form compound atoms (what we would now call molecules) in simple ratios.

Dalton's statements were backed up with much research, even though not all of it was accurate. For example, he insisted that one hydrogen atom combined with one oxygen atom to form water. However, most of his research reflected the same results as other scientists of the time were getting.

Dalton's atomic theory explained much of what scientists were seeing, and so his idea of atoms was accepted relatively quickly. Some scientists even made wooden models of atoms of different elements, to show their different relative sizes.

By 1850, the atomic theory of matter was almost universally accepted and virtually all opposition had disappeared. Dalton's atomic theory was the basis of much of the chemistry done in the rest of the 19th and early 20th centuries.

John Dalton – the man who gave us atoms

ACTIVITY

Imagine that you are John Dalton and that you have just finished writing a book about your ideas on atoms. Write a letter to someone explaining your ideas. You can choose to write to:

- another scientist,
- a member of your family,
- a journalist who is interested in your ideas and who wants to know more about them in order to write a newspaper article for the general public.

John Dalton's eyes (on the watch-glass) were taken out after his death as he requested. He wanted a doctor to check his theory of colour blindness. Unfortunately this theory proved incorrect.

126

Teaching suggestions

Activities

- **Letter writing** – Encourage the students to imagine that they are John Dalton, in the 1700s, after his discoveries about atoms. Ask the students to pick a person to whom he might have written a letter (encourage them to find out actual names of scientists who were alive at the same time, his parents' names, or publications which would have printed his letter at the time). Then ask them to write a letter conveying the excitement of his discoveries, but also in appropriate language for the audience. Students may then also like to 'age' their work, using damp tea bags to stain paper, burning the edges with a candle and could even create a seal using coloured candle wax.
- **Safety:** Be aware that candle wax can cause thermal burns. If the wax gets in contact with the skin, wash under cold water for 10 minutes and seek further medical attention. If the edges of the paper are singed, use a lighted candle on a flame-proof mat, be sure to tie back long hair and keep ties away from the flame. If the paper begins to burn, it could be blown out, or dropped onto the heat-proof mat and allowed to burn out.

- **Information cards** – Encourage the students to research the work of Dalton. Give them index cards: on one side they could summarise the experiment that Dalton did (either diagram or text), and on the reverse detail what he discovered from that particular experiment.
- **Poster** – Scientific research costs a lot of money. Encourage students to find out some sources of funding. Then, with a question and answer session, draw out from the class some positive and negative points about research. Then ask the class to vote whether they think that research should happen. Students could then design and make a poster showing points for and against academic research.

Homework (cut and stick) – Give the students a set of discoveries about the atom and who discovered them in separate boxes on paper. They should then cut out and match the discoverer with the discovery.

Extensions

- **Brainstorm** – Often when a scientist made a discovery, many people were against the new ideas as it contradicted what they already knew. Ask the class to brainstorm what type of people would be against Dalton's ideas and why. Then ask the class to imagine the answers that Dalton could have prepared to counter arguments put forward against his ideas.

Atoms and the future

Deep underneath the Swiss countryside lies a huge maze of tunnels. Inside these tunnels, scientists are working to puzzle out the structure of the atom. They are searching for the particles that make up the protons and neutrons inside each atom.

To find these tiny particles they need to use huge machines. These accelerate particles like electrons and protons up to speeds close to the speed of light. Then the particles smash into each other in a kind of 'subatomic demolition derby'!

This is a particle detector under construction

It's really important that we know as much as we can about atoms. Although it doesn't seem like this knowledge is very useful at the moment, it could lead to important discoveries in the future. And besides, we should try to find out as much as we can about the world around us!

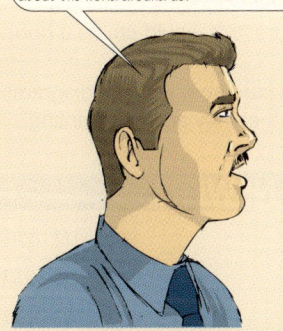

The money that's spent on this kind of research is enormous. We should spend money on APPLIED kinds of scientific research that may be able to help people, not on research that isn't any practical use.

This shows a section of a particle accelerator

ACTIVITY

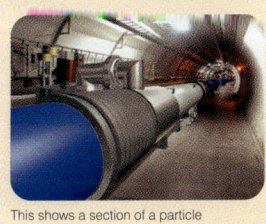

Research like this costs a great deal of money. Who do you agree with?

Design a poster to show your ideas.

- **Time line** – There are philosophers and scientists who have contributed to our knowledge of the structure of the atom. Encourage students to use the Internet and books to create a time line ranging from 400BCE (Democritus) to modern day (quarks and leptons). Students could summarise the discoveries/theories in text or diagrams (e.g. JJ Thomson's plum pudding model is easier described in a diagram). Instead of individuals making their own time line, it could be made into a class effort. Each student, or pair of students, could be given a discovery that they must document. Then all the information could be constructed onto a giant time line spanning the top of the room.
Use PhotoPLUS C2 1.7 'History of the atom' from the GCSE Chemistry CD ROM.

Learning styles
Visual: Preparing the time line for atom discovery.

Interpersonal: Working as a group to prepare resources for the class time line.

Intrapersonal: Writing a letter from Dalton.

ICT link-up
New information about the atomic structure is being discovered at CERN, Europe. Students could use the Internet to find out what CERN is and the discoveries they are making (www.cern.ch).

Special needs
Give the students the names and discoveries of Democritus, John Dalton, Ernest Rutherford, Neils Bohr and James Chadwick, as these scientists discovered parts of the atom as we know it today. They can then use this limited information to make their own time line.

CHEMISTRY — STRUCTURES AND BONDING

SUMMARY ANSWERS

1. a) Proton, neutron, electron.
   b) Proton – positive, neutron – neutral, electron – negative.

2. Diagrams to show the following electronic structures:
   a) 2   b) 2,6   c) 2,8,8,1   d) 2,8,7   e) 2,8,3

3. a) A (Magnesium).
   b) Group 7.
   c) 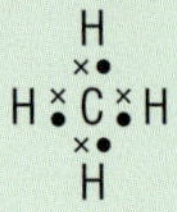

   H
   × •
   H • C × H
   × •
   H   Where C (carbon) = B

   d) 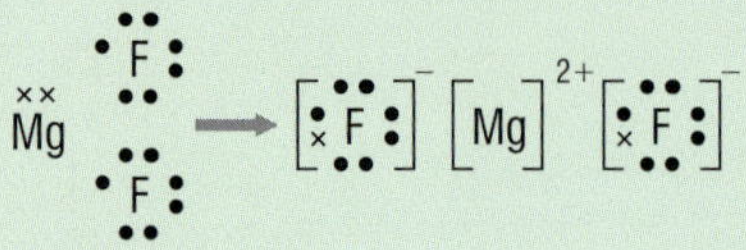

   Mg •• F ••   →   [•• F ••]⁻ [Mg]²⁺ [•• F ••]⁻

   Where Mg = A and F = C

4. a) Atoms held together by sharing a pair of electrons to form a covalent bond, joining two Br atoms together. 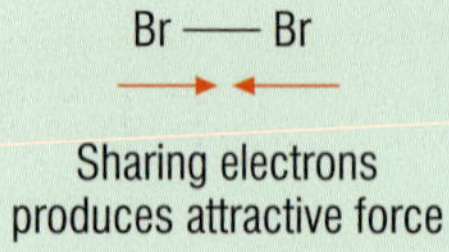

   Br —— Br

   Sharing electrons produces attractive force

   b) Diagram to show a giant lattice of covalent bonds. (See Student Book page 123.)
   c) Diagram to show a giant lattice of Na⁺ and Cl⁻ ions, held together by strong electrostatic attractive forces between opposite charges. (See Student Book page 120.)

5. Diagram to show a giant lattice of positively charged sodium ions held together by delocalised ('sea') of electrons. (See Student Book page 124.) [**HT** only]

Summary teaching suggestions

- **Special needs** – Question 2 requires students to draw their own atomic structures of certain elements. Give these students a framework with the element symbol under the correct amount of shells (circles) so that the students only need to add their crosses on to it.
- **Gifted and talented** – Question 5 is a good example of a higher-level question.
- **Misconceptions** – Often students do not use all the information given to them in an examination question. Question 3 requires candidates to choose examples from those given in the diagrams. However, some students will ignore this information and try to answer the questions immediately and will give chemically correct answers but not be awarded any marks.
- **Learning styles**
  Visual: Questions 2, 4 and 5 require students to draw diagrams, and question 3 requires students to use diagrams to answer the question.
  Interpersonal: Question 4 and 5 lend themselves to class discussion before the students attempt the questions.
- **When to use the questions?**
  - Split the class into groups of three, each member of the team should tackle a different part of question 4. You should time this (3 minutes), encouraging students to use their exercise books and textbooks to help them. Then the papers should be swapped, to the right within the group, and the next student also has time to read the previous answer and amend, then add their own thoughts. This process of passing the paper and correcting previous work continues until the papers are returned to the original owner and the group could then discuss their thoughts about all of the parts.

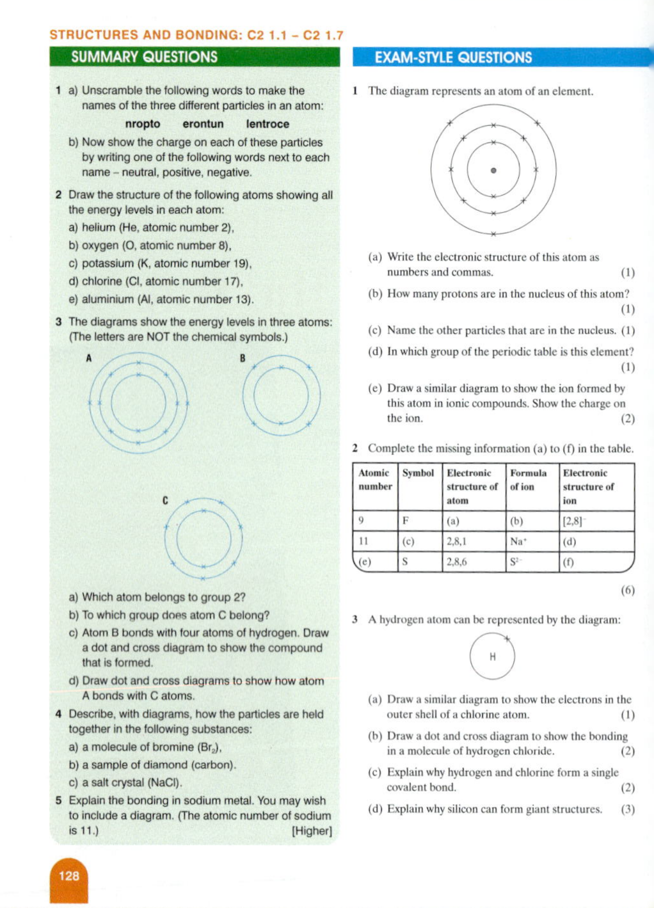

STRUCTURES AND BONDING: C2 1.1 – C2 1.7

SUMMARY QUESTIONS

1. a) Unscramble the following words to make the names of the three different particles in an atom:
      nropto   erontun   lentroce
   b) Now show the charge on each of these particles by writing one of the following words next to each name – neutral, positive, negative.

2. Draw the structure of the following atoms showing all the energy levels in each atom:
   a) helium (He, atomic number 2),
   b) oxygen (O, atomic number 8),
   c) potassium (K, atomic number 19),
   d) chlorine (Cl, atomic number 17),
   e) aluminium (Al, atomic number 13).

3. The diagrams show the energy levels in three atoms: (The letters are NOT the chemical symbols.)

   A   B

   C

   a) Which atom belongs to group 2?
   b) To which group does atom C belong?
   c) Atom B bonds with four atoms of hydrogen. Draw a dot and cross diagram to show the compound that is formed.
   d) Draw dot and cross diagrams to show how atom A bonds with C atoms.

4. Describe, with diagrams, how the particles are held together in the following substances:
   a) a molecule of bromine (Br₂),
   b) a sample of diamond (carbon).
   c) a salt crystal (NaCl).

5. Explain the bonding in sodium metal. You may wish to include a diagram. (The atomic number of sodium is 11.) [Higher]

EXAM-STYLE QUESTIONS

1. The diagram represents an atom of an element.

   (a) Write the electronic structure of this atom as numbers and commas. (1)
   (b) How many protons are in the nucleus of this atom? (1)
   (c) Name the other particles that are in the nucleus. (1)
   (d) In which group of the periodic table is this element? (1)
   (e) Draw a similar diagram to show the ion formed by this atom in ionic compounds. Show the charge on the ion. (2)

2. Complete the missing information (a) to (f) in the table.

Atomic number	Symbol	Electronic structure of atom	Formula of ion	Electronic structure of ion
9	F	(a)	(b)	[2,8]⁻
11	(c)	2,8,1	Na⁺	(d)
(e)	S	2,8,6	S²⁻	(f)

(6)

3. A hydrogen atom can be represented by the diagram:

   H

   (a) Draw a similar diagram to show the electrons in the outer shell of a chlorine atom. (1)
   (b) Draw a dot and cross diagram to show the bonding in a molecule of hydrogen chloride. (2)
   (c) Explain why hydrogen and chlorine form a single covalent bond. (2)
   (d) Explain why silicon can form giant structures. (3)

- Question 1 could be answered by the students creating a labelled diagram of atomic structure, this would create a good revision aid.
- Question 2 could be turned into a card sort, with the diagrams on separate cards to the element that they are representing.

EXAM-STYLE ANSWERS

1. a) 2,8,3 *(1 mark)*
   b) 13 *(1 mark)*
   c) Neutrons *(1 mark)*
   d) 3 *(1 mark)*
   e) Dot at centre with two concentric circles, two crosses on first circle, eight crosses on outer circle, surrounded by brackets with 3+ at top right-hand side.
   (All correct – 2 marks, one error – 1 mark)

2. a) 2,7 *(1 mark)*
   b) F⁻ *(1 mark)*
   c) Na *(1 mark)*
   d) [2,8]⁺ (allow 2,8) *(1 mark)*
   e) 16 *(1 mark)*
   f) [2,8,8]²⁻ (allow 2,8,8) *(1 mark)*

3. a) Cl or dot in centre of circle with seven crosses on the circle. *(1 mark)*
   b) Two circles intersecting, one with H at centre and one with Cl at centre, with a dot and cross at intersection, and six more dots or crosses on circle around Cl. *(2 marks)*
   c) *One mark each for:*
      - Both hydrogen and chlorine need to gain one electron for a stable structure
      - so they share one pair of electrons/can only form one covalent bond. *(2 marks)*

Additional chemistry

4 (a) Draw a dot and cross diagram to show the arrangement of electrons in a magnesium ion. Show the charge on the ion. (3)

(b) Draw a dot and cross diagram to show the arrangement of electrons in an oxide ion. (3)

(c) What is the formula of magnesium oxide? (1)

5 Berzelius (1779–1848) carried out experiments to discover the atomic mass of many elements. He wrote about the fact that bodies combine in definite proportions and that led him to suggest the existence of a cause.

(a) Suggest an observation that Berzelius might have made. (1)

(b) Is what Berzelius wrote a prediction or a hypothesis? Explain your answer. (1)

(c) Berzelius gave oxygen the number 100 to represent its relative atomic mass. He then set out to compare the mass of other elements with oxygen. However, he could not measure these directly because they could not be turned into gases – the temperature needed was too high and he did not have the equipment to do this.

(i) Explain, in general terms, the problem he had. (1)

(ii) Use this example to explain the relationship between technology and science. (1)

6 The diagram represents atoms of potassium in the solid metal.

(a) What is the electronic structure of a potassium atom? (1)

(b) Explain as fully as you can how the atoms are held together in solid potassium metal. (3) [Higher]

HOW SCIENCE WORKS QUESTIONS

How the atomic theory was developed

2,500 years ago, Democritus believed that matter could be broken into smaller and smaller pieces until finally there would be particles that were 'indivisible' – the Greek word for this is *atomos*. He thought they looked like this:

Humphry Davy, who went to Truro Grammar School, discovered many of the elements that we are familiar with in chemistry lessons. He separated potassium, sodium and chlorine. As he couldn't break these elements down any further, he said that this must be the definition of an element.

Dalton became convinced that each element was made of a different kind of atom. He can be credited with the first scientific use of the term 'atom', although the Greeks had used the idea thousands of years before.

Dalton believed that
- the atom must be very small,
- all matter is made from atoms, and
- these atoms cannot be destroyed.

He gave hydrogen the atomic weight of 1, because he knew it to be the lightest atom.

He thought water was made of 1 hydrogen and 1 oxygen atom and therefore predicted that oxygen must have an atomic weight of 7.

Berzelius, a Swedish chemist, tested Dalton's theory experimentally. He correctly found the atomic weights of 40 elements.

a) When was the first theory of the atom put forward? (1)

b) What observation led to the definition of an element? (1)

c) What hypothesis did Dalton come up with? (1)

d) What prediction was made by Dalton? (1)

e) Check in the periodic table whether Dalton's prediction was correct. (1)

f) What was Berzelius' contribution to the atomic theory? (1)

g) Is Dalton's atomic theory completely true? Explain your answer. (1)

129

---

d) *Three from:*
- Silicon has four electrons in its outer shell/highest energy level.
- So it can share four electrons.
- It forms four covalent bonds.
- The covalent bonds between silicon atoms are strong.

(3 marks)

4 a) *One mark each for:*
- Dot or Mg at centre of two concentric circles.
- Two crosses or dots on inner circle, eight dots or crosses on outer circle.
- Surrounded by brackets with 2+ outside top right-hand side.

(3 marks)

b) *One mark each for:*
- Dot or O at centre of two concentric circles.
- Two crosses or dots on inner circle, eight dots or crosses on outer circle
- Surrounded by brackets with 2− outside top right hand side.

(3 marks)

c) MgO (accept $Mg^{2+}O^{2-}$) *(1 mark)*

5 a) E.g. that when compounds are broken down they always do so in the same proportions. *(1 mark)*

b) A hypothesis – it cannot be directly used to design an investigation. *(1 mark)*

c) i) The technology had not been invented to allow him to investigate the science. *(1 mark)*

ii) The idea that science and technology feed from each other. *(1 mark)*

6 a) 2,8,8,1 *(1 mark)*

b) *Three from:*
- The outer electrons move from one atom to the next one/delocalise.
- The (delocalised) electrons form a cloud or 'sea' of electrons.
- The electrons surround positive ions.
- (Delocalised) electrons strongly attract the positive ions.

(3 marks)
[HT only]

Additional chemistry

Exam teaching suggestions

- The questions could be used when the chapter has been completed in a single session. If used in this way, allow 35 minutes (total 35 marks). Alternatively, Q1, Q2 and Q4 could be used after completing spread 1.4, and Q3 after spread 1.5.
- Students should be able to represent atoms and ions in the ways described in the specification. Use of different symbols (dots or crosses) for electrons can be helpful when considering bonding, but students should know that all electrons are identical. Students will not be penalised for using only one symbol in their answers, either dots or crosses, for all electrons in atoms. When drawing diagrams to show bonding, it is usual to show only the electrons in the highest energy level or outer shell.
- Many students think of ionic compounds in terms of pairs or triplets of ions rather than giant structures. It is important in teaching ionic bonding to distinguish between ion formation, which is often described as the transfer of electrons from one atom to another, and the bonding that holds the ions together in a giant lattice.
- When writing formulae for ionic compounds, as in Q4c), students should be encouraged to balance the charges on the ions by using multiples of the ions, but should then write the empirical formula of the compound without any charges. This avoids confusion when showing multiples of ions and the need for brackets around ions and their charges.

HOW SCIENCE WORKS ANSWERS

a) 2,500 years ago.

b) That certain pure substances could not be broken down any further.

c) Dalton's hypothesis was that each element was made of a different kind of atom. That the atom must be very small, that all matter is made from atoms and that these atoms cannot be destroyed.

d) Dalton's prediction was that oxygen must have an atomic weight of 7.

e) Dalton was not correct according to the periodic table, but of course he was not to know!

f) Berzelius tested Dalton's prediction. He found Dalton to be wrong in his prediction.

g) Dalton's atomic theory is largely still correct, but of course the atom has been split!

How science works teaching suggestions

- **Literacy guidance.** Key terms that should be clearly understood: observation, prediction, theory.
- **Higher- and lower-level answers.** Question f) is a higher level question and the answer provided above is also at this level. Questions a) and b) are lower level and the answers provided are also lower level.
- **Gifted and talented.** Able students could find other examples in the history of science on how hypotheses have led to predictions that have been tested and theories amended.
- **How and when to use these questions.** When wishing to develop ideas of how observation leads to hypothesis and then to prediction and testing of that prediction. The questions are probably best used as homework and then discussed in class.
- **Misconceptions.** That a hypothesis is the same as a prediction. To address this: stress the fact that the prediction is based on the hypothesis and is used to test it. If a prediction holds true then that lends support to the hypothesis.
  Another misconception is that observations are just the outcome of investigations and not the stimulus. To address this: this is the equivalent of drawing graphs and not using them to draw conclusions when you analyse your data! Observations, especially unexpected ones, prompt questions. The observation, if repeated when checked, will stimulate an investigation and a new hypothesis is made to explain the observation and then tested.
- **Homework.** The questions are probably best used as homework and then discussed in class.

129

CHEMISTRY STRUCTURES AND PROPERTIES

C2 2.1 Ionic compounds

LEARNING OBJECTIVES

Students should learn that:
- Ionic compounds are solids at room temperature and have high melting points.
- Ionic compounds conduct electricity when they are molten or dissolved in water.

LEARNING OUTCOMES

Most students should be able to:
- State that ionic compounds have high melting points and are solid at room temperature.
- Describe how ionic compounds can conduct when they are molten or dissolved in water.

Some students should also be able to:
- Explain why ionic compounds have high melting points.
- Explain why ionic compounds can conduct electricity when molten or in solution.

Teaching suggestions

- **Special needs**
  - Instead of completing the practical with two ionic compounds, focus only on sodium chloride. This is a chemical that they have everyday experience of and is safe to use.
  - Provide the results' table for the students, so they just have to fill it in.
- **Learning styles**
  Kinaesthetic: Testing the different physical properties of ionic compounds.
  Visual: Looking at images to decide how they are connected.
  Auditory: Listening to explanations of the different physical properties of ionic compounds.
  Interpersonal: Working in groups to explain a certain physical property of ionic compounds.
  Intrapersonal: Making an individual set of revision cards.
- **Homework.** Students could choose an ionic compound and explain why it is used for a specific purpose, e.g. sodium fluoride is used in drinking water. [Fluoride has been found to make teeth stronger and sodium fluoride dissolves easily into the drinking water supply.]

SPECIFICATION LINK-UP   Unit: Chemistry 2.12.2

- Ionic compounds have regular structures (giant ionic lattices) in which there are strong electrostatic forces in all directions between oppositely charged ions. These compounds have high melting points and high boiling points.
- When melted or dissolved in water, ionic compounds conduct electricity because the ions are free to move and carry the current.

Students should use their skills, knowledge and understanding of 'How Science Works':
- to relate the properties of the substances named in this unit to their uses.
- to suggest the type of structure of a substance given its properties.

Lesson structure

STARTER

Pictures – Show students different images of sodium chloride (an ionic lattice, someone putting salt onto their chips, a chemical storage bottle of sodium chloride). Ask the students to work out what all the pictures have in common. (5 minutes)

List – Ask students to make a list of as many ionic substances as they can. Through question and answer, build up a list on the board and ask the students what they all have in common, other than that they have the same bonding [all will be compounds, most examples given will probably consist of a metal bonded to a non-metal]. (10 minutes)

Anagrams – Give the students this set of anagrams on the board; they should work out the key word and then define it:
- noi [Ion – a charged particle made when an atom loses or gains electrons]
- eeontrcl [Electron – negative particle that orbits the nucleus of an atom]
- ttalcei [Lattice – a 3D arrangement of particles in a giant structure]
- conii dobn [Ionic bond – the electrostatic force of attraction between oppositely charged ions] (10 minutes)

MAIN

- There are many examples of ionic compounds in everyday life, but rarely have students considered the properties of these substances. Encourage them to investigate the properties of sodium chloride and potassium chloride.
- Students should first design a table to record information about the appearance, hardness, melting point and conductivity in different states. As it will be near impossible to melt these substances using a Bunsen burner, encourage students to use reference material to find out in which states these substances will conduct.
- Give the students four same-coloured index cards. On one side, they should write a key physical property (high melting point, soluble in water and conducts in (aq) or (l)). Then on the reverse of each card, they should explain that property using key scientific terms and at least one labelled diagram.
- The fourth card should be a title card about ionic bonding. The cards could then be hole punched in a corner, as could the front of the student's exercise book. Using a piece of string the cards could be secured to the book and removed to add other revision cards about bonding.

PLENARIES

AfL (Assessment for Learning) – Give students an examination question about the properties of ionic compounds. Time the students (about 1 minute per mark). Then ask them to swap their answers with a partner, and give out mark schemes. Encourage the students to mark the work, as it is presented, no discussions about 'what they really meant'. Then swap the papers back, and you could collect in the marks. (10 minutes)

Summary – Split the class into three groups. Ask each team to explain why ionic compounds have certain physical properties (soluble in water, high melting point, conduct electricity when (l) or (aq)). Give each group a few minutes to come up with their explanations, then ask each group to read these out to the class. (10 minutes)

Practical support

Testing conductivity

Equipment and materials required

Sodium chloride, potassium chloride, hand lens, mounted needle, spatula, two boiling tubes, boiling tube rack, boiling tube holder, Bunsen burner and safety equipment, two carbon electrodes, lab pack, two crocodile clips, three wires, lamp, beaker, wash bottle with water, glass rod, eye protection.

- The bulb does not light at first but does once the salt dissolves.
- The ions are stuck in position within the giant lattice. However, as the sodium chloride dissolves in water, ions become free to move, carrying charge between the electrodes and the bulb lights up.

Details

Students to investigate the following:

Appearance – Students to look at the crystal through a hand lens and draw a diagram of the crystal.

Hardness – Students to try to scratch the surface with a mounted needle, and view the area using the hand lens.

Melting point – Students to put about half a spatula of the compound into a boiling tube and then hold it just above the blue gas cone in a roaring Bunsen flame. The tube should be at an angle, not pointing at any faces and eye protection should be worn. They should keep it in the flame until they have decided if it has a high/low melting point – the compounds are unlikely to melt. Then they place the boiling tube on a flameproof mat to cool.

Conductivity – Students to put some sodium chloride/potassium chloride crystals into a beaker (to about a depth of 1 cm). They submerge the electrodes and connect them to a lamp and power supply. Then they turn on the power and make observations. Then they add water from the wash bottle (half fill the beaker) and observe. Encourage the students to swirl the beaker to help the ionic compound dissolve. **Safety:** Please note that this electrolysis will produce a small amount of chlorine gas, therefore it should be completed in a well-ventilated area and be aware of students with respiratory problems (e.g. asthma) as the gas can aggravate it.

Solubility – Students to half fill a beaker with warm water from the tap, then add a few crystals and swirl or stir with a glass rod.

ACTIVITY & EXTENSION IDEAS

- Other sets of coloured cards could be given to the students to makes notes about covalent and metallic bonding. These could be added to the set about ionic bonds.
- Students could be encouraged to explain other physical properties of ionic compounds, e.g. crystal structure and hardness in terms of the structure of the ionic lattice.

Answers to in-text questions

a) Attractive electrostatic forces.

b) Because of the strong attractive electrostatic forces holding the oppositely charged ions together.

c) Because the ions are free to move.

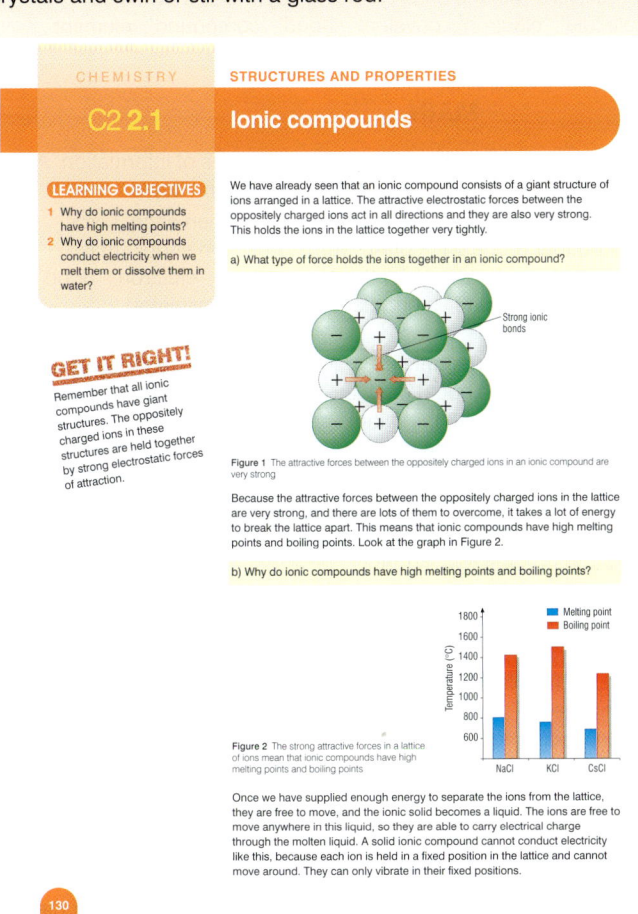

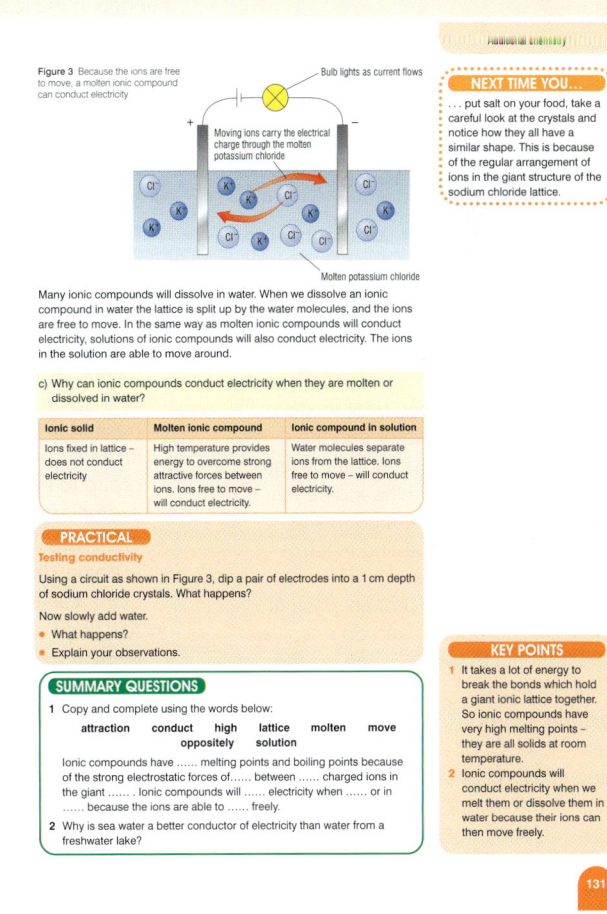

SUMMARY ANSWERS

1. High, attraction, oppositely, lattice, conduct, molten, solution, move.

2. Because it contains dissolved salt (ions).

KEY POINTS

Ask the students to re-write the key points in their own words. This could be in a paragraph, question and answers or changing the bullet points so that it is not just copied.

CHEMISTRY | STRUCTURES AND PROPERTIES

C2 2.2 Simple molecules

LEARNING OBJECTIVES

Students should learn:

- The properties of substances made up of simple molecules.
- The reasons why simple molecular substances have low melting and boiling points. [**HT only**]
- That substances made up of simple molecules do not conduct electricity.

LEARNING OUTCOMES

Most students should be able to:

- Recognise substances made up of simple molecules.
- List examples of substances made up of simple molecules.
- State the physical properties of substances made up of simple molecules.

Some students should also be able to:

- Explain why substances made up of simple molecules have low melting and boiling points. [**HT only**]
- Explain why substances made up of simple molecules do not conduct electricity.

Teaching suggestions

- **Gifted and talented**
  - You, or the students, could put some iodine crystals into a conical flask and seal with a bung. Then heat the flask with running warm water and the iodine will sublime. Then run the flask under cold water and the iodine will solidify again. Ask the students to explain what is happening in terms of intermolecular forces.
  - **Safety:** Be aware of broken glass (if the flask is dropped) and do not allow the students to touch iodine, as the skin will stain.
- **Learning styles**
  Kinaesthetic: Choosing where to stand based on whether they agree or disagree with statements.
  Visual: Creating a mind-map.
  Interpersonal: Working as a group to make a mind-map.
  Intrapersonal: Creating a summary about the properties of simple covalent molecules.
- **Homework.** Find an example of a covalent compound, its melting and boiling point. Then relate this information to a use of it.

SPECIFICATION LINK-UP Unit: Chemistry 2.12.2

- *Substances that consist of simple molecular gases, liquids or solids have relatively low melting points and boiling points.*
- *Substances that consist of simple molecules have only weak forces between the molecules (intermolecular forces). It is these intermolecular forces that are overcome, not the covalent bonds, when the substance melts or boils.* [**HT only**]
- *Substances that consist of simple molecules do not conduct electricity because the molecules do not have an overall electric charge.*

Students should use their skills, knowledge and understanding of 'How Science Works':
- *to relate the properties of the substances named in this unit to their uses.*
- *to suggest the type of structure of a substance given its properties.*

Lesson structure

STARTER

Models – Split the class into small groups. Ask for volunteers to draw the dot and cross diagrams of hydrogen, then instruct the groups to make a model (using a molecular model kit) of this diagram and hold it in the air so that you can easily check. Then repeat with the other simple molecules that the students should know: hydrogen chloride, water, oxygen, ammonia and methane. (15 minutes)

Crosswords – Create a crossword with the answers being key words that will be needed in the lesson: 'molecule', 'electron', 'covalent', 'bond', 'compound', 'element', 'dot and cross'. (10 minutes)

MAIN

- Students often find it difficult to make connections between pieces of information. A mind map can be a very useful tool to help them make links within a topic.
- Split the students into groups of about four, and give them a felt pen each, some Blu Tack, a piece of sugar paper and a pack of A6 word cards. You should make these cards in advance, including key words for this topic: 'atom', 'electron', 'bond', 'covalent', 'melting point', 'boiling point', 'intermolecular forces', 'insulator', 'molecule', 'solid', 'liquid', 'gas'.
- The students should stick two key words onto the page, one should be the start of the sentence the other the end. They should draw an arrow in the correct direction linking the words, then on the arrow write the middle section of the sentence. There is no limit to the number of arrows that can be drawn to and from each. You should circulate during this activity and suggest links by pointing to words and asking the group to consider how they link. Very good pieces could be highlighted as exemplars, and other groups could be encouraged to look at them for ideas.
- There are many covalent compounds that students come into contact with in everyday life, but they have probably not considered the properties of them. Give them a selection of covalently bonded compounds, e.g. water, ethanol, iodine, sulfur.
- Ask them to discuss, in groups, any similarities in appearance [dull]. Then they could experimentally determine the physical properties of this group of substances.
- If it is not possible to complete the practical, students could use data books to obtain melting point, boiling point and conductivity information.

PLENARIES

Stand by – Ask for a volunteer to stand in the centre of the classroom. They should say a statement about simple covalent molecules (for higher ability it could be their own idea, for lower ability there could be statement cards already prepared). The rest of the class decide how much they agree with this statement, the more they agree, the closer they should stand to the person who spoke. (5 minutes)

Summarise – Ask the students to summarise the physical properties of simple molecular compounds and give brief reasons for them in a bullet-point format. (10 minutes)

Additional chemistry

ACTIVITY & EXTENSION IDEAS

- Information from data books including databases such as the CD ROM *RSC Data Book* could be used to get melting point/boiling point/conductivity information. The data for a particular group of covalent compounds could be collected and students could represent this data in a bar chart format. (Or search for conductivity at www.wikipedia.org.)
- Gently heat sulfur in a mineral wool plugged ignition tube. The sulfur should melt. When the sulfur has melted, remove from the heat and take out the plug. In a fume cupboard, tip the sulfur into a beaker of cold water. The sulfur is now plastic and can be pulled into new shapes easily.
- Students should then endeavour to explain why changing its structure could change the properties of this element.
- **Safety:** Be careful not to burn the sulfur – as sulfur dioxide is produced, which is an irritant. Also, the liquid sulphur can cause nasty burns, even if it is run under cold water. (Sulfur is flammable – CLEAPSS Hazcard 96)
- Students could find out how the intermolecular forces between water molecules make ice less dense than liquid water.

Practical support

Conductivity

Equipment and materials required
Beaker, water, carbon electrodes, lamp, power pack, wires, ethanol (flammable – CLEAPSS Hazcard 40), solid wax pieces.

Details
Half-fill a beaker with water and put in the carbon electrodes. Set up a simple circuit with a lamp and power pack, to see if the liquid conducts. Repeat the experiment with ethanol and solid wax pieces. (Keep ethanol away from any naked flames.)

Melting and boiling points

Equipment and materials required
Boiling tubes, boiling tube rack, boiling tube holder, Bunsen burner and safety equipment, thermometer, water, wax, eye protection.

Details
Ask students to predict whether covalent compounds have low or high melting/boiling points and why they think this. Get the students to prepare a results table.
They need to put a small piece of wax into a boiling tube and heat in a blue flame, noting the temperature that the wax begins to melt.
They then put about a 1 cm depth of water into a boiling tube and heat in a blue Bunsen flame, noting the temperature of boiling.

KEY POINTS

Students could create a limerick to remember these two key points.

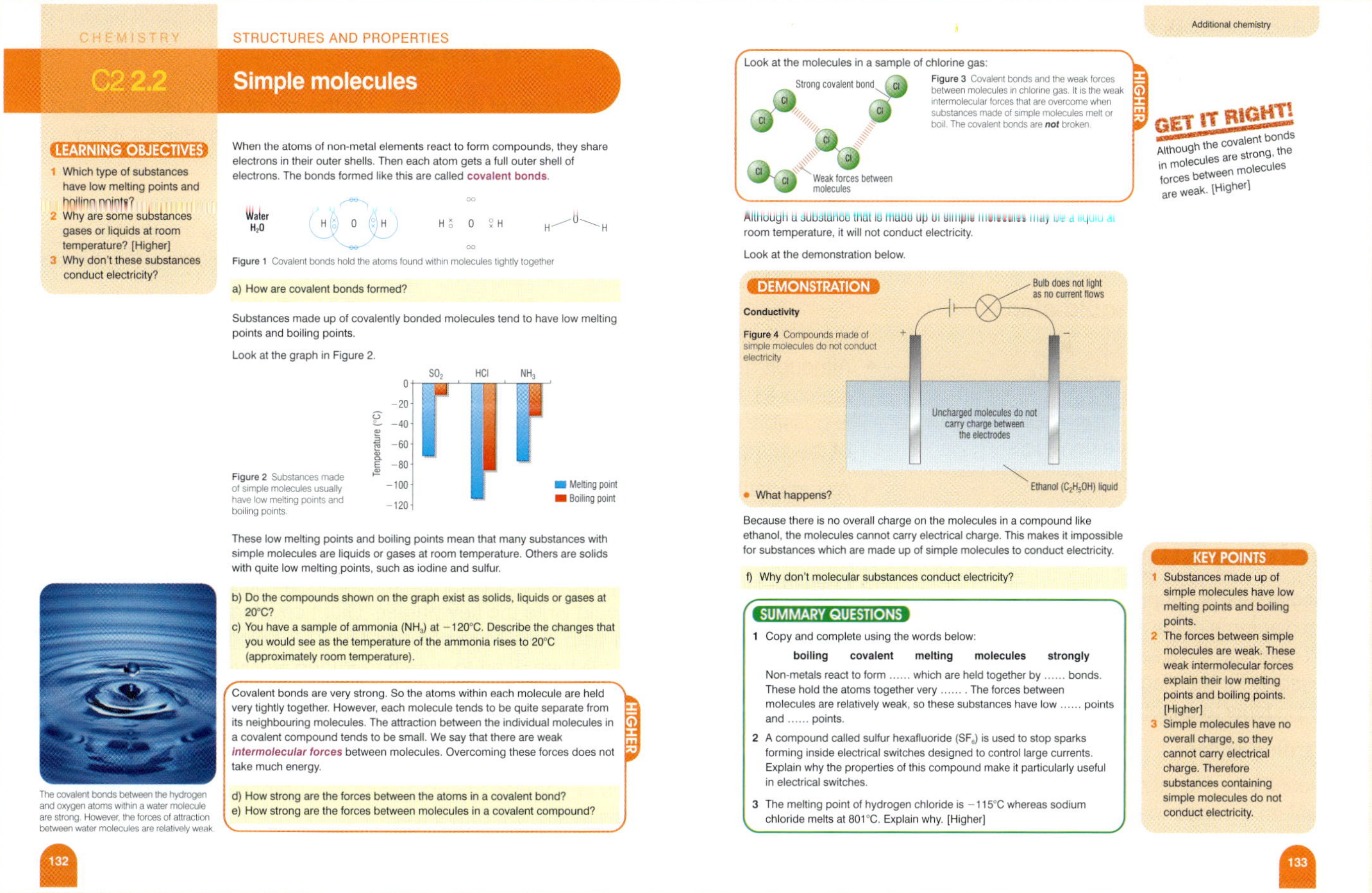

CHEMISTRY — STRUCTURES AND PROPERTIES

C2 2.2 Simple molecules

LEARNING OBJECTIVES
1. Which type of substances have low melting points and boiling points?
2. Why are some substances gases or liquids at room temperature? [Higher]
3. Why don't these substances conduct electricity?

When the atoms of non-metal elements react to form compounds, they share electrons in their outer shells. Then each atom gets a full outer shell of electrons. The bonds formed like this are called **covalent bonds**.

Figure 1 Covalent bonds hold the atoms found within molecules tightly together

a) How are covalent bonds formed?

Substances made up of covalently bonded molecules tend to have low melting points and boiling points.

Look at the graph in Figure 2.

Figure 2 Substances made of simple molecules usually have low melting points and boiling points.

These low melting points and boiling points mean that many substances with simple molecules are liquids or gases at room temperature. Others are solids with quite low melting points, such as iodine and sulfur.

b) Do the compounds shown on the graph exist as solids, liquids or gases at 20°C?
c) You have a sample of ammonia (NH$_3$) at −120°C. Describe the changes that you would see as the temperature of the ammonia rises to 20°C (approximately room temperature).

Covalent bonds are very strong. So the atoms within each molecule are held very tightly together. However, each molecule tends to be quite separate from its neighbouring molecules. The attraction between the individual molecules in a covalent compound tends to be small. We say that there are weak **intermolecular forces** between molecules. Overcoming these forces does not take much energy.

The covalent bonds between the hydrogen and oxygen atoms within a water molecule are strong. However, the forces between water molecules are relatively weak.

d) How strong are the forces between the atoms in a covalent bond?
e) How strong are the forces between molecules in a covalent compound?

Look at the molecules in a sample of chlorine gas:

Figure 3 Covalent bonds and the weak forces between molecules in chlorine gas. It is the weak intermolecular forces that are overcome when substances made of simple molecules melt or boil. The covalent bonds are **not** broken.

GET IT RIGHT!
Although the covalent bonds in molecules are strong, the forces between molecules are weak. [Higher]

Although a substance that is made up of simple molecules may be a liquid at room temperature, it will not conduct electricity.

Look at the demonstration below.

DEMONSTRATION
Conductivity

Figure 4 Compounds made of simple molecules do not conduct electricity

- What happens?

Because there is no overall charge on the molecules in a compound like ethanol, the molecules cannot carry electrical charge. This makes it impossible for substances which are made up of simple molecules to conduct electricity.

f) Why don't molecular substances conduct electricity?

SUMMARY QUESTIONS

1 Copy and complete using the words below:
   boiling   covalent   melting   molecules   strongly
   Non-metals react to form …… which are held together by …… bonds. These hold the atoms together very …… . The forces between molecules are relatively weak, so these substances have low …… points and …… points.

2 A compound called sulfur hexafluoride (SF$_6$) is used to stop sparks forming inside electrical switches designed to control large currents. Explain why the properties of this compound make it particularly useful in electrical switches.

3 The melting point of hydrogen chloride is −115°C whereas sodium chloride melts at 801°C. Explain why. [Higher]

KEY POINTS
1. Substances made up of simple molecules have low melting points and boiling points.
2. The forces between simple molecules are weak. These weak intermolecular forces explain their low melting points and boiling points. [Higher]
3. Simple molecules have no overall charge, so they cannot carry electrical charge. Therefore substances containing simple molecules do not conduct electricity.

SUMMARY ANSWERS

1 Molecules, covalent, strongly, melting, boiling.

2 It is a (simple) molecular substance so it doesn't conduct electricity, it has a low boiling point so it is a gas at normal temperatures.

3 To separate the oppositely charged sodium and chloride ions requires a lot of energy to overcome the strong electrostatic forces of attraction operating in every direction. In hydrogen chloride, there are only weak forces of attraction between individual HCl molecules so they require far less energy to separate them (no covalent bonds are broken in the process of melting.) [**HT** only]

Answers to in-text questions

a) By sharing pairs of electrons.
b) Gases.
c) It would be a solid to start with but at about −80°C it would melt into a liquid. Then at about −35°C it would boil to form ammonia gas. At 20°C it remains a gas.
d) Very strong.
e) Weak (compared to the forces between atoms held together by a covalent bond).
f) There are no charged particles to carry the electric current.

CHEMISTRY · STRUCTURES AND PROPERTIES

C2 2.3 Giant covalent substances

LEARNING OBJECTIVES

Students should learn:

- That not all covalent compounds are made of simple molecules.
- Some of the physical properties of substances with giant covalent structures.
- Why diamond is hard and graphite is slippery.
- Why graphite conducts electricity. [HT only]

LEARNING OUTCOMES

Most students should be able to:

- List examples of substances with giant covalent structures.
- Recognise giant covalent structures.
- State the physical properties of graphite and diamond.
- Explain the physical properties of diamond and graphite, such as melting point and hardness, in terms of their structures.

Some students should also be able to:

- Explain in detail what a giant covalent structure is.
- Explain why graphite conducts electricity. [HT only]

Teaching suggestions

- **Special needs.** Supply these students with diagrams of the structure of diamond and graphite. On a separate sheet include the labels for the diagram and encourage the students to annotate their work.
- **Learning styles**
  Kinaesthetic: Handling samples of giant covalent compounds.
  Visual: Creating an A-map.
  Auditory: Listening to explanations of the key words.
  Interpersonal: Working in groups explaining key terms.
  Intrapersonal: Making a poster to contrast the properties of carbon allotropes.
- **Homework.** Students could find out a use for graphite and explain which property makes it suitable to this use.
- **ICT link-up.** Use C2 2.3 'Giant covalent' from the GCSE Chemistry CD ROM.

SPECIFICATION LINK-UP   Unit: Chemistry 2.12.2

- *Atoms that share electrons can also form giant structures or macromolecules. Diamond and graphite (forms of carbon) and silicon dioxide (silica) are examples of giant covalent structures (lattices) of atoms. All the atoms in the structure are linked to other atoms by strong covalent bonds and so they have high melting points.*
- *In diamond each carbon atom forms four covalent bonds with other carbon atoms in a rigid, giant covalent structure, so diamond is very hard.*
- *In graphite, each carbon atom bonds to three others, forming layers. The layers are free to slide over each other and so graphite is soft and slippery.*
- *In graphite, one electron from each carbon atom is delocalised. These delocalised electrons allow graphite to conduct heat and electricity.* [HT only]

Students should use their skills, knowledge and understanding of 'How Science Works':

- *to relate the properties of the substance named in this unit to their uses.*
- *to suggest the type of structure of a substance given its properties.*

Lesson structure

STARTER

List – Show students different images of diamonds – in the raw state, in jewellery, and on a saw. Ask the students to list different uses of diamonds, and then ask for a few suggestions. (5 minutes)

Word search – Give students a word search about covalent bonding; however do not include the words. Encourage students to think about the topic and use the double page spread in the students' book to work out which words they should be finding. (10 minutes)

MAIN

- Although graphite and diamond are both carbon, they have completely different structures. Give students some graphite to handle (this may be a bit messy!) and if it is possible samples of diamonds to study. Brainstorm the different properties of each of these materials, but explain they are the same element.
- Ask students to make a poster to contrast the properties of these two substances and explain them in terms of their structures.
- Students could use the textbook for information to create an A-map about giant covalent structures. They should select three colours. In the centre of the page, in one colour only, they should write the key phrase 'Giant covalent structures' and draw a small image that might help them to remember this. This colour is then not used again. The second colour is then used to create four long, wavy lines. Following the contour of the line, the student should write 'formation', 'graphite', 'diamond' and 'silica' on separate lines, each including an image.
- Each idea is then added to, with a third colour, again with wavy lines. Each line again should contain key words or phrases to summarise that branch of thought, and include an image to help the student remember.
- Encourage the students to complete one branch before moving to the next.

PLENARIES

Explain – Split the students into pairs, and give them a pack of cards with key terms on it: 'graphite', 'diamond', 'silica', 'delocalised electrons', 'lattice'. The cards should be face down in front of the group. Each student should take it in turns to take a card and try to explain the key term, but the guesser must draw a labelled diagram to match the key term. (10 minutes)

Models – Show the students molecular models of diamond and graphite. Ask them to list down the similarities and the differences. Ask for a volunteer to scribe onto the board. Then through questions and answers, build up bullet points onto the board. (10 minutes)

ACTIVITY & EXTENSION IDEAS

- Graphite is used in pencil leads. Encourage students to research how the different hardness (e.g. H and HB) of pencils is achieved.
- Students could research into other allotropes of carbon, e.g. Bucky balls and Bucky tubes.

Answers to in-text questions

a) Giant covalent (lattice).
b) High melting and boiling points.
c) The layers of carbon atoms can easily slide over each other.
d) These are delocalised (free) electrons.

CHEMISTRY — STRUCTURES AND PROPERTIES
C2 2.3 Giant covalent substances

LEARNING OBJECTIVES
1. How do substances with giant covalent structures behave?
2. Why is diamond hard and graphite slippery?
3. Why can graphite conduct electricity? [Higher]

While most non-metals react and form covalent bonds which join the atoms together in molecules, a few form very different structures. Instead of joining a small number of atoms together in individual molecules, the covalent bonds form large networks of covalent bonds. We call networks like this **giant covalent structures**. They are sometimes called macromolecules or giant molecular structures.

Substances such as diamond, graphite and silicon dioxide have giant covalent structures.

Figure 1 The structures of diamond and silicon dioxide (sand)

All of the atoms in these giant lattices are held together by strong covalent bonds in both diamond and silicon dioxide. This gives these substances some very special properties. They are very hard, they have high melting points and boiling points and they are chemically very unreactive.

a) What do we call the structure of compounds which contain lots (millions) of atoms joined together by a network of covalent bonds?
b) What kind of physical properties do these substances have?

Figure 2 The large attractive forces in a giant lattice of covalently bonded atoms means that these compounds have high melting points and boiling points

DID YOU KNOW?
Diamond is the hardest natural substance that we know. Artificial diamonds can be made by heating pure carbon to very high temperatures under enormous pressures. The 'industrial diamonds' made like this are used in the drill bits which oil companies use when they drill through rocks looking for oil.

Figure 3 Hard, shiny and transparent – diamonds make beautiful jewellery

We don't always find carbon as diamonds – another form is graphite (well known as the 'lead' in a pencil). In graphite, carbon atoms are arranged in giant layers. There are only weak forces between the layers so they can slide over each other quite easily.

c) Why is graphite slippery?

HIGHER
Another important property of graphite comes from the fact that there are free electrons within its structure. These free electrons allow graphite to conduct electricity, which diamond – and most other covalent compounds – simply cannot do. We call the free electrons found in graphite **delocalised electrons**. They behave rather like the electrons in a metallic structure.

The carbon atoms in graphite's layers are arranged in hexagons. So each carbon atom bonds to three others. (See Figure 4.) This leaves one spare outer electron on each carbon atom. It is this electron that becomes delocalised along the layers of carbon atoms.

d) Why can graphite conduct electricity?

Fullerenes
Apart from diamond and graphite, there are other different molecules that carbon can produce. In these structures the carbon atoms join together to make large cages which can have all sorts of weird shapes. Chemists have made shapes looking like balls, onions, tubes, doughnuts, corkscrews and cones!

Chemists discovered carbon's ability to behave like this in 1985. We call the large carbon molecules containing these cage structures **fullerenes**. They are sure to become very important in nanoscience applications. (See pages 138 and 139.)

Figure 4 The giant structure of graphite. When you write with a pencil, some layers of carbon atoms slide off the 'lead' and are left on the paper.

GET IT RIGHT!
Giant covalent structures are held together by covalent bonds throughout the structure.

Figure 5 The first fullerene to be discovered contained only 60 carbon atoms, but chemists can now make **giant fullerenes** which contain many thousands of carbon atoms. Scientists can now place other molecules inside these carbon cages. This has exciting possibilities, including the delivery of drugs to specific parts of the body.

SUMMARY QUESTIONS

1 Copy and complete using the words below:

   atoms   boiling   carbon   hard   high   layers   slide   soft

   Giant covalent structures contain many …… joined by covalent bonds. They have …… melting points and …… points. Diamond is a very …… substance because the …… atoms in it are held strongly to each other. However, graphite is …… because there are …… of atoms which can …… over each other.

2 Graphite is sometimes used to reduce the friction between two surfaces that are rubbing together. How does it do this?

3 Explain in detail why graphite can conduct electricity but diamond cannot. [Higher]

KEY POINTS
1 Some covalently bonded substances contain giant structures.
2 These substances have high melting points and boiling points.
3 The giant structure of graphite contains layers of atoms that can slide over each other which make graphite slippery. The atoms in diamond have a different structure and cannot slide like this – so diamond is a very hard substance.
4 Graphite can conduct electricity because of the delocalised electrons along its layers. [Higher]

SUMMARY ANSWERS

1 Atoms, high, boiling, hard, carbon, soft, layers, slide.

2 The graphite is used to coat the two surfaces. As they rub together the layers of atoms in the graphite slip over each other, reducing the friction.

3 Graphite can conduct electricity because of the delocalised (free) electrons in its structure. These arise because each carbon is only bonded to 3 other carbon atoms. This leaves one electron to become delocalised. However, in diamond all 4 outer electrons on each carbon atom are involved in covalent bonding so there are no delocalised electrons. [**HT** only]

DID YOU KNOW?

Life Gem is a company that offers to cremate pets and humans in a special way, which turns them into diamonds. Encourage students to use the Internet to look up this idea.

KEY POINTS

Ask the students to copy out the key points and highlight any key words in their notes.

CHEMISTRY STRUCTURES AND PROPERTIES

C2 2.4 Giant metallic structures

LEARNING OBJECTIVES

Students should learn:

- That metals conduct electricity and heat, and can be bent and shaped.
- Why metals can be bent and shaped.
- Why metals can conduct electricity and heat. [**HT only**]

LEARNING OUTCOMES

Most students should be able to:

- State the physical properties of metals.
- Match the uses of certain metals with specific properties.
- Explain in detail why metals are malleable and ductile.

Some students should also be able to:

- Explain why metals conduct electricity and heat in terms of delocalised electrons in their structures. [**HT only**]

Teaching suggestions

- **Learning styles**

  Kinaesthetic: Standing up or sitting down to show the answer to questions.

  Visual: Using magazine images to create a poster to explain metal properties.

  Auditory: Listening to explanations of the statement 'metal ions in a sea of electrons'.

  Interpersonal: Working in groups explaining the statement 'metal ions in a sea of electrons'.

  Intrapersonal: Making a poster to explain metal properties.

- **ICT link-up.** Set up flexi-cam and connect to a digital projector or a TV. Then focus in on the bubble raft experiment. Using the image you can then explain how this experiment relates to the structure of metals.

Answers to in-text questions

a) Because the layers of atoms can slide over each other when sufficient force is applied.

b) By delocalised electrons from the outer energy levels of the metal atoms.

c) Through the delocalised electrons being able to move through the metal lattice.

SPECIFICATION LINK-UP Unit: Chemistry 2.12.2

- Metals conduct heat and electricity because of the delocalised electrons in their structure. [**HT only**]
- The layers of atoms in metals are able to slide over each other and so metals can be bent into shape.

Students should use their skills, knowledge and understanding of 'How Science Works':

- to relate the properties of the substances named in this unit to their uses.
- to suggest the type of structure of a substance given its properties.

Lesson structure

STARTER

Circle of truth – This is an interactive, self-marking exercise designed to be used on an interactive whiteboard. To create this activity, open board-specific interactive whiteboard software, or PowerPoint®. Firstly, in a text box, type in the title: 'Which are properties of metals?' Then in a small font size, and in separate text boxes, write the wrong answers e.g.: 'dull', 'brittle' and 'insulator'. Then draw a circle, you may wish to add the text 'circle of truth' and group the objects. This circle should occlude the previously written text, i.e. the wrong answers. Then, in separate text boxes write the correct answers: 'ductile', 'malleable', 'conductor', 'shiny' and 'sonorous'. To use this activity, ask the students for volunteers to come to the board and suggest an answer to the question [Which are the properties of metals?]. They should then move (by dragging) the circle to their answer. If they are correct the answer is still visible; if it is incorrect, then the circle will cover the answer. (5 minutes)

Flash boards – Give the students A4 whiteboards (or laminated paper), a washable pen and eraser. Ask the students to draw an electronic diagram of a metal of their choice, and then hold their answer up to you (these should be dot and cross diagrams). Instant praise can be given. Students can also play the game and use their textbook to help them or look at other people's answer and teacher response. Then ask the students to draw a diagram of a metal structure (as shown in the text book). You could pose other questions about metals. (5 minutes)

MAIN

- Metals are used in everyday life, but often students do not consider which properties make it useful for certain jobs. Give the students adverts or catalogues to look through.
- Ask the students to pick items that use metals and cut them out. They could then make a poster using these items, explaining which part is metal.
- Students could then explain the useful property in terms of metallic bonding. It is important that each poster contains an example of a metal conducting heat, a metal conducting electricity, a metal being ductile and a metal being malleable.
- Metal properties can be modelled in a variety of ways. Show the students any pre-made molecular models that the school may have. Soap bubbles can be used to represent metal atoms and show ductility and malleability.
- Students should then explain their results relating the model to metallic bonding.
- Show the students Animation C2 2.4 'Metals' from the GCSE Chemistry CD ROM.

ACTIVITY & EXTENSION IDEAS

- Metals atoms stack in different layers, e.g. ABAB or ABCABC. Encourage students to find out different atoms arrangements in different metals.
- Some metals are more useful for certain jobs, but substitutes are used, e.g. silver is the best metal electrical conductor, but it degrades easily; so other metals, e.g. gold, are used for satellites. Ask students to find other interesting uses and facts about metals.

Additional chemistry

Practical support
Blowing bubbles

Equipment and materials required
Petri dish, pointed end of a dropping pipette, dropping pipette, soap solution, rubber tubing to connect to gas tap.

Details
Students should, using the pipette, blow similar-sized bubbles into the Petri dish. They observe and then blow different-sized bubbles using a normal dropping pipette and observe.

KEY POINTS

Pick famous people (either in the wider world or the school community) and put their names into a bag. Ask for volunteers to come to pick out a name, they should then read the key points in character.

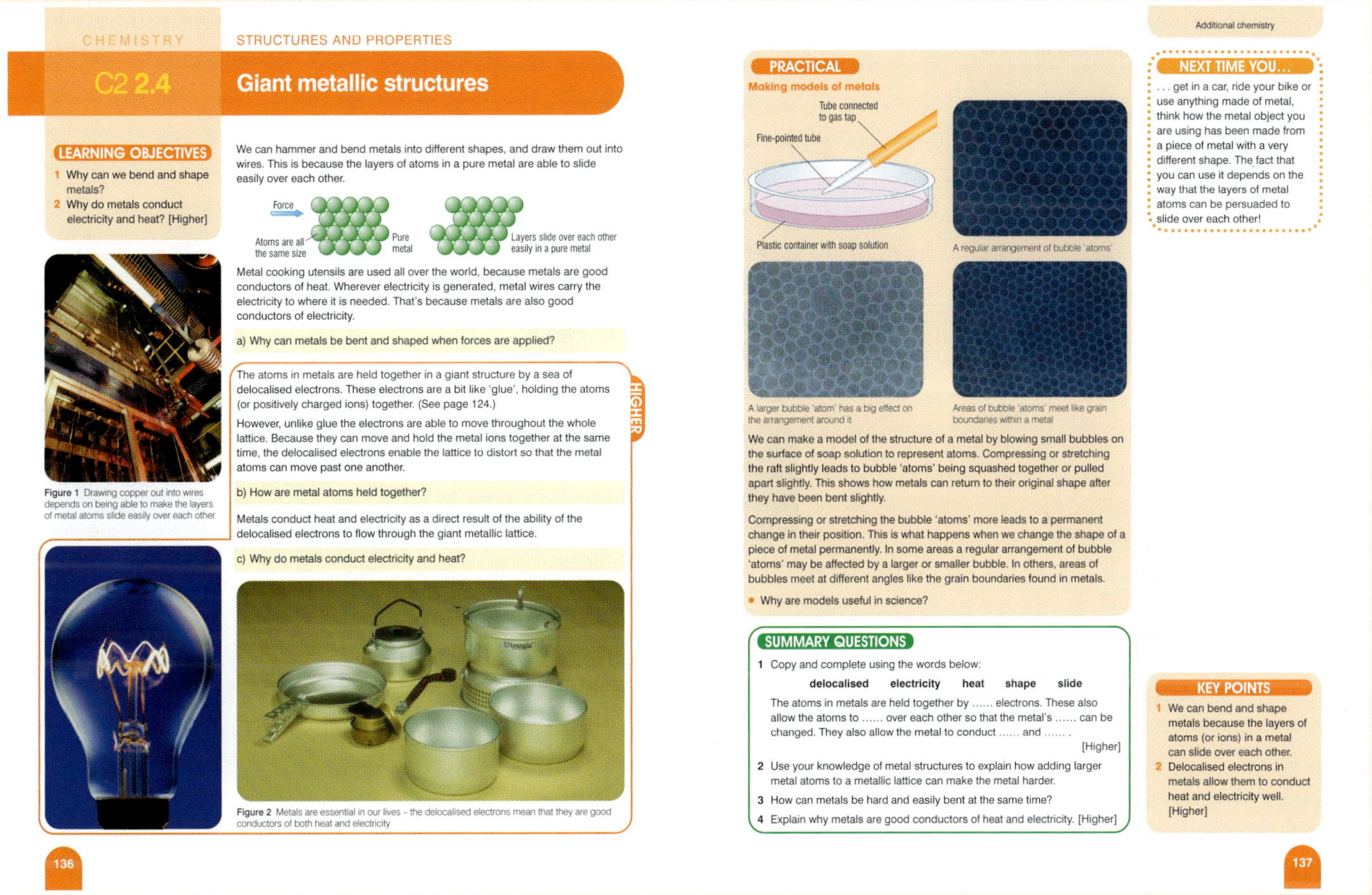

CHEMISTRY — STRUCTURES AND PROPERTIES

C2 2.4 Giant metallic structures

LEARNING OBJECTIVES
1 Why can we bend and shape metals?
2 Why do metals conduct electricity and heat? [Higher]

We can hammer and bend metals into different shapes, and draw them out into wires. This is because the layers of atoms in a pure metal are able to slide easily over each other.

Metal cooking utensils are used all over the world, because metals are good conductors of heat. Wherever electricity is generated, metal wires carry the electricity to where it is needed. That's because metals are also good conductors of electricity.

a) Why can metals be bent and shaped when forces are applied?

The atoms in metals are held together in a giant structure by a sea of delocalised electrons. These electrons are a bit like 'glue', holding the atoms (or positively charged ions) together. (See page 124.)

However, unlike glue the electrons are able to move throughout the whole lattice. Because they can move and hold the metal ions together at the same time, the delocalised electrons enable the lattice to distort so that the metal atoms can move past one another.

b) How are metal atoms held together?

Metals conduct heat and electricity as a direct result of the ability of the delocalised electrons to flow through the giant metallic lattice.

c) Why do metals conduct electricity and heat?

Figure 1 Drawing copper out into wires depends on being able to make the layers of metal atoms slide easily over each other

Figure 2 Metals are essential in our lives – the delocalised electrons mean that they are good conductors of both heat and electricity

PRACTICAL
Making models of metals

We can make a model of the structure of a metal by blowing small bubbles on the surface of soap solution to represent atoms. Compressing or stretching the raft slightly leads to bubble 'atoms' being squashed together or pulled apart slightly. This shows how metals can return to their original shape after they have been bent slightly.

Compressing or stretching the bubble 'atoms' more leads to a permanent change in their position. This is what happens when we change the shape of a piece of metal permanently. In some areas a regular arrangement of bubble 'atoms' may be affected by a larger or smaller bubble. In others, areas of bubbles meet at different angles like the grain boundaries found in metals.

- Why are models useful in science?

SUMMARY QUESTIONS
1 Copy and complete using the words below:
   delocalised   electricity   heat   shape   slide
   The atoms in metals are held together by …… electrons. These also allow the atoms to …… over each other so that the metal's …… can be changed. They also allow the metal to conduct …… and …… . [Higher]
2 Use your knowledge of metal structures to explain how adding larger metal atoms to a metallic lattice can make the metal harder.
3 How can metals be hard and easily bent at the same time?
4 Explain why metals are good conductors of heat and electricity. [Higher]

NEXT TIME YOU…
… get in a car, ride your bike or use anything made of metal, think how the metal object you are using has been made from a piece of metal with a very different shape. The fact that you can use it depends on the way that the layers of metal atoms can be persuaded to slide over each other!

KEY POINTS
1 We can bend and shape metals because the layers of atoms (or ions) in a metal can slide over each other.
2 Delocalised electrons in metals allow them to conduct heat and electricity well. [Higher]

PLENARIES

Explain – Split the class into small groups to discuss a phrase. Bonding in metals can be described as 'metal ions in a sea of electrons'. Encourage the students to explain what this statement means. Choose some groups to feedback to the rest of the class. (5 minutes)

True or false – Ask the students to stand up if they think the fact is true, and remain seated if they think the fact is false.
- All metals are conductors of heat. [True]
- Metals are the best conductors of heat. [False – diamond is a better conductor at room temperature.]
- Metals are listed on the left of the periodic table. [True]
- Metals are ductile and dull. [False]
- The free electrons in metals allow the material to conduct electricity and heat. [True]
(5 minutes)

SUMMARY ANSWERS

1 Delocalised, slide, shape, heat (electricity), electricity (heat). [**HT** only]

2 This helps to stop the layers of metal atoms sliding over each other.

3 Because the atoms are held tightly together, so the metal resists sudden changes to its shape. However, force applied carefully in the right way will change the shape of the metal as the layers of atoms slide over each other.

4 The delocalised electrons in their structures carry the charge through a metal when it conducts electricity, and the energy through it when it conducts heat. [**HT** only]

CHEMISTRY | STRUCTURES AND PROPERTIES

C2 2.5 Nanoscience and nanotechnology

SPECIFICATION LINK-UP
Unit: Chemistry 2.12.2

- Nanoscience refers to structures that are 1–100nm in size, of the order of a few hundred atoms. Nanoparticles show different properties to the same materials in bulk and have a high surface area to volume ratio which may lead to new computers, new catalysts, new coatings, highly selective sensors, and stronger and lighter construction materials.

Students should use their skills, knowledge and understanding of 'How Science Works':

- to evaluate developments and applications of new materials, e.g. nanomaterials, smart materials.

CHEMISTRY | STRUCTURES AND PROPERTIES

C2 2.5 Nanoscience and nanotechnology

The science of tiny things – what can we do?

Nanoscience
Nanoscience is a new and exciting area of science. 'Nano' is a prefix like 'milli' or 'mega'. While 'milli' means 'one-thousandth', 'nano' means 'one-thousand-millionth' – so nanoscience is the science of really tiny things.

What is nanoscience?
Our increasing understanding of science through the 20th century means that we now know that materials behave very differently at a very tiny scale. When we arrange atoms and molecules very carefully at this tiny scale, their properties can be truly remarkable.

Nanoscience at work

Glass can be coated with titanium oxide nanoparticles. Sunshine triggers a chemical reaction that breaks down dirt which then lands on the window. When it rains the water spreads evenly over the surface of the glass washing off the dirt.

Socks that are made from a fabric which contains silver nanoparticles never smell!

A type of lizard called a gecko can hang upside down from a sheet of glass. That's because the hairs on its feet are so tiny they can use the forces that hold molecules together. Scientists can make sticky tape lined with tiny nano-hairs that work in the same way.

Using nanoscience, health workers may soon be able to test a single drop of blood on a tiny piece of plastic no bigger than a ten pence piece. The tiny nanolab would replace individual tests for infectious diseases such as malaria and HIV/AIDS. On a larger scale these tests are both time-consuming and costly.

Nanoscience can do some pretty amazing things – these toy eyes are being moved using a tiny current from an electric battery.

But some nanoscience is pure science fiction – tiny subs that travel through your blood to zap cancer cells with a laser; self-reproducing nanobots that escape and cover the Earth in 'grey goo' – only in airport novels!

138

Teaching suggestions

Activities
- **Scientific ethics** – Write each of the headlines onto flip-chart paper and put on each wall of the classroom.
- Split the group into pairs and ask them to consider each headline in turn and discuss the issues. Then allow the teams to circulate around the papers to mark on their thoughts.
- Now split the class into quarters and give each set the flip-chart paper for the headline they are considering. Allow this large group to make a 3 minute long presentation about their issue, considering whether it is possible and if we should do it. (This relates to 'How Science Works': the questions science can and cannot answer.)
- To extend this activity, students could make a PowerPoint® presentation to illustrate their talk. They could then present their work, and at the end there should be a question section, where the audience can put points to the group about their issue.

- **Poster** – Show the students examples of the RSC poster campaign 'Not all chemist wear white coats'. Then ask students to design their own poster with nanotechnology in mind.
- **PhotoPlus** – Show students the PhotoPLUS C2 2.5 'Nanotechnology' from the GCSE Chemistry CD ROM.

Homework
- **Definitions** – Ask students to define the terms 'nanoscience', 'nanometer' and 'nanoparticles'. Their definition should include a text definition and a labelled diagram.

Extension
- **New materials** – Encourage students to research how nanotechnology could impact on new computers, catalysts, coatings, sensors and construction materials. They could use the Internet to find one example of how nanotechnology has made improvements in the aforementioned areas.
(See www.nano.org.uk or search for 'nanotechnology applications'.)

Additional chemistry

The science of tiny things – what should we do?

IT'S ALL GOING GREY GOO…!
Boffins working on nanorobots reckon that there's a real danger that one day they will learn to reproduce.
When that happens, if the tiny creatures escape from the lab they may devour everything in sight, covering the world in grey goo…
A leading scientist in nanotechnology has warned that…

THE END OF THE LINE FOR DOCTORS? R.I.P. G.Ps?!?
It could be the end of the line for your family doctor if nanotechnology carries on developing at this rate.
One day it may be possible to inject tiny robots into your blood. They'll work out what's wrong with you, send a message to a control centre outside your body and call for reinforcements to deal with what's wrong!

2010 WARRIORS
THE US Army is developing nanotech suits – thin uniforms which are flexible and tough enough to withstand bullets and blasts.
The uniforms would have GPS guidance systems and live satellite feeds of the battlefield piped directly into the soldier's brain. There is also a built-in air conditioning system to keep the body temperature normal. Inside the suit a full range of bio-sensors will send medical data back to a medical team.
Yesterday, a spokesman for…

NANOTECHNOLOGY GIVES CLEAN WATER
One-sixth of the world's population has no access to clean, safe water, and two million children die each year from water-related diseases. But nanoscience may come to the rescue. Nano-membranes are portable and easily-cleaned systems that purify, detoxify and desalinate water far better than ordinary filters. Not only that – they are cheap too!

ACTIVITY
Whenever we are faced with a possible development in science there are two possible questions – what **can** we do? and what **should** we do?
Look at the ideas on the previous page and the four headlines on this page. Ask yourself these two questions about **one** of the headlines – and present your answers to your group.

- The ideas could be listed on the board and at the end of the lesson, students could vote which one they think is the best development. Then ask a few students why they voted the way they did.

Learning styles
Kinaesthetic: Handling zeolites and models of zeolites.

Visual: Creating a poster about nanotechnology.

Auditory: Listening to opinions from other people.

Interpersonal: Working in a group to make a presentation.

Intrapersonal: Defining key terms.

Gifted and talented
School might have some examples of natural zeolites and structures of them. Ask students to research the role of zeolites and nanotechnology in developing new catalysts.

Special needs
The definitions and the key words could be supplied to these students; they could then match them up.

ICT link-up
Images of nanoparticles can be found by completing an image search on Google. These images could be shown or printed out for them to use in their written work.

CHEMISTRY STRUCTURES AND PROPERTIES

SUMMARY ANSWERS

1 a) D b) A c) B d) C

2 The ionic compound is sealed in a container with two electrodes and placed in the reactor. It is connected into an electrical warning circuit. If the temperature reaches 800 °C in the reactor the compound will melt, conducting electricity and activating the alarm.

3 a) **Giant covalent:** graphite, silicon dioxide.
   Giant ionic: aluminium oxide, sodium bromide.
   Molecular: hydrogen chloride, carbon dioxide.
   Metallic: copper, nickel.

   b) Graphite – it conducts electricity even though it is a giant covalent compound, because the structure contains delocalised electrons.

4 Metals and graphite conduct electricity because both contain delocalised (free) electrons that can flow and carry an electric current. Layers of atoms in graphite are held together only weakly by these delocalised electrons, so the layers are able to slide easily over each other, making graphite soft. Although layers of atoms can slide over each other in metals, this does not happen so easily, and metals are therefore hard.

[HT only]

Summary teaching suggestions

- **Special needs** – Question 1 could be turned into a cut and stick activity, if you type in the sentences into Word (ensure the font is suitable, e.g. 14 point Comic Sans) and print them out. Cut the sentences in the same place as in the Student Book. The students can then physically match them up and stick them directly into their books.

- **When to use the questions?**
  - Question 3 can be used in a class exercise. Split the class into four groups and give each a specialism (giant covalent, giant ionic, molecular, metallic). Their job is to use the table to decide which substances belong to their group and why. Each group should then feedback verbally to the class. It would add something to have these substances in sealed containers so that the students could look at them if they wished.
  - These questions could be used as homework, as questions 1 and 2 match section 2.1 'Ionic compounds'.
  - These questions could be used as test preparation, where the students attempt the questions for half of the lesson. Then, in the second half, answers are given out and students mark each others' work.

- **Learning styles**
  Visual: Question 3 involves transferring data from one table to another table.
  Auditory: Question 4 could be used in a class discussion.

- **Misconceptions** – Often students are adamant that covalent bonds are weaker than ionic bonds and this is why simple molecular substances have a low melting point. It is vital that they understand that when you melt a simple molecular substance, no covalent bonds are broken; just the weak intermolecular forces of attraction between molecules. Stress to students that ionic bonds are about the same strength as covalent bonds.

EXAM-STYLE ANSWERS

1 a) good (1 mark)
  b) poor (1 mark)
  c) small molecules (1 mark)
  d) ionic (1 mark)
  e) poor (1 mark)
  f) covalent (1 mark)
  g) giant (1 mark)

2 a) *Three from:*
   - (Very) hard.
   - Melts at 1610 °C/high melting point.
   - Does not conduct electricity when molten. (3 marks)

   Do not accept: 'it forms crystals' – molecular solids are crystalline or 'insoluble in water' – many molecular substances are insoluble.

  b) Covalent (1 mark)
   One from:
   - Silicon and oxygen are non-metals.
   - Silicon and oxygen both need to gain electrons. (1 mark)

3 a) *Three from:*
   - Good conductor of heat.
   - Does not corrode/is not attacked by food or water or acids.
   - Can be bent/pressed into shape.
   - Is not brittle/does not break/is hard.
   - High melting point/does not melt at cooking temperatures. (3 marks)

   Do not allow 'good conductor of electricity'

  b) *One mark each for:*
   - Conduction of electricity.
   - Conduction of heat. (2 marks)

  c) *Two from:*
   - Layers of atoms slide over each other.
   - Atoms slip into new positions.

Additional chemistry

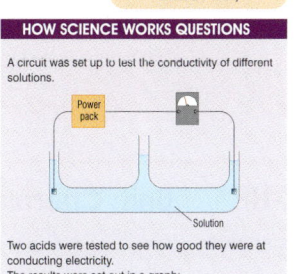

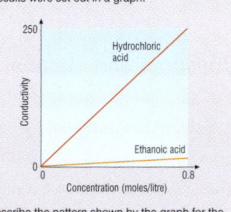

Exam teaching suggestions

- Q1 should not be attempted until this chapter has been completed. Q6 could be used after spread 2.2, Q2 after 2.3 and Q3 after 2.4. Allow 35 minutes for the complete set of questions with a total of 35 marks.
- Many students find it difficult to distinguish between intermolecular forces and covalent bonds. In particular many believe that covalent bonds are broken when liquids become gases. Q6d) should identify problems with these ideas.
- Q2 and Q3 require the identification of appropriate evidence in support of concepts about structures. These questions could be used as the basis for pair or small group discussions to produce exemplar answers. Note especially the 'do not accept' points in the mark scheme, which could form the basis of further discussion. The relationship between the number of marks and the number of points needed in answers can also be emphasised here.
- Q3c) requires a clear understanding of metal structures to achieve full marks. There are several ways in which this can be expressed and the mark scheme has more marking points than the marks available. Students sometimes give too much information in answers, leading to contradictions or loss of clarity. Students should be encouraged to use diagrams when explaining structures.

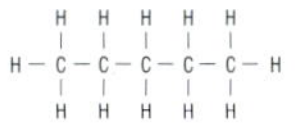

HOW SCIENCE WORKS ANSWERS

a) As the concentration of the hydrochloric acid increases so too does the conductivity.
b) Yes, because the graph shows a positive linear relationship in which the straight line does go through (0,0).
c) i) The graph for ethanoic acid is just above 0 and increases very slightly.
   ii) The slope is always below that of hydrochloric acid.
d) None – we only have evidence for two acids.
e) Bar chart.
f) No – we cannot go beyond the data we have.

How science works teaching suggestions

- **Literacy guidance.** Key terms that should be clearly understood: conclusions, patterns.
- **Higher- and lower-level answers.** Question b) is a higher level question and the answers provided above are also at this level. Question a) is lower level and the answer provided is also lower level.
- **Gifted and talented.** Able students could gather data on the conductance of other acids. They might consider why an acid might be a good or a poor conductor.
- **How and when to use these questions.** When wishing to develop skills associated with interpretation of data from graphs. The questions could be used for homework or in the lesson for individual work.
- **Misconceptions.** That any straight line can be described as directly proportional. To address this, state that this is only true for lines passing through (0,0). Give the students two straight line graphs, one passing through the origin, the other intercepting the y-axis above zero. Then ask the students to use the lines to see if doubling a value of x will result in a doubling of the value of y. Only the straight line through the origin will. If still in doubt, let the students try their own straight lines to test out by substitution.
- **Special needs.** Some help will be needed to understand the term conductivity.
- **ICT link-up.** The Internet could be researched to gather more data to help to answer question e) e.g. search for 'conductance of acids' or 'conductivity of acids'.

- Atoms stay bonded together because of delocalised electrons.
- Atoms remain in position when force removed. *(2 marks)*
  [**HT** only]

4 a) One each for:
- Particles or structures about 1 nanometre in size/between 1 and 100 nm.
- Containing a few hundred atoms. *(2 marks)*

b) Any two points or specific examples from:
- Have different properties to same materials in bulk.
- Can be used to make new types of devices, e.g. computers/processors/sensors.
- New catalysts/coatings/construction materials. *(2 marks)*

c) One each for:
- Much larger surface area (than bulk materials).
- Exposes more atoms to air/increases rate of reaction.
  (2 marks)

5 a) e.g. increased sale of mobile phones. *(1 mark)*
b) e.g. don't use up much natural resources because of small size of devices. *(1 mark)*
c) e.g. warn fire fighters if their protective clothing is getting too hot as it will change colour at a particular temperature. *(1 mark)*

6 a) Atoms (of carbon and hydrogen). *(1 mark)*
b) Covalent *(1 mark)* bonds *(1 mark)* *(2 marks)*
c) Two from:
- Its particles/molecules have no charges.
- It has no ions.
- It is made of molecules.
- It is covalently bonded.
- Its electrons cannot move from molecule to molecule. *(2 marks)*

d) Any two points from:
Molecules have enough energy to move apart/escape from the liquid/overcome intermolecular forces/but covalent bonds are not broken. *(2 marks)*
[**HT** only]

CHEMISTRY　　HOW MUCH?

C2 3.1　Mass numbers

LEARNING OBJECTIVES

Students should learn:

- The relative masses of sub-atomic particles.
- That atoms have a mass number.
- That some atoms can have isotopes.

LEARNING OUTCOMES

Most students should be able to:

- Define mass number.
- Use the periodic table to get mass numbers for any atom.
- State a definition for isotopes.

Some students should also be able to:

- Use information from the periodic table to work out the number of neutrons an atom has.
- Explain how isotopes are different.

Teaching suggestions

- **Special needs.** These students may find it difficult to find the key words to match with the definitions. Therefore, write a list of key words onto the board so they can use these throughout the lesson.
- **Gifted and talented.** Students could draw diagrams for the three hydrogen isotopes (hydrogen, deuterium, tritium).
- **Learning styles**

  Kinaesthetic: Voting by using thumb position during the true or false starter.

  Visual: Creating a spider diagram to summarise the information.

  Auditory: Listening to key terms and associating other facts.

  Interpersonal: Working in pairs, e.g. in 'association' plenary.

  Intrapersonal: Defining key terms.

- **Homework.** Students could find out an example of an isotope pair. Ask them to record the symbols, with its proton and mass number, and state the numbers of sub-atomic particles in the atoms of each isotope.

SPECIFICATION LINK-UP　　Unit: Chemistry 2.12.3

- Atoms can be represented as shown:

  Mass number　　$^{23}_{11}$Na
  Atomic number

- The relative masses of protons, neutrons and electrons are:

Name of particle	Mass
Proton	1
Neutron	1
Electron	Very small

- The total number of protons and neutrons in an atom is called its mass number.
- Atoms of the same element can have different numbers of neutrons: these atoms are called isotopes of that element.

Lesson structure

STARTER

Definitions – Give the students the definitions on the board. They should match each with a key word:

- A positive particle in an atom's nucleus. [Proton]
- A neutral particle with a relative mass of 1. [Neutron]
- The sub-atomic particle that is found in energy levels. [Electron]
- Atoms with the same number of protons, but different number of neutrons. [Isotope]
(5 minutes)

True or false – If students agree with these statements they should show a thumbs up sign, if they disagree their thumbs should point downwards, and if they don't know their thumbs should be horizontal.

- Atoms are charged particles. [False]
- Electrons are found in energy levels or shells. [True]
- Electrons have a negative charge. [True]
- Protons are in the nucleus of an atom. [True]
- Neutrons are found in shells around the nucleus. [False] (5 minutes)

MAIN

- The structure of the atom can be summarised into a spider diagram. Encourage the students to include information about atomic mass, sub-atomic particles, isotopes and uses of isotopes.
- Students could be asked to include a key in their diagram. For example, use specific colours for key terms: red – proton, green – neutron, blue – electron, yellow – atom, purple – isotope.
- Students need to be able to use the periodic table to work out the number of each sub-atomic particle in an atom. With a question and answer session, draw out how the periodic table can be used to supply information about an atom.
- Show the students how to calculate the number of each sub-atomic particle using mass number and proton number.
- Then ask the students to design a table to record the number of each sub-atomic particle in the first 20 elements. Ask them to then complete their table.

PLENARIES

Think – On the board, write the symbol for carbon-12 and carbon-14 isotopes. Ask the students to use the periodic table and their knowledge of isotopes to list all the similarities between the atoms and all their differences. [Similarities – same number and arrangement of electrons, same number of protons in the nucleus, same chemical properties, same atomic/proton number. Differences – different number of neutrons in the nucleus, different mass numbers, different physical properties.] (10 minutes)

Association – Split the class into pairs, each student should face their partner. All students on the right should start first, saying a word or phrase about the lesson. Then the next person says another fact/key word based on the lesson. The activity swaps between partners until all the facts are exhausted. If a student hesitates or repeats previous statements then they have lost the association game. (10 minutes)

ACTIVITY & EXTENSION

- Students could use the Internet to research some uses of isotopes, e.g. in medicine.
- Students could research 'heavy water', D_2O, and how its properties differ from normal water.

CHEMISTRY — **HOW MUCH?**

C2 3.1 Mass numbers

LEARNING OBJECTIVES
1. What are the relative masses of protons, neutrons and electrons?
2. What is an atom's mass number?
3. What are isotopes?

As we saw earlier on, an atom consists of a nucleus containing positively charged protons, together with neutrons which have no charge. The negatively charged electrons are arranged in energy levels (shells) around the nucleus.

Every atom has the same number of electrons orbiting its nucleus as it has protons in its nucleus. The number of protons that an atom has is its **atomic number**.

The mass of a proton and a neutron are the same. Another way of putting this is to say that the *relative mass* of a neutron compared with a proton is 1. Electrons are far, far smaller than protons and neutrons – their mass is negligible. Because of this, the mass of an atom is concentrated in its nucleus. You can ignore the tiny mass of the electrons when it comes to thinking about the mass of an atom!

Type of sub-atomic particle	Relative mass
proton	1
neutron	1
electron	negligible (very small)

a) How does the number of electrons in an atom compare to the number of protons?
b) How does the mass of a proton compare to the mass of a neutron?
c) How does the mass of an electron compare to the mass of a neutron or proton?

Mass number

Almost all of the mass of an atom is found in the nucleus, because the mass of the electrons is so tiny. We call the total number of protons and neutrons in an atom its **mass number**.

When we want to show the atomic number and mass number of an atom we do it like this:

Mass number $^{12}_{6}C$ (carbon) $^{23}_{11}Na$ (sodium)
Atomic number

We can work out the number of neutrons in the nucleus of an atom by subtracting its atomic number from its mass number. The difference is the number of neutrons:

mass number − atomic number = number of neutrons

For the two examples here, carbon has 6 protons and a mass number of 12, so the number of neutrons is (12 − 6) = 6.

Sodium, on the other hand, has an atomic number of 11 but the mass number is 23, so (23 − 11) = 12. In this sodium atom there are 11 protons and 12 neutrons.

d) How do we calculate the number of neutrons in an atom?

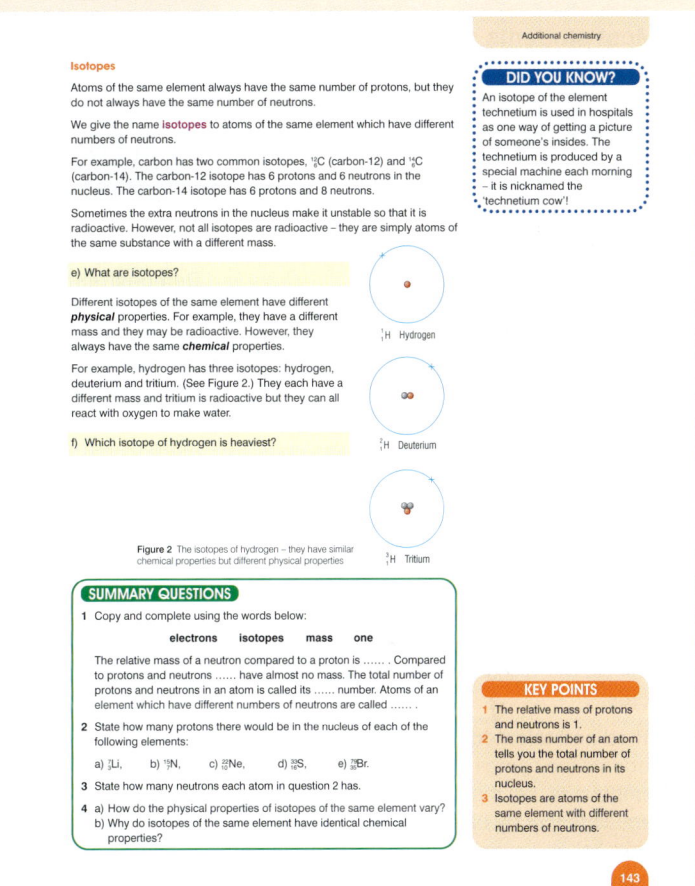

Figure 1 Chemists use the atomic number and the mass number of an element in many ways

Isotopes

Atoms of the same element always have the same number of protons, but they do not always have the same number of neutrons.

We give the name **isotopes** to atoms of the same element which have different numbers of neutrons.

For example, carbon has two common isotopes, $^{12}_{6}C$ (carbon-12) and $^{14}_{6}C$ (carbon-14). The carbon-12 isotope has 6 protons and 6 neutrons in the nucleus. The carbon-14 isotope has 6 protons and 8 neutrons.

Sometimes the extra neutrons in the nucleus make it unstable so that it is radioactive. However, not all isotopes are radioactive – they are simply atoms of the same substance with a different mass.

e) What are isotopes?

Different isotopes of the same element have different **physical** properties. For example, they have a different mass and they may be radioactive. However, they always have the same **chemical** properties.

For example, hydrogen has three isotopes: hydrogen, deuterium and tritium. (See Figure 2.) They each have a different mass and tritium is radioactive but they can all react with oxygen to make water.

f) Which isotope of hydrogen is heaviest?

$^{1}_{1}H$ Hydrogen
$^{2}_{1}H$ Deuterium
$^{3}_{1}H$ Tritium

Figure 2 The isotopes of hydrogen – they have similar chemical properties but different physical properties

DID YOU KNOW?
An isotope of the element technetium is used in hospitals as one way of getting a picture of someone's insides. The technetium is produced by a special machine each morning – it is nicknamed the 'technetium cow'!

SUMMARY QUESTIONS

1. Copy and complete using the words below:

   electrons   isotopes   mass   one

   The relative mass of a neutron compared to a proton is …… . Compared to protons and neutrons …… have almost no mass. The total number of protons and neutrons in an atom is called its …… number. Atoms of an element which have different numbers of neutrons are called …… .

2. State how many protons there would be in the nucleus of each of the following elements:
   a) $^{7}_{3}Li$,   b) $^{15}_{7}N$,   c) $^{20}_{10}Ne$,   d) $^{32}_{16}S$,   e) $^{80}_{35}Br$.

3. State how many neutrons each atom in question 2 has.

4. a) How do the physical properties of isotopes of the same element vary?
   b) Why do isotopes of the same element have identical chemical properties?

KEY POINTS
1. The relative mass of protons and neutrons is 1.
2. The mass number of an atom tells you the total number of protons and neutrons in its nucleus.
3. Isotopes are atoms of the same element with different numbers of neutrons.

SUMMARY ANSWERS

1. One, electrons, mass, isotopes.

2. a) protons = 3
   b) protons = 7
   c) protons = 10
   d) protons = 16
   e) protons = 35

3. a) neutrons = 4
   b) neutrons = 8
   c) neutrons = 12
   d) neutrons = 17
   e) neutrons = 44

4. a) The atoms have a different mass and they may be radioactive.
   b) Because they have identical electronic structures.

Answers to in-text questions

a) Number of electrons = number of protons.
b) Mass of proton = mass of neutron.
c) Mass of electron is much less than the mass of a proton or neutron.
d) Number of neutrons = mass number minus atomic number.
e) Isotopes are atoms of the same element with different numbers of neutrons (or words to that effect).
f) Tritium, $^{3}_{1}H$.

KEY POINTS

Make cards containing parts of the sentences. The students could then arrange the word tiles to make up the key points. This activity can be made easier by splitting each sentence into just three parts.

CHEMISTRY   HOW MUCH?

C2 3.2 Masses of atoms and moles

LEARNING OBJECTIVES

Students should learn:

- That the masses of atoms can be compared by their relative atomic masses.
- That the relative formula mass of compounds can be calculated.

LEARNING OUTCOMES

Most students should be able to:

- Give a definition of relative formula mass.
- Calculate relative formula mass if its formula and the relative atomic mass are given.

Some students should also be able to:

- Give a full definition of relative atomic mass. [HT only]
- Explain what a mole is.

Teaching suggestions

- **Special needs.** Provide the students with a pre-cut out cube template that is also ready scored. To help further, add some information already on it, for example the titles or prose with missing words.
- **Gifted and talented.** Give these students the names of different compounds. Let them work out the formula (either by using the text book or using dot and cross diagrams). Then encourage them to use the periodic table to get the A_r before working out the M_r.
- **Learning styles**
  Kinaesthetic: Matching up cards.
  Visual: Creating revision cube on this topic.
  Auditory: Listening to other students describing key words.
  Interpersonal: Discussing how different samples relate to each other.
  Intrapersonal: Finding the key words in a word search.

SPECIFICATION LINK-UP   Unit: Chemistry 2.12.3

- The relative atomic mass of an element (A_r) compares the mass of atoms of the element with the carbon-12 isotope. It is an average value for the isotopes of the element. [HT only]
- The relative formula mass (M_r) of a compound is the sum of the relative atomic masses of the atoms in the numbers shown in the formula.
- The relative formula mass of a substance, in grams, is known as one mole of that substance.

Students should use their skills, knowledge and understanding of 'How Science Works':

- to calculate chemical quantities involving formula mass (M_r).

Lesson structure

STARTER

Demonstration – Have a mole of different substances pre-measured in sealed containers, e.g. 12 g of carbon, 24 g of magnesium. Allow the students to handle different samples. Explain to these students that all these examples have something in common – but what? Encourage the students to use the Student Book and discuss in small groups how these samples relate to each other. Hopefully they will realise that these are all examples of moles. Then ask students for hands up if they can tell you the mass of, e.g., 1 mole of carbon (and hold up the sample) etc. Repeat for all the samples that you have. (10 minutes)

Word search – Give the students a word search for the key words that they will be using in the lesson: 'relative', 'atomic', 'mass', 'formula', 'mole', 'atom'. (5 minutes)

MAIN

- Students need to be able to obtain A_r from the periodic table and calculate M_r. Give the students a set of cards of different elements (single atoms and molecules) and compound formulas. On separate cards, write numbers that represent A_r or M_r.
- Students should complete calculations and match the formula with its A_r and M_r. They should also decide if the number represents A_r or M_r. This could be made into a competition, by splitting the class into small teams, the first group to correctly match all the cards may get a prize.
- Students need to be able to define the key terms: 'relative atomic mass', 'relative formula mass' and 'moles'.
- Give the students a template of a cube. They should write definitions of relative atomic mass, moles and relative formula mass on three faces. On the remaining faces, they should include a worked example of calculations relating to this topic using lots of colours.
- Then they cut out the template and score the lines to create sharp folds and stick the cube together.

PLENARIES

Difference – Ask the students to explain the difference between the symbols A_r and Ar. Choose a volunteer to explain to the class. [Ar is the symbol for the element argon, A_r is the shorthand notation for relative atomic mass]. (5 minutes)

In the bag – Put the key words: 'relative atomic mass', 'relative formula mass' and 'mole' into a colourful bag. Ask for three volunteers to come to the front and remove a word in turns. After they have removed their word, they should show the class the word and explain what it means. You should interject with a question and answer session to help rectify any misconceptions. (5 minutes)

Teaching suggestions – continued

- **Homework**
  Ask students to work out the mass of a mole of the following:
  - Oxygen atoms [16 g]
  - Oxygen molecules [32 g]
  - Water molecules [18 g]

  Encourage the students to show their working.

- **ICT link-up.** Celebrate mole day, there are lots of resources on www.moleday.org.

ACTIVITY & EXTENSION IDEAS
- Give students a set of timed questions to calculate relative formula masses of different substances.
- Find out how Avogadro's number was discovered.

Additional chemistry

CHEMISTRY C2 3.2 HOW MUCH?
Masses of atoms and moles

LEARNING OBJECTIVES
1 How can we compare the mass of atoms? [Higher]
2 How can we calculate the mass of compounds from the elements they are made from?

Chemical equations show you how many atoms of the reactants we need to make the products. But when we actually carry out a chemical reaction we need to know what amounts to use in grams or cm³. You might think that a chemical equation would also tell you this.

For example, does the equation:

$$Mg + 2HCl \rightarrow MgCl_2 + H_2$$

mean that we need twice as many grams of hydrochloric acid as magnesium to make magnesium chloride?

Unfortunately it isn't that simple. The equation tells us that we need twice as many hydrogen and chlorine atoms as magnesium atoms – but this doesn't mean that the mass of hydrochloric acid will be twice the mass of magnesium. This is because atoms of different elements have different masses.

To turn equations into something that we can actually use in the lab or factory we need to know a bit more about the mass of atoms.

a) Why don't chemical equations tell us how much of each reactant to use in a chemical reaction?

Relative atomic masses

The mass of a single atom is so tiny that it would be impossible to use it in calculations. To make the whole thing manageable we use a much simpler way of thinking about the masses of atoms. Instead of working with the **real** masses of atoms we just focus on the **relative** masses of atoms of different elements. We call these **relative atomic masses** (A_r).

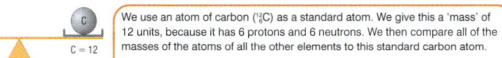

[HIGHER]
We use an atom of carbon ($^{12}_{6}C$) as a standard atom. We give this a 'mass' of 12 units, because it has 6 protons and 6 neutrons. We then compare all of the masses of the atoms of all the other elements to this standard carbon atom.

The mass of an atom found by comparing it with the $^{12}_{6}C$ atom is called its relative atomic mass (A_r).

The relative atomic mass of an element is usually the same as, or very similar to, the mass number of that element. The A_r takes into account any isotopes of the element. The relative atomic mass is the average mass of the isotopes of the element in the proportions in which they are usually found (compared with the standard carbon atom).

When atoms change into ions they either lose or gain electrons. However, for all practical purposes the mass of electrons isn't worth bothering about. So the 'relative ionic mass' of an ion is exactly the same as the relative atomic mass of that element.

b) What do we call the mass of an atom compared with the mass of an atom of carbon-12?

Figure 1 The A_r of carbon is 12. Compared with this, the A_r of helium is 4 and the A_r of magnesium is 24

Relative atomic mass	Relative ionic mass
Na 23	Na⁺ 23
O 16	O²⁻ 16
Mg 24	Mg²⁺ 24

Relative formula masses

We can use the A_r of the various elements to work out the **relative formula mass (M_r)** of chemical compounds. This is true whether the compounds are made up of molecules or collections of ions. A simple example is a substance like sodium chloride. We know that the A_r of sodium is 23 and the A_r of chlorine is 35.5. So the relative formula mass of sodium chloride (NaCl) is:

$$23 + 35.5 = 58.5$$
$$A_r\ Na\quad A_r\ Cl\quad M_r\ NaCl$$

Another example is water. Water is made up of hydrogen and oxygen. The A_r of hydrogen is 1, and the A_r of oxygen is 16. Water has the formula H₂O, containing two hydrogen atoms for every one oxygen, so the M_r is:

$$(1 \times 2) + 16 = 18$$
$$A_r\ H \times 2\quad A_r\ O\quad M_r\ H_2O$$

c) What is the relative formula mass of hydrogen sulfide, H₂S?
(A_r values: H = 1, S = 32)

Moles

Saying or writing 'relative atomic mass in grams' or 'relative formula mass in grams' is rather clumsy. So chemists have a shorthand word for it – **mole**.

They say that the relative atomic mass in grams of carbon (i.e. 12 g of carbon) is a mole of carbon atoms. One mole is simply the relative atomic mass or relative formula mass of any substance expressed in grams. A mole of any substance always contains the same number of particles.

Figure 2 We know how many actual atoms or molecules a mole contains, thanks to an Italian count born in the 18th century, Amedeo Avogadro. He worked out that a mole of any element or compound contains 6.02×10^{23} atoms, ions or molecules. That's 602 000 000 000 000 000 000 000! This is called **Avogadro's number**.

DID YOU KNOW?
One mole of soft drinks cans would cover the surface of the Earth to a depth of 200 miles!

We can use the same approach with relatively complicated molecules like sulfuric acid, H₂SO₄. Hydrogen has a A_r of 1, the A_r of sulfur is 32 and the A_r of oxygen 16. This means that the M_r of sulfuric acid is:

$$(1 \times 2) + 32 + (16 \times 4) = 2 + 32 + 64 = 98$$

GET IT RIGHT!
You don't have to remember Avogadro's number! But practise calculating the mass of one mole of different substances from relative atomic masses that you are given.

SUMMARY QUESTIONS

1 Copy and complete using the words below:

   atomic   carbon-12   elements   formula   number

   We measure the masses of atoms by comparing them to the mass of one atom of .... The relative .... mass of an element is usually almost the same as its mass .... We calculate the relative .... mass of a compound from the relative atomic masses of the .... in it.

2 The equation for the reaction of magnesium and fluorine is:

   $$Mg + F_2 \rightarrow MgF_2$$

   a) How many moles of fluorine molecules react with one mole of magnesium atoms?
   b) What is the relative formula mass of MgF₂? (A_r values: Mg = 24, F = 19)

3 The relative atomic mass of oxygen is 16, and that of magnesium is 24. How many times heavier is a magnesium atom than an oxygen atom?

KEY POINTS
1 We compare the masses of atoms by measuring them relative to atoms of carbon-12. [Higher]
2 We work out the relative formula mass of a compound from the relative atomic masses of the elements in it.
3 One mole of any substance always contains the same number of particles.

SUMMARY ANSWERS

1 Carbon-12, atomic, number, formula, elements.

2 a) 1
  b) 62

3 1.5 times heavier.

Answers to in-text questions

a) Because the atoms of different elements have different masses.

b) Its relative atomic mass.

c) 34

DID YOU KNOW?

If you drew a line that was as long in millimetres as Avogadro's number, it would stretch from the Sun to the Earth and back 2 million times!

KEY POINTS

Students could make a poem with three verses, one to reflect each key point.

145

CHEMISTRY — HOW MUCH?

C2 3.3 Percentages and formulae

LEARNING OBJECTIVES

Students should learn:
- How to calculate the percentage mass of an element in a compound.
- How to calculate the formula of a compound from the percentage composition. **[HT only]**

LEARNING OUTCOMES

Most students should be able to:
- Calculate the percentage composition of an element in a compound.

Some students should also be able to:
- Calculate the formula of a compound if the percentage composition of the elements is given. **[HT only]**

Teaching suggestions

- **Special needs.** These students will often struggle with calculations. Provide them with a writing frame to help them.
- **Gifted and talented.** Students could be given more complex empirical formula type questions to attempt.
- **Learning styles**
  Kinaesthetic: Experimentally determining the formula of magnesium oxide.
  Visual: Interpreting concept cartoon.
  Auditory: Listening to the answers to questions.
  Interpersonal: Working in pairs to give AfL (Assessment for Learning).
  Intrapersonal: Completing calculations.
- **Homework.** Ask: 'Which of the following compounds contains the highest proportion of oxygen?' Encourage the students to calculate the percentage composition and to show their working.
  - CO [57% O]
  - C_2H_4OH [36% O]
  - CH_3COOH [53% O]
- **ICT link-up.** Download a template for a self-marking exercise where students choose their answers from menus. These templates use Excel and are found at www.chemit.co.uk.

SPECIFICATION LINK-UP   Unit: Chemistry 2.12.3

- The percentage of an element in a compound can be calculated from the relative mass of the element in the formula and the relative formula mass of the compound.

Students should use their skills, knowledge and understanding of 'How Science Works':
- to calculate chemical quantities involving percentages of elements in compounds.
- to calculate chemical quantities involving empirical formulae. **[HT only]**

Lesson structure

STARTER

Measurement – Show the students different mass values on balances. Ask them to note to the nearest two decimal places the values shown. Read out the answers and ask the students to put up their hands if they got them all right, one wrong, two wrong etc. Approach students that have been having difficulty and help them to see why they recorded the wrong answer. (5 minutes)

Concept cartoon – Show the students a concept cartoon to highlight the conservation of mass theory. Ask them to discuss the cartoon in small groups, and then feedback to the rest of the class. (5 minutes)

MAIN

- To complete calculations there is often a set order of steps involved. Choose an example question to calculate the percentage composition of an element and write out each step onto separate cards.
- Encourage the students to order the cards and copy out the worked example correctly. Then give the students other examples to work out themselves.
- Then the same idea can be repeated, but for generating a formula of a compound from percentage composition data instead.
- Give the students two flash cards. On one side they should write how to calculate the percentage composition of an element, and on the reverse they should make up some questions of their own.
- On the second card they should write how to generate the formula on one side, and on the reverse some questions.
- The students can then work out the answers and write them upside down on their revision card.
- Students could experimentally determine the formula of magnesium oxide. This requires them to be able to read a balance accurately to 2 decimal places.
- They should design their own results table and show all their working to generate the formula. They should calculate the mass of magnesium used (mass of initially full crucible – empty crucible). Then they should calculate the mass of oxygen in the compound (mass of crucible after heating – mass of initially full crucible).
- Once the mass of each element in the compound is known the formula can be calculated as detailed in the Student Book.

PLENARIES

On the spot – Ask for a volunteer to stand at the front of the class, and give the other students scrap paper. Read out questions to the volunteer and they should say their answer. The rest of the class then writes a number and holds it up to show whether they strongly disagree (1) or strongly agree (10) with the answer. You could reveal the true answer. (10 minutes)

Calculation – Ask the students to calculate the percentage composition of each element in ammonia. They should recall the formula of ammonia from previous work. [N = 82%; H = 18%] (5 minutes)

AfL (Assessment for Learning) – In pairs, students swap their revision cards and tackle each other's questions and check their answers. They should be encouraged to feedback any problems that they are having to their partner. (10 minutes).

146

Practical support

Determining the formula of magnesium oxide

Equipment and materials required
Small strips of magnesium ribbon (flammable), ceramic crucibles and lids, Bunsen burner and safety equipment, tongs, pipe clay triangle, tripod, accurate balance, eye protection.

Details
Students to note the mass of the crucible and lid, and then twist the magnesium ribbon into a coil shape and put into the crucible. Also note the new mass of the crucible, and put onto the pipe clay triangle. Heat strongly in a blue Bunsen flame, and lift the lid gently and occasionally to boost the oxygen flow. They must not lift the lid up high, as some of the product will be lost. When the lid is lifted and there is no white light, then the reaction is complete.

Then turn off the Bunsen and allow the crucible to cool, noting the mass of the crucible at the end of the reaction.

Safety: Eye protection should be worn throughout the reaction and students should be warned that the crucible will retain heat for a surprising amount of time and may crack. Magnesium is flammable – CLEAPSS Hazcard 59.

ACTIVITY & EXTENSION IDEAS

Students could try to calculate the water of crystallisation in certain formulae, e.g. $CuSO_4.5H_2O$.

SUMMARY ANSWERS

1 Compound, dividing, relative formula mass, hundred.

2 35%

3 PCl_3 [**HT** only]

Answers to in-text questions

a) 25%

b) SO_3

KEY POINTS

Before the lesson begins, select five famous people and write their names on a piece of paper and attach them to the underside of five chairs in the class. Then ask students to check under their chairs; if they have a famous person, they should read out the key point in the style of the famous person to the rest of the class.

147

CHEMISTRY   HOW MUCH?

C2 3.4   Equations and calculations

LEARNING OBJECTIVES

Students should learn:

- That chemical equations can give information about the relative numbers of reacting particles and products formed in a reaction. [**HT** only]
- That chemical equations can be used to calculate reacting masses. [**HT** only]

LEARNING OUTCOMES

Most Higher Tier students should be able to:

- Interpret how many moles of reactants/products are shown in a balanced equation. [**HT** only]
- Balance symbol equations. [**HT** only]
- Use a balanced symbol equation to calculate the mass of reactants or products. [**HT** only]

Teaching suggestions

- **Special needs.** These students will find the calculations difficult. Give them half-finished calculations, where they need to add numbers into the working out to generate the answers. Also peer mentoring could be used, where the students are split into pairs, where the higher attaining student supports the lower attaining.
- **Learning styles**
  Kinaesthetic: Completing the card loop.
  Auditory: Listening to other students in group work.
  Interpersonal: Working in groups to give AfL (Assessment for Learning).
  Intrapersonal: Completing calculations.
- **Homework.** Ask students to go through the work and pick out the key terms (e.g. reactant, product, mass). They should then define these key terms.

SPECIFICATION LINK-UP   Unit: Chemistry 2.12.3

- *The masses of reactants and products can be calculated from balanced symbol equations.* [**HT** only]

Students should use their skills, knowledge and understanding of 'How Science Works':

- *to calculate chemical quantities involving reacting masses.* [**HT** only]

Lesson structure

STARTER

Multiple-choice – Give each student three coloured flash cards, e.g. blue, green and red. Then create a few multiple-choice questions, one per slide on PowerPoint® with three answers, each one written in a different colour to match the flash cards. This could also be achieved using Word or whiteboard software. Then show each question in turn and the students should hold up the card that represents the answer that they think is correct. (5 minutes)

Chemical equations – Ask the students to complete the following chemical equations:

1. magnesium + [oxygen] → magnesium oxide
2. methane + oxygen → [carbon dioxide] + water
3. zinc + copper sulfate → [copper] + [zinc sulfate]
4. [sodium hydroxide] + hydrochloric acid → sodium chloride + water

To extend this activity, you could ask the students to say what type of reaction each of the above represents [1 oxidation; 2 combustion/oxidation; 3 displacement; 4 neutralisation]. Then students could turn these into balanced symbol equations. (10 minutes)

MAIN

- Students need to be able to work out the masses of different substances in balanced symbol equations. Create a card loop by drawing a rectangle 10 cm by 15 cm. Draw a dotted line to make a square 10 cm by 10 cm. In the square write out questions that involve balancing equations and calculating reacting masses. Then in the rectangle 5 cm by 10 cm write an answer (not one that matches the question on the card). Ensure that the questions match with answers on other cards so that a loop is made.
- Give the question loop set to small groups of students and allow them to complete the card sort. Then encourage the students to pick two of the questions and answers to copy out into their book, but show their working out stage by stage (as demonstrated in the Student Book).
- Split the class into pairs, and on separate pieces of paper write enough calculation questions for one per group. Give out the questions and allow the students to start to answer for three minutes (timed using a stopwatch). Then ask the students to hand the paper to another group.
- Give the next group three minutes to correct the previous work and then continue with the answer.
- Repeat this a number of times until there has been enough time for the answers to be completed. Then return the paper back to the 'owners' where they should copy up the question and the full answer.
- Use the Simulation C2 3.4 'Equations' from the GCSE Chemistry CD ROM.

PLENARIES

AfL (Assessment for Learning) – Give students some calculations, but instead of tackling the questions encourage them to create the mark scheme. Ask the students to work in small groups discussing the question and devising the marking points, and include alternative answers that could still be given credit, and those that definitely should not be awarded marks. (10 minutes)

Reflection – Ask students to think about the objectives for today's lesson. Ask them to consider if they have been met, and discuss this in small groups. Ask a few groups to feed back to the rest of the class, explaining how they know that they have met the objectives. (5 minutes)

ACTIVITY & EXTENSION IDEAS

- Students could include state symbols in more complex balanced symbol equations.
- Students may attempt industrial-sized calculations (involving tonnes). This would involve them multiplying up the masses of the different components.

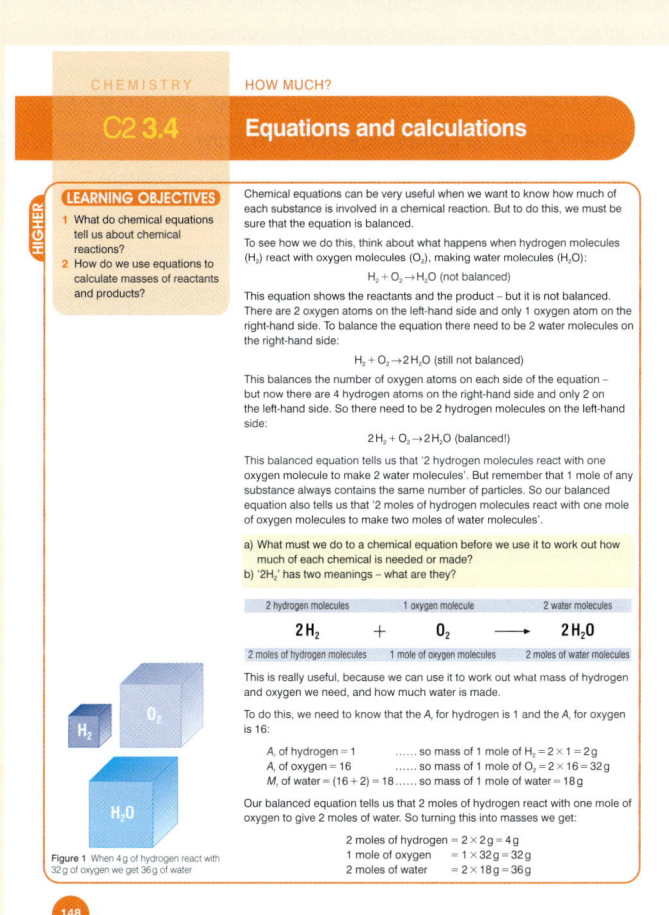

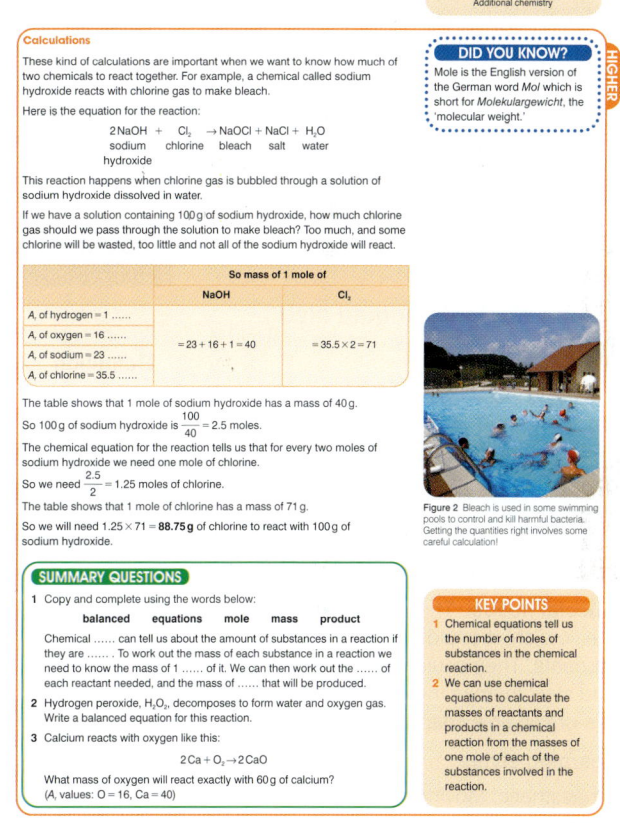

Additional chemistry

CHEMISTRY — HOW MUCH?
C2 3.4 Equations and calculations

LEARNING OBJECTIVES
1. What do chemical equations tell us about chemical reactions?
2. How do we use equations to calculate masses of reactants and products?

Chemical equations can be very useful when we want to know how much of each substance is involved in a chemical reaction. But to do this, we must be sure that the equation is balanced.

To see how we do this, think about what happens when hydrogen molecules (H_2) react with oxygen molecules (O_2), making water molecules (H_2O):

$$H_2 + O_2 \rightarrow H_2O \text{ (not balanced)}$$

This equation shows the reactants and the product – but it is not balanced. There are 2 oxygen atoms on the left-hand side and only 1 oxygen atom on the right-hand side. To balance the equation there need to be 2 water molecules on the right-hand side:

$$H_2 + O_2 \rightarrow 2H_2O \text{ (still not balanced)}$$

This balances the number of oxygen atoms on each side of the equation – but now there are 4 hydrogen atoms on the right-hand side and only 2 on the left-hand side. So there need to be 2 hydrogen molecules on the left-hand side:

$$2H_2 + O_2 \rightarrow 2H_2O \text{ (balanced!)}$$

This balanced equation tells us that '2 hydrogen molecules react with one oxygen molecule to make 2 water molecules'. But remember that 1 mole of any substance always contains the same number of particles. So our balanced equation also tells us that '2 moles of hydrogen molecules react with one mole of oxygen molecules to make two moles of water molecules'.

a) What must we do to a chemical equation before we use it to work out how much of each chemical is needed or made?
b) '$2H_2$' has two meanings – what are they?

2 hydrogen molecules	1 oxygen molecule	2 water molecules
$2H_2$	$+ \quad O_2$	$\rightarrow \quad 2H_2O$
2 moles of hydrogen molecules	1 mole of oxygen molecules	2 moles of water molecules

This is really useful, because we can use it to work out what mass of hydrogen and oxygen we need, and how much water is made.

To do this, we need to know that the A_r for hydrogen is 1 and the A_r for oxygen is 16:

A_r of hydrogen = 1 ...... so mass of 1 mole of H_2 = 2 × 1 = 2 g
A_r of oxygen = 16 ...... so mass of 1 mole of O_2 = 2 × 16 = 32 g
M_r of water = (16 + 2) = 18 ...... so mass of 1 mole of water = 18 g

Our balanced equation tells us that 2 moles of hydrogen react with one mole of oxygen to give 2 moles of water. So turning this into masses we get:

2 moles of hydrogen = 2 × 2 g = 4 g
1 mole of oxygen = 1 × 32 g = 32 g
2 moles of water = 2 × 18 g = 36 g

Figure 1 When 4 g of hydrogen react with 32 g of oxygen we get 36 g of water

---

Calculations

These kind of calculations are important when we want to know how much of two chemicals to react together. For example, a chemical called sodium hydroxide reacts with chlorine gas to make bleach.

Here is the equation for the reaction:

$$2NaOH + Cl_2 \rightarrow NaOCl + NaCl + H_2O$$
sodium hydroxide | chlorine | bleach | salt | water

This reaction happens when chlorine gas is bubbled through a solution of sodium hydroxide dissolved in water.

If we have a solution containing 100 g of sodium hydroxide, how much chlorine gas should we pass through the solution to make bleach? Too much, and some chlorine will be wasted, too little and not all of the sodium hydroxide will react.

	So mass of 1 mole of	
	NaOH	Cl_2
A_r of hydrogen = 1		
A_r of oxygen = 16	= 23 + 16 + 1 = 40	= 35.5 × 2 = 71
A_r of sodium = 23		
A_r of chlorine = 35.5		

The table shows that 1 mole of sodium hydroxide has a mass of 40 g.

So 100 g of sodium hydroxide is $\frac{100}{40} = 2.5$ moles.

The chemical equation for the reaction tells us that for every two moles of sodium hydroxide we need one mole of chlorine.

So we need $\frac{2.5}{2} = 1.25$ moles of chlorine.

The table shows that 1 mole of chlorine has a mass of 71 g.

So we will need 1.25 × 71 = **88.75 g** of chlorine to react with 100 g of sodium hydroxide.

DID YOU KNOW?
Mole is the English version of the German word *Mol* which is short for *Molekulargewicht*, the 'molecular weight.'

Figure 2 Bleach is used in some swimming pools to control and kill harmful bacteria. Getting the quantities right involves some careful calculation!

SUMMARY QUESTIONS

1. Copy and complete using the words below:

   balanced   equations   mole   mass   product

   Chemical ...... can tell us about the amount of substances in a reaction if they are .... To work out the mass of each substance in a reaction we need to know the mass of 1 ...... of it. We can then work out the ...... of each reactant needed, and the mass of ...... that will be produced.

2. Hydrogen peroxide, H_2O_2, decomposes to form water and oxygen gas. Write a balanced equation for this reaction.

3. Calcium reacts with oxygen like this:

   $$2Ca + O_2 \rightarrow 2CaO$$

   What mass of oxygen will react exactly with 60 g of calcium?
   (A_r values: O = 16, Ca = 40)

KEY POINTS
1. Chemical equations tell us the number of moles of substances in the chemical reaction.
2. We can use chemical equations to calculate the masses of reactants and products in a chemical reaction from the masses of one mole of each of the substances involved in the reaction.

SUMMARY ANSWERS

1. Equations, balanced, mole, mass, product.

2. $2H_2O_2 \rightarrow 2H_2O + O_2$

3. 24 g

Answers to in-text questions

a) Balance it.

b) '2 hydrogen molecules' and '2 moles of hydrogen molecules'.

KEY POINTS

Ask the students to copy out the key points, then encourage them to illustrate each of the key points by using a worked example of a calculation.

CHEMISTRY   HOW MUCH?

C2 3.5 Making as much as we want

LEARNING OBJECTIVES

Students should learn:

- That the amount of product made can be expressed as a yield.
- How to calculate percentage yield. [**HT** only]
- That different factors affect yield.
- What atom economy is and why it is important.
- How to calculate atom economy. [**HT** only]

LEARNING OUTCOMES

Most students should be able to:

- Give a definition for yield.
- List factors that affect yield.
- Explain why atom economy is important.

Some students should also be able to:

- Calculate percentage yield. [**HT** only]
- Calculate atom economy. [**HT** only]

Teaching suggestions

- **Special needs.** The different steps in the flow chart could be given to the students. They could then cut them out and stick them in the correct order into a pre-drawn flow chart outline.
- **Learning styles**

   Kinaesthetic: Moving to show the order of a calculation.

   Visual: Creating a flow chart to explain how to tackle a calculation.

   Auditory: Listening to others in group work.

   Interpersonal: Working in a group to answer a series of questions.

   Intrapersonal: Defining percentage yield and reflecting on factors affecting yield.

- **Homework.** Ask students to explain why it is important for a company to maximise its yield.
- **Science @ work.** Industry has to reduce the energy consumption and raw materials to keep costs down and make more profit. However, it also has positive effects for the environment. Often chemical plants use the heat from exothermic reactions elsewhere in manufacture of products or even to heat the offices!

SPECIFICATION LINK-UP   Unit: Chemistry 2.12.3

- Even though no atoms are gained or lost in a chemical reaction it is not always possible to obtain the calculated amount of a product because:
   - the reaction may not go to completion because it is reversible
   - some of the product may be lost when it is separated from the reaction mixture
   - some of the reactants may react in ways different to expected reaction.
- The amount of product obtained is known as the yield. When compared with the maximum theoretical amount as a percentage, it is called the percentage yield. [**HT** only]
- The atom economy (atom utilisation) is a measure of the amount of starting materials that end up as useful products. It is important for sustainable development and for economic reasons to use reactions with high atom economy.

Students should use their skills, knowledge and understanding of 'How Science Works':

- to calculate chemical quantities involving percentage yield. [**HT** only]
- to calculate the atom economy for industrial processes and be able to evaluate sustainable development issues related to this economy. [**HT** only]

Lesson structure

STARTER

Definition – Ask the students to explain what a yield and atom economy is and how it can be calculated. They could use the Student Book to help them. (5 minutes)

Mirror words – Ask the students to work out these key words that will be used in the lesson:

- stnatcaer [reactants]
- stcudorp [products]
- dleiy [yield]
- egatnecrep [percentage]
- noitaluclac [calculation] (5 minutes)

MAIN

- Split the class into teams of about five pupils. Prepare ten questions for each group – they could be written on colour-coded paper. The questions should be face-down on a front desk.
- A volunteer from each group should retrieve their first question and take it back to their table, and the team should complete the calculation. As soon as they have an answer, they take it to you to be checked.
- If they are correct, then they can get their next question, if they are incorrect they should try again, with help where needed. The team to complete all the questions correctly first could win a prize.
- Ask Higher Tier students to look carefully at the worked example for calculating the yield and atom economy. Ask them to draw two flow charts to show the steps of how to complete these calculations.
- Then give the students a number of questions that they can answer using their flow charts to help them.
- Discuss the importance of maximising percentage yield and atom economy to support sustainable development. Students can then list the advantages.

150

Additional chemistry

PLENARIES

Steps – On the board, write a question that involves the calculation of a yield (an example could be used from the Student Book). Put each separate number or mathematical procedure onto separate sheets of A3 paper and arrange them on the floor in the wrong order. Ask for a volunteer to stand on the starting number and move onto the next sheet physically showing the order of the calculation. The student should be encouraged to describe how they would do the calculation as they stand on the different pieces of paper. (5 minutes)

What's the question? – Give students an answer to a yield or atom economy question, including full calculations. Encourage the students to work in small groups to generate questions that match the answer given. (10 minutes)

List – In reality, no reaction ever produces the theoretical yield. Ask the students to think about why this is so, and note their ideas on a spider diagram in their books. Then ask them to contribute to an exhaustive diagram on the board – they should amend their own to ensure all the points are included and are correct. (15 minutes)

CHEMISTRY C2 3.5 HOW MUCH?
Making as much as we want

LEARNING OBJECTIVES
1 What do we mean by the yield of a chemical reaction and what factors affect it?
2 How do we calculate the yield of a chemical reaction? [Higher]
3 What is atom economy and why is it important?
4 How do we calculate atom economy? [Higher]

Many of the substances that we use every day have to be made from other chemicals, using complex chemical reactions. Food colourings, flavourings and preservatives, the ink in your pen or computer printer, the artificial fibres in your clothes – all of these are made using chemical reactions.

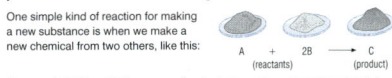

One simple kind of reaction for making a new substance is when we make a new chemical from two others, like this:

A + 2B → C
(reactants)   (product)

If we need 1000 kg of C it seems quite simple for us to work out how much A and B we need to make it. As we saw earlier in this chapter, all we need to know is the relative formula masses of A, B and C.

a) How many moles of B are needed to react with each mole of A in this reaction?
b) How many moles of C will this make?

If we carry out our reaction, it is very unlikely that we will get as much of C as we think. This is because our calculations assumed that *all* of A and B would be turned into C. We call the amount of product that a chemical reaction produces its **yield**.

Calculating percentage yield
Rather than talking about the yield of a chemical reaction in grams, kilograms or tonnes it is much more useful to talk about its **percentage yield**. This compares the amount of product that the reaction *really* produces with the maximum amount that it could *possibly* produce:

$$\text{percentage yield} = \frac{\text{amount of product produced}}{\text{maximum amount of product possible}} \times 100\%$$

Worked example
Using known masses of A and B, it was calculated that the chemical reaction above could produce 2.5 g of product, C. When the reaction is carried out, only 1.5 g of C is produced.
What is the percentage yield of this reaction?

Solution
$$\text{Percentage yield} = \frac{\text{amount of product produced}}{\text{maximum amount of product possible}} \times 100\%$$
$$= \frac{1.5}{2.5} \times 100\%$$
$$= 60\%$$
The percentage yield is **60%**.

c) How is percentage yield calculated?

Very few chemical reactions have a yield of 100% because:
- The reaction may be reversible (so as products form they react to form the reactants again).
- Some reactants may react to give unexpected products.
- Some of the product may be left behind in the apparatus.
- The reactants may not be completely pure.
- Some chemical reactions produce more than one product, and it may be difficult to separate the product that we want from the reaction mixture.

Atom economy
Chemical companies use chemical reactions to make products which they sell. So it is very important to use chemical reactions that produce as much product as possible. In other words, it is better for them to use chemical reactions with high yields.
Making as much product as possible means making less waste. It means that as much product as possible is being made from the reactants. This is good news for the company's finances, and good news for the environment too.
The amount of the starting materials that end up as useful products is called the **atom economy**. So the aim is to achieve maximum atom economy.

We can calculate percentage atom economy using this equation:

$$\text{percentage atom economy} = \frac{\text{relative formula mass of useful product}}{\text{relative formula mass of all products}} \times 100$$

Worked example
Ethanol (C_2H_5OH) can be converted into ethene (C_2H_4) which can be used to make poly(ethene).
Solution
$C_2H_5OH \longrightarrow C_2H_4 + H_2O$
M_r values: $(12 \times 2) + (1 \times 4) \quad (1 \times 2) + (16 \times 1)$
$= 28 \quad\quad = 18$
$$\text{percentage atom economy} = \frac{28}{(28+18)} \times 100 = 61\%$$

To conserve the Earth's resources, as well as reduce pollution and waste, industry tries to maximise both atom economy and percentage yield.

SUMMARY QUESTIONS
1 Copy and complete using the words below:
 high   maximum   percentage   product   waste   yield
 The amount of …… made in a chemical reaction is called its …… . The …… yield tells us the amount of product that is made compared to the …… amount that could be made. Reactions with …… yields are important because they make less …… .
2 A reaction produces a product which has a relative formula mass of 80. The total of the relative formula masses of all the products is 120. What is the percentage atom economy of this reaction? [Higher]
3 A reaction that could produce 200 g of product produces only 140 g. What is its percentage yield? [Higher]
4 If the percentage yield for a reaction is 100%, 60 g of reactant A would make 80 g of product C. How much of reactant A is needed to make 80 g of product C if the percentage yield of the reaction is only 75%? [Higher]

SCIENCE @ WORK
Chemical factories (or **plants**) are designed by chemical engineers. It's the job of a chemical engineer to try to ensure that the yield of a chemical reaction means that the plant makes the product safely and economically. It should waste as little energy and raw materials as possible.

Figure 1 When you make and sell large quantities of chemicals, it's important to know the yield of the reactions you are using

KEY POINTS
1 The yield of a chemical reaction describes how much product is made.
2 The percentage yield of a chemical reaction tells us how much product is made compared with the maximum amount that could be made (100%). [Higher]
3 Factors affecting the yield of a chemical reaction include product being left behind in the apparatus and difficulty separating the products from the reaction mixture.
4 It is important to maximise atom economy to conserve resources and reduce pollution.

SUMMARY ANSWERS

1 Product, yield, percentage, maximum, high, waste.
2 67% [**HT** only]
3 70% [**HT** only]
4 80 g [**HT** only]

Answers to in-text questions

a) 2
b) 1
c) (amount of product made ÷ amount of product possible) × 100%

KEY POINTS

Give the students a crossword using key words from the key points, e.g. yield.

151

CHEMISTRY　　　HOW MUCH?

C2 3.6　Reversible reactions

LEARNING OBJECTIVES

Students should learn that:
- Reactions can be reversible.
- The amount of product can be changed in a reversible reaction.

LEARNING OUTCOMES

Most students should be able to:
- Explain what a reversible reaction is, giving an example.
- Recognise a reversible reaction from its word or symbol equation.
- List ways in which the amount of product can be changed in a reversible reaction.

Some students should also be able to:
- Explain ways in which the amount of product can be changed in a reversible reaction. [*HT* only]

Teaching suggestions

- **Special needs.** The sections to form the flow chart to explain the equilibrium system could be made into a cut and stick activity.
- **Learning styles**
  Kinaesthetic: Moving to show the answers to the 'true or false' plenary.
  Visual: Creating a flow chart to explain an equilibrium system.
  Auditory: Listening to the true or false statements.
  Interpersonal: Working in pairs to match key words with their definitions.
  Intrapersonal: Reflecting on their own learning.
- **Homework.** Ask students to find one further example of an equilibrium reaction and write a word and symbol equation to represent it.

Answers to in-text questions

a) The reaction goes in the forward direction only.
b) The reaction is reversible.
c) The two rates are equal.

SPECIFICATION LINK-UP　Unit: Chemistry 2.12.3

- *In some chemical reactions, the products of the reaction can react to produce the original reactants. Such reactions are called reversible reactions and are represented by:*
  $$A + B \rightleftharpoons C + D$$
  For example: ammonium chloride $\rightleftharpoons$ ammonia + hydrogen chloride
- *When a reversible reaction occurs in a closed system, equilibrium is reached when the reactions occur at exactly the same rate in each direction.* [*HT* only]
- *The relative amounts of all the reacting substances at equilibrium depends on the conditions of the reaction.* [*HT* only]

Lesson structure

STARTER

Card sort – Create a card sort for the students to match the key words with their definitions. Put the cards into envelopes and give each pair of students a set to sort out on their desk. Then ask students to pick three new words and write them in their book, including the definition.
Reactants – starting substances in a chemical reaction.
Products – substances left at the end of a chemical reaction.
Reversible reaction – where the reactants make the products and the products make the reactants.
Closed system – where no reactants or products can get in or out.
Equilibrium – when the reactants are making the products at the same rate as the products making the reactants. (10 minutes)

Reflection – Ask students to draw a table with three columns headed: 'What I already know', 'What I want to know', 'What I know now'. Encourage the students to look at the title of the page and the objectives. Then ask them to fill in the first column with bullet points of facts they already know about the topic. Then ask them to think of questions that they think they need to have answered by the end of the lesson and note these in the second column. (10 minutes)

MAIN

- Heating ammonium chloride causes thermal decomposition to form ammonia and hydrogen chloride. This reaction can be completed experimentally in the lab by heating ammonium chloride in a boiling tube, then relating this to reversible reactions. Encourage the students to focus their attention on the cool part of the boiling tube, and ask them to explain in the form of a flow chart what is happening in the boiling tube.
- Hydrated copper sulfate is blue, and on heating it loses its water of crystallisation. This is a reversible reaction on the addition of water. Students could complete this practical and then explain why it is a reversible reaction.
- Show students the Animation C3 3.6 'Reversible energy' from the GCSE Chemistry CD ROM.

PLENARIES

Reflection – Ask students to review their starter table ('Reflection') and use a different colour pen/pencil to correct any misconceptions from the start of the lesson. Then ask the students to answer the questions that they posed. If they can't, encourage them to talk in small groups, consult the Student Book, and if necessary ask you. Finally, students should record, in bullet-point format, any other facts that they have picked up during the lesson, in the last column. (10 minutes)

True or false – On separate sheets of sugar paper, write the words 'true' and 'false'. Then stick them on opposite sides of the classroom. Read out statements. Students should stand next to the wall to represent their answer. If they don't know, they should stand in the centre of the room.
All chemical reactions are reversible. [False]
A closed system has no mass change. [True]
Equilibrium can only happen in closed systems. [True]
A double-headed arrow in an equation shows that it is a non-reversible reaction. [False]
In a reversible reaction, reactants make products and products make reactants. [True]
(5 minutes)

Practical support

Heating ammonium chloride

Equipment and materials required
A boiling tube, boiling tube holder, Bunsen burner and safety equipment, mineral wool, spatula, ammonium chloride, eye protection.

Details
Put about half a spatula of ammonium chloride into a boiling tube and insert a mineral wool plug at the top. Gently heat in a Bunsen flame.

Safety: Eye protection should be worn at all times. As acidic hydrogen chloride gas and alkaline ammonia gas are produced, the mineral plug must be used and the reaction should be carried out in a well-ventilated room. Ammonium chloride is harmful – CLEAPSS Hazcard 9.

Heating copper sulfate

Equipment and materials required
A boiling tube, boiling tube holder, Bunsen burner and safety equipment, spatula, hydrated copper sulfate, wash bottle, eye protection.

Details
- Put about half a spatula of hydrated copper sulfate into a boiling tube and heat gently on a Bunsen flame until the colour change to white is complete. Remove from the heat and allow the boiling tube to cool. Then add a few drops of water and observe.
- **Safety:** Be careful to allow the boiling tube to cool before adding water as the glass could crack. Eye protection should be worn throughout this experiment. Copper sulfate is harmful – CLEAPSS Hazcard 27.

ACTIVITY & EXTENSION IDEAS

- The colour changes produced by indicators are reversible reactions. Students could find out (experimentally or using secondary resources) the colours different indicators go in acidic/neutral/alkaline solutions.
- Chromate ions form an equilibrium mixture with dichromate ions. These substances were used in the first breathalysers. Encourage students to find out the chemical reactions that occurred in these early testers.

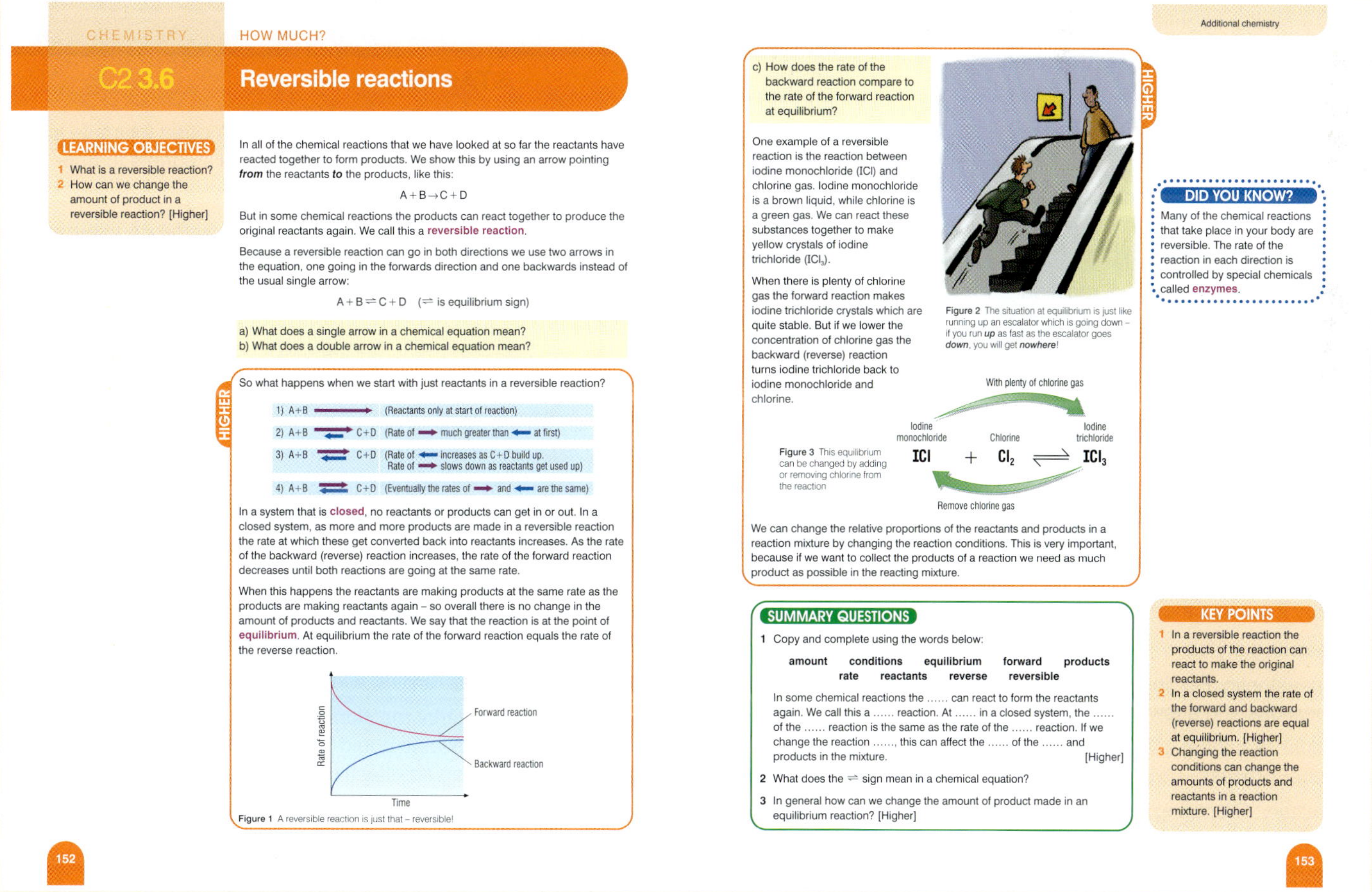

CHEMISTRY — HOW MUCH?

C2 3.6 Reversible reactions

LEARNING OBJECTIVES
1. What is a reversible reaction?
2. How can we change the amount of product in a reversible reaction? [Higher]

In all of the chemical reactions that we have looked at so far the reactants have reacted together to form products. We show this by using an arrow pointing *from* the reactants *to* the products, like this:

$$A + B \rightarrow C + D$$

But in some chemical reactions the products can react together to produce the original reactants again. We call this a **reversible reaction**.

Because a reversible reaction can go in both directions we use two arrows in the equation, one going in the forwards direction and one backwards instead of the usual single arrow:

$$A + B \rightleftharpoons C + D \quad (\rightleftharpoons \text{ is equilibrium sign})$$

a) What does a single arrow in a chemical equation mean?
b) What does a double arrow in a chemical equation mean?

HIGHER

So what happens when we start with just reactants in a reversible reaction?

1) A+B ⟶   (Reactants only at start of reaction)
2) A+B ⇌ C+D   (Rate of ⟶ much greater than ⟵ at first)
3) A+B ⇌ C+D   (Rate of ⟶ increases as C+D build up. Rate of ⟵ slows down as reactants get used up)
4) A+B ⇌ C+D   (Eventually the rates of ⟶ and ⟵ are the same)

In a system that is **closed**, no reactants or products can get in or out. In a closed system, as more and more products are made in a reversible reaction the rate at which these get converted back into reactants increases. As the rate of the backward (reverse) reaction increases, the rate of the forward reaction decreases until both reactions are going at the same rate.

When this happens the reactants are making products at the same rate as the products are making reactants again – so overall there is no change in the amount of products and reactants. We say that the reaction is at the point of **equilibrium**. At equilibrium the rate of the forward reaction equals the rate of the reverse reaction.

Figure 1 A reversible reaction is just that – reversible!

c) How does the rate of the backward reaction compare to the rate of the forward reaction at equilibrium?

One example of a reversible reaction is the reaction between iodine monochloride (ICl) and chlorine gas. Iodine monochloride is a brown liquid, while chlorine is a green gas. We can react these substances together to make yellow crystals of iodine trichloride (ICl₃).

When there is plenty of chlorine gas the forward reaction makes iodine trichloride crystals which are quite stable. But if we lower the concentration of chlorine gas the backward (reverse) reaction turns iodine trichloride back to iodine monochloride and chlorine.

Figure 2 The situation at equilibrium is just like running up an escalator which is going down – if you run *up* as fast as the escalator goes *down*, you will get nowhere!

Figure 3 This equilibrium can be changed by adding or removing chlorine from the reaction.

$$\text{Iodine monochloride} \quad ICl + Cl_2 \rightleftharpoons ICl_3 \quad \text{Iodine trichloride}$$

We can change the relative proportions of the reactants and products in a reaction mixture by changing the reaction conditions. This is very important, because if we want to collect the products of a reaction we need as much product as possible in the reacting mixture.

SUMMARY QUESTIONS

1 Copy and complete using the words below:

amount   conditions   equilibrium   forward   products
rate   reactants   reverse   reversible

In some chemical reactions the …… can react to form the reactants again. We call this a …… reaction. At …… in a closed system, the …… of the …… reaction is the same as the rate of the …… reaction. If we change the reaction ……, this can affect the …… of the …… and products in the mixture. [Higher]

2 What does the ⇌ sign mean in a chemical equation?

3 In general how can we change the amount of product made in an equilibrium reaction? [Higher]

DID YOU KNOW?
Many of the chemical reactions that take place in your body are reversible. The rate of the reaction in each direction is controlled by special chemicals called **enzymes**.

KEY POINTS
1. In a reversible reaction the products of the reaction can react to make the original reactants.
2. In a closed system the rate of the forward and backward (reverse) reactions are equal at equilibrium. [Higher]
3. Changing the reaction conditions can change the amounts of products and reactants in a reaction mixture. [Higher]

SUMMARY ANSWERS

1. Products, reversible, equilibrium, rate, forward (reverse), reverse (forward), conditions, amount, reactants.
2. The reaction is reversible.
3. Change the conditions or add reactants and/or remove products.

DID YOU KNOW?
Enzymes are biological catalysts made of proteins. Proteins work best in optimum conditions, if the body strays too far from this ideal the enzyme proteins denature and no longer have an effective active site.

KEY POINTS
Split the class into three groups and give each group a key point. They should generate reasons to why their point is the most important of the three. Then encourage the students to debate the issue.

CHEMISTRY

HOW MUCH?

C2 3.7 Making ammonia – the Haber process

LEARNING OBJECTIVES

Students should learn that:

- Ammonia is an important chemical.
- How ammonia can be made.
- How waste from ammonia production can be minimised.

LEARNING OUTCOMES

Most students should be able to:

- State a use for ammonia.
- Name the raw materials for the Haber process.
- Write the word equation for the production of ammonia.
- Quote the reaction conditions to make ammonia.
- Explain how waste is minimised.

Some students should also be able to:

- Complete a balanced symbol equation for the production of ammonia. [**HT** only]
- Explain the choice of reaction conditions for the production of ammonia. [**HT** only]

Teaching suggestions

- **Special needs.** A simple script for the factory tour could be provided to the students. However, the paragraphs could be in the wrong order. Students should then order the information and copy it out into their own work.

- **Learning styles**

  Kinaesthetic: Finding the partners for questions and answers.

  Visual: Watching a video about the Haber process.

  Auditory: Preparing and listening to audio revision.

  Interpersonal: Working in small groups to make a script for a factory tour.

  Intrapersonal: Finding elements and compounds in text.

- **Homework.** Ammonia is an important chemical: ask students to find three uses for ammonia.

- **ICT link-up.** There are a number of models for the Haber process available. In some of them, it is possible for students to vary conditions and view the effect that it has on yield.

SPECIFICATION LINK-UP   Unit: Chemistry 2.12.3

- Although reversible reactions may not go to completion they can still be used efficiently in continuous industrial processes, such as the Haber process that is used to manufacture ammonia.
- The raw materials for the Haber process are nitrogen and hydrogen. Nitrogen is obtained from the air and hydrogen may be obtained from natural gas or other sources.
- The purified gases are passed over a catalyst of iron at a high temperature (about 450°C) and high pressure (about 200 atmospheres). Some of the hydrogen and nitrogen reacts to form ammonia. The reaction is reversible so ammonia breaks down again into nitrogen and hydrogen:

  nitrogen + hydrogen $\rightleftharpoons$ ammonia

- On cooling, the ammonia liquefies and is removed. The remaining hydrogen and nitrogen is re-cycled.
- The reaction conditions are chosen to produce a reasonable yield of ammonia quickly. [**HT** only] (See pages 178–9)

Lesson structure

STARTER

Video – Show a video about the industrial production of ammonia. A good example is the RSC *Industrial Chemistry* video (from RSC www.rsc.org). Ask the students to note down the raw materials and reaction conditions. (10 minutes)

DART (Directed Activity Relating to Text) – Ask the students to study the double-page spread and make a list of all the elements and compounds that are mentioned. [**Elements** – nitrogen, hydrogen, iron; **Compounds** – ammonia, nitrates, methane.] (5 minutes)

MAIN

- Show students the Simulation C2 3.7 'Making Ammonia' from the GCSE Chemistry CD ROM and allow them to explore the resource if possible.
- Ask students if they have ever been to a factory tour like 'Cadbury World' or 'Wedgwood'. Ask a few students to recall their experiences of the visit. Split the class into small groups and ask them to prepare a tour guide for a factory tour of an ammonia plant.
- Encourage them to write a script for the guide including what they should point out to the guests. They could even include diagrams or images of certain sections.
- The students could extend this activity by making a visitor guidebook.
- The Haber process in an important industrial reaction met at many levels in chemistry. Other scientific posters commercially available could be shown to students to give them ideas on how to approach designing an effective poster.
- Encourage them to make a poster to highlight the important aspects of the Haber process, including a balanced symbol equation.
- Encourage students to create their own script for an audio revision guide. Their section should last no more than 3 minutes.
- NB The Higher Tier statement in the specification regarding choice of operating conditions for the Haber process is covered in more detail on pages 178–9 in the Student Book. The concepts introduced in C2 Chapters 4 and 5 really need to be covered before students can understand fully the conditions chosen. Then higher attaining students can discuss in detail the sometimes conflicting factors affecting rate of reaction, yield, safety and economics of the process.

PLENARIES

Questions and answers – Give each student a slip of paper (about A5 in size). Ask them to write a question and its answer on the paper about the Haber process and reversible reactions. Then ask them to cut each answer free from the question and give them to you. Now give a question and answer to each student but they should not match. Read the first question out, the student with the correct answer should read it out, then read their question and so on around the room. (10 minutes)

Flow chart – Give the students an outline of a flow chart to show the process of making ammonia. Encourage them to add labels to summarise the reaction. (5 minutes)

Performance – Students could perform their own audio revision piece for the Haber process. They could record theirs using digital technology and this could be put onto the school web site to help others with revision. (15 minutes)

ACTIVITY & EXTENSION IDEAS

Before the Haber process was invented, ammonia had already been discovered and was being used for a variety of things including fertilisers. Ask the students to research where this ammonia came from [urine].

CHEMISTRY — HOW MUCH?

C2 3.7 Making ammonia – the Haber process

LEARNING OBJECTIVES
1. Why is ammonia important?
2. How do we make ammonia?
3. How can we make ammonia without wasting raw materials?

We need plants – for food, and as a way of providing the oxygen that we breathe. Plants need nitrogen to grow, and although this gas makes up about 80% of the air around us, plants cannot use it because it is very unreactive.

Instead, plants absorb soluble nitrates from the soil through their roots. When we harvest plants these nitrates are lost – so we need to replace them. Nowadays we usually do this by adding nitrate fertilisers to the soil. We make these fertilisers using a process invented nearly 100 years ago by a young German chemist called Fritz Haber.

a) Why can't plants use the nitrogen from the air?
b) Where do plants get their nitrogen from?

Figure 1 Plants are surrounded by nitrogen in the air. They cannot use this nitrogen, and rely on soluble nitrates in the soil instead. We supply these by spreading fertiliser on the soil.

The Haber process

The Haber process provides us with a way of turning the nitrogen in the air into ammonia. We can use ammonia in many different ways. One of the most important of these is to make fertilisers.

The raw materials for making ammonia are:
- nitrogen from the air, and
- hydrogen which we get from natural gas (containing mainly methane, CH_4).

The nitrogen and hydrogen are purified and then passed over an iron catalyst at high temperatures (about 450°C) and pressures (about 200 atmospheres). The product of this chemical reaction is ammonia.

c) What are the two raw materials needed to make ammonia?

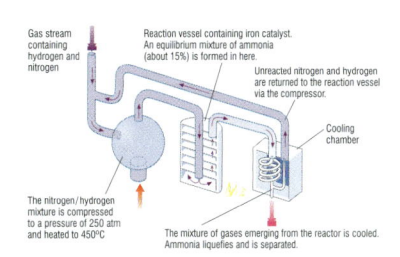

Figure 2 The Haber process

The reaction used in the Haber process is reversible, which means that the ammonia breaks down again into hydrogen and nitrogen. To reduce this, we have to remove the ammonia by cooling and liquefying it as soon as it is formed. We can then recycle any hydrogen and nitrogen that is left so that it has a chance to react again.

$$N_2 + 3H_2 \rightleftharpoons 2NH_3 \quad (450°C \text{ and } 200 \text{ atm})$$

Nitrogen   Hydrogen   Ammonia

By removing the ammonia that forms we can reduce the rate of the backwards reaction. This helps to stop the ammonia that is formed from breaking down into nitrogen and hydrogen.

We carry out the Haber process in conditions that have been carefully chosen to give a reasonable yield of ammonia as quickly as possible. (See pages 178–9.)

d) How is ammonia removed from the reaction mixture?
e) How do we make sure the reactants are not wasted?

SUMMARY QUESTIONS

1 Copy and complete using the words below:

air   fertilisers   gas   450   hydrogen   iron   liquefying
nitrogen   removed   200

Ammonia is an important chemical used for making ……. . The raw materials are ……. from the ……. and ……. from natural ……. . These are reacted at about ……. °C and ……. atmospheres pressure using an ……. catalyst. Ammonia is ……. from the reaction mixture before it can break down into the reactants again by ……. the gas.

2 Draw a flow diagram to show how the Haber process is used to make ammonia.

KEY POINTS
1. Ammonia is an important chemical for making other chemicals, including fertilisers.
2. Ammonia is made from nitrogen and hydrogen in the Haber process.
3. We carry out the Haber process under conditions which are chosen to give a reasonable yield of ammonia as quickly as possible.
4. Any unused nitrogen and hydrogen are recycled in the Haber process.

SUMMARY ANSWERS

1 Fertilisers, nitrogen, air, hydrogen, gas, 450, 200, iron, removed, liquefying.

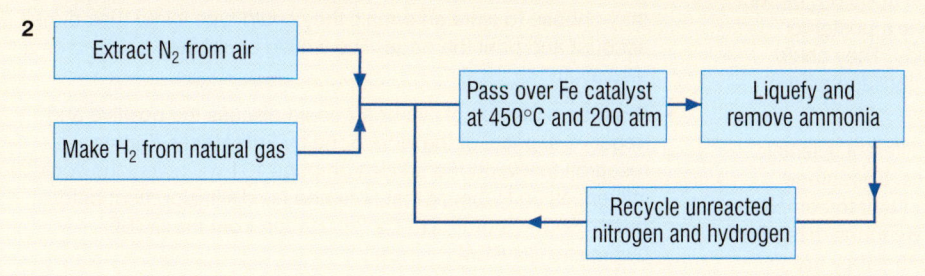

2 Extract N_2 from air → Pass over Fe catalyst at 450°C and 200 atm → Liquefy and remove ammonia
  Make H_2 from natural gas → (joins above)
  Recycle unreacted nitrogen and hydrogen

Answers to in-text questions

a) Because it is very unreactive.
b) From nitrates in the soil, absorbed through their roots.
c) Nitrogen and hydrogen.
d) The gases are cooled down and ammonia is liquefied/condensed and run off.
e) The unreacted nitrogen and hydrogen are recycled into the reaction vessel.

KEY POINTS

Give each key word an action, e.g. for Haber clap hands. Then read out the passage and the students can put in the actions.

CHEMISTRY — HOW MUCH?

C2 3.8 Aspects of the Haber process

SPECIFICATION LINK-UP
Unit: Chemistry 2.12.3

Students should use their skills, knowledge and understanding of 'How Science Works':

- ... to evaluate sustainable development issues related to atom economy. [**HT** only]

This spread can be used to revisit the following substantive content already covered in this chapter:

- Although reversible reactions may not go to completion they can still be used efficiently in continuous industrial processes, such as the Haber process that is used to manufacture ammonia.

CHEMISTRY — HOW MUCH?

C2 3.8 Aspects of the Haber process

Using reversible reactions – 'green' chemistry

- Using relative atomic masses we can work out the relative formula mass of compounds so that we know the mass of 1 mole

- Balanced chemical equations show us the number of moles of reactants and products in reactions

- We can make more products from a reversible reaction by removing them as they are formed

- The yield of a chemical reaction tells us how much product a reaction will REALLY give us compared with what it could POSSIBLY give us

- We use chemical equations to work out what mass of each reactant we need to make as much product as we want

- Some chemical reactions go both ways – they are REVERSIBLE

- Processes with a high percentage atom economy are more profitable and are better for sustainable development

- By carefully choosing chemical reactions and the conditions, we can make as much product from a chemical reaction as possible – with as little waste as possible

ACTIVITY

Look at the ideas on this page. Use them to design a poster about 'Crafty Chemists', showing how chemistry helps us to use chemical reactions which make as much of what we want as efficiently as possible.

156

Teaching suggestions

Activities

- **Poster** – Show the students some thought-provoking posters about innovative use of chemistry, e.g. upd8 (at upd8.org.uk) or RSC (at www.rsc.org). Encourage them to make a poster to highlight the use of chemistry to maximise yields. They could make their poster using a desktop publishing package on the computer.

- **Letter/e-mail** – Show the students images of different scientific laboratories from modern-day research facilities. Encourage them to work out a list of reasons why it is important to complete weapons research and a converse list of why weapons research should be halted. Ask the students to imagine that they are either:
  – A brilliant young chemist, and write an e-mail or letter explaining to a friend that you will be taking this position.
  – A friend of a scientist working in the facility, and write an e-mail or letter outlining why you do not think they should work in this job.

If the student is writing a letter, encourage them to use correct letter format and they could even write their letter onto paper. If they choose to write an e-mail, they could type it into their e-mail account and print the page. The writing could then be used as a display.

- **Discuss** – Groups of five or six could discuss the positive and negative aspects of the work done by Fritz Haber. Further research following the articles on page 131 will reveal the societal influences on Haber at that time and his disillusionment before death. Show PhotoPLUS C2 3.8 'Haber' from the GCSE Chemistry CD ROM.

Homework

- **Location** – Ask the students to find a location of an ammonia plant and detail the reasons why it is positioned there.

Fritz Haber – a good life or a bad one?

Der Newswen
Donnerstag 14. Oktober 1920

Fritz Haber – German Patriot

Early on in the First World War both sides became bogged down in trench warfare. Fritz Haber focused on what he could do to bring about German victory. He thought that poison gas would penetrate the strongest defences, allowing Germany to win the war.

Poison gases were already available as unwanted by-products of chemical processes. Haber experimented with these gases to find those suitable to use on the battlefield. He focused on chlorine gas.

The Germans used chlorine for the first time on 22nd April 1915, against French and Algerian troops in Belgium. They released 200 tonnes of gas which rolled into the allied lines. The allied soldiers choked in agony, and slowly died. The gas cloud tinted everything a sickly green. Those who could escape the cloud fled in panic.

The soldier Wilfrid Owen wrote:

GAS! Gas! Quick, boys! – An ecstasy of fumbling,
Fitting the clumsy helmets just in time;
But someone still was yelling out and stumbling
And floundering like a man in fire or lime.
Dim, through the misty panes and thick green light
As under a green sea, I saw him drowning.
In all my dreams, before my helpless sight,
He plunges at me, guttering, choking, drowning.

19th November 1920 1d   Palestine becomes British mandate – page 4

Tragedy of Clara Haber

Clara Haber had graduated as the first woman from the University of Breslau in Germany in 1900. At this time many professors were still against female students. She married Fritz Haber in 1901. Clara could not continue her research work because she was a woman. Instead, she contributed to her husband's work, although her support was never mentioned. Because of her support Haber was promoted very quickly.

Clara was deeply opposed to warfare, and especially to the use of science in war. She called Haber's work a 'perversion of science'. Unable to stop him, Clara committed suicide in May 1915. Her death was never annouced in the newspapers.

League of Nations holds first meeting in Geneva, Switzerland

ACTIVITY

A new laboratory has been set up to develop a new chemical to be used as a weapon.

Either: As a brilliant young chemist you have been invited to go and work in this laboratory. Write a letter or e-mail to a friend explaining why you are planning to accept this invitation.

Or: A friend has been invited to go and work in this laboratory. Write a letter or e-mail to this friend explaining why you think they should not go and work in this laboratory.

Extension

Spot the difference – Show the students images of different scientific laboratories throughout the ages, including modern-day research facilities. Ask them to work in pairs and note down all the similarities and all the differences. Feedback to the class using question and answer session.

Learning styles

Visual: Looking at different images of laboratories.

Auditory: Listening to other students' work.

Interpersonal: Working in pairs on posters.

Intrapersonal: Penning letters and e-mails.

ICT link-up

Get images of different laboratories from a Google image search. Then project them onto the interactive whiteboard and mark the differences (perhaps in red) and the similarities (maybe in green).

Gifted and talented

Split the class into groups of about six. They are to imagine that they are being commissioned by an international chemical company to site an ammonia plant and decide on its working conditions. The chemical company is multinational, so the group can site the plant anywhere in the world, but they need to reason out all of their decisions, including running conditions of the plant. The group could then create a persuasive 5-minute presentation of their proposal.

CHEMISTRY   HOW MUCH?

SUMMARY ANSWERS

1 a) B   b) A   c) D   d) C

2 a) 44 g
   b) 28 g
   c) 100 g
   d) 94 g
   e) 206 g

3 a) 0.5
   b) 0.1
   c) 0.01

4 $AlBr_3$ [HT only]

5 56% [HT only]

6 a) A reaction that can go in either direction, i.e. products → reactants as well as reactants → products.
   b) An 'ordinary' reaction is normally regarded as going in one direction only, i.e. the 'forward' direction.
   c) About 450°C and 200 atmospheres in presence of iron catalyst.

Summary teaching suggestions

- **Special needs** – Question 1 could be made into a card sort, allowing the students to match up the start and end of sentences and then writing them out once they make sense.
- **When to use the questions?**
  - These questions could be used for revision at the end of the topic.
  - Question 6 could make a good extended homework piece. The students could be encouraged to answer this question in an essay style. Then the following lesson, they could swap their scripts with another student who could be provided with a marking scheme. Students could then assess each others' work.
  - Questions 2, 3, 4 and 5 are further examples of calculation questions, and could be used as an extension or for homework during lessons 3.2–3.4.
- **Learning styles**
  Kinaesthetic: Question 1 lends itself to being completed with a card sort.
  Interpersonal: Question 6 could be completed through a class discussion before students pen their own answers.
  Intrapersonal: Questions 2, 3, 4 and 5 lend themselves to individuals completing their own work.
- **Misconceptions** – Question 4 requires students to generate the formula of a compound after being given the mass of each element. Students often forget to calculate the number of moles of each element first and just complete a formula based on the ratio of the masses instead.

EXAM-STYLE ANSWERS

1 a) One each for:
   - Atoms of the same element/with the same number of protons/same atomic number.
   - But different numbers of neutrons/different mass numbers.
   (2 marks)
   b) 1 proton *(1 mark)*, 1 electron *(1 mark)*, 2 neutrons *(1 mark)*
   c) 20 – *correct answer gains 2 marks.*
      One mark can be gained for showing correct working: $(2 \times 2) + 16$

2 a) 152 – *correct answer gains 2 marks.*
      One mark can be gained for showing correct working:
      $56 + 32 + (16 \times 4)$
   b) 36.8% – *correct answer gains 2 marks (accept 37% or 36.84%)*
      One mark can be gained for showing correct working:
      $56 \times 100/152$

   c) 0.074 g – *correct answer gains 2 marks (accept 0.0737 g or 0.07 g or correct answer based on answer to part (b) – error carried forward)*
      One mark can be gained for showing correct working:
      e.g. $0.2 \times 36.8/100$

3 a) Reversible reaction. *(1 mark)*
   b) i) A is air *(1 mark)* B is methane or natural gas. *(1 mark)*
      ii) Catalyst. *(1 mark)*
      iii) One from:
         - Reverse reaction takes place.
         - Ammonia breaks down to form nitrogen and hydrogen.
         (1 mark)
      iv) They are recycled/returned to the reactor. *(1 mark)*

4 a) 2 *(1 mark)*
   b) 1 *(1 mark)*
   c) 111 g – *correct answer gains 2 marks.*
      One mark can be gained for showing correct working: e.g.
      $40 + (35.5 \times 2)$
   d) 100 g – *correct answer gains 2 marks.*
      One mark can be gained for showing correct working:
      e.g. $40 + 12 + (16 \times 3)$
   e) 66.7% – *correct answer gains 2 marks (accept 66.67 or 67 or correct answer based on answers to part d) and part c) – error carried forward).*
      One mark can be gained for correct working:
      e.g. $(7.4 \times 100)/(10 \times 111/100)$ [HT only]

5 a) 104 g – *correct answer gains 2 marks.*
      One mark can be gained for showing correct working: e.g. 2×52
   b) Using aluminium: 50.5% – *correct answer gains 2 marks.*
      One mark can be gained for correct working:
      e.g. $(104 \times 100)/(104 + 102)$
      Using carbon: 61.2% – *correct answer gains 2 marks.*
      One mark can be gained for correct working:
      e.g. $(208 \times 100)/(208 + 132)$

Additional chemistry

(a) How many moles of hydrochloric acid react with one mole of calcium carbonate? (1)
(b) How many moles of calcium chloride are produced from one mole of calcium carbonate? (1)
(c) What is the mass of calcium chloride that can be made from one mole of calcium carbonate? (2)
(d) What is the mass of one mole of calcium carbonate? (2)
(e) A student reacted 10 g of calcium carbonate with hydrochloric acid and collected 7.4 g of calcium chloride. What was the percentage yield? (2)
[Higher]

5 Chromium can be obtained from chromium oxide, Cr_2O_3, by reduction with aluminium or carbon. For the first reaction, chromium is mixed with aluminium and ignited in a crucible. The reaction using carbon is done at high temperatures in a low-pressure furnace. The equations for the reactions are:

$Cr_2O_3 + 2Al \rightarrow 2Cr + Al_2O_3$
$2Cr_2O_3 + 3C \rightarrow 4Cr + 3CO_2$

(a) Calculate the maximum mass of chromium that can be obtained from one mole of chromium oxide. (2)
(b) Calculate the percentage atom economy for both reactions to show which reaction has the better atom economy. (4)
(c) Suggest one advantage and one disadvantage of using carbon to manufacture chromium. (2)
[Higher]

6 Ibuprofen is used as a pain killer throughout the world. You might know it as Nurofen or Ibuleve. The traditional way to manufacture ibuprofen involved a lot of chemical reactions and produced a lot of waste. The atom economy was just 32%.
Recently it became possible for any pharmaceutical (drug) company to make ibuprofen. As there was a lot of money to be made, the race was on to find the most economic way to make it. This meant cutting down waste. The new method involves catalysts, some of which can be completely recovered and do not go out as waste. The atom economy is increased to 77%, partly because only the active form of ibuprofen is made. This also means that lower doses are needed and they take a shorter time to kill any pain.
Evaluate the two methods of manufacture in terms of the social, economic and environmental issues involved.
[Higher] (6)

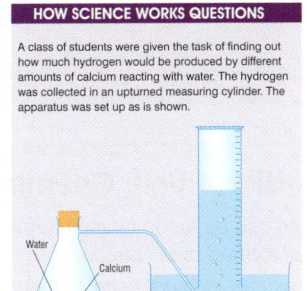

HOW SCIENCE WORKS QUESTIONS

A class of students were given the task of finding out how much hydrogen would be produced by different amounts of calcium reacting with water. The hydrogen was collected in an upturned measuring cylinder. The apparatus was set up as is shown.

Different amounts of calcium were weighed. Each piece was put separately into the flask and the bung put on as quickly as possible. The reaction was left to finish and the volume of hydrogen measured.

The results of the different groups are in the table below.

Mass of Ca (g)	Volume of hydrogen (cm³)				
	A	B	C	D	E
0.05	25	26	27	18	26
0.10	55	53	55	55	52
0.15	85	86	81	89	84
0.20	115	117	109	116	113
0.25	145	146	148	141	140

a) Produce a table to show the mean for all of the groups for each mass of calcium used. (5)
b) Why is the mean often a more useful set of results than any one group? (1)
c) What is the range of volumes when 0.25 grams of calcium are used? (1)
d) What is the sensitivity of the balance used to weigh out the calcium? (1)
e) How could you determine which group had the most accurate results? (1)
f) Look at the method described. Is there any possibility of a systematic error? If so, say how this error could arise. (1)

159

Percentage atom economies can be calculated from the relative mass of useful product compared with the relative mass of all the atoms in either the reactants or the products, because equations are balanced. Students should be aware that this could be done by either method. Calculating atom economies of different routes to products is a good basis for research and discussion.

HOW SCIENCE WORKS ANSWERS

a)

Mass of Ca (g)	Mean volume, hydrogen (cm³)
0.05	26
0.1	54
0.15	85
0.2	114
0.25	144

Note D for 0.05 g is an anomaly and has been omitted from the calculation.

b) The mean is a more useful result because it is likely to be more accurate.
c) The range of volumes when 0.25 grams of calcium are used – 140 cm³ to 148 cm³.
d) The sensitivity of the balance used to weigh out the calcium is at least 0.05 g.
e) The group which was closest to the mean could be considered the one with the most accurate results. A better way would be to calculate the theoretical volume produced and then compare the different groups.
f) Placing the bung on the flask after the reaction has started will produce a systematic error.

How science works teaching suggestions

- **Literacy guidance.** Key terms that should be clearly understood: mean, range, sensitivity, accuracy, systematic error.
- **Higher- and lower-level answers.** Question e) is a higher-level question and the answers provided above are also at this level. Question b) is lower level and the answer provided is also lower level.
- **Gifted and talented.** Able students could consider how to calculate a theoretical value and whether they have enough information to do this.
- **How and when to use these questions.** When wishing to develop table skills and range and mean calculations. How to assess accuracy. The questions could be part individual and part class discussion depending on the level of understanding of the ideas.
- **Misconceptions.** That all results must be used to calculate a mean. To address this: give an example where this would be obviously incorrect. For example, a student investigating a candle burning under a beaker gets the timings 39 seconds, 43 seconds, 40 seconds and 3 seconds. In fact, on the last repeat test the beaker accidently knocked the candle over into the sand tray. Should the student add 39 + 43 + 40 + 3, then divide by 4 to get the mean value? Would it be 'cheating' to leave out the last result?
Another misconception is that range is quoted as a single figure. To address this stress how much more information quoting the minimum and maximum values gives us. For example, ask a student the range of ages of their brothers and/or sisters. An answer such as '11 years' is not as useful as 'From 8 years old to 19 years old'.
- **Homework.** Question a) could be set as homework.
- **Special needs.** For these students the table could be reduced to columns C, D and E.

c) One advantage from:
- Better atom economy.
- More economical/carbon costs less than aluminium/aluminium has to be produced by electrolysis.
- No solid waste to dispose of. (1 mark)

One disadvantage from:
- Produces carbon dioxide/greenhouse gas/global warming.
- Needs more vigorous conditions for the reduction to take place. (1 mark)
[HT only]

6 Social e.g. lower doses OR quicker action in stopping pain (2 marks)
economic e.g. cheaper to manufacture, therefore more profits or cheaper to buy (2 marks)
environmental e.g. higher atom economy (2 marks)
The above could be explained by reference to the two methods of manufacture of ibuprofen. If a non-comparative statement is made then maximum 1 mark for each. [HT only]

Exam teaching suggestions

- Allow 40 minutes for the questions on this chapter, which have a total of 41 marks. Q1 could be set after 3.2, Q2 after 3.3, Q4 and Q5 after 3.5, and Q3 at the end of the chapter.
- Most candidates are able to calculate relative formula masses successfully. Questions similar to Q2 invariably appear as parts of larger structured questions in examinations, and candidates should be encouraged to look for and attempt these straightforward calculations. To give additional practice and variety, get pairs or small groups to set each other similar questions on substances for which they have found the formulas in books or on the Internet. The competition can get quite fierce! They can also be used as the basis for comparing the usefulness of compounds such as metal ores, fertilisers and food supplements.
- Students should be encouraged to read calculation questions carefully to check if answers need to include units. Units may be given in the answer space for lower demand questions, but are often not given in higher-tier questions. If a relative mass is asked for, there will be no units, as in Q2a). The mass of an amount in moles requires units, usually grams, as in Q4, parts c) and d).

159

CHEMISTRY   RATES OF REACTION

C2 4.1   How fast?

LEARNING OBJECTIVES

Students should learn:

- That chemical reactions can happen at different rates.
- That the rate of a chemical reaction can be measured.

LEARNING OUTCOMES

Most students should be able to:

- State a definition for the rate of reaction.
- List ways that the rate can be measured.

Some students should also be able to:

- Suggest a method for measuring the rate in a specified reaction.
- Explain why a particular method of measuring the rate is suitable for a specified reaction.

Teaching suggestions

- **Special needs.** Graph paper can be confusing for these students. Therefore supply them with squared paper, with the scales already drawn on. Once the students have plotted their graph, you could supply these statements (in the wrong order) for students to copy onto their graph.
  - Start of reaction.
  - Fast rate of reaction.
  - Slow rate of reaction.
  - End of reaction.
- **Learning styles**
  Kinaesthetic: Completing the gas collection practical.
  Visual: Watching the disappearing cross.
  Auditory: Listening to discussions in groups.
  Intrapersonal: Finding the definition for rate of reaction.
  Interpersonal: Working in groups discussing decisions.
- **ICT link-up.** The disappearing cross experiment relies on a person deciding when they think the cross disappears and this introduces errors. A light sensor and data logger could be set up, where a plot of the light intensity could be made. When the light intensity gets to a certain level the result (time) is noted by reading off the graph.
  (See www.rogerfrost.com.)

SPECIFICATION LINK-UP   Unit: Chemistry 2.12.4

- The rate of a chemical reaction can be found by measuring the amount of a reactant used or the amount of product formed over time:

$$\text{Rate of reaction} = \frac{\text{Amount of reactant used or amount of product formed}}{\text{Time}}$$

Students should use their skills, knowledge and understanding of 'How Science Works':

- to interpret graphs showing the amount of product formed (or reactant used up) with time, in terms of the rate of the reaction.

Lesson structure

STARTER

Fast or slow – Give each student a piece of paper with 'fast' on one side and 'slow' on the other. Then show them different images of chemical reactions, e.g. rusting, baking a cake, cooking an egg, magnesium reacting with acid, neutralisation, etc. They should look at the image and decide if the rate is fast or slow and hold up the card to demonstrate their answer. Images could be shown using a data projector and having a separate image per PowerPoint® slide. (5 minutes)

Cut and stick – Explain to students what 'rate of reaction' is. Then give the students different magazines and catalogues. Their task is to cut out an example of a reaction with a fast rate and a slow rate. They then compare their findings with a small group (about five students), and they choose the best from their selection. Students could then make a class montage on sugar paper. (15 minutes)

MAIN

- In most chemical reactions that are used to study rate, a gas is made. In order for students to interpret information about a reaction a graph should be produced. Using the reaction between magnesium and acid, get students to plot a graph to show the production of hydrogen over two minutes. Ask them to then annotate their graph to explain the shape. They should include information as to why the graph starts at 0 cm³ of gas and about the shape of the graph.

- The reaction between hydrochloric acid and sodium thiosulfate is the classic example used to highlight how light can be used to measure the rate of reaction. Students could complete this experiment themselves and reflect on the technique. Alternatively, this could be completed as a class demonstration. Draw the black cross onto an OHT and put onto an OHP. Choose a student to be in charge of the stopwatch. Then put the reaction vessel onto the cross, and ask students to raise their hands when they think the cross has gone. When most of the hands are raised, stop the watch and note the time.

- Let class interact with the Simulation C2 4.1 'How fast?' from the GCSE Chemistry CD ROM.

PLENARIES

Card sort – Make a set of eight cards, four with diagrams showing how rate of reaction can be measured (mass change, gas collection by displacement in a measuring cylinder, gas collection in a gas syringe, disappearing cross), four with examples of reactions that can be measured using these techniques (magnesium + acid, calcium carbonate + acid, sodium thiosulfate + acid, hydrogen peroxide + manganese dioxide). Ask the students to match the methods with reactions, encourage them to discuss their work in small groups, then feedback to the class in a question and answer session. [Note: Only the sodium thiosulfate reaction can be measured using the disappearing cross, however the other three reactions can be measured with any of the remaining methods.] (15 minutes)

Graph interpretation – Show students a graph of rate of reaction of a particular reaction. Ask them to interpret the graph and explain the shape of the curve. (5 minutes)

Practical support

Measuring the mass of a reaction mixture
Equipment and materials required
Marble chips, 1 M hydrochloric acid (irritant – CLEAPSS Hazcard 47), 250 ml conical flask, top-pan balance, cotton wool, stopwatch, measuring cylinder, eye protection.

Measuring the volume of gas given off
Equipment and materials required
Marble chips, 1 M hydrochloric acid (irritant – CLEAPSS Hazcard 47), 250 ml conical flask, bung fitted with delivery tube, about 50 cm length of rubber tubing, 100 ml gas syringe (ensure syringe plunger is free-moving), gas syringe holder, boss, stand, stopwatch, measuring cylinder, eye protection.

Measuring the light transmitted through a solution
Equipment and materials required
Two measuring cylinders, stopwatch, paper with large cross in the centre, conical flask, beaker, 0.2 M sodium thiosulfate, 0.2 M hydrochloric acid (irritant), eye protection.

Safety: During this experiment, sulfur dioxide is produced which is toxic and can trigger asthmatic attacks, therefore this should be completed in a well-ventilated room. Once the reaction is complete, the mixture should be disposed of down a well-flushed sink, preferably in a fume cupboard.

Demonstration of the reaction between magnesium and acid
Equipment and materials required
1 M hydrochloric acid (irritant – CLEAPSS Hazcard 47), strips of 1 cm magnesium (flammable – CLEAPSS Hazcard 59), test tube, eye protection.

ACTIVITY & EXTENSION IDEAS

After the students have watched the demonstration of the reaction between magnesium and acid, allow them to experiment with the different methods for measuring rate of reaction detailed in 'Practical support'. They will need a supply of the hydrochloric acid and magnesium strips (and eye protection). The aim of this activity is for the students to decide which is the most informative method. [Hopefully they will realise that the balances available are not sensitive enough, there is not a precipitate formed so the disappearing cross is useless, but collection of gas is the most accurate if a gas syringe is used.]

Answers to in-text questions

a) How fast the reactants are turned into products.

b) In order to understand (and control) how fast chemicals are made.

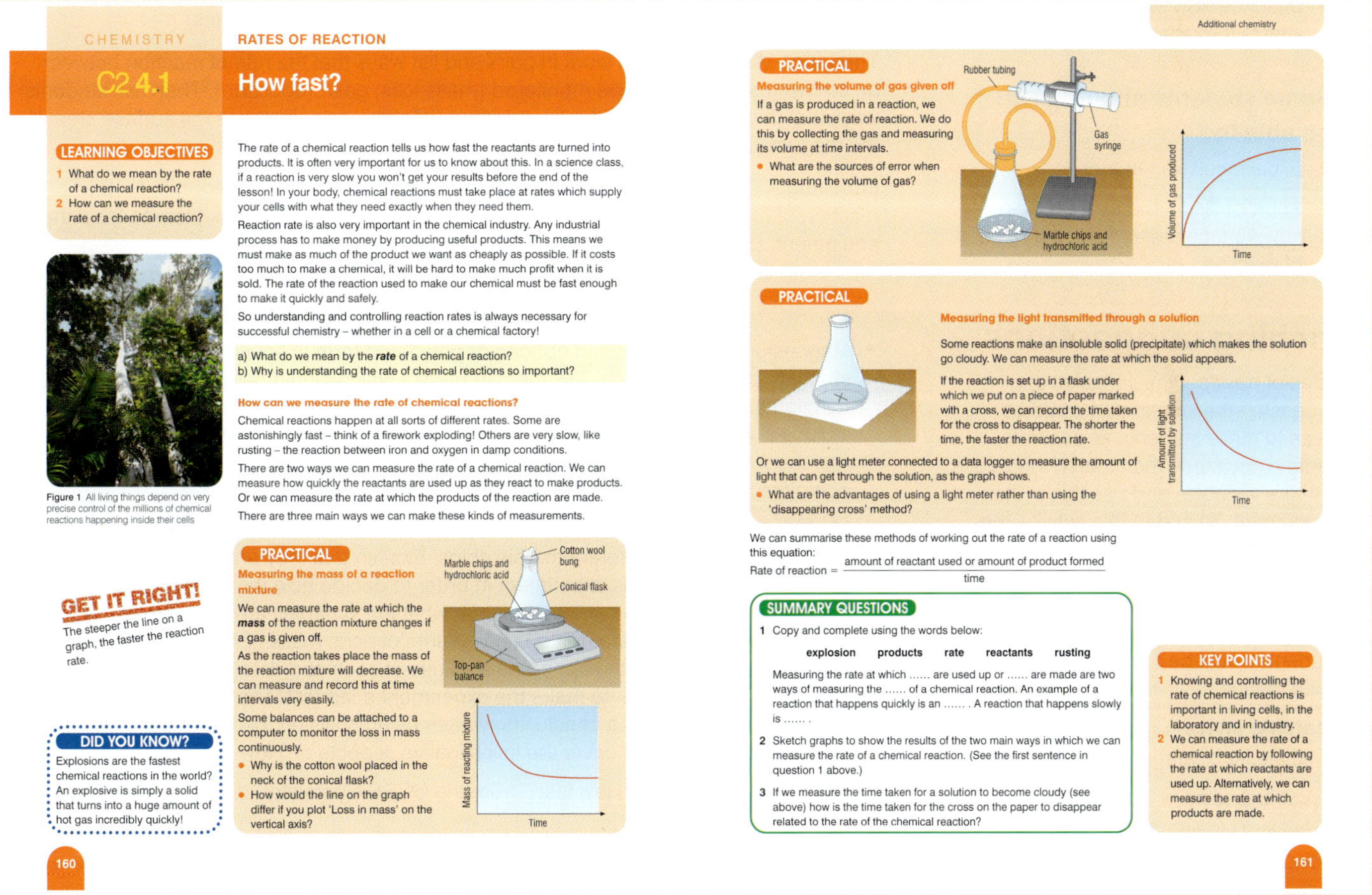

SUMMARY ANSWERS

1 Reactants, products, rate, explosion, rusting.

2 Graphs like those at bottom of page 160 and top of page 161 in Student Book.

3 The shorter the time taken for the cross to disappear, the faster the rate of the reaction.

KEY POINTS

Students could start a spider diagram using the key points from this spread. Then at the end of each lesson during this chapter, encourage students to add the new key points to their diagram.

DID YOU KNOW?

The biggest conventional bomb has a mass of 9752 kg and is known as 'MOAB' (Massive Ordnance Air Blast). It differs from most bombs as it doesn't explode on impact, it has its own parachute and explodes just above the ground.

CHEMISTRY

RATES OF REACTION

C2 4.2 Collision theory

LEARNING OBJECTIVES

Students should learn:
- That different factors affect the rate of reaction.
- That rates of reaction can be explained using collision theory.
- That collision theory can be used to explain the effect of surface area on the rate of reaction.

LEARNING OUTCOMES

Most students should be able to:
- List the factors that affect the rate of reaction.
- Recall a definition for collision theory.
- Describe how surface area affects the rate of reaction.

Some students should also be able to:
- Explain collision theory.
- Apply collision theory to explain how surface area affects the rate of reaction.

Teaching suggestions

- **Special needs.** The variables and suggested measurements could be given to these students as separate cards. They could then match the values with the variables and use this in their experiment. To add to this activity, the variable that must be kept constant could be written in one colour, and the independent and dependent variables could be in another colour. Then the students could be asked what the colour code means.

- **Learning styles**
  Kinaesthetic: Completing the practicals.
  Visual: Labelling of a diagram.
  Auditory: Listening to discussions in groups.
  Intrapersonal: Creating a bullet-point list about collision theory.
  Interpersonal: Working in groups and discussing decisions.

- **Homework.** A bath bomb is mainly a metal carbonate and an acid. When they are put into water a neutralisation reaction happens. As the two reactants dissolve, they can collide and react. Ask students to explain why a bath bomb takes a long time to react with water, but if it is crumbled up it reacts more quickly.

SPECIFICATION LINK-UP   Unit: Chemistry 2.12.4

- The rate of a chemical reaction increases:
  – if the temperature increases
  – if the concentration of dissolved reactants or the pressure of gases increases
  – if solid reactants are in smaller pieces (greater surface area)
  – if a catalyst is used.
- Chemical reactions can only occur when reacting particles collide with each other with sufficient energy. The minimum amount of energy particles must have to react is the activation energy.

Lesson structure

STARTER

Word search – Create a word search using key words that students will use in this lesson spread ('collision theory', 'temperature', 'concentration', 'surface area', 'catalyst', 'particle', 'activation', 'energy'). This activity could be extended by asking students to write eight sentences each involving one of the key words. (10 minutes)

Thinking – Ask students to work in pairs and list ways that the rate of reaction between an acid and a metal could be monitored [mass loss, gas production]. Then ask students ways that this reaction could be speeded up [heat the acid, increase the surface area of the magnesium, increase the concentration of the acid]. (10 minutes)

Labelling – Give students a diagram of the equipment used to monitor rate for the reaction of marble with acid, when mass loss is being measured. Ask them to label the equipment. (5–10 minutes)

MAIN

- Magnesium is often found in ribbons or powdered form in schools. Show the students samples of each. Ask them to predict which would have the fastest rate of reaction and why (using collision theory to explain). In their prediction, they should include a word equation (balanced symbol equation for higher attaining students) to represent the reaction and what observations they would expect. They could then complete the experiment and see if their prediction was correct.

- Marble chips come in a variety of sizes, but each size is within a range. Show the students samples of different marble chips. Explain that they are going to investigate the mass lost during this experiment in order to decide how the surface area affects the rate. Encourage students to consider what the variables are in the experiment [time, temperature, concentration and volume of acid, mass of marble]. Students should then decide on the appropriate values of each and detail which variables should be kept constant to make the experiment a fair test. The investigation should then be completed and a conclusion written using collision theory. This provides an excellent opportunity to cover the investigative aspects of 'How Science Works'.

- Use Simulation C2 4.2 'How fast?' from the GCSE Chemistry CD ROM.

PLENARIES

Demonstration – For this demo you will need an iron nail, iron wool, iron filings, tongs, heat-proof mat, Bunsen burner, spatula, eye protection. Show students the iron nail, iron wool and iron filings. Ask them what reaction will happen when the iron is put in the flame and ask for a volunteer to write the word equation on the board [iron + oxygen → iron oxide]. Ask the students to predict which will combust most quickly and why. Then demonstrate each type of iron in the flame, i.e. hold the nail into the blue flame using tongs; then hold a small piece of iron wool into the flame using tongs; finally sprinkle a few iron filings from a spatula into the flame. (10 minutes)

Summarise – Ask students to make a bullet-point list of facts about the collision theory. (5 minutes)

Practical support

Which burns faster – ribbon or powder?

Equipment and materials required
Bunsen burner and safety equipment, 2 cm length of magnesium ribbon (flammable – CLEAPSS Hazcard 59), magnesium powder (flammable), spatula, tongs, stopwatch, eye protection.

Details
Hold the end of the magnesium ribbon with tongs. Put the tip of the ribbon in the top of the blue gas cone. As soon as the ribbon ignites, remove from the flame and observe. Then sprinkle about half a spatula of magnesium directly into the blue flame (held at an angle) and observe.

Safety: Eye protection should be worn throughout this practical. Magnesium oxide powder will be made and may enter the air; this could irritate airways and therefore the reaction should be completed in a well-ventilated room. When magnesium ribbon burns, a very bright white light is produced. This can blind if people look at it directly. Therefore encourage students to look past the reaction or alternatively use specialised blue glass/plastic to mute the light.

Investigating surface area

Equipment and materials required
Conical flask, dilute hydrochloric acid (1M – irritant – CLEAPSS Hazcard 47), cotton wool, top-pan balance, marble chips of different sizes, measuring cylinder, stopwatch, eye protection.

Details
Wash and dry the marble chips (to remove the powder from the surface). Measure out about 1 g of marble chips of a certain size into a conical flask. Eye protection should be worn at this point. Add 25 ml of acid and put in the cotton wool plug. Put the reaction vessel onto the top-pan balance and observe the mass change over time. Repeat the experiment with different-sized marble chips.

- Control variables are: Concentration of acid, volume of acid, time, temperature.

ACTIVITY & EXTENSION IDEAS

- Students could complete an evaluation about the calcium carbonate and acid reaction. For example, the problems that they might have found may have been: 'the same mass of marble in each experiment could not be achieved due to natural variation in the marble', 'mass was lost before the reaction vessel was put on the balance', 'the balances aren't very accurate in order to get enough information to draw graphs', etc. Students could then consider ways to change the method to try to reduce these problems and ultimately the errors in the experiment.

- Get sports bibs for students to wear, representing different reactant particles. Then ask them to create and act out a play to describe collision theory.

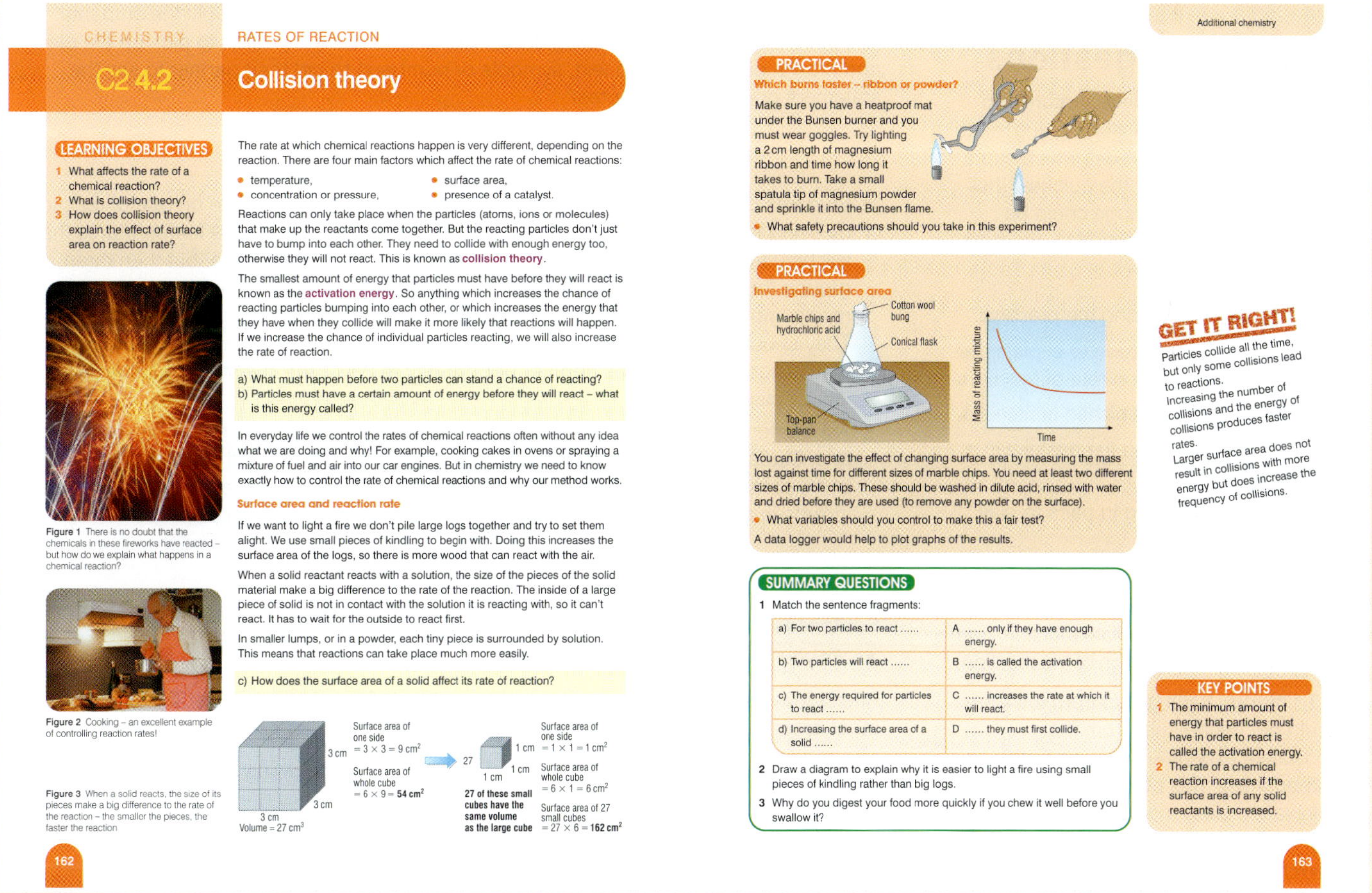

SUMMARY ANSWERS

1 a) D b) A c) B d) C

2 [Students should draw a diagram clearly explaining/showing that cutting a solid into smaller pieces increases its surface area.]

3 Because you have increased its surface area.

Answers to in-text questions

a) The particles must collide.

b) The activation energy.

c) Increasing the surface area increases the rate of the reaction.

KEY POINTS

Students could copy out the key points, representing them in the form of a labelled diagram.

CHEMISTRY RATES OF REACTION

C2 4.3

The effect of temperature

LEARNING OBJECTIVES

Students should learn:

- That changing temperature affects the rate of reaction.

LEARNING OUTCOMES

Most students should be able to:

- Describe how increasing the temperature of a reaction increases the rate.
- List reasons why increasing the temperature increases the rate.

Some students should also be able to:

- Explain how and why changing the temperature changes the rate of reaction.

Teaching suggestions

- **Special needs.** Link temperature and rate of reaction with dissolving sugar into tea. Ask students to predict which cup of tea will dissolve sugar the quickest [hot tea]. This physical change could be demonstrated or completed by the class.

- **Learning styles**
  Kinaesthetic: Completing the practical.
  Visual: Creating a cartoon to explain the effect of temperature on rate of reaction.
  Auditory: Listening to finished sentences.
  Intrapersonal: Spotting the mistake in a sentence.
  Interpersonal: Working in pairs to play 'Pictionary'.

- **Homework.** Ask students to write a brief account in terms of being a reactant particle in a 50°C thiosulfate reaction, from the start to the completion of the reaction.

- **ICT link-up.** Each group from the class could put their results from the thiosulfate experiment into an Excel spreadsheet. This could then be used to calculate a class mean quickly and plot a graph of these results. (See www.rogerfrost.com.)

Answers to in-text questions

a) Because the particles collide more often and have more energy, so when they collide it is more likely that they will have at least the activation energy required for the reaction.

b) The rate roughly doubles.

c) The time decreases.

SPECIFICATION LINK-UP   Unit: Chemistry 2.12.4

- The rate of reaction increases if the temperature increases.
- Increasing the temperature increases the speed of the reacting particles so that they collide more frequently and more energetically. This increases the rate of reaction.

Students should use their skills, knowledge and understanding of 'How Science Works':
- to interpret graphs showing the amount of product formed (or reactant used up) with time, in terms of the rate of reaction.

Lesson structure

STARTER

What is in the bag? – In a brightly coloured bag, put in key words on separate pieces of paper: 'collision theory', 'temperature', 'particles', 'collision', 'rate'. Then ask for a volunteer to come to the front and remove a key word. They can then explain what that words means. If the student struggles, allow them to go back to their seat and look through the Student Book and talk to neighbours; invite them back at the end of the starter. In total, ask five volunteers to explain each of the words in turn. (10 minutes)

Pictionary – Create packs of cards with these statements on: 'increase temperature', 'collision', 'particle', 'reactant', 'product', 'rate', 'chemical reaction'. Split the students into pairs and give them a pack of cards. Ask them to take it in turns to pick up the card and draw a picture (with no text, symbols or numbers) to get their partner to say the statement or word. (10 minutes)

MAIN

- Students could experimentally determine the effect of temperature on rate of reaction by using the sodium thiosulfate reaction. As a class decide on five temperatures that will be used. In small groups each temperature is completed once, but then three groups (or the whole class) could pool their results and take a mean, making the results more reliable. Students could plot a scatter graph, drawing a line of best fit. They should then use their graph and their knowledge of collision theory to draw a conclusion. This provides another opportunity to cover the investigative aspects of 'How Science Works'.

- Ask students to draw a cartoon to show the effect of heating up a reaction in terms of its rate. Students could be encouraged to personify the particles and make a fun depiction of the reaction. To help them, the cartoon framework could be given with statements to include in a box below their images, in order to explain what is happening.

PLENARIES

Sentences – In small groups ask the students to finish the following sentence:
- 'As you heat up a reaction . . .'

After a few minutes ask the groups to read out their finished sentences. Then choose the most accurate and scientific sentence and give that group a prize. (10 minutes)

Spot the mistake – Ask students to spot the error in the following sentence:
- 'When temperature is dropped, particles have more energy but move around less and so the rate of reaction stays the same.' [When temperature is dropped, the particles have less energy and the rate of reaction will reduce.] (5 minutes)

SUMMARY ANSWERS

1 Rate, quickly, collide, energy, rise, doubles, reducing, decreases, chemical, off.

2 Because it is at a higher temperature in the pressure cooker which speeds up the chemical reactions that make food cook.

3 Muscles rely on chemical reactions to produce movement, so a reduction in temperature reduces the rate of these reactions, making the animal move more slowly.

Additional chemistry

Practical support

Reacting magnesium and hydrochloric acid at different temperatures

Equipment and materials required

Ice bath, test tube rack, hot water bath, 1 M hydrochloric acid (irritant – CLEAPSS Hazcard 47), 1 cm magnesium strips (flammable – CLEAPSS Hazcard 59), calcium carbonate, two measuring cylinders, six test tubes, thermometer, eye protection.

Details

Wearing eye protection, measure out 2 ml of acid into each test-tube, put two test tubes in an ice bath, two in a test tube rack and two in a hot water bath. Allow the test tubes to rest in the water/ice baths for about 5 minutes to get to the appropriate temperature. Students can check the temperature of the acid using the thermometer. Add one strip of magnesium to each of the different temperatures of acid. Allow the students to observe the reaction and comment on the rate at different temperatures, encouraging them to decide how they are determining the rate [amount of bubbles produced]. Keep the lab well ventilated.

Repeat the reaction with one marble chip (calcium carbonate) in each test tube.

The effect of temperature on rate of reaction

Equipment and materials required

Two measuring cylinders, stopwatch, paper with large cross in the centre, conical flask, beaker, 0.2 M sodium thiosulfate, 0.2 M hydrochloric acid (irritant), ice bath, water bath/hot plate, thermometer, eye protection.

Details

Measure 10 ml of acid (eye protection should be worn) and 10 ml of sodium thiosulfate in separate clean measuring cylinders and reduce or increase the temperatures of these solutions using ice baths/water baths/hot plates. Choose temperatures that are easy to attain, e.g. 10°C, 20°C, 30°C, 40°C, 50°C; at least five need to be completed in order that a graph can be drawn. Place the beaker on the centre of the large cross; first add the sodium thiosulfate to the beaker. Then add the acid and start the stopwatch and swirl to mix the solutions. Stop the clock when the cross disappears and note the time.

Safety: During this experiment, sulfur dioxide is produced which is toxic and can trigger asthmatic attacks, therefore this should be completed in a well-ventilated room. Once the reaction is complete, the mixture should be disposed of down a well-flushed sink, preferably in a fume cupboard. Also acid will be warmed making it more dangerous.

ACTIVITY & EXTENSION IDEAS

- **Studying more reactions** – Other reactions could be studied at three different temperatures, e.g. magnesium and acid, calcium carbonate and acid. A circus of the three practicals could be set up and students could rotate around them finding out that rate of reaction is always increased on heating the reactions.

KEY POINTS

If there are any EFL (English as a Foreign Language) students present, the key points could be translated into another language. Alternatively you could ask the Modern Foreign Languages department to translate them into a different language, and students could then read each statement and see if they can match it to the English version.

CHEMISTRY — RATES OF REACTION

C2 4.3 The effect of temperature

LEARNING OBJECTIVES

1. How does changing temperature affect the rate of reactions?

When we increase the temperature of a reaction it always increases the rate of the reaction. Collision theory tells us why this happens – there are two reasons.

Both of these reasons are related to the fact that when we heat up a mixture of reactants the particles in the mixture move more quickly.

1 Particles collide more often

When we heat up a substance, energy is transferred to the particles that make up the substance. This means that they move faster. And when particles move faster they have more collisions. Imagine a lot of people walking around in the school playground. They may bump into each other occasionally – but if they start running around, they will bump into each other even more often!

2 Particles collide with more energy

Particles that are moving quickly have more energy, which means that the collisions they have are much more energetic. It's just like two people who collide when they are running about as opposed to just walking into each other!

When we increase the temperature of a reaction, the particles have more collisions and they have more energy. This speeds up the reaction in two ways – the particles will collide more often and they have more energy when they do collide.

Both of these changes increase the chance that two molecules will react. Around room temperature, if we increase the temperature of the reaction by 10°C the rate of the reaction will roughly double.

a) Why does increasing the temperature increase the rate of a reaction?
b) How much does a 10°C rise in temperature increase reaction rate at room temperature?

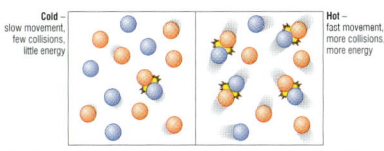

Figure 1 Moving faster means it's more likely that you'll bump into someone else – and the bump will be harder too!

Cold – slow movement, few collisions, little energy

Hot – fast movement, more collisions, more energy

Figure 2 More collisions with more energy – both of these increase the rate of a chemical reaction as the temperature increases

This change in reaction rate is why we use fridges and freezers – because reducing the temperature slows down the rate of a chemical reaction. When food goes bad it is because of chemical reactions. Reducing the temperature slows down these reactions, so the food goes off much less quickly.

PRACTICAL

The effect of temperature on rate of reaction

Time how long it takes for the cross to disappear when viewed from above

Sodium thiosulfate solution and dilute hydrochloric acid

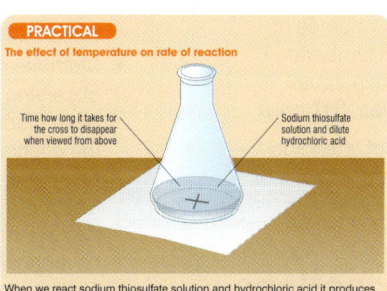

When we react sodium thiosulfate solution and hydrochloric acid it produces sulfur. This makes the solution go cloudy. We can record the length of time it takes for the solution to go cloudy at different temperatures.

- Which variables do you have to control to make this a fair test?
- Why is it difficult to get accurate timings by eye in this investigation?
- How can you improve the reliability of the data you collect?

The results of an investigation like this can be plotted on a graph:

The graph shows how the time for the solution to go cloudy changes with temperature.

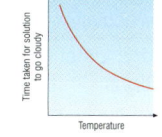

c) What happens to the time it takes the solution to go cloudy as the temperature increases?

SUMMARY QUESTIONS

1 Copy and complete using the words below:

chemical   collide   decreases   doubles   energy   off
quickly   rate   reducing   rise

When we increase the temperature of a reaction, we increase its …… . This makes the particles move more …… so they …… more often and they have more …… . At room temperature, a temperature …… of about 10°C roughly …… the reaction rate. This explains why we use fridges and freezers – because …… the temperature …… the rate of the …… reactions which make food go …… .

2 Water in a pressure cooker boils at a much higher temperature than water in a saucepan because it is under pressure. Why does food take longer to cook in a saucepan than it does in a pressure cooker?

3 Use your knowledge of the effect of temperature on chemical reactions to explain why cold-blooded animals like reptiles or insects may move very slowly in cold weather.

NEXT TIME YOU…

…turn the heat up when you're cooking a meal, remember that you're increasing the rate at which chemical reactions are happening!

KEY POINTS

1 Reactions happen more quickly as the temperature increases.
2 A 10°C increase in temperature at room temperature roughly doubles the rate of a reaction.
3 The rate of a chemical reaction increases with temperature because the particles collide more often and they have more energy.

CHEMISTRY | RATES OF REACTION

C2 4.4 The effect of concentration

LEARNING OBJECTIVES

Students should learn:
- That changing the concentration of reactants changes the rate of reaction.
- That changing the pressure of reacting gases changes the rate of reaction.

LEARNING OUTCOMES

Most students should be able to:
- State the effect on the rate if the concentration of reactants is increased or decreased.
- Describe what we mean by gas pressure.
- State the effect on the rate if pressure is changed in a reaction involving gases.

Some students should also be able to:
- Recall a definition for concentration. [HT only]
- Explain the effect of changing concentration on the rate in terms of collision theory.
- Explain that equal volumes of gases at the same temperature and pressure contain equal numbers of particles. [HT only]
- Explain the effect of changing pressure on the rate in terms of collision theory.

Teaching suggestions

- **Learning styles**
  Kinaesthetic: Completing the practical.
  Visual: Completing the graph in the starter activity.
  Auditory: Listening to other student's definitions.
  Intrapersonal: Creating a poster.
  Interpersonal: Working in groups to discuss the merits of different posters.
- **Homework.** Ask students to explain how pressure affects rate of reaction.
- **ICT link-up.** Arrange for class to use a selection of the simulations available on the GCSE Chemistry CD ROM that cover the effect of concentration on rates of reaction.

SPECIFICATION LINK-UP Unit: Chemistry 2.12.4

- *The rate of a chemical reaction increases if the concentration of dissolved reactants or the pressure of gases increases.*
- *Increasing the concentration of reactants in solutions and increasing the pressure of reacting gases also increases the frequency of collisions and this increases the rate of reaction.*
- *Concentrations of solutions are given in moles per cubic decimetre (mol/dm³). Equal volumes of solutions of the same molar concentration contain the same number of moles of solute, i.e. the same number of particles.* [**HT only**]
- *Equal volumes of gases at the same temperature and pressure contain the same number of molecules. (Candidates will not be expected to find concentrations of solutions or volumes of gases in this unit.)* [**HT only**]

Students should use their skills, knowledge and understanding of 'How Science Works':
- *to interpret graphs showing the amount of product formed (or reactant used up) with time in terms of the rate of reaction.*

Lesson structure

STARTER

Demonstration – Show the students a bottle of undiluted squash. Then put half into a large beaker and add water. Ask the students which container has the most concentrated drink in and how they know. Then ask the students to work in pairs to come up with a definition of concentration. Ask each pair to come to the board and write down their definition. Ask the whole class to consider the definitions and refer to the Student Book to write their own definition of concentration into their notes. (10 minutes)

Graph – Give students an unfinished graph (time, concentration) with two curved lines to show reactants and products. Ask students to complete the axis labels (including units) and briefly explain the shape of the two curves. (5 minutes)

MAIN

- Students can experimentally determine the effect of concentration on rate by observing the reaction between marble chips and acid. At this point, moles have been introduced to students but not their calculation in volume. Therefore to change the concentration the volume of the acid should be diluted with water, but the volume of the mixture should remain constant in order that the reaction is a fair test. Encourage the students to plot all the curves on the same axis. Then ask students to explain their results using collision theory. (This offers another excellent opportunity to cover any investigative aspect of 'How Science Works'.)
- Give students an A4 sheet of paper and ask them to split in it half. On one side they should explain how concentration affects rate and on the other how pressure affects rate. In each section they should define the key word (concentration/pressure) and include one labelled diagram. Ensure that students do not put their name on the front of the poster. (See plenary 'Exhibition'.)

PLENARIES

Act – Split students into small groups of about five, and ask them to design a sketch to highlight that by raising concentration the rate of reaction increases. Circulate around the room and pick two groups to share their sketch with the whole class. (20 minutes)

Demonstration – For this demonstration iron wool, tongs, deflagration spoon, a gas jar of oxygen and a Bunsen burner and safety equipment is needed. Using a safety screen between the class and the demonstration (plus eye protection), hold some iron wool into a blue Bunsen flame using tongs. Then put some iron wool on a deflagration spoon, heat until it is glowing in the top of a blue gas cone. Then quickly put the wool into a gas jar of oxygen. Ask students, in small groups, to explain which reaction was more vigorous and why. Then choose a few students to feedback into the class. (10 minutes)

Exhibition – Get all the students' posters and lay them out on the side benches, and give each a number. Put students in small groups and ask them to rate each poster out of 10 in terms of presentation, accuracy of science and easiest to understand. Then ask them to total up the scores and feedback which is the best poster overall and that student could get a prize. (15 minutes)

ACTIVITY & EXTENSION IDEAS

- Ask students to explain why changing the pressure of a reaction mixture only affects a reaction with gas phase chemicals.
- Once the graph of the production of gas has been drawn, students could be shown how to calculate a numerical value for rate. The graph should be a curve, they choose a particular time and draw a tangent to this point on the curve. Then they work out the gradient (change in vertical value/change in horizontal value) and this is the rate measured in units that refer to volume of gas/time.
- Introduce the idea that [chemical] means the concentration of the chemical.
- Use Simulation C2 4.5 'Rates of Reaction' from the GCSE Chemistry CD ROM.

Additional chemistry

Practical support

Investigating the effect of concentration on rate of reaction

Equipment and materials required

Marble chips, 1 M hydrochloric acid (irritant – CLEAPSS Hazcard 47), 250 ml conical flask, top-pan balance, cotton wool, stopwatch, measuring cylinder, eye protection.

Details

Put about 5 marble chips into the bottom of a conical flask. Measure out 25 ml of acid (wear eye protection), and put into the conical flask, and put a piece of cotton wool in the neck. Quickly place on the balance and take a reading, start the stopwatch. Measure the mass of the conical flask every 10 seconds for 2 minutes.

Repeat for different concentrations.

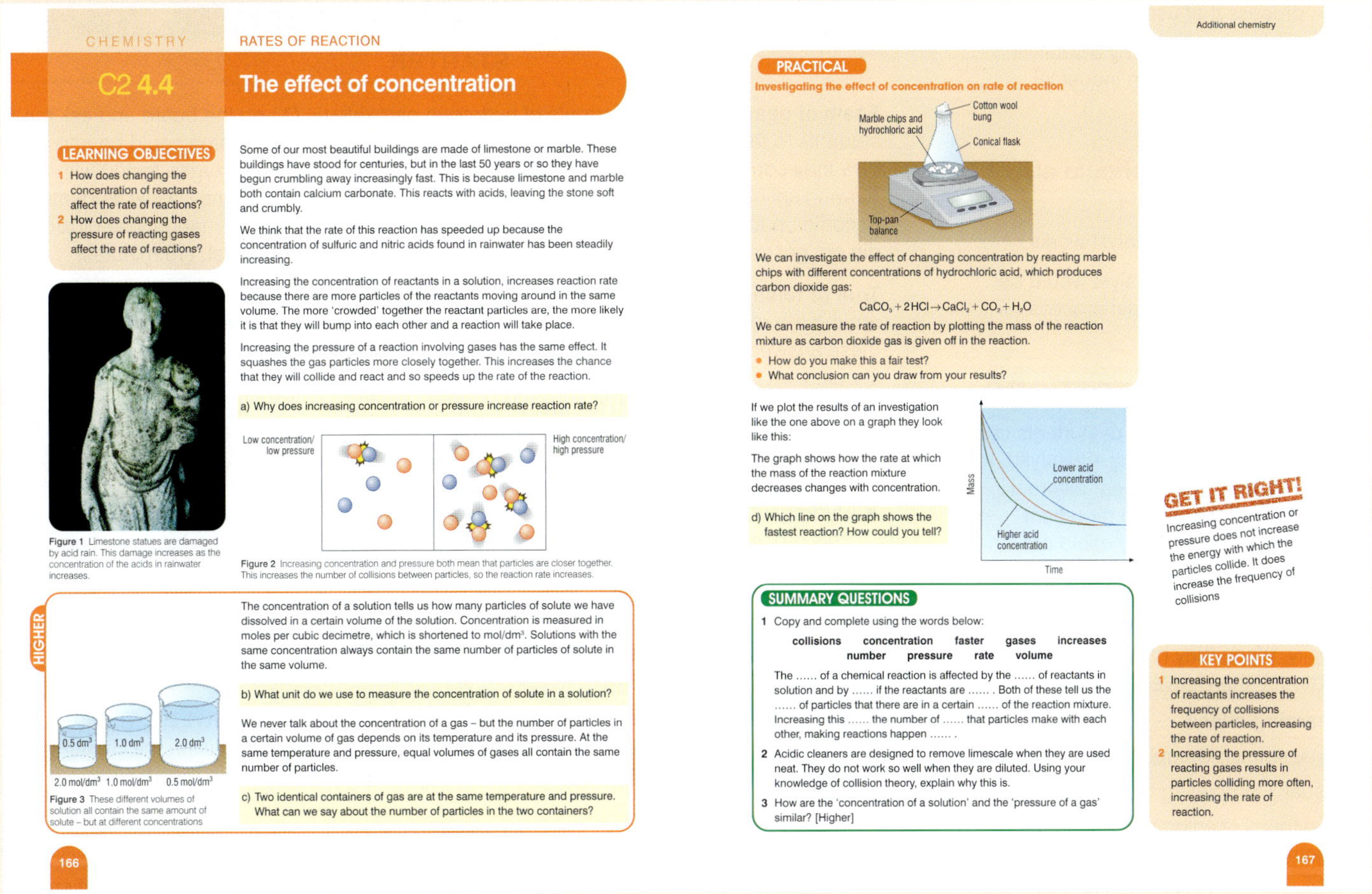

CHEMISTRY — **RATES OF REACTION**

C2 4.4 The effect of concentration

LEARNING OBJECTIVES
1. How does changing the concentration of reactants affect the rate of reactions?
2. How does changing the pressure of reacting gases affect the rate of reactions?

Some of our most beautiful buildings are made of limestone or marble. These buildings have stood for centuries, but in the last 50 years or so they have begun crumbling away increasingly fast. This is because limestone and marble both contain calcium carbonate. This reacts with acids, leaving the stone soft and crumbly.

We think that the rate of this reaction has speeded up because the concentration of sulfuric and nitric acids found in rainwater has been steadily increasing.

Increasing the concentration of reactants in a solution, increases reaction rate because there are more particles of the reactants moving around in the same volume. The more 'crowded' together the reactant particles are, the more likely it is that they will bump into each other and a reaction will take place.

Increasing the pressure of a reaction involving gases has the same effect. It squashes the gas particles more closely together. This increases the chance that they will collide and react and so speeds up the rate of the reaction.

a) Why does increasing concentration or pressure increase reaction rate?

Figure 1 Limestone statues are damaged by acid rain. This damage increases as the concentration of the acids in rainwater increases.

Figure 2 Increasing concentration and pressure both mean that particles are closer together. This increases the number of collisions between particles, so the reaction rate increases.

HIGHER

The concentration of a solution tells us how many particles of solute we have dissolved in a certain volume of the solution. Concentration is measured in moles per cubic decimetre, which is shortened to mol/dm^3. Solutions with the same concentration always contain the same number of particles of solute in the same volume.

b) What unit do we use to measure the concentration of solute in a solution?

We never talk about the concentration of a gas – but the number of particles in a certain volume of gas depends on its temperature and its pressure. At the same temperature and pressure, equal volumes of gases all contain the same number of particles.

c) Two identical containers of gas are at the same temperature and pressure. What can we say about the number of particles in the two containers?

Figure 3 These different volumes of solution all contain the same amount of solute – but at different concentrations.

PRACTICAL
Investigating the effect of concentration on rate of reaction

We can investigate the effect of changing concentration by reacting marble chips with different concentrations of hydrochloric acid, which produces carbon dioxide gas:

$$CaCO_3 + 2HCl \rightarrow CaCl_2 + CO_2 + H_2O$$

We can measure the rate of reaction by plotting the mass of the reaction mixture as carbon dioxide gas is given off in the reaction.

- How do you make this a fair test?
- What conclusion can you draw from your results?

If we plot the results of an investigation like the one above on a graph they look like this:

The graph shows how the rate at which the mass of the reaction mixture decreases changes with concentration.

d) Which line on the graph shows the fastest reaction? How could you tell?

SUMMARY QUESTIONS

1. Copy and complete using the words below:

   collisions   concentration   faster   gases   increases
   number   pressure   rate   volume

   The ...... of a chemical reaction is affected by the ...... of reactants in solution and by ...... if the reactants are .... Both of these tell us the ...... of particles that there are in a certain ...... of the reaction mixture. Increasing this ...... the number of ...... that particles make with each other, making reactions happen ....

2. Acidic cleaners are designed to remove limescale when they are used neat. They do not work so well when they are diluted. Using your knowledge of collision theory, explain why this is.

3. How are the 'concentration of a solution' and the 'pressure of a gas' similar? [Higher]

GET IT RIGHT!

Increasing concentration or pressure does not increase the energy with which the particles collide. It does increase the frequency of collisions.

KEY POINTS

1. Increasing the concentration of reactants increases the frequency of collisions between particles, increasing the rate of reaction.
2. Increasing the pressure of reacting gases results in particles colliding more often, increasing the rate of reaction.

SUMMARY ANSWERS

1. Rate, concentration, pressure, gases, number, volume, increases, collisions, faster.

2. There are more particles in the acid to collide with limescale particles when the cleaner is more concentrated, so increasing the rate of reaction.

3. Both concentration of a solution and pressure of a gas give an indication of the number of particles (of solute or gas) present in a given volume. [**HT** only]

Answers to in-text questions

a) Because there are more particles in the same volume, making collisions more likely.

b) Moles per cubic decimetre (mol/dm^3).

c) They are the same.

d) The higher acid concentration (green line) showed the fastest reaction because the line is steepest initially (or it finished reacting first).

KEY POINTS

Ask students to summarise the points further, maybe using arrows, chemical shorthand and mathematical symbols to represent words e.g.:

↑ [reactants] ⇒ ↑ collisions ⇒ ↑ rate

CHEMISTRY — RATES OF REACTION

C2 4.5 The effect of catalysts

LEARNING OBJECTIVES

Students should learn:
- That catalysts affect the rate of reaction.
- That catalysts are used in many industrial reactions.

LEARNING OUTCOMES

Most students should be able to:
- Give a definition for a catalyst.
- Give an example of an industrial process that uses a catalyst.
- List the reasons why a catalyst may be used in an industrial process.

Some students should also be able to:
- Explain how a catalyst works.
- Explain why a catalyst would be used in an industrial process.

SPECIFICATION LINK-UP   Unit: Chemistry 2.12.4

- The rate of a chemical reaction increases if a catalyst is used.
- Catalysts change the rate of chemical reactions but are not used up during the reaction. Different reactions need different catalysts.
- Catalysts are important in increasing the rates of chemical reactions used in industrial processes to reduce costs.

Students should use their skills, knowledge and understanding of 'How Science Works':
- to interpret graphs showing the amount of product formed (or reactant used up) with time, in terms of the rate of the reaction.

Lesson structure

STARTER

Foam of death – Write the formula of hydrogen peroxide (H_2O_2) on the board and ask the students to think about what the products of the decomposition reaction could be and how they could be tested [water, tested with cobalt chloride paper; oxygen tested with a glowing splint]. See 'Practical support'; when the foam has dried slightly, allow students to come up to the foam and re-light a glowing splint. Explain that the manganese dioxide did not get used up in the reaction, but sped it up and this is a catalyst. (15 minutes)

True or false – Give each student a statement about catalysts. Then they must walk around the room and ask five people if they think the statement is true or false. Based on these answers, the student should decide if the statement is true or false. Each student should then read their statement to the class and say if they think it is true or false and then you give feedback. (10 minutes)

MAIN

- Hydrogen peroxide is unstable in sunlight and will decompose into oxygen and water. This process is relatively slow, but a number of catalysts can be used to speed up this reaction: chopped fresh celery; chopped fresh liver; manganese dioxide. Encourage students to investigate the gas production using the different catalysts to decide which is the best. They should take a set of results for each catalyst and draw all the lines of best fit on the same graph, giving more coverage of the investigative aspects of 'How Science Works'.

- Give students a sheet of A4 paper and ask them to fold it in half (portrait). They should create 10 questions on the left-hand side about catalysts, using the Student Book for inspiration. Then on the right-hand side, they should write the answers.

PLENARIES

Catalytic converter – Get an old catalytic converter (from a scrap yard) and have it cut into slices (maybe in technology). Clean out the deposits then hand out the slices (they look like a honey comb) to the students and let them handle the pieces. The students should be encouraged to discuss in small groups what the visual aid could be used for. Ask each group to feedback their thoughts and then share with the students that it is a catalytic converter used on a car exhaust to remove pollutant gases. (10 minutes)

Poem – Encourage the students to create an eight-line poem, where the first letters of each line spell 'catalyst'. Then choose some students to read their poem to the rest of the class. (20 minutes)

AfL (Assessment for Learning) – To continue the poem activity, ask students to swap their poem with a partner. If the student feels that there is some incorrect science, they should amend the work using a pencil. Once they have worked on the poem, it should be returned to its owner and they should then review any comments that have been made. (10 minutes)

Teaching suggestions

- **Special needs.** A line of students could be formed (representing a catalyst), then other students could wear different coloured sports bibs to represent reactant particles. They could act out how a catalyst works, i.e. the reactants get held by the catalyst and then they can link to form the compound more easily. When they have linked, the 'product' then leaves.

- **Learning styles**
  Kinaesthetic: Completing the practicals.
  Visual: Completing the graph.
  Auditory: Listening to other student's poems.
  Intrapersonal: Creating a question and answer sheet.
  Interpersonal: Working in pairs to reflect on each other's work.

- **ICT link-up.** Excel could be used to plot a graph quickly of the different results.

- **Homework.** Students could find out the name of one catalyst and the reaction it is used in.

Practical support

Foam of death

Equipment and materials required
100 vol. hydrogen peroxide (corrosive – CLEAPSS Hazcard 50), one-litre measuring cylinder, washing-up bowl, washing-up liquid, manganese dioxide (harmful), spatula, cobalt chloride paper, splints, eye protection and gloves.

Details
Stand a one-litre measuring cylinder in a washing-up bowl. Add a good dash of washing-up liquid, and about 100 ml of 100 vol. H_2O_2. Add a spatula of manganese(IV) oxide and allow the students to observe.

Safety: Wear eye protection and be aware of skin burns. Manganese(IV) oxide – see CLEAPSS Hazcard 60.

Investigating catalysis

Equipment and materials required
Stand, boss, gas syringe holder, gas syringe, 10 vol. hydrogen peroxide (irritant), manganese dioxide (harmful), celery, liver, white tile, knife, stopwatch, conical flask, bung, delivery tube, about a 25 cm length of rubber tube, measuring cylinder, spatula, eye protection.

Details
Measure out 25 ml of hydrogen peroxide and put it into the conical flask, eye protection should be worn. Finely chop some celery and put into the flask. Quickly connect the bung to the gas syringe and note the volume of gas produced every 10 seconds for 2 minutes. Repeat with chopped liver, and repeat with a spatula of manganese(IV) oxide. Other transition metal oxides can also be investigated.

- The catalyst.
- Bar chart because the independent variable is categoric (and dependent variable is continuous).

Safety: Be aware of irritation caused by the hydrogen peroxide, wash under cold water and it should dissipate. Make sure the syringe plunger is free-moving.

ACTIVITY & EXTENSION IDEAS

- Catalysts change the rate of reaction, however at this level of chemistry we concentrate on their speeding up properties. Encourage students to research inhibitors (negative catalysts), e.g. in petrol.
- Encourage students to represent the reactions studied as balanced symbol equations. However, ensure that the condition of the reaction (including the catalyst) is listed on the arrow.
- Ask students to consider why hydrogen peroxide is kept in a brown or black bottle away from light. [Light activated decomposition into water and oxygen.]
- For students going on to take GCSE Chemistry (C3) the idea of activation energy and its reduction using a catalyst can be introduced.

CHEMISTRY — **RATES OF REACTION**

C2 4.5 The effect of catalysts

LEARNING OBJECTIVES
1. How do catalysts affect the rate of chemical reactions?
2. Why are catalysts used in so many industrial reactions?

Sometimes we need to change the rate of a reaction but this is impossible using any of the ways we have looked at so far. Or sometimes a reaction might be possible only if we use very high temperatures or pressures – which can be very expensive. However we can speed chemical reactions up another way – by using a special substance called a **catalyst**.

a) Apart from using a catalyst, what other ways are there of speeding up a chemical reaction?

A catalyst is a substance which increases the rate of a chemical reaction but it is not affected chemically itself at the end of the reaction. It is not used up in the reaction, so it can be used over and over again to speed up the conversion of reactants to products.

We need to use different catalysts with different reactions. Many of the catalysts we use in industry are transition metals or their compounds. For example, iron is used in the Haber process, while platinum is used in the production of nitric acid.

Catalysts are often very expensive because they are made of precious metals. But it is often cheaper to use a catalyst than to pay for all the energy needed for higher temperatures or pressures in a reaction.

b) How is a catalyst affected by a chemical reaction?

Figure 1 Catalysts are all around us, in the natural world and in industry. Our planet would be very different without them.

Figure 2 The transition metals platinum and palladium are used in the catalytic converters in cars

Some catalysts work by providing a surface for the reacting particles to come together. They lower the activation energy needed for the particles to react. This means that more of the collisions between particles result in a reaction taking place. We normally use catalysts in the form of powders, pellets or fine gauzes. This gives the biggest possible surface area for them to work.

c) Why is a catalyst divided up into pellets more effective than a whole lump of the catalyst?

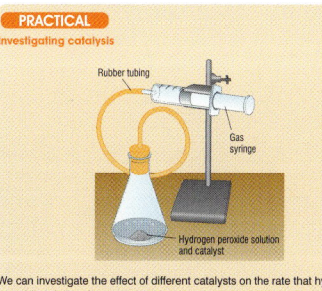

PRACTICAL

Investigating catalysis

We can investigate the effect of different catalysts on the rate that hydrogen peroxide solution decomposes:

$$2H_2O_2 \rightarrow 2H_2O + O_2$$

The reaction produces oxygen. We can collect this in a gas syringe using the apparatus shown above.

We can investigate the effect of many different substances on the rate of this reaction. Examples include manganese(IV) oxide and potassium iodide.

- State the independent variable in this investigation. (See page 2.)

A simple table of the time taken to produce a certain volume of oxygen can then tell us which catalyst makes the reaction go fastest.

- What type of graph would you use to show the results of your investigation? Why? (See page 13.)

Apart from speeding up a chemical reaction, the most important thing about a catalyst is that it does not get used up in the chemical reaction. We can use a tiny amount of catalyst to speed up a chemical reaction over and over again.

SUMMARY QUESTIONS

1. Copy and complete using the words below:

   activation   energy   increases   more   react

   A catalyst ...... the rate of a chemical reaction. It does this by reducing the ...... energy needed for the reaction. This means that ...... particles have enough ...... to ....

2. Solid catalysts used in chemical plants are often shaped as tiny beads or cylinders with holes through them. Why are they made in this shape?

3. Why is the number of moles of catalyst needed to speed up a chemical reaction very small compared to the number of moles of reactants?

DID YOU KNOW?
The catalysts used in chemical plants eventually become 'poisoned' so that they don't work any more. This happens because impurities in the reaction mixture combine with the catalyst and stop it working properly.

KEY POINTS
1. A catalyst speeds up the rate of a chemical reaction.
2. A catalyst is not used up during a chemical reaction.

SUMMARY ANSWERS

1. Increases, activation, more, energy, react.
2. This increases their surface area.
3. Because the catalyst is not used up in the reaction.

Answers to in-text questions

a) Increasing temperature, surface area, concentration (if reactants are in solution) or pressure (if reactants are gases).

b) It is unaffected.

c) Because it has greater surface area.

KEY POINTS

Put the key points onto an index card, underlining the key words. As an extension, a key for the important words could be given to the students, e.g. always write catalyst in red etc.

CHEMISTRY — RATES OF REACTION
C2 4.6 Catalysts in action

SPECIFICATION LINK-UP
Unit: Chemistry 2.12.4

Students should use their skills, knowledge and understanding of 'How Science Works':

- to explain and evaluate the development, advantages and disadvantages of using catalysts in industrial processes.

This spread can also be used to revisit the following substantive content already covered in this chapter:

- Catalysts change the rate of chemical reactions but are not used up during the reaction. Different reactions need different catalysts.
- Catalysts are important in increasing the rate of chemical reactions used in industrial processes to reduce costs.

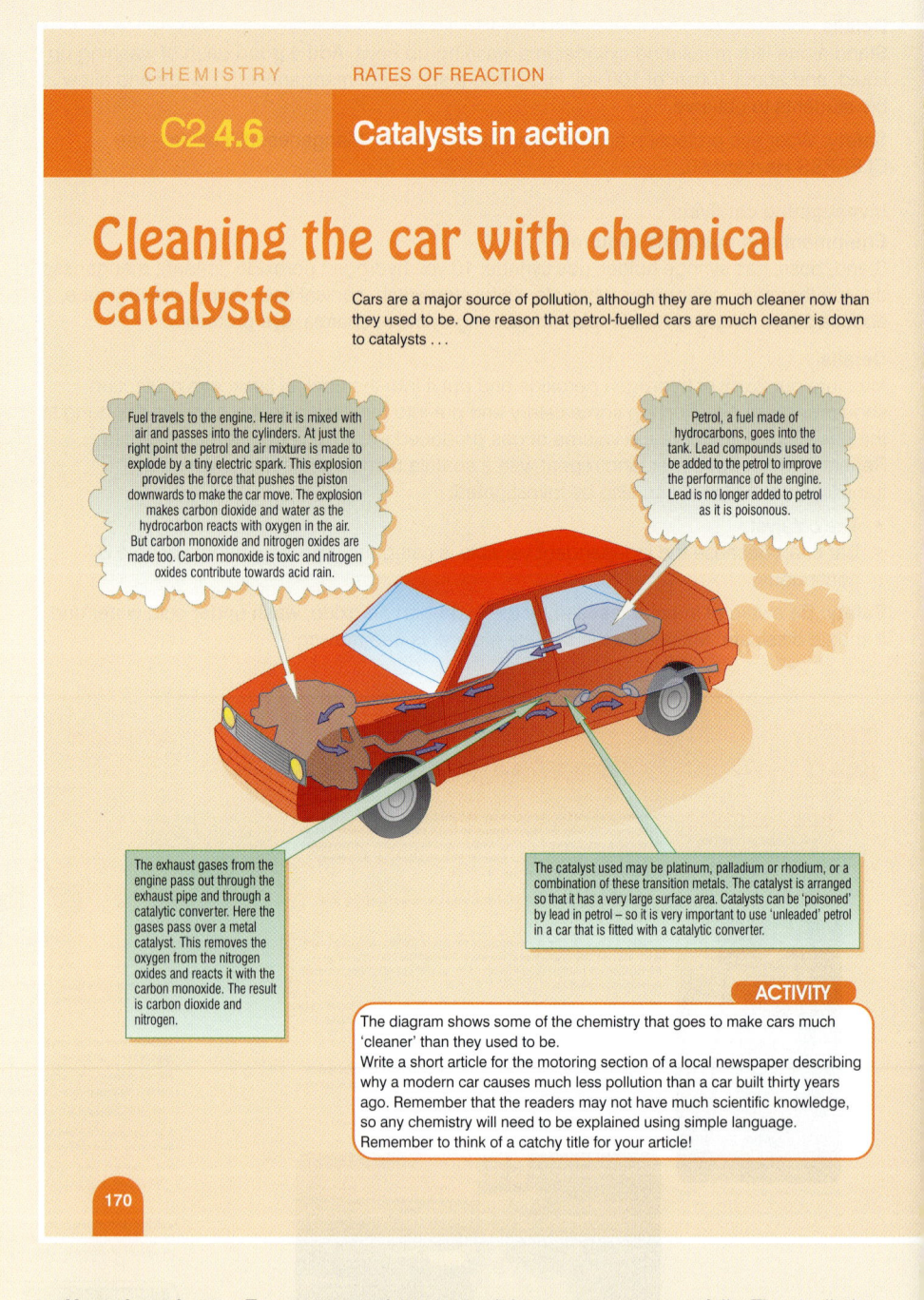

CHEMISTRY — RATES OF REACTION
C2 4.6 Catalysts in action

Cleaning the car with chemical catalysts

Cars are a major source of pollution, although they are much cleaner now than they used to be. One reason that petrol-fuelled cars are much cleaner is down to catalysts…

Fuel travels to the engine. Here it is mixed with air and passes into the cylinders. At just the right point the petrol and air mixture is made to explode by a tiny electric spark. This explosion provides the force that pushes the piston downwards to make the car move. The explosion makes carbon dioxide and water as the hydrocarbon reacts with oxygen in the air. But carbon monoxide and nitrogen oxides are made too. Carbon monoxide is toxic and nitrogen oxides contribute towards acid rain.

Petrol, a fuel made of hydrocarbons, goes into the tank. Lead compounds used to be added to the petrol to improve the performance of the engine. Lead is no longer added to petrol as it is poisonous.

The exhaust gases from the engine pass out through the exhaust pipe and through a catalytic converter. Here the gases pass over a metal catalyst. This removes the oxygen from the nitrogen oxides and reacts it with the carbon monoxide. The result is carbon dioxide and nitrogen.

The catalyst used may be platinum, palladium or rhodium, or a combination of these transition metals. The catalyst is arranged so that it has a very large surface area. Catalysts can be 'poisoned' by lead in petrol – so it is very important to use 'unleaded' petrol in a car that is fitted with a catalytic converter.

ACTIVITY

The diagram shows some of the chemistry that goes to make cars much 'cleaner' than they used to be.

Write a short article for the motoring section of a local newspaper describing why a modern car causes much less pollution than a car built thirty years ago. Remember that the readers may not have much scientific knowledge, so any chemistry will need to be explained using simple language. Remember to think of a catchy title for your article!

170

Teaching suggestions

Activities

- **Newspaper article** – Show students the car sections of a local or national newspaper (or search an online newspaper). Ask the students to imagine that they have been commissioned to write an article about pollution due to cars. Explain that the article should be biased, stating why motorcars of today are not as bad for the environment as previous models. Remind students that they should 'tone down' the science as the audience of the newspaper may not have a scientific background. Some students could then produce their article on a desktop publishing package.

- **News broadcast** – Encourage students to read the news reports carefully. Then split the class into small groups of about three students. Their task is to produce a small news piece (no more than 5 minutes) looking at the future of enzymes in industry. Students could complete some of their own research on enzymes using the Internet. They could then complete their broadcast while being recorded using a camcorder. The video could then be uploaded onto the school's Internet site, or used as a starter in future lessons about enzymes.

- **Presentation** – Split the class into four groups and give each team a different title from these: 'What are enzymes and how are they used in an industrial process?'; 'Enzymes and foods'; 'Enzymes and cleaning'; 'Enzymes and babies'.

Each group should produce an A5 informative leaflet about their topic and a short presentation to highlight the key points of their topic. The leaflets should be collected and photocopied, so that each student has a full record of how the enzyme works. The groups could give their presentations to the rest of the class. Assessment for Learning (AfL) could be incorporated into this activity, by giving students a sheet of marking points to award each group. These sheets can then be given to the relevant groups to inform them about their work.

ENZYMES – CLEVER CATALYSTS THAT ARE GETTING EVERYWHERE

ENZYMES MAKE CLOTHES CLEANER AND CLASSIER!

For years we've been used to enzymes helping to get our clothes clean. Biological washing powders contain tiny molecules that help to literally 'break apart' dirt molecules such as proteins at low temperatures. But why stop there? Why not make washing powders that help to repair clothes and make them like new? Searching the surface of fabric for any tears or breaks in the fibres, enzymes could join these back together, while other enzymes might look for frayed or 'furry' bits of fabric and could makes these smooth again. And not only that . . . . . .

ENZYMES TO THE RESCUE

Everyone knows how upsetting it is to cut yourself. And it can be a pain to have to wear a sticking plaster until your body has repaired your skin. But enzymes may be the answer to this. By choosing the right enzyme mixture we may one day be able to mend cuts and other damage to our skin simply by painting a liquid onto our skin. But until then . . . . . .

SAY 'AAAHH' FOR THE ENZYME!

Those lengthy waits for the results of a blood test to come back could soon be a thing of the past. By combining biological molecules like enzymes with electronics, scientists reckon that they can make tiny measuring probes that will enable doctors to get an instant readout of the level of chemicals in your blood. These sensors are so tiny that it is possible to take more than a dozen measurements at the same time, doing away with the need for lots of tests.

SCIENTISTS MAKE ENZYMES MAKE COMPUTER

Scientists announced today that they are close to making a biological computer made of enzymes and DNA. The tiny device could change the face of computing in the future, which up until now has been based on electronic devices made from silicon. The idea of using DNA in computers first took off in 1994, when a scientist in California used it to solve a maths problem. Computers made from DNA would be so tiny that a trillion of them could fit in a single drop of water.

ACTIVITY

There is more than a grain of truth in all of these ideas about enzymes. Use some or all of these news reports to produce a short piece for the 'and finally' slot in a TV news broadcast. Remember to use your knowledge of catalysts to explain why enzymes are important in all of these developments.

Homework
- **Enzymes** – Ask students to create a spider diagram about the effects of using an enzyme in an industrial process. If the class have studied Unit Biology 2 12.6 in the Specification on enzymes, they could be asked to integrate that work into their spider diagram.

Extension
- **Making yoghurt** – Enzymes are used to make yoghurt. If a room swap can be arranged to a food technology room, students could experiment with making yoghurt: many recipes are available from the Internet, although some schools may have their own yoghurt-making machine, which contains its own instructions.

Learning styles
Kinaesthetic: Completing the 'Making yoghurt' extension activity.

Visual: Preparing a spider diagram about the use of enzymes in industry.

Auditory: Listening to other students' presentations.

Intrapersonal: Writing a newspaper article.

Interpersonal: Working as a group to produce broadcasts.

ICT link-up
The Internet can be used to gain additional information about enzymes. Search in Google for 'uses of enzymes'. Show Animation C2 4.6 'Catalytic converter' from the GCSE Chemistry CD ROM.

Special needs
Give the students cards with pros and cons of using enzymes in an industrial process. They should then sort them into two lists and stick them into their notes.

Gifted and talented
Encourage these students to research how enzymes actually work (link with the biology component), in particular how active sites make the protein specific.

CHEMISTRY   RATES OF REACTION

SUMMARY ANSWERS

1 Lines drawn to link left-hand side and right-hand side columns as follows:
   a) A and C   b) A   c) B   d) B

2 a) Measure volume of gas or mass of reaction mixture.
   b) Three of: increase concentration of acid; increase surface area of magnesium; increase temperature of reaction mixture; add a catalyst.
   c) Increasing concentration/surface area increases number of collisions between reactants; increasing temperature increases number of collisions between reactants and the energy possessed by reacting particles; catalyst lowers activation energy.

3 a) [Graph.]
   b) It is double.
   c) It is double.
   d) Investigation 2 uses acid with twice the concentration of that in investigation 1 (rate and volume of gas double) with at least enough marble chips to react fully with the acid in each case.

Summary teaching suggestions

- **ICT link up** – Question 3 could be used with a graphing package, e.g. Excel, allowing the students to plot a graph using ICT. Alternatively, the graph could be created in advance and then displayed so that students can check their own work.

- **Special needs** – Question 1 could be prepared as a cut and paste question. However, there should be as many reactions as methods of measuring (i.e. some of the second column needs to be repeated), as this could lead to confusion.

- **Misconceptions** – Students often use the terms: 'molecules', 'ions', 'particles', 'elements' and 'compounds' interchangeably. It is important that they realise that the term 'particles' is generic, but the other words have specific meaning. Thus, if they are used incorrectly, they can make answers chemically wrong even if the student is well aware of the collision theory response.

- **Learning styles**
  Auditory: Questions 2 and 3 lend themselves to a class discussion before each student pens their own answer.
  Visual: Question 3 allows the production of a graph.
  Kinaesthetic: Using a card sort, or cut and stick activity, to answer question 1 allows this activity to appeal to these learners.

- **When to use the questions?**
  - As a revision aid at the end of the topic.
  - Question 1 could be used as homework or a plenary to lesson 4.1.
  - Questions 2 and 3 could be used as homework to consolidate learning from lessons 4.2–4.
  - Students could be encouraged not to answer the questions but to create a mark scheme. They should critically consider all the answers that could be awarded a mark and also answers that are close but should not be given any credit.

RATES OF REACTION: C2 4.1 – C2 4.6

SUMMARY QUESTIONS

1 Select from A, B and C to show how the rate of each reaction, a) to d), could be measured.
   a) Gas evolved from reaction mixture
   b) Mass of reaction mixture changes
   c) Precipitate produced
   d) Colour of solution changes

   A Measure mass
   B Measure light transmitted
   C Measure volume

2 A student carried out a reaction in which she dropped a piece of magnesium ribbon in sulfuric acid with a concentration of 1 mol/dm³.
   a) Suggest *one* way in which the student could measure the rate of this reaction.
   b) Suggest *three* ways in which the student could increase the rate of this reaction.
   c) Explain how each of these methods changes the rate of the reaction.

3 The following results show what happened when two students investigated the reaction of some marble chips with acid.

Time (seconds)	Investigation 1 Volume of gas produced (cm³)	Investigation 2 Volume of gas produced (cm³)
0	0	0
30	5	10
60	10	20
90	15	30
120	20	40
150	25	50
180	28	57
210	30	59
240	30	60

   a) Plot a graph of these results with time on the *x*-axis.
   b) After 30 seconds, how does the rate of the reaction in investigation 2 compare with the rate of reaction in investigation 1?
   c) How does the final volume of gas produced in investigation 2 compare with the final volume of gas produced in investigation 1?
   d) Suggest how the reaction in investigation 2 differs from the reaction in investigation 1. Explain your answer.

EXAM-STYLE QUESTIONS

1 Marble chips (calcium carbonate) react with hydrochloric acid as shown in the equation.

$$CaCO_3(s) + 2HCl(aq) \rightarrow CaCl_2(aq) + H_2O(l) + CO_2(g)$$

Some students investigated the effect of the size of marble chips on the rate of this reaction. They did the reactions in a conical flask, which they put onto a balance connected to a computer to record their results. They used three different sizes of marble chips and kept all of the other conditions the same. The graphs show the total mass of the flask and reaction mixture plotted against time for the three experiments.

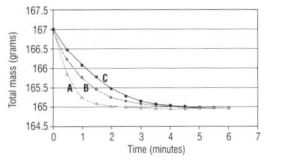

   (a) Which curve, **A**, **B** or **C**, shows the results for the fastest reaction? (1)
   (b) Which curve, **A**, **B** or **C**, shows the results for the largest marble chips? (1)
   (c) Explain, using collision theory, why changing the size of marble chips changes the rate of reaction. (2)
   (d) (i) Use curve **A** to describe how the rate of reaction changes from the start to the finish of the reaction. (3)
       (ii) Explain why the rate of reaction changes in this way. (2)

2 A student investigated the reaction between magnesium ribbon and hydrochloric acid.

$$Mg(s) + 2HCl(aq) \rightarrow MgCl_2(aq) + H_2(g)$$

The student reacted 20 cm³ of two different concentrations of hydrochloric acid with 0.050 g of magnesium. All other conditions were kept the same. The student's results are shown in the table on the next page.

EXAM-STYLE ANSWERS

1 a) A (1 mark)
  b) C (1 mark)
  c) One mark each for:
     - Smaller chips have larger surface area.
     - So more (acid) particles collide with the solid/more collisions.
     Accept converse explanation. (2 marks)
  d) i) One mark each for:
     - Begins rapidly/high rate at start.
     - Rate decreases with time/gets slower.
     - Until it stops/stops after 3 minutes. (3 marks)
     ii) Two from:
     - Concentration of acid greatest at start so highest rate.
     - Concentration of acid decreases as it is used up, so rate decreases.
     - Reaction stops when all acid has been used. (2 marks)

2 a) Volume of gas (1 mark)
  b) e.g. volume of acid/magnesium; temperature of acid (1 mark)
  c) Suggestion linked to b) e.g. use same volume of acid for each concentration of acid. (1 mark)
  d) Suitable scales for axes chosen and both labelled. (1 mark)
     Correct plotting of points for both concentrations (+/− half small square). (2 marks)
     Smooth lines drawn through all points on each curve (no daylight). (1 mark)
  e) i) Doubles the rate/goes twice as fast. (1 mark)
     ii) Slope/gradient of line for concentration 2 mol per dm³ is twice as steep as slope/gradient of other line. (2 marks)
     Accept slope/gradient is steeper *for 1 mark.*
     Accept reaction with concentration 2 mol per dm³ stopped after 4–5 minutes, other reaction after 9 minutes *for 1 mark.*
     Accept after one minute reaction with concentration 2 mol per dm³ produced 15 cm³ of gas, other reaction 30 cm³ *or similar comparison for 1 mark.*

Additional chemistry

HOW SCIENCE WORKS QUESTIONS

This student's account of an investigation into the effect of temperature on the rate of a reaction was found on the Internet.

I investigated the effect of temperature on the rate of a reaction. The reaction was between sodium thiosulfate and hydrochloric acid. I set up my apparatus as in this diagram.

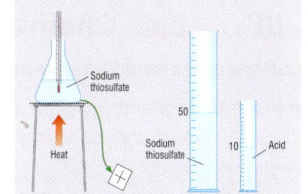

The cross was put under the flask. I heated the sodium thiosulfate to the temperature I wanted and then added the hydrochloric acid to the flask. I immediately started the watch and timed how long it took for the cross to disappear.

My results are below.

Temperature of the sodium thiosulfate	Time taken for the cross to disappear
15	110
30	40
45	21

My conclusion is that the reaction goes faster the higher the temperature.

a) Suggest a suitable prediction for this investigation. (1)
b) Describe one safety feature that is not mentioned in the method. (1)
c) Suggest some ways in which this method could be improved. For each suggestion, say why it is an improvement. (10)
d) Suggest how the table of results could be improved. (1)
e) Despite all of the problems with this investigation, is the conclusion appropriate? Explain your answer. (1)

Concentration of acid (moles per dm³)	Time (minutes)	0	1	2	3	4	5	6	7	8	9	10
1.0	Volume of gas (cm³)	0	15	24	31	37	41	44	46	47	48	48
2.0	Volume of gas (cm³)	0	30	39	45	47	48	48	48	48	48	48

(a) Name the dependent variable. (1)
(b) Suggest a control variable. (1)
(c) Suggest how the student might have controlled this variable. (1)
(d) Plot these results on the same axes, with time on the horizontal axis and volume of gas on the vertical axis. Draw a smooth line for each concentration. Label each line with the concentration of acid. (4)
(e) (i) What is the effect of doubling the concentration on the rate of reaction? (1)
(ii) Explain how the graphs show this effect. (2)
(iii) Explain this effect in terms of particles and collision theory. (2)
(f) Explain why the total volume of hydrogen is the same for both reactions. (2)
(g) Draw a labelled diagram of the apparatus you would use to do this experiment. (3)

3 Hydrogen peroxide solution is colourless and decomposes very slowly at 20°C.

$$2H_2O_2(aq) \rightarrow 2H_2O(l) + O_2(g)$$

Manganese(IV) oxide, a black powder, is a catalyst for the reaction.
(a) Explain what the word catalyst means. (2)
(b) What would you **see** if manganese(IV) oxide was added to hydrogen peroxide solution? (1)
(c) Describe briefly one way that you could show that manganese(IV) oxide was acting as a catalyst. (2)
(d) Explain, using particle and collision theory, how a solid catalyst works. (2)
(e) Hydrogen peroxide solution stored at 10°C decomposes at half the rate compared to when it is stored at 20°C. Explain, in terms of particles, why the rate of the reaction changes in this way. (3)

173

- Q1, parts b) and c) can be used to check that students are clear about the relationship between the size of pieces of reagents and their surface area. Part d) probes their understanding of rate. They should have been taught that rate is an amount divided by time and is the slope of amount versus time graphs. Some students only think in terms of overall rate of a reaction, i.e. the time it takes to go to completion, but they should understand that rates may be calculated at any time during a reaction.
- In Q2 it is the difference in the initial rates that allows the comparison of rate at different concentrations. The concentration of the second reaction is double that of the first reaction at the start of the reactions. It remains so over a short time period, about one minute in this case, and this is sometimes used to measure initial rates in investigations such as the reaction of sodium thiosulfate with hydrochloric acid and iodine clock experiments. Q2 parts a) to c) relate to 'How Science Works'.
- Literacy skills are important in answers requiring explanations. When explaining how the rate of a reaction depends upon collisions, as in Q2e)(iii), many students do not make it clear in their answers that it is an increase in the frequency of collisions that causes an increase in the rate. Commonly, students simply refer to more collisions without mentioning time, leaving examiners to infer that they mean frequency. Definitions, like that of a catalyst in Q3a), should be well rehearsed. A common slip here is for students to write that catalysts 'are not used in the reaction', when they mean 'not used up in the reaction'. It may be better to say that the catalyst remains at the end of the reaction.

HOW SCIENCE WORKS ANSWERS

a) e.g. The higher the temperature, the more quickly the cross will disappear.
b) e.g. Wear eye protection or do not heat solution above 50°C or dispose of solutions in fume cupboard.
c) Ways in which the method could have been improved include:
   - There should have been more temperatures chosen, so that the pattern could have been seen in the results.
   - The range could have been wider, so that the effect of higher and lower temperatures could have been noted.
   - The volume and concentration of the two reactants should be known, to make sure that the method is valid.
   - The hydrochloric acid should have been heated to the desired temperature as well, to ensure that the reaction took place at the stated temperature.
   - Data logging could have been used to detect the end point, it is difficult to tell accurately when the cross disappears.
   - The solutions should be continually stirred, to ensure validity.
   - A water bath should have been used to control the temperature.
d) Include units in the table.
e) It is not possible to tell because the evidence is not reliable. (Also accept an answer that indicates that the conclusion is appropriate because there are large differences between the results at different temperatures (assuming the timings were taken in seconds.)

How science works teaching suggestions

- **Literacy guidance**
  - Key terms that should be clearly understood: controls, validity.
  - Question c) expects a longer answer, where students can practise their literacy skills.
- **Higher- and lower-level answers.** Question c) is a higher-level question and the answers provided above are also at this level. Question d) is lower level and the answer provided is also lower level.
- **Homework.** High attaining students could tackle the questions for homework. Others could bring in suggestions for the brainstorming session.
- **Special needs.** You could take these students through the practical as a demonstration and ask them how they would set up the experiment.

---

iii) Increasing concentration means more particles per cm³ *(1 mark)*
so the frequency of collisions increases. *(1 mark)*

f) All of the magnesium was used up in both reactions *(1 mark)*
because there was excess hydrochloric acid. *(1 mark)*

g) One mark each for:
- Side arm test tube or conical flask containing reactants.
- Gas syringe or inverted measuring cylinder/burette full of water in trough of water.
- Sealed system with bung and delivery tube correctly connected. *(3 marks)*

3 a) A substance that speeds up a chemical reaction *(1 mark)* but is not used up in the reaction/remains at the end of the reaction. *(1 mark)*

b) Rapid fizzing/effervescence/lots of bubbles of gas. *(1 mark)*

c) One mark each for:
- Remove/filter catalyst from products/water.
- Add it to fresh hydrogen peroxide to show it will work again OR dry it and weigh it to show none has been used up. *(2 marks)*

d) It provides a surface for the reactants to come together. *(1 mark)*
It lowers the activation energy needed for the particles to react. *(1 mark)*

e) One mark each for:
- Increasing temperature causes particles to move faster
- so they collide more frequently
- and they collide with more energy. *(3 marks)*

Exam teaching suggestions

- The questions on this chapter total 36 marks, and should take students about 35 minutes to complete in a single session. Q1 could be used after completing spread 4.2, Q2 after 4.4 and Q3 after 4.5.

173

CHEMISTRY   ENERGY AND REACTIONS

C2 5.1 Exothermic and endothermic reactions

LEARNING OBJECTIVES

Students should learn:

- That energy is involved in chemical reactions.
- That energy changes in a chemical reaction can be measured.

LEARNING OUTCOMES

Most students should be able to:

- State a definition for exothermic and endothermic reactions.
- List one example of an exothermic and endothermic reaction.
- Recognise an endothermic or exothermic reaction when data is given.
- Describe how a reaction can be monitored for its energy changes.

Some students should also be able to:

- Explain the difference between exothermic and endothermic reactions.

Teaching suggestions

- **Special needs.** The information needed to be detailed on the posters could be given to the students. However, they would need to decide which poster it is referring to, before copying it out onto their work.
- **Learning styles**

  Kinaesthetic: Using a calorimeter to record the energy changes of a reaction.

  Visual: Preparing posters about energy changes in a reaction.

  Auditory: Listening to different reactions and deciding whether they are exothermic or endothermic.

  Intrapersonal: Making detailed observations about the sherbet reaction.

  Interpersonal: Working as a group to explain observations from the neutralisation experiment.

- **Homework.** Students could list one exothermic reaction and one endothermic reaction that they could not live without and state why.

SPECIFICATION LINK-UP   Unit: Chemistry 2.12.5

- When chemical reactions occur, energy is transferred to or from the surroundings.
- An exothermic reaction is one that transfers energy, often as heat, to the surroundings. Examples of exothermic reactions include combustion, many oxidation reactions and neutralisation.
- An endothermic reaction is one that takes in energy, often as heat, from the surroundings. Endothermic reactions include thermal decompositions.

Lesson structure

STARTER

Sherbet – Give students a sherbet sweet before they enter the room. Ask students to detail what their observations are as they eat it. Then, using questions and answers, get feedback from the students and ask them if they think the reaction is chemical/physical and exo-/endothermic (these words should be defined by the students looking back at their previous work and using the Student Book). (5 minutes)

Cut and stick – Pictures of different reactions could be given to students. They firstly need to make themselves aware of the definitions of exothermic and endothermic reactions. They could then cut up the pictures and arrange them in a table to detail the energy changes shown in the reactions. (10 minutes)

MAIN

- The energy changes of a reaction can be recorded using a coffee cup calorimeter. Explain to the students that most reactions show their energy change in the form of heat, and that the reaction needs to be well insulated to prevent heat loss to the surroundings. Then ask students to complete the displacement reaction between zinc powder and copper sulfate solution. Students should design their own results table and record their results in order to draw a graph. They should be reminded that the scales do not have to start at 0 (and the y-axis will probably start at about 15°C). Students may struggle in drawing the line of best fit for this reaction; you could show how to do this on the board. There are many whole investigations that this can be developed into to extend the 'How Science Works' concepts already covered.
- Students could be given an A5 sheet of blue paper. They should then write a definition of endothermic onto the blue paper and include examples of endothermic reactions. A similar poster could then be created for exothermic reactions on red paper.

PLENARIES

Exo-/endothermic – Give the students a blue card with the word 'endothermic' written on, and a red card with the word 'exothermic' printed on. Then read out these reactions and ask the students to decide if they are exo- or endothermic, displaying the card to represent their answer:

- Thermal decomposition of marble. [Endothermic]
- Combustion of methane. [Exothermic]
- Neutralisation of hydrochloric acid and sodium hydroxide. [Exothermic]
- Rusting of an iron nail. [Exothermic]
- Thermal decomposition of copper carbonate. [Endothermic]

This activity could be extended by asking the students to complete word or symbol equations for the reactions. Also these reactions could be demonstrated by you, or they could be shown using photographs or a video via a digital projector. (5 minutes)

Demonstration – Use a data logger to plot the temperature changes in a neutralisation reaction. Display the temperature graph using a digital projector. In small groups, students should decide whether the reaction is exothermic or endothermic and say how they could tell. Then choose a few students to feedback to the class. (10 minutes)

Practical support
Investigating energy changes
Equipment and materials required
Polystyrene coffee cup, polystyrene lid with two holes in, a mercury thermometer (0–50°C), copper sulfate 1 M (harmful), zinc powder (flammable), spatula, balance, measuring cylinder, stopwatch, stirrer, eye protection.

Details
Wear eye protection and measure 25 ml of copper sulfate solution into the coffee cup. Measure the temperature every 30 seconds for 5 minutes. Then add 1 g of zinc to the cup and quickly put on the lid and stir constantly. Take the temperature every 10 seconds for 10 minutes.

- Repeat the measurements more than once or repeat using a different thermometer or a temperature sensor or check your results with those of another group.

Safety: Make students aware that they are using a mercury thermometer for accuracy, but that this contains a risk and they should be careful not to leave them by the edge of the bench. You should be aware of where the mercury spillage kit is and how to use it. Copper sulfate is harmful – CLEAPSS Hazcard 27. Zinc powder is flammable – CLEAPSS Hazcard 107.

Demonstration of neutralisation reaction
Equipment and materials
Burette, measuring cylinder, burette holder, stand, 1 M sodium hydroxide (corrosive), 1 M hydrochloric acid (irritant), universal indicator (flammable), magnetic stirrer, conical flask, magnetic stirrer bar, temperature probe, interface, computer, digital projector, white tile, filter funnel, eye protection.

Details
Measure 25 ml of sodium hydroxide into a conical flask and add a few drops of indicator. Place the flask onto the magnetic stirrer and add the bar. Fill the burette with hydrochloric acid using the filter funnel. Position the burette over the conical flask and add the temperature probe to the flask, taking care that it doesn't hit the stirrer. Set the graph to take data for about 2 minutes and begin stirring. Start the data collection. Turn on the flow of acid to the flask and observe.

This activity can be extended by adding a pH probe and comparing the temperature rise with the pH of the solution.

Additional chemistry

DID YOU KNOW?
When people suffer sports injuries cold packs can be used to alleviate the pain and swelling. These also use a reaction, but it takes in heat energy from its surroundings. Cold packs work by having two reactants that are separated and when you break an inner bag, it allows them to mix and the associated temperature change is then produced.

Answers to in-text questions
a) Exothermic.
b) Endothermic.
c) Respiration, burning (or other reaction releasing energy).
d) Thermal decomposition, photosynthesis (or other reaction that absorbs energy).

KEY POINTS
Ask the students to imagine that they work for a marketing company. They are to make a poster to encourage students to think about science in their everyday lives (like the RSC posters 'Scientists don't always wear white coats'). Their poster should include all the key points.

CHEMISTRY
ENERGY AND REACTIONS

C2 5.1 Exothermic and endothermic reactions

LEARNING OBJECTIVES
1. How is energy involved in chemical reactions?
2. How can we measure the energy transferred in a chemical reaction?

Whenever chemical reactions take place, energy is involved. That's because energy is always transferred as chemical bonds are broken and formed.

Some reactions transfer energy *from* the reacting chemicals *to* the surroundings. We call these **exothermic** reactions. The energy transferred from the reacting chemicals often heats up the surroundings. This means that we can measure a rise in temperature as the reaction happens.

Some reactions transfer energy *from* the surroundings *to* the reacting chemicals. We call these **endothermic** reactions. Because they take in energy from their surroundings, these reactions cause a drop in temperature as they happen.

a) What do we call a chemical reaction that gives out heat?
b) What do we call a chemical reaction that absorbs heat from its surroundings?

Exothermic reactions
Fuels burning are an obvious example of exothermic reactions, but there are others which we often meet in the chemistry lab.

Neutralisation reactions between acids and alkalis are exothermic. We can easily measure the rise in temperature using simple apparatus (see opposite).

Similarly, heat is released when we add water to white anhydrous copper(II) sulfate (anhydrous means 'without water'). This reaction makes blue hydrated copper(II) sulfate crystals. The reaction gives out heat – it is an exothermic reaction.

Respiration is a very special kind of burning. It involves reacting sugar with oxygen inside the cells of every living thing. This makes the energy needed for all the reactions of life, and also makes water and carbon dioxide as waste products. Respiration is another exothermic reaction.

c) Give two examples of exothermic reactions.

Figure 1 When a fuel burns in oxygen, energy is transferred to the surroundings. We usually don't need a thermometer to know that there is a temperature change!

DID YOU KNOW?
Chemical handwarmers use an exothermic chemical reaction to keep your hands warm on cold days.

Figure 2 All warm-blooded animals rely on exothermic reactions to keep their body temperatures steady

Endothermic reactions
Endothermic reactions are much less common than exothermic ones.

When we dissolve some ionic compounds like potassium chloride or ammonium nitrate in water the temperature of the solution drops.

Thermal decomposition reactions are also endothermic. An example is the decomposition of calcium carbonate to form calcium oxide and carbon dioxide. This reaction only takes place if we keep heating the calcium carbonate strongly. It takes in a great deal of energy from the surroundings.

The most important endothermic reaction of all is **photosynthesis**. This is the reaction in which plants turn carbon dioxide and water into sugar and oxygen, using energy from the Sun.

Figure 3 When we eat sherbet we can feel an endothermic reaction! Sherbet dissolving in the water in your mouth takes in energy – giving a slight cooling effect.

d) Name two endothermic reactions.

PRACTICAL
Investigating energy changes

The thermometer is used to measure the temperature change which takes place during the reaction.
Chemicals are mixed in the cup. The insulation reduces the rate at which energy can enter or leave the contents of the cup.
Styrofoam cup

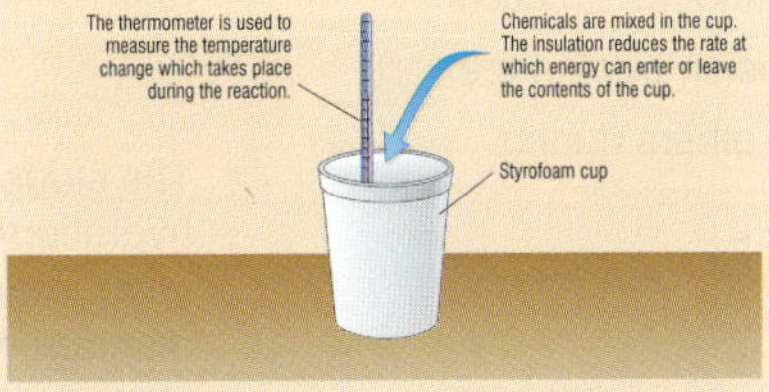

We can use very simple apparatus to investigate the energy changes in reactions. Often we don't need to use anything more complicated than a Styrofoam drinks cup and a thermometer.

- State two ways in which you could make the data you collect more reliable.

GET IT RIGHT!
Remember that exothermic reactions involve energy EXiting (leaving) the reacting chemicals so the surroundings get hotter. In endothermic reactions energy moves INTO (sounds like 'endo'!) the reacting chemicals, so the surroundings get colder.

SUMMARY QUESTIONS
1 Copy and complete using the words below:

broken   endothermic   exothermic   made   neutralisation
photosynthesis   respiration   thermal decomposition

Chemical reactions involve energy changes as bonds are …… and …… . When a chemical reaction releases energy we say that it is an …… reaction. Two important examples of this kind of reaction are …… and …… . When a chemical reaction takes in energy we say that it is an …… reaction. Two important examples of this kind of reaction are …… and …… .

2 Potassium chloride dissolving in water is an endothermic process. What might you expect to observe when potassium chloride dissolves in water?

KEY POINTS
1 Energy may be transferred to or from the reacting substances in a chemical reaction.
2 A reaction where energy is transferred from the reacting substances is called an exothermic reaction.
3 A reaction where energy is transferred to the reacting substances is called an endothermic reaction.

SUMMARY ANSWERS

1 Broken, made, exothermic, neutralisation, respiration, endothermic, thermal decomposition, photosynthesis.

2 Condensation forming on outside of the walls of the container in which the solution is being made as a result of the decrease in temperature.

175

CHEMISTRY — ENERGY AND REACTIONS

C2 5.2 Energy and reversible reactions

LEARNING OBJECTIVES

Students should learn:

- That energy is involved in reversible reactions.
- How altering the temperature when reactions are at equilibrium produces a change. [HT only]

LEARNING OUTCOMES

Most students should be able to:

- Recall the test for water.
- Recognise that if the forward reaction is exothermic, the reverse reaction will be endothermic.
- Recognise that if the forward reaction is endothermic, the reverse reaction will be exothermic.
- That the energy used or released in either direction are the same amount.

Some students should also be able to:

- Explain how temperature changes will affect the equilibrium mixture. [HT only]

Teaching suggestions

- **Learning styles**
  Kinaesthetic: Completing the practical.
  Visual: Creating a revision book page.
  Auditory: Listening to others during group work.
  Intrapersonal: Writing own answers to questions.
  Interpersonal: Working as a group and considering group dynamics.

- **ICT link-up.** Set up a flexi-cam or video camera. This can be used to show exemplar work quickly and easily to the rest of the class.

- **Homework.** Students could tackle each group's exemplar question from their revision page.

SPECIFICATION LINK-UP   Unit: Chemistry 2.12.5

- If a reversible reaction is exothermic in one direction it is endothermic in the opposite direction. The same amount of energy is transferred in each case. For example:

  hydrated copper sulfate (blue) ⇌ anhydrous copper sulfate (white) + water
  (endothermic / exothermic)

  The reverse reaction can be used to test for water.

- When a reversible reaction occurs in a closed system, equilibrium is reached when the reactions occur at exactly the same rate in each direction. [HT only]
- The relative amounts of all the reacting substances at equilibrium depend on the conditions of the reaction. [HT only]
- If the temperature is raised, the yield from the endothermic reaction increases and the yield from the exothermic reaction decreases. [HT only]
- If the temperature is lowered, the yield from the endothermic reaction decreases and the yield from the exothermic reaction increases. [HT only]

Lesson structure

STARTER

Group dynamics – Give each student a questionnaire to find out what type of team player they are, e.g. leader, recorder, ideas generator, etc. These sorts of questionnaires are available from management recruitment books and courses. Explain to students what type of group works and set them the task of forming their own group with at least one of each type of person. (15 minutes)

Questions – Give each student an A4 whiteboard (or laminated sheet of paper), a washable pen and eraser. Then ask them the following series of questions, the student should note down their answer and show you for immediate assessment. If the student is unsure of the answer, they could refer to the Student Book or wait for other students to hold up their answer and then use these responses to inform their answer.

- What is the symbol to show a reversible reaction? [⇌]
- Give an example of a reversible reaction. [The Haber process, hydration of dehydrated copper sulfate, thermal decomposition of ammonium chloride.]
- What does exothermic mean? [Energy is given out in the reaction.]
- What happens to the temperature in an endothermic reaction? [Temperature decreases.] (10 minutes)

MAIN

- The students can experimentally complete the reversible reaction of hydration/dehydration of copper sulfate crystals. Before the experiment is completed, encourage the students to think about how they will record their results (table, diagram, flow chart, paragraphs, bullet points, etc.). Once the practical is completed, show the exemplar work to the rest of the class and explain why it is a good way to record the results.

- Ask students to imagine that they have been commissioned by a top publisher to create a GCSE science revision book. Show students a selection of revision materials and ask them to discuss in groups what they like and dislike about the material. Explain that they have an A4 page spread in a book to explain energy and reversible reactions. They must include a worked examination question and an extra question for the reader to attempt, with the answers upside down on the page. Students could work in small teams to complete this task, allowing them to calve up the task as they desire.

PLENARIES

Objectives – Ask students to try to answer the questions posed by the objectives. (10 minutes)

Crossword – Create a crossword with the answers taken from this double-page spread (words could include: 'reversible', 'endothermic', 'exothermic', 'energy', 'equilibrium', 'closed', 'hydrated', 'water'). There are many free sites via the Internet, which can be used to create your own crossword. Then ask students to complete the crossword. (10–15 minutes)

Practical support

Energy changes in a reversible reaction

Equipment and materials required

Hydrated copper sulfate (harmful – CLEAPSS Hazcard 27), spatula, Bunsen burner and safety equipment, dropping pipette, water, boiling tube, boiling tube holder, eye protection.

Details

Eye protection should be worn throughout this practical. Put a spatula of copper sulfate crystals into a boiling tube. Using the boiling tube holder, hold the boiling tube just above the blue flame of the Bunsen burner. The tube should be held at an angle and out of the direction of people's faces. Do not overheat. Once the visible change is complete, allow the tube to cool. Add a few drops of water. Be aware that water added directly to the boiling tube, may crack it.

Demonstration of making cobalt chloride paper

Equipment and materials required

Filter paper, cobalt chloride (toxic), 50 ml beaker, stirring rod, wash bottle and water and a spatula, Bunsen burner, (desiccator), eye protection.

Details

Add half a spatula of cobalt chloride crystals, add water and stir until it dissolves. Soak some filter paper in the solution. Take care drying the paper using a yellow Bunsen flame and it will become blue (dehydrated), add water and it will become pink (hydrated).

Explain that the paper should be kept out of air in a desiccator as the air contains water and will turn the paper pink. A desiccator could be shown to the students and they could research how it works.

Safety: Wear eye protection. Keep cobalt chloride off skin (avoid handling papers with fingers.) Wash hands after use. (See CLEAPSS Hazcard 25.)

Additional chemistry

ACTIVITY & EXTENSION IDEAS

- Add state symbols to the symbol equation for the dehydration/hydration of cobalt chloride/copper sulfate.
- Cobalt chloride is usually made into paper for use in practicals to test for water. This can be shown to the students. See 'Practical support'.

Answers to in-text questions

a) Amount of energy released in one direction is the same as the amount of energy absorbed in the other direction.

b) Water.

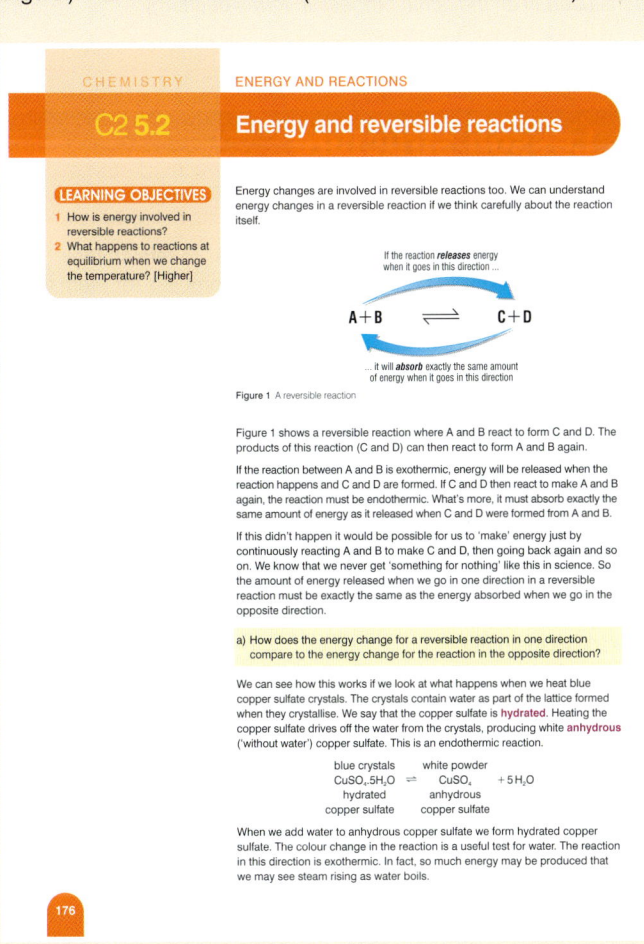

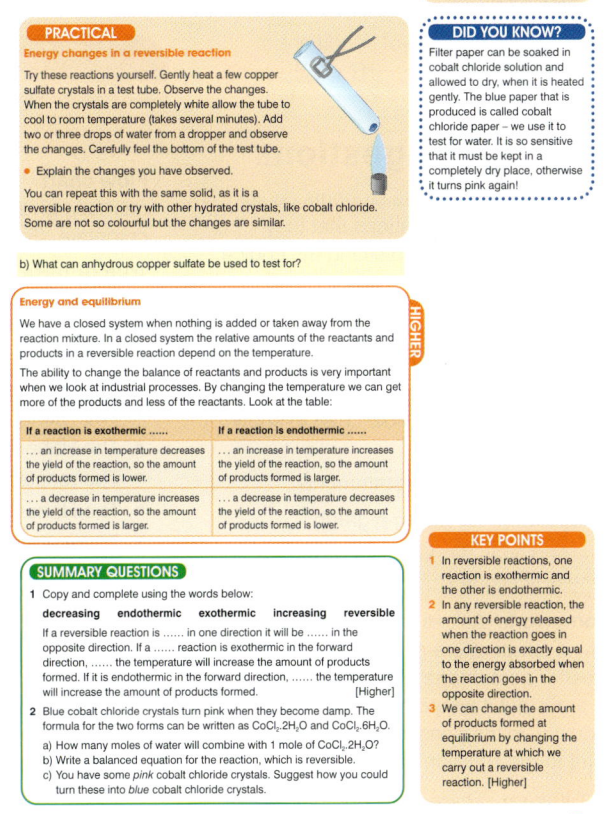

SUMMARY ANSWERS

1 Exothermic (endothermic), endothermic (exothermic), reversible, decreasing, increasing. [HT only]

2 a) 4

b) $CoCl_2.2H_2O + 4H_2O \rightleftharpoons CoCl_2.6H_2O$

c) Heat them (gently) to drive off the water.

KEY POINTS

Encourage the students to copy out the key points onto flash cards. They can then create a bank of the key points on separate cards to use for revision.

CHEMISTRY — ENERGY AND REACTIONS

C2 5.3 More about the Haber process

LEARNING OBJECTIVES

Students should learn:

- The conditions used in the Haber process. (See C2 3.7 for students taking the Foundation Paper.)
- Why these conditions are chosen. [**HT** only]

LEARNING OUTCOMES

Most students should be able to:

- State the operating temperature and pressure used in the Haber process. (See C2 3.7 for students taking the Foundation Paper.)

Some students should also be able to:

- Explain the effects of changing temperature and pressure in a given reversible reaction. [**HT** only]
- Justify the choice of conditions in the Haber process. [**HT** only]

Teaching suggestions

- **Special needs.** These students could be given a set of questions that they must answer when explaining the choice of temperature and pressure.
- **Learning styles**
  Kinaesthetic: Moving the true/false sign to show the answer.
  Visual: Completing a flow chart to show the Haber process.
  Auditory: Listening to statements.
  Intrapersonal: Drawing a graph.
  Interpersonal: Working in a group to assess fictitious student answers.
- **Homework.** Ask students to explain why a temperature of 0°C would achieve a better percentage yield in the Haber process but it would not be used by industry. In their answer they need to refer to the collision theory.
- **ICT link-up.** There are a number of simulations available for the Haber process. These allow students to change the conditions to investigate the affect on yield. One such simulation could be projected onto an interactive whiteboard, teams could then come to the board and change the temperature and pressure separately in order to get their own set of results to plot the graphs.

SPECIFICATION LINK-UP   Unit: Chemistry 2.12.5

- *The relative amounts of all the reacting substances at equilibrium depend on the conditions of the reaction.* [**HT** only]
- *If the temperature is raised, the yield from the endothermic reaction increases and the yield from the exothermic reaction decreases.* [**HT** only]
- *If the temperature is lowered the yield from the endothermic reaction decreases and the yield from the exothermic reaction increases.* [**HT** only]
- *In gaseous reactions, an increase in pressure will favour the reaction that produces the least number of molecules as shown by the symbol equation for that reaction.* [**HT** only]
- *These factors, together with reaction rates, are important when determining the optimum conditions in industrial processes, including the Haber process.* [**HT** only]
- *It is important for sustainable development as well as economic reasons to minimise energy requirements and energy wasted in industrial processes. Non-vigorous conditions means less energy is used and less is released into the environment.*

Students should use their skills, knowledge and understanding of 'How Science Works':

- *to describe the effects of changing the conditions of temperature and pressure on a given reaction or process.*
- *to evaluate the conditions used in an industrial process in terms of energy requirements.*

Lesson structure

STARTER

Flow chart – Students have already encountered the Haber process. To refresh their memory, give the students an unfinished flow chart of the industrial process for them to complete. (5 minutes)

True or false – Create two A4 sheets of paper, one with 'True' written on and the other with 'False'. Then secure these onto each side of the classroom. Read out the following statements and students should then stand by the poster that shows their response. If they are unsure, they could stand in the centre or move more towards one side than the other to show how sure they are of their answer.

- The Haber process makes ammonia. [True]
- The Haber Process is a reversible reaction. [True]
- The reactants for the Haber process are natural gas and air. [False]
- The Haber process is carried out at room temperature and pressure. [False]
- There are more moles of gas on the products' side than the reactants' side in the Haber process. [False] (10–15 minutes)

MAIN

- Give the students data for the yield of the Haber process at different temperatures and different pressures. Students could then plot two graphs to show the trend in yield as these variables change. Higher attaining students could have two *x*-axis scales and plot the data onto one graph. They could then be encouraged to use the graphs to make conclusions about how temperature and pressure affects this reaction. Students could then be encouraged to explain these trends using information from the Student Book.
- Split the class into two teams. One group should explain the choice of temperature in the industrial Haber process and the other should describe the choice of pressure. The groups should decide how they will present their explanations to the class – as a presentation, using the board, just speaking, as a poster, etc. It is up to the group to decide.

178

PLENARIES

Explanations – Each half of the class should explain the choice of temperature and pressure in the industrial Haber process. (10 minutes)

AfL (Assessment for Learning) – Give students an examination question on this topic and three fictitious student answers. Students should work in small groups discussing the responses and put them in order according to the number of marks that they would give. Then using question and answer you could gain feedback from the whole class and reveal the positive and negative points of the answers. (15 minutes)

ACTIVITY & EXTENSION IDEAS

- Industrial Chemistry (from www.rsc.org) which includes the Haber process could be shown to remind students of the reaction.

Additional chemistry

CHEMISTRY — ENERGY AND REACTIONS

C2 5.3 More about the Haber process

LEARNING OBJECTIVES
1. Why do we use a temperature of 450°C for the Haber process?
2. Why do we use a pressure of about 200 atmospheres for the Haber process?

We saw on the previous page that the temperature at which we carry out a reversible reaction can affect the amount of the products formed at equilibrium. But if the reaction we are carrying out involves gases, pressure can be very important too.

Many reversible reactions which involve gases have more moles of gas on one side of the equation than on the other. By changing the pressure at which we carry out the reaction we can change the amount of products that we produce. Look at the table below:

If a reaction produces a larger volume of gases ……	If a reaction produces a smaller volume of gases ……
… an increase in pressure decreases the yield of the reaction, so the amount of products formed is lower.	… an increase in pressure increases the yield of the reaction, so the amount of products formed is larger.
… a decrease in pressure increases the yield of the reaction, so the amount of products formed is larger.	… a decrease in pressure decreases the yield of the reaction, so the amount of products formed is lower.

To see how this is useful we can look at the Haber process which we met earlier. (See pages 154 and 155.)

a) Look at the table above. How does increasing the pressure affect the amount of products formed in a reaction which produces a larger volume of gas?

The economics of the Haber process

The Haber process involves the reversible reaction between nitrogen and hydrogen to make ammonia:

$N_2 + 3H_2 \rightleftharpoons 2NH_3$ ($\rightleftharpoons$ is the equilibrium symbol)

Energy is released during this reaction, so it is exothermic. As the chemical equation shows, there are 4 moles of gas ($N_2 + 3H_2$) on the left-hand side of the equation. But on the right-hand side there are only 2 moles of gas ($2NH_3$). This means that the volume of the reactants is much greater than the volume of the products. So an increase in pressure will tend to produce more ammonia.

b) How does the volume of the products in the Haber process compare to the volume of the reactants?

To get the maximum possible yield of ammonia in the Haber process, we need to make the pressure as high as possible. But high pressures need expensive reaction vessels and pipes which are strong enough to withstand the pressure. Otherwise there is always the danger that an explosion may happen.

In the Haber process we have to make a compromise between using very high pressures (which would produce a lot of ammonia) and the expense of building a chemical plant which can withstand those high pressures. This compromise means that we usually carry out the Haber process at between 200 and 350 atmospheres pressure.

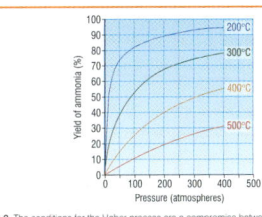

Figure 1 It is expensive to build chemical plants that operate at high pressures

Figure 2 The conditions for the Haber process are a compromise between getting the maximum amount of product in the equilibrium mixture and getting the reaction to take place at a reasonable rate

The effect of temperature on the Haber process is more complicated than the effect of pressure. The forward reaction is exothermic. So if we carry it out at low temperature this would increase the amount of ammonia in the reaction mixture at equilibrium.

But at a low temperature, the rate of the reaction would be very slow. That's because the particles would collide less often and would have less energy. To make ammonia commercially we must get the reaction to go as fast as possible. We don't want to have to wait for the ammonia to be produced!

To do this we need another compromise. A reasonably high temperature is used to get the reaction going at a reasonable rate, even though this reduces the amount of ammonia in the equilibrium mixture.

We also use an iron catalyst to speed up the reaction. (Since this affects the rate of reaction in both directions, it does not affect the amount of ammonia in the equilibrium mixture.)

SUMMARY QUESTIONS

1 Copy and complete using the words below:

  decreases   exothermic   fewer   increasing   left   pressure   released

  The Haber process is …… so energy is …… during the reaction. This means that …… the temperature …… the amount of ammonia formed. Increasing the …… will increase the amount of ammonia formed, because there are …… moles of gas on the right-hand side of the equation than on the ……-hand side.

2 Look at Figure 2.
  a) What is the approximate yield of ammonia at a temperature of 500°C and 400 atmospheres pressure?
  b) What is the approximate yield of ammonia at a temperature of 500°C and 100 atmospheres pressure?
  c) What is the approximate yield of ammonia at a temperature of 200°C and 400 atmospheres pressure?
  d) What is the approximate yield of ammonia at a temperature of 200°C and 100 atmospheres pressure?
  e) Why is the Haber process carried out at around 200 to 350 atmospheres and 450°C?

DID YOU KNOW?
The Haber process is really called the Haber–Bosch process, since Fritz Haber found out how to make ammonia from nitrogen and hydrogen but Carl Bosch carried out the work to find the best conditions for the reaction. Bosch carried out 6500 experiments to find the best catalyst for the reaction.

KEY POINTS
1 The Haber process uses a pressure of around 200 to 350 atmospheres to increase the amount of ammonia produced.
2 Although higher pressures would produce more ammonia, they would make the chemical plant too expensive to build.
3 A temperature of about 450°C is used for the reaction. Although lower temperatures would increase the amount of ammonia at equilibrium, the ammonia would be produced too slowly.

SUMMARY ANSWERS

1 Exothermic, released, increasing, decreases, pressure, fewer, left. **[HT only]**

2 a) 32%
  b) 10%
  c) 95%
  d) 82%
  e) This combines optimum conditions for rate of reaction, amount of ammonia at equilibrium and cost. **[HT only]**

Answers to in-text questions

a) It decreases the amount of product formed.
b) It is smaller.

KEY POINTS

Create a word search involving key words from this section. However, do not share the words with the students, they should refer to the key points section to decide on which words that they could find. For lower ability students the number of words to be found in the search could be given, along with their first letter.

CHEMISTRY | ENERGY AND REACTIONS

C2 5.4 Industrial dilemmas

SPECIFICATION LINK-UP
Unit: Chemistry 2.12.5

Students should use their skills, knowledge and understanding of 'How Science Works':

- to describe the effects of changing the conditions of temperature and pressure on a given reaction or process.
- to evaluate the conditions used in an industrial process in terms of energy requirements.

This spread can also be used to revisit the following substantive content already covered in this chapter:

- It is important for sustainable development as well as economic reasons to minimise energy requirements and energy wasted in industrial processes. Non-vigorous conditions means less energy is used and less is released into the environment.

CHEMISTRY | ENERGY AND REACTIONS

C2 5.4 Industrial dilemmas

How can we make as much chemical as possible...

ABC Laboratory Consultants
Haber House • Drudge Street • Anywhere • AD13 4FU

Dear Sirs

We are planning to build a factory to produce our new chemical, which has the secret formula AB. We are including some data sheets giving details of the reaction we shall be using to produce this chemical, and would like you to advise us about the best reaction conditions (temperature, pressure etc) to use to get as much AB as we can as cheaply as possible. We should like you to present your ideas in a short presentation to be held in your offices in two weeks' time.

Signed

BRIEFING SHEET 1

Project number: 45AB/L1670-J4550K
Specification: R MST3K 65 L7

Brief prepared by J K Rolling
Checked by L Skywalker

CHECKED

The equation for the reaction is:

$A_2B_2 \rightleftharpoons 2AB$

Both A_2B_2 and AB are gases. These are not their real formulae, which are secret. But the reaction does involve making two moles of product from one mole of reactants.

BRIEFING SHEET 2

Project number: 45AB/L1670-J4550K
Specification: R MST3K 65 L7

Brief prepared by J K Rolling
Checked by L Skywalker

CHECKED

The graph shows the amount of AB in the equilibrium mixture at different temperatures.

[Graph: % of AB at equilibrium (y-axis, 0–80) vs Temperature (°C) (x-axis, 0–400), showing a decreasing curve]

ACTIVITY

Working in teams, decide what you will advise Consolidated Chemicals to do about the conditions for the reaction. Prepare a presentation with your advice – the whole team should contribute to this. The following questions may help you:

- How does the amount of product change with temperature?
- How does the volume of the gases in the reaction change as AB is made from A_2B_2?
- What conditions may affect the reaction, and how?

Teaching suggestions

Activities

- **Presentation** – Split the class into groups of about five and ask all but one group to imagine that they are a group of chemical consultants. Their job is to use the brief set out in the Student Book to generate a proposal for what the chemical conditions should be for this reaction. Their proposal should include a bullet-pointed list to summarise their recommendations. Students could be encouraged to use a presentation package such as PowerPoint® to enhance their proposal. The remaining group should be told to imagine that they are the chemical company; they should write a list of what they are looking for from their contractors. This team could be encouraged to design a pro forma to help judge the presentations and come up with a list of questions that they could ask the groups. Their final job is to decide, with reasons, which group they would employ. Students could then give the presentations, while the company director group takes notes and gives at least one question to the group, which they must respond to. Finally the company director group could give feedback to each team and announce the winners of the contract. You may wish to give a prize for the winning team.

- **Report** – Students should work in small groups of about three. Their task is to consider whether or not it would be possible to go to other worlds and bring back resources for use on Earth. Students should be encouraged to brainstorm their ideas, maybe on a large piece of sugar paper. They could use secondary resources, such as the Internet and library books, for this task; a room swap to the library could be advantageous. Students should continue their discussions and research until they have a clear idea of whether it would be possible, and higher attaining students may like to predict which resources we could bring back from where and the timescale for this to occur. Each team could then compile a report on their work. Some students may struggle writing a report and it may be worth consulting with the English department to see if they have any help sheets to give guidance for this task.

Additional chemistry

... and what happens when the raw materials run out?!

SUPERMARKET

NO MORE TINNED FOOD IN STOCK

Due to the world shortage of metals our suppliers have told us that there will be no more deliveries of tinned food. Until further notice.

London today saw some of the worst rioting as people struggled to get their hands on the last deliveries to be made to the shops. The world shortage of minerals has really begun to bite now, with the supplies of raw materials like copper and zinc running low and prices going through the roof. As oil supplies dwindle too, the lights are going out all over London...

'What do we do when our resources run low?'

The world population grows all the time. It grows in its demands for a better lifestyle as well. Why shouldn't everyone have access to cars, computers and the latest electrical goodies? Yet all this growth means greater use of our natural resources – chemicals, minerals, oil. Minerals and metals don't replace themselves as carefully managed living resources do. So either we will have to find alternative materials, or alternative sources of the minerals we have been using...

'SPACE IS THE ANSWER!!'

The Bugle says 'get into space to find more minerals!!' It must be obvious even to our dim-witted leaders that we need to go and explore. Just as explorers in the past found new lands and new riches, we must go into space to find minerals on other planets! We can then bring them back to Earth so that we can make the things we need!'

ACTIVITY

There are many technical problems that have to be solved to allow us to travel to other planets in the Solar System. But imagine that they could be overcome. Could we really travel to other worlds to find new resources and bring them back to Earth?

Work in teams. You have been asked to produce a report for a government department about the possibility of using the Moon and nearby planets as a source of minerals. You need to consider not only the practical aspects of this but also the economics and the politics too. For example, in 1969 American astronauts landed on the Moon. So does this mean that the USA owns the Moon? Who will decide who owns the minerals on Mars or on the Moon?

Homework

Find out – The higher the pressure, the more product is formed in the Haber process. Show students images of pressure vessels used in the lab and by industry. Encourage students to find out the safety and cost implications of running a system under high pressure.

Extension

Find out – Ask students to find out about another industrial process and its reaction conditions (e.g. metal extractions or The Contact Process). Higher attaining students could be encouraged to explain the choice of these reaction conditions.

Learning styles

Visual: Creating the presentation on chemical conditions.

Auditory: Listening to presentations by other students.

Intrapersonal: Discovering the cost and safety implications of using pressure vessels.

Interpersonal: Working as small groups in the report writing or presentation activities.

Special needs

- Give these students a pack of cards with details about the AB reaction. The cards should include explanations for temperature and pressure changes, information about costs and safety. Students can then use these as prompts to create their presentation.
- A similar set of cards could be used with prompts about the exploitation of other worlds for their resources, or a part-finished spider diagram to help them form their ideas.

Gifted and talented

Split the class in half, one side is to argue that humans will exploit other planets' resources and the other will argue that they will not. Allow the students to research the facts and then hold a debate on the matter.

ICT link-up

Students could use a word-processing package to type up their report.

CHEMISTRY — ENERGY AND REACTIONS

SUMMARY ANSWERS

1 Lines drawn to link left-hand and right-hand columns as follows:
   a) B and C   b) A and D

2 [Students should describe a way in which the temperature change can be measured when known amounts of sherbet dissolve in water.]

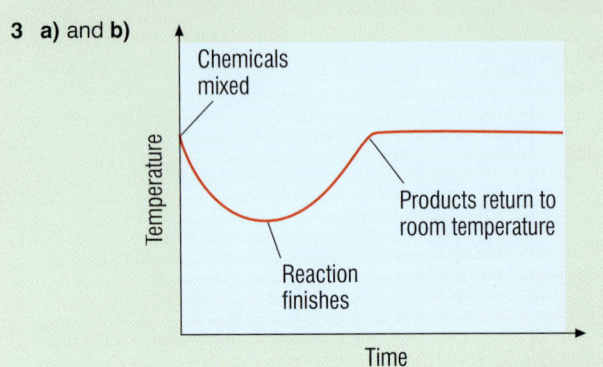

3 a) and b)

Graph: Temperature (y-axis) vs Time (x-axis). Labels: "Chemicals mixed", "Reaction finishes", "Products return to room temperature".

4 a) $X(g) + 2Y(g) \rightleftharpoons 3Z(g)$
   b) i) No change.
      ii) Increase.
   c) i) Decrease.
      ii) Increase.
   d) Better (because it would cost less) to get 10% of product in 25 seconds rather than waiting 3 times as long to get twice the amount of product. [HT only]

Summary teaching suggestions

- **Special needs** – Prepare a table with two columns – exothermic and endothermic. On a separate sheet of paper create a cut and paste activity using the statements from question 1. Students can then cut out the sentences and put them in the correct column of the table.

- **Learning styles**
  Visual: Question 2 involves the drawing of a diagram and question 3 involves the drawing of a graph.
  Auditory: Question 4 could be read out to students, and they note their answers on A4 whiteboards (or laminated paper) and hold them up to you for assessment.
  Interpersonal: Question 2 lends itself to a discussion before each student pens their own answer.

- **When to use the questions?**
  - As a revision resource.
  - Questions 1 and 4 could be turned into multiple-choice questions and displayed on slides. The answers could then be colour-coded, and each student could be given different coloured cards to correspond to the answers. Then you could refer to the question and the students hold up their cards to represent their answer.

ENERGY AND REACTIONS: C2 5.1 – C2 5.4

SUMMARY QUESTIONS

1 Select from A, B, C and/or D to describe correctly exothermic and endothermic reactions.
   a) In an exothermic reaction ……
   b) In an endothermic reaction ……
   A …… we may notice a decrease in temperature.
   B …… energy is released by the chemicals.
   C …… we may notice an increase in temperature.
   D …… energy is absorbed by the chemicals.

2 'When sherbet sweets dissolve in your mouth this is an endothermic process.' Devise an experiment to test your statement. Use words and diagrams to describe clearly what you would do.

3 Two chemicals are mixed and react endothermically. When the reaction has finished, the reaction mixture is allowed to stand until it has returned to its starting temperature.
   a) Sketch a graph of temperature (y-axis) v time (x-axis) to show how the temperature of the reaction mixture changes.
   b) Label the graph clearly and explain what is happening wherever you have shown the temperature changing.

4 A chemical reaction can make product Z from reactants X and Y. Under the reaction conditions, X, Y and Z are gases.
   X, Y and Z react in the proportions 1:2:3. The reaction is carried out at 250°C and 100 atmospheres. The reaction is reversible, and it is exothermic in the forward direction.
   a) Write an equation for this (reversible) reaction.
   b) How would increasing the pressure affect
      i) the amount of Z formed,
      ii) the rate at which Z is formed?
   c) How would increasing the temperature affect
      i) the amount of Z formed,
      ii) the rate at which Z is formed?
   d) A 10% yield of Z is obtained in 25 seconds under the reaction conditions. To get a 20% yield of Z under the same conditions takes 75 seconds. Explain why it makes more sense economically to set the reaction up to obtain a 10% yield rather than a 20% yield. [Higher]

EXAM-STYLE QUESTIONS

1 Match each of (a) to (g) with one of the following:
   endothermic reaction   exothermic reaction
                  no reaction
   (a) Burning petrol in a car engine.
   (b) Respiration in living cells.
   (c) Boiling water.
   (d) Converting limestone into calcium oxide.
   (e) Switching on an electric light bulb.
   (f) Reducing lead oxide with carbon to produce lead.
   (g) Carbon dioxide combining with water in cells of green plants. (7)

2 When heated continuously, pink cobalt chloride crystals can be changed into blue crystals.
   $$CoCl_2 \cdot 6H_2O \rightleftharpoons CoCl_2 \cdot 2H_2O + 4H_2O$$
   pink   blue
   (a) What does the symbol $\rightleftharpoons$ tell you about this reaction? (1)
   (b) How can you tell that the reaction to produce blue crystals is endothermic? (1)
   (c) i) How could you change the blue crystals to pink crystals? (1)
      ii) What temperature change would you observe when this is done? (1)
   (d) Suggest how the colour changes of these crystals could be used. (1)

3 The equation for the main reaction in the Haber process to make ammonia is:
   $$N_2 + 3H_2 \rightleftharpoons 2NH_3$$
   The table shows the percentage yield of the Haber process at different temperatures and pressures.

Pressure (atm)	Temp. (°C) 0	100	200	300	400	500
400	99	91	78	55	32	20
200	96	87	66	40	21	12
100	94	79	50	25	13	6
50	92	71	36	16	5	2

   (a) Why does the yield of ammonia decrease with increased temperature? (2)
   (b) Why does the yield of ammonia increase with increased pressure? (2)

EXAM-STYLE ANSWERS

1 a) Exothermic reaction. (1 mark)
   b) Exothermic reaction. (1 mark)
   c) No reaction. (1 mark)
   d) Endothermic reaction. (1 mark)
   e) No reaction. (1 mark)
   f) Exothermic reaction. (1 mark)
   g) Endothermic reaction. (1 mark)

2 a) It is reversible. (1 mark)
   b) It has to be heated continuously. (1 mark)
   c) i) Add water. (1 mark)
      ii) It would get hot/temperature rises. (1 mark)
   d) As a test for water. (1 mark)

3 a) Formation of ammonia is exothermic/forward reaction is exothermic. (1 mark)
   So increase in temperature favours reverse reaction/increase in temperature causes more ammonia to decompose. (1 mark)
   b) For forward reaction, 4 moles of gas produces 2 moles of gas. (1 mark)
   An increase in pressure favours reaction that produces smaller number of molecules of gas. (1 mark)
   c) These are compromise conditions (explained somewhere in answer). (1 mark)
   200 atm is as high as economically possible/higher pressure would need much stronger plant/need more energy/would be more dangerous. (1 mark)
   450°C is needed so that reaction is quite fast/so that catalyst works. (1 mark)
   d) Better as line graphs on the same axes. (1 mark)
   [HT only]

Additional chemistry

- The Haber process is used as an example again in this part of the specification, but questions will be set on other industrial processes that candidates are not expected to be familiar with. This will assess their understanding of the principles in this part of the specification and their ability to apply them in new situations (Assessment Objective 2).
- Q5 is based on concepts embedded in 'How Science Works'.

HOW SCIENCE WORKS ANSWERS

a) Graph drawn should be fully labelled, with units. The plots need to be correct and a line of best fit drawn. The temperature needs to be on the *x*-axis and time taken on the *y*-axis.

b) As the temperature increases, the time taken decreases. The reduction in time gets less as the temperature gets higher.

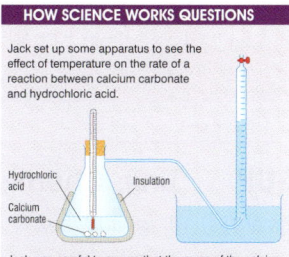

c) Jack controlled the mass of the calcium carbonate, the concentration and the volume of the hydrochloric acid.

d) Jack could not control the temperature change.

e) The changing temperature could be called a systematic error. It is related to the rate of the reaction, it being exothermic. Students might argue that it is a random error because it is not constant. The difference is not greatly important, but for able students might be worthy of discussion.

f) No because the pattern is difficult to detect.

g) It is not possible to judge the precision of results because there are no actual results shown, (he has only shown the average time taken) the variation of which would indicate precision.

h) Yes. There is no other data, e.g., from secondary sources to establish reliability. However the pattern shown looks convincing and fits in with accepted theory.

How science works teaching suggestions

- **Literacy guidance**
  - Key terms that should be clearly understood: control, error, precision, reliability.
  - Question h) expects a longer answer, where students can practise their literacy skills.
- **Higher- and lower-level answers.** Questions b), e), f), g) and h) are higher-level questions. The answers for these have been provided at this level. Question d) is lower level and the answer provided is also at this level.
- **Gifted and talented.** Able students could suggest how the variable temperature might be taken into account, for example in the plotting of the graph.
- **How and when to use these questions.** The questions could be used when wishing to develop graph-drawing skills or when an understanding of sensitivity, precision and reliability needs to be developed.
  The questions should be tackled for homework and reviewed in a class plenary.
- **Homework.** For lower-ability students, the graph might be drawn for homework.
- **Special needs.** For these students the axes of the graph could be drawn and labelled to get them started.

---

4 a) The catalyst. *(1 mark)*

b) Use heat from (exothermic) reaction to heat reactants/use heat produced elsewhere in the chemical plant, e.g. to make steam to drive pumps. *(1 mark)*

c) It uses less energy/uses smaller amounts of finite resources to produce energy. *(1 mark)*
Less energy is released into the environment. *(1 mark)*

5 a) Any reasonable suggestion – wrapped in cotton wool. *(1 mark)*

b) It is a variable she has not controlled. *(1 mark)*
OR she does not know if it is the heat in the acid that is raising the temperature. *(2 marks)*

c) No she measured the temperature of the two liquids. *(1 mark)*

d) She could have used the indicator to note when the reaction had finished. *(1 mark)*

Exam teaching suggestions

- Allow about 30 minutes for the four questions on this chapter, totalling 29 marks. Q1 and Q2 could be done after 5.2 and the other questions when the chapter has been completed. Q3 would appear only on a higher-tier paper.
- In Q1, students should be familiar with common examples of exothermic and endothermic reactions and should be able to differentiate physical changes from chemical reactions. Students could be encouraged to suggest and classify other everyday changes, perhaps in the form of a 'day in my life' sequence, listing things that happen from getting up in the morning until going to bed at night.
- Some students find questions on reversible reactions difficult, or avoid them in exams because they look complicated. Familiarity and consistent logic help students to understand what happens in these reactions. Simulations can be helpful for many students, especially when considering the effects of changes in conditions.

CHEMISTRY   ELECTROLYSIS

C2 6.1 Electrolysis – the basics

LEARNING OBJECTIVES

Students should learn:

- That ionic compounds can undergo electrolysis.
- Which substances can be electrolysed.
- The products of electrolysis.

LEARNING OUTCOMES

Most students should be able to:

- State a definition for electrolysis.
- Recognise which compounds will undergo electrolysis.
- Add state symbols to an equation.
- Predict the products of molten electrolysis.

Some students should also be able to:

- Explain how electrolysis occurs.

Teaching suggestions

- **Special needs.** Give the students the parts of the flow chart for the decomposition of lead bromide, but in the wrong order. These students can then cut them up and stick them into their own diagram in their notes.
- **Learning styles**
  Kinaesthetic: Completing the electrolysis practical.
  Visual: Drawing a labelled diagram of the electrolysis equipment.
  Auditory: Listening to explanations of different words.
  Intrapersonal: Defining key words.
  Interpersonal: Working in pairs to note information about chemicals.
- **Homework.** Ask students to find out two different materials that can be used to make electrodes and then give examples of a use for each electrode material.
- **ICT link-up.** Often it is difficult for students to see a demonstration in a fume cupboard. If the reaction can be filmed beforehand it could be shown to students. Alternatively set up flexicam or a camcorder connected to a TV or digital projector to show the demonstration magnified in real time.

SPECIFICATION LINK-UP   Unit: Chemistry 2.12.6

- *The state symbols in equations are (s), (l), (g) and (aq).*
- *When an ionic substance is melted or dissolved in water, the ions are free to move about within the liquid or solution.*
- *Passing an electric current through ionic substances that are molten or in solution breaks them down into elements. This process is called electrolysis.*
- *During electrolysis, positively charged ions move to the negative electrode, and negatively charged ions move to the positive electrode.*

Lesson structure

STARTER

Anagram – As a title write: 'cysistrollee'. Explain to the students that they are going to study this topic, but the letters are jumbled up. Encourage them to find out the word [electrolysis] and write this as the title, followed by a brief definition [splitting-up a compound using electricity]. (10 minutes)

Observations – In sealed containers show the students an ampoule of bromine, a sample of lead and lead bromide. In pairs, ask students to make a list about everything that they know about these chemicals and encourage them to use the periodic table and list the mass etc. Draw a three-column table on the board, each headed with the different chemical and ask groups for pieces of information to fill in the table. Then ask the students how lead and bromine could be made from lead bromide. (10 minutes)

MAIN

- A classic demonstration of electrolysis involved the decomposition of lead bromide. This is chosen, as it is an ionic solid with a relatively low melting point. The reaction does produce lead and bromine and therefore should be completed in a fume cupboard. Demonstrate the experiment and use questions and answers to extract observations from the students. Then ask them to draw a diagrammatic flow chart, including a symbol equation to represent the demonstration.
- Students could complete their own electrolysis experiment, however this cannot be completed for a molten liquid, a solution must be used. To prevent any confusion due to water producing oxygen or hydrogen, copper chloride solution should be used. Students could be given a set of questions to consider as they complete the reaction to channel their thoughts.
- Use Simulation C2 6.1 'Electrolysis' from the GCSE Chemistry CD ROM.

PLENARIES

Taboo – Create a set of cards with the key words: 'electricity', 'electrolysis', 'electrolyte', 'electrode', 'decompose'. Below each key word list three further words that would aid in explaining the main word. Give the pack of cards to groups of three. Each person should take it in turns to pick a card and try to explain the main word, without using the taboo words. The person who managed to explain the most words (without using any taboo words) is the winner. (10 minutes)

Definitions – Ask students to define the key words: 'electrolysis', 'electrolyte', 'decompose', 'anode', 'cathode', 'electrode' in their books. Higher attaining students could define the term, then use it correctly in a sentence. (10 minutes)

Diagram – Ask students to draw a labelled diagram of the equipment needed to complete a simple electrolysis. (5 minutes)

Answers to in-text questions

a) Using an electric current to break down a substance.
b) Electrolyte.   **c)** Negative electrode (Cathode).   **d)** Positive electrode (Anode).

Additional chemistry

Practical support

Demonstration of the electrolysis of lead bromide

Equipment and materials required
Ceramic evaporating basin, lead bromide (toxic – CLEAPSS Hazcard 57), spatula, tongs, Bunsen burner and safety equipment, tongs, two carbon electrodes, lamp, three wires, two crocodile clips, lab pack, fume cupboard, tripod, pipe-clay triangle, eye protection, protective gloves.

Details
Half-fill the evaporation basin with lead bromide and submerge the ends of the electrodes. Connect the electrodes into the circuit involving the lamp and the lab pack. Put the evaporation basin on the pipe-clay triangle above the Bunsen burner. Ignite the Bunsen burner and heat the lead bromide strongly, turn on the lab pack and observe. Once the lamp is on, the electricity is flowing, this will only occur when the ions are free to move, i.e. the lead bromide is molten. Point out the vapour (bromine is toxic – CLEAPSS Hazcard 15). The reaction is heated so the halogen is released as a gas not as a liquid, which is its state at room temperature. The molten lead will collect at the bottom of the basin. Switch off the Bunsen and use the tongs to tip the molten lead onto the flame-proof mat to show the students.

Safety: Eye protection should be worn during this demonstration and it should be completed in a fume cupboard. Pregnant women should not use lead bromide. Anhydrous zinc chloride (corrosive – CLEAPSS Hazcard 108) melts at a lower temperature than lead bromide so can be used as an alternative.

Electrolysis of copper chloride solution

Equipment and materials required
Beaker, two carbon electrodes, lamp, three wires, two crocodile clips, lab pack, 1 M copper chloride solution (harmful – CLEAPSS Hazcard 27), eye protection.

Details
Half-fill the beaker with copper chloride solution and immerse the tips of the electrodes. Connect the electrodes in a simple circuit with the lab pack and lamp. Start the current and observe, chlorine (toxic) should be smelt at the anode, and copper should be deposited at the cathode. As soon as the observations are complete the lab pack should be switched off.

Safety: Eye protection should be worn throughout the practical. This experiment should be completed in a well-ventilated room as the chlorine could irritate asthmatics.

ACTIVITY & EXTENSION IDEAS

- Show students a simulation of the reaction detailing the particles.
- Students could complete electrolysis of other halides that involve a metal below hydrogen in the reactivity series, e.g. zinc chloride. By using this select group of compounds, students do not need to use the table of discharge to determine the products. The experiment is identical to that for copper chloride, as detailed in 'Practical support'.

SUMMARY ANSWERS

1 Anode, cathode, negative, ions, move, solution, molten.

2 a) Copper at −; iodine at +.
  b) Potassium at −; bromine at +.
  c) Sodium at −; fluorine at +.

3 [Words/diagrams explain how ions carry charge.] If ions are not free to move (as they are not in a solid because they are held in position by strong electrostatic forces) no current can flow in the circuit.

KEY POINTS

Ask students to copy out the objectives with the key point that best answers the question alongside it.

CHEMISTRY | ELECTROLYSIS

C2 6.1 Electrolysis – the basics

LEARNING OBJECTIVES
1 What is electrolysis?
2 What types of substances can we electrolyse?
3 What is made when we electrolyse substances?

The word electrolysis means 'splitting up using electricity'. In electrolysis we use an electric current to break down (or **decompose**) a substance made of ions into simpler substances. We call the substance broken down by electrolysis the **electrolyte**.

a) What is electrolysis?
b) What do we call the substance broken down by electrolysis?

We set up an electrical circuit for electrolysis that has two electrodes which dip into the electrolyte. The electrodes are conducting rods. One of these is connected to the positive terminal of a power supply, the other is connected to the negative terminal.

We normally make the electrodes out of an unreactive (or **inert**) substance like graphite or platinum. This is so they do not react with either the electrolyte or the products made during electrolysis. We use the name **anode** for positive electrode, while we call the negative electrode the **cathode**.

During electrolysis, positively charged ions move to the negative electrode (cathode) and negative ions move to the positive electrode (anode).

When the ions reach the electrodes they can lose their charge and be deposited as elements. Depending on the compound being electrolysed, gases may be given off or metals deposited at the electrodes.

Figure 1 The first person to explain electrolysis was Michael Faraday, who worked on this and many other problems in science nearly 200 years ago. His work formed the basis of an understanding of electrolysis that we still use today.

DEMONSTRATION
The electrolysis of lead bromide
This demonstration needs a fume cupboard because bromine is toxic and corrosive.

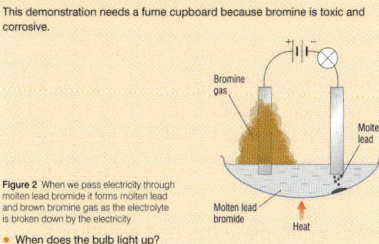

Figure 2 When we pass electricity through molten lead bromide it forms molten lead and brown bromine gas as the electrolyte is broken down by the electricity
- When does the bulb light up?

Figure 2 shows how electricity breaks down lead bromide into lead and bromine:

lead bromide → lead + bromine
$PbBr_2(l) → Pb(l) + Br_2(g)$

Lead bromide is an ionic substance which does not conduct electricity when it is solid. But when we melt it the ions can move freely towards the electrodes.

The positive lead ions move towards the cathode, while the negatively charged bromide ions move towards the anode. Notice how the state symbols in the equation tell us that the lead bromide and the lead are molten. The '(l)' stands for 'liquid', while bromine is given off as a gas, shown as '(g)'.

c) Which electrode do positive ions move towards during electrolysis?
d) Which electrode do negative ions move towards during electrolysis?

Many ionic substances have very high melting points. This can make electrolysis very difficult or even impossible. But some ionic substances dissolve in water, and when this happens the ions can move freely.

When we dissolve ionic substances in water to electrolyse them it is more difficult to predict what will be formed. This is because water also forms ions, and so the product at the anode and the cathode is not always exactly what we expect.

When we electrolyse a solution of copper bromide in water, copper ions move to the negative electrode (cathode) and the bromide ions move to the positive electrode (anode). Copper bromide is split into its two elements at the electrodes:

copper bromide → copper + bromine
$CuBr_2(aq) → Cu(s) + Br_2(aq)$

In this case the state symbols in the equation tell us that the copper bromide is dissolved in water, shown as '(aq)'. The elements that are produced are solid copper, shown as '(s)', and bromine which remains dissolved in the water – '(aq)'.

Covalent compounds cannot be split by electrolysis.

SUMMARY QUESTIONS

1 Copy and complete using the words below:

anode   cathode   ions   molten   move
       negative   solution

In electrolysis the ...... is the positive electrode while the ...... is the ...... electrode. For the current to flow, the ...... must be able to ...... between the electrodes. This can only happen if the substance is in ...... or it is ....

2 Predict the products formed at each electrode when the following compounds are melted and then electrolysed:
a) copper iodide
b) potassium bromide
c) sodium fluoride.

3 Solid ionic substances do not conduct electricity. Using words and diagrams explain why they conduct electricity when molten or in solution.

FOUL FACTS
Electrolysis is also a way of getting rid of unwanted body hair. A small electric current is passed through the base of each individual hair to be removed. The hair is destroyed by chemical changes caused by the electric current which destroy the cells that make the hair grow.

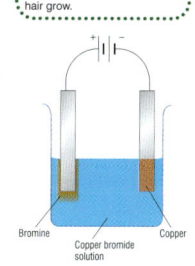

Figure 3 If we dissolve copper bromide in water we can decompose it by electrolysis. Copper metal is formed at the cathode, while brown bromine appears in solution around the anode.

KEY POINTS
1 Electrolysis involves splitting up a substance using electricity.
2 Ionic substances can be electrolysed when they are molten or in solution.
3 In electrolysis positive ions move to the negative electrode (cathode) and negative ions move to the positive electrode (anode).

CHEMISTRY   ELECTROLYSIS

C2 6.2 Changes at the electrodes

LEARNING OBJECTIVES

Students should learn:

- That electrons are transferred during electrolysis.
- That electrolysis can be represented in half equations. [**HT** only]
- That water affects electrolysis.

LEARNING OUTCOMES

Most students should be able to:

- Recall the transfer of electrons at the anode and cathode.
- Recognise oxidation and reduction at electrodes.
- Predict the products of electrolysis.

Some students should also be able to:

- Explain the transfer of electrons in electrolysis.
- Construct half equations. [**HT** only]
- Explain how water affects the products of electrolysis.

Teaching suggestions

- **Learning styles**

  Kinaesthetic: Completing a card sort activity.

  Visual: Annotating the digital photograph of the electrolysis play.

  Auditory: Listening to questions and answers to guess a key word.

  Intrapersonal: Completing half equations.

  Interpersonal: Working as a class to act out the particle movement in electrolysis.

- **Homework.** Ask students to complete the following symbol equation and half equations:
  $2FeCl_3(aq) \rightarrow [2Fe(s)] + [3Cl_2(g)]$
  Anode: $[2Cl^-(aq)] \rightarrow Cl_2(g) + 2e^-$
  Cathode: $[Fe^{3+}(aq) + 3e^-] \rightarrow Fe(s)$

- **ICT link-up.** Digital photographs could be taken of the electrolysis play. These could then be used in the classroom to remind students of the play. If a photograph is displayed on an interactive whiteboard, then annotations could be added in front of the class.

SPECIFICATION LINK-UP   Unit: Chemistry 2.12.6

- At the negative electrode positively charged ions gain electrons (reduction) and at the positive electrode negatively charged ions lose electrons (oxidation).
- If there is a mixture of ions, the products formed depend on the reactivity of the elements involved.
- Reactions at electrodes can be represented by half equations, for example:

$$2Cl^- \rightarrow Cl_2 + 2e^-$$ [**HT** only]

Students should use their skills, knowledge and understanding of 'How Science Works':

- to predict the products of electrolysing solutions of ions.
- to complete and balance supplied half equations for the reactions occurring at the electrodes during electrolysis. [**HT** only]

Lesson structure

STARTER

Card sort – Give the key words (oxidation, reduction and redox) and their definitions on separate cards. Students should sort the cards to match the key words with their definitions. (5 minutes)

Poem – Encourage the students to create a little poem or saying to help them remember that oxidation is the loss of electrons and happens at the anode, meanwhile reduction is the gain of electrons and occurs at the cathode. To help students, direct their attention to the 'Get it right section' of the Student Book. Encourage a few students to read out their work. The best one could then be copied by all the students into their notes. (15 minutes)

MAIN

- Show the students a sample of potassium chloride and ask them to predict the products of the reaction if the compound was molten. Encourage a student to write the balanced symbol equation on the board.

- Now ask pairs of students to predict the products if a solution of potassium chloride were electrolysed. Ask each group their thoughts and why they came to this idea. Then allow the students to complete the experiment to find out it they were correct. Encourage students to note their work in the form of a fully labelled diagram, including half equations and brief notes to explain where the hydrogen comes from. (Note that half equations are Higher Tier content.)

- Students could act out an electrolysis experiment. They could wear black bibs and make a line to represent the electrodes and wires in the circuit. Polystyrene balls could be used as electrons, two students could stand by a bucket of balls – one student giving them out and one putting them into the bucket (this represents the power source). Different coloured bibs (blue – cations, red – anions) could be used to create the solution. The circuit could then 'run' under your instructions. Students could then use the play to describe what happens in terms of particles at the anode and cathode.

PLENARIES

What am I? – On sticky labels write the following words: 'redox', 'reduction', 'oxidation', 'reduced', 'oxidised', 'half equation'. Split the students into teams of six and give each a word and ask them to stick it on their forehead (but they should not know what their word is). Each student then takes it in turns to ask his or her group questions, which the team can only respond with 'yes' or 'no'. The aim is for each student to guess their word. (10 minutes)

Half equations – Ask students to complete the half equations as detailed in question 2 of the summary questions. Then encourage the students to create three more examples of half equations of their choice. [**HT** only] (10 minutes)

Practical support
Electrolysis of potassium chloride
Equipment and materials required
Beaker, two carbon electrodes, lamp, three wires, two crocodile clips, lab pack, saturated solution of potassium chloride, test tube, splint, eye protection.

Details
Half-fill the beaker with potassium chloride solution and immerse the tips of the electrodes. Connect the electrodes in a simple circuit with the lab pack and lamp. Start the current and observe, chlorine (toxic – CLEAPSS Hazcard 22) should be smelt at the anode, and bubbles (hydrogen – flammable – CLEAPSS Hazcard 48) should be observed at the cathode. As soon as the observations are complete the lab pack should be switched off. The hydrogen could be collected in a test tube under displacement, and tested with a lighted splint.

Safety: Eye protection should be worn throughout the practical. This experiment should be completed in a well-ventilated room as the chlorine could irritate asthmatics.

ACTIVITY & EXTENSION IDEAS
Use Simulation C2 6.1 from the GCSE Chemistry CD ROM which shows particle movement in electrolysis.

Answers to in-text questions
a) Electron(s) are transferred from the ion to the electrode.

b) Electron(s) are transferred to the ion from the electrode.

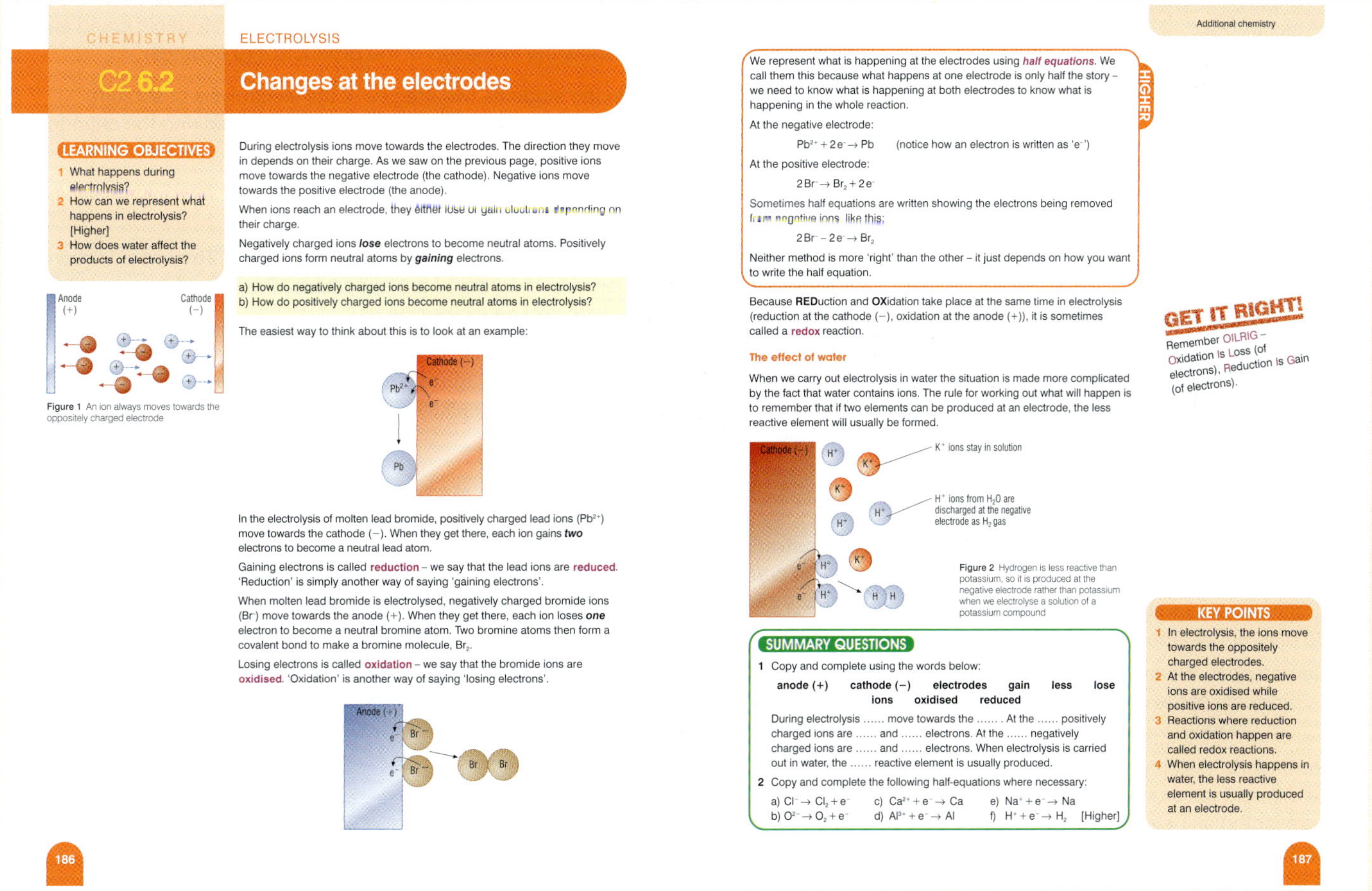

CHEMISTRY
C2 6.2 ELECTROLYSIS
Changes at the electrodes

LEARNING OBJECTIVES
1. What happens during electrolysis?
2. How can we represent what happens in electrolysis? [Higher]
3. How does water affect the products of electrolysis?

During electrolysis ions move towards the electrodes. The direction they move in depends on their charge. As we saw on the previous page, positive ions move towards the negative electrode (the cathode). Negative ions move towards the positive electrode (the anode).

When ions reach an electrode, they either lose or gain electrons, depending on their charge.

Negatively charged ions **lose** electrons to become neutral atoms. Positively charged ions form neutral atoms by **gaining** electrons.

a) How do negatively charged ions become neutral atoms in electrolysis?
b) How do positively charged ions become neutral atoms in electrolysis?

The easiest way to think about this is to look at an example:

Figure 1 An ion always moves towards the oppositely charged electrode

In the electrolysis of molten lead bromide, positively charged lead ions (Pb^{2+}) move towards the cathode (−). When they get there, each ion gains **two** electrons to become a neutral lead atom.

Gaining electrons is called **reduction** – we say that the lead ions are **reduced**. 'Reduction' is simply another way of saying 'gaining electrons'.

When molten lead bromide is electrolysed, negatively charged bromide ions (Br^-) move towards the anode (+). When they get there, each ion loses **one** electron to become a neutral bromine atom. Two bromine atoms then form a covalent bond to make a bromine molecule, Br_2.

Losing electrons is called **oxidation** – we say that the bromide ions are **oxidised**. 'Oxidation' is another way of saying 'losing electrons'.

We represent what is happening at the electrodes using *half equations*. We call them this because what happens at one electrode is only half the story – we need to know what is happening at both electrodes to know what is happening in the whole reaction.

At the negative electrode:
$$Pb^{2+} + 2e^- \rightarrow Pb$$ (notice how an electron is written as 'e⁻')

At the positive electrode:
$$2Br^- \rightarrow Br_2 + 2e^-$$

Sometimes half equations are written showing the electrons being removed from negative ions, like this:
$$2Br^- - 2e^- \rightarrow Br_2$$

Neither method is more 'right' than the other – it just depends on how you want to write the half equation.

Because **RED**uction and **OX**idation take place at the same time in electrolysis (reduction at the cathode (−), oxidation at the anode (+)), it is sometimes called a **redox** reaction.

The effect of water
When we carry out electrolysis in water the situation is made more complicated by the fact that water contains ions. The rule for working out what will happen is to remember that if two elements can be produced at an electrode, the less reactive element will usually be formed.

- K^+ ions stay in solution
- H^+ ions from H_2O are discharged at the negative electrode as H_2 gas

Figure 2 Hydrogen is less reactive than potassium, so it is produced at the negative electrode rather than potassium when we electrolyse a solution of a potassium compound

GET IT RIGHT!
Remember OILRIG – Oxidation Is Loss (of electrons), Reduction Is Gain (of electrons).

SUMMARY QUESTIONS
1 Copy and complete using the words below:

   anode (+)   cathode (−)   electrodes   gain   less   lose
   ions   oxidised   reduced

During electrolysis …… move towards the ……. At the …… positively charged ions are …… and …… electrons. At the …… negatively charged ions are …… and …… electrons. When electrolysis is carried out in water, the …… reactive element is usually produced.

2 Copy and complete the following half-equations where necessary:
a) $Cl^- \rightarrow Cl_2 + e^-$ c) $Ca^{2+} + e^- \rightarrow Ca$ e) $Na^+ + e^- \rightarrow Na$
b) $O^{2-} \rightarrow O_2 + e^-$ d) $Al^{3+} + e^- \rightarrow Al$ f) $H^+ + e^- \rightarrow H_2$ [Higher]

KEY POINTS
1. In electrolysis, the ions move towards the oppositely charged electrodes.
2. At the electrodes, negative ions are oxidised while positive ions are reduced.
3. Reactions where reduction and oxidation happen are called redox reactions.
4. When electrolysis happens in water, the less reactive element is usually produced at an electrode.

SUMMARY ANSWERS
1 Ions, electrodes, cathode (−), reduced, gain, anode (+), oxidised, lose, less.

2 a) $2Cl^- \rightarrow Cl_2 + 2e^-$
   b) $2O^{2-} \rightarrow O_2 + 4e^-$
   c) $Ca^{2+} + 2e^- \rightarrow Ca$
   d) $Al^{3+} + 3e^- \rightarrow Al$
   e) $Na^+ + e^- \rightarrow Na$
   f) $2H^+ + 2e^- \rightarrow H_2$ [**HT** only]

KEY POINTS
Ask students to copy the key points and to write any word that has a positive charge in red (e.g. oxidation, positive, anode,) and any with a negative charge in blue.

CHEMISTRY | ELECTROLYSIS

C2 6.3 Electrolysing brine

LEARNING OBJECTIVES

Students should learn:
- That brine can be electrolysed.
- The uses of the products of the electrolysis of brine.

LEARNING OUTCOMES

Most students should be able to:
- Recall the products of the electrolysis of brine.
- List some uses of the products of the electrolysis of brine.

Some students should also be able to:
- Explain how brine can be electrolysed.
- Generate half equations for the electrolysis of brine. [HT only]

Teaching suggestions

- **Gifted and talented.** The Solvay process uses sodium chloride. Students could research the industrial production of sodium carbonate and sodium hydrogencarbonate using this method.
- **Learning styles**
  Kinaesthetic: Completing the electrolysis of sodium chloride practical.
  Visual: Writing and assembling a magazine article.
  Auditory: Listening to uses of the products of electrolysis of brine, then deciding which product it refers to.
  Intrapersonal: Spotting the difference in two different pictures.
  Interpersonal: Working in pairs to predict the products of the electrolysis of sodium chloride.
- **Homework.** Ask the students to find out the different uses of chlorine in the UK, represented as percentages. Then ask the students to display the information as a pie chart. For lower ability students, the data could be given and they could plot a bar chart.
- **ICT link-up.** Students could use desktop publishing packages to produce their article. They could be encouraged to use photographs of the industrial processes using the Internet, or they could use a digital camera to take images in the lab to be used in their article.

SPECIFICATION LINK-UP Unit: Chemistry 2.12.6

- The state symbols in equations are (s), (l), (g) and (aq).
- The electrolysis of sodium chloride solution produces hydrogen and chlorine. Sodium hydroxide solution is also produced. These are important reagents for the chemical industry.

Students should use their skills, knowledge and understanding of 'How Science Works':
- to predict the products of electrolysing solutions of ions.
- to explain and evaluate processes that use the principles described in this unit.
- to complete and balance supplied half equations for the reactions occurring at the electrodes during electrolysis. [HT only]

Lesson structure

STARTER

Predict – Ask students to work in pairs to predict the products of electrolysis of molten sodium chloride and a solution of sodium chloride. Higher attaining students could also complete half equations to show the formation of the products. (10 minutes)

Spot the difference – Show the students two images of the electrolysis of sodium chloride solution from the GCSE Chemistry CD ROM. Students should ring the changes in the second picture, e.g. labels missing/incorrect. (5 minutes)

MAIN

- Students can complete their own electrolysis of sodium chloride. They could record their observations in a colourful diagram of the apparatus. They could also annotate the formation of the products and detail their uses.
- Show students different popular science magazines, from *New Scientist* to *Horrible Science*. Ask the students to write a magazine article for a popular science magazine to explain the importance of the chloro-alkali industry (search for 'electrolysis of salt' or 'chloro-alkali').

PLENARIES

Demonstration – Show the electrolysis of sodium chloride solution in a Petri dish. This could be completed on an OHP and the colours of the universal indicator solution can be clearly seen. Take care not to spill solution into OHP. Ask the students to explain the observations. (10 minutes)

Uses – Give the students separate cards with the words 'hydrogen', 'chlorine' and 'sodium hydroxide' printed on. Read out the following uses of the products of electrolysis of sodium chloride solution, students should then hold up the card to show which product is used for that specific use:

- Margarine [hydrogen]
- PVC [chlorine]
- Bleach [sodium hydroxide, chlorine]
- Soap [sodium hydroxide]
- Paper [chlorine, sodium hydroxide]
- Rayon fibres [sodium hydroxide]
- Detergents [sodium hydroxide, chlorine]
- Purification of aluminium ore [sodium hydroxide]
- Hydrochloric acid manufacture [chlorine, hydrogen] (10 minutes)

Additional chemistry

Practical support

Electrolysing brine in the lab

Equipment and materials required
Beaker or electrolysis cell, saturated sodium chloride solution, two carbon electrodes, two crocodile clips, two wires, lab pack, litmus paper, water, 2 test tubes, splint, matches, gloves, eye protection.

Details
Half-fill the beaker with the sodium chloride solution and submerge one end of the carbon electrodes. Using the wires and crocodile clips, connect to the lab pack. Wearing gloves, fill the test-tube with the solution and hold, inverted with the neck in the solution over the cathode (the carbon electrode attached to the black terminal of the lab pack). Put on eye protection and start the electrolysis. Once the test-tube is full of gas, put a gloved finger to seal the tube, and remove from the water, test the gas with a lighted splint (a pop should be heard). While the gas is being collected, using a damp piece of litmus paper, test the gas at the anode. Hold the litmus paper over the anode and observe.

Safety: This practical produces chlorine gas (CLEAPSS Hazcard 22 – could irritate asthmatics) and should only be completed in a well-ventilated area, and once the products have been tested the equipment should be switched off. The solution produces sodium hydroxide and this is why gloves should be worn to collect the gas by displacement.

ACTIVITY & EXTENSION IDEAS

- Show students the industrial electrolysis of brine using a video, e.g. RSC *Industrial Chemistry*.
- Electrolysis of brine occurs in two main ways: membrane cell, and mercury cathode cell. Students could research these methods using the Internet.
- Students could complete the electrolysis of sodium chloride in a beaker and collect the gas produced at the cathode under displacement. This gas could be tested with a lighted split. A damp piece of litmus paper can be used to test the gas at the anode. See 'Practical support'.

SUMMARY ANSWERS

1 Hydrogen (chlorine), chlorine (hydrogen), sodium hydroxide, sodium chlorate(I), hydrochloric.

2 **a)** $2NaCl(aq) + 2H_2O(l) \rightarrow 2NaOH(aq) + Cl_2(g) + H_2(g)$ **[HT only]**

b) Sodium is formed at the negative electrode with molten sodium chloride whereas hydrogen is formed there with sodium chloride solution. We also get sodium hydroxide solution formed when we electrolyse the solution.

Answers to in-text questions

a) Chlorine, hydrogen, sodium hydroxide solution.

b) Water treatment, making bleach, making plastics (PVC).

c) Hardening vegetable oils, making hydrochloric acid.

d) Making soap and paper, making bleach (with chlorine), pH control.

KEY POINTS

Give students a diagram of the electrolysis of brine. They should then annotate their diagram so that it contains all the information from the key points.

CHEMISTRY | ELECTROLYSIS

C2 6.4 Purifying copper

LEARNING OBJECTIVES

Students should learn that:
- Copper needs to be purified.
- Electrolysis is used to purify copper.

LEARNING OUTCOMES

Most students should be able to:
- State how copper is purified using electrolysis.

Some students should also be able to:
- Explain what happens at the electrodes during purification of copper.
- Construct the half equations for the purification of copper. [HT only]

Teaching suggestions

- **Special needs.** Students could be given the labels to cut and stick onto their diagram of the electrolysis of copper.
- **Learning styles**
  Kinaesthetic: Completing the purification of copper activity.
  Visual: Creating a poster to contrast the observations from the experiment.
  Auditory: Listening to predictions of products from each group.
  Intrapersonal: Assessing other students' work.
  Interpersonal: Working in pairs to generate a labelled diagram of copper purification.
- **Homework.** Ask students to use the AfL (Assessment for Learning) feedback to make any corrections to their work.

SPECIFICATION LINK-UP Unit: Chemistry 2.12.6

- The state symbols in equations are (s), (l), (g) and (aq).
- Copper can be purified by electrolysis using a positive electrode made of impure copper and a negative electrode of pure copper in a solution containing copper ions.

Students should use their skills, knowledge and understanding of 'How Science Works':
- to predict the products of electrolysing solutions of ions.
- to explain and evaluate processes that use the principles described in this unit.
- to complete and balance supplied half equations for the reactions occurring at the electrodes during electrolysis. [HT only]

Lesson structure

STARTER

Connections – Show the students three photographs of copper-containing objects (search the Internet for water pipes, an electrical circuit and a copper roof). Ask the students to consider what all the pictures have in common. Then feedback to the class with questions and answers. (5–10 minutes)

Prediction – Students could predict the products of electrolysis of copper sulfate if:
- Graphite electrodes are used. [Copper and oxygen]
- Copper electrodes are used. [Copper and copper ions]

Ask students to talk in small groups about their predictions and then encourage each group to feedback to the whole class, in order to generate a whole class prediction. To extend students further, ask them to attempt to write half equations for each electrode. (10 minutes)

MAIN

- Supply students with the parts of a diagram of the electrolysis of copper for purification. They should assemble the full diagram from the pieces and then label the image, including explanations to explain how copper is purified in this process.
- Students can complete their own purification of copper, in order to compare active and inert electrodes; encourage the students to work in pairs. One student will complete the electrolysis with carbon electrodes, meanwhile the second student could complete the electrolysis with copper electrodes. Once the practical is up and running, the pair can make observations and comments together. Students could be given an A4 sheet of paper, which they could fold in half (landscape). On each side they should draw a labelled diagram of the apparatus (one with carbon electrodes and one with copper electrodes). Then they need to explain the observations at each electrode (including half equations for students taking the Higher Tier paper).
- Students could be encouraged to draw how copper is purified in a cartoon-strip style. To guide students, ask them to use the key words, e.g. electrolysis, electrode, electron, sludge, at least once. More artistic students may wish to personify the ions and electrons to make the cartoon more amusing.
- Use Simulation C2 6.4 'Purifying copper' from the GCSE Chemistry CD ROM.
- The electrolysis of copper sulfate solution provides a good opportunity to develop investigative aspects of 'How Science Works'. For example, students could investigate the factors that might affect the rate of electrolysis.

PLENARIES

I went to the shops... – Sit the students in a circle, the first student says 'I went to the shops to buy...' (insert a copper object here). The next student repeats the first and adds another copper-containing item onto their list. This continues around the circle. (5 minutes)

AfL (Assessment for Learning) – Lay the cartoons on the side bench of the room, with an A4 sheet of paper at one side. Ask each student to study all the cartoon strips and comment on the scientific accuracy of the work, by noting their thoughts on the paper. (10–15 minutes)

Practical support

Comparing electrodes

Equipment and materials required
Two beakers, 1 M copper sulfate solution (harmful), two carbon electrodes, two copper electrodes, six wires, two lab packs, four crocodile clips, eye protection.

Details
Wear eye protection throughout this practical. Half-fill each beaker with copper sulfate solution. Add the electrodes to each beaker, ensuring that one end is submerged into the liquid, while the other is free of the solution. The two carbon electrodes should be added to the first beaker and, using the wires and crocodile clips, connected to the lab pack. Meanwhile, add the two copper electrodes to the second beaker and connect to the second lab pack.

Safety: Copper sulfate is harmful – CLEAPSS Hazcard 27.

ACTIVITY & EXTENSION IDEAS

- Students could research into the use of electrolysis to plate other metals (electroplating) or colouring aluminium using anodising.
- Students could watch a video on industrial copper refining, e.g. *Industrial Chemistry* from RSC.

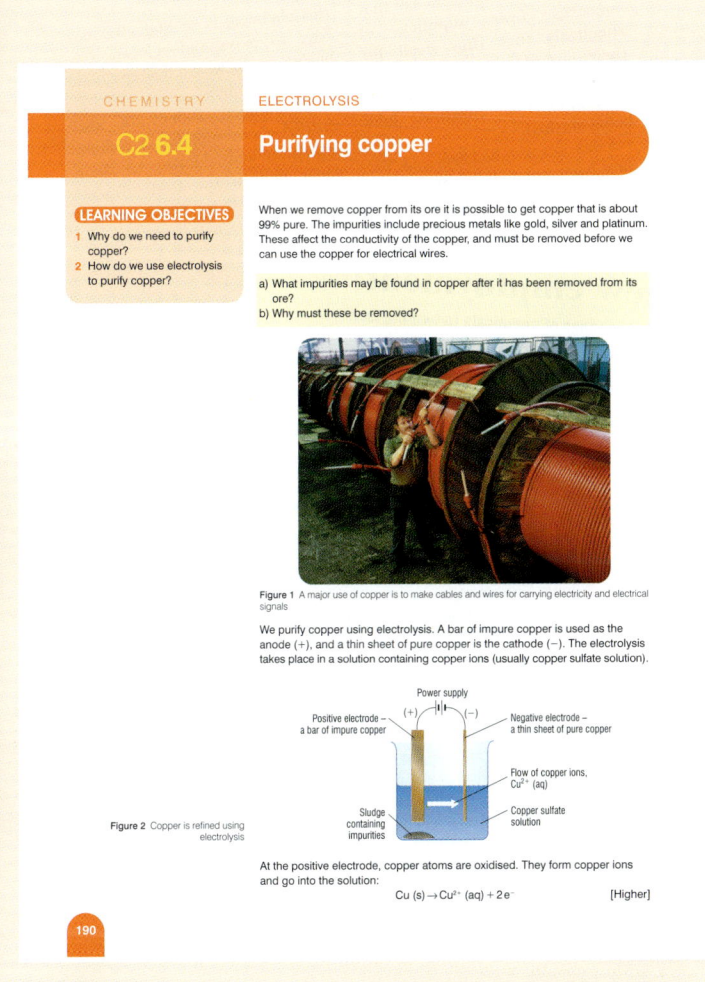

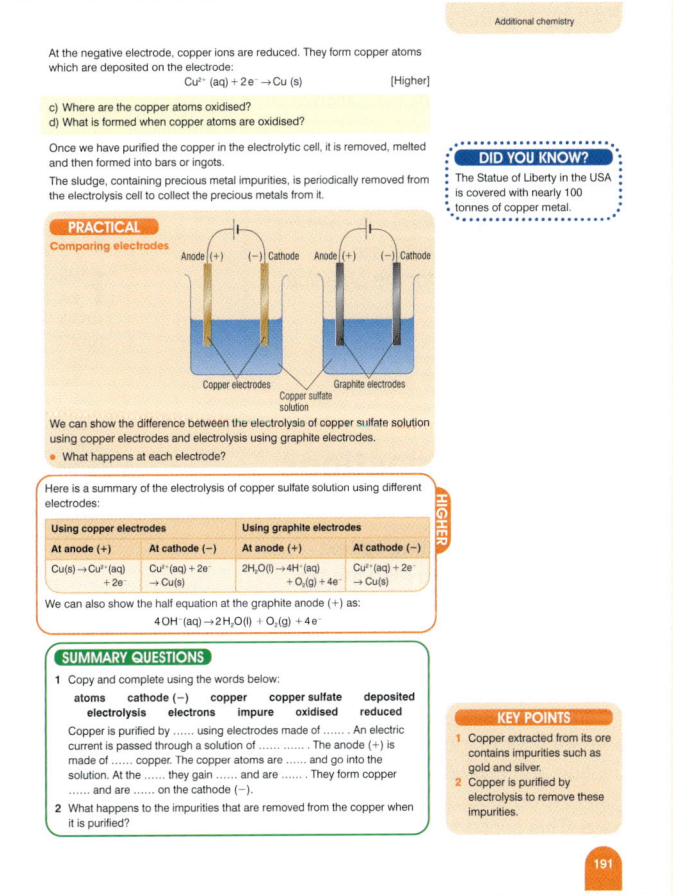

CHEMISTRY — ELECTROLYSIS

C2 6.4 Purifying copper

LEARNING OBJECTIVES
1. Why do we need to purify copper?
2. How do we use electrolysis to purify copper?

When we remove copper from its ore it is possible to get copper that is about 99% pure. The impurities include precious metals like gold, silver and platinum. These affect the conductivity of the copper, and must be removed before we can use the copper for electrical wires.

a) What impurities may be found in copper after it has been removed from its ore?
b) Why must these be removed?

Figure 1 A major use of copper is to make cables and wires for carrying electricity and electrical signals

We purify copper using electrolysis. A bar of impure copper is used as the anode (+), and a thin sheet of pure copper is the cathode (−). The electrolysis takes place in a solution containing copper ions (usually copper sulfate solution).

Figure 2 Copper is refined using electrolysis

At the positive electrode, copper atoms are oxidised. They form copper ions and go into the solution:
$$Cu(s) \rightarrow Cu^{2+}(aq) + 2e^-$$ [Higher]

At the negative electrode, copper ions are reduced. They form copper atoms which are deposited on the electrode:
$$Cu^{2+}(aq) + 2e^- \rightarrow Cu(s)$$ [Higher]

c) Where are the copper atoms oxidised?
d) What is formed when copper atoms are oxidised?

Once we have purified the copper in the electrolytic cell, it is removed, melted and then formed into bars or ingots.

The sludge, containing precious metal impurities, is periodically removed from the electrolysis cell to collect the precious metals from it.

PRACTICAL
Comparing electrodes

We can show the difference between the electrolysis of copper sulfate solution using copper electrodes and electrolysis using graphite electrodes.
- What happens at each electrode?

Here is a summary of the electrolysis of copper sulfate solution using different electrodes:

Using copper electrodes		Using graphite electrodes	
At anode (+)	At cathode (−)	At anode (+)	At cathode (−)
$Cu(s) \rightarrow Cu^{2+}(aq) + 2e^-$	$Cu^{2+}(aq) + 2e^- \rightarrow Cu(s)$	$2H_2O(l) \rightarrow 4H^+(aq) + O_2(g) + 4e^-$	$Cu^{2+}(aq) + 2e^- \rightarrow Cu(s)$

We can also show the half equation at the graphite anode (+) as:
$$4OH^-(aq) \rightarrow 2H_2O(l) + O_2(g) + 4e^-$$

SUMMARY QUESTIONS
1. Copy and complete using the words below:
   atoms   cathode (−)   copper   copper sulfate   deposited   electrolysis   electrons   impure   oxidised   reduced

   Copper is purified by …… using electrodes made of …… . An electric current is passed through a solution of …… …… . The anode (+) is made of …… copper. The copper atoms are …… and go into the solution. At the …… they gain …… and are …… . They form copper …… and are …… on the cathode (−).

2. What happens to the impurities that are removed from the copper when it is purified?

DID YOU KNOW?
The Statue of Liberty in the USA is covered with nearly 100 tonnes of copper metal.

KEY POINTS
1. Copper extracted from its ore contains impurities such as gold and silver.
2. Copper is purified by electrolysis to remove these impurities.

SUMMARY ANSWERS

1. Electrolysis, copper, copper sulfate, impure, oxidised, cathode (−), electrons, reduced, atoms, deposited.
2. They are removed from the sludge, purified and sold.

DID YOU KNOW?

The depth of the copper on the Statue of Liberty is 2.5 mm, and the monument has a height from base to torch of 46 m. In addition to copper, the Statue of Liberty also contains 125 tonnes of steel, making its total mass 225 tonnes.

Answers to in-text questions

a) Precious metals like gold, silver and platinum.
b) These metals affect the electrical conductivity of the copper.
c) At the anode (+)/positive electrode.
d) Copper ions (Cu^{2+})

KEY POINTS

Ask students to add information to the key points so that they produce two paragraphs about these topics.

CHEMISTRY — ELECTROLYSIS
C2 6.5 To build or not to build?

SPECIFICATION LINK-UP
Unit: Chemistry 2.12.6

Students should use their skills, knowledge and understanding of 'How Science Works':

- To explain and evaluate processes that use the principles described in this unit.

This spread can be used to revisit the following substantive content covered in this chapter:

- Passing an electric current through ionic substances that are molten or in solution breaks them down into elements. This process is called electrolysis.
- The electrolysis of sodium chloride solution produces hydrogen and chlorine. Sodium hydroxide solution is also produced. These are important reagents for the chemical industry.

Teaching suggestions

Activities

- **Directed activity relating to text** – Encourage students to read the two biased pieces of writing – one from BrineCo and the other from a pressure group. Ask students to complete questions 1–3 in note form. Then put the students into pairs and ask them to compare their responses. Using question and answer, feedback from the class to form a complete answer on the board. This section could be lead by one pair (a scribe and a person fielding the comments from the rest of the class).
- **Newspaper article** – Students should be reminded that news items should be impartial, and that newspapers and broadcasters risk prosecutions if they are found to be bias. Show students examples of articles and get them to underline in different colours the two sides of the argument. This could be completed using an OHT or interactive whiteboard. Then encourage students to use information from the book to write their own page lead in a local newspaper (about 250 words) about BrineCo. They should also consider the type of images that they would like to use in their article. Encourage students to take quotes from the book to use in their articles.

CHEMISTRY — ELECTROLYSIS
C2 6.5 To build or not to build?

Unemployment in Newtown may rise!

Two big local employers say that concerns over supplies of chemicals that they need for their factories mean that they may have to close. This will lead to hundreds of Newtown jobs being slashed.

A director of Allied Fats said 'We have been worried about supplies of hydrogen to our plant for some time since the cost of transporting this chemical is so high. We may have to close and relocate our business somewhere nearer to our present suppliers.'

Consolidated Paper are also worried about supplies of sodium hydroxide and chlorine to their paper mill in the town. Tracey Wiggins, the MP for Newtown, said 'This would be a tragedy for the town.'

Hope for new employment!

Following concerns about supplies of chemicals to two big local employers, we can exclusively reveal that a deal is being struck that would bring a manufacturer of these chemicals to Newtown.

BrineCo, one of the largest chemical companies in the country, is currently in talks with the council about building a big new plant to produce chemicals in a new factory near the town. BrineCo already manufacture chlorine and sodium hydroxide at other plants in the UK.

Local MP Tracey Wiggins said 'This would be a wonderful opportunity for workers and their families in Newtown and the surrounding area.'

QUESTIONS
Look at the two leaflets produced by BrineCo and by the local pressure group GREEN.
1. Make a list of the differences between the two maps on the leaflets.
2. How is BrineCo trying to persuade people that their factory is a good idea?
3. How is GREEN trying to persuade people that the factory is *not* a good idea?

ACTIVITY
Write an editorial for the local newspaper in which you examine both sides of the argument for bringing the BrineCo factory to the town. The final part of your editorial should come down on one side or the other – but you must argue your point logically. You may also decide that the factory should go ahead, but on a different site. Can *you* persuade local people that *you* are the voice of reason?

- **Debate** – Split the class into half, one group should be acting as the brine company and the other as the protestors. Give the students time to conduct further research about the impact of such a plant in a local area. Then hold a debate on the issue. Following the debate, ask all the students to vote on whether they think that the plant should/should not get permission to trade.

Homework

- **Hydrogen as a fuel** – Hydrogen is another product of the electrolysis of brine. Encourage students to find out how it can be used as a fuel, and the environmental implications of doing this.

Extensions

- **Research** – Ask students to find out the location of one brine electrolysis plant (anywhere in the world). They could then list the benefits of the chosen site.
- **Saponification** – Sodium hydroxide is used to make soap. Students could research how to do this (using the Internet) and they could make their own soaps.

Additional chemistry

BrineCo working for you!

BrineCo produce chlorine and sodium hydroxide solution by passing electricity through brine (salt solution). This is called **electrolysis**.

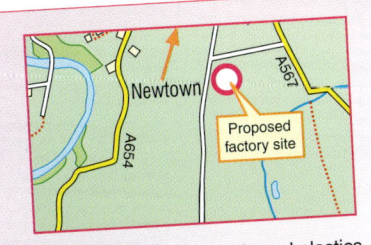

The chlorine that we make is used to make paper, chemicals and plastics, and for treating water to kill bacteria. Sodium hydroxide solution is sold to companies making paper, artificial fibres, soaps and detergents.

Our new factory can bring many benefits to Newtown. Consolidated Paper will be a major user of BrineCo's chemicals, and Allied Fats will buy the hydrogen produced by our factory.

This will give both companies a cheaper supply of raw materials than they have at present. *Think carefully about BrineCo's proposals – they mean a secure future for you and your children.*

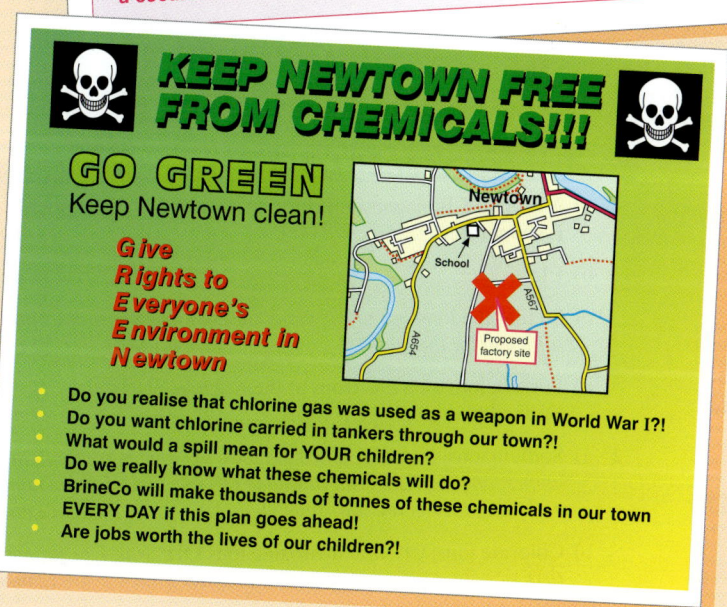

Proposed factory site

KEEP NEWTOWN FREE FROM CHEMICALS!!!

GO GREEN Keep Newtown clean!

Give
Rights to
Everyone's
Environment in
Newtown

- Do you realise that chlorine gas was used as a weapon in World War I?!
- Do you want chlorine carried in tankers through our town?!
- What would a spill mean for YOUR children?
- Do we really know what these chemicals will do?
- BrineCo will make thousands of tonnes of these chemicals in our town EVERY DAY if this plan goes ahead!
- Are jobs worth the lives of our children?!

Learning styles

Kinaesthetic: Making soap.

Visual: Preparing a newspaper article.

Intrapersonal: Researching into hydrogen as a fuel.

Interpersonal: Working as a team in a debate.

ICT link-up

Desktop publishing packages could be used by students to create their newspaper articles. The Internet could be used, to add images. The work could then be printed and put on display.

Special needs

All the advantages and disadvantages of the electrolysis plant could be written on separate cards. These students could then sort them into two lists before jotting them down in their notes.

Teaching assistant

The teaching assistant could be the team leader of half of the class, meanwhile the teacher could lead the other half. This would aid the students in preparing their arguments for their debate.

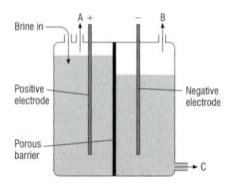

CHEMISTRY   ELECTROLYSIS

SUMMARY ANSWERS

1. a) B b) A c) B d) A e) B f) A

2. **Negative electrode:** sodium, calcium, zinc, aluminium.
   Positive electrode: iodide, fluoride, oxide, bromide.

3. a) $2H_2O \rightarrow 2H_2 + O_2$
   b) **Cathode (−):** $2H^+ + 2e^- \rightarrow H_2$
      Anode (+): $4OH^- \rightarrow O_2 + 2H_2O + 4e^-$
   c) 1 mole.
   d) The power supply.   [HT only]

4. a) $K^+ + e^- \rightarrow K$
   b) $Ba^{2+} + 2e^- \rightarrow Ba$
   c) $2I^- \rightarrow I_2 + 2e^-$
   d) $2O^{2-} \rightarrow O_2 + 4e^-$ [HT only]

5. Description with object to be plated made negative (cathode) in solution containing metal ions (e.g. $CuSO_4$ solution for copper plating). To keep concentration of metal ions in solution constant, an anode made of the metal to be plated should be used.   [HT only]
   Half equation: $Cu^{2+} + 2e^- \rightarrow Cu$

Summary teaching suggestions

- **Special needs** – Question 1 could be prepared as a cut and stick activity. A blank table with two columns – anode and cathode could be supplied to the students. Then the statements could be given on a separate sheet of paper. Students could cut up the statements and stick them into the appropriate column in the table. To extend this activity, all positive words (e.g. anode) could be underlined in red, whereas all negative words could be underlined in blue.

- **Gifted and talented** – Students could be encouraged to write a full method, including safety, for question 5. These students may also be allowed to complete their practical.

- **Learning styles**
  Auditory: Question 5 lends itself to a class discussion before each student tries to write their own answer.
  Visual: Questions 2 and 5 involve creating a table or diagrams.
  Kinaesthetic: If question 1 is turned into a cut and stick activity, this will appeal to these learners.

- **When to use the questions?**
  - These questions could be used as a test preparation, where for half of the lesson the students attempt the questions. Then, in the second half, answers are given out and students mark each others' work.
  - Question 1 is a good review question to check understanding of electrolysis. This could be used after lesson 6.2 as a plenary or homework.
  - Both questions 1 and 2 could be used as a kinaesthetic activity. Stick the two column headings on opposite sides of the room (e.g. for question 1, anode and cathode). Then give each student a statement and they should stand in the group that they think they belong to.

EXAM-STYLE ANSWERS

1. a) **A** bromine, **B** magnesium chloride, **C** hydrogen, **D** copper, **E** copper ions.   (5 marks)
   b) Electrolyte.   (1 mark)
   c) So that the ions can move (*'ions cannot move in solids' is not sufficient for the mark*).   (1 mark)
   d) Positive ions gain electrons at the negative electrode. (1 mark)
      Reduction is gaining electrons.   (1 mark)

2. a) Sodium ions, Na^+ and hydrogen ions, H^+ (*one mark for both names, one mark for both formulae OR one mark for one name and formula – ignore (aq) state symbols*).   (2 marks)
   b) Chloride ions, Cl^-, and hydroxide ions OH^- (*mark as for part (a)*).   (2 marks)
   c) A is chlorine (1 mark) B is hydrogen (1 mark)   (2 marks)
   d) *Four from:*
      - Positive (hydrogen and sodium) ions are attracted to negative electrode.
      - Hydrogen is less reactive than sodium.
      - Hydrogen ions are reduced/gain electrons to hydrogen atoms.
      - Two hydrogen atoms combine to form hydrogen molecules.
      - Hydrogen ions are replaced by more water ionising.
                                                         (4 marks)
   e) Sodium hydroxide.   (1 mark)

3. a) *One mark each for:*
      - Tin ions (Sn^{2+}) from solution gain electrons/are reduced.
      - Tin atoms are formed.
      - Tin is deposited on the electrode.   (3 marks)
   b) *One mark each for:*
      - Tin atoms lose electrons/are oxidised.
      - Tin ions (Sn^{2+}) are formed.
      - Tin ions (Sn^{2+}) go into the solution/electrolyte. (3 marks)

Additional chemistry

3 Mild steel can be electroplated with tin in the laboratory. The diagram shows the apparatus used.

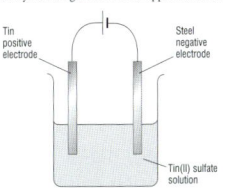

(a) Explain what happens at the negative electrode to deposit tin on the steel. (3)
(b) What happens to tin at the positive electrode? (3)
(c) Why does the concentration of the tin(II) sulfate solution not change during the electrolysis? (2)
(d) Some food cans are made of mild steel coated with tin. Suggest **two** reasons why tin plated steel is chosen for this use. (2)

4 A student was interested in electrolysis. He knew that a current passes through a copper sulfate solution. With copper electrodes some of the copper would come away from one electrode and move to the other. He thought that there would be the same amount of copper leaving one electrode as attached to the other electrode. He set up his equipment and weighed each electrode several times over a 25 minute period. His results are in this table:

Loss in mass of positive electrode in 5 minutes (g)	Gain in mass of negative electrode in 5 minutes (g)	Time (mins)
0.027	0.021	5
0.022	0.027	10
0.061	0.030	15
0.001	0.025	20
0.025	0.027	25

(a) What evidence is there for an anomalous result? (1)
(b) What was the range for the results at the negative electrode? (1)
(c) What evidence is there to support the student's prediction? (1)
(d) Comment on the reliability of the results. (1)

HOW SCIENCE WORKS QUESTIONS

Hydrogen – the new petrol?

Hydrogen could be a very important fuel for personal transport. However, there are many practical problems to be solved.

Mikael came up with the idea of using the Sun's energy to produce hydrogen from sea water. The apparatus used was similar to what you might have seen in your school laboratory. However, he used a solar cell to produce a voltage to drive the electrolysis. Mikael left the electrolysis for the same time for each solution used.

The results are shown below.

Solution used	Volume of hydrogen (cm³)			mean
Sea water	33	27	45	

a) Calculate the mean volume of hydrogen produced. (1)
b) What do these results tell us about the precision of the method used? Explain your answer. (1)
c) What probably caused the variation in the student's results? (1)
d) Mikael's teacher dismissed the research saying, 'It could never come to anything that might produce large volumes of hydrogen.' Why do you think the teacher thought this? (1)
e) Mikael's dad thought it was a brilliant idea and a chance to make some money! He pictured a huge factory turning out millions of tonnes of hydrogen and millions of pounds of money! He quizzed Mikael about his results. He asked Mikael if he was telling the whole truth. Why was it important that Mikael was telling the whole truth about his investigation? (1)
f) What might be Mikael's next step towards becoming a millionaire? (1)

---

c) As tin ions are removed from the solution at the negative electrode they are replaced from the positive electrode (1 mark)
by equal numbers of ions going into the solution. (1 mark)

d) Any two from:
- Tin prevents iron from rusting.
- Tin is not corroded by the atmosphere/water.
- Tin is not attacked/corroded by food/no toxic substances go into food.
- Tin plate is cheaper than pure tin.
- Mild steel is stronger than tin (so cans can be thinner/use less metal). (2 marks)

4 a) For the +ve electrode the reading at 15 minutes is very high and that at 20 minutes very low. (1 mark)
b) 0.021 g to 0.030 g (1 mark)
c) After 25 minutes the +ve electrode has lost the same mass as the −ve electrode has gained. (1 mark)
d) The repeats are not similar over each 5 minute period and therefore the reliability is not good. (1 mark)

Exam teaching suggestions

- The questions on this chapter have a total of 34 marks and should take students about 35 minutes to complete. Q1 could be set after completing spread 6.2, Q2 after 6.3, and Q3 after 6.4.
- In Q1, students should be encouraged to look at all of the information in the table and not just focus on the missing parts. The other information should help them to predict or confirm any answers they are unsure about. This applies to all questions that require a table to be completed.

- State symbols are not essential in Q2, because the focus is on the ions. There is effectively half a mark for each answer to parts a) and b) of this question, but half marks are not used in GCSE, so the mark scheme reflects this. Part d) has a maximum of four marks, but there are five marking points available. Students could discuss and produce exemplar answers to this question. Questions of this type are often used to assess quality of written communication, and this could be applied here, using the correct scientific terms or correct sequencing of ideas as the criteria.
- Candidates are not expected to have met tin plating before, but should apply their knowledge and understanding of the electrolysis of copper(II) sulfate to this process. Q4 is based on concepts drawn from the 'How Science Works' content in the specification.

HOW SCIENCE WORKS ANSWERS

a) The mean volume of hydrogen produced is 35 cm³.
b) The precision is not good. The results are too widely spread around the mean.
c) The variation in the level of sunlight is likely to have caused the variation in the student's results.
d) The results are on a very small scale and do not necessarily indicate that they could be used on a large scale.
e) The results are more credible if the whole truth is told.
f) Mikael should get someone else to repeat his results, to increase their reliability.

How science works teaching suggestions

- **Literacy guidance**
  - Key terms that should be clearly understood: precision, conclusions, credibility of data.
  - The question expecting a longer answer, where students can practise their literacy skills is: d).
- **Higher- and lower-level answers.** Question b) is a higher-level question and the answer provided above is also at this level. Question a) is lower level and the answer provided is also lower level.
- **Gifted and talented.** Able students could suggest how the reliability of Mikael's results might be further enhanced by using a different technique to collect more gas.
- **How and when to use these questions.** When wishing to encourage students to see their own work as being part of a bigger picture. The questions could be tackled in small discussion groups.
- **Homework.** The questions could be used for homework.
- **Special needs.** A teacher-led discussion could be conducted to lead through the ideas.

195

CHEMISTRY   ACIDS, ALKALIS AND SALTS

C2 7.1 Acids and alkalis

LEARNING OBJECTIVES

Students should learn:

- How solutions can be acidic or alkaline.
- That acidity can be measured.

LEARNING OUTCOMES

Most students should be able to:

- List the properties of acids and alkalis.
- Give an example of an acid and alkali.
- Recognise if a chemical is an acid or alkali if the pH is given.
- Recognise a neutralisation reaction.

Some students should also be able to:

- Explain in terms of ions what an acid and alkali are.

Teaching suggestions

- **Special needs.** The method to test the alkalinity of different household chemicals could be given in labelled diagrams to these students, but in the wrong order. They could sort out the steps before completing the practical.
- **Learning styles**

  Kinaesthetic: Completing the practical testing of pH.

  Visual: Putting data into a table.

  Auditory: Listening to people's explanations about the cryptic sentence.

  Intrapersonal: Creating a poster about the pH scale.

  Interpersonal: Designing an investigation in pairs.

- **Homework.** Ask students to find out how to make an indicator at home and write a bullet-point method on how to make it, e.g. using elderberries, cranberries or red cabbage.
- **ICT link-up.** Make a coloured universal indicator pH scale on interactive whiteboard software or PowerPoint®. Invite the students to label weak/strong acid/alkali and neutral chemicals. Then show images of different things, e.g. stomach acid, then drag and drop the images onto the pH scale.

SPECIFICATION LINK-UP   Unit: Chemistry 2.12.6

- Hydrogen ions $H^+(aq)$ make solutions acidic and hydroxide ions $OH^-(aq)$ make solutions alkaline. The pH scale is a measure of the acidity or alkalinity of a solution.
- The state symbols in equations are (s), (l), (g) and (aq).

Lesson structure

STARTER

Table – Ask students to draw a three-columned table, with titles: 'acid', 'base', 'neutral'. They should then list as many things about each group as they can, including examples. Then draw a similar table on the board, and ask each student in turn to write a piece of information into the table. (5–10 minutes)

Think – On the board, write the sentence: 'All alkalis are bases but not all bases are alkali.' Ask students to work in pairs to explain this sentence. Feedback ideas from the class. (10–15 minutes)

MAIN

- Ask students to create a colourful poster to display the universal indicator chart. A common misconception is starting the chart from pH1, but it should actually start from pH0 and point out that we can also have negative pH values. Students could then use secondary sources of data to put everyday and lab examples of chemicals onto their poster.
- Students could test a variety of chemicals using universal indicator to find out their pH. Encourage them to design their own results table for the experiment. Then ask them to draw conclusions from their results. Hopefully, they will realise that, with everyday chemicals, some acids can be eaten, whereas most alkalis are cleaning products.
- Students could design and carry out their own investigation to determine the alkalinity of different household cleaning products. Encourage students to work in pairs to plan their experiment. They could use a variety of methods, including universal indicator, digital pH probes or data loggers.

PLENARIES

5,4,3,2,1 – Ask students to list the names of 5 everyday acids, 4 lab based bases, 3 properties of acids, 2 properties of alkalis and 1 example of a neutral chemical. (5–10 minutes)

Review – Show students the table that the class made. Ask them to look carefully and consider any mistakes. Discuss the mistakes and make amendments. Then ask students to copy out three facts from the table and add a new fact that they have learned from the lesson into their notes. (10–15 minutes)

Practical support

Testing pH of various chemicals

Equipment and materials required
Dimple tiles, beaker of water, dropping pipettes, samples of acids (irritants/harmful), alkalis (irritants/harmful), neutral chemicals and buffer solutions (irritants/harmful), universal indicator solution (flammable), universal indicator paper, scissors, eye protection.

Details
Wear eye protection throughout the practical, and wash hands in cold water if any of the solutions get onto the skin. Be aware that universal indicator will stain the skin for about three days.

Put a few drops of each type of solution in separate dimples. Either add a few drops of universal indicator solution or a small square of universal indicator paper. Compare the colour of the paper or solution with the given colour chart (each brand of universal indicator will go a different colour at each pH value, so it is important to compare with the appropriate chart). Put dropping pipette into beaker of water when finished.

Investigating household cleaning products

Equipment and materials required
Different cleaning products (irritant/harmful), beakers, stirring rods, pH probes, pH data logger and equipment, universal indicator (flammable), dropping pipette, dimple tile, eye protection.

Details
Wear eye protection and put a small amount of cleaning product on a dimple tile. Add a few drops of water if the product is a solid. Then add universal indictor and compare with the colour chart. Alternatively, put the cleaning product into a beaker and submerge the calibrated pH probe (either digital or data logger) and note the reading.

Safety: If the cleaning product gets onto skin, wash well with cold water. Be aware that some cleaning products may be 'corrosive' and 'toxic' – avoid these.

ACTIVITY & EXTENSION IDEAS
- Ask students to find out how electricity can be used to measure pH.
- Ask students to research and find out different indicators that can be used to test for acids and bases.
- Students could complete mole calculations on the balanced symbol equations.

Answers to in-text questions
a) A base is a chemical that can neutralise acids.
b) An alkali is a base that is soluble in water.
c) H^+ ions/hydrogen ions.
d) OH^- ions/hydroxide ions.

CHEMISTRY
C2 7.1
Acids and alkalis

ACIDS, ALKALIS AND SALTS

LEARNING OBJECTIVES
1 Why are solutions acidic or alkaline?
2 How do we measure acidity?

Acids and bases are an important part of our understanding of chemistry. They play a vital part inside us and for all other living things too.

What are acids and bases?
When we dissolve a substance in water we make an **aqueous solution**. The solution may be acidic, alkaline or neutral, depending on the chemical we have dissolved. **Bases** are chemicals which can neutralise **acids**.

Alkalis are bases which dissolve in water. Pure water is **neutral**.

a) What is a base?
b) What is an alkali?

Acids include chemicals like citric acid, sulfuric acid and ethanoic acid. All acids taste very sour, although many acids are far too dangerous to put in your mouth. We use acids in many chemical reactions in the laboratory. Ethanoic acid (vinegar) and citric acid (the sour taste in citric fruit, fizzy drinks and squashes) are acids which we regularly eat.

One acid that we use in the laboratory is hydrochloric acid. This is formed when the gas hydrogen chloride (HCl) dissolves in water:

$$HCl (g) \xrightarrow{water} H^+ (aq) + Cl^- (aq)$$

All acids form H^+ ions when we add them to water – it is hydrogen ions that make acids acidic. Hydrogen chloride also forms chloride ions (Cl^-). The '(aq)' symbol shows that the ions are in an 'aqueous solution'. In other words, they are dissolved in water.

c) What ions do all acids form when we add them to water?

Bases are the opposite of acids in the way they react. Because alkalis are bases which dissolve in water they are the bases which we use most commonly. For example, sodium hydroxide solution is often found in our school laboratories. Sodium hydroxide solution is formed when we dissolve solid sodium hydroxide in water:

$$NaOH (s) \xrightarrow{water} Na^+ (aq) + OH^- (aq)$$

All alkalis form hydroxide ions (OH^-) when we add them to water. It is hydroxide ions that make a solution alkaline.

d) What ions do all alkalis form when we add them to water?

Measuring acidity
Indicators are special chemicals which change colour when we add them to acids and alkalis. Litmus paper is one well-known indicator, but there are many more. These include some natural ones like the juice of red cabbage or beetroot.

Figure 1 Acids and bases are all around us, in many of the things we buy at the shops, in our schools and factories – and inside us too

Figure 2 Some common laboratory acids

We use the **pH scale** to show how acid or alkaline a solution is. The scale runs from 0 (most acidic) to 14 (most alkaline). **Universal indicator** is a very special indicator made from a number of dyes. It turns different colours at different values of pH. Anything in the middle of the pH scale (pH 7) is **neutral**, neither acid nor alkali.

Universal indicator pH solution		
0		Very acidic
1	Hydrochloric acid	
2	Lemon juice	
3	Orange juice / Vinegar	
4		
5	Black coffee	Slightly acidic
6	Rainwater	
7	Pure water	Neutral
8	Sea water / Baking soda	
9	Milk of magnesia / Soap	Slightly alkaline
10		
11		
12	Washing soda	
13		
14	Oven cleaner / Sodium hydroxide	Very alkaline

Figure 3 The pH scale tells us how acid or alkaline a solution is

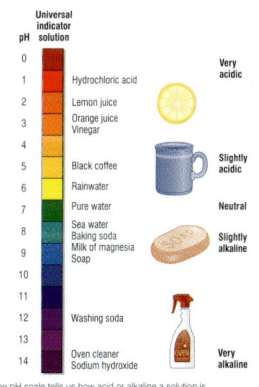

A H^+ ion is simply a hydrogen atom that has lost an electron – in other words a proton. So another way of describing an acid is to say that it is a 'proton donor'.

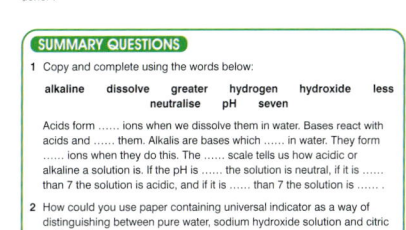

SUMMARY QUESTIONS
1 Copy and complete using the words below:

alkaline   dissolve   greater   hydrogen   hydroxide   less
neutralise   pH   seven

Acids form …… ions when we dissolve them in water. Bases react with acids and …… them. Alkalis are bases which …… in water. They form …… ions when they do this. The …… scale tells us how acidic or alkaline a solution is. If the pH is …… the solution is neutral, if it is …… than 7 the solution is acidic, and if it is …… than 7 the solution is …… .

2 How could you use paper containing universal indicator as a way of distinguishing between pure water, sodium hydroxide solution and citric acid solution?

PRACTICAL
Which is the most alkaline product?

Compare the alkalinity of various cleaning products.

You can test washing-up liquids, shampoos, soaps, hand-washing liquids, washing powders/liquids and dishwasher powders/tablets.

You might be able to use a pH sensor and data logger to collect your data.

- What are the advantages of using a pH sensor instead of universal indicator solution or paper?

KEY POINTS
1 Acids are substances which produce H^+ ions when we add them to water.
2 Bases are substances that will neutralise acids.
3 An alkali is a soluble base. Alkalis produce OH^- ions when we add them to water.
4 We use the pH scale to show how acidic or alkaline a solution is.

SUMMARY ANSWERS
1 Hydrogen, neutralise, dissolve, hydroxide, pH, seven, less, greater, alkaline.
2 The paper would turn green in water, blue in sodium hydroxide solution and red/orange in citric acid solution.

KEY POINTS
Ask students to copy out the key points, but to colour-code them. Each word that is a base, colour in blue or purple, each acid word colour in red, yellow or orange and each neutral word colour in green.

CHEMISTRY — ACIDS, ALKALIS AND SALTS

C2 7.2 Making salts from metals or bases

LEARNING OBJECTIVES

Students should learn:

- That acids and bases can be neutralised.
- Which products are made in a neutralisation reaction.
- That salts can be made using neutralisation.

LEARNING OUTCOMES

Most students should be able to:

- Define neutralisation.
- Name the salt formed if the acid and alkali are given.
- Complete symbol equations including state symbols.
- Write the ionic equation for neutralisation.
- Write general word equations for neutralisation reactions.

Teaching suggestions

- **Special needs.** Provide these students with a skeleton structure of the equations. Then each additional piece of information could be made into a card. Each card should have a separate chemical and then the students try to create the equations, using Blu-tack to secure the cards.

- **Learning styles**

  Kinaesthetic: Completing a neutralisation practical.

  Visual: Creating A6 revision cards.

  Auditory: Listening to other student's answers.

  Intrapersonal: Completing equations.

  Interpersonal: Trying to complete a neutralisation in pairs.

- **Homework.** Students to find three uses for a neutralisation reaction (e.g. antacids, reduction of acidity of soils, to remove harmful gases from factory emissions).

- **ICT link-up**

  There are many simulations of neutralisation. Search Google for 'neutralisation/animation/simulation'.

SPECIFICATION LINK-UP   Unit: Chemistry 2.12.6

- Soluble salts can be made from acids by reacting them with:
  - metals – not all metals are suitable, some are too reactive and others are not reactive enough.
  - insoluble bases – the base is added to the acid until no more will react and the excess solid is filtered off.
  - alkalis – an indicator can be used to show when the acid and alkali have completely reacted to produce a salt solution.
- The particular salt produced in any reaction between an acid and a base or alkali depends on:
  - the acid used (hydrochloric acid produces chlorides, nitric acid produces nitrates, sulfuric acid produces sulfates).
  - the metal or base or alkali.
- Salt solutions can be crystallised to produce solid salts.
- Metal oxides and hydroxides are bases. Soluble hydroxides are called alkalis.

Students should use their skills, knowledge and understanding of 'How Science Works':

- to suggest methods to make a named salt.

Lesson structure

STARTER

Table – Ask students to complete the following table:

Name of acid	Name in salt	Example
Hydrochloric	[Chloride]	[Sodium chloride]
[Nitric]	Nitrate	[Copper nitrate]
Sulfuric	Sulfate	[Calcium sulfate]

Show the incomplete table on the board and ask different students to fill in the missing data. (10 minutes)

Experiment – Ask students to complete a neutralisation reaction in pairs. The first group to get exactly green is the winner and a prize could be given. (10 minutes)

MAIN

- Students have frequently had the experience of neutralisation of an acid with an alkali. However, they may not have had the experience using an insoluble base. Show the students some copper oxide and allow them to try to dissolve it in water. Then allow students to prepare copper sulfate crystals (toxic) using this method. Encourage the students to write up the method in a brief bullet-point format and summarise the reaction in a general word equation.

- Give each student three index cards. These can be made out of three different coloured pieces of card about A6 in size. In the top right-hand corner hole-punch all the cards. On the front of each card the student should write a general word equation. Then on the reverse a specific example, including a method and an equation for the reaction. Once all of the cards have been completed, they can be joined together with a treasury tag or a piece of string. These can then be tied to their notes and used for revision for examination.

PLENARIES

Copy and complete – Ask students to copy and complete the following prose. Students should be encouraged to use the most scientific word they can think of to complete the paragraph.

'Soluble [salts] can be made by reacting [acids] and bases or [alkalis]. Metal oxides and hydroxides are [bases]. Alkalis are [soluble] hydroxides.' (5 minutes)

Additional chemistry

Chemical equations – Ask students to complete the following equations (they get progressively more difficult). Time the students for five minutes and assure them that it doesn't matter how far they get. When the notes are marked it will give an idea of the level that each student is working at:

- Acid + alkali → [salt] + [water]
- [Acid] + [metal] → metal salt + hydrogen
- Acid + [base] → salt + [water]
- [Sodium hydroxide] + [nitric acid] → sodium nitrate + water
- Sulfuric acid + zinc → [zinc sulfate] + hydrogen
- [2HCl(aq)] + [Ca(s)] → $CaCl_2$ [(aq)] + H_2 [(g)] (5–15 minutes)

Practical support

Preparing copper sulfate crystals

Equipment and materials required
Copper oxide (harmful), 1 M sulfuric acid (irritant), stirring rod, beaker, Bunsen burner, tripod, gauze, filter funnel, filter paper, evaporating basin, spatula, measuring cylinder, conical flask, eye protection.

Details
Add a spatula of copper oxide to a beaker, then add 25 ml of sulfuric acid. Stir the reaction mixture well and note any observations [colour change of liquid from colourless to blue]. Warm the mixture gently on a tripod and gauze. Do not allow to boil. Let the mixture containing excess black copper oxide cool down. Fold the filter paper and put into the funnel in the neck of a conical flask. Filter the mixture. Collect the filtrate and put into an evaporating basin. Leave the liquid in a warm place for a few days to allow the crystals to form.

Safety: Eye protection should be worn throughout this practical. This reaction makes copper sulfate which is harmful – CLEAPSS Hazcard 27. (Sulfuric acid – CLEAPSS Hazcard 98.)

ACTIVITY & EXTENSION IDEAS

- Students could be encouraged to generate general symbol equations using M as any metal.
- Students could be shown how to generate the ionic equation for neutralisation from first principles. They could then use the method to check other examples and prove that the same ionic equation is always generated.
- Students could complete mole calculations on the balanced symbol equations.

Answers to in-text questions

a) Salt and hydrogen.
b) Salt and water.
c) Zinc sulfate.

KEY POINTS

Split the class into three groups and give each group a different key point. They then need to come up with reasons why their key point is the most important. Then hold the debate!

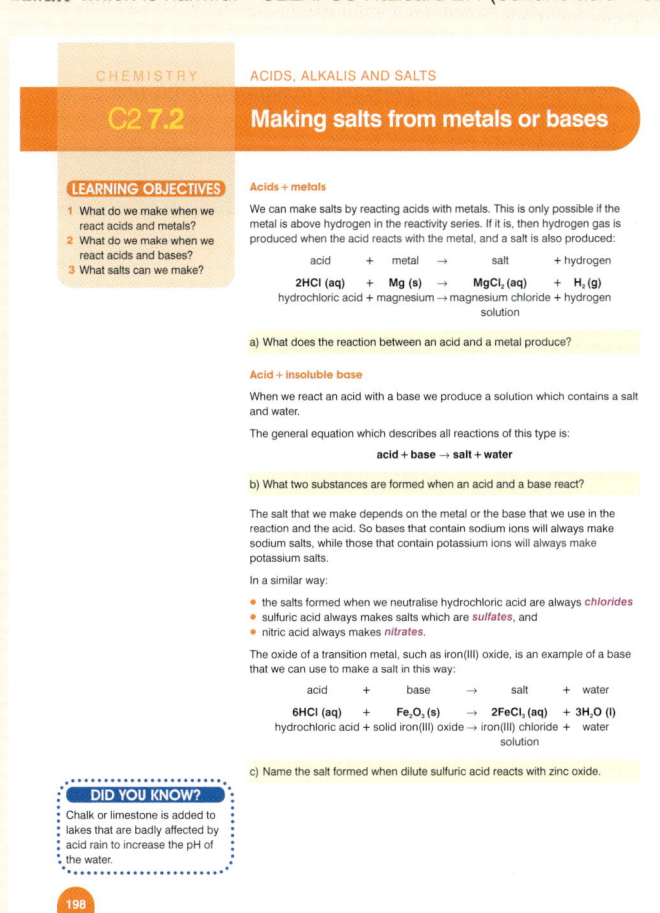

CHEMISTRY — ACIDS, ALKALIS AND SALTS

C2 7.2 Making salts from metals or bases

LEARNING OBJECTIVES
1. What do we make when we react acids and metals?
2. What do we make when we react acids and bases?
3. What salts can we make?

Acids + metals

We can make salts by reacting acids with metals. This is only possible if the metal is above hydrogen in the reactivity series. If it is, then hydrogen gas is produced when the acid reacts with the metal, and a salt is also produced:

acid + metal → salt + hydrogen
2HCl (aq) + Mg (s) → $MgCl_2$ (aq) + H_2 (g)
hydrochloric acid + magnesium → magnesium chloride solution + hydrogen

a) What does the reaction between an acid and a metal produce?

Acid + insoluble base

When we react an acid with a base we produce a solution which contains a salt and water.

The general equation which describes all reactions of this type is:

acid + base → salt + water

b) What two substances are formed when an acid and a base react?

The salt that we make depends on the metal or the base that we use in the reaction and the acid. So bases that contain sodium ions will always make sodium salts, while those that contain potassium ions will always make potassium salts.

In a similar way:
- the salts formed when we neutralise hydrochloric acid are always *chlorides*
- sulfuric acid always makes salts which are *sulfates*, and
- nitric acid always makes *nitrates*.

The oxide of a transition metal, such as iron(III) oxide, is an example of a base that we can use to make a salt in this way:

acid + base → salt + water
6HCl (aq) + Fe_2O_3 (s) → $2FeCl_3$ (aq) + $3H_2O$ (l)
hydrochloric acid + solid iron(III) oxide → iron(III) chloride solution + water

c) Name the salt formed when dilute sulfuric acid reacts with zinc oxide.

DID YOU KNOW?
Chalk or limestone is added to lakes that are badly affected by acid rain to increase the pH of the water.

PRACTICAL

1. Add insoluble copper oxide to sulfuric acid and stir. Warm gently on a tripod and gauze (do not boil).
2. The solution turns blue as the reaction occurs, showing that copper sulfate is being formed
3. When the reaction is complete, filter the solution to remove excess copper oxide
4. We can evaporate the water so that crystals of copper sulfate are left

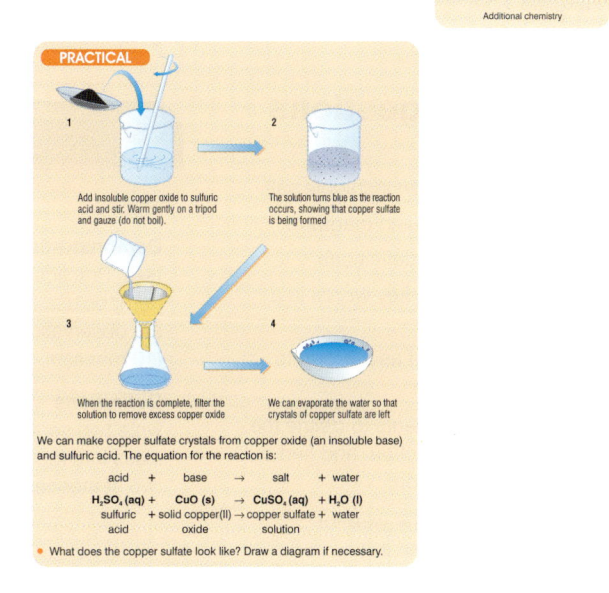

We can make copper sulfate crystals from copper oxide (an insoluble base) and sulfuric acid. The equation for the reaction is:

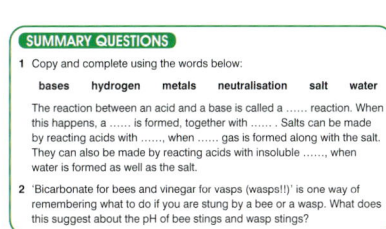

acid + base → salt + water
H_2SO_4 (aq) + CuO (s) → $CuSO_4$ (aq) + H_2O (l)
sulfuric acid + solid copper(II) oxide → copper sulfate solution + water

- What does the copper sulfate look like? Draw a diagram if necessary.

SUMMARY QUESTIONS

1. Copy and complete using the words below:

   bases   hydrogen   metals   neutralisation   salt   water

   The reaction between an acid and a base is called a …… reaction. When this happens, a …… is formed, together with …… . Salts can be made by reacting acids with ……, when …… gas is formed along with the salt. They can also be made by reacting acids with insoluble ……, when water is formed as well as the salt.

2. 'Bicarbonate for bees and vinegar for vasps (wasps!!)' is one way of remembering what to do if you are stung by a bee or a wasp. What does this suggest about the pH of bee stings and wasp stings?

KEY POINTS
1. When we react an acid with a base a neutralisation reaction occurs.
2. The reaction between an acid and a base produces a salt and water.
3. Salts can also be made by reacting a metal with an acid. This reaction also produces hydrogen gas as well as a salt.

SUMMARY ANSWERS

1. Neutralisation, salt, water, metals, hydrogen, bases.
2. Bee stings are acidic and wasp stings are alkaline.

CHEMISTRY   ACIDS, ALKALIS AND SALTS

C2 7.3 Making salts from solutions

LEARNING OBJECTIVES

Students should learn that:

- Salts can be made from an acid and alkali.
- Insoluble salts can be made.
- Unwanted ions can be removed from solutions.

LEARNING OUTCOMES

Most students should be able to:

- Record a method to make soluble salts.
- Record a method to make insoluble salts.
- State what a precipitation reaction is and recognise examples.

Some students should also be able to:

- Suggest a method for making a named salt.
- Explain what precipitation is in terms of ions involved.

Teaching suggestions

- **Learning styles**
  Kinaesthetic: Making an insoluble salt.
  Visual: Drawing a labelled diagram.
  Auditory: Listening to definitions.
  Intrapersonal: Finding key words in a word search.
  Interpersonal: Working as a group to determine definitions.
- **Homework.** Ask students to define the term 'precipitation reaction' and find out two uses of this reaction.
- **ICT link-up.** Search the web for 'word search generator' e.g. www.puzzlemaker.school.discovery.com, to make an exercise about acids and bases.

FOUL FACTS

Nitrogen is needed by plants, to synthesis the proteins in stalks and leaves.

Answers to in-text questions

a) acid + alkali → salt + water
b) A precipitation reaction.

SPECIFICATION LINK-UP   Unit: Chemistry 2.12.6

- In neutralisation reactions, hydrogen ions react with hydroxide ions to produce water. This reaction can be represented by the equation:

$$H^+(aq) + OH^-(aq) \rightarrow H_2O(l)$$

- Insoluble salts can be made by mixing appropriate solutions of ions so that a precipitate is formed. Precipitation can be used to remove unwanted ions from solutions, for example in treating water for drinking or in treating effluent.
- Soluble salts can be made from acids by reacting them with:
  – metals – not all metals are suitable, some are too reactive and others not reactive enough.
  – insoluble bases – the base is added to the acid until no more will react and the excess solid is filtered off.
  – alkalis – an indicator can be used to show when the acid and alkali have completely reacted to produce a salt solution.
- Ammonia dissolves in water to produce an alkaline solution. It is used to produce ammonium salts. Ammonium salts are important as fertilisers.
- The state symbols in equations are (s), (l), (g) and (aq).
- The particular salt produced in any reaction between an acid and a base or alkali depends on:
  – the acid used (hydrochloric acid produces chlorides, nitric acid produces nitrates, sulfuric acid produces sulfates).
  – the metal or base or alkali.

Students should use their skills, knowledge and understanding of 'How Science Works':

- to suggest methods to make a named salt.
- to explain and evaluate processes that use the principles described in this unit.

Lesson structure

STARTER

Demonstration – The solubility of ammonia can be shown using the fountain reactions (see 'Practical support'). Show the students and ask them to note their observations – perhaps use a scribe to jot them onto the board as you complete the demonstration. Then the observations can be used as a starting point for discussion about solubility. (10 minutes)

Definitions – Ask students to define the terms 'soluble' and 'insoluble'. Then ask them to write two sentences each using one of the key words. After about five minutes split the class into four groups and ask each group to come up with their definitive definitions and two sentences. Then ask each group to feedback to the class their work. (10 minutes)

MAIN

- Students could show experimentally that ammonia is very soluble and makes an alkali. They could then record this experiment with a fully labelled diagram to explain the observations. Then encourage them to include information about what ammonium hydroxide can be used for.
- Students could make an insoluble salt. Encourage them to record this in a step-by-step method including an equipment list. Also the students could generate the word equation or balanced symbol equation.

PLENARIES

Method – Ask students to briefly explain how they would make the following salts:

- Sodium chloride [Neutralisation between sodium hydroxide and hydrochloric acid, then evaporate the water.]
- Lead iodide [Reaction between lead nitrate and sodium iodide, filter and collect the solid wash with distilled water and dry.] (10 minutes)

Practical support

Making an insoluble salt

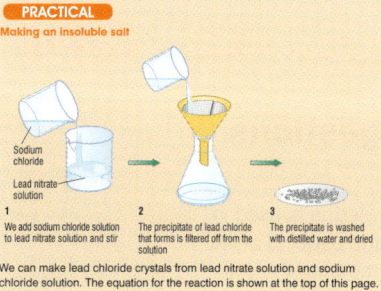

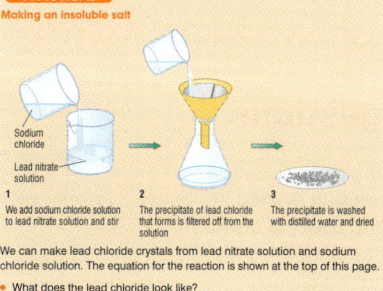

Equipment and materials required

0.01 M lead nitrate solution (toxic), sodium chloride solution, beaker, measuring cylinder, conical flask, filter funnel, filter paper, distilled water, eye protection.

Details

Measure 10 ml of sodium chloride and 5 ml of lead nitrate into a test tube. Gently shake, and then filter the mixture and wash through with distilled water. Remove the filter paper and allow the solid to dry. This is the insoluble salt.

Safety: Eye protection should be worn throughout, and hands should be thoroughly washed after the experiment has been completed. Pregnant women should be aware that lead salts can affect unborn children – CLEAPSS Hazcard 57.

ACTIVITY & EXTENSION IDEAS

- Students could act out a precipitation reaction, where each student represents an ion.
- Mole calculations could be completed from balanced symbol equations.
- Students could test the solubility of salts at different temperatures and plot solubility curves (see 'Practical support'). Secondary data could be obtained to compare the solubility of different chemicals, e.g. from *RSC Data book* or search the Internet for 'solubility data'.

Word search – Create a word search, but students need to answer questions to determine the words that they need to find:

- A method for removing pollutants from water. [Precipitation]
- When a solute will dissolve into a solvent, it is described as . . . [Soluble]
- Chalk is described as this it will not dissolve in water. [Insoluble]
- A chemical with a pH < 7 [Acid]
- A soluble base. [Alkali]
- The name of the chemical reaction between a hydrogen ion and hydroxide ion. [Neutralisation] (10 minutes)

SUMMARY ANSWERS

1 Acid (Alkali), alkali (acid), water, insoluble, soluble, precipitation, solid, metal, polluted.

2 **a)** nitric acid + potassium hydroxide → potassium nitrate + water

b) lead nitrate + potassium bromide → lead bromide + potassium nitrate

KEY POINTS

Ask students to make three questions that could be answered by each key point.

CHEMISTRY — ACIDS, ALKALIS AND SALTS

C2 7.4 It's all in the soil

SPECIFICATION LINK-UP
Unit: Chemistry 2.12.6

Students should use their skills, knowledge and understanding of 'How Science Works':

- To explain and evaluate processes that use principles described in this unit.

This spread can be used to revisit the substantive content below:

- ... Precipitation can be used to remove unwanted ions from solutions, for example in treating water for drinking or in treating effluent.

CHEMISTRY — ACIDS, ALKALIS AND SALTS

C2 7.4 It's all in the soil

The importance of rotation

No, nothing to do with rotating YOU! This is about not growing the same vegetables in the same place two years running. If you do this you are likely to find two problems.

First, pests and diseases which live on the particular vegetables will increase, and you will have real problems.

Second, growing the same crop in the same place year after year will lead to the soil becoming unbalanced, with the level of some nutrients becoming too low.

Getting the right amount of acid

When the soil in your garden is too acid or alkaline, nutrients present in the soil become locked-up or unavailable. Acidic soil has a 'pH' that is too low (less than 7) while alkaline soil has a 'pH' that is too high. In fact, a decrease of just one pH unit means that the soil is ten times more acidic!

Getting the pH right is the same as applying fertiliser since it 'unlocks' plant nutrients which are already present.

ACTIVITY

Although there is a lot of chemistry in gardening, it is not often that it is explained clearly (or correctly!). Your job is to write an article for a gardening newspaper or a leaflet for a local garden centre.
It should describe the chemistry behind getting the pH of the soil correct by testing it and then adding the necessary chemicals. You can even use simple chemical equations (especially word equations) if this helps you to explain things more clearly.

Testing your soil

You can find out the pH of your soil by testing it with a simple soil testing kit. This will tell you how acidic or alkaline your soil is.

Follow the instructions in the kit, which usually involves mixing a little soil with some water and testing it with some special paper. The colour that the paper turns will tell you if your soil has a 'pH' that is too low or too high.

What to add . . . ?

If your soil has the wrong 'pH' you'll need to do something about it. Unless you live on chalky soil it's very unusual for the pH of soil to be too high. This is because adding fertiliser usually makes soil acidic. So the most common thing that you'll need to do every so often to keep your soil with a 'neutral pH' is to add lime.

Lime is made by heating limestone to decompose it. Lime reacts with acid in the soil, making it neutral. You can buy lime from your local garden centre.

Teaching suggestions

Activities

- **Article** – Science knowledge is used in a lot of different jobs and aspects of life. Gardeners often put lime onto the soil (to increase pH) and add fertilisers. Gardeners know from past experience that these methods create healthier plants, but may not be aware of the science behind this. Ask students to imagine that they have been commissioned to write an article explaining the science of gardening. To help students, show them the gardening section in the local newspaper or some information leaflets from the local gardening centre.

- **Report** – A blue flag award for a beach is prestigious and helps tourism in an area. However, beaches can be polluted in a variety of different ways, heavy metals are just one form of pollution. Split the class into small groups of about three. They are to write a report to advise a council on how to remove heavy metals from polluted water. Students should include methods for this, but also a simplified explanation for non-scientists. Cleaning up pollution is an expensive task; therefore students could also consider how the pollution occurred and thus how it can be prevented. Students should also build into their reports a cost structure and whom they recommend should pay.

Homework

- **Research** – Encourage students to find out the chemical processes involved in purifying water for drinking purposes. They could display the processes as a flow chart.

Extension

- **Making a fertiliser** – Students could make ammonium sulfate, see 'Practical support'.
- **Natural fertilisers** – A number of plants have nitrogen-fixing bacteria in root nodules. Encourage students to find out how these plants provide their own fertilisers and how farmers can utilise them in crop rotations.
- **Which is the best fertiliser?** – Ask students to research the active chemical in a number of fertilisers (e.g. ammonium nitrate, ammonium phosphate). Also students could find out which minerals plants need and why. They should then decide which is the best fertiliser and why. Higher attaining students could complete mole calculations to show the percentage composition of nitrogen in different fertilisers, in order to find out which is the best fertiliser.

Blue flag beaches

The idea of a way of showing clearly that a beach is clean was put forward in 1987, when 244 beaches from 10 countries were awarded a flag to show that the beach met certain standards. As far as water quality goes, these standards include:

- the cleanliness of the water must comply with the EU Bathing Water Directive,
- no industrial effluent or sewage discharges may affect the beach area,
- there must be local emergency plans to cope with pollution accidents.

In 2005 there were nearly 2500 blue flag beaches worldwide.

ACTIVITY

The town council of a seaside resort wishes to apply for a 'blue flag' for their beach. However, they have been told that they must get rid of a large amount of heavy metal pollution in the water discharged through the town's sewage system. The heavy metals come from a large factory near the town, which is a very important local employer.

Your job is to act as a consultant to the town council to advise them of the best way to go about cleaning up the effluent in order to be able to apply for a blue flag.

Write a report to the council explaining what they should do. You will need to explain the chemistry to them in simple terms (they should be able to understand simple word equations), and you will need to suggest who will pay for the treatment – whether this should be the local people (through their local taxes), the factory producing the pollution, or even the visitors to the town (through higher prices for their accommodation and other holiday costs).

Additional chemistry

Cleaning up industrial effluent

A lot of wastewater from industry contains salts of heavy (transition) metals dissolved in it. Before this can be discharged these must be removed. The simplest way of removing the metal ions is to raise the pH of the solution. The hydroxide ions in the alkaline solution then react with the metal ions, producing metal hydroxides. The hydroxides of most heavy metals are very insoluble. So these form a precipitate which can be removed from the wastewater before it is discharged into a river or into the sea.

203

Practical support

Making ammonium sulfate

Equipment and materials required

A burette, stand, boss, clamp, conical flask, measuring cylinder, 1 M ammonia solution (CLEAPSS Hazcard 6), 1 M sulfuric acid (irritant – CLEAPSS Hazcard 98), glass rod, litmus paper, evaporating dish, funnel, eye protection.

Details

Wearing eye protection, students should measure 25 ml of ammonia solution into a conical flask and fill the burette with sulfuric acid. Add 1 ml of the acid into the conical flask and swirl the mixture. Then they remove a drop on a glass rod and touch litmus paper and observe the colour. Keep adding 1 ml of acid at a time until the litmus paper just turns pink, then the reaction is complete. Transfer the reaction mixture to an evaporating dish and allow the water to evaporate. The white crystals left behind are the ammonium sulfate fertiliser.

Learning styles

Kinaesthetic: Making a fertiliser.

Visual: Creating a flow chart to show the purification of drinking water.

Intrapersonal: Completing calculations on percentage composition of different fertilisers.

Interpersonal: Working as a small group to prepare a report.

ICT link-up

A data logger could be used to show the pH changes in the neutralisation reaction to make the fertiliser ammonium sulfate.

Special needs

Instead of writing an article about the science behind gardening, the class could be split into groups of three. Each group could be given the task to make three posters with different focuses: soil pH, rotation, and fertilisers. Students could arrange their own group as they wish, e.g. each student taking responsibility for a poster, or splitting each poster into tasks and each student working on all the posters.

CHEMISTRY — ACIDS, ALKALIS AND SALTS

SUMMARY ANSWERS

1 a) C b) A c) E d) B e) F f) D

2 Beaker 1: OH^- and H^+
Beaker 2: O^{2-} and $2H^+$
Beaker 3: Pb^{2+} and $2Cl^-$

3 a) Hydrogen.

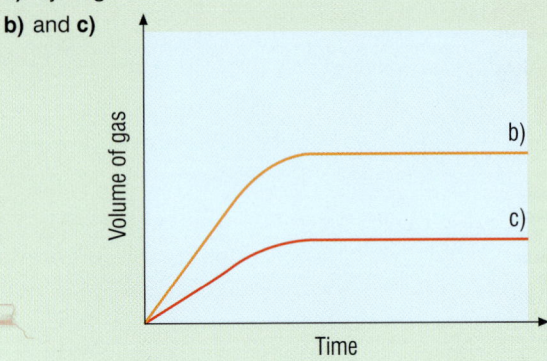

b) and c)

[Graph: Volume of gas (y-axis) against Time (x-axis); curve b) rises steeply and plateaus higher, curve c) rises with half the slope and plateaus lower.]

[Line on graph has half the initial slope of the first line, producing half as much hydrogen.]

4 a) $2KOH(aq) + H_2SO_4(aq) \rightarrow K_2SO_4(aq) + 2H_2O(l)$

b) $ZnO(s) + 2HNO_3(aq) \rightarrow Zn(NO_3)_2(aq) + H_2O(l)$

c) $Ca(s) + 2HCl(aq) \rightarrow CaCl_2(aq) + H_2(g)$

d) $Ba(NO_3)_2(aq) + Na_2SO_4(aq) \rightarrow BaSO_4(s) + 2NaNO_3(aq)$

Summary teaching suggestions

- **Special needs** – Question 4 could have the reactants already written out on a worksheet in the form of a word equation. There should be two lines for each product. Then a list of the chemicals should be displayed to the students. Each student then uses the list to decide which chemical should go on which line.
- **Gifted and talented** – Students could write balanced symbol equations, including state symbols for the reactions in question 2.
- **Learning styles**
  Kinaesthetic: Question 1 could be turned into a card sort.
  Visual: Question 3 allows students to sketch a graph.
  Auditory: Question 2 lends itself to a discussion before students try to answer the question.
  Intrapersonal: Question 4 allows students to work on chemical equations as individuals.
- **When to use the questions?**
  - Question 1 is a good indicator of language used in this section. It would be useful as a plenary or homework after lesson 7.1 had been taught.
  - Students could attempt the questions in the first half of the lesson. They could then swap their work with a neighbour, who should then try to mark the work, putting on suggestions for amendments. In the last ten minutes of the lesson, the work could be returned to the owner in order to make amendments and additions.
  - Question 4 is a good question to use after lessons 7.2 and 7.3 have been taught, as this utilises the general equations introduced in these two lessons.
  - Question 1 could be used to verbally assess the understanding of the key words.

ACIDS, ALKALIS AND SALTS: C2 7.1 – C2 7.4

SUMMARY QUESTIONS

1 Match the halves of the sentences together:

a) A base that is soluble in water ……	A …… a pH of exactly 7.
b) Pure water is neutral with ……	B …… form OH^- ions when they dissolve in water.
c) Acids are substances that ……	C …… is called an alkali.
d) Alkalis are substances that ……	D …… is acidic.
e) Indicators are substances that ……	E …… produce H^+ ions when they dissolve in water.
f) A solution with a pH less than 7 ……	F …… change colour when we add them to acids and alkalis.

2 The table shows the ions in substances in three pairs of beakers. Copy the table and draw lines between the ions that react in each beaker.

Beaker 1	Na^+	OH^-		H^+	Cl^-
Beaker 2	Cu^{2+}	O^{2-}		H^+	H^+	SO_4^{2-}
Beaker 3	Pb^{2+}	NO_3^-	NO_3^-	Cu^{2+}	Cl^-	Cl^-

3 A student carried out an investigation in which she dropped a piece of magnesium ribbon into some acid. She measured the total amount of gas that had been produced every 10 seconds and plotted this on a graph. At the end of the reaction some magnesium ribbon remained that had not reacted.
a) What gas does this reaction produce?
b) Sketch a graph of volume of gas (y-axis) against time (x-axis) that this student could have obtained.
c) Sketch another line on the graph to show the results that might be obtained if the student repeated this investigation, using the same acid but diluted so that its concentration was half of that used in the first investigation.

4 Write chemical equations to describe the following chemical reactions. (Each reaction forms a salt.)
a) Potassium hydroxide (an alkali) and sulfuric acid.
b) Zinc oxide (an insoluble base) and nitric acid.
c) Calcium metal and hydrochloric acid.
d) Barium nitrate and sodium sulfate (this reaction produces an insoluble salt – hint: all sodium salts are soluble).

EXAM-STYLE QUESTIONS

1 Magnesium hydroxide, $Mg(OH)_2$, is used in many antacids for relieving acid indigestion.
(a) Magnesium hydroxide is slightly soluble in water.
 (i) Give the formulae of the ions produced when it dissolves. (2)
 (ii) Give a value for the pH of the solution it forms. (1)
(b) Write a word equation for the reaction of magnesium hydroxide with hydrochloric acid. (2)
(c) Write a balanced symbol equation for the reaction. (2)
(d) Suggest why sodium hydroxide would not be suitable for use as a cure for indigestion. (2)

2 Copper(II) sulfate crystals can be made from an insoluble base and sulfuric acid.
(a) Name the insoluble base that can be used to make copper(II) sulfate. (1)
(b) Describe how to make a solution of copper(II) sulfate from $25\,cm^3$ of dilute sulfuric acid so that all of the acid is used. (3)
(c) Describe how you could make crystals of copper(II) sulfate from the solution. (3)

3 Salts are formed when acids react with alkalis.
(a) Complete the word equation:
 acid + alkali → ……… + ……… (2)
(b) What type of reaction takes place when an acid reacts with an alkali? (1)
(c) (i) Name the acid and alkali used to make potassium nitrate. (2)
 (ii) What would you use to show when the acid had completely reacted with the alkali? (1)
 (iii) Write a balanced symbol equation for the reaction that takes place. (2)

EXAM-STYLE ANSWERS

1 a) i) $OH^-(aq)$ and $Mg^{2+}(aq)$ *(2 marks)*
 ii) Any value between 8 and 12. *(1 mark)*

b) magnesium hydroxide + hydrochloric acid → magnesium chloride + water.
(1 mark for reactants, 1 mark for products) *(2 marks)*

c) $Mg(OH)_2 + 2HCl \rightarrow MgCl_2 + 2H_2O$
(1 mark for all correct formulae, 1 mark for balancing) *(2 marks)*

d) Sodium hydroxide is very (strongly) alkaline/has very high pH. *(1 mark)*
It is corrosive/it will damage skin or flesh *(1 mark)*
(do not accept just 'dangerous' or 'harmful').

2 a) Copper Oxide (copper(II) oxide). *(1 mark)*

b) *One mark each for:*
- Add copper(II) oxide to (warm) acid a little at a time.
- Until no more will dissolve/excess solid remains.
- Filter off the (excess) solid. *(3 marks)*

c) *One mark each for:*
- Heat/boil the solution.
- To evaporate some (but not all) of the water.
- Allow to cool.
- Filter off crystals.
- Allow to dry at room temperature/allow water to evaporate at room temperature. *(3 marks)*

3 a) Salt *(1 mark)* + water *(1 mark)* *(2 marks)*

b) Neutralisation *(1 mark)*

c) i) Potassium hydroxide *(1 mark)* + nitric acid *(1 mark)* *(2 marks)*
 ii) An indicator. *(1 mark)*
 iii) $KOH + HNO_3 \rightarrow KNO_3 + H_2O$ *(2 marks all correct, 1 mark for correct formulae with incorrect balancing).*

Additional chemistry

Exam teaching suggestions

- Allow students 40 minutes to do all five questions, with a total of 43 marks. Q1, Q2 and Q3 could be set after completing 7.2, Q4 after 7.3.
- In Q1, students are expected to apply their knowledge of acids and bases. Writing word equations and balanced symbol equations for reactions should be practised as often as possible and there are plenty of opportunities in teaching this topic. In part d) students should know that specific reasons are expected rather than simple ideas, such as 'it is harmful'.
- The preparation of a salt is separated into two parts in Q2. This approach could be helpful in teaching and revising this topic, making the learning more manageable, more bite-sized. Using bulleted answers to questions of this type can help students ensure that they are writing the required number of marking points and can help them focus on the essential steps, cutting out unnecessary statements.
- Summary equations, like that in Q3a) should be thoroughly learnt by students. Small cards or posters displayed in the room where they work or revise will help them remember such essential facts. These can be prepared in class and students can help each other to produce very effective learning aids.
- Q4 requires students to apply their knowledge to a new situation. They should be encouraged to attempt questions like this and not be put off by the unknown. Focusing on the key words helps. Any reasonable answer will usually gain credit.

HOW SCIENCE WORKS QUESTIONS

Chemistry to help!

Modern living produces enormous quantities of wastewater. Most of this can be treated in sewage works by biological processes. Sometimes biology cannot solve all of the problems. Chemistry is needed.

Phosphates are one such problem. You might have seen patches of stinging nettles near to old farms. These are due to the high concentrations of phosphates produced in animal (and human!) waste. This is a real problem when you have farms producing beef. In parts of USA they rear cattle with very little land.

The waste would normally be put on the land. It would cost a lot of money to transport the waste back to the farms that produced the feed. The waste is therefore dumped. The problem is that the high concentration of the phosphates causes water pollution problems.

Removing the phosphates at the sewage works by adding iron(III) chloride is also expensive. The wastewater therefore is treated with struvite, a magnesium salt that precipitates the phosphates.

Use these notes and your experience to answer these questions.

a) What are the economic issues associated with the disposal of animal waste? (2)
b) What are the environmental issues associated with the disposal of animal waste? (2)
c) What are the ethical issues associated with the use of chemistry to solve the problems of pollution? (1)
d) Who should be making the decisions about using chemistry to solve these problems? Explain your answer. (1)
e) Struvite can become a problem by precipitating out and blocking water pipes. What extra information would be useful to those using struvite? (1)

---

4 The effluent from nickel plating works is treated with sodium carbonate to precipitate nickel ions from the solution. The precipitate is separated from the solution by settlement in a tank. Filtration is not usually used as the main method of removing the precipitate, but can be used to remove small amounts of solids from the effluent after settlement.
   (a) Write a word equation for the reaction between nickel sulfate solution and sodium carbonate solution. (2)
   (b) Name the precipitate that is formed. (1)
   (c) How is most of the precipitate removed from the effluent? (1)
   (d) Suggest one reason why filtration is not used to remove most of the precipitate. (1)
   (e) Why is it necessary to remove metal ions like nickel from effluents? (1)

5 There are four main methods of making salts:
   A Acid + metal
   B Acid + insoluble base
   C Acid + alkali
   D Solution of salt A + solution of salt B
   (a) A student wanted to make some sodium sulfate.
       (i) Which method would be the best one to use? (1)
       (ii) Explain why you chose this method. (3)
       (iii) Name the reagents you would use. (2)
       (iv) Write a word equation for the reaction. (1)
   (b) Another student wanted to make some magnesium carbonate.
       (i) Which method would you use for this salt? (1)
       (ii) Explain why you chose this method. (2)
       (iii) Name the reagents you would use. (2)
       (iv) Write a word equation for the reaction. (1)

HOW SCIENCE WORKS ANSWERS

a) Economic issues: cost of transport of waste away from farm to where it can be used; cost of treating the waste on the farm; cost of treatment if it leaks into the water supply; is it still profitable to rear the cattle in this way?
b) Environmental issues: pollution of water supplies; survival of plants where it is dumped; use of fossil fuels to transport waste to where it can be used.
c) Ethical issues: should humans be using animals in such an artificial way to produce 'cheap' food?
d) Scientists should provide the evidence, and society in the shape of government should make the decisions.
e) Exactly how much struvite is needed to remove a quantity of phosphates – then none is left to block up the drains.

How science works teaching suggestions

- **Literacy guidance.** Key terms that should be clearly understood: ethical, environmental, economic.
- **Higher- and lower-level answers**
  - Higher-level answers are expected from c).
  - Lower-level answers are expected from d).
- **Gifted and talented.** Able students could review the responsibility of chemists for the environment.
- **How and when to use these questions.** When wishing to develop the meaning of ethical, economic and environmental issues. Also, the limitations of science in answering some important questions.
  The questions should be a stimulus for whole-class discussion.
- **Homework.** For homework, ask students to research one other topic that relates to the role of the chemist in either improving or reducing the quality of the environment.
- **ICT link-up.** The Internet could be a source for further information to research the economic, environmental and ethical issues.

---

4 a) nickel sulfate + sodium carbonate → nickel carbonate + sodium sulfate.
      (1 mark for reactants, 1 mark for products) (2 marks)
   b) Nickel carbonate (1 mark)
   c) By allowing it to settle/settlement in a tank. (1 mark)
   d) Filters will clog up/need frequently changing/filters are more expensive. (1 mark)
   e) (Nickel) metal ions are toxic/poisonous/harmful to living things. (1 mark)

5 a) i) C; acid + alkali (1 mark)
      ii) *Three from:*
          - Sodium sulfate is soluble (so cannot use D).
          - Sodium oxide is soluble in water/a soluble base (so cannot use B).
          - Sodium hydroxide is an alkali (so C is suitable).
          - Sodium metal is too reactive (to use safely with acid, so cannot use A). (3 marks)
      iii) Sodium hydroxide (1 mark)
           Sulfuric acid (1 mark)
      iv) sodium hydroxide + sulfuric acid → sodium sulfate + water (1 mark)

   b) i) D; solution of salt A + solution of salt B (1 mark)
      ii) *Two from:*
          - Magnesium carbonate is insoluble.
          - Magnesium carbonate reacts with acids.
          - There is no suitable acid that can be used. (2 marks)
      iii) Any soluble magnesium salt e.g. magnesium chloride. (1 mark)
           Any soluble carbonate (alkali metal carbonate) e.g. sodium carbonate. (1 mark)
      iv) Depends on their choice of reactants. (1 mark)

205

CHEMISTRY — ACIDS, ALKALIS AND SALTS

C2 Examination-Style Questions

Examiner's comments

Allow 40 minutes to complete all of the questions if done in a single session. Q1 and Q2 could be set after completing C2 2, Q3 after C2 3, Q4 after C2 4 and Q5 after C2 6.

Q6 is best left until the end of the unit.

Questions will be set in contexts that are unfamiliar to candidates. These questions will provide candidates with information so that they can apply their skills, knowledge and understanding (Assessment Objective 2). Candidates do not need to learn any substantive content outside the current specifications that appear in questions given as examples in specimen assessment materials, or from previous examination papers.

Many candidates do not attempt calculations or they give up at the first problem they encounter. Encourage students to attempt all parts of a problem, and to use whatever answer they get for the next step to benefit from error carried forward (e.c.f.) marks.

Answers to Questions

1. (a) hydrogen chloride
   (b) neon
   (c) diamond
   (d) sodium chloride
   (e) magnesium   *(1 mark each, total 5 marks)*

2. (a) Li or dot at centre of two concentric circles, inner circle with two dots/crosses, outer circle with one dot/cross. *(all correct = 2 marks, one error or omission = 1 mark)*

   (b) F or dot at centre of two concentric circles, inner circle with two dots/crosses, outer circle with seven dots/crosses. *(all correct = 2 marks, one error or omission = 1 mark)*

   (c) Lithium ion: EITHER Li$^+$ or [Li]$^+$ OR Li at centre of circle with two dots/crosses (with brackets) and $^+$ at top right-hand side.   *(1 mark)*
   Fluoride ion: EITHER F at centre of two concentric circles with two dots/crosses on inner circle and eight dots/crosses on outer circle (surrounded by brackets) with $^-$ at top right-hand side OR F surrounded by eight dots/crosses with $^-$ at top right-hand side.   *(2 marks)*
   (It is acceptable to show only the outer electrons in bonding diagrams)

3. (a) 13
   (b) 2,8,3
   (c) 8
   (d) [2,8]$^{2-}$ *(allow 2,8)*
   (e) 39
   (f) K$^+$
   (g) 18
   (h) [2,8,8]$^-$ *(allow 2,8,8)*   *(1 mark each, total 8 marks)*

   continues opposite ›

EXAMINATION-STYLE QUESTIONS

1. Match these substances with the descriptions (a) to (e):

   diamond, hydrogen chloride, magnesium, neon, sodium chloride

   (a) A compound made of small molecules.
   (b) A gas at room temperature made of single atoms.
   (c) A giant lattice of atoms that are covalently bonded.
   (d) An ionic solid with a high melting point.
   (e) A giant lattice that conducts electricity when it is solid.   *(5 marks)*

   See pages 130–7

2. (a) Draw a dot and cross diagram to show the electron arrangement of a lithium atom, atomic number 3.   *(2 marks)*
   (b) Draw a dot and cross diagram to show the electron arrangement of a fluorine atom, atomic number 9.   *(2 marks)*
   (c) Draw dot and cross diagrams to show the ions in lithium fluoride.   *(3 marks)*

   See pages 116–19

3. Complete the table that shows information about some atoms.

Symbol	Atomic number	Mass number	Number of protons	Number of neutrons	Electron arrangement of atom	Formula of ion	Electron arrangement of ion
Al	13	27	(a)	14	(b)	Al^{3+}	[2,8]$^{3+}$
O	8	16	8	(c)	2,6	O^{2-}	(d)
K	19	(e)	19	20	2,8,8,1	(f)	[2,8,8]$^+$
Cl	17	35	17	(g)	2,8,7	Cl$^-$	(h)

   (8 marks)

   See pages 114–21, 142

4. A student added 20g of marble chips to 50cm^3 of dilute hydrochloric acid in a conical flask. The flask was put onto a balance. The table shows the mass of gas that was given off. Some marble chips were left in the flask at the end of the reaction.

Mass of gas given off (g)	0	0.14	0.27	0.38	0.47	0.51	0.57	0.59	0.60
Time (minutes)	0	1.0	2.0	3.0	4.0	5.0	6.0	7.0	8.0

   (a) Plot a graph of the results. Put time on the horizontal axis and mass lost on the vertical axis. Draw a smooth line through the points, omitting any result that is anomalous.   *(5 marks)*
   (b) The rate of this reaction decreases with time. Explain how you can tell this from the graph.   *(1 mark)*

   The student decided to extend his work to see if temperature affected the rate at which the gas was produced.

   (c) (i) Suggest one control variable he should use.

   See pages 163–5

   GET IT RIGHT!
   It is important to express yourself clearly in answers that require explanations. In Question 4(b), you should make it clear that the gradient or slope of the graph shows the rate of reaction at that time. Also, if you are asked how collisions affect the rate of reaction, it is not enough to say there are more collisions. It is the frequency of collisions (the number of collisions per second) that the rate depends upon.

206

BUMP UP THE GRADE

Students should be encouraged to read and attempt all parts of each question. Questions do not necessarily become more difficult towards the end, and may contain some easier parts. These should not be missed!

206

GET IT RIGHT!

It is important that students express themselves clearly in answers that require explanations. They do not always make it clear in their answers that they understand it is the gradient or slope of the graph that shows the rate of reaction at a particular time, and that the rate decreases as the reaction proceeds. Also, when explaining how collisions affect the rate of reaction, it is not enough to say there are more collisions. It is the frequency of collisions (the number of collisions per second) that the rate depends upon, and so the number of collisions needs to be related to the time for full marks.

(ii) Describe how he would control that variable. *(2 marks)*
(d) Suggest a suitable range of temperatures he could use. *(1 mark)*
(e) Suggest a suitable interval between temperatures. *(1 mark)*
(f) Use the first set of data to suggest a suitable length of time to leave the reaction. *(1 mark)*

5 Complete the table that shows information about the electrolysis of different substances. Carbon electrodes were used.

See pages 186–7

Substance	Positive ions present	Negative ions present	Product at negative electrode	Product at positive electrode
Molten magnesium chloride	Mg^{2+}	Cl^-	magnesium	(a)
Aqueous solution of potassium chloride	K^+ H^+	(b)	hydrogen	chlorine
Dilute sulfuric acid	(c)	SO_4^{2-} OH^-	hydrogen	oxygen
Aqueous solution of copper(II) sulfate	Cu^{2+} H^+	SO_4^{2-} OH^-	(d)	(e)

(5 marks)

6 Ammonium sulfate $(NH_4)_2SO_4$, is an important fertiliser. It is made by reacting ammonia solution with sulfuric acid. The reaction can be represented by the equation:

$$H_2SO_4(aq) + 2NH_4OH(aq) \rightarrow (NH_4)_2SO_4(aq) + 2H_2O(l)$$

See pages 196, 200

(a) How can you tell from the equation that ammonium sulfate is soluble? *(1 mark)*
(b) (i) Which ions make the sulfuric acid solution acidic? *(1 mark)*
   (ii) Which ions make the ammonia solution alkaline? *(1 mark)*
   (iii) What name is used to describe the reaction between these ions? *(1 mark)*
(c) A student made 15.4 g of ammonium sulfate from 0.2 moles of sulfuric acid.
   (i) What is the mass of one mole of ammonium sulfate? *(2 marks)*
   (ii) What mass of ammonium sulfate can be made from 0.2 moles of sulfuric acid, according to the equation? *(1 mark)*
   (iii) What was the percentage yield of ammonium sulfate obtained by the student? *(2 marks)* [Higher]

See pages 148–50

GET IT RIGHT!
In calculations, always give your answer to an appropriate number of significant figures or decimal places (usually 2 or 3 significant figures or one or two decimal places).

> continues from previous page

4 (a) *One mark each for:*
   - Both axes labelled.
   - Suitable scales used.
   - All points correctly plotted (+/− half small square).
   - Smooth line through points.
   - Omitting point at 5 minutes. *(5 marks)*

(b) Slope/gradient decreases with time OR slope/gradient/line is steeper at the beginning or becomes less steep or levels off. *(1 mark)*

(c) (i) E.g. concentration of acid; size of marble chips. *(1 mark)*
   (ii) Linked to the above e.g. ensure that the same concentration of acid is used for each temperature. *(1 mark)*

(d) E.g. 20°C to 60°C – reasonable within practical and safety limits. *(1 mark)*

(e) At least five, equally spaced. *(1 mark)*

(f) About four minutes. *(1 mark)*

5 (a) chlorine *(1 mark)*

(b) Cl^- and OH^- *(accept with correct state symbols, i.e. aq)* *(1 mark)*

(c) H^+ *(accept H_3O^+, $H^+(aq)$, $H_3O^+(aq)$)* *(1 mark)*

(d) copper *(1 mark)*

(e) oxygen *(1 mark)*

6 (a) Its state symbol is (aq)/it is aqueous. *(1 mark)*

(b) (i) Hydrogen ions/H^+/$H^+(aq)$/H_3O^+/$H_3O^+(aq)$. *(1 mark)*

   (ii) Hydroxide ions/OH^-/$OH^-(aq)$. *(1 mark)*

   (iii) Neutralisation. *(1 mark)*

(c) (i) 132 g *(2 marks for correct answer with units)* *(correct working, e.g. $(14 + 4) \times 2 + 32 + (16 \times 4)$ gains 1 mark)*

   (ii) 26.4 g *(1 mark)*

   (iii) 58.3% *(2 marks for correct answer)* *(correct working, e.g. $15.4 \times 100/26.4$ (e.c.f. from (ii) can gain 2 marks)*
   [**HT** only]

CHEMISTRY

C3 | Further chemistry

Key Stage 3 curriculum links

The following link to **'What you already know'**:

- That elements are shown in the periodic table and consist of atoms, which we can represent using chemical symbols.
- How elements vary widely in their physical properties, including appearance, state at room temperature, magnetic properties and thermal and electrical conductivity, and how these properties can be used to classify elements as metals or non-metals.
- How elements combine through chemical reactions to form compounds with a definite composition.
- To represent compounds by formulae and summarise reactions by word equations.
- About the displacement reactions that take place between metals and solutions of salts of other metals.
- How metals and bases, including carbonates, react with acids, and what the products of these reactions are.
- About some everyday applications of neutralisation.
- To identify patterns in chemical reactions.

QCA Scheme of work
8E – Atoms and elements
8F – Compounds and mixtures
9E – Reactions of metals and metal compounds
9F – Patterns of reactivity

Links with Units C1 and C2
11.1 – How do rocks provide building materials?
11.1 – How do rocks provide metals and how are metals used?
12.1 – How do sub-atomic particles help us to understand the structures of substances?
12.2 – How do structures influence the properties and uses of substances?
12.6 – How can we use ions in solutions?

Chapters in this unit
- Development of the periodic table
- More about acids and bases
- Water
- Energy calculations
- Analysis

RECAP ANSWERS

1. a) Carbon.
   b) Hydrogen.
   c) Nitrogen.
   d) Oxygen.
   e) Sodium.
   f) Iron.
2. Groups.
3. Sodium chloride.
4. A substance that forms a solution with a pH of less than 7.
5. They form a neutral solution.
6. Hydrogen gas.
7. Crystals of sodium chloride will form in the beaker.

CHEMISTRY

C3 | Further chemistry

What you already know

Here is a quick reminder of previous work that you will find useful in this unit:

- The elements are shown in the periodic table and consist of atoms, which we can represent using chemical symbols.
- The properties of elements, compounds and mixtures can be used to classify them.
- Elements combine through chemical reactions to form compounds.
- We can represent compounds by formulae and we can summarise reactions by word equations.
- Displacement reactions take place between metals and solutions of salts of other metals.
- Metals and bases react with acids.
- Some everyday applications of neutralisation such as indigestion tablets.
- We can identify patterns in chemical reactions.

Filter beds like these are used to purify water

Lime is used to raise the pH of acidic soil

RECAP QUESTIONS

1. What elements do the following symbols represent?
   a) C b) H c) N d) O e) Na f) Fe
2. What do we call the columns of elements in the periodic table?
3. Complete the word equation: sodium + chlorine →
4. What is an acid?
5. What is formed when alkalis react with acids?
6. What gas is produced when magnesium reacts with dilute hydrochloric acid?
7. A small volume of sodium chloride solution is left in a beaker on the window sill over the summer holidays. Explain what you will see when you get back after the holidays.

208

Teaching suggestions

What you already know

- **Statements** – Ask students to think about each statement, then to generate a sentence about the topic including a fact that is pertinent to the statements. Refer to the Electronic Resource for C3 opener on the GCSE Chemistry CD ROM 'What you already know'.

- **Mind map** – Students often compartmentalise information and do not apply concepts and skills across different topics. Students could create an A-map to show the topic structure. Ask the students to pick three colours. Choose one colour to write the topic area in the centre of the page and draw a small image

208

Further chemistry

SPECIFICATION LINK-UP
Unit: Chemistry 3

This unit covers the following:

How was the periodic table developed and how can it help us understand the reactions of elements?

The periodic table was developed to classify elements before atomic structure was understood. It is a powerful aid to understanding the properties and reactions of the elements.

What are strong and weak acids and alkalis? How can we find amounts of acids and alkalis in solutions?

Acids and alkalis vary in strength as well as concentration. Titrations can be used to find the amounts of acid or alkali in a solution.

What is in the water we drink?

The water we drink is not pure because it contains dissolved substances. It should be safe to drink, which means it does not contain anything that could cause us harm. Some of the dissolved substances are beneficial to our health but some cause hard water.

How much energy is involved in chemical reactions?

Knowing the amount of energy involved in chemical reactions is useful so that resources are used efficiently and economically. It is possible to measure the amount of energy experimentally or to calculate it. Controlling the amount of energy intake in our diet is important in avoiding obesity.

How do we identify and analyse substances?

A range of chemical tests can be used for the detection and identification of elements and compounds. Instrumental methods that are quick, accurate and sensitive have been developed to identify and measure substances, often in very small samples. These methods are used to monitor products, our health, the environment and in forensic science.

Further chemistry

Making connections

Acids and bases around the home

Stinging nettles are covered with tiny hairs. When you touch a nettle the hairs stick into your skin. They inject an acid into you (called oxalic acid) – this is painful. (See the photo opposite.) It makes a tiny swelling as your body pumps liquid into the area to dilute the acid.

The traditional remedy for nettle stings is rubbing a dock leaf on the sting. But dock leaves are acidic too! It's likely that dock leaves help because rubbing the sting with them releases moist sap from the leaf which is cooling. But people hundreds of years ago had the right idea. They thought that goose dung was a good remedy! And what's so special about goose dung? It's alkaline!

That full-up, bloated feeling that you sometimes get when you've eaten a really big, rich meal can make you feel very uncomfortable. Sometimes the feeling doesn't go away, and you need something to 'settle your stomach'.

Indigestion tablets contain substances such as calcium carbonate. These react with the acid in your stomach to neutralise it and so put a stop to indigestion. Some of these substances produce carbon dioxide when they neutralise the acid – and this has to go somewhere! The quickest way out of the stomach is back up into your mouth ... so you'd better be prepared to say 'pardon me!'

Baking powder is used to make cakes rise. It contains sodium hydrogencarbonate and tartaric acid. They are mixed together as dry powders so they do not react.

In the moist cake mixture the two chemicals react to produce carbon dioxide gas. Cooking the cake speeds up this reaction, and lots of gas bubbles form in the soft cake mixture. As the cake cooks the mixture hardens with the bubbles of gas trapped inside. This makes the cake light and tasty!

ACTIVITY

Chemistry is found all round the home – there are three examples here. But how many people really understand what's happening in these situations?

Design a page to go at the start of a kitchen book that will explain some of the chemistry of cooking, eating and gardening to people who will be using the book.

Chapters in this unit

Development of the periodic table → More about acids and bases → Water → Energy calculations → Analysis

---

- **Flash cards** – Most of the key points can be summarised as definitions (e.g. element) or as word equations. Give the students a selection of A6 sized cards and allow them to write their own revision flash cards, one for each statement,
e.g. sodium hydroxide + hydrochloric acid → water + sodium chloride
Higher attaining students could include chemical examples to highlight facts and write balanced symbol equations.

Recap questions

- **A4 whiteboards** – Give each student an A4 whiteboard (or laminated piece of paper), a washable marker and eraser. Read out the questions and ask them to note their answers and show you for instant feedback. Students can refer to the Student Book to help them, or wait for others to write and show their answers and use this to aid them with their own. This activity has a fun element and allows you to assess the baseline understanding of topics that will be developed.

- **AfL (Assessment for learning)** – Instead of allowing the students to answer the questions, ask the students to work in pairs to generate the mark scheme, including mark allocation. Students should not only consider the 'perfect' answer but all connotations that could be awarded marks, and answers that are close but not worthy of marks.

Making connections (poster)

Many people do not realise that they use chemistry in their everyday life. Ask students to design a poster to show how neutralisation is used in everyday life. The students can choose what audience that they wish the poster to be for, e.g. local library, school, workplace, billboard. Encourage them to think about the language and imagery that they will use and how it relates to the audience. Students could generate their poster using a desktop publishing package.

Have a go! (poster)

Show students some cookbooks and explain that they are to write and design an introductory page for a similar book. Their page needs to explain the chemistry of cooking. Allow students to think about what chemistry is involved in cooking and complete a class brainstorm on the board. Students should then generate their page. This activity could be completed in small groups, where each group member has a different job e.g. artist, researcher, writer, etc.

---

to help them remember the topic (e.g. Chemistry, and a test tube). That colour will no longer be used. With the second colour, draw wavy long lines from the central idea, on each wavy line, following its contour write the topic headings, again including images to help to remember each word, e.g. metal and a picture of a weight. Then using the last colour, add wavy lines from each topic area to put in the fine details about the topic area, each with an image to help to remember (e.g. list the properties of metals on separate lines). This helps students view the topic as a whole. Any missing links can be quickly identified and you can challenge any misconceptions.

CHEMISTRY

DEVELOPMENT OF THE PERIODIC TABLE

C3 1.1

The early periodic table

LEARNING OBJECTIVES

Students should learn:
- The importance of the periodic table.
- That the periodic table has developed since its discovery.

LEARNING OUTCOMES

Most students should be able to:
- Describe how the periodic table was first constructed.

Some students should also be able to:
- Explain why the periodic table is important.
- Explain how the periodic table was discovered.
- Explain why Mendeleev's ordering of the elements was so innovative.

Teaching suggestions

- **Gifted and talented.** Mendeleev was laughed at when he first went to the scientific community with gaps in his table. Ask the students to act out a scene where great scientists were ridiculing Mendeleev at a meeting.
- **Learning styles**
  Kinaesthetic: Sorting the elements into different groupings.
  Visual: Spotting the differences between the original and modern periodic table.
  Auditory: Listening to discussions in groups.
  Interpersonal: Working in groups.
  Intrapersonal: Deciding if a statement is true or false.
- **Homework.** Ask students to find out another way that elements were ordered in the past, e.g. the law of triads.
- **ICT link-up.** The Internet or RSC electronic data book can be used to gain information about the elements. Use Electronic Resource C3 3.1 'periodic table' from the GCSE Chemistry CD ROM.

SPECIFICATION LINK-UP   Unit: Chemistry 3.13.1

- Newlands and then Mendeleev attempted to classify the elements by arranging them in order of their atomic weights. The list can be arranged in a table so that elements with similar properties are in columns, known as Groups. The table is called a periodic table because similar properties occur at regular intervals.
- The early periodic tables were incomplete and some elements were placed in inappropriate Groups if the strict order of atomic weights were followed. Mendeleev overcame some of the problems by leaving gaps for elements that he thought had not been discovered.

Students should use their skills, knowledge and understanding of 'How Science Works':
- to explain how attempts to classify elements in a systematic way, including those of Newlands and Mendeleev, have led through the growth of chemical knowledge to the modern periodic table.

Lesson structure

STARTER

True or false – Ask students to show if they think a statement is true (put their thumbs up), false (their thumbs down), unsure (their thumbs horizontal). You could read out the following statements:
- The periodic table is the only way to classify the elements. [False]
- Most elements are metals. [True]
- Most elements are gases at room temperature. [False]
- The periodic table can be used to make predictions about the products formed in chemical reactions. [True]
- Most non-metallic elements are gases at 20°C. [True]
- The metals are on the right of the periodic table. [False] (5 minutes)

List – Show the students a selection of different elements in sealed Petri dishes. Maybe put a different selection of about 10 on each table. Ask the students to sort the elements into different groups. They might select colour, metal/non-metals, state of matter at 20°C, hazard, increasing atomic number. Ask each group to feedback on how they ordered their elements. (5 minutes)

MAIN

- There have been many attempts to classify the elements, such as Dalton's table, Newlands' law of octaves and Mendeleev's table. Ask the students to imagine that they work for an advertising agency. They are to make an advert for each method of listing elements. Their advert needs to be persuasive, as they want scientists to subscribe to their method of listing the elements.
- In pairs, give the students 20 cards of A6 in size. Ask the students to make a separate card for each of the first 20 elements.
- The card should include the name, symbol, atomic mass of the element, state at 20°C and a little information about its chemical reactions.
- Then ask the students to sort the cards.
- Circulate around the different groups to find out how the students have ordered the cards. Students may choose alphabetical order, increasing mass, groupings in terms of chemical properties.
- Allow the students to 'visit' other groups to find out how they ordered them.
- Ask the students to make a decision on how they would order the first 20 elements and ask them to jot it in their notes with an explanation of their choice.
- Then give the students a mystery element card, only including chemical and physical data. Ask the students to place this into their table.

- Then hold a discussion about how the elements were ordered by each group and draw into the discussion how Mendeleev discovered the periodic table.
- Allow students to contrast their ordering with Mendeleev's table and discuss the leaving of gaps in his table.

PLENARIES

Spot the difference – Show the students Mendeleev's original periodic table. Ask students to contrast this with the current periodic table and make a list of differences. (5–10 minutes)

Think, pair, square – Ask students to think about why the periodic table is important. Then ask students to discuss their answers in pairs and finally in groups of four. Then ask each group of four for a reason why the periodic table is important and list this on the board. (10 minutes)

ACTIVITY & EXTENSION IDEAS

- Allow students to consider the f-block elements and how they fit into the modern periodic table.
- Encourage students to consider why there were gaps in the periodic table proposed by Mendeleev, and how he managed to predict the properties of these chemicals.
- Ask students to write a letter from Mendeleev to explain to a friend his great discovery. Students may even wish to 'age' the paper using tea bags and singe the edges with a candle. They could even melt some candle wax and make a seal.

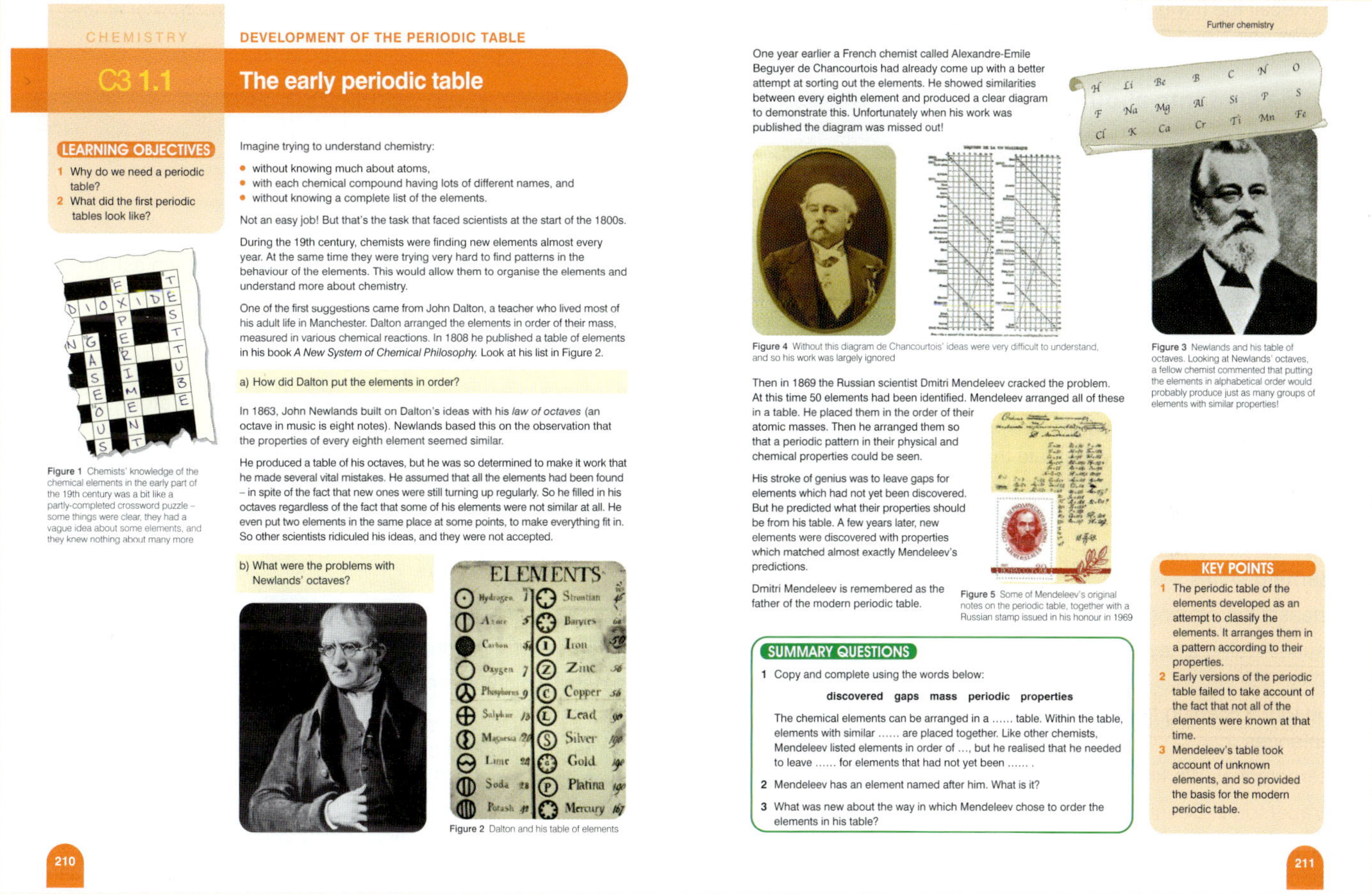

Further chemistry

CHEMISTRY
DEVELOPMENT OF THE PERIODIC TABLE

C3 1.1 The early periodic table

LEARNING OBJECTIVES
1. Why do we need a periodic table?
2. What did the first periodic tables look like?

Imagine trying to understand chemistry:
- without knowing much about atoms,
- with each chemical compound having lots of different names, and
- without knowing a complete list of the elements.

Not an easy job! But that's the task that faced scientists at the start of the 1800s.

During the 19th century, chemists were finding new elements almost every year. At the same time they were trying very hard to find patterns in the behaviour of the elements. This would allow them to organise the elements and understand more about chemistry.

One of the first suggestions came from John Dalton, a teacher who lived most of his adult life in Manchester. Dalton arranged the elements in order of their mass, measured in various chemical reactions. In 1808 he published a table of elements in his book *A New System of Chemical Philosophy*. Look at his list in Figure 2.

a) How did Dalton put the elements in order?

In 1863, John Newlands built on Dalton's ideas with his *law of octaves* (an octave in music is eight notes). Newlands based this on the observation that the properties of every eighth element seemed similar.

He produced a table of his octaves, but he was so determined to make it work that he made several vital mistakes. He assumed that all the elements had been found – in spite of the fact that new ones were still turning up regularly. So he filled in his octaves regardless of the fact that some of his elements were not similar at all. He even put two elements in the same place at some points, to make everything fit in. So other scientists ridiculed his ideas, and they were not accepted.

b) What were the problems with Newlands' octaves?

Figure 1 Chemists' knowledge of the chemical elements in the early part of the 19th century was a bit like a partly-completed crossword puzzle – some things were clear, they had a vague idea about some elements, and they knew nothing about many more

Figure 2 Dalton and his table of elements

One year earlier a French chemist called Alexandre-Emile Beguyer de Chancourtois had already come up with a better attempt at sorting out the elements. He showed similarities between every eighth element and produced a clear diagram to demonstrate this. Unfortunately when his work was published the diagram was missed out!

Then in 1869 the Russian scientist Dmitri Mendeleev cracked the problem. At this time 50 elements had been identified. Mendeleev arranged all of these in a table. He placed them in the order of their atomic masses. Then he arranged them so that a periodic pattern in their physical and chemical properties could be seen.

His stroke of genius was to leave gaps for elements which had not yet been discovered. But he predicted what their properties should be from his table. A few years later, new elements were discovered with properties which matched almost exactly Mendeleev's predictions.

Dmitri Mendeleev is remembered as the father of the modern periodic table.

Figure 4 Without this diagram de Chancourtois' ideas were very difficult to understand, and so his work was largely ignored

Figure 3 Newlands and his table of octaves. Looking at Newlands' octaves, a fellow chemist commented that putting the elements in alphabetical order would probably produce just as many groups of elements with similar properties!

Figure 5 Some of Mendeleev's original notes on the periodic table, together with a Russian stamp issued in his honour in 1969

SUMMARY QUESTIONS

1 Copy and complete using the words below:

  discovered   gaps   mass   periodic   properties

  The chemical elements can be arranged in a …… table. Within the table, elements with similar …… are placed together. Like other chemists, Mendeleev listed elements in order of …, but he realised that he needed to leave …… for elements that had not yet been …… .

2 Mendeleev has an element named after him. What is it?

3 What was new about the way in which Mendeleev chose to order the elements in his table?

KEY POINTS

1. The periodic table of the elements developed as an attempt to classify the elements. It arranges them in a pattern according to their properties.
2. Early versions of the periodic table failed to take account of the fact that not all of the elements were known at that time.
3. Mendeleev's table took account of unknown elements, and so provided the basis for the modern periodic table.

SUMMARY ANSWERS

1 Periodic, properties, mass, gaps, discovered.

2 Mendelevium.

3 He left gaps for elements that were as yet undiscovered.

Answers to in-text questions

a) In order of their mass.

b) He assumed that all elements had been found, so that some elements in an octave were not similar to the others.

KEY POINTS

Start a spider diagram using the key points from this spread. Then at the end of each lesson during this chapter, encourage students to add the new key points to their diagram.

CHEMISTRY   DEVELOPMENT OF THE PERIODIC TABLE

C3 1.2 The modern periodic table

LEARNING OBJECTIVES

Students should learn:

- That elements fit into groups.
- That there are patterns of behaviour in groups.

LEARNING OUTCOMES

Most students should be able to:

- Label the main groups of the periodic table.
- Determine which group a given element belongs to.
- Recall the trend in reactivity in Groups 1 and 7.

Some students should also be able to:

- Explain why the chemical properties are similar in a group.
- Explain why reactivity changes in Groups 1 and 7. [**HT** only]

Teaching suggestions

- **Special needs.** The students could be given a prompt card with questions/statements to help them complete their periodic table. Their outline could also include a key, which they need to just add colour to.
- **Learning styles**
  Kinaesthetic: Sorting the cards.
  Visual: Adding a key to the periodic table.
  Auditory: Listening to different students' sentences.
  Interpersonal: Working in pairs.
  Intrapersonal: Defining key terms.
- **ICT link-up.** Use Simulation C3 1.2 'periodic table' from the GCSE Chemistry CD ROM.
- **Homework.** Ask students to create a rhyme or mnemonic to help them remember the patterns of reactivity in Groups 1 and 7.

SPECIFICATION LINK-UP   Unit: Chemistry 3.13.1

- *When electrons, protons and neutrons were discovered early in the 20th century, the periodic table was arranged in order of atomic (proton) numbers. When this was done all elements were placed in appropriate groups.*
- *The modern periodic table can be seen as an arrangement of the elements in terms of their electronic structures. Elements in the same Group have the same number of electrons in their highest occupied energy level (outer shell).*
- *The trends in reactivity within Groups in the periodic table can be explained because the higher the energy level:*
  – *the more easily electrons are lost*
  – *the less easily electrons are gained.*   [**HT** only]

Students should use their skills, knowledge and understanding of 'How Science Works':

- *to explain why scientists regarded a periodic table of the elements first as a curiosity, then as a useful tool, and finally as an important summary of the structure of atoms.*

Lesson structure

STARTER

Labelling an atom – Give the students a diagram of a helium atom, just the size of A6. All the students then add as many labels and information as they can. Then ask them to swap with a partner, who should mark the information and make any amendments. Students can then stick this into their notes. (10 minutes)

Definitions – Ask students to define the following terms:

- Atomic number [same as proton number, the number of protons in an atom].
- Mass number [number of protons and neutrons in an atom].
- Isotope [atoms with the same proton number, but different mass number, i.e. a different number of neutrons]. (5 minutes)

MAIN

- Give students a blank A3 periodic table and a selection of colours. Ask them to label each group (1 to 0) and add extra names if they can (e.g. alkali metals).
- Then ask the students to detail which elements are metals, non-metals, liquids and gases by developing their own key.
- Also ask students to work out the electronic structure of the first 20 elements and note them in the appropriate box, e.g. Ca 2.8.8.2.
- Finally ask students to determine any relationship between electronic structure and position in the periodic table. Hopefully they will realise that the number of outer shell electrons is the same as the group number and that the number of shells is the same as the period number.
- Alternatively, give the students a pack of cards with the electronic structure of the first 20 elements. Ask them to order the cards in the form of the periodic table. Then challenge the students to work out the connection between the group number and the electronic structure.
- State the trends in reactivity in Groups 1 and 7. Then ask the students to explain the trends in prose, using electronic structures. The explanation for the trends in reactivity is Higher Tier content.

PLENARIES

Copy and complete – Ask students to copy and complete the following two sentences with as much scientific detail and language as possible:

- The reactivity in Group 1 . . .
- The reactivity in Group 7 . . .

Then ask a few students to read out and share their sentences. (10 minutes)

Answering objectives – Split the students into pairs, and ask them to read the learning objectives from the Student Book. Then ask the groups to generate an answer to each of the questions, asking each pair to note their answer on the board. Then allow the students time to read all the answers and take a vote as to which is the best response. Finally, ask all the students to copy the objective and the chosen answer from the board into their notes. (15 minutes)

ACTIVITY & EXTENSION IDEAS

- Students could wear sports bibs to represent the different sub-atomic particles in an atom. This drama then can be used to physically explain the effect of shielding on the outer electrons and its effect on reactivity.
- Ask students to find the trends in reactivity of some other groups of the periodic table.

CHEMISTRY — DEVELOPMENT OF THE PERIODIC TABLE

C3 1.2 The modern periodic table

LEARNING OBJECTIVES
1 How do the elements fit into groups in the periodic table?
2 What are the patterns of behaviour within the groups?

Using the relative atomic mass of elements was the only option available to Mendeleev at that time. His periodic table produced patterns which were recognised and accepted, but it had its limitations.

If we put the elements in order of the mass of their atoms, most elements end up in a group which behave in a similar way. But not all elements do this.

For example, argon atoms have a greater atomic mass than potassium atoms. This would mean that argon (a noble gas) would get grouped with extremely reactive metals such as sodium and lithium. And potassium (an extremely reactive metal) would be put with the noble gases. So argon would go in front of potassium in the periodic table, even though its atoms are heavier.

DID YOU KNOW?
The alkali metal caesium reacts explosively with cold water, and reacts with ice at temperatures above −116°C.

a) Find another pair of elements that get placed in the wrong order if atomic masses are used. (Refer to the periodic table on the next page.)

Once scientists began to find out more about atoms at the start of the 20th century, they could solve the problem described above. The structure of the atom was the key to developing the modern periodic table.

We now arrange the elements in order of their atomic (proton) number. This puts them all in exactly the right place in the periodic table. Their patterns of physical and chemical properties show this.

The periodic table is now a reliable model. It arranges the elements in groups with similar properties. It also provides us with an important summary of the structure of the atoms of all the elements.

b) How are elements arranged in the modern periodic table?

Going up and down the groups

Elements in the same group of the periodic table have similar properties. That's because their atoms have the same number of electrons in the highest occupied (outer) energy level.

HIGHER
Reactivity INCREASES going down the group – as the atoms get bigger the single electron in the outer energy level is attracted less strongly to the positive nucleus. This is because it is further away from the nucleus, and the inner shells of electrons screen it from the positive charge on the nucleus. The outer electron is easier to lose, so elements lower down the group are MORE reactive.

Group 7
Reactivity DECREASES going down the group – as the atoms get bigger an electron added to the outer energy level is attracted less strongly to the positive nucleus. This is because it is further away from the nucleus, and the inner shells of electrons screen it from the positive charge on the nucleus. An extra electron is less easily attracted into the outer shell, so elements lower down the group are LESS reactive.

Within a group, the properties of the elements are affected by the number of lower energy levels underneath the outer level. As we go down a group the number of occupied energy levels increases, and the atoms get bigger. This means that the outer electrons are further from the positive nucleus. There are also more energy levels between them and the nucleus.

This has two effects:
- the larger atoms **lose** electrons **more** easily,
- the larger atoms **gain** electrons **less** easily.

In both cases this happens because the outer electrons are further away from the nucleus. Not only that, the inner energy levels 'screen' or 'shield' the outer electrons from the positive charge in the nucleus. We can see this effect with the alkali metals and the halogens. (See the boxes on the left.)

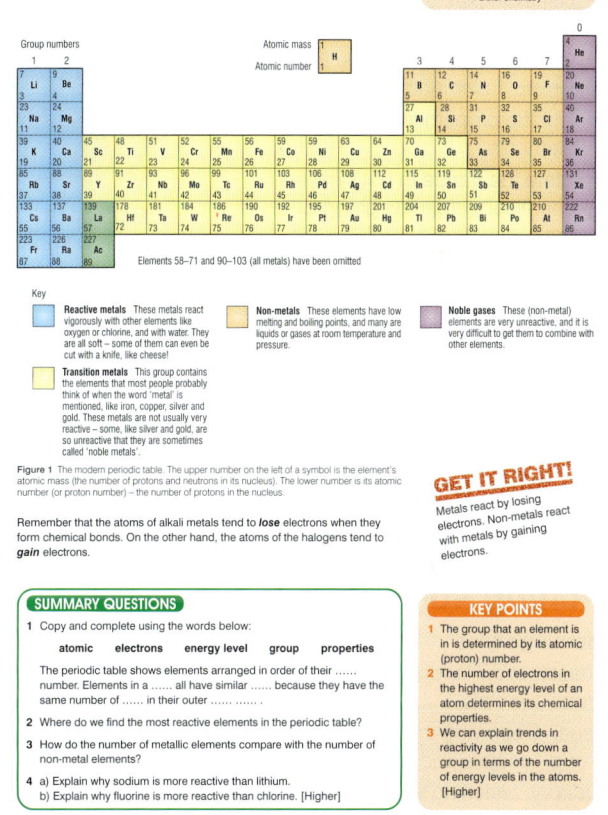

Figure 1 The modern periodic table. The upper number on the left of a symbol is the element's atomic mass (the number of protons and neutrons in its nucleus). The lower number is its atomic number (or proton number) – the number of protons in the nucleus.

Remember that the atoms of alkali metals tend to **lose** electrons when they form chemical bonds. On the other hand, the atoms of the halogens tend to **gain** electrons.

GET IT RIGHT!
Metals react by losing electrons. Non-metals react with metals by gaining electrons.

SUMMARY QUESTIONS

1 Copy and complete using the words below:

atomic   electrons   energy level   group   properties

The periodic table shows elements arranged in order of their …… number. Elements in a …… all have similar …… because they have the same number of …… in their outer …… …… .

2 Where do we find the most reactive elements in the periodic table?

3 How do the number of metallic elements compare with the number of non-metal elements?

4 a) Explain why sodium is more reactive than lithium.
  b) Explain why fluorine is more reactive than chlorine. [Higher]

KEY POINTS
1 The group that an element is in is determined by its atomic (proton) number.
2 The number of electrons in the highest energy level of an atom determines its chemical properties.
3 We can explain trends in reactivity as we go down a group in terms of the number of energy levels in the atoms. [Higher]

SUMMARY ANSWERS

1 Atomic, group, properties, electrons, energy level.

2 At the bottom of Group 1 and the top of Group 7.

3 There are many more metallic elements than non-metallic elements.

4 a) Sodium's outer electron is further from the attractive force of the nucleus and is therefore more easily lost than lithium's. (Sodium's outer electron is also shielded by more inner electrons than lithium's.)

  b) An extra electron is attracted into the outer shell more strongly in fluorine's small atoms where the outer shell is nearer the attractive force of the nucleus than in chlorine. [HT only]

DID YOU KNOW?

Francium is also a Group 1 metal, but very little is known about it as it is radioactive with a very short half life.

KEY POINTS

Give the students a word search, but not a list of words to find. All the missing words should be found in the key points.

Answers to in-text questions

a) Iodine and tellurium.

b) In order of their atomic (proton) number.

CHEMISTRY   DEVELOPMENT OF THE PERIODIC TABLE

C3 1.3 Group 1 – the alkali metals

LEARNING OBJECTIVES

Students should learn:

- The physical and chemical properties of Group 1 elements.
- That the properties of the Group 1 elements change depending on their position in the group.

LEARNING OUTCOMES

Most students should be able to:

- List examples of Group 1 elements.
- Give an alternative name for Group 1 elements.
- List the properties of Group 1 elements.
- State the trends in physical and chemical properties going down the group.

Some students should also be able to:

- Generate balanced symbol equations for the reaction of Group 1 elements with water. [**HT** only]
- Explain the observations for the reactions of Group 1 elements with water.

Teaching suggestions

- **Learning styles**
  Kinaesthetic: Handling samples of Group 1 metals.
  Visual: Observing the reaction between Group 1 metals and water.
  Auditory: Listening to partner in group work.
  Interpersonal: Working in pairs.
  Intrapersonal: Reflecting on their own understanding of a topic.
- **Homework.** Ask students to find out three uses of Group 1 metals. They should detail which metal is used for what purpose and if it is in a compound, the formula should be included.
- **ICT link-up.** Using PowerPoint®, put each student's name on a separate slide. Then make the slide show to be shown in a constant loop with 0 seconds between each slide. Start the show, when you press 'pause' one name will be shown, ask this student a property of metals. Press 'pause' again and the names will continue to flash. To select further names, just press 'pause'. This technique can be used to randomly select names, or weight names by not including a student or including them on more than one slide.

SPECIFICATION LINK-UP   Unit: Chemistry 3.13.1

- The elements in Group 1 of the periodic table (known as the alkali metals):
  – are metals with low density (the first three elements in the Group are less dense than water)
  – react with non-metals to form ionic compounds in which the metal ion carries a charge of +1. The compounds are white solids that dissolve in water to form colourless solutions
  – react with water releasing hydrogen
  – form hydroxides that dissolve in water to give alkaline solutions.
- In Group 1, the further down the group an element is:
  – The more reactive the element
  – The lower its melting point and boiling point.

Lesson structure

STARTER

Reflection – Ask the students to make a three-column table with the titles: 'what I already know', 'what I want to know' and 'what I know now'. Ask the students to fill in the first two columns using bullet points and the learning objectives to help them. (5 minutes)

List – Ask students to list all the properties of metals. Then ask random students to name one of the properties, and draw up an exhaustive list on the board. (5 minutes)

Observations – Put a small piece of the Group 1 metals in oil-filled vials. These should then be put on a cotton wool bed in a sealed and labelled glass dish. Ask the students to look at the samples and detail how they are hazardous, and how they are stored to reduce the risk. Use question and answer to get feedback from the students about how the metals are kept under oil to stop them reacting on contact with the oxygen and water in the air. You can also explain that they are stored in a flame-resistant lockable cupboard in school. **Safety** – Make sure these samples are returned to the technician at the end of the lesson. (10 minutes)

MAIN

- Ask students to predict the products of the reaction between the Group 1 metals and water (with universal indicator solution added). Encourage students to also suggest the observations and what causes them.
- Then demonstrate the reaction, using question and answer to draw out from the students the observations and how they relate to the balanced symbol equation.
- Give the students an exercise to look up the melting points of the alkali metals and to present the data in a table. Then ask them to display the data graphically, justifying their choice [bar chart]. Higher attaining students can plot melting points against atomic numbers. Use this to revise 'How Science Works' concepts of 'types of variable' and 'how to present data'.
- Show students some revision guides and examination papers. Ask students to work in pairs to create an A3 spread for a revision book to review the objectives detailed.
- Students should include a set of examination questions and their answers in their work. Once the students have planned their work, they could use desktop publishing packages to present it.

PLENARIES

Reflection – Ask students to review their table from the starter. Using a different colour pen, they should make any amendments in light of the lesson, and write the answers to the questions posed in the second column. If they cannot answer these questions, encourage the students to consult the Student Book, other students and finally you. Then ask the students to fill in the final column with any other facts that they have learned. (10 minutes)

214

Practical support

Reactions of alkali metals with water

Equipment and materials required
Group 1 metals (lithium, sodium, potassium – flammable, corrosive), white tile, filter paper, spatula, tweezers, water trough, water, universal indicator solution (flammable), safety screen.

Details
- **Safety:** You should wear eye protection and there should be safety screens between the water trough and the students. Be sure not to get the metal on the skin – if this does happen, remove with paper or tweezers and wash the affected area well with cold water. CLEAPSS Hazcards: lithium 58, sodium 88, potassium 76.

- Half-fill the trough of water and add enough universal indicator solution so that the colour is clearly visible. Cut a small piece of lithium (no more than 3 mm). Wipe off the excess oil and put into the solution of universal indicator. Repeat with the other metals.

Questions – Give students ten '1 mark' questions, getting progressively harder. Using a stopwatch, give the students 5 minutes to answer as many questions as they can. Explain that the questions get progressively harder and they should just to do as many as they can. After 5 minutes the students can mark their own work, with you reading out the answers. Then ask the students to put up their hands if they attempted 10 questions, attempted 9, etc., and finally if they got 10 questions correct, or 9, etc. This gives instant feedback about understanding. (15 minutes)

AfL (Assessment for Learning) – Give each pair of students a review sheet containing a table. Each team should rate another couple's revision page for its layout, attractiveness, ease of reading, scientific correctness, meeting objectives, examination practice. Each area should be awarded a mark out of ten and the total mark recorded. Once the assessment has been completed, the review sheet and work should be passed back to the 'authors' for them to consider their work. (10 minutes)

ACTIVITY & EXTENSION IDEAS

- Students can complete flame tests with solutions of Group 1 metal salts (e.g. sodium chloride), on an inoculating loop to determine the metal ion by the flame colour.
- Video footage of the reaction of rubidium and caesium with water can be shown to the students.

Answers to in-text questions

a) Li^+

b) lithium + water → lithium hydroxide + hydrogen
$2Li (s) + 2H_2O (l) \rightarrow 2LiOH (aq) + H_2 (g)$

CHEMISTRY — DEVELOPMENT OF THE PERIODIC TABLE

C3 1.3 Group 1 – the alkali metals

LEARNING OBJECTIVES
1. How do the Group 1 elements behave?
2. How do the properties of the Group 1 elements change with their position in the group?

We call the first group (Group 1) of the periodic table the **alkali metals**. This group consists of the metals lithium, sodium, potassium, rubidium, caesium and francium. The first three are the only ones you will usually have to deal with, as the others are extremely reactive. Francium is radioactive as well!

Properties of the alkali metals

All of the alkali metals are very reactive. They have to be stored in oil to stop them reacting with oxygen in the air. Their reactivity increases as we move down the group. So lithium is the least reactive alkali metal and francium the most reactive.

All of the alkali metals have a very low density for metals. In fact lithium, sodium and potassium will all float on water. The alkali metals are also all very soft, so we can cut them with a knife. They have the silvery, shiny look of typical metals when we first cut them. However, they quickly go dull as they react with oxygen in the air to form a layer of oxide.

The Group 1 metals also melt and boil at relatively low temperatures (for metals). As we go down the group, the melting points and boiling points get lower and lower.

The properties of this rather unusual group of metals are the result of their electronic structure. The alkali metals all have one electron in their highest energy level, which gives them similar properties. It also makes them very reactive, as they only need to lose one electron to obtain a stable electronic structure.

They react with non-metals, losing their single outer electron and forming a metal ion carrying a 1+ charge, e.g. Na^+, K^+. They always form ionic compounds.

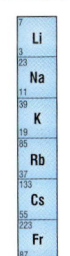

Figure 1 The alkali metals (Group 1)

a) What is the formula of a lithium ion?

Reaction with water

When we add lithium, sodium or potassium to water the metal floats on the water, moving around and fizzing. The fizzing happens because the metal reacts with the water to form hydrogen gas. Potassium reacts so vigorously with the water that the hydrogen produced in the reaction catches fire. It burns with a lilac flame.

The reaction between an alkali metal and water also produces a metal hydroxide. The hydroxides of the alkali metals are all soluble in water, producing a colourless solution with a high pH. (Universal indicator turns purple.)

Figure 2 The alkali metals have to be stored under oil

Figure 3 Lithium and potassium reacting with water (the lithium is on the right of the trough)

This is how the alkali metals got their name – they all form hydroxides which dissolve in water to give strongly alkaline solutions:

sodium + water → sodium hydroxide + hydrogen
$2Na (s) + 2H_2O (l) \rightarrow 2NaOH (aq) + H_2 (g)$

potassium + water → potassium hydroxide + hydrogen
$2K (s) + 2H_2O (l) \rightarrow 2KOH (aq) + H_2 (g)$

b) Write the word and symbol equations for the reaction of lithium with water.

Other reactions

The alkali metals also react vigorously with other non-metals such as chlorine. They produce metal chlorides which are white solids. These all dissolve readily in water to form colourless solutions.

These reactions get more and more vigorous as we go down the group. That's because it becomes easier to lose the single electron in the outer shell to form ions with a 1+ charge. (See page 212.)

sodium + chlorine → sodium chloride
$2Na (s) + Cl_2 (g) \rightarrow 2NaCl (s)$

They react in a similar way with fluorine, bromine and iodine. All of the compounds of the alkali metals are ionic, so they form crystals. All of their compounds also dissolve easily in water.

DEMONSTRATION
Reactions of alkali metals with water

The reaction of the alkali metals with water can be explored by dropping small pieces of the metal into water. This must be done with great care, using a large volume and surface area of water. That's because the reaction is so vigorous, releasing a large amount of energy and hydrogen gas too.

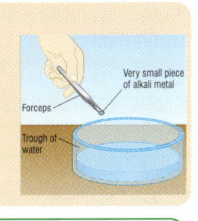

DID YOU KNOW?
Caesium is used in atomic clocks as a way of measuring time very accurately. One second is defined as: *the duration of 9 192 631 770 cycles of microwave light absorbed or emitted by the hyperfine transition of caesium-133 atoms in their ground state undisturbed by external fields . . . !!*

SUMMARY QUESTIONS

1 Copy and complete using the words below:

alkali metals   alkaline   bottom   ionic   less   reactive   top

The Group 1 elements are also known as the …… ……. They are very ……, producing …… solutions when reacted with water. Lithium, at the …… of the group, is …… reactive than caesium, near the …… of the group. These elements always form …… compounds.

2 Francium is the element right at the bottom of Group 1. What do you think would happen if it was dropped into water?

3 Write a balanced equation for the reaction of caesium with iodine. [Higher]

KEY POINTS
1. The elements in Group 1 of the periodic table are called the alkali metals.
2. The metals all react with water to produce hydrogen and an alkaline solution containing the metal hydroxide.
3. The reactivity of the alkali metals increases as we go down the group.

SUMMARY ANSWERS

1 Alkali metals, reactive, alkaline, top, less, bottom, ionic

2 It would explode.

3 $2Cs + I_2 \rightarrow 2CsI$

KEY POINTS

Ask students to copy out the learning objective questions from the Student Book, and answer them using only the key points.

CHEMISTRY | DEVELOPMENT OF THE PERIODIC TABLE

C3 1.4 Group 7 – the halogens

LEARNING OBJECTIVES

Students should learn:
- The chemical properties of Group 7 elements.
- That the properties of the Group 7 elements change depending on their position in the group.

LEARNING OUTCOMES

Most students should be able to:
- List examples of Group 7 elements.
- Give an alternative name for Group 7.
- List the properties of Group 7 elements.
- State the trends in physical and chemical properties in the group.

Some students should also be able to:
- Generate balanced symbol equations for the reaction of Group 7 elements with another non-metal, e.g. hydrogen. [**HT** only]
- Explain the relative reactivity of Group 7 elements. [**HT** only]

Teaching suggestions

- **Special needs.** Give the students the steps for the method in a pictorial flow chart. The students should cut out and stick the steps into the correct order to generate their own method.
- **Learning styles**
  Kinaesthetic: Carrying out the displacement reactions.
  Visual: Completing an advertising spread.
  Auditory: Listening to explanation of displacement reactions.
  Interpersonal: Working in small groups.
  Intrapersonal: Completing chemical equations.
- **ICT link-up.** Using halogens is quite hazardous and you may not wish to allow the students to complete the displacement reactions themselves. You could demonstrate them in test tubes and project the image using a flexi-cam connected to a digital projector or TV. This allows the image to be enlarged for the whole class to see easily.
- **Homework.** Ask students to explain the trend in reactivity in Group 7. They could be encouraged to illustrate their answer with symbol equations and information about the electronic structure of the atoms/ions.

SPECIFICATION LINK-UP Unit: Chemistry 3.13.1

- The elements in Group 7 of the periodic table (known as halogens):
  - have coloured vapours
  - consist of molecules that are made up of pairs of atoms
  - form ionic salts with metals in which the chloride, bromide or iodide ion (halide ion) carries a charge of −1
  - form molecular compounds with other non-metallic elements.
- In Group 7, the further down the group an element is:
  - the less reactive the element
  - the higher its melting point and boiling point.
- A more reactive halogen can displace a less reactive halogen from an aqueous solution of its salt.

Lesson structure

STARTER

Explain – Ask the students to work in small groups to explain the difference between halogens and halides. Ask each group to write their explanation on the board. Then with the help of the students, select the most appropriate explanation for all the students to note in their books. (10 minutes)

Definitions – Write these definitions on the board and ask the students to determine which word the statements are describing:
- The other name for Group 7 elements. [Halogen]
- A 1− ion made from halogens. [Halide ion]
- A reaction when a more reactive element takes the place of a less reactive element in its compound. [Displacement]
- Halogens exist as '2-atom' molecules, another name for this. [Diatomic molecules]
(5 minutes)

MAIN

- Students can compare the reactivity of halogens using the displacement reaction between halogen and halide solutions of iodine, bromine and chlorine.
- Ask students to think about the definition of a displacement reaction (maybe take the students back to displacement reactions of metal and metal ion solutions completed in Year 9).
- Then ask them to write a bullet-point method and equipment list for this reaction. Check the plans for safety, and then encourage the students to design an appropriate results table and allow them to complete the experiment.
- In small groups, encourage the students to discuss their results and use a question and answer session to determine a class-wide conclusion [reactivity decreases as you go down the group and a more reactive halogen will displace a less reactive halide from its compounds].
- Ask students to imagine that they are part of the advertising branch of a large chemical company. They are to design a magazine advert for a science publication explaining what halogens are, their properties and uses, in order to increase sales.

PLENARIES

Reflection – Ask the students to consider one fact that they revised in the lesson and one new fact that they learned in the lesson. Select a few students to share their facts with the rest of the class. (5 minutes)

Practical support

Displacement reactions between halogens

Equipment and materials required
Dimple tiles, six dropping pipettes, 0.1% chlorine water (toxic gas may be released), 0.1% bromine water (harmful), solution of iodine in potassium iodide (hazardous), 0.1 mol/dm³ solutions of potassium chloride, potassium bromide, potassium iodide.

Details
- **Safety:** Wear eye protection and keep the halogen solutions in a fume cupboard. These reactions may produce toxic fumes and should be completed in a well-ventilated area. CLEAPSS Recipe Cards: potassium iodide 55; potassium chloride 51; gas solutions 28. CLEAPSS Hazcards: chlorine 22; bromide 15.
- Into three separate dimples put three drops of potassium chloride solution, then put three drops of each halogen solution into each of the dimples and observe. Note that the same halogen and halide will not react, but some students may try to complete this experiment. Repeat the above with potassium bromide and potassium iodide.

SUMMARY ANSWERS

1 Halogens, top, most, less, molecules, two, covalent, ionic.
2 E.g. $2Na + Cl_2 \rightarrow 2NaCl$;
$2Na + Br_2 \rightarrow 2NaBr$ [**HT** only]

Answers to in-text questions

a) Their melting points and boiling points increase.

b) hydrogen + fluorine → hydrogen fluoride

c) I^-

d) Bromine is more reactive than iodine. Therefore it displaces iodine, and the solution will turn a brownish colour.

ACTIVITY & EXTENSION IDEAS

- Students could research the uses of halogens and halides.
- Students could complete an experiment to research into the acidity and bleaching affect of halogens. Put three pieces of universal indictor paper onto a white tile, and add a few drops of a weak solution of chlorine, bromine and iodine solution and observe.
- A demonstration of the reaction of chlorine with iron could be completed for the students.
- The reaction of silver halides with light could be studied. This reaction could also be considered for its commercial application, e.g. in photography.

CHEMISTRY C3 1.4 — Group 7 – the halogens

LEARNING OBJECTIVES
1. How do the Group 7 elements behave?
2. How do the properties of the Group 7 elements change with their position in the group?

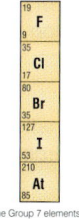

Properties of the halogens
The halogens are a group of poisonous non-metals which all have coloured vapours. They are fairly typical non-metals:
- they have low melting points and boiling points,
- they are also poor conductors of heat and electricity.

The halogens all look different. At room temperature fluorine is a very reactive, poisonous, pale yellow gas, while chlorine is a reactive, poisonous dense green gas.

It is important to be able to detect chlorine if it is given off. It has a very distinctive smell – you'll recognise it from some swimming pools. But it is much safer to hold a piece of damp litmus paper in an unknown gas. If the damp litmus paper is bleached, the gas is chlorine.

Bromine is a dense, poisonous dark orange-brown liquid which vaporises easily – it is volatile. Iodine is a poisonous dark grey crystalline solid which produces violet-coloured vapour when we heat it.

As elements, the halogens all exist as molecules made up of pairs of atoms, joined together by covalent bonds.

Figure 1 The Group 7 elements

	F—F (F₂)	Cl—Cl (Cl₂)	Br—Br (Br₂)	I—I (I₂)
Melting Point (°C)	−220	−101	−7	114
Boiling Point (°C)	−188	−35	59	184

Figure 2 The halogens all form molecules made up of pairs of atoms, joined by a covalent bond – we call this type of molecule a **diatomic** molecule.

a) What patterns can you spot in the physical properties of the halogens as you go down Group 7?

Reactions of the halogens

FOUL FACTS
Many early chemists were badly hurt or even killed as they tried to make pure fluorine, which they called 'the gas of Lucifer'. It was finally produced by the French chemist Henri Moissan, who died aged just 55 – his life was almost certainly shortened by his work with fluorine.

The way the halogens react with other elements and compounds is a direct result of their electronic structure. They all have a highest energy level containing seven electrons. So they need just one more electron to achieve a stable arrangement.

This means that the halogens take part in both ionic and covalent bonding. It also explains why the halogens get less reactive as we go down the group. That's because the outer electrons get further away and are more and more shielded from the nucleus. (See page 212.)

b) Write a word equation for the reaction between hydrogen and fluorine.

How the halogens react with hydrogen

$F_2(g) + H_2(g) \rightarrow 2HF(g)$	Explosive even at −200°C and in the dark
$Cl_2(g) + H_2(g) \rightarrow 2HCl(g)$	Explosive in sunlight/slow in the dark
$Br_2(g) + H_2(g) \rightarrow 2HBr(g)$	300°C + platinum catalyst
$I_2(g) + H_2(g) \rightleftharpoons 2HI(g)$	300°C + platinum catalyst (very slow, reversible)

The halogens all react with metals. They gain a single electron to give them a stable arrangement of electrons, forming ions with a 1− charge, e.g. F^-, Cl^-, Br^-.

c) Write down the formula of an iodide ion.

In these reactions ionic salts, which we call *metal halides*, are formed. Some examples of these are sodium chloride (NaCl), iron(III) bromide (FeBr₃) and magnesium iodide (MgI₂). (See Figure 3.)

When we react the halogens with other non-metals, both sets of atoms share electrons to gain a stable electronic structure. Therefore their compounds with non-metals contain covalent bonds. (See Figure 4.)

Examples of these compounds are hydrogen chloride (HCl) and tetrachloromethane (CCl₄).

Displacement reactions between halogens
We can use a more reactive halogen to displace a less reactive halogen from solutions of its salts.

Bromine displaces iodine from solution because it is more reactive than iodine, while chlorine will displace both iodine and bromine.

For example, chlorine will displace bromine if we bubble the gas through a solution of potassium bromide:

$$Cl_2 + 2KBr \rightarrow 2KCl + Br_2$$

d) What would happen if bromine was added to a solution of potassium iodide?

Obviously fluorine, the most reactive of the halogens, would displace all of the others. However, it reacts so strongly with water that we cannot carry out any displacement reactions in aqueous solutions.

SUMMARY QUESTIONS
1 Copy and complete using the words below:

covalent   halogens   ionic   less   molecules   most   top   two

Group 7 elements are also called the ……. Fluorine, at the …… of the group, is the …… reactive, while iodine is much …… reactive. All of these elements exist as …… made up of …… atoms. They react with other non-metals to form …… compounds and with metals to form …… compounds.

2 The halogens react with the alkali metals to form ionic compounds. Chose any ONE alkali metal and any TWO halogens and write balanced equations for the possible reactions. [Higher]

GET IT RIGHT!
In Group 7, reactivity decreases as you go down the group but in Group 1 it increases going down the group.

Figure 3 When we react a halogen and a metal, the metal donates electrons to the halogen and ionic bonds are formed between the ions produced

Figure 4 When we react a halogen with a non-metal they share electrons to form covalent bonds within the resulting molecules

PRACTICAL
Displacement reactions
Add bromine water to potassium iodide solution in a test tube. Then try some other combinations of solutions of halogens and potassium halides.
- Explain your observations.

KEY POINTS
1 The halogens exist as diatomic molecules.
2 The halogens all form ions with a single negative charge.
3 The halogens form covalent compounds by sharing electrons with other non-metals.
4 The reactivity of the halogens decreases going down the group.

KEY POINTS

Ask students to copy out each key point and to illustrate it with a diagram, e.g. key point 3 as a dot and cross diagram of H—Cl.

Chemical equations – Ask students to copy and complete the following equations (the equations get progressively more difficult):

bromine + hydrogen → [hydrogen bromide]
F_2 + [H_2] → $2HF$
Cl_2 + [$2KI$] → $2KCl + I_2$
Br_2 + $2KCl$ → [no reaction]

(10 minutes)

CHEMISTRY

DEVELOPMENT OF THE PERIODIC TABLE

C3 1.5 The transition elements

LEARNING OBJECTIVES

Students should learn:

- The properties of transition metals.
- The type of reactions that transition metals will be involved in.

LEARNING OUTCOMES

Most students should be able to:

- List examples of transition metals.
- List the properties of transition metals.
- State the general properties of transition metal compounds.
- State that transition metals can form more than one type of ion and work out the formula of their compounds from information provided.

Some students should also be able to:

- Give reasons for the use of transition metals for specific tasks.
- Explain why the transition metals lie between Groups 2 and 3 in the periodic table. [**HT** only]
- Generate balanced symbol equations for the reactions of transition metals. [**HT** only]

Teaching suggestions

- **Special needs.** The cube template could contain some information such as fill in the gaps prose, unfinished bullet points and unlabelled diagrams. Students can then complete the cube rather than generate all the material themselves.
- **Learning styles**
  Kinaesthetic: Determining the properties of transition metals in practical work.
  Visual: Looking at images of transition metal uses.
  Auditory: Listening to previous facts.
  Interpersonal: Working as a class to derive a list of facts about transition metals.
  Intrapersonal: Listing to information about transition metals.
- **Homework.** Ask students to find out which transition metals or their compounds are used in the following: Haber process [Fe], Contact process [vanadium oxide], making margarine [Ni] and nitric acid production [Pt/Rh].

SPECIFICATION LINK-UP   Unit: Chemistry 3.13.1

- In the periodic table between Groups 2 and 3 is a block of elements known as transition elements. These elements are all metals.
- The transition elements have similar properties and some special properties because a lower energy level (inner shell) is being filled in the atoms of the elements between Groups 2 and 3. This is because the third energy level can hold up to 18 electrons, once two electrons have occupied the fourth level. [**HT** only]
- Compared with the elements in Group 1, transition elements:
  – have higher melting points (except for mercury) and higher densities
  – are stronger and harder
  – are much less reactive and so do not react as vigorously with water and oxygen.
- Many transition elements have ions with different charges, form coloured compounds, and are useful as catalysts.

Lesson structure

STARTER

Images – Show the students different interesting images of transition metals being used, e.g. gold covering the sun visor of an astronaut, chromium compounds being used in a breathalyser, coloured gem stones. Ask the students to look at the pictures and find the connection. (5 minutes)

Word search – Give the students a word search with all the words being the physical properties of metals. Higher attaining students could write a definition for the words found. (10 minutes)

MAIN

- Give the students a template of a cube on an A4 piece of card. On each of the six faces, students could be encouraged to put a different piece of information (physical properties, chemical properties, specific uses, information about transition compounds, position in the periodic table, alloys).
- Students should be encouraged to use colour and summarise the information in an easy to digest format, then cut out the cube template, scoring in the appropriate positions and using glue, stick the cube together.
- Students need to be aware of the properties of transition metals and their compounds. On a large poster of the periodic table, put samples of different transition metals and transition metal compounds.
- Allow the students to look at the exhibition and to draw visible conclusions.
- Then let the students use different metals to test their properties and contrast them with Group 1 metals. Set up a circus of five stations with different transition metal elements, allowing the students to rotate around the circus using an activity card placed at each station with the method to complete the practical.
- Once all the activities have been tried, encourage the students to write a bullet-point list of the properties of transition elements.
- Then ask the students to contrast these properties with that of Group 1 metals and write a few sentences to explain the similarities and differences.

PLENARIES

5,4,3,2,1 – Ask students to create the following list: 5 properties of transition metals, 4 symbols of transition metals, 3 magnetic transition metals, 2 different copper ions, 1 example of a transition metal alloy. (5 minutes)

Facts – Ask students to think about a fact from the lesson. Choose one student to say their fact, then the next student should repeat the first fact and then their own fact. This activity can continue around the classroom. (10 minutes)

218

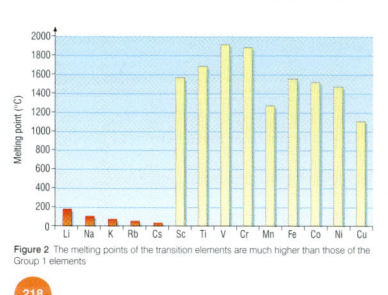

Teaching suggestions continued

- **ICT link-up.** Using a graphing package, e.g. Excel, information about conductivity of transition metals could be plotted onto a scatter graph (atomic/proton number against conductivity). Data can be sourced from the Internet or the RSC Electronic Data book. Use ELS C3 1.5 'Transition Elements' from the GCSE Chemistry CD ROM.

Practical support

Investigating transition metals

Equipment and materials required

Samples of different transition metals, two crocodile clips, three wires, lamp, lab pack, boiling tubes, boiling tube holders, Bunsen burner and safety equipment, beaker, water, 1 mol/dm³ acid (corrosive/irritant), white tile, dropping pipette, spatula, tongs, magnets.

Details

Allow students to handle the metals to find out that they are malleable, ductile and lustrous. They can check if the metal is magnetic using the magnet. Allow students to place in water and observe if there is any reaction and comment on the density. Wearing eye protection, put the metal on a white tile then add a drop of acid and observe. Still wearing eye protection, connect the metal with the crocodile clip into a simple circuit. If the lamp shines this is a positive result for conduction. Be aware that the metal might get hot in the circuit.

ACTIVITY & EXTENSION

- Students could find out the transition metals that cause the colours of gemstones.
- Students could find out about crystal field theory and how it relates to the colours of transition metal complexes.

SUMMARY ANSWERS

1 Two, three, densities, melting, conductors, less, coloured.

2 a) $FeCl_2$, $FeCl_3$
   b) iron(II) chloride, iron(III) chloride.

3 $4V + 5O_2 \rightarrow 2V_2O_5$ [HT only]

Answers to in-text questions

a) Malleable.
b) Nickel(II) chloride.

DID YOU KNOW?

Titanium, another transition metal, is used in alloys to pin bones. This is because the alloy can be made sterile, will not be rejected by the body and is a strong and lightweight material.

KEY POINTS

Students could copy the key points onto separate revision cards (A6 size). On the card, they could include a small image and colours to aid memory.

CHEMISTRY | DEVELOPMENT OF THE PERIODIC TABLE

C3 1.6 Finding and creating new elements

SPECIFICATION LINK-UP
Unit: Chemistry 3.13.1

This spread can be used to revisit the following statements covered in this chapter:

- Newlands and then Mendeleev attempted to classify the elements by arranging them in order of their atomic weights. The list can be arranged in a table so that elements with similar properties are in columns, known as Groups. The table is called a periodic table because similar properties occur at regular intervals.

- The early periodic tables were incomplete and some elements were placed in inappropriate Groups if the strict order of atomic weights were followed. Mendeleev overcame some of the problems by leaving gaps for elements that he thought had not been discovered.

Students should use their skills, knowledge and understanding of 'How Science Works':

- to explain how attempts to classify elements in a systematic way, including those of Newlands and Mendeleev, have led through the growth of chemical knowledge to the modern periodic table.

- to explain why scientists regarded a periodic table of the elements first as a curiosity, then as a useful tool, and finally as an important summary of the structure of atoms.

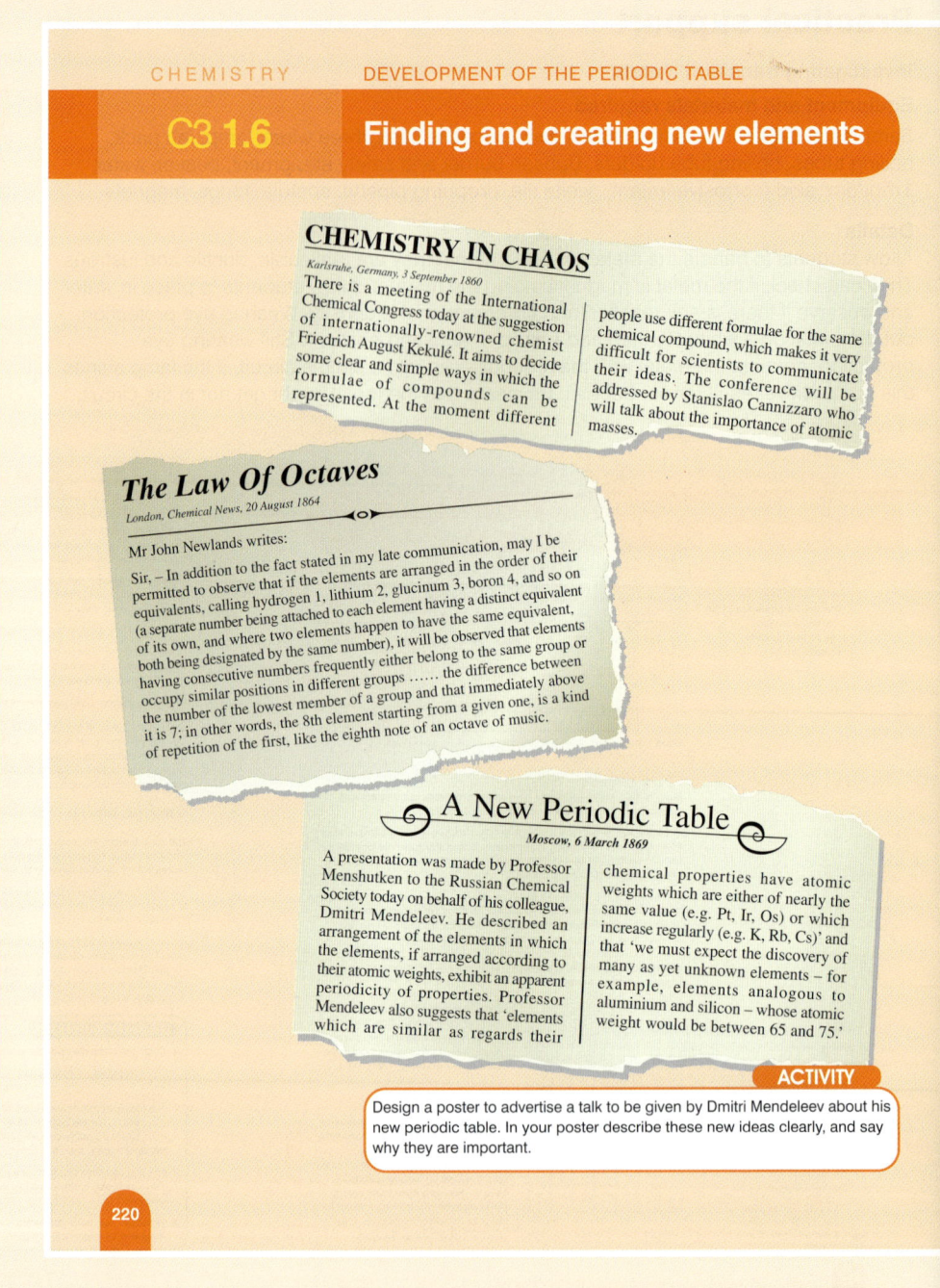

CHEMISTRY | DEVELOPMENT OF THE PERIODIC TABLE

C3 1.6 Finding and creating new elements

CHEMISTRY IN CHAOS
Karlsruhe, Germany, 3 September 1860

There is a meeting of the International Chemical Congress today at the suggestion of internationally-renowned chemist Friedrich August Kekulé. It aims to decide some clear and simple ways in which the formulae of compounds can be represented. At the moment different people use different formulae for the same chemical compound, which makes it very difficult for scientists to communicate their ideas. The conference will be addressed by Stanislao Cannizzaro who will talk about the importance of atomic masses.

The Law Of Octaves
London, Chemical News, 20 August 1864

Mr John Newlands writes:

Sir, – In addition to the fact stated in my late communication, may I be permitted to observe that if the elements are arranged in the order of their equivalents, calling hydrogen 1, lithium 2, glucinum 3, boron 4, and so on (a separate number being attached to each element having a distinct equivalent of its own, and where two elements happen to have the same equivalent, both being designated by the same number), it will be observed that elements having consecutive numbers frequently either belong to the same group or occupy similar positions in different groups …… the difference between the number of the lowest member of a group and that immediately above it is 7; in other words, the 8th element starting from a given one, is a kind of repetition of the first, like the eighth note of an octave of music.

A New Periodic Table
Moscow, 6 March 1869

A presentation was made by Professor Menshutken to the Russian Chemical Society today on behalf of his colleague, Dmitri Mendeleev. He described an arrangement of the elements in which the elements, if arranged according to their atomic weights, exhibit an apparent periodicity of properties. Professor Mendeleev also suggests that 'elements which are similar as regards their chemical properties have atomic weights which are either of nearly the same value (e.g. Pt, Ir, Os) or which increase regularly (e.g. K, Rb, Cs)' and that 'we must expect the discovery of many as yet unknown elements – for example, elements analogous to aluminium and silicon – whose atomic weight would be between 65 and 75.'

ACTIVITY
Design a poster to advertise a talk to be given by Dmitri Mendeleev about his new periodic table. In your poster describe these new ideas clearly, and say why they are important.

Teaching suggestions

Activities

- **Poster** – Explain to students that universities hold guest lectures for the academic community and interested parties to attend. Show students some posters advertising these (maybe some applicable to themselves, sixth-form study and ones for graduates). Ask the students to work in pairs to note down the information that must be contained on such as poster [venue, date, time, title of the lecture]. Then explain that the pairs should imagine that it is 1869 and Mendeleev is going to visit their local university, and give a guest lecture about his 'new' periodic table. Students could age the paper using tea bags, singe the edges with a candle and make a seal with candle wax. On their poster, students should be encouraged to use text that is inviting and include some facts about why the table is so important.

- **Radio** – Scientists believe that there are a finite number of elements. There have been about 100 (92) naturally occurring elements discovered. However, with the advent of nuclear power more elements have been made and discovered on Earth. A continued search for new materials and sub-atomic particles means that discoveries are still occurring today. Impress upon the students the expense of this type of research and hold a discussion about why this type of research is still carried out. Then split the students into small teams and encourage them to write a script for a radio interview about this topic. The segment should last no longer than 5 minutes. Encourage students to think about the argument and, either make it balanced or biased. However they should decide this at the outset. Allow students to perform their radio slot. This could be digitally recorded and played back to other classes or used on the school web site.

Homework

Summary – Ask students to make a bullet-pointed list of the main points about the law of octaves and the modern periodic table.

Further chemistry

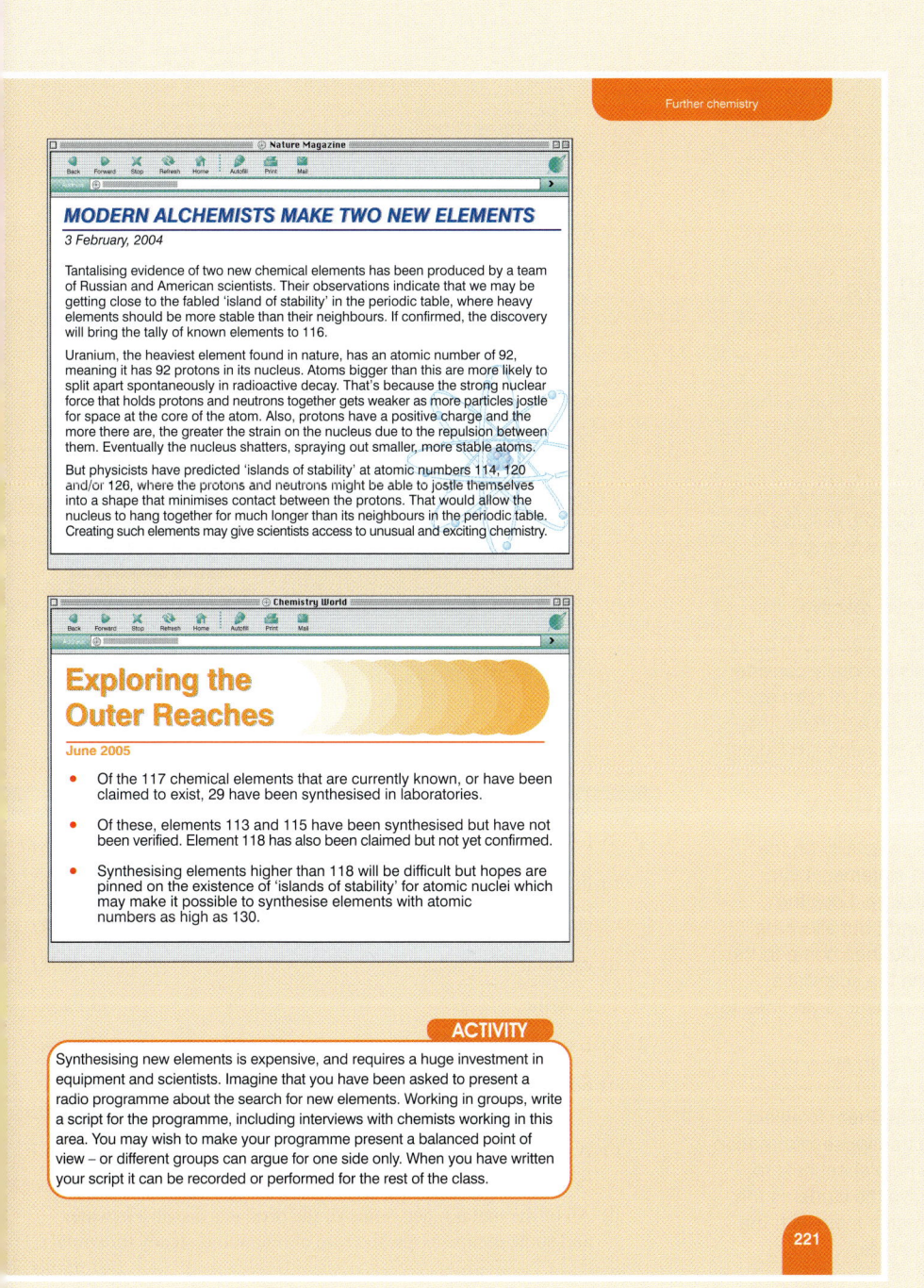

MODERN ALCHEMISTS MAKE TWO NEW ELEMENTS
3 February, 2004

Tantalising evidence of two new chemical elements has been produced by a team of Russian and American scientists. Their observations indicate that we may be getting close to the fabled 'island of stability' in the periodic table, where heavy elements should be more stable than their neighbours. If confirmed, the discovery will bring the tally of known elements to 116.

Uranium, the heaviest element found in nature, has an atomic number of 92, meaning it has 92 protons in its nucleus. Atoms bigger than this are more likely to split apart spontaneously in radioactive decay. That's because the strong nuclear force that holds protons and neutrons together gets weaker as more particles jostle for space at the core of the atom. Also, protons have a positive charge and the more there are, the greater the strain on the nucleus due to the repulsion between them. Eventually the nucleus shatters, spraying out smaller, more stable atoms.

But physicists have predicted 'islands of stability' at atomic numbers 114, 120 and/or 126, where the protons and neutrons might be able to jostle themselves into a shape that minimises contact between the protons. That would allow the nucleus to hang together for much longer than its neighbours in the periodic table. Creating such elements may give scientists access to unusual and exciting chemistry.

Exploring the Outer Reaches
June 2005

- Of the 117 chemical elements that are currently known, or have been claimed to exist, 29 have been synthesised in laboratories.
- Of these, elements 113 and 115 have been synthesised but have not been verified. Element 118 has also been claimed but not yet confirmed.
- Synthesising elements higher than 118 will be difficult but hopes are pinned on the existence of 'islands of stability' for atomic nuclei which may make it possible to synthesise elements with atomic numbers as high as 130.

ACTIVITY

Synthesising new elements is expensive, and requires a huge investment in equipment and scientists. Imagine that you have been asked to present a radio programme about the search for new elements. Working in groups, write a script for the programme, including interviews with chemists working in this area. You may wish to make your programme present a balanced point of view – or different groups can argue for one side only. When you have written your script it can be recorded or performed for the rest of the class.

Extensions
- **Research** – There are many other ways that the elements were classified in the past, e.g. the law of triads. Encourage students to find out other examples and why they were superseded by other ideas.
- **Areas of the periodic table** – The periodic table can be split into blocks [s, p, d and f]. Encourage the students to find out the names of the blocks and why they are called this [the shape of the highest electron-occupied energy orbital/sub-shell].

- **Graphs** – Ask students to find out data about the periodic table, e.g. the number of metallic v. non-metallic elements. Encourage the students to display these facts using different statistical methods, e.g. charts, graphs, averages and percentages. (This relates to: 'How Science Works': presenting data.)

Learning styles
Visual: Making a poster.

Auditory: Listening to other students' radio presentations.

Interpersonal: Working as a group.

Intrapersonal: Summarising the main points of ordering elements.

ICT link-up
The graphs could be completed using Excel and the data from a database, such as the RSC electronic data book or Internet sites.

Special needs
Give the students the sections of the radio interview/broadcast but in the wrong order. They could then sort the statements and perform the broadcast.

CHEMISTRY — DEVELOPMENT OF THE PERIODIC TABLE

SUMMARY ANSWERS

1. A2 B3 C1

2. Groups are columns of elements, periods are rows.

3.
   a) sodium + water → sodium hydroxide + hydrogen
   b) caesium + chlorine → caesium chloride
   c) aluminium + fluorine → aluminium fluoride
   d) hydrogen + chlorine → hydrogen chloride
   e) bromine + potassium iodide → potassium bromide + iodine

4.
   a) $2Na(s) + 2H_2O(l) \rightarrow 2NaOH(aq) + H_2(g)$
   b) $2Cs(s) + Cl_2(g) \rightarrow 2CsCl(s)$
   c) $2Al(s) + 3F_2(g) \rightarrow 2AlF_3(s)$
   d) $H_2(g) + Cl_2(g) \rightarrow 2HCl(g)$
   e) $Br_2(aq) + 2KI(aq) \rightarrow 2KBr(aq) + I_2(aq)$ [HT only]

5.
   a) F–H (dot and cross diagram)
   b) Cl–Cl (dot and cross diagram)
   c) [Na]⁺ [I]⁻ (dot and cross diagram)

6.
   a) Alkali metals are not very dense, they are soft, reactive metals, compared to the transition metals, which are denser, harder and less reactive.
   b) The transition metals are stronger and less reactive.

7. Zinc has many of the properties of transition metals, but it does not form coloured ions in solution. Chemists generally consider that it is not a transition element because it does not form at least one ion with a partially filled sub-shell of d electrons (the generally accepted definition of a transition element). [HT only]

Summary teaching suggestions

- **ICT link-up** – Question 1 could be used as an activity on the interactive whiteboard. Type in the separate statements into boxes in interactive whiteboard specific software. Lock the named scientist into place (make background), but allow the other data to be able to move. Students could then come to the board and move the discovery to match with the scientist's name. Alternatively, students could use the pens to draw lines to connect the pieces of data

- **Special needs** – Question 3 will be quite difficult. Allow the students to complete the word equations themselves, maybe putting a list of the products onto the board for them to select from. Some students may even struggle to transpose information from the board into their notes, therefore a help sheet next to them may be more useful. For question 4 give the students the balanced symbol equations. They should match them with the correct word equation and copy it into their notes.

- **Learning styles**
  Kinaesthetic: Using a card sort or cut and stick activity to answer question 1 allows this activity to appeal to these learners.
  Auditory: Questions 6 and 7 lend themselves to a class discussion before each student pens their own answer.
  Visual: Question 5 allows diagrams to be given as answers.

- **When to use the questions?**
  - As a revision aid at the end of the topic.
  - Students could be encouraged not to answer the questions but to create a mark scheme. They should critically consider all the answers that could be awarded a mark, and also answers that are close but should not be given any credit.
  - Split the students into teams of about eight, and give each one a piece of A4 paper. Ask them to read the first part of question 6 and write sentence to start the answer. Then pass the paper to the right. The next student reads the response so far and then corrects it and adds to it. This is repeated until all the students have seen each sheet of paper. Repeat this with the second part of the question. Then allow students to use their A4 paper to help them answer the question in prose in their own notes.

222

DEVELOPMENT OF THE PERIODIC TABLE: C3 1.1 – C3 1.6

SUMMARY QUESTIONS

1. Link each scientist (A–C) with his idea (1–3).

A	Newlands	1	Arranged the elements in order of their masses.
B	Mendeleev	2	Produced the 'law of octaves'.
C	Dalton	3	Produced the periodic table on which our modern table is based.

2. What is the difference between a **group** and a **period** in the periodic table?

3. Write down word equations for the following reactions:
   a) sodium and water
   b) caesium and chlorine
   c) fluorine and aluminium
   d) chlorine and hydrogen
   e) bromine and potassium iodide solution.

4. Write down balanced chemical equations for the reactions in question 3. [Higher]

5. Draw dot and cross diagrams (draw the outer energy shell electrons only) to show the bonding in the following substances:
   a) hydrogen fluoride
   b) chlorine
   c) sodium iodide.

6.
   a) How are the properties of the transition elements different to the properties of the alkali metals?
   b) Why are the transition elements more useful than the alkali metals as structural materials (materials used to make things)?

7. Most chemists consider that zinc is not a transition element. Find out more about the properties of zinc and its compounds and suggest why zinc may not be called a transition element. [Higher]

EXAM-STYLE QUESTIONS

Use a periodic table (on page 213 of Student Book or on the AQA Data Sheet) to help you to answer these questions.

1. Choose elements from the list to match the descriptions (a) to (e).

   aluminium   astatine   bromine   caesium
   chromium   fluorine   lithium   magnesium

   (a) A liquid at room temperature with a brown vapour.
   (b) A metal that floats on water.
   (c) A transition element.
   (d) The most reactive element in Group 1.
   (e) The most reactive element in Group 7. (5)

2. Some students observed sodium reacting with water. They wrote down these observations.
   (a) The metal turned into a silver ball.
   (b) The metal moved around on the surface of the water.
   (c) A fizzing sound was heard.
   (d) The metal gradually disappeared.

   Write down one deduction you can make from each of these observations. (4)

3. Part of Mendeleev's periodic table is shown below.

	Group 1	Group 2	Group 3	Group 4	Group 5	Group 6	Group 7	Group 8
Period 1	H							
Period 2	Li	Be	B	C	N	O	F	
Period 3	Na	Mg	Al	Si	P	S	Cl	
Period 4	K Cu	Ca Zn	? ?	Ti ?	V As	Cr Se	Mn Br	Fe Co Ni
Period 5	Rb Ag	Sr Cd	Y In	Zr Sn	Nb Sb	Mo Te	? ?	Ru Rh Pd

   (a) (i) Write the symbols of the three elements in Group 1 of Mendeleev's table that are not in Group 1 of the modern periodic table. (1)
   (ii) Where are these elements placed in the modern table? (2)
   (iii) Suggest one reason why Mendeleev put all of these elements in the same group. (1)

222

EXAM-STYLE ANSWERS

1.
   a) bromine (1 mark)
   b) lithium (1 mark)
   c) chromium (1 mark)
   d) caesium (1 mark)
   e) fluorine (1 mark)

2.
   a) Exothermic reaction/heat produced/metal melts. (1 mark)
   b) Sodium is less dense than water/gas given off moves metal. (1 mark)
   c) A gas is given off/gas produced by reaction (1 mark) *(cannot deduce it is hydrogen).*
   d) All of the metal reacts/some of the products dissolve in water and some escape as gas/the rate of reaction is steady *(not rapid)*. (1 mark)

3.
   a) i) H, Cu, Ag. (all correct for 1 mark)
      ii) H at the top of the table/on its own. (1 mark)
      Cu and Ag in the transition elements. (1 mark)
      iii) They have similar chemical properties/all form 1+ ions/ they appear every 8 elements in a list arranged in order of atomic mass. (1 mark)
   b) The noble gases/inert gases/Group 0 *(not Group 8)*. (1 mark)
   c) i) Atomic weight *(accept relative atomic mass).* (1 mark)
      ii) Atomic number (proton number). (1 mark)
   d) To allow for elements that had not yet been discovered. (1 mark)
      So that elements were in (correct) groups according to their properties. (1 mark)

Further chemistry

HOW SCIENCE WORKS QUESTIONS

(b) Which group of elements in the modern periodic table is completely missing from Mendeleev's table? (1)

(c) (i) In what order did Mendeleev place the elements in his table? (1)
   (ii) In what order are elements in the modern periodic table? (1)

(d) Explain why Mendeleev left the gaps shown by question marks (?) in his table. (2)

4 The table shows the numbers of protons and neutrons in ten different atoms.

Atom	A	E	G	J	L	M	Q	R	T	X
Number of protons	9	11	12	17	17	18	19	20	22	24
Number of neutrons	10	12	12	18	20	22	20	20	26	28

(a) Which are atoms of elements in Group 1?
(b) Which is an atom of a noble gas?
(c) Which are atoms of transition elements?
(d) Which two atoms are isotopes of the same element?
(e) Which atoms have the same mass number?
(f) Write the formula of the ion formed by atom E.
(g) Write the formula of the ion formed by atom L.
(h) Write the formula of the compound formed when A reacts with R. (8)

5 This question is about the halogens, Group 7 in the periodic table.
(a) Write down one similarity and one difference in the electronic structures of the elements going down Group 7 from fluorine to astatine. (2)
(b) How does the reactivity of the halogens change going down the group? (1)
(c) Explain this change in reactivity in terms of atomic structure. (3)

[Higher]

Tony is starting an investigation into the halogens. He has been told about the order in which different halogens appear in the periodic table and from that has devised a method for seeing which is the most reactive. He has chosen you as his partner! It all sounds very complex. Tony says he is going to use four test tubes.

In tube 1 he is going to put a few crystals of potassium iodide into some chlorine water – a colour change would prove that chlorine is more reactive than iodine.

In tube 2 he is going to put a few crystals of potassium iodide into some bromine water – a colour change would prove that bromine is more reactive than iodine.

In tube 3 he is going to put a few crystals of potassium chloride into some bromine water – a colour change would prove that bromine is more reactive than chlorine.

In tube 4 he is going to put a few crystals of potassium bromide into some chlorine water – a colour change would prove that chlorine is more reactive than bromine.

Tony quickly carries out the first reaction and then decides that it would be a good idea if you produced a table for his results.

a) Make a table to show what is being mixed and leave room for the results. (3)
b) The results were that tubes 1 and 2 went dark brown. Tube 3 showed no change of colour and tube 4 went yellow in colour. Now complete your table with these results. (1)
c) You told Tony that you thought 'it could have been the water that changed the first two dark brown'. What could he do to prove that it was not the water? (1)
d) Is the dependent variable categoric, continuous, discrete or ordered? (1)
e) Can you see a pattern from these results? If so, state the pattern. (1)

223

Further chemistry

Exam teaching suggestions

The questions could be used for homework or as a test when the chapter has been completed. Allow 30 minutes if done under test conditions. Q3 could be done after completing C3.1.2, Q2 after C3.1.3. Students should be encouraged to refer to a periodic table, such as the one provided on the Data Sheet used in the examinations, when they are answering questions.

In Q2, students are asked to make deductions from observations. Some students go too far in questions of this type, and suggest answers based on their knowledge rather than on the information provided. Making valid deductions is an important skill.

When teaching the historical aspects of the periodic table it is important that students know the limitations under which the scientists that proposed the early tables were working, especially that nothing was known about atomic structure at that time. In examinations, students often give answers as though Newlands and Mendeleev knew about electrons and atomic numbers. Students could compare accounts of the developments from different textbooks and other sources. The original table produced by Mendeleev was rather different to that in Q3, and would provide a good basis for discussion.

Students should know the trends in reactivity within groups in the periodic table and should be able to explain how these are related to electronic structures. Many students think that the trends are the same for all groups and do not make the distinction between metals and non-metals. Check that they can respond adequately to longer questions requiring explanations, such as Q5c).

4 a) E and Q (both correct for 1 mark)
  b) M (1 mark)
  c) T and X (both correct for 1 mark)
  d) J and L (both correct for 1 mark)
  e) M and R (both correct for 1 mark)
  f) E^+ (1 mark)
  g) L^- (1 mark)
  h) RA_2 (1 mark)

5 a) All have seven electrons (same number of electrons) in outer shell/energy level. (1 mark)
    Each atom has one extra shell/energy level or atoms have more electrons going down the group. (1 mark)
  b) They get less reactive (going down the group). (1 mark)
  c) Three from:
    - Halogens react by gaining electrons.
    - Electrons are more strongly attracted by atoms at the top of the group.
    - Atoms at the top are smaller/outer electrons are closer to nucleus.
    - Atoms at the bottom have more shells/energy levels.
    - More electrons/shells means more shielding (of outer electrons). (3 marks)
    [HT only]

HOW SCIENCE WORKS ANSWERS

a) and b)

Chemicals used	Final colour
Chlorine water + potassium iodide	Dark brown
Bromine water + potassium iodide	Dark brown
Bromine water + potassium chloride	No change
Chlorine water + potassium bromide	Yellow

c) He could add water to the potassium iodide – a control.
d) The dependent variable is categoric.
e) Chlorine, bromine, iodine.

How science works teaching suggestions

- **Literacy guidance**
  - Key terms that should be understood: categoric, control, pattern, dependent and independent variable.
- **Higher- and lower-level answers.** Questions c) and e) are higher-level questions. The answers for these have been provided at this level. Question d) is lower-level.
- **Gifted and talented.** Able students could consider why it would not be possible to use fluorine in this investigation.
- **How and when to use these questions.** When wishing to develop table construction skills and determining patterns in less familiar ways. Also that categoric variables do have their uses. The questions could be tackled in small groups.
- **Homework.** The questions could be set for homework.
- **Special needs.** For these students you could use cards with the names of the elements on and show the reactions that are occurring.

223

CHEMISTRY

MORE ABOUT ACIDS AND BASES

C3 2.1 Strong and weak acids/alkalis

LEARNING OBJECTIVES

Students should learn:

- That water is involved in acidity and alkalinity.
- That certain ions are responsible for acidity and alkalinity.
- The difference between strong and weak acids or alkalis.

LEARNING OUTCOMES

Most students should be able to:

- State a definition for acid and alkali in terms of ions produced in aqueous solutions.
- State a definition for strong and weak acids or alkalis.
- List some common examples of strong and weak acids and alkalis.

Some students should also be able to:

- Explain the difference between strong and weak acids or alkalis.
- Explain neutralisation in terms of ions.
- Define acids and bases as proton donors or acceptors. [**HT** only]

Teaching suggestions

- **Gifted and talented.** In some cases it is very important that the pH remains constant, e.g. in the blood. Encourage students to find out what a buffer solution is and how it works.
- **Learning styles**

  Kinaesthetic: Holding up cards to classify acids/alkalis.

  Visual: Highlighting key words in answers to questions.

  Auditory: Listening to chemical names.

  Interpersonal: Working in groups to determine a method for finding out which is a strong and which is a weak acid.

  Intrapersonal: Answering a series of questions.

- **Homework.** Other than the examples used in the lesson, encourage the students to find a further example of a strong acid, weak acid, strong alkali and weak alkali.

SPECIFICATION LINK-UP   Unit: Chemistry 3.13.2

- Water must normally be present for a substance to act as an acid or as a base.
- Acids produce hydrogen ions in aqueous solution. The H^+ ion is a proton. In water this proton is hydrated and is represented by $H^+(aq)$.
- Alkalis produce $OH^-(aq)$ ions in aqueous solutions.
- An acid can be defined as a proton donor. A base can be defined as a proton acceptor. [**HT** only]
- Acids and alkalis are classified by the extent of their ionisation in water.
  – A strong acid or alkali is one that completely ionises in water. Examples of strong acids are hydrochloric, sulfuric and nitric acids. Examples of strong alkalis are sodium and potassium hydroxide.
  – A weak acid or alkali is only partially ionised in water. Examples of weak acids are ethanoic, citric and carbonic acids. An example of a weak alkali is ammonia solution.

Lesson structure

STARTER

Explain – Ask students to explain how they would find out which of two acids (of equal concentration) is strong and which is weak [pH scale/common reactions]. Give students time to think about it individually. Then split the class into four groups. Ask each group to decide on the method and feedback to the class. (15 minutes)

Definitions – Ask students to define the following key terms: acid, alkali, base, strong and weak. Encourage the students to use previous work and the Student Book to help them. (10 minutes)

MAIN

- Students can use universal indicator to determine the pH of a solution and thus infer whether it is strongly or weakly acidic/alkaline.
- Carefully explain the difference between strong and weak acids as opposed to concentrated and dilute solutions of acids. Ask how they can have a solution of a strong acid (high degree of dissociation) but with a relatively high pH value, e.g. 5 [very dilute solution].
- Another method for comparing the strength of acids is to consider their reaction with a metal e.g. magnesium ribbon. Give students a selection of mystery acids (of equal concentration) labelled A to E and ask them to put the acids in order, from weakest to strongest.
- Give the students a set of 20 questions about the topic. Encourage them to answer each question in full.
- Then ask each student to review their work and highlight in red the words acidic, acid or an example of an acid. Then use blue for alkaline, alkali, base or an example of a base.

PLENARIES

Classification – Give students a set of four cards, a red card with the word 'acid' on it, a blue card with 'alkali' and a white card with 'strong' on one side and 'weak' on the other. Read out the names of the following solutions. After each one, the students should hold up two cards to describe the acid/alkali.

- Ammonia solution [weak alkali] • Sulfuric acid [strong acid] • Potassium hydroxide [strong alkali] • Citric acid [weak acid] • Nitric acid [strong acid]
- Hydrochloric acid [strong acid] • Sodium hydroxide [strong alkali]
- Ethanoic acid [weak acid] • Carbonic acid [weak acid] (5 minutes)

Spot the mistake – Ask students to spot the mistake in the following statement:

'An example of a solution of a weak acid is 0.00001 mol/dm³ hydrochloric acid'. [Weak refers to a low degree of *ionisation*, whereas 0.00001 mol/dm³ is a low *concentration*.] (5 minutes)

Answers to in-text questions

a) A proton donor.

b) A proton acceptor.

c) Two of: hydrochloric, sulfuric, nitric acids.
Two of: lithium, sodium, potassium, calcium, magnesium hydroxides.

d) Two of: citric, ethanoic, carbonic, ascorbic acids.
Ammonia.

Practical support

Comparing a strong and a weak acid

Equipment and materials required

Magnesium strips about 5 mm in length (flammable), five different 1 mol/dm³ solutions of acids labelled A–E (e.g. hydrochloric acid, sulfuric acid, ethanoic acid, tartaric acid, citric acid – corrosive or irritants), measuring cylinder (10 cm³), 5 test tubes, test-tube rack, stopwatch. CLEAPSS Hazcards: magnesium 59; hydrochloric acid 47; sulfuric acid 98; ethanoic acid 38.

Details

Wearing eye protection, measure out equal volumes of acids into each of 5 test tubes in a rack. Drop a piece of magnesium ribbon into each beaker simultaneously. Then order the acids in terms of how vigorous the reaction is. To make this method quantitative, the students could time how long it takes for the magnesium to fully react. However, in the weak acids this could take a very long time, so a cut-off point of about 5 minutes should be used. If students spill the acid onto their skin or clothes they should wash it well in cold water.

ACTIVITY & EXTENSION

- Students could use a pH probe to measure the acidity of different solutions.

- Students could be encouraged to find out which acid is naturally in rain (weak acid, carbonic) and how it is formed. They could then go on to find out/revise how acid rain differs [contains strong acids like nitric and sulfuric acid] and how it affects the environment.

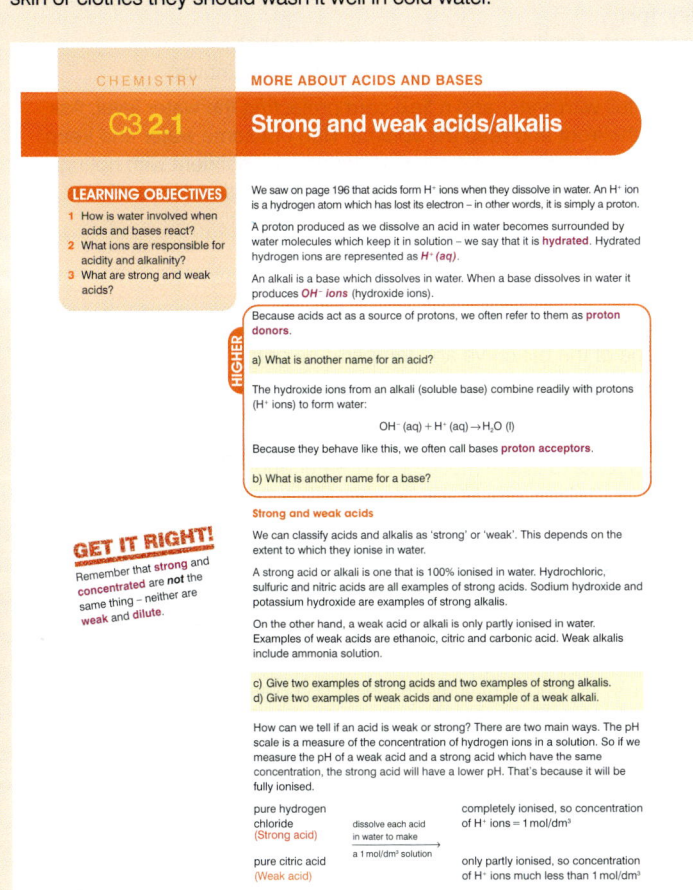

SUMMARY ANSWERS

1 Hydrogen, protons, alkali, hydroxide, water.

2 By measuring their pH (a strong acid has a lower pH than a weak acid), or observing their rates of reaction with a metal such as magnesium (the reaction is quicker with a strong acid).

3 a) Hydrogen – a lighted splint causes the gas to burn with a squeaky pop.

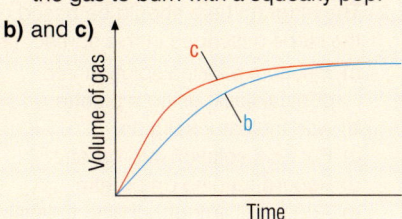

b) and c) [graph: Volume of gas vs Time, curve c above curve b]

KEY POINTS

Students could be encouraged to translate the key points into text language. The more artistic students could then draw a mobile phone with the display showing the points.

225

CHEMISTRY   MORE ABOUT ACIDS AND BASES

C3 2.2 Titrations

LEARNING OBJECTIVES

Students should learn:

- That accurate measurements can be taken in a neutralisation reaction.
- That there are methods for determining the completion of a neutralisation reaction.

LEARNING OUTCOMES

Most students should be able to:

- State the definition of a titration, end point and indicator.
- Safely carry out a simple titration.

Some students should also be able to:

- Explain qualitatively what is happening in a titration.
- Choose a suitable indicator for a titration, including the cases of strong acid + weak alkali and a weak acid + a strong alkali. [HT only]

SPECIFICATION LINK-UP   Unit: Chemistry 3.13.2

- The volumes of acid and alkali solutions that react with each other can be measured by titration using a suitable indicator:
  - strong acid + strong alkali – any acid–base indicator
  - strong acid + weak alkali – methyl orange indicator [**HT** only]
  - weak acid + strong alkali – phenolphthalein indicator. [**HT** only]

Lesson structure

STARTER

Crossword – Give students a crossword made from the following clues:
- A substance that is a proton donor. [acid]
- A substance that can dissolve in water and is a base. [alkali]
- When neutralisation is complete. [end point]
- End points are shown using a solution of one of these. [indicator]
- A measure of acidity. [pH]
- Used to measure accurately a definite, specific volume. [pipette]
- Used to measure accurately a variety of volumes. [burette] (10 minutes)

Volume – Set up a burette full with water and a flexi-cam projecting the water level. Ask for a volunteer to come to the front and read the volume. Run out some water and keep asking random students to read the volume until all students are confident with noting the volume from a burette. By having the flexi-cam, all students can see the meniscus and scale, and can participate in reading the volume. (5 minutes)

MAIN

- Using a data logger, an acid–base titration can be demonstrated to the class. Ask students to predict shape of the pH curve and temperature graph.
- Complete the titration and discuss the shape of the curve and contrast this with the prediction.
- Students can complete their own titration. To help them get used to using the equipment, allow the students to fill the pipettes with water and practise getting the meniscus to the line. Also students can fill the burette with water and practise running it out at different rates and noting the volume. Discuss accuracy, precision, reliability and repeat readings with the students, as well as designing an appropriate results table (this relates to: 'How Science Works').

PLENARIES

Safety – Give students a series of images of titrations being completed unsafely, e.g. no eye protection, etc. Ask the students to discuss the safety issues in the images and explain why they are problems. Pick a few groups to feedback about each image. (10 minutes)

Graph – Give students a titration curve for a strong acid/weak alkali titration. Ask the students to label strongly acidic/alkaline, weakly acidic/alkaline, when pH = 7 and describe briefly the shape of the curve. Students could be encouraged to colour code the curve to show the pH changes. (15 minutes)

Teaching suggestions

- **Special needs.** To help the students read the volume on the burette, give them a sheet of white paper. Make two cuts (about 3 cm long and parallel to each other about 2 cm away). Slot this over the top of the burette and this makes the scale easier to read.

- **Learning styles**
  Kinaesthetic: Carrying out a titration.
  Visual: Labelling a titration graph.
  Auditory: Listening to other students' responses.
  Interpersonal: Working in small groups to pick out safety issues.
  Intrapersonal: Completing a crossword.

- **Homework.** Students could draw a pictorial flow chart to explain the step-by-step method of a titration.

- **ICT link-up.** Show the students footage of the use of a pipette, burette and titrations. This is available from *Practical A-level Chemistry*, CD-ROM from the RSC (or search the Internet for 'titration video'.)

Answers to in-text questions

a) The final solution will be acidic.
b) The final solution will be alkaline.
c) An indicator.

SUMMARY ANSWERS

1 Neutralisation, acid, end point, indicator.
2 The diagram here should be based on the steps described in this spread, i.e.
   a) Measure alkaline solution into conical flask, using a pipette.
   b) Add indicator solution.
   c) Put acid solution into burette.
   d) Record reading on burette.
   e) Add small amount of acid to flask.
   f) Check colour of indicator – if it has changed, go to **g)**, if not, go back to **e)**.
   g) Read burette.
   h) Repeat **a)** to **g)** until consistent readings obtained.
3 Indicator A is better because the colour change is much more distinctive.

226

Practical support

Carrying out a titration

Equipment and materials required
Stand, boss, clamp, 1 mol/dm³ hydrochloric acid (irritant), 1 mol/dm³ sodium hydroxide (corrosive), pipette, pipette filler, burette, funnel, conical flask, dropping pipette, phenolphthalein, wash bottle, white tile. CLEAPSS Hazcards: hydrochloric acid 47; sodium hydroxide 91; phenolphthalein 32. Titrations: see CLEAPSS Handbook/CD-ROM section 13.8.

Details
Wearing eye protection, rinse all equipment with reagents. Using a pipette and filler, measure 25 cm³ of sodium hydroxide into a conical flask. Add a few drops of indicator to the conical flask and put it onto a white tile. Fill the burette with acid, remove the funnel and position the tap over the conical flask. Run in the acid, swirling the flask all the time. When the indicator has changed colour, stop the tap and note the volume. This is the rough titration to give an idea of the volume needed. Wash the conical flask thoroughly and add a fresh sample of 25 cm³ of sodium hydroxide and indicator. Quickly run in the acid (5 cm³ less than the titre of the rough titration). Add the acid drop wise, swirling between drops. When the colour change begins to persist, using the wash bottle, rinse around the conical flask and the end of the burette. Now add half drops at a time, washing the acid from the bottom of the burette, until the colour change lasts for 10 seconds. Note the volume, and repeat three times or until there are two concordant (within 0.1 of each other) results.

Using a data logger to investigate titrations

Equipment and materials required
pH probe, temperature probe, interface, data logger, stand, boss, clamp, computer, data projector, 1 mol/dm³ hydrochloric acid (irritant), 1 mol/dm³ sodium hydroxide (corrosive), pipette, pipette filler, burette, funnel, conical flask, dropping pipette, phenolphthalein, magnetic stirrer, magnetic stirrer bar.

Details
Wearing chemical splash-proof eye protection, measure 25 cm³ of sodium hydroxide using the pipette. Add a few drops of phenolphthalein and a magnetic stirrer bar. Put the conical flask onto the magnetic stirrer, and submerge the two data probes. Connect the ICT equipment and set the run to last 2 minutes. Fill the burette with acid and put the tap over the conical flask. Start the stirrer and recording data. Add the acid from the burette at a steady flow rate. (Be aware of what to do if alkali gets into the eye.)

ACTIVITY & EXTENSION IDEAS

- There are many indicators that can be used in acid–base titrations. Encourage students to find out a list of different indicators and their pH range. E.g. The range of phenolphthalein is pH 8.2–10.0 whereas methyl orange's range is 3.2–4.4.

- Show students titration curves for strong/weak, weak/weak and strong/strong titrations. Using an indicator chart, discuss which indicators could be used in each example. Note: For weak/weak there is no suitable indicator.

- Ask students to plan their own titration to find out the percentage of ascorbic acid (vitamin C) that there is in a specific tablet; or which type of vinegar (ethanoic acid) is the most concentrated.

KEY POINTS
Students could generate three questions to which each key point would be an answer.

CHEMISTRY — MORE ABOUT ACIDS AND BASES

C3 2.3 Titration calculations

LEARNING OBJECTIVES

Students should learn:

- How to calculate concentration from reacting volumes. [HT only]
- How to calculate the amount of acid or alkali used in a neutralisation reaction. [HT only]

LEARNING OUTCOMES

Most students should be able to:

- Complete straightforward calculations involving concentration. [HT only]
- Complete calculations with results from a titration involving simple ratios. [HT only]

Some students should also be able to:

- Carry out more complex titration calculations. [HT only]

Teaching suggestions

- **Special needs.** Give the students the lines of working out for each question, but in the wrong order, or incomplete. Allow the students to cut and stick them in the correct order and fill in the missing information.
- **Gifted and talented.** Allow these students to tackle titration questions from AS level papers.
- **Learning styles**
  Kinaesthetic: Completing the question card sort.
  Visual: Generating a flow chart to help with answering calculation questions.
  Auditory: Listening to questions for bingo.
  Interpersonal: Working in small groups.
  Intrapersonal: Completing calculations.
- **Homework.** Ask students to write their own titration examination question and mark scheme.

SPECIFICATION LINK-UP   Unit: Chemistry 3.13.2

- If the concentration of one of the reactants is known, the results of a titration can be used to find the concentration of the other reactant. [HT only]

Students should use their skills, knowledge and understanding of 'How Science Works':

- to calculate the chemical quantities in titrations involving concentrations (in moles or mass per unit volume) and masses. [HT only]

Lesson structure

STARTER

Find – Ask students to use the Student Book to find out all the formulae that will be used in this double-page spread. Then ask a few students to write on the board the formulae and the units that each variable is measured in, e.g. number of moles (mol) = mass (g)/A_r (10 minutes)

Anagrams – Write the following anagrams onto the board for the students to unscramble:

- tittirason [titrations]
- sleom [moles]
- eumolv [volume]
- rationcentnoc [concentration]
- ionculatcal [calculation]

This activity can be extended by encouraging students to define each of the key words. (5 minutes)

MAIN

- Create a card sort made up of 30 questions and their answers on separate cards. The questions should range from easy questions, such as what is concentration measured in, to calculation questions from the worked examples and summary questions.
- This activity can be differentiated by giving fewer questions to lower attaining students, also students could work in teams. Students should match the questions with their answers.
- Then ask students to pick five of the questions and copy them into their notes, including their answers. One of the five should be a calculation question, and the students should be encouraged to show their working out to arrive at the answer.
- Demonstrate how to complete a calculation from a titration, by building up the steps on the board.
- Encourage students to generate a flow chart to help them answer this type of question, showing in the correct order all the steps that need to be followed.
- Then give the students a few calculation questions, which they should then answer, using their flow chart to help them.

PLENARIES

Calculations – Give the students an A4 whiteboard (or laminated paper), washable pen and eraser. Show a calculation question onto the board and students should try to answer the question, write it on the board and hold it up to you for instant feedback. Encourage students to report the answers including the units. Unsure students can play the game and wait until other students have answered the question before penning their own. (10 minutes)

Bingo – Make bingo cards with six answers on the card, including: key words e.g. moles; units e.g. grams; and numbers to answer simple calculations. Then ask questions, the students cross off the answer if it appears on their bingo card. The first student to call 'house' (with all the answers) is the winner and could get a prize. (5 minutes)

Teaching suggestions continue

- **ICT link-up.** Generate multiple-choice questions, one per PowerPoint® slide in a single slide show. Play the question slideshow and allow small groups to go to the interactive whiteboard to try to answer the sequence of questions. Time each group, and give the group that correctly answers the questions fastest a small prize.

  Use Interactive C3 2.3 'Titration Calculations' from the GCSE Chemistry CD ROM.

ACTIVITY & EXTENSION IDEAS

Allow students to actually complete a titration with different combinations of strong/weak acids and bases and use the titres to complete the calculations.

Safety: See Practical support C3 2.2

CHEMISTRY — MORE ABOUT ACIDS AND BASES

C3 2.3 Titration calculations

LEARNING OBJECTIVES
1. How can we calculate concentrations from reacting volumes?
2. How can we calculate the amount of acid or alkali needed in a neutralisation reaction?

We describe the concentration of a solute in a solution in terms of the number of moles of solute dissolved in one cubic decimetre of solution. We write these units as **moles per cubic decimetre** or **mol/dm³** for short. So if we know the amount of substance dissolved in a certain volume of a solution, we can work out the concentration of the solution.

As an example, imagine that we make a solution of sodium hydroxide in water by dissolving exactly 40 g of sodium hydroxide to make exactly 1 dm³ of solution. We know that the mass of 1 mole of sodium hydroxide (NaOH) is the sum of the atomic masses of sodium, oxygen and hydrogen, i.e. 23 + 16 + 1 = 40 g. So we know that the solution contains exactly 1 mole of sodium hydroxide in exactly 1 dm³ of solution — and the concentration of sodium hydroxide in the solution is therefore 1 mol/dm³.

Worked example 1
But what if we use exactly 40 g of sodium hydroxide to make exactly 500 cm³ of solution instead of 1 dm³? (Remember that 1 dm³ = 1000 cm³.)

Solution
To find the concentration of the solution we must work out how much sodium hydroxide there would be in exactly 1000 cm³ (1 dm³) of solution if the proportions of sodium hydroxide and water stayed the same.
40 g of NaOH are dissolved in 500 cm³ water, so
$\frac{40}{500}$ g of NaOH would be dissolved in 1 cm³ of solution, and
$\frac{40}{500} \times 1000$ g = **80 g** of NaOH would be dissolved in 1000 cm³ of solution.
The mass of 1 mole of NaOH is 40 g,
so 80 g of NaOH is 80 ÷ 40 moles = **2 moles**.
2 moles of NaOH are dissolved in 1 dm³ of solution. So the concentration of NaOH in the solution is **2 mol/dm³**.

Sometimes we know the concentration of a solution and need to work out the mass of solute in a certain volume.

Worked example 2
What mass of H₂SO₄ is there in 250 cm³ of 1 mol/dm³ sulfuric acid (H₂SO₄)?

Solution
In 1 dm³ there would be 1 mole of H₂SO₄.
The mass of 1 mole of H₂SO₄ is (2 × 1) + 32 + (4 × 16) = 98 g, so
in 1000 cm³ of solution there would be 98 g of H₂SO₄, and
in 1 cm³ of solution there are $\frac{98}{1000}$ g of H₂SO₄, so
in 250 cm³ of solution there are $\frac{98}{1000} \times 250$ g of H₂SO₄ = **24.5 g** of H₂SO₄
There is **24.5 g of H₂SO₄** in 250 cm³ of 1 mol/dm³ sulfuric acid.

Titration calculations

In a titration we always have one solution with a concentration which we know accurately. We put this in the burette. We put the other solution, which contains a known substance but with an unknown concentration, in a conical flask. We do this using a pipette to ensure that we know the volume of this solution in the flask. The result from the titration is used to calculate the number of moles of the substance in the solution in the conical flask.

Worked example 3
A student put 25.0 cm³ of sodium hydroxide solution with an unknown concentration into a conical flask using a pipette. The sodium hydroxide reacted with exactly 20.0 cm³ of 0.50 mol/dm³ hydrochloric acid added from a burette. What was the concentration of the sodium hydroxide solution?

Solution
The equation for this reaction is:

$$NaOH\,(aq) + HCl\,(aq) \rightarrow NaCl\,(aq) + H_2O\,(l)$$

This equation tells us that 1 mole of NaOH reacts with 1 mole of HCl.
The concentration of the HCl is 0.50 mol/dm³, so
0.50 moles of HCl are dissolved in 1000 cm³ of acid, and
$\frac{0.50}{1000}$ moles of HCl are dissolved in 1 cm³ of acid, therefore
$\frac{0.50}{1000} \times 20.0$ moles of HCl are dissolved in 20.0 cm³ of acid.

There are 0.010 moles of HCl dissolved in 20.0 cm³ of acid.

The equation for the reaction tells us that 0.010 moles of HCl will react with exactly 0.010 moles of NaOH. This means that there must have been 0.010 moles of NaOH in the 25.0 cm³ of solution in the conical flask. To calculate the concentration of NaOH in the solution in the flask we need to calculate the number of moles of NaOH in 1 dm³ of solution.
0.010 moles of NaOH are dissolved in 25.0 cm³ of solution, so
$\frac{0.010}{25}$ moles of NaOH are dissolved in 1 cm³ of solution, and there are
$\frac{0.010}{25} \times 1000 = 0.40$ moles of NaOH in 1000 cm³ of solution.

The concentration of the sodium hydroxide solution is 0.40 mol/dm³.

SUMMARY QUESTION
1. In a titration, a 25.0 cm³ sample of nitric acid (HNO₃) reacted exactly with 20.0 cm³ of 0.40 mol/dm³ sodium hydroxide solution.
   a) Write down a balanced equation for this reaction.
   b) Calculate the number of moles of sodium hydroxide added.
   c) Write down the number of moles of HNO₃ in the acid.
   d) Calculate the concentration of the nitric acid.

Figure 1 From results like these we can work out the concentration of the unknown solution

KEY POINTS
1. To calculate the concentration of a solution
   - calculate the mass (in grams) of solute in 1 cm³ of solution,
   - calculate the mass (in grams) of solute in 1000 cm³ of solution,
   - convert the mass (in grams) to moles.
2. To calculate the mass of solute in a certain volume of solution
   - calculate the mass (in grams) of the solute there is in 1 dm³ of solution,
   - calculate the mass (in grams) of solute in 1 cm³ of solution,
   - calculate the mass (in grams) of solute there is in the given volume of the solution.

SUMMARY ANSWER

1. a) $HNO_3(aq) + NaOH(aq) \rightarrow NaNO_3(aq) + H_2O(l)$
   b) 0.008 moles
   c) 0.008 moles
   d) 0.32 mole/dm³ [HT only]

KEY POINTS

Give the students the key terms, e.g. mass and concentration, on separate cards. Split the class into small groups and give each team some Blu-Tack, sugar paper, pens and a pack of cards. Get the students to generate a mind map of these points by choosing two cards, one to be the first word of the sentence and the other to be the last word. Draw an arrow between the cards to show the flow of the sentence and write the middle words of the sentence on the arrow. Each word can have as many arrows going into or coming out of it as is needed. Encourage the students to use all the key words at least once.

CHEMISTRY

MORE ABOUT ACIDS AND BASES

C3 2.4 How ideas about acids and bases developed

SPECIFICATION LINK-UP
Unit: Chemistry 3.13.2

Students should use their skills, knowledge and understanding of 'How Science Works':

- to evaluate the contributions of Arrhenius, Lowry and Brønsted to our understanding of acid–base behaviour. [**HT** only]
- to suggest why the work of some scientists, for example Arrhenius, took much longer to be accepted than the work of others, for example, Lowry and Brønsted. [**HT** only]

CHEMISTRY

MORE ABOUT ACIDS AND BASES

C3 2.4 How ideas about acids and bases developed

Joseph Priestley

Alkali
The word 'alkali' is derived from Arabic *al qalīy*, meaning the 'calcined ashes'. This refers to the original source of alkalis, which were made from wood ash. The reaction of fats with alkalis produced from wood ash to produce soap (a process called 'saponification') has been known for thousands of years.

Hydrochloric acid
Joseph Priestley discovered hydrogen chloride gas in 1772, when he reacted concentrated sulfuric acid with sodium chloride. When he dissolved the gas in water it produced an acidic solution which became known as muriatic acid. This is from the Latin word *muria*, meaning brine (salt solution).

Lavoisier

Lavoisier's ideas
One of the first attempts to explain the behaviour of acids was in 1778, when the French chemist Lavoisier published his ideas about acids, burning and the air. In particular, Lavoisier argued that part of the air was responsible for the behaviour of acids. He called this gas *oxygen*, from the Greek meaning 'acid-forming'.

Doubts about oxygen and acid
The great British chemist Sir Humphry Davy heated charcoal to high temperatures with HCl and did not get any reaction, and certainly did not see any oxygen produced.

In 1810 Davy wrote:

Sir Humphry Davy

> One of the singular facts I have observed on this subject, and which I have before referred to, is, that charcoal, even when ignited to whiteness in oxymuriatic or muriatic acid gases, by the Voltaic battery, effects no change in them; if it has been previously freed from hydrogen and moisture by intense ignition in vacuo. This experiment, which I have several times repeated, led me to doubt the existence of oxygen in that substance.

It was not long before Davy concluded that hydrogen, rather than oxygen, is the important element in acids.

The important link – acids and hydrogen
It was the German chemist Justus von Liebig who produced the first really useful definition of acids in 1838. He described them as compounds containing hydrogen which could react with a metal to produce hydrogen gas. This definition was not bettered for more than 50 years – although at this time no-one could explain what a base is, other than to describe it as a substance that neutralises an acid.

Justus von Liebig

230

Teaching suggestions

Activities

- **Timeline** – Encourage students to create a timeline to show how the theories about acids and bases have changed since the eighteenth century. Students could also use the Internet and extend their timeline backwards to include previous people's work. Students should be encouraged to summarise the information to include the date, scientist name and bullet points to form an overview of their contribution. This activity could be used to complete a class timeline display for the classroom. The group could be split into seven teams, one to actually make the timeline and find images of the scientists, and the other six groups could have one discovery each to find out about, summarise and present.

- **Obituary** – When famous people die, often other famous people and commentators discuss the person's life and their achievements. Encourage students to choose a character, maybe a newspaper editor, another famous scientist or perhaps a friend of Arrhenius. Students should then prepare an obituary. This could be a written piece or a presentation for radio or TV. Students should summarise Arrhenius's breakthrough and explain why it took so long for the scientific community to accept his ideas and how he felt about this. Students could then present their obituary to the rest of the class.

- **Specification** – Give the students the above extract from the specification. Encourage students to work in pairs to generate the answer to these two points.

Further chemistry

The breakthrough

The first truly scientific definition of acids and bases was suggested by the Swedish chemist Svante Arrhenius in his PhD thesis in 1884.

Arrhenius suggested that when acids, bases and salts dissolve in water they separate either partly or completely into charged particles called ions in a process called **dissociation**. According to Arrhenius, all the similarities seen between acids with very different formulae were due to the hydrogen ions they produce when dissolved in water. Similarly, he argued that the common properties of bases are due to the fact that they all produce hydroxide ions in solution.

These ideas were seen as revolutionary at the time. The University of Uppsala was very reluctant to give Arrhenius his doctorate, and finally gave him a fourth rank pass – a disgrace which meant he could not get a professorship. Arrhenius kept describing his ideas to other scientists, but older chemists completely rejected his ideas – they were convinced that molecules could not split up and certainly could not carry an electric charge.

Fortunately some of his younger colleagues began to see that Arrhenius's ideas could help explain the results they were getting from their experiments. More and more data built up supporting the new theory and eventually Arrhenius was given credit for the great breakthrough he had made. In 1903, Svante Arrhenius was finally awarded the Nobel Prize for his work.

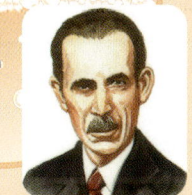

Svante Arrhenius

The modern way of thinking

Although Arrhenius's theory has been and still is extremely useful, it has some limitations. His definition of acids and bases is limited to situations in which water is present. However, many reactions which appear to be acid–base reactions occur in solvents other than water, when there is no water present at all. For example, think about the reaction between the two gases hydrogen chloride and ammonia. This reaction produces white fumes, made of tiny crystals of ammonium chloride:

$$HCl\ (g) + NH_3\ (g) \rightarrow NH_4Cl\ (s)$$

According to Arrhenius's definition of an acid the reaction between these two gases is not neutralisation because it does not take place in aqueous solution. But it is clearly the same reaction that occurs between HCl and NH_3 in aqueous solution.

This problem was recognised in 1923 by the Danish chemist Johannes Brønsted and the British chemist Thomas Lowry.

Working independently they each produced a much more general definition of acids and bases – that an acid is a **proton donor** and a base is a **proton acceptor**.

This definition explains reactions like the one above as well as aqueous acid–base reactions. The ideas of Lowry and Brønsted were accepted very quickly, because they built on the foundation of Arrhenius's theories which were by now well accepted, and they also helped to explain observations which Arrhenius's ideas could not.

Johannes Brønsted

Thomas Lowry

ACTIVITY

Using the ideas in this spread, write and illustrate a timeline which describes the development of ideas about acids since the late 18th century.

ACTIVITY

Write an obituary for Svante Arrhenius explaining his ideas and describing why you think it took much longer for his ideas to be accepted than those of Brønsted and Lowry. [Higher]

Homework

- **Definitions** – Ask students to note the different definitions of acid and base as they have developed over time.

Extension

- **This is your life** – Encourage students to generate a 'This is your life' book for the three great scientists Arrhenius, Brønsted and Lowry.

Learning styles

Visual: Making a timeline.

Auditory: Listening to other students' radio/TV/newspaper obituaries.

Interpersonal: Working as a group.

Intrapersonal: Defining the key terms acids and bases.

ICT link-up

The Internet can be used to get more information about the three scientists, including pictures of them. Run a search in Google under their names, and click on 'Image' to see their pictures.

Special needs

Give the students the summaries of each section for the timeline. They can then cut and stick them onto their own timeline.

231

CHEMISTRY — MORE ABOUT ACIDS AND BASES

SUMMARY ANSWERS

1 A3 B5 C2 D6 E1 F4

2 a)

```
                Congo red                    Alizarin yellow
                blue → red                   yellow → red

       0   1   2   3   4   5   6   7   8   9  10  11  12  13  14
               ↑                   ↑
       Malachite green         Bromothymol blue
       yellow → blue/green     yellow → blue
```

b) Congo red.

c) Bromothymol blue.

d) Alizarin yellow.

3 Acids dissolve in water to produce H⁺ ions. An H⁺ ion is a proton (as a hydrogen atom is made up of a proton and an electron – so when the electron is lost, it leaves just a proton). Alkalis dissolve in water, producing OH⁻ (hydroxide) ions. These react with H⁺ ions to form water i.e. H⁺ + OH⁻. This can be described as the hydroxide ion 'accepting' a proton (H⁺ ion). **[HT only]**

Summary teaching suggestions

- **Special needs**
  - A lot of students often know the science but can't understand the question and therefore fail to gain marks that they can answer orally to a teacher. You, or LSAs, could read out each question in turn and allow the students time to answer before reading the next. For more competent students, they could carry on without having the questions read out.

- **Learning styles**
  Kinaesthetic: Question 1 lends itself to being turned into a matching activity, either as a cut and stick or a card sort.
  Visual: Question 2a) allows students to answer using a diagram of the pH scale.

- **When to use the questions?**
  - As a revision resource.
  - Question 1 could be used to ensure that students understand the language that is being used in the chapter. This could be completed before the chapter has been studied, and then returned to at the end of the chapter and amended.
  - Each question relates to a different lesson spread, e.g., question 1 relates to lesson 2.1, question 2 relates to lesson 2.2.
  - The questions could be given as part of a plenary session, as homework or as an extension during the lesson.

- **Gifted and talented** – Draw off small groups of about four, to generate the answer to question 3 as a group. Encourage groups to illustrate their answers with examples they look up themselves in secondary sources of information.

MORE ABOUT ACIDS AND BASES: C3 2.1 – C3 2.4

SUMMARY QUESTIONS

1 Copy the table and draw lines to link the terms with the explanations or definitions.

A	An acid	1	Solution containing a high concentration of acid.
B	An alkali	2	An acid that is partly ionised when dissolved in water.
C	Weak acid	3	Dissolves in water to give H⁺(aq) ions.
D	Strong acid	4	Solution containing a low concentration of acid.
E	Concentrated acid	5	Dissolves in water to give OH⁻(aq) ions.
F	Dilute acid	6	An acid that is fully ionised when dissolved in water.

2 Not all indicators change colour at the same pH. The table shows four different indicators and the colour changes that occur as the pH increases.

Indicator	Colour change as pH increases	Approximate pH at which colour change occurs
Malachite green	yellow → blue/green	1
Congo red	blue → red	4
Bromothymol blue	yellow → blue	7
Alizarin yellow	yellow → red	11

a) Draw a pH scale which runs from 0 to 14 and draw on it labelled arrows to show where each indicator changes colour.

In the following questions, all solutions have a concentration of 1 mol/dm³.

b) Which indicator could be used to distinguish between a solution containing a strong acid and one containing a weak acid?

c) Which indicator could be used to distinguish between a solution containing a weak acid and one containing a weak alkali?

d) Which indicator could be used to distinguish between a solution containing a strong alkali and one containing a weak alkali?

3 Explain the statement:
'Acids are proton donors whereas bases are proton acceptors.' **[Higher]**

232

EXAM-STYLE QUESTIONS

1 Ethanoic acid is a weak acid. Some students tested solutions of ethanoic acid and hydrochloric acid. The results are shown in the table.

	Hydrochloric acid	Ethanoic acid
Formula	HCl	CH₃CO₂H
Concentration of solution (mol per dm³)	0.10	0.10
pH	1.0	2.9
Reaction with magnesium ribbon	Vigorous bubbling	Slow stream of bubbles
Volume of sodium hydroxide solution used to exactly neutralise 25 cm³ of acid solution (cm³)	25.0	25.0

(a) Explain, as fully as you can, why the pH of ethanoic acid is higher than the pH of hydrochloric acid. (3)

(b) Explain the difference in the reactions with magnesium ribbon. (2)

(c) Explain why the volumes of sodium hydroxide to neutralise the acids are the same. You should write balanced equations to help with your explanation. The formula of hydrochloric acid is HCl. Use HA for the formula of ethanoic acid. (4)

2 A student carried out a titration to find how much dilute nitric acid was needed to react completely with 25 cm³ of sodium hydroxide solution.

Here are his results:

Test	Volume of dilute nitric acid added (cm³)
1	28.9
2	25.1
3	24.9
4	25.0

(a) The student placed 25 cm³ of sodium hydroxide solution into a conical flask to start with. What piece of apparatus should he use to get exactly 25 cm³ of solution? Choose from the list below: (1)

   a beaker   a pipette   a measuring cylinder

(b) What else would be added to the conical flask before adding any acid? (1)

EXAM-STYLE ANSWERS

1 a) *Three from:*
- Ethanoic acid is a weak acid, but hydrochloric acid is a strong acid.
- Ethanoic acid is only partly dissociated in solution/only some of the ethanoic acid molecules produce hydrogen ions in solution.
- Hydrochloric acid is fully dissociated in solution/all of the hydrochloric acid molecules produce hydrogen ions in solution.
- The concentration of hydrogen ions is lower in ethanoic acid than in hydrochloric acid.
- A higher concentration of hydrogen ions means a lower pH/lower concentration of hydrogen ions means a higher pH.
   (3 marks)

b) Concentration of hydrogen ions is higher for hydrochloric acid/lower for ethanoic acid. *(1 mark)*
So the rate of reaction is faster for hydrochloric acid/slower for ethanoic acid. *(1 mark)*

c) *Four from:*
- HCl + NaOH → NaCl + H₂O.
- HA + NaOH → NaA + H₂O.
- One mole of each acid reacts with one mole of sodium hydroxide.
- HCl → H⁺ + Cl⁻.
- HA ⇌ H⁺ + A⁻ is reversible/only some of the ethanoic acid molecules are ionised.
- As hydrogen ions from ethanoic acid react with the alkali, more ethanoic acid molecules dissociate until all the acid is used.
- One mole of each acid produces one mole of hydrogen ions when fully reacted.
   (4 marks)

2 a) A pipette *(1 mark)*

b) An indicator *(1 mark)*

c) A burette *(1 mark)*

d) Test 1 *(1 mark)*

Further chemistry

HOW SCIENCE WORKS QUESTIONS

You have been asked to design an investigation to find out the changes in pH as you add a strong acid to a strong alkali. You have a burette into which you have been told to add some dilute hydrochloric acid. The flask will contain your sodium hydroxide solution.

You have to add the acid to the alkali and get a reading of the pH as more and more acid is added.

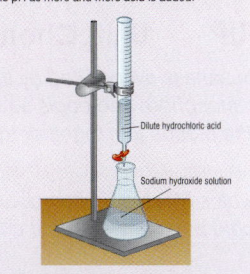

(c) What piece of apparatus would he use to add the dilute nitric acid to the conical flask? (1)
(d) Which test (1 to 4) produced an anomalous result? (1)
(e) How would the student work out how much acid was needed to neutralise 25 cm³ of dilute sodium hydroxide from his results? (2)

3 25.0 cm³ of a solution of sodium carbonate reacted with exactly 20.0 cm³ of 0.2 mol per dm³ of nitric acid. The equation for the reaction is:

$Na_2CO_3 + 2HNO_3 \rightarrow 2NaNO_3 + CO_2 + H_2O$

(a) Name a suitable indicator that could be used to find the end point of this reaction. (1)
(b) Calculate the number of moles of nitric acid in 20.0 cm³ of the solution. (2)
(c) Calculate the number of moles of sodium carbonate in 25.0 cm³ of solution. (1)
(d) Calculate the concentration of sodium carbonate solution in mol per dm³. (2)
(e) Calculate the concentration of the solution in grams per dm³ of anhydrous sodium carbonate. (2)
(A_r values: Na = 23, C = 12, O = 16)
[Higher]

4 25.0 cm³ of a solution containing 4.0 g of sodium hydroxide per dm³ were exactly neutralised by 20 cm³ of a solution of sulfuric acid.
(a) Calculate the concentration of the sodium hydroxide solution in mol per dm³. (2)
(A_r values: Na = 23, O = 16, H = 1)
(b) Calculate the number of moles of sodium hydroxide in 25.0 cm³ of the solution. (2)
(c) Write a balanced equation for the reaction. (2)
(d) Calculate the number of moles of sulfuric acid in 20 cm³ of solution. (1)
(e) Calculate the concentration of the sulfuric acid in mol per dm³. (2)
(f) You have been given 200 cm³ of each of the solutions. Describe how you would carry out a titration to find the volumes of the solutions that react. (6)
[Higher]

a) You have a choice of either using an indicator and recording the colour changes or a pH meter and recording the pH. Which would you choose? Explain your choice. (1)
b) How much acid would you add at a time? Explain your answer. (2)
c) Why would you stir the flask before checking the pH? (1)
d) Why would it be important to repeat the titration at least one more time? (1)
e) How would you present your results? (1)
f) If you knew that both the acid and the alkali were of the same concentration, how might you check the reliability of your results? (1)

---

e) Discard/ignore the result for Test 1/28.9 cm³. (1 mark)
   Add up other results and divide by 3/get mean or average. (1 mark)

3 a) Methyl orange. (1 mark)
   b) 0.004 mol. (2 marks)
      (correct working: 20 × 0.2/1000 gains 1 mark)
   c) 0.002 mol or e.c.f.: (b)/2. (1 mark)
   d) 0.08 mol per dm³ or e.c.f.: (c) × 40. (2 marks)
      (correct working: (c) × 1000/25 gains 1 mark)
   e) 8.48 g per dm³ or e.c.f.: (d) × 106 (2 marks)
      (1 mark for working e.g. Na₂CO₃ = 106 or (d) × incorrect attempt at M_r)
      [HT only]

4 a) 0.10 mol per dm³. (2 marks) (correct working: 4/40 gains 1 mark)
   b) 0.0025 mol or e.c.f. from (a). (2 marks)
      (correct working: 25 × 0.1/1000 gains 1 mark)
   c) $H_2SO_4 + 2NaOH \rightarrow Na_2SO_4 + 2H_2O$. (2 marks)
      (1 mark for correct formulae, 1 mark for correct balancing)
   d) 0.00125 mol or e.c.f.: (b)/2. (1 mark)
   e) 0.0625 mol per dm³ or e.c.f.: (d) × 50. (2 marks)
      (1 mark for working 0.00125 × 1000/20)
   f) Up to six from:
      • Rinse burette with acid.
      • Fill burette with acid.
      • Record reading on burette.
      • Rinse pipette with sodium hydroxide solution.
      • Pipette 25 cm³ of sodium hydroxide solution into flask.
      • Add indicator.
      • Add acid from burette until indicator changes colour.
      • Record burette reading.
      • Calculate volume added/note volume added from burette.
      • Repeat until two titres agree within 0.1 cm³. (6 marks)
      [HT only]

Exam teaching suggestions

These questions would be best tackled after completing the chapter. Foundation-Tier candidates should be able to do Q1) and Q2. Allow 35 minutes for students to attempt all of the questions.

Higher-Tier candidates will be set calculations on concentrations in moles per dm³ and grams per dm³. Foundation-Tier candidates are expected to understand that solutions of equal concentrations in moles per dm³ contain equal molar amounts of solute and that equal volumes of solutions of monobasic acids and alkalis react exactly. They may be asked to interpret simple quantitative data on titrations but will not be asked to do more complex calculations on concentrations in moles per dm³ and grams per dm³.

It is good practice in calculations to show all working. A correct answer with appropriate units will gain full marks even if no working is shown. However, an incorrect answer with no working will gain no marks. So showing steps in the working acts as insurance against a careless mistake on the calculator, and correct working will always gain some marks. An arithmetical error in working is carried forward, (e.c.f.) so students should be encouraged to continue to work through calculations, even if they are not sure about their intermediate answers. Incorrect chemistry in the working, however, will not gain credit.

Students should be encouraged to round numerical answers to an appropriate number of significant figures, but will not be penalised if the answer they give is numerically correct.

HOW SCIENCE WORKS ANSWERS

a) Use the pH meter because it produces a continuous variable, which is more powerful than the categoric variable of a colour change. It will produce greater accuracy than using a colour chart comparison.
b) As little as can be reasonably measured. This produces more plotting points on the graph and therefore a more accurate graph.
c) To ensure that the pH represents the whole of the contents of the flask. It increases the accuracy. This is a potential area for human error and therefore random errors.
d) Increase the accuracy of your method [accept improve reliability].
e) As a graph of the mean pH against the volume of alkali added.
f) You should have a pH of 7 when the same volume of alkali has been added as there is acid in the flask.

How science works teaching suggestions

- **Literacy guidance**
  - Key terms that should be understood: reliability, accuracy, continuous and categoric variables, precision.
  - The question expecting a longer answer, where students can practise their literacy skills: a) and c).
- **Higher- and lower-level answers.** Question f) is a higher-level question and the answers provided above is also at this level. Question d) is lower-level and the answer provided is also lower-level.
- **Gifted and talented.** Able students could consider the likely shape of the graph.
- **How and when to use these questions.** When wishing to develop concepts of accuracy, precision and reliability. The questions could be used as a preliminary to a demonstration.
- **Homework.** The questions could be studied for homework and discussed in class.
- **Special needs.** The students may well need to be shown a titration before appreciating the skills required.
- **ICT link-up.** The data could be collected quickly using data logging equipment.

CHEMISTRY: WATER

C3 3.1 Water and solubility

LEARNING OBJECTIVES

Students should learn:

- The processes involved in the water cycle.
- That many substances dissolve in water and that solutions can be saturated.

LEARNING OUTCOMES

Most students should be able to:

- Describe where rainwater comes from.
- Give examples of substances that can dissolve in water.
- State the units for solubility.
- State a definition for saturated solutions.

Some students should also be able to:

- Explain the water cycle.
- Explain which type of substances are usually soluble.

Teaching suggestions

- **Special needs.** Give the students a set of everyday chemicals, e.g. sugar, salt, coffee, tea bags, wood, soap. Each student should be given a results table with three columns labelled 'substance', 'cold water' and 'hot water'. Students should then put ticks and crosses to show their prediction on whether they think the substance could dissolve. Allow students to complete the practical and record their observations in a different colour on the same table. Then ask students to draw conclusions from their experiment – hopefully students will recognise that the hotter the solvent, the greater the amount of solute that can be dissolved. Note: The difference is only slight with sodium chloride.
- **Gifted and talented.** Students could be encouraged to understand how dissolving differs in different solvents due to the intermolecular forces of attraction between solute particles and solvent particles.

SPECIFICATION LINK-UP   Unit: Chemistry 3.13.3

- Water in rivers, lakes and the oceans is evaporated by the heat of the Sun. This forms water vapour that rises in the atmosphere and cools so that it condenses to form clouds. The water droplets in the clouds join together to produce rain. This is known as the water cycle.
- Many substances dissolve in water. Most ionic compounds are soluble in water. Some molecular substances are soluble but many covalent compounds are insoluble in water.
- The solubility of a solute in water, or any other solvent, is usually given in grams of solute per 100 grams of water (or solvent) at that temperature.
- The solubility of most solutes that are solids increases as the temperature increases.
- A saturated solution is one in which no more solute will dissolve at that temperature. When a hot saturated solution cools some of the solute will separate from the solution.

Lesson structure

STARTER

Definitions – Ask students to define each of the following key words and give an example of each: 'solvent, solution, solute, dissolve'. Ask students to compare their answers in groups of four, and put down two further examples of each word. (5–10 minutes)

Demonstration – Take a very large (1 litre) glass beaker, table-tennis balls, marbles and a large glass rod. Put the table-tennis balls into the glass beaker and add the marbles and stir. Ask the students to think about what they have just been shown and ask them to work in pairs to explain what the model shows. Ask a few groups to feedback to the class about what they think the model shows. [The table-tennis balls represent the solvent, the marbles represent the solute that dissolves to form a mixture of the two spheres, the solution]. Ask about the limitations of the model and how it could be improved. (10 minutes)

MAIN

- In chemistry, like dissolves like. For example, ionic chemicals dissolve in water, as water is polar; whereas covalent compounds dissolve in organic solvents that tend not to be polar.
- Allow students to experiment with different substances and solvents to find out the pattern between solvent and solute. Students may need a hint to consider bonding.
- Ask students to predict the effect of temperature on dissolving. Then ask students to design their own experiment to prove their prediction.

PLENARIES

Diagram – Give students an unlabelled diagram of the water cycle. Allow students to add their own labels. For lower attaining students, the labels could be supplied so that they cut and stick them into position. Use Animation C3 3.1 'Water cycle' from the GCSE Chemistry CD ROM. (5–10 minutes)

AfL (Assessment for Learning) – Give the students an examination question with three fictitious student answers. Ask the students to work in small groups and put the answers in order from weakest to most comprehensive. Students should think about why they have put the answers in that order. Feedback from each group about which they feel is the order of the answers and why. (10 minutes)

Teaching suggestions continued

- **Learning styles**

   Kinaesthetic: Completing the practical on solubility.

   Visual: Labelling the water cycle.

   Auditory: Listening to feedback from groups.

   Interpersonal: Working in small groups.

   Intrapersonal: Defining key words.

- **ICT link-up.** The dissolving practical can be completed as a demonstration on microscope slides. Connect the microscope via flexi-cam to the TV or a data projector to see, at the microscopic level, the chemicals dissolving or otherwise.

- **Homework.** Ask students to name three everyday solutions, their solvent and solute.

Practical support

Solubility experiment

Equipment and materials needed

Copper sulfate crystals (harmful), spatula, sodium chloride crystals, nail varnish (flammable), propanone (flammable and irritant), water, polystyrene beads, test tubes, test-tube racks, two dropping pipettes. (CLEAPSS Hazcards: copper sulphate 27; propanone 85.)

Details

Wearing eye protection, put a crystal of copper sulfate into two test tubes and add water to the first and propanone to the second. Shake the tube and decide if the compound has dissolved in either of the solvent. Repeat the experiment with sodium chloride, nail varnish (put a small amount in the tube and allow to dry) and polystyrene beads.

ACTIVITY & EXTENSION IDEAS

- Students could find out data of the solubility of different solutes at room temperature in water. This data could then be plotted on a bar chart. Ask students to explain why this data is presented as a bar chart, whereas solubility curves on the next spread are line graphs. (This relates to: 'How Science Works' – the independent variable in this case is categoric, i.e. type of solute; whereas in a solubility curve the independent variable is a continuous variable, i.e. temperature.)

- Students could find out data for the solubility of a particular solute in different solvents. This data could be shown in a table/bar chart.

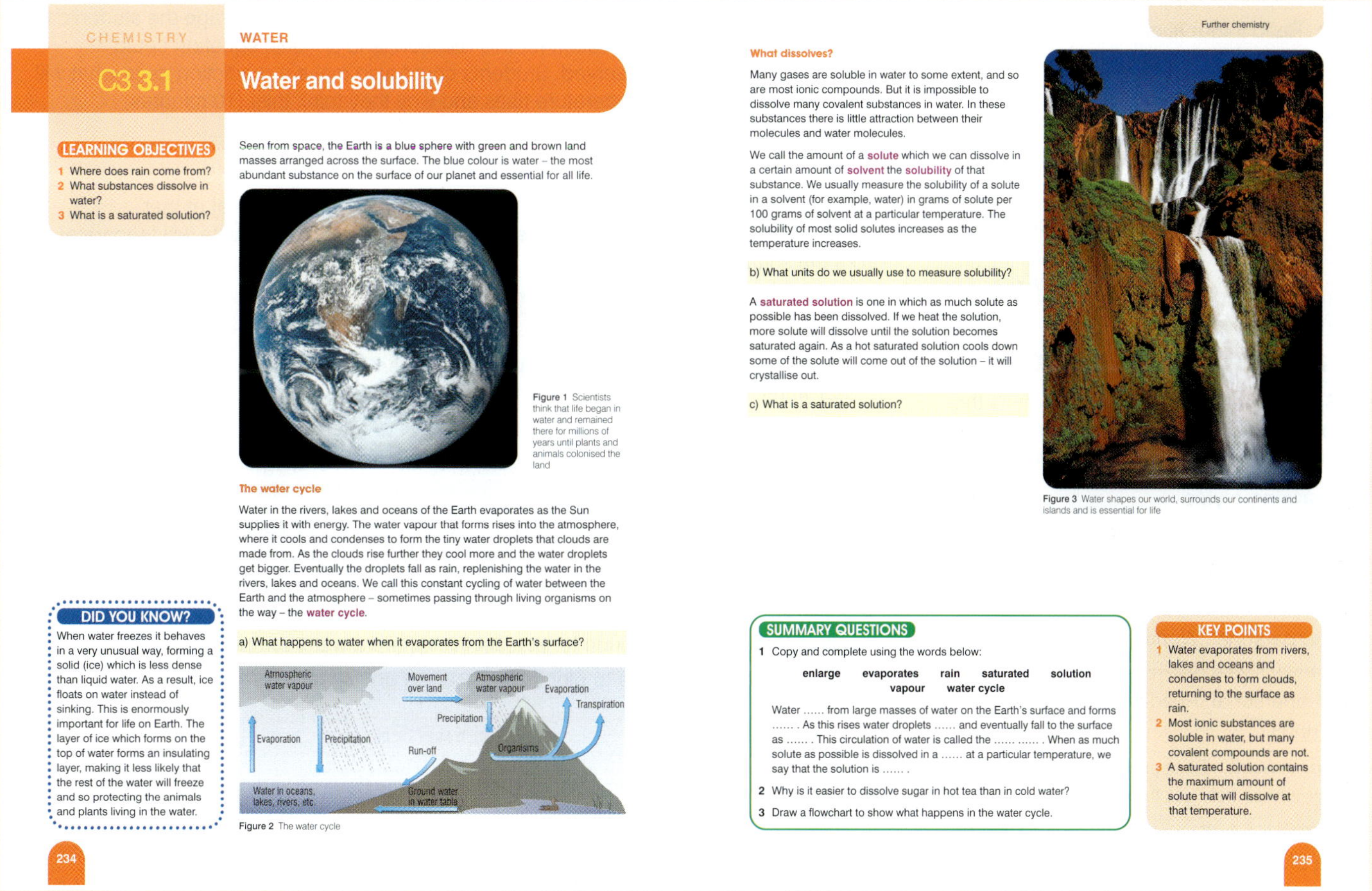

CHEMISTRY — WATER

C3 3.1 Water and solubility

LEARNING OBJECTIVES
1. Where does rain come from?
2. What substances dissolve in water?
3. What is a saturated solution?

Seen from space, the Earth is a blue sphere with green and brown land masses arranged across the surface. The blue colour is water – the most abundant substance on the surface of our planet and essential for all life.

Figure 1 Scientists think that life began in water and remained there for millions of years until plants and animals colonised the land

The water cycle

Water in the rivers, lakes and oceans of the Earth evaporates as the Sun supplies it with energy. The water vapour that forms rises into the atmosphere, where it cools and condenses to form the tiny water droplets that clouds are made from. As the clouds rise further they cool more and the water droplets get bigger. Eventually the droplets fall as rain, replenishing the water in the rivers, lakes and oceans. We call this constant cycling of water between the Earth and the atmosphere – sometimes passing through living organisms on the way – the **water cycle**.

a) What happens to water when it evaporates from the Earth's surface?

DID YOU KNOW?
When water freezes it behaves in a very unusual way, forming a solid (ice) which is less dense than liquid water. As a result, ice floats on water instead of sinking. This is enormously important for life on Earth. The layer of ice which forms on the top of water forms an insulating layer, making it less likely that the rest of the water will freeze and so protecting the animals and plants living in the water.

Figure 2 The water cycle

What dissolves?

Many gases are soluble in water to some extent, and so are most ionic compounds. But it is impossible to dissolve many covalent substances in water. In these substances there is little attraction between their molecules and water molecules.

We call the amount of a **solute** which we can dissolve in a certain amount of **solvent** the **solubility** of that substance. We usually measure the solubility of a solute in a solvent (for example, water) in grams of solute per 100 grams of solvent at a particular temperature. The solubility of most solid solutes increases as the temperature increases.

b) What units do we usually use to measure solubility?

A **saturated solution** is one in which as much solute as possible has been dissolved. If we heat the solution, more solute will dissolve until the solution becomes saturated again. As a hot saturated solution cools down some of the solute will come out of the solution – it will crystallise out.

c) What is a saturated solution?

Figure 3 Water shapes our world, surrounds our continents and islands and is essential for life

SUMMARY QUESTIONS
1. Copy and complete using the words below:

   enlarge   evaporates   rain   saturated   solution
   vapour   water cycle

   Water …… from large masses of water on the Earth's surface and forms ……. As this rises water droplets …… and eventually fall to the surface as ……. This circulation of water is called the …… ……. When as much solute as possible is dissolved in a …… at a particular temperature, we say that the solution is …….

2. Why is it easier to dissolve sugar in hot tea than in cold water?

3. Draw a flowchart to show what happens in the water cycle.

KEY POINTS
1. Water evaporates from rivers, lakes and oceans and condenses to form clouds, returning to the surface as rain.
2. Most ionic substances are soluble in water, but many covalent compounds are not.
3. A saturated solution contains the maximum amount of solute that will dissolve at that temperature.

SUMMARY ANSWERS

1. Evaporates, clouds, enlarge, rain, water cycle, solvent, saturated.
2. Sugar is more soluble in hot water than cold water.
3. Flow chart summarising the cycle on page 234 in the Student Book.

Answers to in-text questions

a) As the air cools, the water vapour forms clouds.

b) Grams of solute per 100 grams of solvent.

c) A solution in which no more solute will dissolve.

KEY POINTS

Give students the words that make up the key points as a card sort. Students should then generate the key points from the cards. The first student to successfully complete the sentences could get a prize.

235

CHEMISTRY WATER

C3 3.2 Solubility curves

LEARNING OBJECTIVES

Students will learn:

- That solubility changes with temperature and how to use solubility curves.
- That cooling a saturated solution results in crystallisation.
- That gases can dissolve in water and factors that affect their solubility.

LEARNING OUTCOMES

Most students should be able to:

- Read data from a solubility curve.
- Give examples of gases that can dissolve in water and uses for this.
- Construct a solubility graph.
- Read information from solubility curves.

Some students should also be able to:

- Explain how solubility changes with temperature and pressure and solve more complex problems using solubility curves.

Teaching suggestions

- **Special needs.** Give these students the axis and scale on squared paper for them the plot the solubility curves.
- **Learning styles**
  Kinaesthetic: Crystallising sugar.
  Visual: Plotting solubility curves.
  Auditory: Listening to feedback.
  Interpersonal: Working in groups to explain observations.
  Intrapersonal: Reading off data from graphs.
- **Homework.** Encourage students to find out where fish get their oxygen.
- **ICT link-up.** The solubility curves could be plotted using a graphs package, e.g. Excel. Use Animation C3 3.1 'Water cycle' from the GCSE Chemistry CD ROM.

SPECIFICATION LINK-UP   Unit: Chemistry 3.13.3

- A saturated solution is one in which no more solute will dissolve at that temperature. When a hot saturated solution cools some of the solute will separate from the solution.
- Many gases are soluble in water. Their solubility increases as temperature decreases and as the pressure increases.
  – Dissolving carbon dioxide in water under high pressure makes carbonated water. When the pressure is released, the gas bubbles out of the solution. Carbonated water is used to make fizzy drinks.
  – Dissolving oxygen is essential for aquatic life. If the temperature of the water increases, the amount of oxygen that is dissolved decreases.

Students should use their skills, knowledge and understanding of 'How Science Works':

- *to interpret solubility curves and explain when crystallisation may occur.*

Lesson structure

STARTER

Demonstration – Show the students the effect of temperature on dissolving of lead chloride crystals. Firstly, the lead chloride needs to be made from the precipitation reaction of dilute hydrochloric acid with lead nitrate solution. Encourage the students to write a balanced symbol equation for this reaction, and an ionic equation could emphasise the change observed. Students could also make a prediction as to what will happen to solubility as temperature rises and why they think this. (10 minutes)

Fill in the gaps – Give the students part of the specification with missing words. Encourage the students to fill in the gaps with the most scientific word that they can:

'A [saturated] solution is one in which no more [solute] will [dissolve] at that temperature. When a hot saturated [solution] cools some of the solute will [separate] from the solution'. (5 minutes)

MAIN

- Ask the students to make a saturated sugar solution in a 50 cm^3 beaker containing hot water. Put a cocktail stick into the solution and leave.
- Then allow the solution to cool as the students predict what the effect will be.
- Ask the students to record their results in a flow chart of diagrams including at least one labelled particle diagram.
- If the reactants and the room are hygienic, the sugar crystals can be eaten from the stick. (Use a food technology room for this.) They can be coloured by adding food colouring to the saturated solution.
- Allow students to use the Internet or data books to find out the solubility of potassium nitrate and sodium chloride for at least five different water temperatures.
- Encourage the students to plot the two curves on the same graph.

PLENARIES

Graph – Ask the students to use the graph that they have already plotted to answer the following questions:

- What is the temperature of the water when the salts are equally soluble? [the temperature where the curves cross]
- Which salt is the most soluble at 10°C? [sodium chloride]
- Which salt is the most soluble at 50°C? [potassium nitrate] (5 minutes)

Explain – Show students some cans of fizzy pop. Ask students to name the solvent [water] and solute [gas, carbon dioxide, and other solid solutes listed on the contents label]. Open one can carefully. Then shake another can and ask the students to predict what will happen, and open the can. Ask students to work in small groups to explain what causes the fizz and why shaking the can caused more fizz to be produced. Ask a few groups to feedback their ideas to the class. (10 minutes)

Practical support

Starter demonstration

Equipment and materials needed
Stand, boss, clamp, Bunsen burner and safety equipment, two boiling tubes, spatula, filter funnel, filter paper, 0.02 mol/dm³ lead nitrate solution (toxic), 0.04 mol/dm³ sodium iodide solution, 2 mol/dm³ hydrochloric acid (irritant). CLEAPSS Hazcards: lead nitrate 57; hydrochloric acid 47.

Details
Wearing eye protection, pour a depth of about 3 cm lead nitrate solution into the boiling tube. Add hydrochloric acid until the boiling tube is half-full and allow the precipitate to settle. To speed up this process, filter the mixture and collect the solid from the filter paper. Put a few lead chloride crystals into another boiling tube and add cold water. Clamp into position over a blue Bunsen flame. Observe the crystals.

Wash hands after experiment.

ACTIVITY & EXTENSION IDEAS

Some re-usable hand warmers, such as those available for camping, are super-saturated solutions. The metal chip inside starts a crystallisation reaction, which releases energy. Show the students one of these hand warmers and, using the Internet, ask them to find out how they work.

C3 3.2 Solubility curves

LEARNING OBJECTIVES
1. How does solubility change with temperature?
2. What happens when we cool a saturated solution?
3. Do gases dissolve in water?

Solubility of solids
The amount of a substance that will dissolve in a solvent is affected by the temperature of the solvent. We can see the effect of temperature on the solubility of solutes by looking at graphs which we call **solubility curves**. A solubility curve shows the amount of a solute which dissolves to produce a saturated solution at any given temperature.

a) What does a solubility curve show?

We can use solubility curves to predict how much solute will form when we cool a hot solution down.

For example, look at the solubility curve of potassium nitrate in Figure 1. You can see that at 80°C, almost 150 g of potassium nitrate will dissolve in every 100 g of water, but at 20°C, only about 35 g will dissolve. That means that as we cool a saturated solution of potassium nitrate down from 80°C to 20°C around 115 g (i.e. 150 g − 35 g) of potassium nitrate will crystallise out of every 100 g of water.

Solubility of gases
There are two main factors which affect the solubility of gases – temperature and pressure. Gases behave in the opposite way to solids when they dissolve in water. As the temperature increases, the amount of gas which will dissolve in a certain volume of water decreases when we keep the pressure constant. On the other hand, if we keep the temperature constant, the solubility of a gas increases as we increase the pressure.

b) What factors affect the solubility of a gas in water?

Figure 1 These solubility curves show the effect of temperature on three different solutes dissolving in water. Notice that the solubility of each one increases as the temperature increases.

Gas	Solubility (g of gas in 100 g of water)			
	0°C	20°C	50°C	100°C
Nitrogen (N₂)	0.0029	0.0019	0.0012	0
Oxygen (O₂)	0.0069	0.0043	0.0027	0
Carbon dioxide (CO₂)	0.335	0.169	0.076	0
Ammonia (NH₃)	89.9	51.8	28.4	7.4

Figure 2 The effect of temperature and pressure on the solubility of gases in water

Why is it important to know about solubility?
There are lots of examples of the way that solubility affects our lives every day. In the kitchen we often need to dissolve solids like sugar in water. This is made easier by heating the water to increase the solubility of the solid.

Outside our homes, the artificial fertilisers that we put on the soil are very soluble in water. They dissolve in rainwater, and can contaminate rivers, lakes and reservoirs.

The nitrate ions in these fertilisers can be very bad for babies and some adults. This means that nitrate levels in drinking water must be carefully monitored by the water companies who supply water to our homes and schools.

Oxygen dissolved in water is essential to keep animals living in water alive. When we pump hot water from the cooling towers of power stations into rivers it contains no chemical pollution.

However, the warm water from the power station increases the temperature of the water in the river. This reduces the amount of oxygen dissolved in it. We call this thermal pollution. It can be very bad for wildlife living in the river, especially fish.

c) Why must drinking water be checked for nitrate levels?
d) Where does nitrate in drinking water come from?

Another example of the importance of dissolved gases is the fizzy drinks that many of us enjoy. The carbonated water we use to make them is produced by dissolving carbon dioxide in water at high pressures before bottling or canning the drink. When we open the can or bottle and release the pressure, the gas comes out of the solution and provides us with 'fizz'!

Lemonade, cola and other sparkling drinks that have been allowed to stand for a while are not very fizzy. That's because they have warmed up and a lot of the carbon dioxide has come out of solution.

Figure 3 Some fish need high levels of oxygen dissolved in the water they live in. They are particularly badly affected if the temperature of the water is raised, reducing the amount of oxygen in solution.

FOUL FACTS
Fizzy drinks make you burp because the carbon dioxide dissolved in them comes out of solution as the drink warms up in your stomach.

SUMMARY QUESTIONS
1. Copy and complete using the words below:

   dissolve   less   more   pressure   solubility   temperature

   The amount of a substance that will ...... in water is shown by a ...... curve. The solubility of gases is affected by ...... and .... Gases are ...... soluble at high temperatures and ...... soluble at high pressures.

2. 125 g of sodium nitrate is dissolved in 100 g of water at 80°C. The solution is then allowed to cool to 35°C. Use the graph in Figure 1 to estimate what mass of sodium nitrate crystals will be present at this temperature.

3. Use the information in the table in Figure 2 to plot a graph of the solubility of oxygen in water at temperatures between 0°C and 50°C. Why are fish kept in a small pond in danger of dying in very hot weather?

KEY POINTS
1. The solubility of most solid solutes increases as the temperature rises.
2. The solubility of gases decreases as the temperature rises.
3. Solubility curves show how the solubility of a substance changes with temperature.

SUMMARY ANSWERS
1. Dissolve, solubility, temperature, pressure, less, more
2. 25–35 g
3. Not enough oxygen can be dissolved in the water as small bodies of water are affected by air temperature more than large bodies of water.

Answers to in-text questions
a) How much solute is needed to make a saturated solution at a given temperature.
b) Temperature and pressure.
c) Nitrate ions can be bad for people.
d) (Artificial) fertilisers.

KEY POINTS
Students could create a limerick to remember these three key points.

CHEMISTRY | WATER

C3 3.3 Hard water

LEARNING OBJECTIVES

Students should learn:

- That water can be described as hard.
- That there are advantages and disadvantages to hard water.

LEARNING OUTCOMES

Most students should be able to:

- Recall a definition for hard water.
- List advantages of hard water.
- List disadvantages of hard water.

Some students should also be able to:

- Explain what makes water hard.
- Explain what happens to soap in hard water.

Teaching suggestions

- **Special needs.** The method for investigating the mass of dissolved chemicals in water could be supplied as a diagrammatic flow chart. Students could also be supplied with an empty results table.
- **Gifted and talented.** These students could be given a selection of different waters. They could plan an investigation to find out which water is the hardest.
- **Learning styles**
  Kinaesthetic: Investigating the mass of dissolved compounds in water.
  Visual: Creating an information card.
  Auditory: Listening to answers to a question.
  Interpersonal: Working in groups to determine observations.
  Intrapersonal: Appreciating the difference between hard and soft water.
- **Homework.** Water hardness can reduce the life of appliances in the home. Ask students to find out how hardness of water can be removed at home.

SPECIFICATION LINK-UP   Unit: Chemistry 3.13.3

- *Soft water readily forms lather with soap. Hard water reacts with soap to form scum and so more soap is needed to form a lather.*
- *Hard water contains dissolved compounds, usually of calcium or magnesium. The compounds are dissolved when water comes into contact with rocks.*
- *Using hard water can increase costs because more soap is needed. When hard water is heated it can produce scale that reduces the efficiency of heating systems and kettles.*
- *Hard water has some health benefits because calcium compounds are good for health.*

Students should use their skills, knowledge and understanding of 'How Science Works':

- *to consider and evaluate the environmental, social and economic aspects of water quality and hardness.*

Lesson structure

STARTER

Soap up – Give students samples of hard and soft water. Ask each student to wash their hands with soap and each type of water in turn and to note their observations. Encourage students to share their ideas in pairs and then in groups of about four. Ask each group to feedback their observations to the class. (10 minutes)

Question – Ask students to answer the following question in as much scientific detail as they can:

- What makes water hard? [dissolved compounds of magnesium and calcium]

Encourage a few students to share their explanations and ask the whole class to copy out the most scientific response from the class. (10 minutes)

MAIN

- Students may find it difficult to understand that the dissolved compounds in the water cause the hardness. Use PhotoPLUS C3 3.3 'Hard water' from the GCSE Chemistry CD ROM.
- Students can experimentally investigate the amount of dissolved compounds in the water. Higher attaining students could design their own experiment, whereas others could be supplied with the method.
- Students should record their information in the appropriate results table and calculate the mass of dissolved substances in the water.
- Discuss the accuracy and errors involved in the experiment (this relates to: 'How Science Works').
- Ask the students to imagine that they have been commissioned by a water company to create a fact file card to be put into an information pack given to schools. Many companies provide educational resources. Show students some information from companies, maybe hard copies or web sites.
- They can use the information on the pages and their card should be an introduction to what causes hard water, its benefits and the problems that it can cause.

PLENARIES

Think – Explain to students that the dissolved chemicals in the water produce scale and scum. Ask students to generate a list of problems that this may cause. Ask each student to write one problem (must be new, i.e. not already listed on the board) onto the board. Ask the students to pick three of the problems to copy into their notes. (10 minutes)

AfL (Assessment for Learning) – Put out the fact file cards onto the side benches. Next to each piece of work leave a table made of two columns headed 'mark' and 'comment'. Ask the students to go around each piece of work, give it a mark in line with the school's marking policy and give a comment. The comment should have at least one piece of praise and one comment for improvement of the work. Allow the students to rotate around the work. Then give each student their comment sheet to review their own work. (15 minutes)

ACTIVITY & EXTENSION IDEAS

- Students could design a label for a bottle of mineral water explaining the health benefits of dissolved minerals and how they get into the water.
- Students could study the packaging of different mineral waters. They could then rate the science content of the labelling. They could also draw pie charts to show the mineral composition of the different waters.
- Students could research into industrial tests for hardness of water, e.g. test strips.
- The hardness of water could be investigated by the amount of standard soap solution that is needed to produce a permanent soap lather. A set volume of the water to be tested should be measured into a conical flask. Then add 1 cm³ of soap, maybe from a burette, and shake the flask. Keep adding 1 cm³ of soap and shaking until a lather of bubbles persists for 10 seconds.
- This experiment can be carried out using micro-scale equipment.

Further chemistry

Practical support

Hard water experiment

Equipment and materials required
Two beakers, measuring cylinder, balance, samples of hard and soft water, Bunsen burner and safety equipment, tripod, gauze, eye protection.
CLEAPSS Recipe Cards 72, 60.

Details
Record the mass of an empty beaker. Measure 100 ml of hard water and put into the same beaker and re-record the mass. While wearing eye protection, boil the water on a tripod and gauze over a blue Bunsen flame until all the water has been removed. Allow the beaker to cool and re-weigh. Repeat the experiment with soft water.

CHEMISTRY / WATER

C3 3.3 Hard water

LEARNING OBJECTIVES
1. What is hard water?
2. What are the advantages and disadvantages of hard water?

Most of us in the developed world take it for granted that we have fresh, clean water piped to our homes. The water which comes out of our taps in different areas of the country may look very similar, but there are some very big chemical differences in it. These differences become obvious when we get washed.

When we wash ourselves with soap, the water in some areas of the country forms a really rich, thick lather easily. But in other parts of the country the water doesn't behave in this way. It is quite difficult to get the bubbles that the soap adverts promise us. This is because the water is **hard**.

Figure 1 Clean water may look the same wherever you are – but appearances can be deceptive

Figure 2 It isn't always easy to get bubbles like this

Hard water not only makes it difficult to wash ourselves, it also makes it difficult to clean the bath or sink when we have finished. This is because hard water contains dissolved compounds which react with the soap to form **scum**. The scum floats on the water and sticks to the bath.

a) Why is it difficult to wash with hard water?

Most hard water contains dissolved calcium and magnesium compounds. These dissolve when streams and rivers run over or through rocks containing calcium and/or magnesium compounds.

Limestone is an example of such a rock. It contains calcium carbonate. As raindrops fall through the air, carbon dioxide dissolves in them. This dissolved carbon dioxide makes rain slightly acidic, even without pollutants like oxides of sulfur and nitrogen. The water in streams and rivers is therefore slightly acidic too. This means that compounds such as calcium carbonate react with the products formed dissolve in the water.

The dissolved minerals are carried into the reservoirs and on into our domestic water supply. It is the dissolved calcium and magnesium ions that react with soap to form scum.

DID YOU KNOW?
Hard water is not too much of a problem when washing clothes, because modern detergents are designed not to produce scum in hard water. But it still causes problems whenever we heat the water because of the scale it produces.

b) What does hard water form when we put soap in it?

Using hard water is expensive because we need to use much more soap. Before soap ever gets anywhere near dirt it first reacts with the dissolved calcium and magnesium ions in the water, forming salts called stearates (the chemical name for scum). It is only when all of the calcium and magnesium ions have reacted with the soap that a lather can begin to form.

sodium stearate + Ca²⁺ and Mg²⁺ ions → calcium stearate + Na⁺ ions
(soap)   calcium and   magnesium stearate   soluble in water
              magnesium salts   precipitate
              ('hardness')   (scum)

As well as forming scum with soap, hard water often leads to **scale** forming in pipes, immersion heaters and other parts of our hot water systems. Pipes can eventually block up. The same scale forms in our kettles, 'furring up' the heating elements and making them much less efficient, because scale is a poor conductor of heat.

c) What does hard water form when we heat it?

$$Ca^{2+}(aq) + 2HCO_3^-(aq) \xrightarrow{heat} CaCO_3(s) + H_2O(l) + CO_2(g)$$
('hardness')   (limescale)

But hard water isn't all bad news. The same dissolved compounds which are bad for our water pipes seem to be good for our health. Calcium ions in drinking water help in the development of strong bones and teeth. There is also evidence which suggests that hard water helps to reduce the incidence of heart disease in people who drink it.

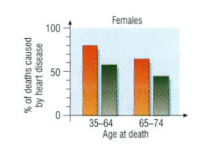

Figure 3 As scale builds up in heating systems and kettles it not only makes them less efficient – it can stop them working completely

Figure 4 The study on which these graphs are based showed that the number of people suffering from heart disease in a Canadian town with a hard water supply was significantly lower than the number with heart disease in a Canadian town with soft water

SUMMARY QUESTIONS

1. Copy and complete using the words below:

    calcium   conductor   efficient   health   magnesium
    scale   scum

    Hard water contains ...... and/or ...... salts. These react with soap to form .... The salts also produce ...... when the water is heated. This is a poor ...... of heat, and makes kettles and water heaters less .... Hard water may be better for human ...... than soft water.

2. Why is the pH of rainwater less than 7?

3. Using words and chemical equations, explain the difference between scale and scum.

KEY POINTS

1. Hard water contains dissolved substances such as calcium and magnesium salts.
2. The calcium and/or magnesium ions in hard water react with soap producing a precipitate called scum.
3. The calcium salts and/or magnesium salts also decompose to form scale when the water is heated.
4. Hard water may have benefits for human health.

SUMMARY ANSWERS

1. Calcium, magnesium, scum, scale, conductor, efficient, health.

2. Because of dissolved carbon dioxide.

3. Scum – produced when soap reacts with the salts in hard water:

    sodium stearate + Ca²⁺ and Mg²⁺ ions → calcium stearate and + Na⁺ ions
    (soap)   calcium and magnesium   magnesium stearate   soluble in water
                      salts ('hardness')   precipitate (scum)

    Scale – produced when hard water is heated:

    $$Ca^{2+}(aq) + 2HCO_3^-(aq) \xrightarrow{heat} CaCO_3(s) + H_2O(l) + CO_2(g)$$
    ('hardness')   (limescale)

Answers to in-text questions

a) Because the soap reacts with the dissolved ions in the water, which reduces the amount of soap available to clean you.

b) Scum.

c) Scale.

KEY POINTS

Ask the students to re-write the key points into their own words. This could be in a paragraph, questions and answers or changing the bullet points so that they are not just copied.

CHEMISTRY • WATER

C3 3.4 Removing hardness

LEARNING OBJECTIVES

Students should learn:

- That hardness can be removed from water.

LEARNING OUTCOMES

Most students should be able to:

- List methods for removing hardness from water.

Some students should also be able to:

- Explain how different methods remove hardness from water.

Teaching suggestions

- **Special needs.** The circus of experiments could be simplified to demonstrating the ion-exchange column and allowing the students to complete the sodium carbonate practical themselves. The methods, advantages and uses could be supplied to the students as a cut and stick activity.
- **Gifted and talented.** Students could design their own experiment to test the effectiveness of the different methods of softening water.
- **Learning styles**
  Kinaesthetic: Completing a circus of experiments.
  Visual: Producing a magazine article.
  Auditory: Listening to questions.
  Interpersonal: Working in groups to explain observations.
  Intrapersonal: Completing DART exercise.
- **ICT link-up.** Ask students to research claims made for water-softening devices sold for the home.
- **Homework.** Ask students to answer the 'Learning objective' question.

SPECIFICATION LINK-UP   Unit: Chemistry 3.13.3

- Hard water can be made soft by removing the dissolved calcium and magnesium ions, this can be done by:
  – adding sodium carbonate, which reacts with the calcium and magnesium ions forming a precipitate of calcium carbonate and magnesium carbonate
  – using an ion exchange column containing hydrogen ions or sodium ions, which replace the calcium and magnesium ions when hard water passes through the column.

Students should use their skills, knowledge and understanding of 'How Science Works':

- to consider and evaluate the environmental, social and economic aspects of water quality and hardness.

Lesson structure

STARTER

DART – Ask students to use the double-page spread in the Student Book and find an example of:

- a positive ion [calcium, magnesium, sodium]
- a negative ion [carbonate]
- a compound [sodium carbonate, calcium carbonate, sodium chloride]
- a common name used to describe a compound [washing soda, scale, salt]. (5 minutes)

Think 'fur' – show the students a furred up element, such as in the base of an old kettle. Ask students to think which ions might have caused this. Ask groups to feedback to the class their thoughts. (10 minutes)

MAIN

- Hardness in water can be permanent or temporary. Create a circus of three different methods to remove hardness from water.
- Allow students to circulate around the different stations removing the hardness using a method card at each station.
- Each student should record in their notes a brief explanation of the method, how successful it is, its advantages, and a use for that method.
- Students could be encourage to write a report on the different methods, including a results table to compare the different methods. ('How Science Works' opportunity.)
- Show students a selection of science magazines. Ask students to imagine that they have been commissioned to write a feature about how water can be softened. Their article should be aimed at a scientific audience and include diagrams. Use ELS C3 3.4 'Hard water' Electronic Resource from the GCSE Chemistry CD ROM.

PLENARIES

AfL (Assessment for Learning) – Give the students an examination question on this topic. Using a stopwatch, time each section (a minute a mark) and give the students time checks for each section of the question. Once all the time has been used, give the students the mark scheme and ask them to mark their own work in a different colour and jot any amendments. (15 minutes)

Earn the right to leave – Ask all students to sit down. Then ask students in turn a question. If they get it correct they can leave the classroom on the bell. If they get it incorrect, pass the question to hands up. Each student has a chance of as many questions as they need to get one correct. (10 minutes)

Diagram – Give the students an unlabelled diagram of an ion-exchange column, and a sheet of information to explain how it works. Ask students to annotate the diagram using the labels provided to explain how this water softening method works. (10 minutes)

Practical support

Methods of removing hardness

Equipment and materials required

Ion-exchange column, hard water, conical flask, soap solution (irritant, may be flammable), sodium carbonate (irritant), filter funnel, filter paper, conical flasks, beaker, tripod, gauze, Bunsen burner and safety equipment, measuring cylinder, spatula.
CLEAPSS Recipe Cards: hard water 72; soap solution 60.

Details

To test the hardness of water, add a measured amount of water into a conical flask. Add 1 ml of soap solution and shake. Repeat, until the foam lasts for 10 seconds or more.

Station 1 – Measure 25 ml of hard water into a beaker. Wearing eye protection, boil the water for about 2 minutes, observe. Allow the water to cool, and test to compare hardness.

Station 2 – Measure 25 ml of hard water into a beaker. Add excess sodium carbonate and filter the mixture. Test to compare hardness.

Station 3 – Measure 25 ml of hard water and run through an ion-exchange column. Test to compare hardness.

ACTIVITY & EXTENSION IDEAS

- Ask students to find out other applications for ion exchange, e.g. for catalysts in zeolites.
- Students could investigate whether 'hard water' tea bags are actually different from 'normal' tea bags.
- Different chemical methods of softening water could be shown to the students. They could research the composition of each product and draw a graph comparing the amount of active ingredient (sodium carbonate).

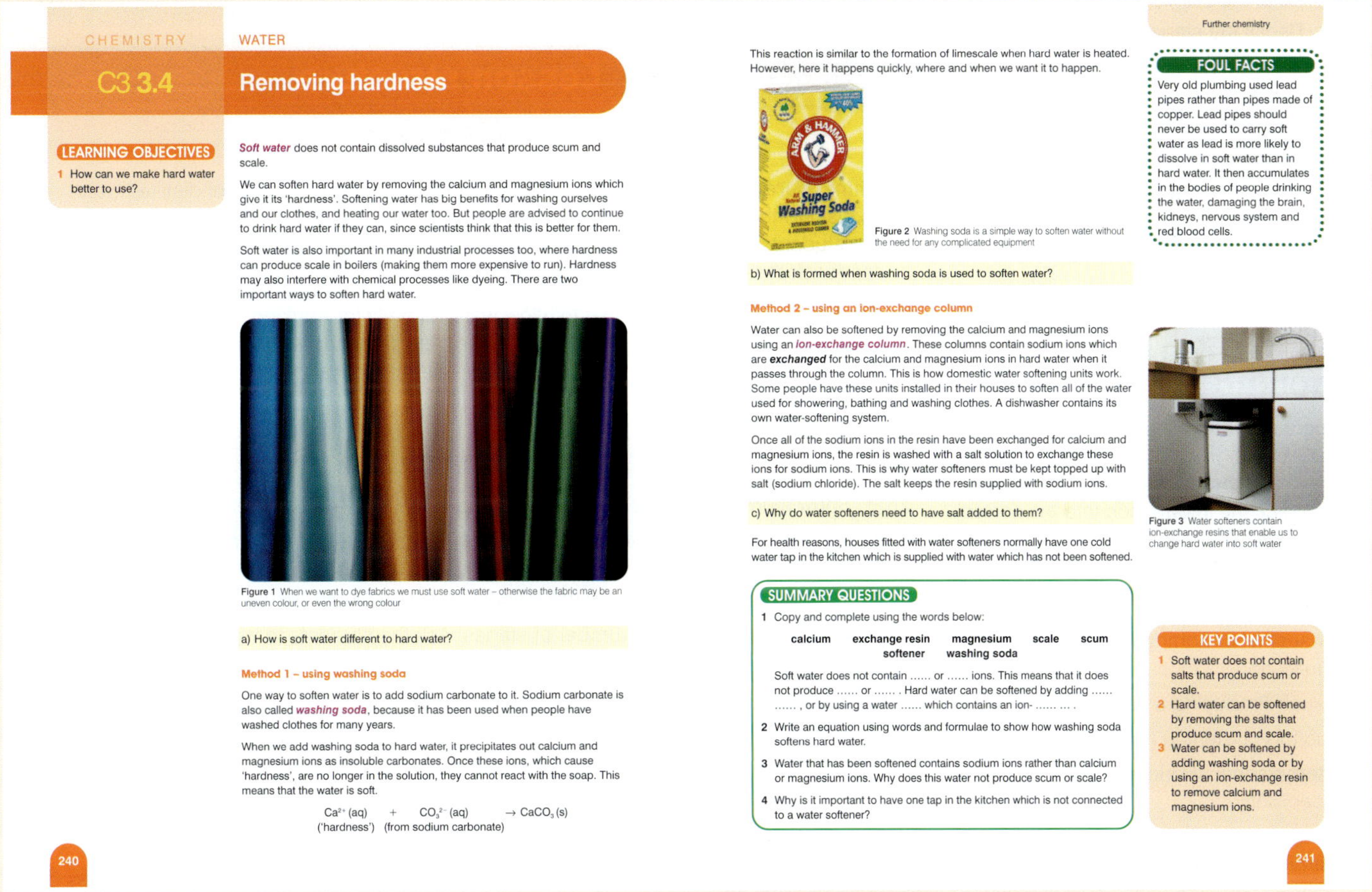

CHEMISTRY — **WATER**

C3 3.4 Removing hardness

LEARNING OBJECTIVES
1 How can we make hard water better to use?

Soft water does not contain dissolved substances that produce scum and scale.

We can soften hard water by removing the calcium and magnesium ions which give it its 'hardness'. Softening water has big benefits for washing ourselves and our clothes, and heating our water too. But people are advised to continue to drink hard water if they can, since scientists think that this is better for them.

Soft water is also important in many industrial processes too, where hardness can produce scale in boilers (making them more expensive to run). Hardness may also interfere with chemical processes like dyeing. There are two important ways to soften hard water.

Figure 1 When we want to dye fabrics we must use soft water – otherwise the fabric may be an uneven colour, or even the wrong colour

a) How is soft water different to hard water?

Method 1 – using washing soda

One way to soften water is to add sodium carbonate to it. Sodium carbonate is also called *washing soda*, because it has been used when people have washed clothes for many years.

When we add washing soda to hard water, it precipitates out calcium and magnesium ions as insoluble carbonates. Once these ions, which cause 'hardness', are no longer in the solution, they cannot react with the soap. This means that the water is soft.

$$Ca^{2+}(aq) + CO_3^{2-}(aq) \rightarrow CaCO_3(s)$$
('hardness') (from sodium carbonate)

This reaction is similar to the formation of limescale when hard water is heated. However, here it happens quickly, where and when we want it to happen.

Figure 2 Washing soda is a simple way to soften water without the need for any complicated equipment

b) What is formed when washing soda is used to soften water?

Method 2 – using an ion-exchange column

Water can also be softened by removing the calcium and magnesium ions using an **ion-exchange column**. These columns contain sodium ions which are *exchanged* for the calcium and magnesium ions in hard water when it passes through the column. This is how domestic water softening units work. Some people have these units installed in their houses to soften all of the water used for showering, bathing and washing clothes. A dishwasher contains its own water-softening system.

Once all of the sodium ions in the resin have been exchanged for calcium and magnesium ions, the resin is washed with a salt solution to exchange these ions for sodium ions. This is why water softeners must be kept topped up with salt (sodium chloride). The salt keeps the resin supplied with sodium ions.

c) Why do water softeners need to have salt added to them?

For health reasons, houses fitted with water softeners normally have one cold water tap in the kitchen which is supplied with water which has not been softened.

Figure 3 Water softeners contain ion-exchange resins that enable us to change hard water into soft water

SUMMARY QUESTIONS

1 Copy and complete using the words below:

calcium   exchange resin   magnesium   scale   scum
softener   washing soda

Soft water does not contain ...... or ...... ions. This means that it does not produce ...... or .... Hard water can be softened by adding .... , or by using a water ...... which contains an ion- ....

2 Write an equation using words and formulae to show how washing soda softens hard water.

3 Water that has been softened contains sodium ions rather than calcium or magnesium ions. Why does this water not produce scum or scale?

4 Why is it important to have one tap in the kitchen which is not connected to a water softener?

FOUL FACTS

Very old plumbing used lead pipes rather than pipes made of copper. Lead pipes should never be used to carry soft water as lead is more likely to dissolve in soft water than in hard water. It then accumulates in the bodies of people drinking the water, damaging the brain, kidneys, nervous system and red blood cells.

KEY POINTS

1 Soft water does not contain salts that produce scum or scale.
2 Hard water can be softened by removing the salts that produce scum and scale.
3 Water can be softened by adding washing soda or by using an ion-exchange resin to remove calcium and magnesium ions.

Answers to in-text questions

a) It does not contain the ions that make the water hard.
b) Calcium carbonate.
c) To replenish supply of sodium ions in the ion-exchange resin.

SUMMARY ANSWERS

1 Calcium/magnesium, magnesium/calcium, scale/scum, scum/scale, washing soda, softener, exchange resin.

2 $Ca^{2+}(aq) + CO_3^{2-}(aq) \rightarrow CaCO_3(s)$
('hardness') (from sodium carbonate) calcium carbonate

3 Sodium salts are soluble.

4 Hard water is better for health than soft water.

FOUL FACTS

Romans used lead water pipes; some historians believe that the fall of the Roman Empire was due to lead toxicity.

KEY POINTS

Ask the students to copy out the key points and highlight any key words in the text.

CHEMISTRY | WATER

C3 3.5 Water treatment

LEARNING OBJECTIVES

Students should learn:

- How water is made safe to drink.
- That there is a difference between pure water and drinking water.

LEARNING OUTCOMES

Most students should be able to:

- List places that drinking water is obtained from.
- Recall the stages that water goes through to make it fit to drink.

Some students should also be able to:

- Explain how water is treated to make it fit to drink.
- Explain the difference between pure water and drinking water.

Teaching suggestions

- **Special needs.** The sections of the flow chart could be given to the students in the wrong order. They could then cut and stick the information into the correct order and add an image for each step to show understanding.

- **Learning styles**

  Kinaesthetic: Sorting the stages of water purification.

  Visual: Producing a flow chart.

  Auditory: Listening to group adverts.

  Interpersonal: Working in pairs to make a decision.

  Intrapersonal: Reflecting on their own learning.

- **Homework.** Ask students to find out where the water comes from in their area, e.g. in the Midlands it comes from the Welsh mountains and is stored in reservoirs.

- **ICT link-up.** The adverts could be recorded on a camcorder. This material could then be transferred to *Windows Movie Maker*. Groups could then add text and manipulate the images to make a discrete advert. The final product could be shown to the students or presented on the school web site.

SPECIFICATION LINK-UP   Unit: Chemistry 3.13.3

- Water of the correct quality is essential for life. For humans, drinking water should have sufficiently low levels of dissolved salts and microorganisms. This is achieved by choosing an appropriate source, passing the water through filter beds to remove any solids and then sterilising with chlorine.
- Water filters contain carbon, silver and ion-exchange resins that can remove some dissolved substances from tap water to improve the taste and quality.
- Pure water can be produced by distillation.

Students should use their skills, knowledge and understanding of 'How Science Works':

- to consider and evaluate the environmental, social and economic aspects of water quality and hardness.

Lesson structure

STARTER

Think 'pure' – Show students a bottle of mineral water and a bottle of distilled water. Explain to the students that both of these waters are fit to drink, but only one is pure. Ask the students to work in pairs to decide which water is pure and why. Ask a few groups to feedback their thoughts to the class. (5 minutes)

Find – Explain to students that to allow water to be fit for drinking there are three main stages: sedimentation, filtration, disinfection. Ask the students to find the chemicals associated with each stage [sedimentation – aluminium sulfate, lime; filter – sand; disinfection – chlorine]. (5 minutes)

MAIN

- Show students a water filter cartridge that is used in the domestic environment.
- Ask the students to work in small groups to generate a TV advert to promote the product, explain its benefits and how it works. Impress on the students that advertising is expensive, so the advert can be no longer than 1 minute.
- Water treatment has a number of stages. Ask the students to write a flow chart to show how ground water is turned into drinking water.
- Students could be encouraged to add a colour code, e.g. colour the chemical stages in red and the physical stages in yellow.
- Use PhotoPLUS C3 3.5 'Treating water' from the GCSE Chemistry CD ROM.

PLENARIES

Sort – Give the students a list of sentences on separate cards to explain the process of water treatment. Time the students as they put the sentences in order. The quickest, correct student could be given a prize. (5 minutes)

Adverts – Each group can show their water cartridge advert to the class. (10 minutes)

Reflection – Ask students to think about one fact that they have revised in the lesson and a new fact that they have learned. Ask a few students to share their thoughts. (5 minutes)

ACTIVITY & EXTENSION IDEAS

- In some countries the water in the taps is not fit to drink, or water may need to be collected by each family from bore holes or rivers. Ask students to find out how this water is made fit to drink.
- Students could use agar plates to test for microorganisms in water. Water collected from puddles or another 'dirty' source could be cleaned using different methods for purification of water, e.g. sterilisation tablets, boiling and filtering. The water should be swabbed and spread over an agar plate, taped and left in a warm place for a week to see if microbes grow. Follow aseptic techniques as described in B3 3.1 Biology Student Book. See CLEAPSS Handbook CD-ROM section 15.2.
- Many water boards offer free visits to treatment works.

Further chemistry

Answers to in-text questions

a) Disinfect it with chlorine.

b) To kill any microbes (e.g. bacteria), i.e. pathogens.

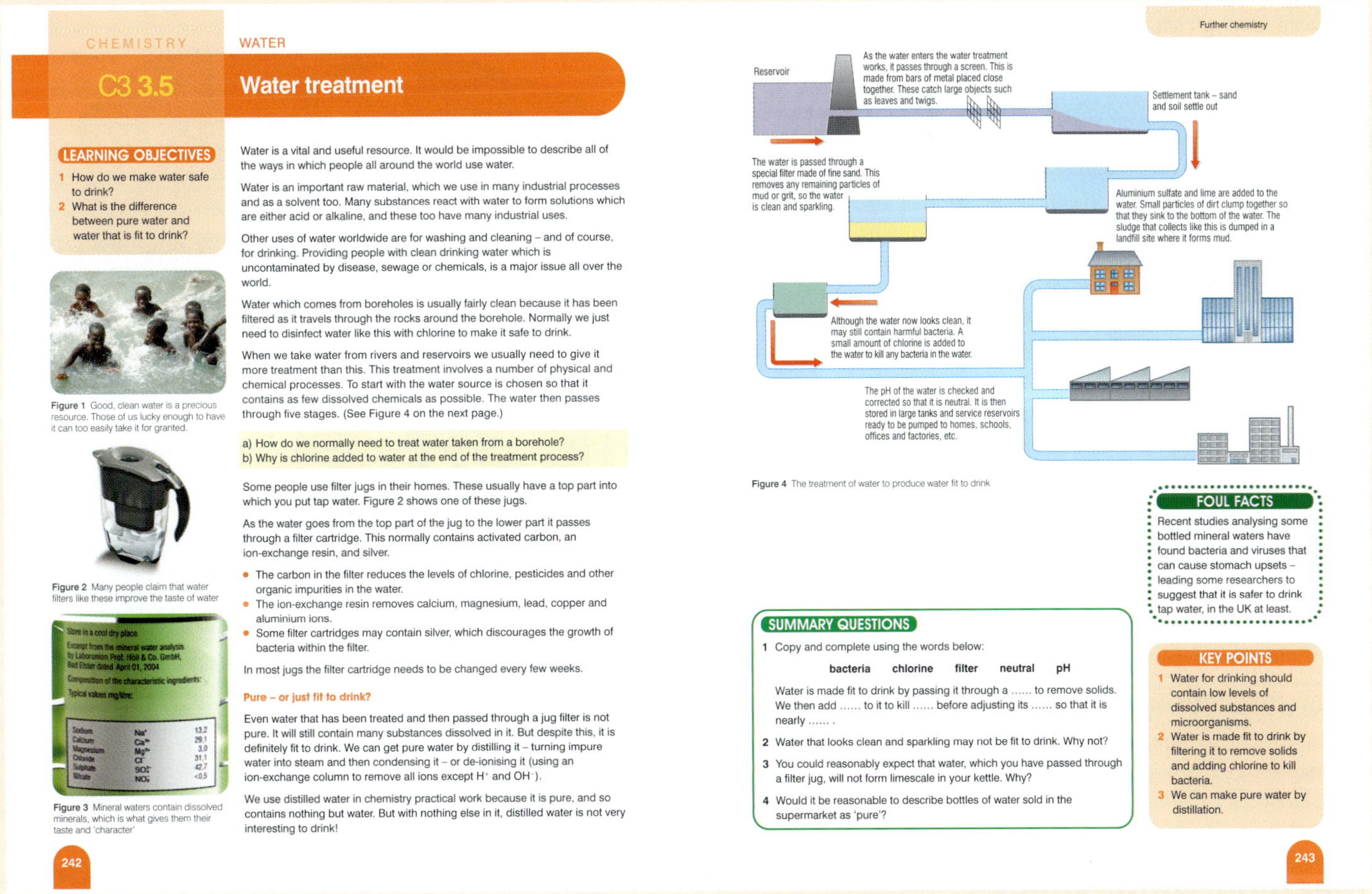

SUMMARY ANSWERS

1. Filter, chlorine, bacteria, pH, neutral.
2. It may contain microbes, e.g. bacteria.
3. Calcium and magnesium ions have been removed from it.
4. Not in the chemical sense as they contain dissolved solids (as the labels show).

KEY POINTS

Split the class into three groups and give each group a different key fact. Ask the groups to find reasons why their fact is the most important from the lesson. Then hold the debate!

243

CHEMISTRY | WATER

C3 3.6 Water fit to drink

SPECIFICATION LINK-UP
Unit: Chemistry 3.13.3

This spread can be used to revisit the following content already covered in this chapter:

- Water of the correct quality is essential for life. For humans, drinking water should have sufficiently low levels of dissolved salts and microorganisms. This is achieved by choosing an appropriate source, passing the water through filter beds to remove any solids and then sterilising with chlorine.

Students should use their skills, knowledge and understanding of 'How Science Works':

- to consider and evaluate the environmental, social and economic aspects of water quality and hardness.

CHEMISTRY | WATER

C3 3.6 Water fit to drink

[Illustration with speech bubbles:]

- I am so tired. Where I have come from is very far, walking with 20 litres on my head. I am old, I have a bad hip and am always tired, carrying this bucket twice a day. I need to get home, I need to rest.
- Look at the queue for the toilet – I'll have to wait at least 5 minutes! They really should put more toilets on these aeroplanes!
- Oh dear, I've dropped my bottle of spring water and I can't find it. I don't want to get dehydrated while I'm flying. Can I have another one please?
- Fetch water? Me?! No, that's women's work.
- Every day I get up at 5:30am to fetch water for my family. I walk to a muddy pool where animals also drink – the water is very dirty, but it doesn't taste so bad. I don't go to school, because it takes about six hours a day to collect enough water for my family and all our animals.
- Young children are particularly affected by dirty water and poor sanitation. Over two million children a year die throughout the world because they have no access to clean water and don't have anywhere safe and clean to go to the toilet. Faeces left lying around are a big health risk when near to houses – and children out searching for water or somewhere to go to the toilet are exposed to attacks by wild animals and being bitten by snakes.

244

Teaching suggestions

Activities

- **Water audit** – Encourage students to estimate how many litres of water they think that they use in a day. Then allow the students to complete their own water audit. In small groups, students should feedback about their water audits and answers. Encourage students to discuss how they feel about these facts. Then ask how many students use: less than, the same as, or more than 178 litres of water.

- **Poster** – Show students different poster campaigns from charities about poor sanitation and water supply on the Internet. To find these run a Google search for the charity and homepage, e.g. Christian Aid, homepage. Other charities with similar campaigns are Red Cross and Save the Children. Encourage students to think about how the posters are persuasive, maybe images, words or a combination of both. Ask students to then design their own poster focusing on the plight of women and children in poor sanitation conditions.

- **Letter** – In a democracy, people can write to their MPs to register their protest. Alternatively people write to the editorial pages in newspapers (examples could be shown to the students). Go through the format of a letter on the board. Then ask students to write their own letter to a local MP (the name could be supplied to the students) highlighting the need for clean water supplies and improved sanitation in the developing world. The letter should clearly state the reasons, and not just be an argument.

Extensions

- **Water audit** – Students could show their results from the water audit activity as a pictogram, with one drawing of a bottle of water representing 10 litres.

- **Tsunami** – The Tsunami that hit Indonesia in 2004 caused a large humanitarian disaster for many reasons. Encourage the students to focus on water and the health problems caused by disruption in the water supply and treatment in this disaster.

Further chemistry

Further chemistry

'When the water starts boiling it is foolish to turn off the heat.' – Nelson Mandela

The world's poorest people are still waiting for the water itself, let alone for it to boil. The 1980s Water Decade failed to secure water and sanitation for all the world's population. Since then there has been a procession of international reports and conferences calling for universal access to these services.

But constant repetition of the fact that 'water is life' has not proved to be enough. More than a billion people are still without safe water and 2.6 billion lack any way to dispose of their excrement in safety and with dignity.

These failures are undermining development: keeping children out of school, stopping adults pursuing their livelihoods, and denying many people good health and in some cases even life.

This is the silent emergency affecting the world today. Unless the delivery of water and sanitation improves significantly the Millennium Development Goal (MDG) to halve world poverty by 2015 will not be met.

Text extract from the 'Getting to Boiling Point' report, published by Water Aid in March 2005

ACTIVITY

a) i) You are going to carry out a water audit. How much water do you use in a day? The water companies estimate that each of us uses on average 178 litres of water each day! Use the table to work out the water use in *your* home:

	Average use (litres)	Number of times per day in your home	Total water use (litres)
Shower – electric	30		
'power shower'	65		
Bath	85		
Flushing the toilet – standard	10		
water-saving flush	6		
Washing hands and cleaning teeth – under running tap	15		
turning tap off	10		
Dishwasher	25		
Washing up in sink	10		
Cooking/drinking	10		
Washing machine	80		
Hose (10 minutes to wash car or water garden)	90		

ii) Now imagine you had to fetch all of this water in 20 litre pots.
What would be the mass of all this water? (1 litre of water = 1 kg)
How many pots would be needed?
Estimate how long it might take if the water supply was 5 km away from your home. Could you use this much water each day?

b) Why are women and children particularly affected by poor sanitation and water supplies? Design a poster as part of a campaign to draw attention to the need to bring clean water and sanitation to villages in the developing world. Use your poster to explain how this will help children especially.

c) Write a letter that you could send to the editor of your local paper, to your MP or to anyone else that you think you might write to about the need for clean water and sanitation in the developing world.
Make your points clearly, and back up your arguments with facts.

Homework

- **Reduce water consumption** – Ask students to find out three ways that water consumption could be reduced by their household, e.g. reducing the water in a toilet cistern, collecting rain water for washing cars and watering the garden, not have the tap running when brushing teeth.

Learning styles

Visual: Preparing a pictogram of personal water shortage.

Interpersonal: Comparing water consumption between students.

Intrapersonal: Writing a letter.

ICT link-up

Information about water and water aid can be found at www.wateraid.org.uk. Use PhotoPLUS C3 3.5 'Treating water'.

Special needs

Students should be given large squared paper with axis and labels already on for the histogram. They can also be given a page of water bottles, for them to colour and cut out the appropriate number to display on their pictogram.

Teaching assistant

Small groups of students could be taken by the teaching assistant to measure out the different volumes of water in buckets to show the volume used in different domestic tasks.

Gifted and talented

Ask these students to find out the water board bill for their house (use www.upmystreet.com). Then ask the students to find out the water charges for the use of a water meter. Ask students to calculate a water meter bill for their house for a quarter. Then they can compare the prices to see if a water meter would produce a saving for their family.

CHEMISTRY   WATER

SUMMARY ANSWERS

1 a) C   b) A, D and E   c) B

2 a) B, solubility decreases as temperature increases.
   b) The solubility of the solid increases with temperature until it reaches a maximum value (possibly at the boiling point of water).
   c) The water will be warmer, so less oxygen will be dissolved in it, and it will support fewer fish.

3 a) One of: calcium or magnesium.
   b) $Ca^{2+}(aq)$ or $Mg^{2+}(aq)$ + $CO_3^{2-}(aq)$ (from sodium carbonate) → $CaCO_3(s)$ calcium carbonate or $MgCO_3(s)$ magnesium carbonate
   ('hardness')

   Hardness is removed as calcium/magnesium ions are precipitated out from the solution by the carbonate ions from the sodium carbonate.

Summary teaching suggestions

- **Special needs** – Turn question 1 into a card sort.
- **Gifted and talented** – Question 3 is a good example of a higher-level question.
- **Learning styles**
  Kinaesthetic: Question 1 could be turned into a card sort.
  Auditory: Question 2 could be used as a discussion piece.
  Visual: Question 2 encourages the students to compare graphs.
  Intrapersonal: Question 3 lends itself to individual work.
- **When to use the questions?**
  - The questions can be used as a revision activity.
  - Question 2b) and c) could be answered using a drag and drop activity on an interactive whiteboard. Import the graphs into board-specific software and make the graph background (lock into place). Then have the labels typed into boxes, to describe the shapes of the graphs. These labels should be at the bottom of the screen. Students then take it turns to move a label into position on the graph.

WATER: C3 3.1 – C3 3.6

SUMMARY QUESTIONS

1 Link the statements a) to c) with options from A to E.

a) Water evaporates from lakes, rivers and oceans, forms clouds and then falls as rain.	A Cause hardness in water.
b) Calcium and magnesium ions.	B Calcium salts.
c) Causes limescale when water is boiled.	C This is the **water cycle**.
	D React with soap to form scum.
	E Exchanged for sodium or potassium ions in a water softener.

2 A student carried out an experiment to measure the solubility of two different substances in water at different temperatures. One of these substances was a crystalline solid, the other was a gas. The two graphs A and B show her results.

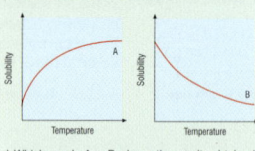

a) Which graph, A or B, shows the results obtained by the student for the solubility of the gas? Explain your answer.
b) Explain the shape of graph A.
c) Warm water from a power station's cooling system is discharged into a river. Use graph B to explain why there are fewer fish in this part of the river than elsewhere along its length.

3 Washing soda is used to soften water, making it easier to get clothes clean. It consists of crystals of sodium carbonate.
a) Name **one** ion which makes water hard.
b) Write a balanced equation for the reaction of washing soda with this ion, showing how the washing soda makes the water soft.

EXAM-STYLE QUESTIONS

1 Fizzy drinks are made using carbonated water.
  (a) Name the gas that is released when a can of fizzy drink is opened. (1)
  (b) Explain why bubbles form in the drink when it has been poured into a glass. (2)
  (c) Why does cooling the can before it is opened reduce the amount of bubbles that are produced? (1)

2 The solubility of potassium chlorate in water at different temperatures is shown in the table.

| Temperature (°C) | 10 | 20 | 30 | 50 | 60 | 80 | 90 |
| Solubility (g per 100 g water) | 5 | 7 | 10 | 19 | 24 | 37 | 46 |

  (a) i) Plot a graph of these results. Put temperature on the horizontal axis and solubility on the vertical axis. Draw a smooth line through the points. (4)
     ii) What do we call the smooth line drawn through points obtained by experiment? (1)
  (b) What does the graph show about how the solubility of potassium chlorate changes with temperature? (1)
  (c) Use your graph to find the solubility of potassium chlorate at 70°C. (1)
  (d) Explain what is meant by a saturated solution. (2)
  (e) A saturated solution of potassium chlorate was made using 100 g of water at 55°C. What mass of potassium chlorate separates when the solution is cooled to 25°C? (2)
  (f) A student wanted to check the solubility of potassium chlorate at 20°C by experiment. The value given in his data book was 7 g per 100 g of water. He did the experiment 4 times. His results are shown below:

Number of experiment	Solubility (g per 100 g of water)
1	5
2	9
3	8
4	6

246

EXAM-STYLE ANSWERS

1 a) Carbon dioxide. (1 mark)
   b) The drink contains dissolved carbon dioxide. (1 mark)
      (when pressure released) carbon dioxide from solution escapes as gas. (1 mark)
   c) Gases are more soluble at lower temperatures. (1 mark)

2 a) i) *One mark each for:*
        - Axes labelled.
        - Suitable scales.
        - Correct plotting (*within half small square*).
        - Smooth line through points (*no gap between line and points*). (4 marks)
      ii) A line of best fit (1 mark)
   b) Solubility increases as temperature increases. (1 mark)
   c) 30 (g per 100 g water) (+/−1). (1 mark)
   d) A solution that contains the maximum amount of dissolved solute (1 mark)
      at a given temperature. (1 mark)
   e) 13 g (+/−1). (2 marks)
      (*correct working, i.e. attempt to find values at 55°C and 25°C and subtract them scores 1 mark*)
   f) i) 5–9 g per 100 g of water. (*1 mark for quoting maximum and minimum values and 1 mark for units*)
      ii) 7 g per 100 g of water (1 mark)
      iii) Good accuracy. (1 mark)
          Close agreement with values from table or data book. (1 mark)
      iv) An anomalous result (1 mark)

3 a) Calcium carbonate, magnesium sulfate, and magnesium chloride. (2 marks)
      (*All three correct for 2 marks, one or two correct gains 1 mark*)
   b) Calcium and/or magnesium ions/salts/compounds (1 mark)
      react with soap/form a precipitate with soap/form an insoluble solid with soap. (1 mark)

246

i) What was the range of his results presented in the table? (2)
ii) Work out the mean (average) value for the solubility of potassium chlorate at 20°C from his results (1)
iii) Comment on the accuracy of the student's results. (2)
iv) The first time he did the test his result came out at 15g per 100g of water. He did not include this in his results table. What is this type of result called? (1)

3 Water from a spring was found to be hard. A sample of 1.0 dm³ of the water was evaporated. The solid residue was analysed and the results are shown in the table.

Name of mineral	Amount (mg)
Calcium carbonate	86
Magnesium sulfate	39
Magnesium chloride	34
Sodium chloride	29
Sodium nitrate	5

(a) Name all the compounds in the table that make this water hard. (2)
(b) Explain why a scum is formed when soap is used with hard water. (2)
(c) (i) Suggest one method that could be used to make this water soft. (1)
    (ii) Explain how this method works. (1)
(d) The calcium carbonate in the residue reacts with hydrochloric acid.
    (i) Write a balanced equation for this reaction. (2)
    (ii) What volume of hydrochloric acid, concentration 0.10 mol per dm³, would react with the calcium carbonate in the residue from 1 dm³ of this water? (3)
(e) Explain why hot water pipes and central heating boilers should be checked regularly in hard water areas. (2)
[Higher]

HOW SCIENCE WORKS QUESTIONS

Yasmin carried out an investigation into the solubility of potassium nitrate. She carefully weighed a beaker. She added 100 cm³ of pure water. She re-weighed the beaker. She then carefully added her potassium nitrate, stirring after adding each amount, until she could see a sediment in the beaker. She then re-weighed the beaker.

She did this with different temperatures of water. Her results were as follows:

At 26°C she added 43 g of potassium nitrate. At 44°C she added 74 g and at 65°C she added 128 g.

a) Produce a table of Yasmin's results. (3)
b) Draw a graph of Yasmin's results. (3)
c) Do you think Yasmin produced enough results? Explain your answer. (1)
d) The work took a very long time and Yasmin did the work very carefully. Should she have done any repeats? Explain your answer. (1)
e) i) Yasmin checked her results against a table of saturation temperatures for potassium nitrate in a data book. Why would she do this? (1)
   ii) Yasmin was quite pleased with her results. The values in the data book were much the same as her own results, except that hers were all slightly higher than the ones in the book. Why might this have happened? (2)

247

Further chemistry

i.e. tolerances of half of the smallest square on the grid. The 'no daylight' rule can be useful for both line graphs and bar charts, i.e. no white space visible between a point and a line or between a gridline and a horizontal or vertical line. However, thick lines should be discouraged! Lines should never be thicker than half of the smallest square on the grid.

Most students are aware of the decrease in solubility of gases with increase in temperature, but it is worth encouraging them to explain the well-known fizzy drink phenomenon clearly in scientific terms. Similarly, they should rehearse their explanations of a saturated solution. Students should know the methods used for softening water in the specification and should be able to explain the chemistry involved in simple terms, but will not be expected to know the details of temporary and permanent hardness. However, interpretative questions may be set in which candidates are given information about these phenomena.

HOW SCIENCE WORKS ANSWERS

a)

Temperature (°C)	Mass of potassium nitrate added (g)
26	43
44	74
65	128

b) Temperature on X axis and mass added on Y axis. All points plotted correctly and axes labelled.

c) No. It is difficult to draw a line of best fit with just three plots. She should have done at least five.

d) She still needs to repeat to improve reliability.

e) i) To check on the reliability and accuracy of her data.
   ii) This is evidence for a systematic error. It could have been that she did not weigh the solution until there was a sediment and this is included in the final weight recorded.

How science works teaching suggestions

- **Literacy guidance**
  - Key terms that should be understood: table drawing and graph plotting, accuracy, reliability, systematic error.
- **Higher- and lower-level answers.** Question e) is a higher-level question and the answers provided above is also at this level. Question a) is lower-level and the answer provided is also lower-level.
- **Gifted and talented.** Higher attaining students could produce a table for the collection of data and for comparison with data book values.
- **How and when to use these questions.** When wishing to develop table and graph drawing skills as well as reliability. Questions a) and b) could be set as homework and the remainder discussed in small groups.
- **Homework.** For homework ask students to prepare the table and graphs.
- **Special needs.** Could be used as a table and graph plotting exercise. Method could be demonstrated.
- **ICT link-up.** There is an opportunity here for students to use spreadsheet software such as Excel for the graph drawing part of the question.

---

c) i) One from:
   • Add sodium carbonate/washing soda.
   • Use ion exchange.
   • Use distillation. (1 mark)
   ii) One mark for corresponding explanation:
   • Removes calcium/magnesium ions from solution *or* removes calcium/magnesium compounds/salts from solution.
   • Exchanges calcium/magnesium ions for other/sodium/ hydrogen ions.
   • Only water evaporates or calcium/magnesium ions/ compounds left in solution. (1 mark)

d) i) $CaCO_3 + 2HCl \rightarrow CaCl_2 + CO_2 + H_2O$. (2 marks all correct) (correct formulae gains 1 mark)
   ii) 17.2 cm³. (3 marks)
   Working marks: e.g. moles $CaCO_3 = 86/1000 \times 1/100$ (1 mark) moles $HCl = 0.00086 \times 2$ (1 mark) (can be gained by e.c.f. from equation written in part (i) or incorrect value for moles $CaCO_3$)

e) Two from:
   • Deposits of scale may form.
   • Pipes may get blocked.
   • Efficiency of heating system is reduced. (2 marks)
   [**HT** only]

Exam teaching suggestions

Q1 and Q2 could be set after completing C3 3.2. Students attempting all of the questions should be allowed 30 minutes. Q1 and Q2 could appear on both Foundation- and Higher-Tier papers. Q3(d) would be only on Higher Tier.

Students for both tiers should be able to draw solubility curves from given data and interpret their graphs. They should be able to find the solubility at a given temperature and calculate the mass of substance that would come out of a saturated solution for a given change in temperature. The usual marking criteria for graphs apply,

247

CHEMISTRY

ENERGY CALCULATIONS

C3 4.1 Comparing the energy produced by fuels

LEARNING OBJECTIVES

Students should learn:

- That the energy produced by different fuels can be measured.

LEARNING OUTCOMES

Most students should be able to:

- Describe a method for measuring the energy in fuels.
- State that food contains energy.

Some students should also be able to:

- Calculate the energy content of a fuel.
- Explain why vegetable oils are used for cooking and as fuels.

Teaching suggestions

- **Gifted and talented**
  - In the calorimetry practical, encourage the students to take the mass of the spirit burner before and after it has been lit, in order to calculate the mass of fuel that has been used. Then see if they can work out the energy produced by the fuel in joules per gram.
  Using the formula:

  energy (J/g) = (50 × 4.2 × change in temperature (°C))/mass of fuel (g)

  will give the amount of energy given per gram of fuel. This may give a different order of fuels to the amount of energy given out in a set amount of time.
  - Students could be given other calculations to complete in order to compare fuels and foods.

- **Learning styles**
  Kinaesthetic: Experimentally comparing fuels.
  Visual: Sorting diagrams to order the method for calorimetry.
  Auditory: Listening to definitions.
  Interpersonal: Working in pairs to evaluate the practical.
  Intrapersonal: Generating own marketing material about vegetable fats.

- **ICT link-up.** Energy change in the experiment could be monitored by a temperature probe with a data logger.

- **Homework.** Depending on the age and activity of humans, they need a different amount of energy from their diet. Ask the students to find out how much energy a child, a pregnant woman, and an old person need.

SPECIFICATION LINK-UP Unit: Chemistry 3.13.4

- *The relative amounts of energy released when substances burn can be measured by simple calorimetry, e.g. by heating water in a glass or metal container. This method can be used to compare the amount of energy produced by fuels and foods.*
- *Energy is normally measured in joules (J). Some dietary information is given in calories, which are equal to 4.2 joules.*
- *Different foods produce different amount of energy. Foods with high proportions of carbohydrates, fats and oils produce relatively large amounts of energy.*
- *Eating food that provides more energy than the body needs can lead to obesity.*
- *The amount of energy produced by a chemical reaction in solution can be found by mixing the reagents in an insulated container and measuring the temperature change of the solution. This method can be used for reactions of solids with water or neutralisation reactions.*

Students should use their skills, knowledge and understanding of 'How Science Works':

- *to compare the energy produced by different fuels and foods.*
- *to consider the social, economic and environmental consequences of using fuels.*

Lesson structure

STARTER

5,4,3,2,1 – Ask students to list 5 fuels, 4 high energy foods, 3 units to measure temperature, 2 products of the combustion of a hydrocarbon, 1 gas needed for combustion. (5 minutes)

Definitions – Read out the following definitions. The students' task is to give the correct key word that they relate to.

- The scientific word for burning. [combustion]
- The unit for measuring energy. [joule]
- A chemical change that involves energy being released. [exothermic]
- A chemical change that involves the gain of oxygen, loss of hydrogen or loss of electrons. [oxidation]
- A chemical that is burned to release useable energy. [fuel] (10 minutes)

MAIN

- Show the students health posters and leaflets that may be found in doctor's surgeries and at supermarkets.
- Ask the students to design their own piece of marketing material (could be a poster, leaflet, sticker, bookmark, advert, etc.) to explain why vegetable fats are an important part of a human's diet. However, the poster should be a balanced piece and also contain information about the health impact of over-consumption of fat.
- Create a cut and stick activity about vegetable oils as fuels. A set of sentences relating to the 'social', 'economic' and 'environmental' impact should be given to the students. They could then sort the sentences into the three groups, and underline disadvantages in red and advantages in green.
- Show students the equipment for calorimetry, and ask them to consider what is the independent variable [fuel] and dependent variable [temperature]. As a class, using question and answer, generate the values for the control variables, e.g. amount of water (50 cm³), distance from flame to calorimeter (5 cm), time (2 minutes). (This relates to: 'How Science Works': types of variable and fair testing.)
- Allow the students to experimentally compare the energy content of two different fuels.
- Give students a diagram of a bomb calorimeter. They should then add labels to explain how it can be used to monitor energy changes in a chemical reaction, e.g. combustion.

Further chemistry

PLENARIES

Evaluation – Ask students to reflect on the calorimetry experiment that they have completed. Tell the students that the experiment is not very reliable, then ask why this is so. [There are a number of reasons, some could include: a lot of energy is lost as heat to the surroundings; the can is heated but this is not taken into account in the calculation.] Ask students to work in pairs to generate amendments to the equipment to minimise this problem [e.g. insulation – around the calorimeter, lid on the calorimeter, use shields to reduce draughts]. Then ask each group to feedback their ideas to the class. (10 minutes)

Card sort – Provide the students with a set of images which, when they are sorted into the correct order, produce a pictorial method of calorimetry. Ask the students to work in pairs to sort the images into the correct order. (5 minutes)

ACTIVITY & EXTENSION

Give the students data of the amount of energy released by different alkanes. Encourage them to show this in a graph (number of carbon atoms, energy released) and draw conclusions from this.

Practical support

Comparing the energy produced by fuels when they burn

Equipment and materials required

Glass beaker/metal can/calorimeter, tripod, gauze, flame-proof mat, spirit burner, paraffin (flammable), ethanol (flammable), thermometer, measuring cylinder, water, stopwatch, eye protection.

Details

Measure 50 cm^3 of water into a calorimeter and place on the tripod. Take the temperature of the water. Light the spirit burner and put on the flame-proof mat, positioned under the calorimeter. Time for 2 minutes, then remove the burner and take the temperature again. (Know how to extinguish a bench fire. See CLEAPSS Hazcard 40 (ethanol); CLEAPSS Handbook CD-ROM section 9.4.3 (spirit burners).)

Answers to in-text questions

a) As a source of energy.

b) Bomb calorimeter.

c) Same quantity of water, known quantity of fuel, starting at the same temperature.

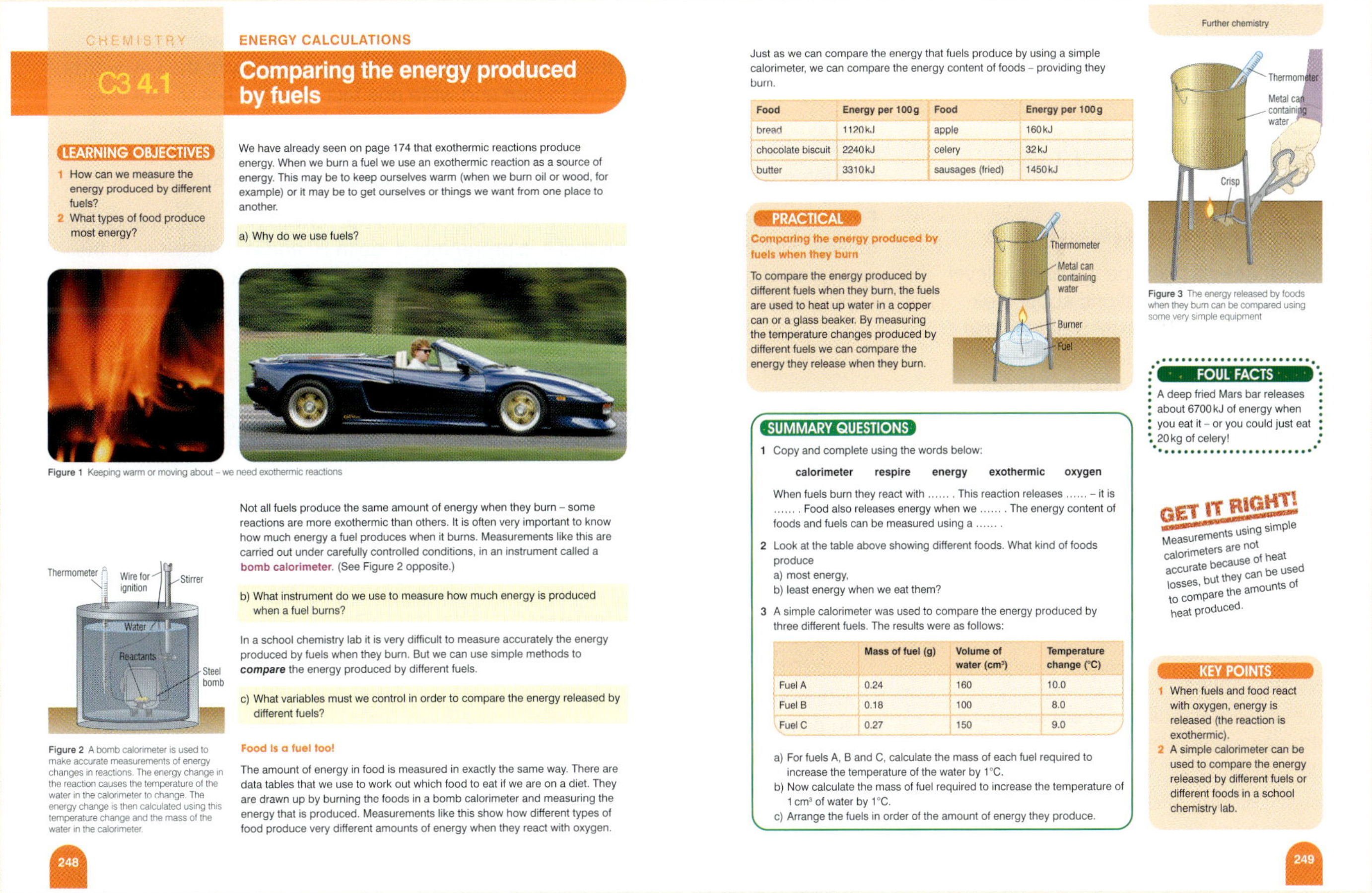

SUMMARY ANSWERS

1 Oxygen, energy, exothermic, respire, calorimeter.

2 a) Foods containing fat and carbohydrate.

  b) Fruit and vegetables.

3 a) A: 0.024 g   B: 0.0225 g   C: 0.030 g

  b) A: 0.000 15 g   B: 0.000 225 g   C: 0.000 20 g

  c) A > C > B

KEY POINTS

Before the lesson begins, put the names of five famous people on pieces of paper under five desks. Then ask students to look under their desk. If they have a famous person's name there, they should read out the key points to the rest of the class in the style of that person.

249

CHEMISTRY — ENERGY CALCULATIONS

C3 4.2 Energy changes in reactions

LEARNING OBJECTIVES

Students should learn:

- That bonds change in a chemical reaction.
- That energy changes in a reaction can be represented on a diagram including the activation energy.

LEARNING OUTCOMES

Most students should be able to:

- State and explain how we can think of reactions as having exothermic and endothermic stages.
- Complete a simple energy level diagram for a chemical reaction.
- Interpret a simple energy level diagram for a chemical reaction.

Some students should also be able to:

- Draw a simple energy level diagram for a chemical reaction.
- Calculate the energy transferred in reactions using a simple energy level diagram. [**HT** only]

Teaching suggestions

- **Special needs.** Provide the energy level diagrams and explanations about their shape on separate cards. Students can then match the explanation with the image and copy them into their notes.
- **Gifted and talented.** These students could use the Internet to find out the ΔH of reaction and add this information onto their diagrams, in order to scale the differences in energies between the reactants and products. They could then use their diagrams to determine which reaction would release the most energy or take in most energy.
- **Learning styles**
  Kinaesthetic: Handling the separate sentence cards, which explain an energy level diagram.
  Visual: Drawing and labelling energy level diagrams.
  Auditory: Listening to pronunciation and definition of ΔH.
  Interpersonal: Working in pairs to generate an energy level diagram.
  Intrapersonal: Completing the missing words in the prose.
- **Homework.** Ask students to write a mnemonic or rhyme to help them remember that energy is used to break bonds and energy is released on making bonds.

SPECIFICATION LINK-UP   Unit: Chemistry 3.13.4

- *During a chemical reaction:*
  – *energy must be supplied to break bonds*
  – *energy is released when bonds are formed.*
  These changes can be represented on an energy level diagram.
- *In an exothermic reaction, the energy released from forming new bonds is greater than the energy needed to break existing bonds.*
- *In an endothermic reaction, the energy needed to break existing bonds is greater than the energy from forming new bonds.*

Students should use their skills, knowledge and understanding of 'How Science Works':

- *to interpret simple energy level diagrams in terms of bond breaking and bond formation (including the idea of activation energy and the effect on this of catalysts).*
- *to calculate the energy transferred in reactions using simple energy level diagrams.* [**HT** only]

Lesson structure

STARTER

List – Ask students to brainstorm everything they know about exothermic and endothermic reactions. On the board, draw two columns headed with the key words. Then ask each student to come in turn and write one fact onto the board, but they cannot repeat something that is already on there. Then ask students to look at the finished list and comment on any amendments that they think are needed (this could be prompted by you saying how many mistakes you can spot). (15 minutes)

Find – Ask students to use the Student Book to find out how to pronounce, and what ΔH means. Students should find that it is pronounced 'delta H' and is a measure of the energy change of a reaction. Encourage students to feedback their findings to the class. (5 minutes)

MAIN

- Create a set of statements about a number of energy transfer diagrams, e.g. these statements relate to the energy level diagram for the formation of carbon dioxide from its elements:
  – Reactants have higher energy than the product.
  – The reactants are carbon and oxygen.
  – There is a relatively small activation energy.
  – The y-axis is energy.
  – Energy is measured in kJ/mol.
  – The product is carbon dioxide.

  Cut out each statement so that they are on separate cards. Give a pack of statements to pairs of students, they should use them to create and label the energy level diagram that it describes.

- Give the students a selection of different reactions and state whether they are exothermic or endothermic. They could then draw their own energy level diagrams to represent these reactions.
- Reactions suitable for this task could include those that have already been met: Haber process [exothermic] and neutralisation [exothermic]; or new ones like: dissolving of ammonium nitrate [endothermic], dissolving of potassium nitrate [endothermic].
- Revise the effect of catalysis on a chemical reaction and introduce the concept of 'lowering the activation energy' by drawing an energy level diagram with and without the use of a catalyst.

PLENARIES

Fill in the missing word – Give the students this excerpt from the specification, with some missing words. Encourage students to complete the prose, using the most scientific word that they can:

- In an [exothermic] reaction, the energy [released] from forming new bonds is greater than the energy needed to [break] existing bonds.
- In an endothermic reaction, the [energy] needed to break existing bonds is [greater] than the energy from [forming] new bonds. (10 minutes)

Diagram – Give the students an unlabelled energy level diagram for the combustion of carbon. They should then add the axis labels, detail which are the reactants and which is the product, annotate the activation energy and finally determine if the reaction is exothermic or endothermic. (5 minutes)

Show – Each pair can show their energy level diagram and explain what reaction it shows, and whether it is exothermic or endothermic. (10 minutes)

ACTIVITY & EXTENSION IDEAS

Students could research to find out the exact amount of activation energy that a particular reaction needs, e.g. complete combustion of carbon. They could then use this information to draw an energy level diagram to scale.

Further chemistry

CHEMISTRY
ENERGY CALCULATIONS

C3 4.2 Energy changes in reactions

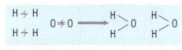

LEARNING OBJECTIVES
1. What happens to the bonds in a chemical reaction?
2. How do we represent energy changes in chemical reactions?
3. What do we mean by activation energy?

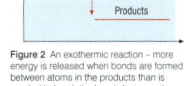

When we carry out a chemical reaction, we can think of the chemical bonds between the atoms in the reactants being broken. Then new chemical bonds can be formed to make the products.

- Because energy has to be supplied to break chemical bonds, breaking bonds is an **endothermic** process – energy is taken in from the surroundings.
- But when new bonds are formed, energy is released – so making bonds is an **exothermic** process.

a) What kind of process is breaking bonds?
b) What kind of process is making bonds?

- In some reactions the energy released when new bonds are formed (as the products of the reaction are made) is more than the energy needed to break the bonds in the reactants. These reactions transfer energy to the surroundings – they are **exothermic**.
- In other reactions the energy needed to break the bonds in the reactants is more than the energy released when new bonds are formed in the products. These reactions involve a transfer of energy from the surroundings to the reacting chemicals – they are **endothermic**.

c) If the energy required to break bonds is greater than the energy released when bonds are made, what kind of reaction is this?

Figure 1 When hydrogen and oxygen react to make water, bonds between hydrogen atoms and between oxygen atoms have to be broken before bonds between oxygen atoms and hydrogen atoms can be formed

GET IT RIGHT!
Remember that **B**reaking bonds a**B**sorbs energy, fo**R**ming bonds **R**eleases energy.

The balance between the energy needed to break bonds and the energy released when new bonds are made is what decides whether a reaction is endothermic or exothermic. We can find out more about what is happening in a particular reaction by looking at energy level diagrams.

Energy level diagrams

Energy level diagrams show us the relative amounts of energy contained in the reactants and the products of a reaction. This energy is measured in **kJ/mol**.

Figure 2 shows the energy level diagram for an exothermic reaction. The products are at a lower energy level than the reactants, so as reactants react to form products energy is released.

The difference between the energy levels of the reactants and the products is the change during the reaction, measured in kJ/mol. We represent this energy change by the symbol ΔH ('delta H'). This simply means 'the difference in energy between the products and the reactants'.

- In an exothermic reaction ΔH is always negative, because the products are at a lower energy level than the reactants. The temperature of the surroundings increases.

Figure 3 on the next page shows the energy level diagram for an endothermic reaction. Here, the products are at a higher energy level than the reactants. As reactants react to form products, energy is absorbed from the surroundings.

Figure 2 An exothermic reaction – more energy is released when bonds are formed between atoms in the products than is needed to break the bonds between the atoms in the reactants

Once again, the difference between the energy levels of the reactants and the products is the energy change during the reaction.

- In an endothermic reaction ΔH is always positive, because the products are at a higher energy level than the reactants. The temperature of the surroundings decreases.

Worked example
We can use a simple calorimeter like the one on page 175 to measure the energy change in a chemical reaction. To do this we use the fact that:
4.2 J of energy raise the temperature of 1 g of water by 1°C
A simple calorimeter is used to measure the energy change in the reaction:
$$A + B \rightarrow C$$
60 cm³ of a solution containing 0.1 moles of A is mixed with 40 cm³ of a solution containing 0.1 moles of B. The temperature of the two solutions before mixing is 19.6°C – after mixing them, the maximum temperature reached is 26.1°C.

Step 1 – calculate temperature change:
temperature change = 26.1°C − 19.6°C
= 6.5°C

Step 2 – calculate energy change:
4.2 J of energy raise the temperature of 1 g of solution by 1°C:
[mass solution = 100 g (assuming that density of solution = density of water, which is true for dilute solutions)]
energy change = 100 g × 4.2 J/g/°C × 6.5°C
= 2730 J
= 2.73 kJ

This is the energy change when 0.1 moles of reactants are mixed – so when 1 mole of reactants are mixed the energy change will be:
= 2.73 kJ × 10
= 27.3 kJ

So this experiment gives the energy change for the reaction:
$$A + B \rightarrow C$$
as −27.3 kJ/mol. (The temperature rises so the reaction is exothermic.)

SUMMARY QUESTIONS

1. Copy and complete using the words below:
   absorbing   formed   positive   released   releases   endothermic
   Breaking bonds involves …… energy, while making bonds …… energy. If more energy is needed to break bonds than is …… when bonds are ……, the reaction is …… and ΔH is …… .

2. Why is energy released in an exothermic reaction?

3. Draw energy level diagrams for the following reactions:
   a) $6CO_2(g) + 6H_2O(g) \rightarrow C_6H_{12}O_6(aq) + 6O_2(g)$; $\Delta H = +2880$ kJ/mol
   b) $H_2(g) + I_2(g) \rightarrow 2HI(g)$; $\Delta H = +26.5$ kJ/mol

Figure 3 An endothermic reaction – more energy is needed to break the bonds between the atoms in the reactants than is released when bonds are formed between atoms in the products

Figure 4 The energy needed to start a reaction is called the **activation energy**. A catalyst lowers the activation energy so that a higher proportion of reactant particles have sufficient energy to react.

KEY POINTS

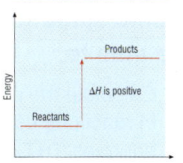

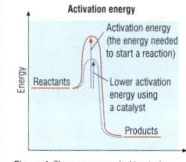

1. In chemical reactions, energy must be supplied to break the bonds between atoms in the reactants.
2. When bonds are formed between atoms in a chemical reaction, energy is released.
3. In an exothermic reaction, the energy released when bonds are formed is greater than the energy absorbed when bonds are broken. The opposite is true for endothermic reactions.
4. ΔH is negative for exothermic reactions. It is positive for endothermic reactions.
5. The minimum amount of energy to start a reaction is called the activation energy.

SUMMARY ANSWERS

1. Absorbing, releases, released, formed, endothermic, positive.

2. The energy released as new bonds are made is greater than the energy absorbed breaking bonds initially.

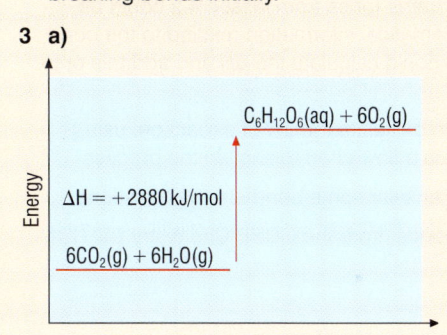

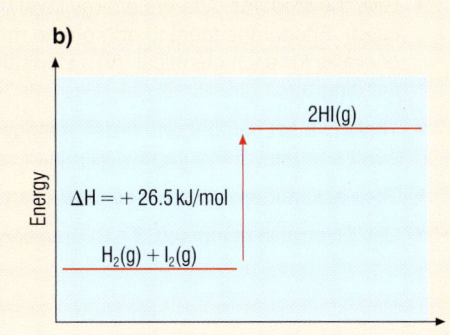

3. a) Energy level diagram: $6CO_2(g) + 6H_2O(g)$ → $C_6H_{12}O_6(aq) + 6O_2(g)$, $\Delta H = +2880$ kJ/mol
   b) Energy level diagram: $H_2(g) + I_2(g)$ → $2HI(g)$, $\Delta H = +26.5$ kJ/mol

KEY POINTS

Encourage the Modern Foreign Languages department to translate the key points into French and German. Then, on cards, supply each key point written in English or a MFL. Students could then group the key points in the different languages together.

Answers to in-text questions

a) Endothermic.
b) Exothermic.
c) Endothermic.

251

CHEMISTRY ENERGY CALCULATIONS

C3 4.3 Calculations using bond energies

LEARNING OBJECTIVES

Students should learn:
- That bond energies can be used to calculate energy changes in a reaction. [**HT** only]

LEARNING OUTCOMES

Most students should be able to:
- State a definition of bond energy.
- Use a data table to get a bond energy.

Some students should also be able to:
- Calculate the energy transferred in reactions using supplied bond energies. [**HT** only]

Teaching suggestions

- **Special needs.** Supply the answers to bond energy calculation questions in discrete lines of working out, in an incorrect order. Students should cut and stick these sentences into the correct order.
- **Gifted and talented.** Some AS-level bond energy questions could be given to these students.
- **Learning styles**

  Kinaesthetic: Making models to represent a chemical reaction.

  Visual: Labelling energy level diagrams with figures and calculations.

  Auditory: Listening to statements to decide if they are true or false.

  Interpersonal: Working in groups to explain how two key terms relate.

  Intrapersonal: Completing calculations using bond energies.

- **Homework.** Ask students to explain why the calculated ΔH is never the same as the actual energy change measured in the reaction.

SPECIFICATION LINK-UP Unit: Chemistry 3.13.4

Students should use their skills, knowledge and understanding of 'How Science Works':
- *to calculate the energy transfer in reactions, using simple energy level diagrams or supplied bond energies.* [**HT** only]

Lesson structure

STARTER

Sort – Write the following sentences on separate cards:
- Reactant bonds break (endothermic).
- Atoms rearrange.
- Product bonds form (exothermic).

Ask students to work in small groups and sort the sentences into the correct order. Then give each group a molecular model kit. Ask them to choose a reaction (the Student Book could help them, e.g. combustion of carbon). Then use the molecular model kit to make models of each stage of a chemical reaction (carbon atoms and oxygen molecules for stage one, free atoms for stage two and carbon dioxide molecules for stage three). Then each group could feedback their thoughts to the whole of the class. (15 minutes)

True or false – Give each child a red and a green card. Read out the following statements. If the students think a statement is true, they should show a green card, if they think it is false, they should show the red card.
- Bond making is exothermic. [True]
- If the reactants have more energy than the products, the reaction is endothermic. [False]
- Ammonia contains three identical bonds. [True]
- Energy is needed to break bonds. [True]
- If ΔH is negative, the reaction takes in energy. [False]
- Bond energy is measured in joules per gram (J/g). [False]
- Bond energy is the energy needed to break the bond between two atoms. [True]

(5 minutes)

MAIN

- On flip-chart paper, write different examination questions that relate to bond energies. The worked example as one could be used.
- Using Blu-Tack, attach the sheets to the wall. Split the students into pairs and give each team a marker pen and a calculator. Ask each pair to start answering one question, and time the students for 3 minutes.
- Then ask the students to move on, they should read the previous work, correct if necessary and add to the answer. Once all the students have attempted each question, give each group a sheet of paper and ask them to copy up the question and what they consider to be the correct working out into their notes.
- Give the students different energy level diagrams (ones from lesson 4.2 could be used). Encourage them to add on the mathematical information relating to the bond energies for each chemical. Also students should calculate the ΔH and add this onto the diagram.
- There is a set number and order of stages to calculate the ΔH of a reaction, using bond energies. Encourage students to create a flow chart to explain the process.
- Then ask students to use their flow chart to answer some bond energy questions.
- Use Electronic resource C3 4.3 'Breaking bonds' from the GCSE Chemistry CD ROM.

PLENARIES

Calculate – Ask students to work out how much energy would be needed to break a molecule of the following into separate atoms:
- methane [1652 kJ/mol]
- ammonia [1173 kJ/mol]
- hydrogen chloride [432 kJ/mol]
- water [928 kJ/mol]. (10 minutes)

Relationship – Bond energies and ΔH are related. Ask students to work in small groups to explain how these terms can be linked. Then ask each group to share their thoughts. (10 minutes)

ACTIVITY & EXTENSION IDEAS

- Encourage students to research to find out how values for bond energies have been generated.
- Students could draw a graph or chart to compare the bond energies of different bonds.
- Students could find out how the C—C, C=C and C≡C compare and why they are different.

Further chemistry

CHEMISTRY C3 4.3 — ENERGY CALCULATIONS

Calculations using bond energies

LEARNING OBJECTIVE
1. How can we use bond energies to calculate energy changes in reactions?

The energy needed to break the bond between two atoms is known as the **bond energy** for that bond.

Bond energies are measured in kJ/mol. We can use bond energies to work out the energy change (ΔH) for many chemical reactions. Before we can do this, we need to have a list of the bond energies for some of the most commonly found chemical bonds:

Bond	Bond energy (kJ/mol)	Bond	Bond energy (kJ/mol)
C—C	347	H—Cl	432
C—O	358	H—O	464
C—H	413	H—N	391
C—N	286	H—H	436
C—Cl	346	O=O	498
Cl—Cl	243	N≡N	945

To calculate the energy change for a chemical reaction we need to work out:
- firstly, how much energy is needed to break the chemical bonds in the reactants, and
- then how much energy is released when the new bonds are formed in the products.

a) What do we mean by the **bond energy** of a chemical bond?

It is very important to remember that the data in the table is the energy required for *breaking* bonds. When we want to know the amount of energy released as these same bonds are formed, the number is the *same* but the sign is *negative*.

For example, the bond energy for a C—C bond is +347 kJ/mol. This means that the bond energy for *forming* a C—C bond is −347 kJ/mol.

b) Is bond making endothermic or exothermic? What about bond breaking?

DID YOU KNOW?
Bond energies in different molecules are remarkably similar, which is why it is possible to use them to calculate energy changes for reactions in this way. However, values do vary slightly depending on the molecule so ΔH worked out like this gives us an approximate value.

Bond breaking
H(g) + H(g)
$\Delta H = +436$ kJ/mol
H—H (g)

Bond making
H(g) + H(g)
$\Delta H = -436$ kJ/mol
H—H (g)

Figure 1 Making and breaking a bond always involves the same *quantity* of energy (but the *sign* is different).

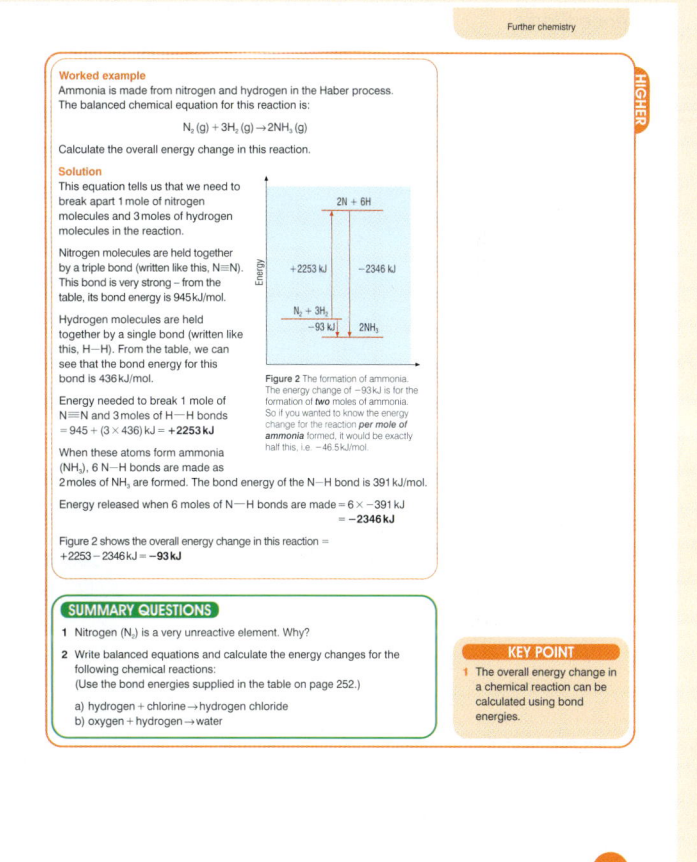

Worked example
Ammonia is made from nitrogen and hydrogen in the Haber process. The balanced chemical equation for this reaction is:

$$N_2(g) + 3H_2(g) \rightarrow 2NH_3(g)$$

Calculate the overall energy change in this reaction.

Solution
This equation tells us that we need to break apart 1 mole of nitrogen molecules and 3 moles of hydrogen molecules in the reaction.

Nitrogen molecules are held together by a triple bond (written like this, N≡N). This bond is very strong – from the table, its bond energy is 945 kJ/mol.

Hydrogen molecules are held together by a single bond (written like this, H—H). From the table, we can see that the bond energy for this bond is 436 kJ/mol.

Energy needed to break 1 mole of N≡N and 3 moles of H—H bonds
= 945 + (3 × 436) kJ = **+2253 kJ**

When these atoms form ammonia (NH₃), 6 N—H bonds are made as 2 moles of NH₃ are formed. The bond energy of the N—H bond is 391 kJ/mol.

Energy released when 6 moles of N—H bonds are made = 6 × −391 kJ
= **−2346 kJ**

Figure 2 shows the overall energy change in this reaction = +2253 − 2346 kJ = **−93 kJ**

Figure 2 The formation of ammonia. The energy change of −93 kJ is for the formation of *two* moles of ammonia. So if you wanted to know the energy change for the reaction *per mole of ammonia* formed, it would be exactly half this, i.e. −46.5 kJ/mol.

SUMMARY QUESTIONS
1. Nitrogen (N₂) is a very unreactive element. Why?
2. Write balanced equations and calculate the energy changes for the following chemical reactions:
   (Use the bond energies supplied in the table on page 252.)
   a) hydrogen + chlorine → hydrogen chloride
   b) oxygen + hydrogen → water

KEY POINT
1. The overall energy change in a chemical reaction can be calculated using bond energies.

SUMMARY ANSWERS

1. The two atoms in a nitrogen molecule are joined by a very strong (triple) bond, with a very large bond energy.

2. a) $H_2(g) + Cl_2(g) \rightarrow 2HCl(g)$
   $\Delta H = -185$ kJ/mol

   b) $O_2(g) + 2H_2(g) \rightarrow 2H_2O(l)$
   $\Delta H = -486$ kJ/mol

Answers to in-text questions

a) The energy needed to break apart the two atoms in the bond.

b) Bond breaking = Endothermic
Bond making = Exothermic.

KEY POINT

Copy out the key point. Then encourage each student to illustrate it by using a worked example of a calculation.

CHEMISTRY ENERGY CALCULATIONS

C3 4.4 Energy balance – how much energy do you use?

SPECIFICATION LINK-UP
Unit: Chemistry 3.13.4

This spread can be used to revisit the following content already covered in this chapter:

- Eating food that provides more energy than the body needs can lead to obesity.

Students should use their skills, knowledge and understanding of 'How Science Works':

- to consider the social, economic and environmental consequences of using fuels.

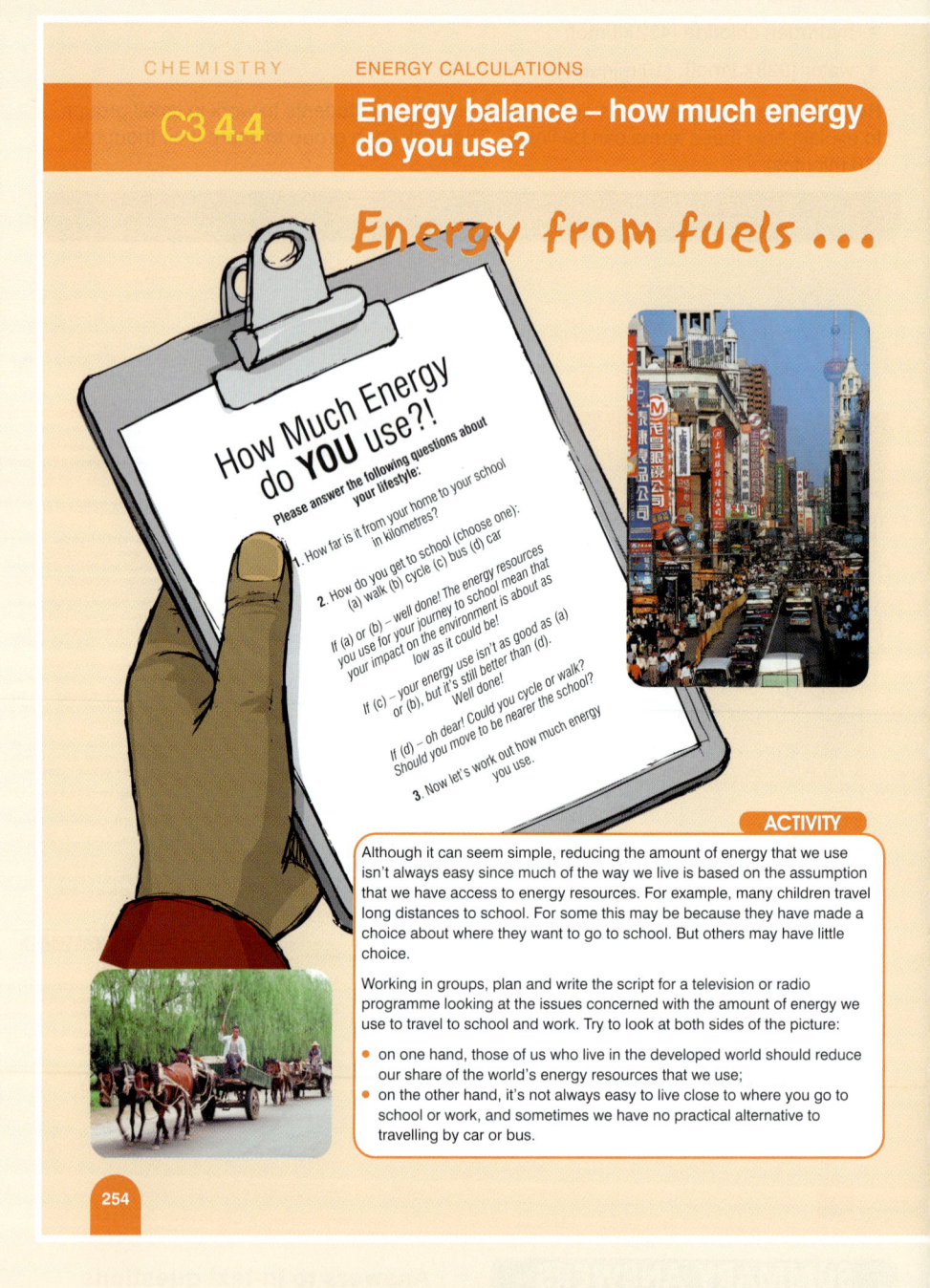

CHEMISTRY ENERGY CALCULATIONS

C3 4.4 Energy balance – how much energy do you use?

Energy from fuels...

How Much Energy do YOU use?!

Please answer the following questions about your lifestyle:

1. How far is it from your home to your school in kilometres?
2. How do you get to school (choose one): (a) walk (b) cycle (c) bus (d) car

If (a) or (b) – well done! The energy resources you use for your journey to school mean that your impact on the environment is about as low as it could be!

If (c) – your energy use isn't as good as (a) or (b), but it's still better than (d).
Well done!

If (d) – oh dear! Could you cycle or walk? Should you move to be nearer the school?

3. Now let's work out how much energy you use.

ACTIVITY

Although it can seem simple, reducing the amount of energy that we use isn't always easy since much of the way we live is based on the assumption that we have access to energy resources. For example, many children travel long distances to school. For some this may be because they have made a choice about where they want to go to school. But others may have little choice.

Working in groups, plan and write the script for a television or radio programme looking at the issues concerned with the amount of energy we use to travel to school and work. Try to look at both sides of the picture:

- on one hand, those of us who live in the developed world should reduce our share of the world's energy resources that we use;
- on the other hand, it's not always easy to live close to where you go to school or work, and sometimes we have no practical alternative to travelling by car or bus.

Teaching suggestions

Activities

- **Script** – Split the students into groups of about four. Explain to them that they are going to write a script for a TV programme or radio programme about travelling to school or work. Students should create a script that includes at least one expert interview and an anchorperson, which focuses on the amount of energy used for these journeys. The article should be balanced, and consider energy usage in the developed and developing world. The images in the Student Book could help students brainstorm the issues of energy usage in different parts of the world. The article should last no longer than 5 minutes. They could perform their script to the rest of the class. This could be recorded and uploaded onto the school web site.
- **Energy from fuels** – Use PhotoPLUS C3 4.4 'Energy from fuels' from the GCSE Chemistry CD ROM.

- **Energy from food, news article** – Obesity is a big issue in the western world, and this disorder is even affecting youngsters. Ask students to imagine that they have been commissioned by a Sunday newspaper to write a feature article. Show some examples of feature articles in different newspapers and magazines. Explain to the class that they must write between 500–1000 words comparing the life of a child in the UK to a child in the developing world. They should include information about the difference in size of the children, even if their food intake is the same.

- **Diary** – Ask students to use information from the pie chart and pictures in the Student Book to empathise with the two students in the developed and developing world. They could be encouraged to write a diary entry for each child.

Extension

Poster – Ask students to create a poster, which could be displayed in a doctor's surgery about the threat of eating too much fat in our diet.

Energy from food...

Child in developing world

Time spent:
- Fetching water
- Doing chores at home
- Working in the fields
- Preparing, cooking and eating food
- School
- Collecting firewood for cooking
- Sleeping

Child in developed world

Time spent:
- Watching TV
- Playing computer games
- School
- Sleeping

About a quarter of the time spent watching TV or playing computer games is spent eating!

ACTIVITY

Where do you go if you're hungry? The larder? The kitchen cupboards? And if they're empty – to the corner shop, or the supermarket?

In the developed world we don't usually find it hard to get food. Most of us don't have to spend our days worrying about how we'll make the next meal, or spend hours collecting the food to make it, or the fuel to cook it. But it isn't the same in the developing world – where many people spend a lot of time and energy just finding the food, water and fuel they need to live.

The two pie charts show how two different children spend their days. They are both lucky – they have enough to eat and a place to sleep.

Write a short feature article for a newspaper or a news website comparing the lives of these two children. In your article, explain why the lives of children in the developed world make it more likely that they will be overweight than children in the developing world. This is true even when we compare children who both have similar amounts to eat.

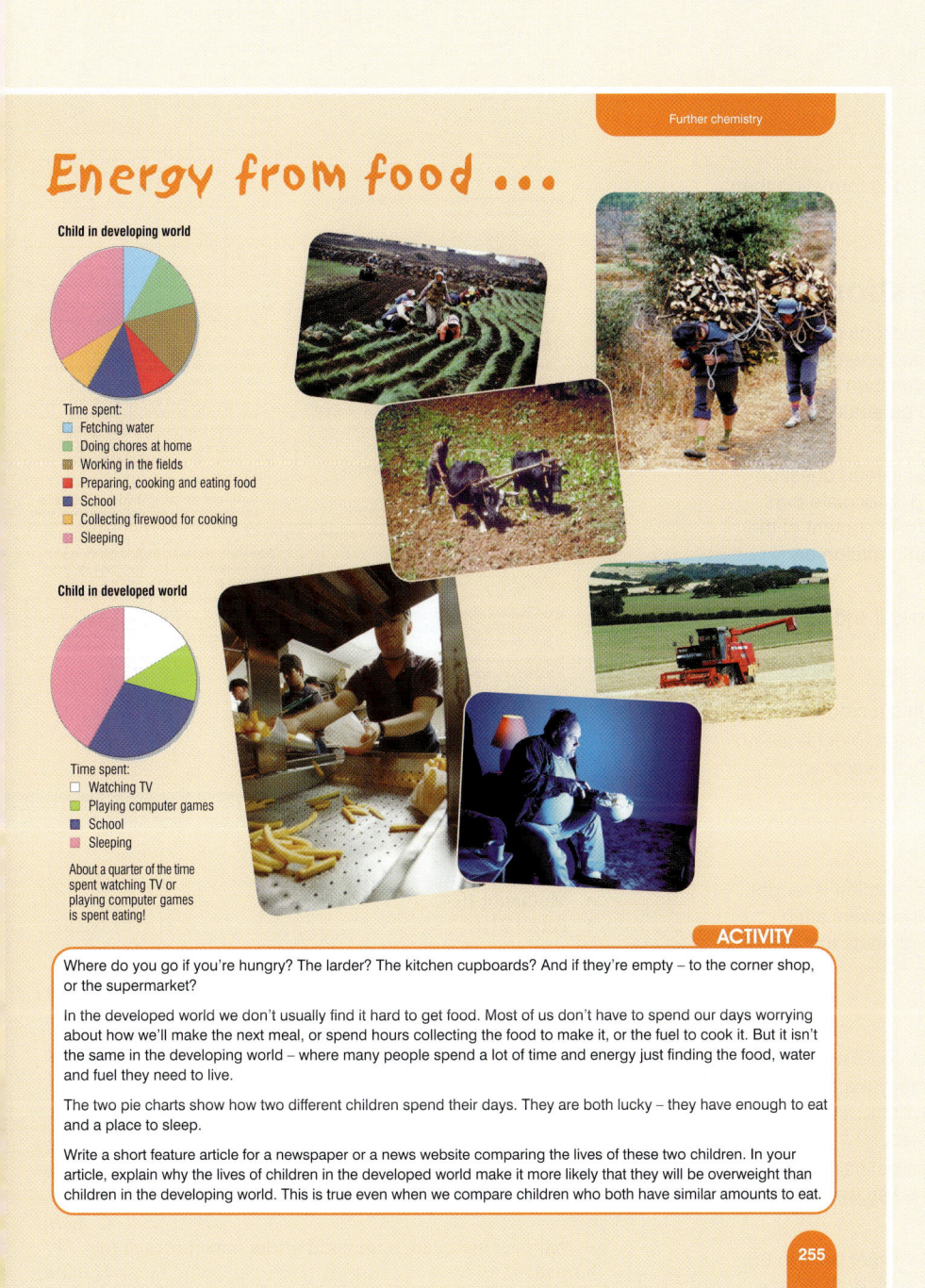

Homework

Questionnaire – Encourage students to ask ten members of their family or friends the questionnaire as detailed in the Student Book. Students could then record the methods of transport as a pie chart and the distance as a bar chart.

Learning styles

Kinaesthetic: Acting out TV scripts.
Visual: Creating a poster about obesity.
Auditory: Listening to other students performing their scripts.
Interpersonal: Working in groups to produce radio/TV scripts.
Intrapersonal: Empathising with different characters to write their diary entries.

Gifted and talented

Students could calculate the number of kilojoules of energy taken to walk to school and contrast this to the amount of energy used by a car for the same distance. Data about the amounts of energy could be found from car specifications at car dealerships, and the amount of energy used for walking could be found on lifestyle Internet sites. Students could then draw a pictogram of the data using food, e.g. cream cakes, as the picture.

Special needs

Hold a class discussion about each of the two children's lives regarding travel to school and food, then give the students a cut and stick activity. The students could sort the statements and stick them around an artist's impression of each child. To help further, there could be the correct number of boxes for statements around each image.

ICT link-up

Students could write up their newspaper article into a desktop publishing package and add images taken from the Internet.

CHEMISTRY — ENERGY CALCULATIONS

SUMMARY ANSWERS

1. a) D b) C c) A d) B

2. a) To break the molecule apart/break the bonds in the molecule.
   b) Bonds are formed when new substances (e.g. CO_2 and water) are formed and energy is given out.
   c) 85 kJ

3. a) −210 kJ/mol
   b) Exothermic – more energy released in bond formation than needed in bond breaking. **[HT only]**

Summary teaching suggestions

- **Special needs** – For question 3a), the calculations could be written out with missing information, e.g. bond energies and the actual answer to the calculation. Students can then use the data table to complete the working out and then generate the final answer.

- **Gifted and talented** – These students could extend question 2c) to find out how much of other foods, e.g. chocolate bars, would equal 1.7×10^3 kJ per 100 g. The calorific content of the foods could be found using the nutritional information on packaging.

- **ICT link-up** – Students could use Excel to detail and calculate their answer for question 3a).

- **Learning styles**
  Kinaesthetic: Question 1 could be turned into a card sort.
  Visual: The data from question 3 could be used to generate an energy level diagram for the decomposition of hydrogen peroxide.
  Auditory: Question 3b) could be used in a class discussion.

- **When to use the questions?**
  - Question 2 could be attempted before this section is taught. Students could then review their previous answers after completing the topic and make any amendments that are necessary.
  - As revision resources.
  - As homework.
  - Instead of answering question 3, students could prepare a mark scheme. This should include how many marks can be obtained and for what information. The scheme should also include answers that would not be accepted.
  - You could create a crossword or word search, using the definitions from question 1 as clues for the key words detailed in the puzzle.

- **Misconceptions** – Students often forget to include units in the answers to their calculations. If units aren't quoted, then they lose one mark.

ENERGY CALCULATIONS: C3 4.1 – C3 4.4

SUMMARY QUESTIONS

1. Match statements a) to d) with the terms labelled A to D in the table below.

a) Reactant required for fuels and food to release energy.	A	bomb calorimeter
b) Reaction in which energy is released.	B	calorie
c) Apparatus used to measure energy change in a reaction.	C	exothermic
d) Unit used to describe the energy released when food is eaten.	D	oxygen

2. When we eat sugar we break it down to produce water and carbon dioxide.
$$C_{12}H_{22}O_{11} + 12O_2 \rightarrow 12CO_2 + 11H_2O$$
   a) Why must your body **supply** energy in order to break down a sugar molecule?
   b) When we break down sugar in our bodies, energy is released. Explain where this energy comes from in terms of the bonds in molecules.
   c) We can get about 1.7×10^3 kJ of energy by breaking down 100 g of sugar.
   If a heaped teaspoon contains 5 g of sugar, how much energy does this produce when broken down by the body?

3. Hydrogen peroxide has the structure H—O—O—H. It decomposes slowly to form water and oxygen.
$$2H_2O_2 \rightarrow 2H_2O + O_2$$
   The table shows the bond energies for different types of bond.

Bond	Bond energy (kJ/mol)
H—O	464
H—H	436
O—O	144
O=O	498

   a) Use the bond energies to calculate the energy change for the decomposition of hydrogen peroxide in kJ/mol.
   b) Is this reaction exothermic or endothermic? Explain your answer. **[Higher]**

EXAM-STYLE QUESTIONS

1. A student burned some liquid fuels using the apparatus shown in the diagram.

The student used the same volume of water and the same starting temperature of the water for each fuel. The student's results are shown in the table.

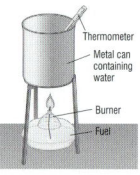

Fuel	Mass of fuel burned (g)	Temperature rise of water (°C)	Temperature rise per gram of fuel burned (°C/g)
Ethanol	2.46	32	13.0
Kerosene	1.30	30	
Methanol	2.40	25	
Petrol	1.80	38	

(a) Calculate the values of the temperature rise per gram of fuel burned that are missing from the table. (3)
(b) Write down the four fuels in order of increasing heat energy produced per gram of fuel according to the experiment. (1)
(c) The student checked the results with some data for fuels in a textbook. The values from the experiment were much lower than the values in the book.
   (i) Suggest one reason why this experiment gives lower results than expected. (1)
   (ii) What sort of error is this? (1)
(d) Suggest one way that the student could change this experiment to make it a fairer comparison. Explain why your suggestion would make it fairer. (2)

2. Two students had snacks. The first table shows what was in each student's snack. The second table gives some nutritional information about the foods.

Student 1	Student 2
100 g French fries	25 g crisps
300 g cola drink	250 g fruit smoothie

EXAM-STYLE ANSWERS

1. a) One mark each for:
   - Kerosene 23.1.
   - Methanol 10.4.
   - Petrol 21.1. *(3 marks)*

   b) Methanol, ethanol, petrol, kerosene.
   (1 mark for all in correct order)

   c) i) Heat losses/not all of heat used to heat water/some heat used to heat container. *(1 mark)*
      ii) Systematic error. *(1 mark)*

   d) *Either:* burn fuels to produce same temperature rise of water *(1 mark)*
   so that heat losses are the same for each fuel. *(1 mark)*
   or: use a special calorimeter that collects more of the heat *(1 mark)*
   so that heat losses are minimised or the same for each fuel burned. *(1 mark)*
   (Accept any other valid suggestion with a correct reason, but **not** burn the same mass of fuel each time.)

2. a) Student 1: 1702 kJ *(2 marks)*
      (working: 1 mark for $1174 + (3 \times 176)$)
      Student 2: 1039 kJ *(2 marks)*
      (working: 1 mark for $(2216/4) + (2.5 \times 194)$)

   b) One mark each for:
      - Student 1's snack has more fat/student 2 has less fat in snack.
      - Student 1's snack has larger mass/student 2's snack has less mass. *(2 marks)*

   c) Causes obesity/causes increase in body weight. *(1 mark)*

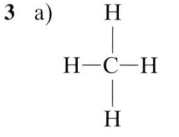

3. a)
```
      H
      |
   H—C—H
      |
      H
```
(all correct: 2 marks)
(one error: 1 mark)

Further chemistry

HOW SCIENCE WORKS QUESTIONS

Bomb calorimeter

Bomb calorimeters are used in research laboratories to calculate the energy in food. You will have tried to do this at some time in school when you burn a crisp or some fuel under a beaker of water and measure the rise in temperature. A bomb calorimeter does the same thing, but better!

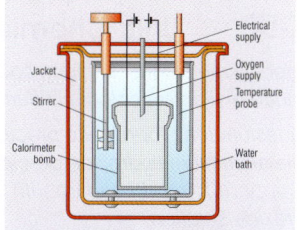

As you can see from this diagram, it is sealed and has its own supply of oxygen. There is a supply of electricity to produce a spark that will ignite the food. The increase in temperature of the water around the bomb is measured.

a) Why is the bomb 'better' than the school method? (1)

b) The bomb is calibrated before it is used by burning a substance with a known energy value. Use this example to explain what is meant by 'calibration'. (1)

Most foods are not tested in a bomb calorimeter. They have their energy value calculated by what is called the 4–9–4 rule. That is, for every gram of protein there are 4 calories of energy; 9 for fats and 4 for carbohydrates. So once you know the content of the food you can simply calculate its energy value.

c) Will the 4–9–4 rule or the bomb calorimeter produce the most valid results? Explain your answer. (1)

d) The bomb calorimeter burns parts of the food that are not digestible, e.g. hair which is protein but cannot be digested. How does this affect your answer to c)? (1)

Food	Energy (kJ per 100g)	Fat (g per 100g)	Protein (g per 100g)	Carbohydrate (g per 100g)
Cola	176	0	0	11
Crisps	2216	34	5.7	53
French fries	1174	15	3.3	34
Fruit smoothie	194	0.5	1.5	20

(a) Calculate the total energy produced by each student's snack. (4)

(b) Student 1's snack produces more energy than the other snack. Suggest **two** reasons why this snack produces more energy. (2)

(c) What is the effect of eating food that provides more energy than the body needs? (1)

3 Methane is used as a fuel. The equation for the complete combustion of methane is:

$$CH_4 + 2O_2 \rightarrow CO_2 + 2H_2O$$

The energy changes for the reaction are shown on the diagram:

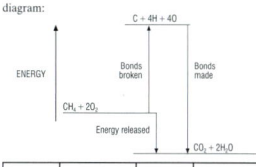

Bond	Bond energy (kJ/mol)	Bond	Bond energy (kJ/mol)
C—H	413	C=O	805
O=O	498	H—O	464

(a) Draw the structure of methane to show all the bonds in methane. (2)

(b) Use the table of bond energies and the energy diagram to calculate:
  (i) the energy to break all the bonds in the reactants. (2)
  (ii) the energy produced when the bonds in the products are made. (2)
  (iii) the energy released by the reaction. (1)

[Higher]

HOW SCIENCE WORKS ANSWERS

a) It gives a more accurate measurement of the energy value of a food.

b) Calibration ensures that the instrument being used is accurate. In this instance the bomb calorimeter is tested against a known chemical to check on the accuracy of its measurements.

c) The bomb calorimeter because it is directly linked to the energy value of the food. The 4–9–4 rule is a rough guide to the energy in different chemicals.

d) The bomb calorimeter is likely to be inaccurate for some foods. It will over-estimate the energy to be passed on to the person eating the food. It is important for people to know this.

How science works teaching suggestions

- **Literacy guidance**
  - Key terms that should be understood: accurate, reliable, valid.
  - The question expecting a longer answer, where students can practise their literacy skills is: d).
- **Lower-level answer.** Question a) is lower level and the answer provided is also lower level.
- **Gifted and talented.** Able students could check out the 4–9–4 rule with the information given on packets of food.
- **How and when to use these questions.** When wishing to develop an awareness of the limitations of different ways of measuring variables.
  The questions could be used in small group discussion.
- **Homework.** Check out the energy levels in different foods and their relationship to carbohydrates, fats and proteins.

b) i) 2648 (kJ) (2 marks)
  (working: (413 × 4) + (498 × 2) gains 1 mark)
  ii) −3466 (kJ) (2 marks)
  (working: (805 × 2) + (464 × 4) gains 1 mark)
  iii) −818 (kJ) (1 mark)
  [**HT** only]

Exam teaching suggestions

Allow 20 minutes for students to attempt all of the questions in a single session. Alternatively, Q1 and Q2 could be set after completing C3 4.1. Q1 and Q2 are Foundation Tier and Q3 is more suitable for Higher-Tier candidates.

Q1 assesses some How Science Works skills, in particular 10.4 and 10.5, that form part of Assessment Objective 2 (AO2) and questions of this type may also be found in Investigative Skills Assessments.

Questions involving bond energy calculations and molar quantities similar to Q3 are considered high demand and so will appear only on Higher-Tier papers. Foundation-Tier papers may contain simpler calculations on energy data, but will not involve bond energy calculations. However, the concepts of bond-breaking and bond-making and simple energy level diagrams should be understood in relation to exothermic and endothermic reactions.

CHEMISTRY ANALYSIS

C3 5.1 Tests for positive ions

LEARNING OBJECTIVES

Students should learn:

- That cations can be experimentally identified.

LEARNING OUTCOMES

Most students should be able to:

- State the positive result for lithium, sodium, potassium, calcium and barium in flame tests.
- State the positive result for aluminium, calcium, copper(II), iron(II)/(III), ammonium and magnesium ions with sodium hydroxide.
- State the positive result for ammonia.

Some students should also be able to:

- Explain how to complete a flame test.
- Explain how to use sodium hydroxide to test for different cations.
- Explain how to test for ammonia gas using litmus paper.
- Interpret results of chemical tests.

Teaching suggestions

- **Special needs.** Test tubes with the transition metal solutions could be set up in advance with labels stuck to them. Students can simply add sodium hydroxide from a pipette to observe the colour change.
- **Learning styles**
  Kinaesthetic: Completing practical tests for ions.
  Visual: Looking at images to find their connection.
  Auditory: Listening to feedback from other students.
  Interpersonal: Working in groups to generate ideas about how to test for ammonia.
  Intrapersonal: Creating a crossword.
- **ICT link-up.** The Bunsen flame tests could be photographed. These images could then be printed out and students could add them to their notes.
- **Homework.** Ask students to find out what colour copper ions turn in a flame test.

SPECIFICATION LINK-UP   Unit: Chemistry 3.13.5

- *Flame tests can be used to identify metal ions. Lithium, sodium, potassium, calcium and barium compounds produce distinctive colours in flame tests.*
- *Aluminium, calcium and magnesium ions form white precipitates with sodium hydroxide solution but only the aluminium hydroxide precipitate dissolves in excess sodium hydroxide solution. Copper(II), iron(II) and iron(III) ions form coloured precipitates with sodium hydroxide solution.*
- *Ammonium ions react with sodium hydroxide solution to form ammonia. Ammonia gas turns damp litmus paper blue.*

Students should use their skills, knowledge and understanding of 'How Science Works':

- *to interpret results of the chemical tests in this specification.*

Lesson structure

STARTER

Images – Show the students a picture of salty water boiling over on a gas hob, a street light and a photograph of sodium burning in oxygen or a sodium flame as it reacts with water (with hydrogen having been ignited). Ask the students to look at the images and decide what they have in common. Encourage them to discuss the images with other students, then feedback the ideas to the class. Reveal to the students that all of the images contain sodium that is heated and causing the yellow colour. (5 minutes)

Think – Explain to students that ammonia is an alkali. Ask students to suggest methods for testing for ammonia. Encourage students to feedback their ideas, as bullet-point notes are made on the board. Explain that if damp red litmus paper turns blue, this is the positive test for ammonia. This could be demonstrated: wearing eye protection, remove the stopper from concentrated ammonia solution (kept in a fume cupboard). Wave the damp red litmus paper over the open neck of the bottle and it should turn blue. As an extension, students could be asked which gas damp litmus paper is also used to test for – if it bleaches, it is the positive test for chlorine. (10 minutes)

MAIN

- Firstly, students could test different known metal solutions to determine the flame colour of lithium, sodium, potassium, calcium and barium.
- Once students can distinguish the difference in the colours, a group of mystery solutions could be given. They should carry out flame tests to determine the positive ion present.
- Students could use sodium hydroxide to test for copper(II), iron(II) and iron(III) ions in unknown solutions.
- A set of three (A6) flash cards could be given to the students. On one side they could write the chemical test [flame, using sodium hydroxide and damp litmus paper]. On the back they could write a step-by-step set of instructions to explain how to conduct each test and what the result would infer.
- The cards could be laminated, and used in a lab to help the students to identify 'mystery' solutions.
- Use Interaction C3 5.1 'Testing for positive ions' from the GCSE Chemistry CD ROM.

PLENARIES

Conclusion – Ask students to conclude what the following compound contained:

'When sodium hydroxide was added to the solution, a white precipitate was formed. On adding excess sodium hydroxide, the precipitate was insoluble. When the solution was tested in a flame, the colour was brick red.' [calcium] (5 minutes)

Crossword – Ask students to create their own crossword that relates to the chemical tests that have been studied in the lesson. To speed the process up, the box frame could be given to the students, so they just need to work out which word goes into what position and generate the clues. (20 minutes)

Practical support

Testing with sodium hydroxide

Equipment and materials required
Three test tubes, 0.1 mol/dm³ sodium hydroxide solution (irritant), three dropping pipettes, test-tube rack, <1.4 mol/dm³ copper(II) chloride (harmful), 1 mol/dm³ iron(II) chloride (harmful), 1 mol/dm³ iron(III) chloride (irritant).

Details
Wearing chemical splash-proof eye protection, add about 1 cm³ of each solution to separate test tubes. Add about 2 cm³ of sodium hydroxide solution to each test tube, agitate the tube and observe.

Flame tests

Equipment and materials required
Inoculating loop (nichrome flame wires, fused onto glass rod handles), Bunsen burner and equipment, nine watch glasses, solutions of lithium chloride (irritant), sodium chloride, potassium chloride, calcium hydroxide (irritant), concentrated hydrochloric acid (corrosive). CLEAPSS Hazcards: lithium chloride 58; sodium salts 95; hydrochloric acid 47; calcium hydroxide 18; sodium hydroxide 91; copper chloride 27; iron compounds 55. Be aware of what to do if alkali gets into the eye.

Details
Wearing chemical splash-proof eye protection, put each of the known solutions into six labelled watch glasses. Then choose three of the solutions to be the mystery solutions and put them into the other three watch glasses labelled A–C. Dip the inoculating loop into the hydrochloric acid and put into the top of the blue gas cone in the roaring Bunsen flame (hottest part). This cleans the loop, but it does produce hydrogen chloride fumes and must be completed in a well-ventilated area. Repeated cleaning does corrode the wire and platinum is the best to use. Alternatively have specific inoculating loops for each solution and this would remove the need to clean them between solutions. It is possible to forgo cleaning and just heat the wire until it is red hot to burn off any of the previous salt. Put the inoculating loop into one solution and shake gently. Then put it into the hottest part of the blue flame, and observe the initial colour. Remove the loop and clean. Repeat with the other solutions.

ACTIVITY & EXTENSION

- Other metal ions could be added to the flame tests, e.g. copper ions.
- Sodium hydroxide could be used to test for magnesium, aluminium and calcium ions (0.1 M). The sodium hydroxide should be added at 1 cm³ at a time, up to 5 cm³ to see if the precipitate re-dissolves (see 'Practical support').

Answers to in-text questions
a) To identify unknown metals.
b) White.

FOUL FACTS
Flame spectroscopy is still used in biochemical labs in hospitals to determine the content of certain metal ions in body fluids.

KEY POINTS
Make a poem with three verses, one to reflect each key fact.

C3 5.1 Tests for positive ions

LEARNING OBJECTIVES
1 How do we identify different positive ions?

One of the problems we face in chemistry is that many substances look very similar to the naked eye. Just telling the difference between elements is hard enough. There are lots of shiny grey metals and one colourless, odourless gas looks much like another!

But once elements have been combined to form compounds the possibilities are simply enormous. To identify unknown substances we have a variety of different tests which can help us to distinguish one substance from another.

Flame tests
Identifying some of the metals in Groups 1 and 2 of the periodic table is made much easier because most of them produce flames with a characteristic colour. To carry out a flame test you:

- put a small amount of the compound to be tested in a platinum wire loop which has been dipped in concentrated hydrochloric acid,
- then hold the loop in the roaring blue flame of a Bunsen burner,
- then use the colour of the Bunsen flame to identify the metal element in the compound.

Figure 1 A flame test can identify a Group 1 or Group 2 metal in a compound. In this case the metal is lithium

Element	Flame colour
lithium	bright red
sodium	golden yellow
potassium	lilac
calcium	brick red
barium	green

a) What do we use flame tests for?

Sometimes we can use the reactions of unknown compounds with **sodium hydroxide solution** to help us with our identification. Aluminium ions, calcium ions and magnesium ions all form **white precipitates** with sodium hydroxide solution. So if we add sodium hydroxide to an unknown compound and a white precipitate forms we know it contains either aluminium, calcium or magnesium ions.

If we add more and more sodium hydroxide then the precipitate formed with aluminium ions dissolves – but a precipitate formed with calcium or magnesium ions will not. Calcium and magnesium ions can be distinguished by a flame test. Calcium ions give a brick red flame but magnesium ions produce no colour at all.

b) What colour precipitate does sodium hydroxide produce with aluminium, calcium and magnesium ions?

Some metal ions form **coloured precipitates** with sodium hydroxide.

- If we add sodium hydroxide solution to a substance containing copper(II) ions a light blue precipitate appears.
- If the substance contains iron(II) ions a 'dirty' green precipitate is produced when sodium hydroxide solution is added.
- When sodium hydroxide solution is added to iron(III) ions, a reddish-brown precipitate is produced.

Figure 2 This distinctive precipitate formed when we add sodium hydroxide solution tells us that Cu²⁺ ions are present

---

Sodium hydroxide solution can also be used to test whether ammonium ions (NH₄⁺) are present in an unknown substance. Ammonium ions react with sodium hydroxide solution to form ammonia and water:

$$NH_4^+ (aq) + OH^- (aq) \rightarrow NH_3 (aq) + H_2O (l)$$

To test for ammonium ions, we add sodium hydroxide solution to a solution of the unknown substance. If ammonium ions are present, ammonia is formed. When we gently warm the solution, ammonia is then driven off as a gas. We can detect this using damp red litmus paper. The red litmus turns blue because ammonia is an alkaline gas.

Figure 3 Sodium hydroxide solution provides a very useful test for many positive ions

PRACTICAL
Identifying positive ions
Try to identify the metal in some unknown compounds.

SUMMARY QUESTIONS
1 Copy and complete using the words below:

ammonia ammonium colours flame hydroxide one precipitates two

The Group ...... and ...... elements produce distinctive ...... when their compounds are placed in a .... Sodium ...... solution can be used to identify metal ions by the ...... that they produce. It can also be used to identify ...... ions, which produce ...... gas when warmed.

2 Draw a flowchart to describe how to carry out a flame test.

3 Copy and complete the table.

Add sodium hydroxide solution	Flame test	Metal ion
nothing observed	lilac	e)
white precipitate	brick red	f)
a)	c)	Fe³⁺
white precipitate which dissolves as more sodium hydroxide solution added	nothing observed	g)
light green precipitate which slowly turns reddish brown	nothing observed	h)
b)	d)	Na⁺

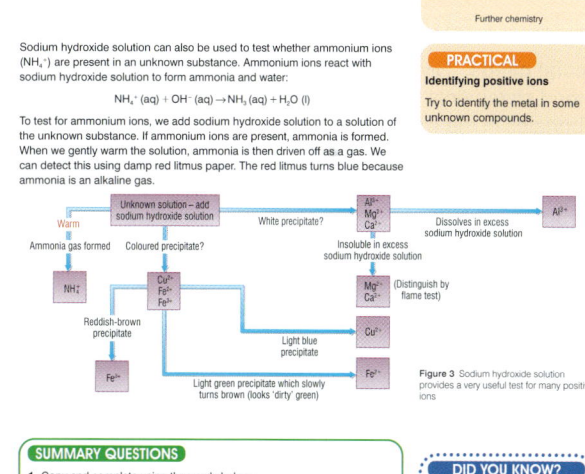

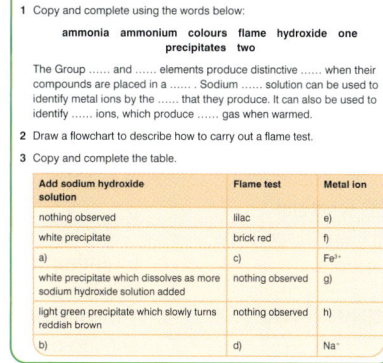

DID YOU KNOW?
Many metals are poisonous in large enough amounts – so it is very important to be able to analyse blood and body tissues for metal ions.

KEY POINTS
1 Group 1 and Group 2 metals can be identified in their compounds using flame tests.
2 Sodium hydroxide solution can be used to identify different metal ions depending on the precipitate that is formed.
3 Ammonium ions produce ammonia when sodium hydroxide solution is added and the solution is warmed gently.

SUMMARY ANSWERS

1 One, two, colours, flame, hydroxide, precipitates, ammonium, ammonia.

2 [Student flow chart.]

3 a) Reddish-brown precipitate b) Nothing observed
  c) Nothing observed d) Golden yellow e) Potassium
  f) Calcium g) Al³⁺ h) Fe²⁺

CHEMISTRY ANALYSIS

C3 5.2 Tests for negative ions

LEARNING OBJECTIVES

Students should learn:

- That anions can be experimentally identified.

LEARNING OUTCOMES

Most students should be able to:

- State the positive result for carbonates.
- State the positive result for halides.
- State the positive result for sulfates.
- State the positive result for nitrates.

Some students should also be able to:

- Explain how to complete tests for carbonates, halides, sulfates and nitrates.
- Interpret results of chemical tests.

Teaching suggestions

- **Special needs.** Give the students the method statements for testing carbonates in the wrong order. They should then sort the sentences to make the method.
- **Learning styles**
  Kinaesthetic: Completing practical tests of chemicals.
  Visual: Labelling the diagram for the test of carbonates.
  Auditory: Listening to time checks when answering examination questions.
  Interpersonal: Working in pairs to find different chemical examples in the Student Book.
  Intrapersonal: Creating a key to identify halides.
- **Homework.** Ask students to summarise the chemical tests in the form of a spider diagram.
- **ICT link-up.** On the RSC web site (www.chemit.co.uk) there are video clips of some of these experiments.

Answers to in-text questions

a) Carbon dioxide.
b) Silver nitrate solution with dilute nitric acid.
c) Barium chloride solution with hydrochloric acid.
d) Add sodium hydroxide solution and aluminium powder then warm gently and test for ammonia.

SPECIFICATION LINK-UP   Unit: Chemistry 3.13.5

- *Carbonates react with dilute acids to form carbon dioxide. Carbon dioxide turns lime water milky.*
- *Copper carbonate and zinc carbonate decompose on heating and can be identified by the distinctive colour changes.*
- *Halide ions in solution produce precipitates with silver nitrate solution in the presence of dilute nitric acid. Silver chloride is white, silver bromide is cream and silver iodide is yellow.*
- *Sulfate ions in solution produce a white precipitate with barium chloride solution in the presence of dilute hydrochloric acid.*
- *Nitrate ions are reduced by aluminium powder in the presence of sodium hydroxide to form ammonia.*
- *Ammonium ions react with sodium hydroxide solution to form ammonia. Ammonia gas turns damp litmus paper blue.*

Students should use their skills, knowledge and understanding of 'How Science Works':

- *to interpret results of the chemical tests in this specification.*

Lesson structure

STARTER

Find – Ask students to work in pairs and use the Student Book spread to find:

- Three examples of an ionic compound. [barium sulfate, copper carbonate, zinc carbonate, silver halide, copper oxide, zinc oxide, barium chloride]
- Two examples of a covalent compound. [carbon dioxide, ammonia]
- One example of a mono-atomic ion. [any halide] (5 minutes)

Recall – Ask students to recall the test for carbon dioxide gas [lime water turns milky] and ammonia [damp red litmus paper turns blue]. (5 minutes)

Label – Give the students an unlabelled diagram of the equipment used to test for carbonates. Students should then annotate the diagram to explain the test. (10 minutes)

MAIN

- Students could try to write a step-by-step method for testing carbonates. Then they could attempt the practical, having been checked for safety, and make any amendments to their method as they try to complete the practical. The students could test calcium, copper and zinc carbonates.
- A circus of all the experiments could be set up, so that students test for carbonates, halides, sulfates and nitrates. Each station should contain a help card with an outline of the method and a diagram. (See 'Practical support'.) Students should design their own results table and note observations at each station.
- Use Interactive C3 5.2 'Testing for negative ions' from the GCSE Chemistry CD ROM.

PLENARIES

Key – Ask students to generate a key for identifying halides. (10 minutes)

Examination questions – Students could be given a set of examination questions on this topic. To help students with their exam preparation, time the students (approximately 1 minute per mark), and give the students an idea when they should be tackling each section of a question. Then show the students the mark scheme and allow them to mark their own work and make any notes that are needed, so that they can use the material for revision at a later date. (15 minutes)

KEY POINTS

Give the students four diagrams of test tubes. They should then add to the image and label the diagram to illustrate each of the four key points.

Practical support

Testing halides

Equipment and materials required
Five different salts containing halides labelled 1–5 (e.g. sodium chloride, sodium iodide, sodium bromide, potassium chloride, potassium bromide), spatula, 5 test tubes, test-tube rack, 2 dropping pipettes, 0.5 mol/dm³ nitric acid (corrosive), 0.05–0.1 mol/dm³ silver nitrate solution, eye protection. CLEAPSS Hazcards: nitric acid 67; silver nitrate 87.

Details
Wearing chemical splash-proof eye protection, put about a quarter of a spatula of a halide into a test tube. Add about 1 cm³ of nitric acid, agitate and add more nitric acid until all of the halide has dissolved. Then add about 1 cm³ of silver nitrate solution and observe the colour of the precipitate to determine the halide in the solution.

Testing sulfates

Equipment and materials required
Test tube, test-tube rack, a sulfate solution (e.g. magnesium sulfate), 1 mol/dm³ hydrochloric acid (irritant), 2 pipettes, 0.2 mol/dm³ barium chloride (toxic), eye protection. CLEAPSS Hazcards: hydrochloric acid 47; barium chloride 10.

Details
Wearing eye protection, put about 1 cm³ of sulfate solution into a test tube. Add about 1 cm³ of acid and then 1 cm³ of barium chloride and observe. The mixture may need agitating for the reaction to complete.

Testing for nitrates

Equipment and materials required
0.5 mol/dm³ sodium hydroxide (corrosive), warm water bath, damp red litmus paper, aluminium powder (flammable), test tube, spatula, two pipettes, a nitrate solution (e.g. sodium nitrate), eye protection. CLEAPSS Hazcards: sodium hydroxide 91; aluminium 01; potassium (sodium) nitrate 82.

Details
Wearing chemical splash-proof eye protection, put about 1 cm³ of nitrate solution in a test tube and add about 1 cm³ of sodium hydroxide. Heat the solution gently in the water bath and test for ammonia. If no ammonia is detected, add a small amount of aluminium powder and continue to test for ammonia.

Testing carbonates

Equipment and materials required
Boiling tube, 2 stands, 2 bosses, 2 clamps, Bunsen burner and safety equipment, test tube, lime water (irritant), copper carbonate (harmful), zinc carbonate, spatula, bung with a hole, delivery tube, eye protection. CLEAPSS Hazcards: lime water 18; copper carbonate 26.

Details
Wearing eye protection, set up the equipment as shown in Figure 1, in the Student Book. In the boiling tube there should be about one spatula full of the carbonate and the test tube should be half filled with lime water. Heat the carbonate with the blue flame and observe the lime water. Once the lime water has changed, lower the test tube so that the delivery tube is not in the lime water, and then remove the heat from the carbonate. This will prevent suck back and thermal shock in the boiling tube. Observe the colour change in the zinc oxide on cooling.

Safety: CLEAPSS Handbook CD-ROM section 13.2.4 (heating substances).

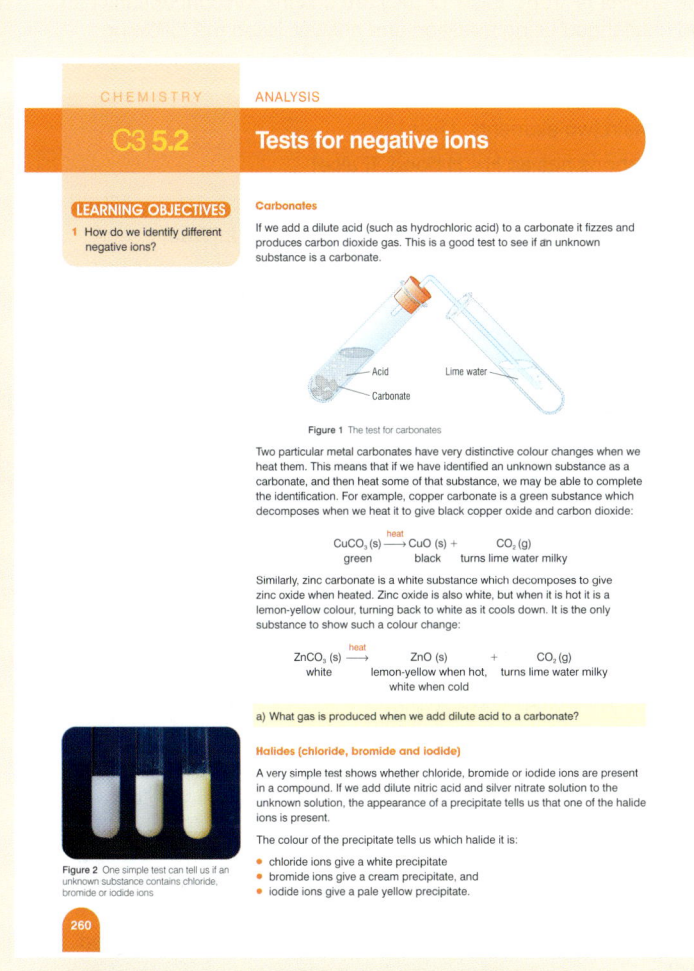

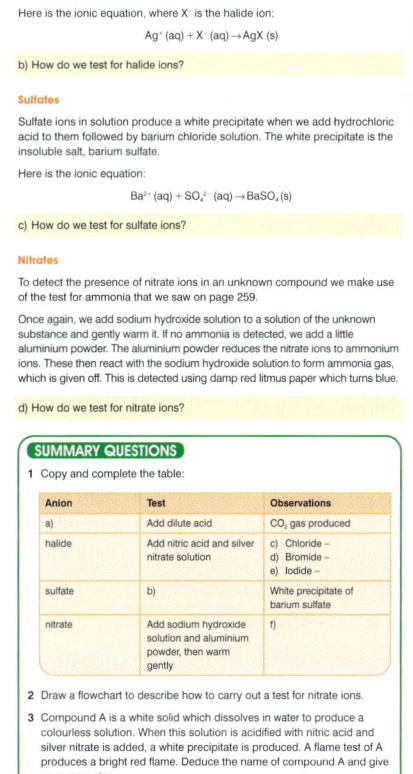

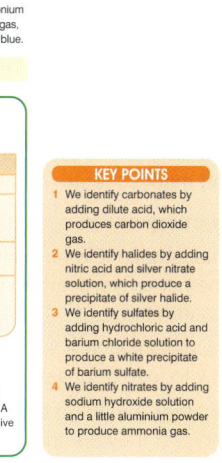

CHEMISTRY
ANALYSIS
C3 5.2 Tests for negative ions

LEARNING OBJECTIVES
1. How do we identify different negative ions?

Carbonates
If we add a dilute acid (such as hydrochloric acid) to a carbonate it fizzes and produces carbon dioxide gas. This is a good test to see if an unknown substance is a carbonate.

Figure 1 The test for carbonates

Two particular metal carbonates have very distinctive colour changes when we heat them. This means that if we have identified an unknown substance as a carbonate, and then heat some of that substance, we may be able to complete the identification. For example, copper carbonate is a green substance which decomposes when we heat it to give black copper oxide and carbon dioxide:

$$CuCO_3(s) \xrightarrow{heat} CuO(s) + CO_2(g)$$
green → black, turns lime water milky

Similarly, zinc carbonate is a white substance which decomposes to give zinc oxide when heated. Zinc oxide is also white, but when it is hot it is a lemon-yellow colour, turning back to white as it cools down. It is the only substance to show such a colour change:

$$ZnCO_3(s) \xrightarrow{heat} ZnO(s) + CO_2(g)$$
white → lemon-yellow when hot, white when cold, turns lime water milky

a) What gas is produced when we add dilute acid to a carbonate?

Halides (chloride, bromide and iodide)
A very simple test shows whether chloride, bromide or iodide ions are present in a compound. If we add dilute nitric acid and silver nitrate solution to the unknown solution, the appearance of a precipitate tells us that one of the halide ions is present.

The colour of the precipitate tells us which halide it is:
- chloride ions give a white precipitate
- bromide ions give a cream precipitate, and
- iodide ions give a pale yellow precipitate.

Figure 2 One simple test can tell us if an unknown substance contains chloride, bromide or iodide ions

Here is the ionic equation, where X⁻ is the halide ion:

$$Ag^+(aq) + X^-(aq) \rightarrow AgX(s)$$

b) How do we test for halide ions?

Sulfates
Sulfate ions in solution produce a white precipitate when we add hydrochloric acid to them followed by barium chloride solution. The white precipitate is the insoluble salt, barium sulfate.

Here is the ionic equation:

$$Ba^{2+}(aq) + SO_4^{2-}(aq) \rightarrow BaSO_4(s)$$

c) How do we test for sulfate ions?

Nitrates
To detect the presence of nitrate ions in an unknown compound we make use of the test for ammonia that we saw on page 259.

Once again, we add sodium hydroxide solution to a solution of the unknown substance and gently warm it. If no ammonia is detected, we add a little aluminium powder. The aluminium powder reduces the nitrate ions to ammonium ions. These then react with the sodium hydroxide solution to form ammonia gas, which is given off. This is detected using damp red litmus paper which turns blue.

d) How do we test for nitrate ions?

DID YOU KNOW?
Silver compounds are sensitive to light – if a silver halide precipitate is left for a few minutes in bright sunlight it slowly turns black as silver metal is formed.

SUMMARY QUESTIONS
1 Copy and complete the table:

Anion	Test	Observations
a)	Add dilute acid	CO₂ gas produced
halide	Add nitric acid and silver nitrate solution	c) Chloride – d) Bromide – e) Iodide –
sulfate	b)	White precipitate of barium sulfate
nitrate	Add sodium hydroxide solution and aluminium powder, then warm gently	f)

2 Draw a flowchart to describe how to carry out a test for nitrate ions.

3 Compound A is a white solid which dissolves in water to produce a colourless solution. When this solution is acidified with nitric acid and silver nitrate is added, a white precipitate is produced. A flame test of A produces a bright red flame. Deduce the name of compound A and give your reasoning.

KEY POINTS
1. We identify carbonates by adding dilute acid, which produces carbon dioxide gas.
2. We identify halides by adding nitric acid and silver nitrate solution, which produce a precipitate of silver halide.
3. We identify sulfates by adding hydrochloric acid and barium chloride solution to produce a white precipitate of barium sulfate.
4. We identify nitrates by adding sodium hydroxide solution and a little aluminium powder to produce ammonia gas.

SUMMARY ANSWERS

1 **a)** Carbonate **b)** Add barium chloride solution and hydrochloric acid **c)** Chloride – white precipitate **d)** Bromide – creamy precipitate **e)** Iodide – pale yellow precipitate **f)** Ammonia gas evolved.

2 [Student flow chart.]

3 Lithium chloride because lithium turns flames red and chloride test is positive if a white precipitate is produced with AgNO₃.

CHEMISTRY / ANALYSIS

C3 5.3 Testing for organic substances

LEARNING OBJECTIVES

Students should learn:
- That there is a simple test for organic compounds.
- That the empirical formula can be calculated using combustion. [HT only]
- That C=C bonds can be experimentally detected.

LEARNING OUTCOMES

Most students should be able to:
- State the positive test result for organic compounds.
- State the positive test result for unsaturated organic compounds

Some students should also be able to:
- Explain the test for organic compounds.
- Calculate the empirical formula from a combustion analysis of a simple organic compound. [HT only]
- Explain what an iodine number is.

SPECIFICATION LINK-UP   Unit: Chemistry 3.13.5

- Organic compounds burn or char when heated in air.
- Unsaturated organic compounds containing a double carbon–carbon bond decolourise bromine water.
- The empirical formula of an organic compound can be found from the masses of the products formed when a known mass of the compound is burned. [HT only]

Students should use their skills, knowledge and understanding of 'How Science Works':
- to interpret results of the chemical tests in this specification.

Lesson structure

STARTER

Similarities and differences – Show the students the structural formulae of ethane and ethene. Ask the students to work in pairs to determine the similarities [same number of carbon atoms, both are hydrocarbons] and differences [different number of hydrogen atoms, ethane is saturated but ethene is unsaturated]. Ask groups to feedback to the class their thoughts to create a list of similarities and differences. (10 minutes)

True or false – In the corner of a classroom put a 'false' sign, then at the other corner on the same wall put a 'true' sign. This wall represents a continuum from true to false, ask students a list of statements and they should stand somewhere on the wall to show if they definitely think the answer is 'true', 'false' or they are unsure. Misconceptions can then be discussed and challenged using question and answer. Read the following statements:
- Combustion is the scientific word for oxidation. [False]
- Hydrocarbons only contain two elements. [True]
- An unsaturated hydrocarbons has an H=H bond. [False]
- Hydrocarbons are organic compounds. [True]
- Empirical formula is the simplest ratio of elements in a compound. [True]
- Molecular, structural and empirical formula are all the same thing. [False] (10 minutes)

MAIN

- Students could be given a selection of saturated and unsaturated hydrocarbons. Their task is to sort them into two groups (saturated and unsaturated).
- Students should be reminded that bromine water is decolourised in unsaturated hydrocarbons. There should be a selection of equipment for the students to use (but not all is needed). The task for the students is to select correctly the appropriate equipment and test the liquids. (See 'Practical support'.)
- Ask students to create a revision poster to explain how an organic compound is tested.
- Also their poster should include a step-by-step guide on how to calculate the empirical formula of an organic compound using combustion analysis. Students should be reminded that colour helps people learn, so their poster should be colourful.

PLENARIES

Calculations – Split the class into groups and give each team one question that involves the calculation of an empirical formula from a combustion analysis. (The example question and summary questions 3 and 4 from the Student Book could be used.) Wait for each group to solve the calculation, then encourage the students to demonstrate how to complete the question on the board and explain each step that they have performed in the calculation. (20 minutes)

Flow chart – Ask students to write a flow chart to explain how to test for unsaturated molecules. (10 minutes)

Complete – Ask students to complete the following sentence: 'An iodine number is . . . .' Then encourage a few students to read their sentence out. The class should vote on the most scientific sentence and the class should then copy it into their notes. (10 minutes)

Teaching suggestions

- **Special needs.** A pictorial flow chart method of using bromine water to test for double carbon bonds can be given to the students. There should only be two red herring pieces of equipment for these students to choose from.
- **Gifted and talented.** These students could be given an organic compound, e.g. ethanol, and they could generate their own examination-style question and mark scheme.
- **Learning styles**

  Kinaesthetic: Experimentally determining whether a hydrocarbon is saturated or unsaturated.

  Visual: Creating a flow chart to explain how to test for unsaturated molecules.

  Auditory: Listening to statements to decide if they are true or false.

  Interpersonal: Working in groups to complete calculation questions.

  Intrapersonal: Completing a sentence about iodine number.

- **Homework.** Ask students to find the iodine number of three fats of their choice.

Practical support

Testing unsaturated compounds

Equipment and materials needed
Test tubes, bungs, test-tube racks, selection of 6 liquid saturated and unsaturated hydrocarbons (flammable), bromine water (harmful and irritant), 6 dropping pipettes, eye protection. CLEAPSS Recipe Card: gas solutions 28. CLEAPSS Hazcard: bromine 15.

Red herring: Flame-proof mat, beaker, conical flask, delivery tube, tripod, pipe-clay triangle, burette, pipette, measuring cylinder, gas syringe, delivery tube.

Details
- Wearing eye protection and in a well-ventilated room, put about 1 cm³ of the hydrocarbon into a test tube. Add about 1 cm³ of bromine water, and put the bung into the test tube. Shake the solution and leave in the test-tube rack.
- Observe to see if there is a colour change.

ACTIVITY & EXTENSION

Students could complete calculations for combustion analysis of organic compounds that contain oxygen as well as carbon and hydrogen.

CHEMISTRY ANALYSIS
C3 5.3 Testing for organic substances

LEARNING OBJECTIVES
1. What simple test can we use to see if a substance is organic?
2. How can we detect carbon–carbon double bonds?
3. How can we find out the empirical formula of an organic compound by burning it? [Higher]

From the earliest days of science people have heated substances to see what happened to them. Two hundred years ago a Swedish chemist called Jöns Jakob Berzelius decided that chemicals could be classified into two groups according to how they behaved when he heated them.

Chemicals that burned or charred on heating came mainly from living things, so Berzelius called these **organic** substances.

In contrast, other substances melted or vaporised when Berzelius heated them. These returned to their original state when they were cooled. Berzelius called these **inorganic** substances.

Our modern definition describes organic chemicals as substances which are based on the element carbon.

a) What is an organic substance?
b) How do organic substances behave when they are heated?

Detecting carbon–carbon double bonds (C═C)

As we saw on page 71, unsaturated hydrocarbons will react with bromine water, producing colourless compounds. This is a good way of testing a hydrocarbon to see if it contains a carbon–carbon double bond.

unsaturated hydrocarbon + bromine water → products
(colourless)   (orange-yellow)   (colourless)

saturated hydrocarbon + bromine water → **no reaction**
(colourless)   (orange-yellow)   (orange-brown)

c) How can we test for a carbon–carbon double bond?

This test is the basis for determining the number of carbon–carbon double bonds in unsaturated oils and fats. The oil is titrated against an iodine solution. (Iodine reacts with carbon–carbon double bonds in exactly the same way as bromine.) The 'iodine number' of the fat is based on the number of molecules of iodine needed to react with all of the carbon–carbon double bonds in one molecule of the fat.

Figure 1 As a rule, organic substances char or burn when heated in air, while inorganic substances do not

Combustion analysis
We can find the empirical formula of an organic compound by burning it and measuring the amounts of the products formed.

Worked example
An organic substance Z contains carbon and hydrogen. A sample of Z is burnt in an excess of oxygen, producing 1.80 g of water and 3.52 g of carbon dioxide. What is the empirical formula of Z?

Solution
Step 1: Calculate moles of CO_2:

The M_r of CO_2 is $12 + (2 \times 16) = 44$ g

Amount of $CO_2 = \frac{3.52}{44} = 0.08$ moles

Step 2: Calculate moles of H_2O:

The A_r of H_2O is $(2 \times 1) + 16 = 18$ g

Amount of $H_2O = \frac{1.80}{18} = 0.10$ moles

Each molecule of carbon dioxide formed requires one carbon atom from a molecule of Z. So for each mole of carbon dioxide formed, Z must contain one mole of carbon atoms.

Amount of C atoms in sample of Z = 0.08 mols

In the same way, each water molecule formed requires two hydrogen atoms from a molecule of Z. So for each mole of water formed, Z must contain two moles of hydrogen atoms.

Amount of H atoms in sample of Z = $0.10 \times 2 = 0.20$ mols

So Z contains carbon atoms and hydrogen atoms in the ratio $0.08 : 0.20 = 2 : 5$.

Therefore the empirical formula of Z is C_2H_5.

SUMMARY QUESTIONS

1. Copy and complete using the words below:

   burn   bromine   char   double

   Organic substances …… or …… when heated. Carbon–carbon …… bonds (C═C) can be detected using …… water.

2. Draw a flowchart for using combustion analysis to work out the empirical formula of a hydrocarbon. [Higher]

3. A hydrocarbon Y is burnt in excess oxygen. It produces 5.28 g of carbon dioxide and 2.16 g of water. What is the empirical formula of Y? [Higher]

4. Substance W contains carbon, hydrogen and oxygen. When 0.23 g of W is burnt in excess oxygen, 0.44 g of carbon dioxide and 0.27 g of water are produced. What is the empirical formula of W? [Higher]

FOUL FACTS
In 1828, the German chemist Friedrich Wöhler heated ammonium cyanate to make urea. He showed that urea made this way was exactly the same as urea which he extracted from dog urine – the first time that an organic substance had been made from an inorganic one.

KEY POINTS
1. Organic compounds burn or char when we heat them.
2. We can work out the empirical formula of an organic compound from the ratio of the products produced when it burns. [Higher]
3. We can detect carbon–carbon double bonds using bromine water.

SUMMARY ANSWERS

1. Burn/char, char/burn, double, bromine.
2. Flow chart [**HT** only]
3. CH_2 [**HT** only]
4. C_2H_6O [**HT** only]

Answers to in-text questions

a) A substance that is based on the element carbon.
b) Decompose or char.
c) A C═C double bond will decolourise bromine water.

KEY POINTS

Ask students to copy out each key point and write a flow chart for each one. The diagram should expand the key point and include a chemical method or an explanation for how to complete the calculation.

CHEMISTRY   ANALYSIS

C3 5.4   Instrumental analysis 1

LEARNING OBJECTIVES

Students should learn:

- That there are a number of methods of modern analysis.
- That elements can be identified using modern analysis techniques.

LEARNING OUTCOMES

Most students should be able to:

- Name some modern analysis techniques.
- List advantages and disadvantages of modern analysis techniques.

Some students should also be able to:

- Explain the technique of atomic absorption spectroscopy. [**HT** only]
- Explain what mass spectrometry can be used for. [**HT** only]

Teaching suggestions

- **Gifted and talented.** Students could try to interpret simple spectra.
- **Learning styles**

  Kinaesthetic: Completing cut and stick activity of advantages and disadvantages of instrumental analysis.

  Visual: Creating a flow chart to explain how different instrumental analysis machines work.

  Auditory: Listening to persuasive arguments.

  Interpersonal: Working in pairs to critically assess each other's work.

  Intrapersonal: Writing a newspaper article about the discovery of a particular instrumental analysis technique.

- **ICT link-up.** The RSC produce a spectroscopy CD ROM that has a video of these machines being used.
- **Homework.** Ask students to find out what an emission spectrum is. [Each atom gives out its own pattern of radiation when the electrons have been excited. The emitted radiation is the emission spectrum.]

SPECIFICATION LINK-UP   Unit: Chemistry 3.13.5

- The development of modern instrumental methods has been aided by the rapid progress in technologies such as electronics and computing.
- Elements and compounds can also be detected and identified using a variety of instrumental methods. Instrumental methods are accurate, sensitive and rapid and are particularly useful when the amount of a sample is very small.
- Some instrumental methods are suited to identifying elements, such as atomic absorption spectroscopy used in the steel industry. Other instrumental methods are suited to identifying compounds, such as infrared spectrometry, ultraviolet spectroscopy, nuclear magnetic resonance spectroscopy, and gas-liquid chromatography. Some methods can be adapted for elements or compounds, such as mass spectrometry. (Details of how the instruments work are not required). [**HT** only]

Students should use their skills, knowledge and understanding of 'How Science Works':

- to evaluate the advantages and disadvantages of instrumental methods of analysis and the features that influence that development.

Lesson structure

STARTER

Cut and stick – Explain to students that using instruments for analysis has advantages and disadvantages. Give the students the six statements as detailed in the bullet points featured in the Student Book. Students should cut out and stick each statement into a two-column table headed with advantages and disadvantages. (10 minutes)

Think – Show students an image of a science lab 100 year ago, and a modern science lab. Ask students to think about why instrumental analysis has only recently developed. Allow students to discuss their ideas as a class. (10 minutes)

MAIN

- Ask students to imagine that they have been commissioned by a steel mill to create a leaflet about their use of instrumental analysis in their industry.
- Their leaflet should be designed for schools to use as an information sheet and should include an activity with answers.
- Students could create a flow chart to detail the stages involved in atomic absorption spectroscopy and mass spectrometry.
- They could imagine that they are a reporter in a newspaper in the past. They should write a news article documenting the discovery of atomic absorption spectroscopy and its uses. Students could use the Internet to find out the date for such an article and people that may have given relevant quotes.

PLENARIES

Persuade – Ask students to work in small groups, and imagine that they are research chemists who have made a new fertiliser. Each group should make a persuasive argument for a board of directors on why they should finance the use of instrumental analysis technique rather than using traditional lab techniques. Allow each group to read out their statement to the rest of the class. (20 minutes)

Paper round – Give each student a piece of A4 paper. Students should work in groups of six. Ask the students to write at the top of the paper an example of instrumental analysis, then fold the paper over and pass to the student at the right. Then on the folded-over paper from another student, ask the next person to write one new fact that they have learned today. Again fold over the paper and pass to the right. Ask the students to continue to fold over and pass the paper after writing a revised fact, an advantage of instrumental analysis, a disadvantage of instrumental analysis and one use for mass spectrometry. After the sixth paper move, ask each student to unfold the paper and read what has been put. Ask a few students to share the work from their paper. Examination technique can be highlighted from this exercise, as some students should have answered in sentences; whereas others may have used just key words which may be ambiguous. (15 minutes)

Further chemistry

AfL (Assessment for Learning) – Ask students to work in pairs to compare their leaflets about instrumental analysis in steel mills. Students should comment (out of 10) on the science content, choice of language, activity and presentation, and award an overall mark out of 40. Students could then make amendments as homework. (10 minutes)

ACTIVITY & EXTENSION IDEAS

- Students could be shown spectra from atomic absorption spectroscopy and mass spectrometry.
- A trip to a local university may be organised to see spectrometers in action.
- Students could use combustion analysis information of a hydrocarbon, coupled with mass spectra information to generate the molecular formula of organic compounds.

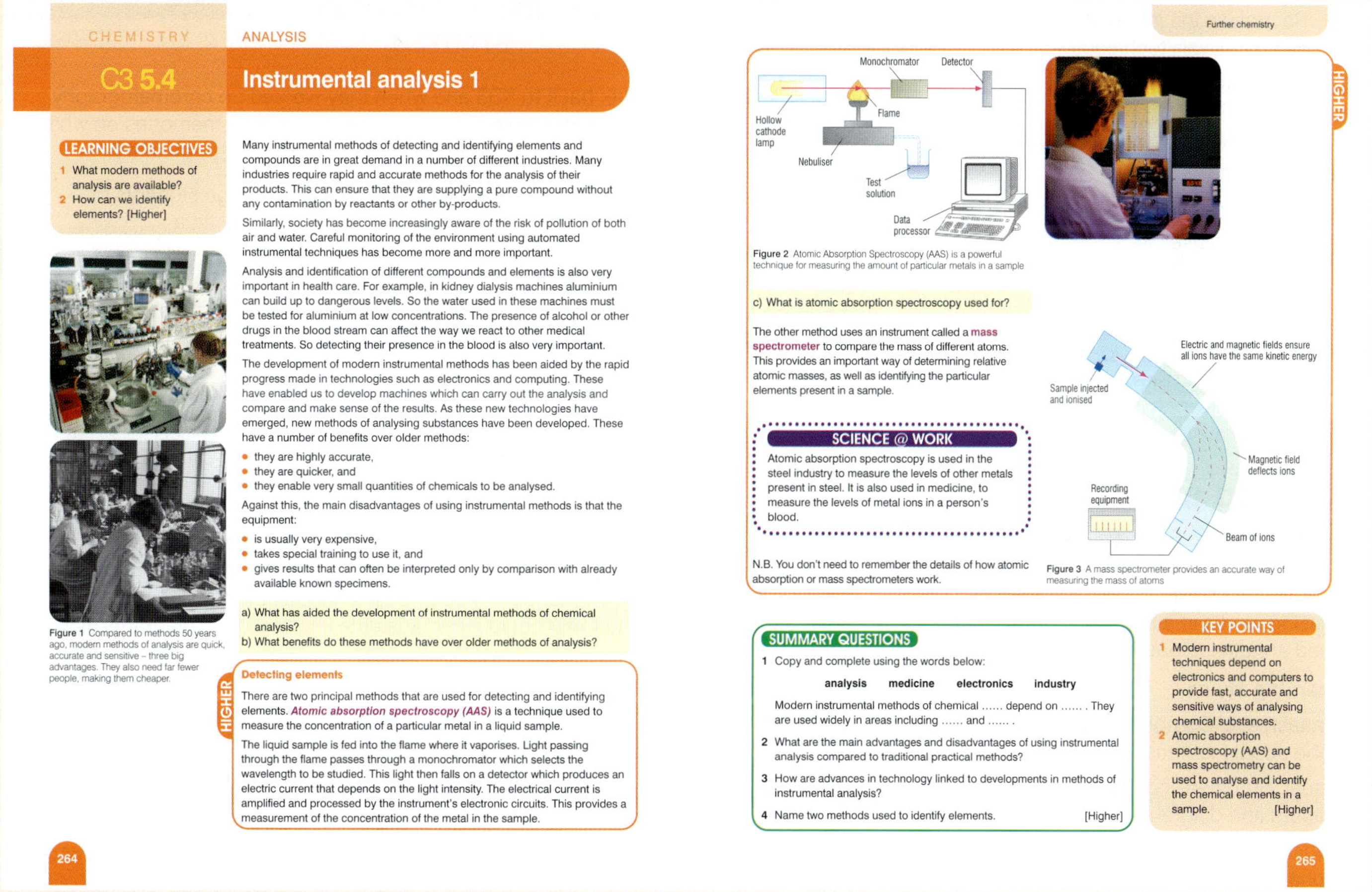

CHEMISTRY — ANALYSIS
C3 5.4 Instrumental analysis 1

LEARNING OBJECTIVES
1 What modern methods of analysis are available?
2 How can we identify elements? [Higher]

Many instrumental methods of detecting and identifying elements and compounds are in great demand in a number of different industries. Many industries require rapid and accurate methods for the analysis of their products. This can ensure that they are supplying a pure compound without any contamination by reactants or other by-products.

Similarly, society has become increasingly aware of the risk of pollution of both air and water. Careful monitoring of the environment using automated instrumental techniques has become more and more important.

Analysis and identification of different compounds and elements is also very important in health care. For example, in kidney dialysis machines aluminium can build up to dangerous levels. So the water used in these machines must be tested for aluminium at low concentrations. The presence of alcohol or other drugs in the blood stream can affect the way we react to other medical treatments. So detecting their presence in the blood is also very important.

The development of modern instrumental methods has been aided by the rapid progress made in technologies such as electronics and computing. These have enabled us to develop machines which can carry out the analysis and compare and make sense of the results. As these new technologies have emerged, new methods of analysing substances have been developed. These have a number of benefits over older methods:
- they are highly accurate,
- they are quicker, and
- they enable very small quantities of chemicals to be analysed.

Against this, the main disadvantages of using instrumental methods is that the equipment:
- is usually very expensive,
- takes special training to use it, and
- gives results that can often be interpreted only by comparison with already available known specimens.

a) What has aided the development of instrumental methods of chemical analysis?
b) What benefits do these methods have over older methods of analysis?

Detecting elements

There are two principal methods that are used for detecting and identifying elements. **Atomic absorption spectroscopy (AAS)** is a technique used to measure the concentration of a particular metal in a liquid sample.

The liquid sample is fed into the flame where it vaporises. Light passing through the flame passes through a monochromator which selects the wavelength to be studied. This light then falls on a detector which produces an electric current that depends on the light intensity. The electrical current is amplified and processed by the instrument's electronic circuits. This provides a measurement of the concentration of the metal in the sample.

Figure 1 Compared to methods 50 years ago, modern methods of analysis are quick, accurate and sensitive – three big advantages. They also need far fewer people, making them cheaper.

Figure 2 Atomic Absorption Spectroscopy (AAS) is a powerful technique for measuring the amount of particular metals in a sample

c) What is atomic absorption spectroscopy used for?

The other method uses an instrument called a **mass spectrometer** to compare the mass of different atoms. This provides an important way of determining relative atomic masses, as well as identifying the particular elements present in a sample.

SCIENCE @ WORK
Atomic absorption spectroscopy is used in the steel industry to measure the levels of other metals present in steel. It is also used in medicine, to measure the levels of metal ions in a person's blood.

N.B. You don't need to remember the details of how atomic absorption or mass spectrometers work.

Figure 3 A mass spectrometer provides an accurate way of measuring the mass of atoms

SUMMARY QUESTIONS
1 Copy and complete using the words below:

   analysis   medicine   electronics   industry

   Modern instrumental methods of chemical …… depend on …… . They are used widely in areas including …… and …… .

2 What are the main advantages and disadvantages of using instrumental analysis compared to traditional practical methods?
3 How are advances in technology linked to developments in methods of instrumental analysis?
4 Name two methods used to identify elements. [Higher]

KEY POINTS
1 Modern instrumental techniques depend on electronics and computers to provide fast, accurate and sensitive ways of analysing chemical substances.
2 Atomic absorption spectroscopy (AAS) and mass spectrometry can be used to analyse and identify the chemical elements in a sample. [Higher]

SUMMARY ANSWERS

1 Analysis, electronics, industry/medicine medicine/industry.

2 Advantages – speed, sensitivity, ability to analyse small samples. Disadvantages – use expensive equipment, training is needed.

3 As technology advances it makes it possible to develop new analytical techniques and to refine existing methods.

4 Atomic absorption spectroscopy and mass spectrometry. [**HT** only]

Answers to in-text questions

a) The development of technologies such as electronics and computing.

b) These methods are highly accurate, quick and can be used with very small quantities of materials.

c) To measure the concentration of a particular metal in a liquid sample.

KEY POINTS

Show students chemical posters such as ones given free to schools from the RSC. Ask students to create a poster, which includes the key points.

CHEMISTRY — ANALYSIS

C3 5.5 Instrumental analysis 2

LEARNING OBJECTIVES

Students should learn:
- That compounds can be identified using modern analysis techniques. [HT only]

LEARNING OUTCOMES

Most students should be able to:
- Name some modern analysis techniques. [HT only]
- Recognise the information a given analysis technique will provide. [HT only]

Some students should also be able to:
- Explain the difference that the medium makes in chromatography. [HT only]
- Explain what chromatography, mass spectrometry, IR spectroscopy, UV/visible spectroscopy and NMR can be used for. [HT only]

SPECIFICATION LINK-UP   Unit: Chemistry 3.13.5

- Other instrumental methods are suited to identifying compounds, such as infrared spectroscopy, ultraviolet spectroscopy, nuclear magnetic resonance spectroscopy, and gas-liquid chromatography. Some methods can be adapted for elements or compounds, such as mass spectrometry.

Students should use their skills, knowledge and understanding of 'How Science Works':
- to evaluate the advantages and disadvantages of instrumental methods of analysis and the features that influence that development.

Lesson structure

STARTER

Think – Ask students to think back to KS3 and when they worked on chromatography. Encourage students to discuss the topic in small groups to jog their memories on what they did. Ask a few students to share their thoughts on the subject. (10 minutes)

Anagrams – Write the following anagrams onto the board. Encourage students to decode the key word, and to extend the activity further, they could write a definition/explanation for each word.
- graphchrotomay [Chromatography]
- mtrupecs [Spectrum]
- metertospecr [Spectrometer]
- poundcom [Compound]
- aentgm [Magnet] (5 minutes)

MAIN

- Give students the template of a cube (each face 5 cm × 5 cm) on A4 card. Students should then summarise each of the instrumental analysis techniques on separate faces. There will be one face left over, this could be a title face, glossary or outline of the advantages and disadvantages of instrumental analysis. Students should be encouraged to use colours and could summarise the information in diagrams as well as text.
- Ask students to complete an alphabet based on instrumental analysis. Students should use their textbooks, work in small groups and will need to be creative to obtain 26 different sentences. For example, H is for hydrogen, which is usually featured in NMR.
- Supply five A6 revision cards to each student. Each card should represent a different instrumental analysis technique. On the front, the student should write five questions, encourage students to try to write in an examination style. Then, on the reverse of the card, students should write a full answer.

PLENARIES

Reading – Ask each group to read out their alphabets of instrumental analysis. (10 minutes)

Sentences – Choose a key word from the double-page spread, e.g. spectra. Then ask students for a number from 1–19, then count down to the appropriate line in the text. Ask another student to pick a number from 1 to the maximum number of words in a sentence, count to this word. Write the randomly chosen word onto the board, with the key word. Students should then try to write a sentence that is scientifically and grammatically correct and contains both words. Select a few students to share their sentences with the rest of the class. Repeat the process with other key words. (10 minutes)

AfL (Assessment for Learning) – Students swap their question cards with another student. Each person should review the questions and with pencil correct any mistakes in the science content of the work. The corrected cards should then be returned to the writer, who should review the comments and make necessary corrections. (15 minutes)

Teaching suggestions

- **Special needs.** Students could be provided with a cube that already has information on it, such as 'fill in the missing words in a prose', diagrams that need annotating and titles, etc.
- **Learning styles**
  Kinaesthetic: Completing a revision cube about instrumental analysis.
  Visual: Summarising information using colours and diagrams.
  Auditory: Listening to different groups' alphabets.
  Interpersonal: Working in groups to recall previous work on chromatography.
  Intrapersonal: Solving anagrams.
- **Homework.** Ask students to find out which instrumental analysis could be used to monitor chemicals in the blood. [IR – ethanol; gas-liquid chromatography – drugs; AAS – electrolytes.]
- **ICT link-up.** There are many cube templates available free on the Internet. Search the Internet for 'cube template'.

ACTIVITY & EXTENSION IDEAS

- Students could research other instrumental techniques e.g. Raman spectroscopy.
- Ask students to find out what solvent is usually used in IR spectroscopy and NMR spectroscopy. Students could also be encouraged to find out why these specific solvents are usually used.

CHEMISTRY **ANALYSIS**

C3 5.5 Instrumental analysis 2

LEARNING OBJECTIVES
1 How can we identify compounds?

There is a very wide range of chemical instruments that we can use to identify unknown chemical compounds. In many cases the instruments use techniques that are simply more sophisticated and automated versions of techniques that we use in the school chemistry lab.

One example of this is **chromatography**, which is used to separate different compounds within a mixture. The technique is based on how well they dissolve in a particular solvent. This determines how far each substance travels across a stationary medium such as a piece of chromatography paper.

We can use:
- **gas-liquid chromatography** to separate compounds that are easily vaporised,
- **gel permeation chromatography** to separate compounds according to the size of their molecules,
- **ion-exchange chromatography** to separate compounds containing differently charged particles, and
- **high-performance liquid chromatography** to separate compounds in solution.

Once the compounds in a mixture have been separated, they may be identified by comparison with the distance moved by known substances.

Alternatively, other instruments may then be used to identify them.

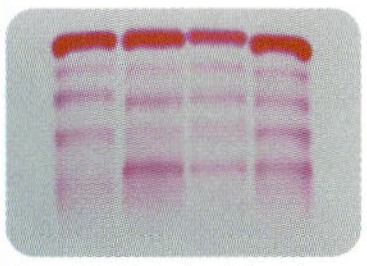

Figure 1 Gel electrophoresis is another type of chromatography. It uses an electric field to separate compounds moving across a gel-covered plate

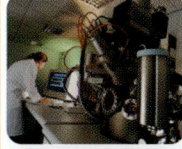

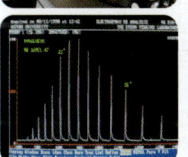

Mass spectrometry can be used to provide information about compounds as well as elements. The mass spectrum of a molecule tells us its relative mass, and can also provide information about its structure because some of the molecules break up as they go through the spectrometer.

Figure 2 Athletes train for years to reach the peak of their performance in the Olympic Games. Instruments are used to carry out rapid automated analysis of the test samples collected during the competition, detecting the presence of illegal drugs that could give an athlete an unfair advantage.

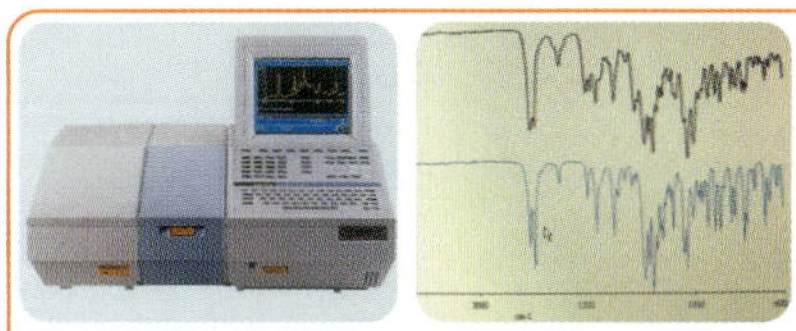

The frequency of infra-red radiation is lower than that of visible light. Molecules can absorb the energy carried by infra-red radiation, which makes the bonds in the molecule vibrate. The frequency of the infra-red radiation that a molecule absorbs depends on the chemical bonds in it – so the **infra-red spectrum** of a compound can provide valuable information about its structure.

The energy carried by visible and ultraviolet light may also be absorbed by compounds, promoting electrons to higher energy levels. **UV-visible spectroscopy** is used with molecules and inorganic ions. It provides us with very limited information about the structure of compounds but is very useful when we want to make quantitative measurements about the amount of a substance that is present, based on the amount of light that a sample absorbs at a particular frequency.

The nuclei of some atoms behave like tiny magnets, and can be affected by a magnetic field. **NMR (nuclear magnetic resonance) spectroscopy** uses radio waves to 'flip' these nuclei in a molecule between different alignments within a strong magnetic field, rather like changing the alignment of a compass needle by pushing it with your finger. If we measure the amount of energy needed to cause this flipping at different frequencies of radio waves, the spectrum produced tells us a great deal about the way that the atoms in the molecule are arranged. NMR spectroscopy is particularly useful for determining the structure of large organic molecules. It is also the basis of the medical imaging technique which we call magnetic resonance imaging.

DID YOU KNOW?
Some athletes are now turning to chemicals found naturally in the body and which can be made in the chemistry laboratory. One of these is erythropoietin (or EPO for short) which increases the number of red blood cells made by the body. Abuse of EPO is impossible to detect, because it is present in everyone's body – so scientists have to measure the number of red blood cells in an athlete's blood instead.

SUMMARY QUESTIONS
1 Copy and complete using the words below:

chromatography energy formula mass spectrometry
mixture

Separating a ...... of compounds uses techniques which are based on .... Identifying compounds once they have been separated then uses techniques like ...., in which the relative ...... mass of the molecule is measured, or other techniques in which the ...... absorbed by the compound is measured.

2 Which of the techniques described on these two pages is *not* used to determine the structure of molecules? Explain your answer.

KEY POINTS
1 Compounds in a mixture can be separated using chromatography.
2 Once separated, compounds can be identified using a variety of instrumental techniques.

SUMMARY ANSWERS

1 Mixture, chromatography, mass spectrometry, formula, energy.

2 Chromatography/electrophoresis – a separation technology.

KEY POINTS

Ask students to expand each key point into a paragraph. The two paragraphs should try to summarise the whole of the double-page spread.

CHEMISTRY / ANALYSIS

C3 5.6 Chemical analysis

SPECIFICATION LINK-UP
Unit: Chemistry 3.13.5

Students should use their skills, knowledge and understanding of 'How Science Works':

- to interpret and evaluate the results of instrumental analysis carried out to identify elements and compounds for forensic, health or environmental purposes.

C3 5.6 Chemical analysis

Paper, ink and forgery

In Germany in 1983 *Stern* magazine published extracts from what they claimed were the diaries of Adolf Hitler. The magazine had paid about $6 million for sixty small handwritten books, which covered the period from 1932 to 1945. At a press-conference in April 1983 the historian Hugh Trevor-Roper said: 'I am now satisfied that the documents are authentic; that the history of their wanderings since 1945 is true; and that the standard accounts of Hitler's writing habits, of his personality and, even, perhaps, of some public events, may in consequence have to be revised.'

But many people were suspicious, and within two weeks the police were on the case. Using chemical analysis, forensic scientists were able to:

- show that the paper on which the diaries were printed contained *blankophor*, a fluorescent whitening substance that was not used in paper until after 1954;
- prove that polyester and viscose, modern polymers, were present in the bindings of the books;
- use chromatography to prove that none of the four different inks used in the diaries were available during Hitler's lifetime.

The diaries were actually written by Konrad Kujau, a well-known forger. Both Kujau and Gerd Heidemann – the journalist who 'discovered' the diaries – were sent to prison for $3\frac{1}{2}$ years.

ACTIVITY
Using the information from this chapter, and any further information you can find, write a newspaper article entitled 'Chemical analysis in action – can we believe our eyes?'

Doping – drugs in sport

The doping classes and methods that are prohibited by most governing bodies of sport are based on those of the World Anti-Doping Agency. However, it is important to note that some of the prohibited substances may vary from sport to sport. It is the athlete's responsibility to know their sport's anti-doping regulations. In cases of uncertainty, it is important to check with the appropriate governing body or UK Sport. Also be sure to read carefully the anti-doping rules adopted by the relevant governing body and international sports federations.

Athletes are advised to check all medications and substances with their doctor or governing body medical officer. All substances should be checked carefully when travelling abroad as many products can, and do, contain different substances to those found in the UK.

ACTIVITY
Chemists are active in the fight to uncover the abuse of drugs in sport. Design a poster which could be displayed in the changing rooms of a sports centre used by young athletes to show them how chemical analysis using sensitive instruments is used to catch the 'drug cheats'.

268

Teaching suggestions

Activities

- **Newspaper article** – Show students a number of science-based articles in newspapers. Study one article to pull out features such as the number of quotes and people who gave them, images and length of text. Explain to students that they have been commissioned by a newspaper to write a similar article with the title: 'Chemical analysis in action – can we believe our eyes?' Students should write a balanced article and obtain real quotes, using the Internet to help them, e.g. companies that make the equipment and academics who use the equipment. Each student should also provide information about the images that they would include in their article.

- **Poster** – There are a number of anti-drug posters that are given to schools. Show some of these posters to the students and discuss who they are aimed at, where they would be put and how they work [shock tactics with imagery, information giving, thought provoking etc.]. Then ask students to design their own poster to be shown in changing rooms to explain how athletes who take drugs are caught.

- **Table** – Ask students to draw two tables with three columns labelled 'goals', 'rights' and 'duties'. Students should work in small groups and complete each table for the characters James and Nelson. They may find that some of the statements are the same for the boys. Once the tables have been completed, each team should then prepare advice for the boys. Encourage each group to read out their advice to the rest of the class.

Further chemistry

Teenzine
A Difficult Choice?
the BIG debate

It can be a tough road to the top in any field – and nowhere is it tougher than in athletics. The route from the school athletics field to the Olympic gold medal winners' podium is full of hard work, and you may need to make some difficult choices too.

So how far would you go to get into a sports team?

- try harder in school sports lessons
- go along to training sessions outside school
- trip up competing athletes to try to injure them
- get your parents to pay for private coaching
- skip homework to work in a fast-food restaurant to earn money to pay for private coaching
- steal money to pay for private coaching
- follow a special diet
- take a 'herbal supplement' that your coach recommends to improve your performance
- take drugs which a fellow competitor says doubled her performance

When we are faced with decisions like these we need to think about what we *can* do. Once we know this, we must decide what we *should* do.

Science is very useful for the first type of question. For example, if we want to know whether drugs or diet can affect our performance as an athlete, science can provide answers. Science can also tell us whether a particular substance is likely to be bad for us.

But science is not helpful when we want to know how we *should* behave – so we need to look elsewhere. One way of helping us to make decisions about our behaviour is to think about *goals*, *rights* and *duties*.

A *goal* is something we want to achieve – for example, to be the fastest person in the 200 metres. One way of judging someone's behaviour is to look at why they behave in the way they do – in other words, to look at their goals.

Our *rights* refer to the way that we can expect to be treated – for example, we may be able to say what we think, a right that is called our *freedom of speech*.

And *duties* describe the way that we should behave – for example, the duty to tell the truth.

Duties, rights and goals are often linked. If you are accused of a crime you have a *right* to a lawyer who has a *duty* to try to get you acquitted – which is the lawyer's *goal*.

But it can get complicated. What about the case of a dying patient, who asks his doctor not to keep him alive any longer? Does the doctor have a *duty* to do as the patient asks because that patient has the *right* to decide how and when to die? Or is the doctor's *duty* to ignore the patient's wishes because of the *goal* of preserving life?

ACTIVITY
James is a member of the school swimming squad. Nelson wants to get into the squad. Draw up a table to show the **goals, rights** and **duties** that you think James and Nelson each have. How do you think that these two young people **should** behave. What advice would **you** give them and why?

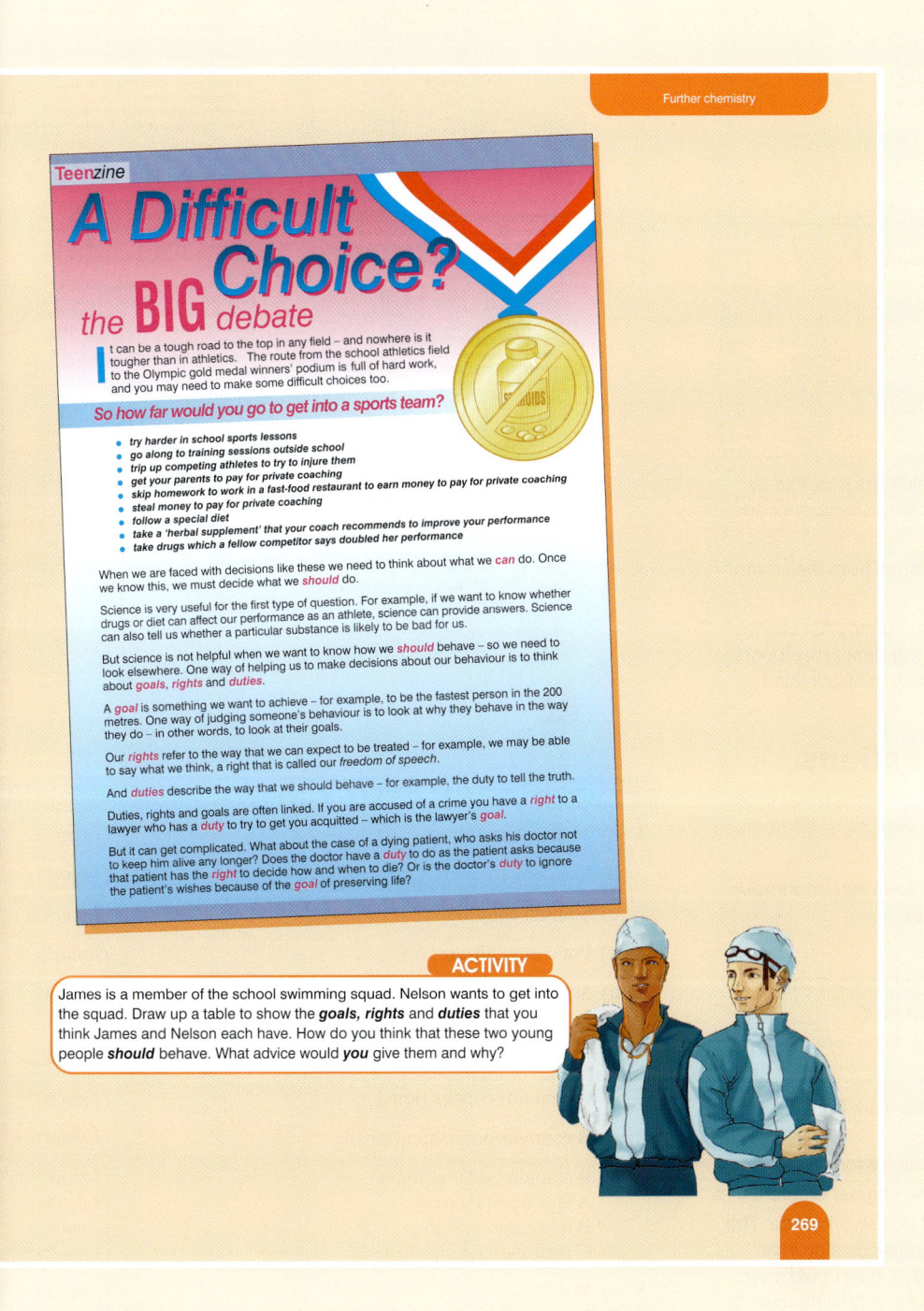

Extensions
- **Drugs** – Ask students to find a list of banned substances that athletes cannot take. They could also find out the reasons why the drugs are taken by sports people and their side effects.
- **Problem page** – Ask students to prepare a fictitious letter to a problem page about the temptation to take drugs to improve athletic performance. Students should then draft the answer from the agony aunt.

Homework
- **Drug cheat** – Ask students to find one example of a sports person that has been caught for taking drugs and the punishment that was given.

Learning styles
Kinaesthetic: Completing cut and stick the goals, rights and duties.

Visual: Creating a poster about doping issues.

Auditory: Listening to advice from different groups.

Interpersonal: Working in groups to complete a table on goals, rights and duties.

Intrapersonal: Writing a newspaper article about instrumental analysis.

Special needs
Students could be given statements for goals, rights and duties. They could cut and stick these statements into the correct parts of the table.

ICT link-up
Newspapers often have archives on the Internet of previous stories. These databases could be used to obtain newspaper articles about athletes who have been part of doping controversy.

CHEMISTRY   ANALYSIS

SUMMARY ANSWERS

1

Add dilute acid	Add sodium hydroxide solution and warm	Add sodium hydroxide solution and warm – then add aluminium	Flame test	Substance
Nothing observed	Nothing observed	Gas evolved turns damp red litmus paper blue after aluminium added	Golden yellow	e) Sodium nitrate
Fizzing – gas turns lime water milky	Gas evolved turns damp universal indicator paper blue	Nothing observed	Nothing observed	f) Ammonium carbonate
a) Fizzing – gas turns lime water milky	b) White precipitate immediately on adding solution	c) White precipitate immediately on adding solution	d) Brick red	Calcium carbonate

2 a) By comparing the bands on the samples it is possible to decide whether the sample from the crime scene matches that from on the suspects.

b) B – Bands from DNA analysis match those from the scene of the crime.

c) Samples may be contaminated, matching may not always be perfect. [See www.abpischools.org.uk/resources/poster-series/pcr/dnatrial.asp for more information about this.]

Summary teaching suggestions

- **Special needs** – For question 1, a help sheet of the missing text could be prepared. Students then choose from the statements to complete the table.
- **Gifted and talented** – Some schools may have electrophoresis kits that could be demonstrated to students.
- **Learning styles**
  Kinaesthetic: Question 1 could be turned into a card sort.
  Visual: Question 1 involves completion of a table.
  Auditory: Question 2c) could be used as a discussion piece.
- **When to use the questions?**
  - Question 1 can be used to summarise the work from lesson 5.1.
  - Question 2 could be used as homework for lessons 5.5 and 5.6.
  - The questions could be used to revise the chapter before a test.
  - Question 2 could make a good extended homework piece. The students could be encouraged to answer this question in an essay/report style. Then the following lesson, they could swap their scripts with another student who could be provided with a marking scheme. Students could then assess each other's work.

EXAM-STYLE ANSWERS

1 a) Magnesium sulfate. *(1 mark)*

   b) Copper carbonate. *(1 mark)*

   c) Sodium chloride. *(1 mark)*

   d) Potassium nitrate. *(1 mark)*

2 a) Solid A is insoluble and solid B is soluble. *(1 mark)*

   b) Solid A is a base/reacts with acid to produce a (soluble) salt.
   (1 mark)

   c) C contains copper (ions). *(1 mark)*

   d) B contains potassium (ions). *(1 mark)*

   e) B contains sulfate (ions). *(1 mark)*
   A is copper(II) oxide. *(1 mark)*
   B is potassium sulfate. *(1 mark)*
   C is copper(II) nitrate. *(1 mark)*

3 a) Y *(1 mark)*

   b) V *(1 mark)*

   c) W *(1 mark)*

   d) Z *(1 mark)*

   e) X *(1 mark)*
   [**HT** only]

4 a) Detects elements *(1 mark)* and measures their concentrations.
   (1 mark)

   b) *Three from:*
   - It is rapid/gives results very quickly.
   - It is (very) accurate.
   - It uses (very) small samples.
   - It is sensitive/specific/measures or detects many elements.
   (3 marks)

   c) Development of computers/electronics. *(1 mark)*
   [**HT** only]

(a) Finding the concentration of caffeine in a soft drink.
(b) Finding the formula of an organic compound.
(c) Finding the amounts of alkanes in petrol.
(d) Finding the amount of lead in a sample of water.
(e) Showing which trans fatty acids are in margarine.
(5)
[Higher]

4 Read the information about steel and answer the questions (a) to (c).

> Very small changes in the amounts of elements in steel can affect its properties. Atomic emission spectroscopy is an instrumental method of analysis that helps to ensure steels have exactly the correct composition. A small sample of the steel from the furnace is placed in the instrument. Each element present emits light of a particular wavelength and the intensity of the light is proportional to the concentration of the element in the steel. A computer processes the results so that the steel-maker knows almost instantly and very accurately the composition of the steel. Any adjustments can be made before the steel is poured out of the furnace.

(a) What does atomic emission spectroscopy detect and measure? (2)
(b) Give **three** reasons why atomic emission spectroscopy is more useful in the steel industry than traditional laboratory methods of analysis. (3)
(c) Suggest one advance in technology that has helped the rapid development of instrumental methods of analysis. (1)
[Higher]

HOW SCIENCE WORKS QUESTIONS

Atomic absorption spectroscopy and the space shuttle

One of the world's most amazing sights is the space shuttle taking off from Cape Canaveral Space Center. The rockets must deliver the shuttle into orbit. It is essential that they are reliable and that they are re-usable. They are therefore tested to establish their reliability. However, like a car engine they do show signs of wear after use. Atomic absorption spectroscopy (AAS) can identify that wear, by analysing the exhaust gases from the rockets.

AAS will identify the presence of iron, nickel, cobalt, copper and silver. Any increase in these elements suggests engine wear.

a) Who should carry out these tests? Explain your answer. (2)
b) How might the invention of AAS be used to improve engine design for the space shuttle? (1)
c) How else might this technology be used? (1)
d) On 28 January 1986 the Challenger space shuttle blew up just over a minute into its flight. An 'O ring' on the solid rocket booster had broken. All seven crew members were killed.

AAS can only detect engine wear. It is for the judgement of the scientists to decide if that wear is dangerous. Make the decision too soon and space travel becomes too expensive. Make the decision too late and astronauts die. What are the ethical issues around such a decision? (2)

Exam teaching suggestions

There are 23 marks for the questions on this chapter, so allow 25 minutes if the questions are done in a single session. Q1 and Q2 could be set after completing C3 5.2.

Students should know the tests listed in the specification and should be able to interpret the results of these tests. Q1 and Q2 assess these abilities and students usually enjoy the challenge of investigative aspects of analysis. They should be encouraged to tackle as many problems of this type as possible and there are many examples in traditional textbooks. Such questions can form the basis for discussion and group work. They can be carried out practically, assuming they can be done safely, and can provide the basis for competitions between groups in a class. The more practical experience that students have of these tests, the better.

Students should be aware of the use of instrumental methods of chemical analysis in monitoring manufactured goods, our health and the environment. They do not need to know details of the methods, but should know the main methods that are used. Questions will provide information or data and students will be expected to apply their skills of interpretation as in Q4. They should be trained to look for key words in the information provided and use the information in their answers, supplemented by any specific knowledge they may have. Use as many resources as possible to develop students' skills in answering this type of question.

HOW SCIENCE WORKS ANSWERS

a) Independent scientists who are fully trained in the use of the equipment and who have no bias.
b) E.g. engines might be compared for the rate at which they deteriorate.
c) To analyse wear in aircraft engines.
d) [Some open-ended discussions around the importance of space travel and the dangers involved and possibly uses of resources and pollution.]

Ideas of evidence teaching suggestions

- **Literacy guidance**
  - Key terms that should be understood: bias, technology, ethical issues.
  - Question d) expects a longer answer, where students can practise their literacy skills.
- **Higher- and lower-level answers.** Questions b) and d) are higher-level questions. The answers for these have been provided at this level. Questions a) and c) are lower-level and the answers provided are lower-level.
- **Gifted and talented.** Able students could suggest how to establish standards for the wear of jet engines and how these can be related to the AAS results, e.g. testing an engine to destruction and measuring the exhaust output of the elements stated.
- **How and when to use these questions.** When wishing to develop how science links to technology and the ethics involved in technological developments. The questions are best used for group discussion.
- **Homework.** Able students could prepare a speech, for or against space travel.
- **ICT link-up.** Students could research the Internet for the science behind the Challenger and the Columbia space shuttle disasters.

CHEMISTRY — FURTHER CHEMISTRY

C3 Examination-Style Questions

Examiner's comments

Students will need about 35 minutes to complete all of the questions if done in a single session. Question 1 could be done on completing Chapter 1 and Question 2 after completing Chapter 2. Question 3 could be done when Chapter 4 has been completed.

Questions 1, 3 and 6 are suitable for all candidates. Questions 2 and 4 are intended for Higher-Tier candidates, although parts (a) to (c) in Question 2, should be accessible to Foundation-Tier candidates.

When a question begins with the word 'suggest', it implies that there may be more than the required number of acceptable responses. Students should use reasoning to produce the best answers based on the information in the question and their own knowledge.

Answers to Questions

1. (a) Atomic (proton) numbers. *(1 mark)*

    (b) Electrons. *(1 mark)*

    (c) *Two from:*
    - There are eight electrons in the outer shell/highest energy level (for the elements in these periods).
    - So every ninth element has the same number of electrons in the highest energy level/outer shell.
    - Chemical properties depend on the number of electrons in the highest energy level/outer shell.

    (2 marks)

    (d) Group 0/the noble gases were missing/had not been discovered. *(1 mark)*

2. (a) Titration. *(1 mark)*

    (b) Burette. *(1 mark)*

    (c) An indicator *(accept any named indicator)*. *(1 mark)*

    (d) To increase reliability. *(1 mark)*

    (e) 0.008 moles *(2 marks)*
    (working: $0.5 \times 16/1000$ gains 1 mark)

    (f) 0.016 moles (or answer to (e) $\times 2$). *(1 mark)*

    (g) 0.64 moles/dm^3 (or answer to (f) $\times 40$) *(2 marks)*
    (working: answer to (f) $\times 1000/25$ gains 1 mark)

    (h) 25.6 g/dm^3 (or answer to (g) $\times 40$) *(2 marks)*
    (working: (g) $\times$ attempt at M_r gains 1 mark)

EXAMINATION-STYLE QUESTIONS

1. In the modern periodic table, the elements in periods 2 and 3 have similar chemical properties every ninth element. *See pages 210–13, 218*

    (a) Complete the sentence: In the modern periodic table, elements are arranged in order of their …… *(1 mark)*

    (b) Complete the sentence: The chemical properties of an element depend upon the number of …… in the highest energy level (outer shell) of its atoms. *(1 mark)*

    (c) Explain why the chemical properties are repeated every ninth element in these two periods. *(2 marks)*

    (d) Why did Newlands and Mendeleev find that the properties repeated every eighth element? *(1 mark)*

2. 25.0 cm^3 of sodium hydroxide solution reacted with 16.0 cm^3 of 0.50 mol per dm^3 sulfuric acid. The equation for the reaction is: *See pages 226–9*

    $$2NaOH + H_2SO_4 \rightarrow Na_2SO_4 + H_2O$$

    (a) Name the method that could be used to find these reacting volumes. *(1 mark)*

    (b) Name the apparatus you would use to add the acid to the alkali. *(1 mark)*

    (c) What would you need to add to the solution to find the end point of the reaction? *(1 mark)*

    (d) Explain why it would be advisable to repeat the method more than once. *(1 mark)*

    (e) Calculate the number of moles of sulfuric acid in 16.0 cm^3 of the solution. *(2 marks)*

    (f) How many moles of sodium hydroxide were in 25.0 cm^3 of solution? *(1 mark)*

    (g) Calculate the concentration of the sodium hydroxide solution in moles per dm^3. *(2 marks)*

    (h) Calculate the concentration of the sodium hydroxide solution in grams per dm^3. *(2 marks)*
    (A_r values: Na = 23, O = 16, H = 1) *[Higher]*

---

3. (a) Hydrogen. *(1 mark)*

    (b) Petrol. *(1 mark)*

    (c) Sugar. *(1 mark)*

    (d) *Two from:*
    - (Relatively) high energy output per gram or per cm^3.
    - Burn easily.
    - Can be easily controlled/fed into engine/piped from storage.

    continues opposite ▶

GET IT RIGHT!

Check all calculations. Go through your working a second time. Use estimation to make sure your answer is a reasonable value. Always include units where necessary.

BUMP UP THE GRADE

Grade A candidates use technical vocabulary with fluency, applying their knowledge in a range of tasks and unfamiliar situations. Practise these skills by discussing and talking through answers to get the words right before writing them down. Then get someone else to check that your writing is scientific, in a sensible order and is clearly expressed. If your writing is not clear, redraft.

---

3 The table gives information about some fuels. All of the fuels, except for hydrogen, are organic compounds.

See pages 248–9

Name of fuel	Energy produced per gram (kJ/g)	Volume of 1 gram at 20°C and 1 atm (cm³)
Coal	25	1.35
Ethanol	27	0.79
Hydrogen	120	12000
Petrol	44	0.72
Sugar	17	1.58
Vegetable oil	38	0.93
Wood	15	0.70

(a) Which fuel produces the most energy per gram? *(1 mark)*
(b) Which of the liquid fuels produces most energy per cm³? *(1 mark)*
(c) Which of the solid fuels produces the least energy per cm³? *(1 mark)*
(d) Suggest **two** reasons why liquid fuels are used for road vehicles. *(2 marks)*
(e) Hydrogen could be used as a fuel for cars.
  (i) Suggest **two** reasons why hydrogen would be a good choice of fuel. *(2 marks)*
  (ii) Suggest **two** reasons why hydrogen is not more widely used as a fuel for cars. *(2 marks)*
(f) Describe an experiment you could do to compare the energy produced by the liquid fuels in the table. Give only the essential steps and explain how you would make the experiment a fair test. Explain why it is not possible to obtain accurate values for the energy produced by the fuels in your experiment. *(6 marks)*

4 An organic compound contains carbon and hydrogen only. A sample of the compound was burnt completely. It produced 1.32 g of carbon dioxide and 0.72 g of water. What is the empirical formula of the compound? Show all of your working. *(4 marks)*
(A_r values: C = 12, O = 16, H = 1) **[Higher]**

See page 263

> *continues from previous page*

- Can be easily stored (in a tank/at ordinary temperatures).
  (Answers could be advantages or comparisons with solids or gases.) *(2 marks)*

(e) (i) *Two from:*
  - High energy output per gram.
  - Produces only water when burnt/no harmful gases so no pollution.
  - Produces no carbon dioxide so no global warming/greenhouse effect. *(2 marks)*

(ii) *Two from:*
  - Has a very large volume (at ordinary temperatures and pressures).
  - Needs very large tanks or high-pressure tanks that are heavy.
  - Leaks easily/hard to contain/greater risk of explosion.
  - Expensive to produce in large quantities. *(2 marks)*

(f) *One mark each for:*
  - Burn known or measured mass of fuel.
  - In a simple calorimeter or under a metal can/beaker containing water.
  - Measure the temperature rise of water.
  - Repeat for different fuels.
  - Use same conditions each time, e.g. same starting temperature of water/same temperature rise/same sized flame/same apparatus *(the same amount of fuel is not important and on its own is not worth a mark)*.
  - The values obtained are not accurate because heat is lost/not all of the heat raises the temperature of the water. *(6 marks)*

4 Moles carbon dioxide = 1.32/44 = 0.03. *(1 mark)*
Moles water = 0.72/18 = 0.04. *(1 mark)*
Moles hydrogen in compound = 0.04 × 2 = 0.08. *(1 mark)*

Empirical formula is C_3H_8. *(1 mark)*
(working: 1 mark can be gained for attempt at mass/relative formula mass; arithmetical errors from first two steps can be carried forward.)

Notes